THE MODERN LAW OF
RESTITUTION

THE MODERN LAW OF RESTITUTION

Gerard McMeel, BCL, MA (Oxon)

Lecturer in Law, University of Bristol

Barrister, Guildhall Chambers

BLACKSTONE
PRESS LIMITED

First published in Great Britain 2000 by Blackstone Press Limited, Aldine Place, London W12 8AA. Telephone: (020) 8740 2277
www.blackstonepress.com

© Gerard McMeel, 2000

ISBN: 1 85431 939 6

British Library Cataloguing in Publication Data
A CIP catalogue record for this book is available from the British Library

Typeset by Montage Studios Limited, Horsmonden, Kent
Printed and bound in Great Britain by Antony Rowe Limited, Chippenham and Reading

Contents

PART A — FOUNDATIONS

1.1 Restitution in the map of the law   1.2 The structure of the unjust enrichment enquiry   1.3 Pervasive themes   1.4 Enrichment

2.1 Theoretical foundations   2.2 Historical foundations   2.3 *In personam* and *in rem*   2.4 Common law and equity   2.5 Quasi-contract 2.6 Rescission   2.7 Tracing and claiming   2.8 Conclusion

PART B — DEFECTIVE TRANSFERS

3.1 Theoretical foundations   3.2 Mistake and ignorance   3.3 Fact and law   3.4 The ground for restitution   3.5 Restrictions on recovery 3.6 Special problems of mistake of law   3.7 Contributory negligence 3.8 Non-money benefits   3.9 Practical issues

PART H — DEFENCES

PART I — PRACTICAL MATTERS

Preface

Whereas in the 1980s the fashionable plaintiff alleged that he or she had suffered loss as a result of another's negligence, by the end of the 1990s the fashionable claimant sought restitution for unjust enrichment. The acknowledgement that English law recognises a law of restitution based upon a principle of unjust enrichment has transformed private law.

A lawyer who completed his or her substantive legal education in 1990 may find the changes in the intervening decade somewhat startling. He or she may think that obligations arise only as a result of contract or tort; the modern position is that the law of obligations has at least three components: contract, tort and restitution. This lawyer might be dimly aware that the law permits recovery of mistaken payments subject to numerous restrictions; in the modern law generous rights of recovery are allowed in respect of both money and non-money benefits. He or she may have a strong conviction that the law's characteristic response to civil wrongdoing is compensation; in the modern law the victims of wrongdoing are increasingly entitled to elect between compensation or a measure based upon the gains made by the wrongdoer as a result of his conduct. He or she may be familiar, and yet uncomfortable, with the language of *money had and received* and *constructive trusts*; in the modern law, archaic language is being jettisoned and replaced by a new vocabulary of 'grounds for restitution', 'subjective devaluation' and 'incontrovertible benefit'. These examples can be mulitplied.

It is worth pausing to ask why private law has been transformed so rapidly? The answer, it is suggested, is that the modern developments were necessary. Restitution performs a corrective function where contracts fail and wealth goes astray. Five typical fact scenarios underlie most of the modern case law. First, a trusted company officer or senior employee embezzles corporate funds or a company either perpetrates or is a victim of a massive fraud which pushes it into insolvency. Secondly, a husband suborns his wife to give security over her share of the matrimonial home so that the bank will prop up his ailing business. Thirdly, cases of mortgage fraud, where banks or building societies have lent money to borrowers whose ability to repay is dubious and where the underlying security proves not to be as valuable as it was supposed to be. Fourthly, interest-rate swap contracts and other transactions entered into by local authorities in order to evade central government restrictions upon borrowing. Fifthly, cases where persons abstract or invade the property of another without seeking the owner's consent, and make considerable profits or gains thereby. Many of the cases involve fall-out from the recession and property crash of the late 1980s. Such cases demonstrate the problems thrown up by an advanced capitalist society.

English transactional law has the remarkable feature that it is largely judge-made. It has a highly developed structure for ascertaining what the terms of the transaction are and what the remedies for the breach of an undertaking should be. In contrast, its resources for dealing with the fall-out of failed transactions and for assisting those seeking to trace misdirected funds were less well developed. The modern law has been forged by close cooperation between an active judiciary and the body of distinguished legal academics. Unjust enrichment and restitution have been a focus of scholarly and innovative thinking in the leading university law schools over the last few decades. This has forced the recognition of unjust enrichment as the explanation of a large and distinct body of substantive law. Further, it has provided the materials which the judiciary needed for dealing with increasingly complex cases.

This book focuses upon the *modern* law of restitution. The House of Lords only recognised unjust enrichment as the foundation of the law of restitution in early 1991. This book concentrates upon the formative years of the modern law. The authorities discussed predominantly come from the 1990s. Earlier case law before the recognition of unjust enrichment as the governing principle must always be treated with circumspection. The path-breaking work was by Goff and Jones and Professor Birks. Their contributions, together with the contributions of other scholars, have great authority. Recent treatises on subrogation, tracing and resulting and constructive trusts have facilitated the exposition of the modern law. Restitution has overcome its early twentieth century identity crisis. A new generation of scholars is seeking to identify and occasionally delimit the application of the principle of unjust enrichment.

An important theme of this work is that this comparatively new body of law need not be regarded as unsettling the foundations of established principles drawn from provinces of contract, tort, equitable obligations and property law. Where unjust enrichment reasoning intersects and potentially conflicts with an established body of law, restitutionary reasoning should only prevail if the older doctrine is unprincipled or incoherent; where older doctrine is based upon well-established principle or sound policy it should prevail. In particular, in the context of contract and other consensual transactions the law of restitution plays a subsidiary function. Unjust enrichment reasoning must never subvert a voluntarily assumed allocation of risk. Restitution has no role to play where the transfer of benefits is governed by a subsisting and enforceable contract. This is the *primary of contract* or *subsidiarity* principle. It should be considered in every case.

It is hoped that this book will be of use to two different constituencies. First, practitioners who wish to acquaint themselves with the theory and detailed principles of this modern body of law. Secondly, students of the subject in the university law schools, whether final year undergraduates or postgraduates. It is hoped that the style and structure of the book will make it accessible to both.

For the benefit of the former, the last five chapters seek briefly to address some of the issues of practice which arise in the context of restitution. The recent civil justice reforms make it difficult for anybody, whether academic or practitioner, to venture into print in this area. However, it is a striking feature of modern restitution cases that the substantive and adjectival law have developed at different speeds. English law developed and refined the procedural mechanisms to cope with the growing number of claims in respect of misdirected funds in the 1970s and 1980s, such as freezing injunctions and ancillary orders. In contrast, the judges only began to develop and refine the substantive principles of restitution in the late 1980s and 1990s. Many of the difficult modern cases have arisen as a result of matters of practice. The law on this topic is still bedevilled by the comparative immaturity of the subject.

I have incurred a number of debts of gratitude. First, to the ever-efficient Rachel Nee who typed the manuscript. Secondly, to the practitioners who have attended my weekend LL.M course on Restitution at the University of Bristol over the last few years. The impetus for this book, and many of the ideas in it, have derived from those enjoyable sessions. And lastly, to Victoria, for the invaluable benefit of her support and encouragement.

I have attempted to trace developments up to the end of the 1990s.

Gerard McMeel
Bellevue, Clifton
March 2000

Table of Cases

Table of Statutes

Table of Secondary Legislation

Abbreviations of the Principal Works Cited

Andrews	Neil Andrews, *Principles of Civil Procedure*, London: Sweet & Maxwell, 1994.
Anson	J. Beatson, *Anson's Law of Contract*, 27th edn, Oxford: Oxford University Press, 1998.
Beatson	J. Beatson, *The Use and Abuse of Unjust Enrichment*, Oxford: Clarendon Press, 1991.
Birks	Peter Birks, *An Introduction to the Law of Restitution*, revised paperback edition, Oxford: Clarendon Press, 1989.
Birks (1992)	Peter Birks, *Restitution — The Future*, Sydney: The Federation Press, 1992.
Birks (1995)	Peter Birks (ed.), *Laundering and Tracing*, Oxford: Clarendon Press, 1995.
Burrows (1991)	Andrew Burrows (ed.), *Essays on the Law of Restitution*, Oxford: Clarendon Press, 1991.
Burrows	Andrew Burrows, *The Law of Restitutuion*, London: Butterworths, 1993.
Burrows (1998)	Andrew Burrows, *Understanding the Law of Obligations — Essays on Contract, Tort and Restitution*, Oxford: Hart Publishing, 1998.
Chambers	Robert Chambers, *Resulting Trusts*, Oxford: Clarendon Press, 1997.
Cornish	W. R. Cornish, Richard Nolan, J. O'Sullivan and G. Virgo (eds), *Restitution Past, Present & Future — Essays in Honour of Gareth Jones*, Oxford: Hart Publishing, 1998.
Dawson	J. Dawson, *Unjust Enrichment — A Comparative Analysis*, Boston: Little, Brown and Company, 1951.

Finn
P. D. Finn (ed.), *Essays on Restitution*, Sydney: The Law Book Company, 1989.

Goff and Jones
Lord Goff of Chieveley and Gareth Jones, *The Law of Restitituion*, 5th edn, London: Sweet & Maxwell, 1998.

McInnes
Mitchell McInnes, *Restitution: Development in Unjust Enrichment*, Sydney: LBC Information Services, 1996.

Mitchell
Charles Mitchell, *The Law of Subrogation*, Oxford: Clarendon Press, 1994.

Rose (1996)
F. D. Rose (ed.), *Consensus ad Idem — Essays on the Law of Contract in Honour of Guenter Treitel*: London: Sweet & Maxwell, 1996.

Rose (1997)
Francis Rose (ed.), *Failure of Contracts — Contractual, Restitutionary and Proprietary Consequences*, Oxford: Hart Publishing, 1997.

Rose (1998)
Francis Rose, *Restitution and Banking Law*, Oxford: Mansfield Press, 1998.

Smith L.C. or *Smith's Leading Cases*
Sir Thomas Chitty, Bart., Alfred Denning and Cyril Harvey, *Smith's Leading Cases or a Selection of Leading Cases on Various Branches of the Common Law with notes by John William Smith*, 13th edn, London: Sweet & Maxwell, 1929 (2 volumes).

Skelton
A. Skelton, *Restitution and Contract*, Oxford: Mansfield Press, 1998.

Smith
Lionel D. Smith, *The Law of Tracing*, Oxford: Clarendon Press, 1997.

Winfield
Percy Winfield, *The Province of the Law of Tort*, Cambridge: Cambridge University Press, 1931.

PART A

FOUNDATIONS

1   Unjust Enrichment and Restitution

1.1   RESTITUTION IN THE MAP OF THE LAW

Modern legal systems generally promote the freedom to transact. Citizens are empowered by facilitative rules to trade goods, services and other manifestations of wealth. It is a significant insight of any refined jurisprudential theory that such power-conferring rules constitute a substantial component of a mature legal order. Therefore much of the traditional law curriculum is concerned with the regulation of transactions. Pre-eminent in transactional law is the law of contract with its sub-species: sales, carriage, employment, and so on. In addition, consider the law of trusts, together with the rules on gift, assignment and negotiation of commercial instruments. Consensual transfers of wealth, both discrete and relational, constitute the web of social relations which we term the market economy. The freedom to transact, which is the hallmark of a liberal society, evidences the respect for autonomy and choice which characterises such a community. This commitment to choice and transactional freedom further necessitates a legal regime in response to movements of value which were not the result of a free and informed choice. If the law has a role to play in facilitating transactions and promoting the freedom to deploy wealth, it follows that it must provide a regime for reversing non-voluntary transfers and unscrambling defective transactions. Modern technology has, if anything, multiplied the possible routes by which wealth can go astray. In response the modern law deploys the principle against unjust enrichment which yields that body of doctrine known as the law of restitution.

Over 50 years ago in *Fibrosa Spolka Akcyjna v Fairbairn Lawson Combe Barbour Ltd* [1943] AC 32, Lord Wright proclaimed (at 61):

> It is clear that any civilized system of law is bound to provide remedies for cases of what has been called unjust enrichment or unjust benefit, that is to prevent a man from retaining the money of or some benefit derived from another which it is against conscience that he should keep. Such remedies in English law are

generically different from remedies in contract or in tort, and are now recognized to fall within a third category which has been called quasi-contract or restitution.

The location of unjust enrichment in the map of the law is our initial concern. The main substantive components of civil law are property, obligations and the rules governing the status of persons. Property law supplies a stable element: defining and constituting the interests which persons can have in things. It supplies the benchmark of what constitutes wealth in a society. Property must be distinguished from obligations. The duties (and the correlative rights) owed by citizens to each other are the concern of the law of obligations. The category of obligations can in turn be further subdivided. First, the law of wrongs draws upon the community's standards to identify a person's legally protected interests: in bodily integrity, in earning capacity, in reputation, in property and in other economic interests. Torts and equitable wrongs provide remedies for interference with and wrongfully caused harm to such interests. Remedies for wrongdoing promote stability, or at least aim to restore the equilibrium. Secondly, in contrast, the institution of contract provides the dynamic component: persons contract out their labour by hand or by brain, in order to obtain the wealth to buy the essential and non-essential goods and services they desire. Most of this transacting is done utilising that universal repository of value: money.

Symmetry necessitates a role for a third category of obligations here: restitution for unjust enrichment. Just as the law gives effect to consensual dispositions of value, so to it must reverse what can be broadly described as non-consensual transfers of wealth. Further, the law intervenes to prevent persons profiting from wrongdoing. Consequently, the law recognises two main categories of restitution. First, *autonomous unjust enrichment*, where the defendant has received wealth from the claimant, and the latter disputes the former's entitlement to that benefit. Secondly, *restitution for wrongs*, where the defendant obtains a benefit as a result of a breach of duty owed to the claimant. In contract and tort the law recognises both primary and secondary obligations. A party to a contract must perform what he has undertaken to do (primary obligation) or else pay damages for the consequences to the other party (secondary obligation). Similarly, a driver must exercise reasonable care and skill on the highway (primary obligation) or else pay damages to any person injured as a result of the driver's negligence (secondary obligation). In restitution the picture is slightly more complicated, however. In cases of autonomous unjust enrichment there is no need to demonstrate any breach of a primary legal obligation. Receipt engenders liability. 'It is sufficient to say restitution is not a fault-based remedy' (*Banque Financière de la Cité* v *Parc (Battersea) Ltd* [1999] 1 AC 221, at 227 *per* Lord Steyn). In contrast, in restitution for wrongs it is necessary to show the breach of a primary legal duty, albeit one from another category of the law of obligations, such as conversion or breach of fiduciary duty.

A number of concrete examples can be given. First, consider an employer whose clerk makes a mistake and overpays his employees. Can the employer recover? What happens if the employees have frittered away their unexpected bonus? Secondly, consider a company which is defrauded by one of its officers who diverts wealth away from the business. Can it recover from the ultimate recipients of the value derived from its assets? Thirdly, consider the spouse who is imposed upon by her husband to provide a guarantee to the bank in a vain attempt to keep his ailing business afloat. Can the bank enforce its security? Fourthly, consider the purchaser of a second-hand car who subsequently discovers it is stolen property. Can he recover the purchase price from the seller? Fifthly, consider the infamous murderess who profits from the publication of a book which details her crimes. Can she be made to disgorge the royalties to the victims' families? These examples of shifting wealth and profiting from wrongdoing provide some of the concerns of the law of restitution.

Lord Steyn has observed, 'unjust enrichment ranks next to contract and tort as part of the law of obligations. It is an independent source of rights and obligations' *Banque Financière de la Cité* v *Parc (Battersea) Ltd* [1999] 1 AC 221, at 227). Unjust enrichment is a close neighbour of contract as they are both concerned with transactions. In contradistinction to contract, however, where obligations are self-imposed, restitution shares with tort the characteristic that its obligations are imposed by law irrespective of consent. The acceptance of a tripartite division of the heart of the law of obligations is a comparatively recent development. As Dawson has commented (at 39–40):

> It seems clear that the Anglo-American legal system has come late to the problems of restitution. This tardiness is only relative. Therefore it appears that the prevention of unjust enrichment as a distinct and independent motive for judicial action is apt to be recognised late in any legal system after provision has been made for primary institutions through which societies organise.

In English law, the 1990s saw a triptych of landmark House of Lords' decisions. First, in *Lipkin Gorman* v *Karpnale Ltd* [1991] 2 AC 548, the principle of unjust enrichment was recognised as the foundation of claims in restitution. Secondly, in *Westdeutsche Landesbank Girozentrale* v *Islington London Borough Council* [1996] AC 669, the implied contract fiction which had bedevilled the subject and stunted its growth was emphatically rejected. Thirdly, *Banque Financière de la Cité* v *Parc (Battersea) Ltd* [1999] 1 AC 221 adopted the analytical methodology to the structure of the unjust enrichment enquiry which was promoted in leading scholarly works. According to Lord Steyn (at 227) four questions arise:

(1) Has [the defendant] benefited or been enriched?
(2) Was the enrichment at the expense of [the claimant]?
(3) Was the enrichment unjust?
(4) Are there any defences?

1.2 THE STRUCTURE OF THE UNJUST ENRICHMENT ENQUIRY

Helpful though this recognition of a four-stage test is, it is proposed in this work to develop and refine the enquiry. A seven-stage approach is suggested:

1.   Has the defendant been benefited or enriched (the *'enrichment* question')?

2.   Was the benefit at the expense of the claimant (the *'at the expense of* question')?

3.   Was the transfer of value pursuant to an apparently binding contract, gift, trust or other dispositive act (the *'contractual'* or *'transactional matrix question'*)?

4.   Is retention of the benefit by the defendant unjustified (the *'ground for restitution'* or *'unjust factor question'*)?

5.   What is the appropriate quantum of recovery (the *'measure of relief* question')?

6.   Which form should restitutionary relief take: personal or proprietary (the *'nature of relief* question')?

7.   Can the defendant raise a defence to extinguish and diminish the claimant's prima facie right to restitution (the *'defences* question')?

Often only one or two of these issues will be in dispute in a particular case. The relevance of each of the questions will be introduced here, and then the relevant issues to which they give rise will be used as tools of analysis throughout the text to explain and criticise the authorities. Owing to the immaturity of the subject, a persistent problem is that one of these vital steps has been overlooked in a particular case.

1.2.1   Enrichment

Restitution is concerned with benefit-based liabilities and therefore satisfying the test of enrichment is the most basic element of the cause of action. There are five main species of value which are relevant. First and most commonly, enrichment takes the form of the receipt of money. Secondly, the defendant may be enriched by the receipt of property. Thirdly, he may benefit as the recipient of services. Fourthly, the defendant may be enriched by the discharge of a valid obligation which he owed or would have necessarily incurred. Further, the law recognises the profits of wrongdoing as constituting a relevant benefit.

The benefit received will normally form the ceiling to any restitution claim. Money provides no difficulty in terms of valuation. In contrast the receipt of property or services presents problems as the value of any benefit to the defendant may be debatable. Here the law seeks to reconcile the tension between the interests of claimant and defendant. The former will generally favour an objective valuation of the benefit conferred. The latter will probably insist that any benefit was of little or no subjective value to him. These difficulties have yet to be successfully confronted in the case law. To date, non-money claims in restitution are rare and yield little sophisticated discussion. The discharge of obligations presents its own difficulties, in that the law takes a restrictive view as to when payment can effectively extinguish a debt or obligation owed by another. Different problems arise with the concept of benefit in the sphere of profiting from wrongdoing. In this context it may be arguable that some profits are too remote from the initial breach of duty to the claimant. These difficulties will be addressed below (at 1.4) and at relevant stages during the course of the text.

1.2.2 At the expense of

In *Chase Manhattan Bank NA* v *Israel-British Bank (London) Ltd* [1981] Ch 105, Goulding J observed (at 125): 'Unjust enrichment cannot be a complete cause of action in itself, for ... it does not identify the plaintiff'. Accordingly in *Kleinwort Benson Ltd* v *Birmingham City Council* [1997] QB 380, Evans LJ supplied the missing link (at 393): '"At his expense" in my judgment, serves to identify the person by or on whose behalf the payment was made and to whom the repayment is due'. Dawson, commenting upon a general statement of restitutionary principle, has stated that: '[It] suggests an element of causation; it implies a type of enrichment that is caused (and perhaps also measured) by another's loss.' This component of the cause of action provides the link between defendant and claimant. It has long been recognised that there is a crucial ambiguity at the heart of restitution. Winfield, writing over 50 years ago, observed (at 121):

> there are some instances of waiver of tort in order to sue in a quasi-contractual action in which the situation is more accurately described by saying that the defendant has reaped a benefit by inflicting an injury on the plaintiff, not that the plaintiff has 'conferred' a benefit on the defendant.

Therefore the 'at the expense of' enquiry can be satisfied in one of two alternative ways. First, the claimant demonstrates a corresponding plus and minus: the defendant has been benefited to a degree that precisely matches the diminution in the claimant's wealth, and that benefit can be identified as passing from the claimant to the defendant. Secondly, the claimant can demonstrate that the defendant benefited by committing a wrong against him and thereby in breach of a legal duty owed to the claimant. Such a cause of action arises outside the law of restitution, in the law of wrongs: This leads to a significant bifurcation in the subject between the former category, termed *autonomous* or *subtractive* unjust enrichment, and the latter category termed *restitution for wrongs*. This stark division was first proposed in doctrinal writings (Birks, 99, 313) and has now won acceptance in the case law: *Macmillan Inc.* v *Bishopsgate Investment Trust plc (No. 3)* [1995] 1 WLR 978, at 988–989 *per* Millett J, reversed on other grounds [1996] 1 WLR 387; *Halifax Building Society* v *Thomas* [1996] Ch 217, at 224 *per* Peter Gibson LJ; *Banque Financière de la Cité* v *Parc (Battersea) Ltd* [1999] 1 AC 221, at 226 *per* Lord Steyn; *Portman Building Society* v *Hamlyn Taylor Neck* [1998] 4 All ER 202, at 206 *per* Millett LJ. In *Kleinwort Benson Ltd* v *Birmingham City Council* [1997] QB 380, Morritt LJ traced the history of the 'at the expense of' requirement, and identified the originator of the phrase as Ames, 'The History of Assumpsit' (1888) 2 Harv LR 1, 64 (at 401–2).

1.2.3   Contractual or transactional matrix

Sometimes wealth goes astray in a legal vacuum. For example, a credit may simply be attributed to the wrong bank account. Perhaps more commonly, however, wealth is transferred pursuant to an apparently binding contract or other transactional arrangement. In such circumstances it is necessary to ascertain whether the conditions establishing the invalidity of the apparently binding transfer have been made out. In some circumstances, such as mistaken intention, the rule for invalidating the contractual obligation is more stringent than the rule governing restitutionary relief. Therefore the law provides that restitutionary relief is not available where there is a subsisting contract between the parties which, by its express or implied terms, regulates the transfer of the disputed benefit, unless and until the contract is avoided or discharged in accordance with the rules of contract law. As Lord Goff stated in *Dimskal Shipping Co. SA* v *International Transport Workers' Federation, The Evia Luck (No. 2)* [1992] 2 AC 152, at 165: 'before the [plaintiff] could establish any right to recover the money, they had first to avoid the relevant contract. Until this was done, the money in question was paid under a binding contract and so was irrecoverable in restitution.'

The primacy of contractual techniques in resolving disputes about transfer of benefits is long established: *Weston* v *Downes* (1778) 1 Dougl. 24, 99 ER 19; *Toussaint* v *Martinnant* (1787) 2 TR 100, 100 ER 55; *Gompertz* v *Denton* (1832) 1 C & M 207, 149 ER 376, *Smith's Leading Cases* II, 9. Where the contract remains binding, its provisions remain operative in respect of the return or retention of benefits and the parties are confined to any remedies for breach of contract they may have (*Pan Ocean Shipping Co. Ltd* v *Creditcorp Ltd, The Trident Beauty* [1994] 1 WLR 161). Further, even when a contract is terminated for breach or pursuant to an express termination clause its provisions may, as a matter of construction, still govern the question whether there was a conditional or an unconditional transfer of benefits (*Stocznia Gdanska SA* v *Latvian Shipping Co.* [1998] 1 WLR 574). This restriction on the reach of restitution may be described as the *primacy of contract* or the *subsidiarity* principle. Further, it recognises in the hierarchy of norms in civil obligations that the courts respect the parties' own determination as to whether a transfer of wealth is conditional or unconditional. Similar principles are applied by analogy to other dispositive acts such as gifts and express trust. Subsidiarity recognises that restitution's corrective function does not undermine well-established rules and limitations upon when a binding contract, or other disposition of wealth, is set aside for some defect in its formation or otherwise proves ineffective. Clearly the rules on restitution closely interact and overlap with the vitiating factors in contract law and analogous rules in respect of other transactions, such as the presumptions of resulting trust and advancement in respect of apparent gifts.

The dangers posed for legal advisers who overlook the threshold question of the contractual matrix are starkly illustrated by *Portman Building Society* v *Hamlyn Taylor Neck* [1998] 4 All ER 202. The plaintiff building society was the victim of a mortgage fraud, and sued the solicitors who acted both for itself and for the mortgagor. The society had remitted money to the solicitors, which was in turn, upon the society's instructions, forwarded to the vendor's solicitors in return for a conveyance of the property. The mortgagor defaulted. The society claimed restitution of the money on the ground that it was paid under an operative mistake of fact. It believed that its condition that the property be used solely for residential purposes had been complied with. In fact it was intended that it would be used as a boarding house. The claim was doomed from the start. The society conceded it had never revoked the solicitors' authority to pay over the money. Crucially, it never sought to set aside the transaction on the grounds of misrepresentation, mistake or some other factor. Rather it affirmed the transaction by enforcing its security over the property. Millett LJ concluded (at 208):

> The continuing validity of the transaction under which the money was paid to the firm is, in my judgment, fatal to the society's claim. The obligation to make restitution must flow from the ineffectiveness of the transaction under which the money was paid and not from a mistake or misrepresentation which induced it. It is fundamental that, where the money is paid under a legally effective transaction, neither misrepresentation nor mistake vitiates consent or gives rise by itself to an obligation to make restitution. The recipient obtains a defeasible right to the money, which is divested if the payer rescinds or otherwise withdraws from the transaction. If the payer exercises his right of rescission in time and before the recipient deals with the money in accordance with those instructions, the obligation to make restitution may follow.

For academic scepticism about subsidiarity and the primacy of contract, see Birks in Rose (1996), 179, at 187–93; Barker (1995) 15 OJLS 457, at 459–63 and Smith (1999) 115 LQR 245.

1.2.4   Grounds for restitution

'Restitutionary liability is triggered by a range of unjust factors or grounds of restitution' (*Banque Financière de la Cité* v *Parc (Battersea) Ltd* [1999] 1 AC 221, at 227 *per* Lord Steyn). Much of the law of restitution is concerned with the vital question of whether or not the defendant should be made to give up the benefit received. This ingredient of the cause of action is described as either the *unjust factor* or the *ground for restitution*. What the former term lacks in elegance it may make up for in precision. It emphasises that we are only concerned with the fourth stage of the enquiry. It makes clear that the other questions must still be addressed. In contrast, *ground for restitution* appears more all-encompassing. While the latter phrase is generally preferred in this book, it should always be recalled that ground for restitution is concerned *only* with the fourth stage of the enquiry. On the autonomous side of the subject our concern is generally with the integrity of the claimant's decision to transfer. The burden of proof is upon the claimant to establish some concrete ground for recovering the benefit. This is in contrast to the approach of civil law systems which respond, as Dawson observes (at 6): 'by adopting a legal technique which in certain large classes of transactions requires justification for retention of the gain'. English law requires the claimant to prove affirmatively a sufficient defect in his transmissive consent, or some other ground for restitution. The deep structure of the law of restitution derives from the principle of unjust enrichment. However, this is not an abstract principle, aspiring to effect perfect justice or dependent upon the moral convictions of the particular judge. Rather restitution is a body of positive law derived from the judicial responses to concrete fact situations in the decided cases. In *Kleinwort Benson Ltd* v *Birmingham City Council* [1997] QB 380, Evans LJ commented (at 387): 'Notwithstanding its roots in natural justice and equity, the principle does not give the courts a discretionary power to order repayment whenever it seems in the circumstances of a particular case just and equitable to do so.'

The 'skeleton of principle' (Birks, 1) discerned by Peter Birks in his seminal work has proved highly influential. His terminology and taxonomy are largely followed in this work (as indeed they are followed by most scholars, and increasingly by the judiciary). The Birks bifurcation of the subject into the super-categories of *subtractive* or *autonomous* unjust enrichment and *restitution for wrongs* has already been adverted to. The most prominent examples of grounds for restitution constitute a category within *subtractive unjust enrichment* termed *non-voluntary transfer*. These include factors such as mistake, misrepresentation, duress, undue influence and other examples of imposition. Birks describes these as being a sub-category of *non-voluntary transfer* which he labels *vitiation*. This is contrasted with the second sub-species of non-voluntary transfer which is termed *qualification* (Birks, 101). The latter type of claim arises where a consensual transfer is freely entered into, but the transfer of wealth is conditional, either upon the occurrence of some requested counter-performance or upon the occurrence of some other event. In addition to non-voluntary transfer, there exist miscellaneous other grounds for restitution which have been labelled *policy-motivated restitution* (Birks, 105). In contrast, whereas the foregoing grounds are concerned with the integrity of the claimant's decision-making process, there are in addition some streams of authority which suggest a claim may be based in some circumstances upon the defendant's state of mind at the time of receipt. Such cases may be broadly categorised as cases of *unconscientious receipt* or, in Birks's scheme, *free acceptance* (Birks, 104).

On the *restitution for wrongs* side of the subject, the cause of action in the law of wrongs provides the basis of the ground for restitution. In addition it will be necessary to show that the wrong in question is of the type to which a restitutionary response is appropriate and that in the circumstances of the case the defendant should be made to disgorge. Further, this work argues for the existence of a third super-category of unjust enrichment, which is concerned with apportioning *complex entitlements* and *complex liabilities* in multi-party cases.

The experience of the last 10 years has been the growing liberalisation of the grounds of restitution. Traditional restrictions upon the right to recover money and benefits have been questioned, and tested to see whether they are consistent with the underlying principle of unjust enrichment. The most telling prediction of the 1990s was that of Lord Goff in *Lipkin Gorman* v *Karpnale Ltd* [1991] 2 AC 548. Commenting on the 'beneficial' consequences of the recognition of change of position as a defence, his Lordship observed (at 581): 'It will enable a more generous approach to be taken to the recognition of the right to restitution, in the knowledge that the defence is, in appropriate cases, available.' Since then the mistake of law bar has been judicially abrogated (*Kleinwort Benson Ltd* v *Lincoln City Council* [1999] 2 AC 349). A new right of restitution against public authorities has been recognised (*Woolwich Equitable Building Society* v *Inland Revenue Commissioners* [1993] AC 70). Similarly, the traditional requirement that a failure of consideration must be *total* is being scrutinised (*Westdeutsche Landesbank Girozentrale* v *Islington London Borough Council* [1996] AC 669; *Goss* v *Chilcott* [1996] AC 778).

1.2.5   Measure of relief: value received or value surviving?

'How much?' is the question that a client with a greater or lesser degree of willingness is keen to ask. Leaving aside for now the question of defences which may extinguish or diminish a prima facie claim, there appear to be two potential measures for restitution claims in cases of subtractive unjust enrichment. First and most commonly, the *value received* by the defendant at the claimant's expense. Secondly and alternatively, the claimant may seek to reach beyond the veil of receipt and make a claim to the *value surviving* in the defendant's hands (Birks, 75–77). The latter claim is more rare but has on occasion succeeded. The motivation for such a claim is either to obtain priority upon the defendant's insolvency, or to lay claim to profits in the hands of the defendant which derive from the value initially received. The former motive leads to an overlap with the next question. Such a claim to value surviving may be accompanied by a prayer for proprietary relief. In such cases the value surviving is typically less than the value received, but the claimant switches to a proprietary claim to some value surviving in order to recover a particular item of property or a share in a particular item of property, which thereby removes that thing from the insolvent estate and from the *pari passu* rule of distribution for unsecured creditors. The latter motive typically involves a sum greater than the value received but which is identifiably derived from value received. Such claims have succeeded and may be accompanied by a declaration of proprietary relief, although this is not essential where the defendant is not insolvent.

Where restitution is a response to acquisitive wrongdoing, different problems of quantification exist. The benefit may be measured by the net profits obtained by the wrongdoer. Alternatively the measure may be expense saved, such as the rent or hire which the claimant might have obtained for wrongfully detained property. Principles of remoteness of gain may limit the measure of recovery.

1.2.6   Nature of relief: personal or proprietary?

The two questions as to the nature and measure of relief are often closely linked in practice, but remain analytically distinct. The law of restitution is predominantly a component of the law of obligations and yields in most cases (including historically all claims at common law) a personal judgment sounding in debt. There are, in contrast, cases where the duty to make restitution has been rendered more stringent by superimposing a proprietary claim in the shape of a trust or a charge over assets in the hands of the defendant. These claims originated in equity. The grounds for granting such a proprietary relief remain controversial and are considered in Chapter 30.

1.2.7 Defences

In *Lipkin Gorman* v *Karpnale Ltd* [1991] 2 AC 548 Lord Goff asserted (at 578):

> The recovery of money in restitution is not, as a general rule, a matter of discretion for the court. A claim to recover money at common law is made as a matter of right; and even though the underlying principle of recovery is the principle of unjust enrichment, nevertheless, where recovery is denied, it is denied on the basis of legal principle.

Where the claimant has made out a successful prima facie cause of action the defendant may still be able to defeat or diminish that claim by relying upon on one of the established restitutionary defences. It is no defence that the payee of money honestly believed that he was entitled to the benefit received. Such a broad defence would contradict the underlying principle of unjust enrichment. Honest receipt was authoritatively rejected by the House of Lords in *Kleinwort Benson Ltd* v *Lincoln City Council* [1999] 2 AC 349, at 384–85 *per* Lord Goff of Chieveley. The two main defences grounded on principle are good faith purchase, which wholly extinguishes a restitutionary claim, and good faith change of position, which may diminish or extinguish such a claim. Both defences were recognised in the landmark case of *Lipkin Gorman* v *Karpnale Ltd* (above). Previously the development of defences in the law of restitution had proceeded in a haphazard way, in the shadow of doubts about the conceptual basis and unity of this substantive part of the subject.

Good faith purchase is of the utmost significance in the law of obligations as a whole, because it is one of the doctrines which marks the boundaries of the province of the law of contract and the law of restitution. It protects security of receipt and in particular indirect recipients who have received wealth under a valid and effective exchange and in good faith. For example, in *Lipkin Gorman* a solicitor had raided the client account to feed his addiction to gambling. The recipient casino had to disgorge to the firm its net winnings at his expense, because it had provided no lawful consideration for its receipt of stolen money. However, it is clear, that if the rogue had spent the money which he siphoned from the client account on an expensive foreign car at a showroom in nearby Park Lane, or at regular lunches at the Ritz, both the garage and the Ritz would be immune from actions in restitution as bona fide purchasers of stolen currency. Good faith purchase is also a manifestation of the principle that restitution has no role to play in respect of wealth passing under a valid and effective contract.

Good faith change of position protects the security of receipt of a person who is enriched, but whose circumstances change as a result of being benefited so that it would be inequitable to order restitution of some or all of the enrichment. Change of position may operate *pro tanto*, that is the diminution of the claimant's entitlement to recover is in proportion to the defendant's expenditure in reliance upon the receipt. The House of Lords in *Lipkin Gorman* first explicitly recognised the defence was a general one in the law of restitution, but left its boundaries to be decided on a case by case basis. In that case change of position reduced the defendant casino's liability to the net sums received taking into account winnings paid out, not the total sums gambled.

There are also a number of policy-motivated defences which are of immense practical significance: compromise, submission to an honest claim and limitation. More controversial are the suggested defences of estoppel, ministerial receipt and passing on. The first two of these may have been subsumed within change of position. The last-named supposed defence appears to be inconsistent with the basic premise of restitutionary relief. Lastly, illegality or public policy may preclude a restitutionary claim.

1.3 PERVASIVE THEMES

In addition to the structure of analysis discussed in the preceding section, Professor Birks in *An Introduction to the Law of Restitution*, also identified a number of recurring themes for the modern law. These themes have been developed in his subsequent writings. Some of them will be introduced here. First, Birks consistently argues that there is no analytical distinction between so-called direct and indirect recipients. Secondly, the unjust factors in relation to money and non-money claims should be the same. This is the imperative of symmetry. Thirdly, where a transaction is unwound in which each party has transferred benefits to the other, there should be mutual restitution. In such cases, there should be no restitution without counter-restitution.

1.3.1 Direct and indirect recipients

Does the law of restitution draw a sharp distinction between direct and indirect recipients of wealth? Suppose A pays B £100 by mistake and B subsequently transfers £100 to C. Can A elect to sue either B or C? In both cases there is an operative ground for restitution: the mistake indicates a defect in the integrity of the claimant's transmissive consent. If it can be shown that C was enriched at the expense of A, that is the £100 was identifiably derived from the wealth subtracted from A, there appears to be no reason why A could not elect to sue C instead of B, subject to rules ensuring that A cannot achieve double recovery. It is submitted that in the modern law of restitution there is in principle no difference between direct and indirect recipients as far as establishing a cause of action is concerned: Birks, 138–9; 445–7; Birks [1989] LMCLQ 296, at 306–8. A contrary view has been expressed

that the law of restitution (or at least a quasi-contractual component of it) is subject
to a privity restriction preventing recovery against remoter recipients. This is alluded
to in some older cases (see Winfield, 134–38, 161–62). However, the supposed
restriction is unsound and inconsistent with the principle against unjust enrichment.
For an example of such privity reasoning see *In Re J Leslie Engineers Co.
Ltd (in liquidation)* [1976] 1 WLR 292, at 299 *per* Oliver J; and compare Burrows,
at 45–54. The decision in the House of Lords in *Banque Financière de la Cité* v *Parc
(Battersea) Ltd* [1999] 1 AC 221 suggests that indirect recipients are equally
amenable to claims in unjust enrichment: Lord Steyn stigmatized as 'pure
formalism' an attempt to raise the indirect route of the money, by the interposition
of a third party, as a bar to recovery (at 227). Such privity reasoning has no home in
the modern law, whether in unjust enrichment or contract law.

While no distinction is drawn in principle, in practice recovery against remoter
recipients is difficult to achieve given two overlapping factors. First, returning to our
original example, if the transfer of £100 from B to C was pursuant to the terms of a
valid and binding contract, restitution has no role to play unless and until that
contract is set aside. Secondly, the indirect recipient will have the benefit of the
restitutionary defences of good faith purchase and good faith change of position (see
1.2.7). Good faith purchase is a total defence to a restitutionary claim for money
brought against an indirect recipient who has exchanged some value for the
enrichment received and did so without notice of any defects in the transferor's
intentions. If the transfer between B and C was a valid gift, C will be able to rely upon
the defence of good faith change of position to extinguish or diminish A's claim to
the extent that the money has been spent in reliance upon the receipt. In contrast,
restitutionary claims will succeed against remoter recipients in the following cases:

(a)   where the recipient is a volunteer;

(b)   where the recipient gave value in exchange for the enrichment, but that value
is worthless in the eyes of the law, as in *Lipkin Gorman* v *Karpnale Ltd* [1991] 2 AC
548;

(c)   where the recipient acted in bad faith or had notice of the circumstances
giving rise to the right to restitution.

1.3.2   Symmetry

The predominant role of money claims in the existing case law tends to marginalise
claims to non-money benefits. As will be seen in the next chapter, in the primitive
precursor to the modern law of restitution, namely the common law of quasi-
contract, there were different forms of action in respect of money and non-money
claims. In respect of money claims the courts had identified nominate grounds for
restitution, such as mistake, compulsion and failure of consideration. In contrast, in
respect of non-money claims there was little or no explicit reference to the relevant
unjust factor. Birks (at 7) argues that the grounds for restitution should be the same
whatever the species of benefit:

there is in reality a perfect theoretical symmetry between claims in respect of money and claims in respect of other subject-matter. The grounds for restitution are the same, whatever the benefit received by the defendant. However, non-money plaintiffs win more rarely because, even when equipped with a good ground for restitution, they often cannot establish that the defendant was enriched as unequivocally as though he had received money.

Birks's scheme, however, appears to envisage one possible asymmetrical pocket of case law. Where free acceptance operates as an unjust factor, it is solely concerned with non-money benefits. In the wake of this call for symmetry, much academic scholarship in the area of unjust enrichment is concerned with characterising and classifying the ground of restitution in non-money cases. The creative reinterpretation of older authority so that it can been accommodated within the modern structure is more prevalent in restitution than in other fields of law. Birks has subsequently criticised authorities such *Rover International Ltd* v *Cannon Film Sales Ltd* [1989] 1 WLR 912, which have treated money and non-money claims as though the underlying cause of action differs. See Birks (1992), 86–96 or Birks (1990) 2 JCL 227. The courts in practice seem to concentrate upon the ground for restitution or unjust factor question. It does not negate the difficulties of enrichment which will obtain in respect of non-money benefits. These will be returned to below in 1.4.

1.3.3   No restitution without counter-restitution

Where a contract or other transaction is held to be ineffective there is the possibility that each party may have conferred benefits upon the other. A contract may be voidable because it was the result of misrepresentation or duress of one of the parties. Or the supposed contract may be void *ab initio* by reason of incapacity or public policy. The characteristic response of the modern law, once it has identified a ground for restitution such as mistake, compulsion or failure of consideration, is to effect mutual restitution. This is the regime imposed by statute in respect of frustrated contracts (Law Reform (Frustrated Contracts) Act 1943). Similarly the process of rescission developed both at common law and in equity in the context of pre-contractual representations. In older cases it was often stated that a bar to the remedy of rescission was that it was impossible to effect *restitutio in integrum*. Where the benefit conferred consists of money, counter-restitution in kind is always possible. However, where the benefit consists of goods or services issues of valuation may prove more difficult. In *Boyd & Forrest* v *Glasgow & South-Western Railway Company* [1915] SC (HL) 20, the House of Lords appeared to deny that the services could ever be restored. The more modern trend is not to insist on counter-restitution *in specie*, but to allow counter-restitution in money. Birks originally considered that counter-restitution impossible operated as a defence: Birks, 415–24. Birks argued (at 416): 'The crucial question is, therefore, whether the courts will allow pecuniary counter-restitution, to balance what cannot be returned *in specie*.'

The modern approach is best characterised by *O'Sullivan* v *Management Agency and Music Ltd* [1985] QB 428. A pop musician was entitled to rescind his management, publishing, service and recording agreements with the defendant companies on the ground of undue influence. The court ordered a complex restitutionary solution. The defendant had to account for profits, and to restore copyrights in materials and deliver up master tapes (subject to the rights of good faith purchasers). In return, the defendant companies were entitled to an allowance of reasonable remuneration, including a profit element for all the work done in promoting the plaintiff's career. Consider also *Cheese* v *Thomas* [1994] 1 WLR 129 (discussed in 32.4). Accordingly, it can be argued that the modern law and the position of Birks has moved from one which recognises a bar to relief based on counter-restitution to a modern principle of promoting mutual restitution. There should be no restitution, without counter-restitution. There remain some difficult authorities, such as *Guinness plc* v *Saunders* [1990] 2 AC 663, discussed by Birks, 'Restitution without counter-restitution' [1990] LMCLQ 330. The case is further discussed below at 12.2.

1.4   ENRICHMENT

The identification of an enrichment or benefit received by the defendant is a threshold question in the law of restitution. It draws a divide between the comparatively well-developed realm of money claims and the immature and sporadic authority on non-money claims. There is only one sophisticated judicial discussion of the topic. In *BP Exploration (Libya) Ltd* v *Hunt (No. 2)* [1979] 1 WLR 783, Robert Goff J observed (at 799):

> it is always necessary to bear in mind the difference between awards of restitution in respect of money payments and awards where the benefit conferred by the plaintiff does not consist of a payment of money. Money has the peculiar character of a universal medium of exchange. By its receipt, the recipient is inevitably benefited; and (subject to problems arising from such matters as inflation, change of position and the time value of money) the loss suffered by the plaintiff is generally equal to the defendant's gain, so that no difficulty arises concerning the amount to be repaid. The same cannot be said of other benefits, such as goods or services. By their very nature, services cannot be restored; nor in many cases can goods be restored, for example where they have been consumed or transferred to another. Furthermore the identity and value of the resulting benefit to the recipient may be debatable. From the very nature of things, therefore, the problem of restitution in respect of such benefits is more complex than in cases where the benefit takes the form of a money payment.

Money proves relatively unproblematic. Its receipt is always inevitably or incontrovertibly beneficial. More problematic are claims concerning the receipt of goods and services. Here the claimant is met by the argument of 'subjective devaluation': Birks, 109–14. Two famous Victorian judicial *dicta* summarise this problem. First, in *Taylor* v *Laird* (1856) 25 LJ Ex 329 Pollock CB famously observed (at 332): 'One cleans another's shoes, what can the other do but put them on?'

Secondly, and more forthrightly, in *Falcke* v *Scottish Imperial Insurance Co.* (1886) 34 Ch D 234, Bowen LJ stated (at 238): 'Liabilities are not to be forced upon people behind their backs anymore than you can confer a benefit upon man against his will.' Such personal preferences must be respected in a community which values personal autonomy. The enrichment issue in respect of goods and services received has to be resolved in a way which respects individual choice. Simple recourse to an objective test of value would negate the freedom to transact and would also result in serious tension with the principles and policy of the law of contract.

A number of ways of circumventing the individualistic argument of subjective devaluation have been proposed. Predominantly these are free acceptance (see 1.4.2) and incontrovertible benefit (see 1.4.3). The argument from subjective devaluation has now received recognition in the case law. In *Ministry of Defence* v *Ashman* [1993] 2 EGLR 102 and *Ministry of Defence* v *Thompson* [1993] 2 EGLR 107, the Court of Appeal allowed deserted forces' spouses to rely upon subjective devaluation to reduce claims for restitutionary damages for trespass. It should be noted that the argument was used in the context of restitution for wrongs, rather than subtractive unjust enrichment and that the argument from subjective devaluation did not extinguish a claim but only diminished it. For further discussion see 25.4. Distinct but related problems arise where the enrichment takes the form of discharge of a debt, or the discharge of an obligation of the defendant which he will have necessarily have incurred. Lastly, the defendant may have benefited by profiting from wrongdoing.

1.4.1 Request

Where the defendant has requested goods or services it will usually be concluded that he is under a contractual obligation to pay for them. The fact that no price was agreed does not negate contractual responsibility. If there is an otherwise complete express contract for services but no price is specified, a reasonable charge is payable under statute (Supply of Goods and Services Act 1982, s. 15). Similarly, if there is an express contract for the sale of goods but the price is not determined by the parties, a reasonable price is payable (Sale of Goods Act 1979, s. 8). However, the arrangement may lack the necessary certainty for it to be held to be a valid contract. In such a case the request may still give rise to a claim in restitution for the goods and services rendered. For example, in *British Steel Corporation* v *Cleveland Bridge & Engineering Co. Ltd* [1984] 1 All ER 504, it was held that no valid bilateral or unilateral contract had been entered into for the supply of goods. The terms relating to the timing of delivery and the sequence of delivery were never agreed with sufficient certainty. Despite this, a request to manufacture and deliver gave rise to a restitutionary obligation to pay a reasonable sum.

In the modern law the request must be a genuine one which is explicit or obviously implicit. The history of the subject has been bedevilled by fictional uses of the word 'request'. In *Falcke* v *Scottish Imperial Insurance Co.* (1886) 34 Ch D 234, Bowen LJ stated that he abstained from 'using the word "request" more than is necessary, for fear of plunging myself into all the archaic embarrassments connected with the cases about requests' (at 249). Therefore it is necessary to tread carefully when alleging a request as the basis of a claim for the reasonable value of goods and services rendered. In practice, most cases where there is an explicit request are forced into the category of contract law.

1.4.2   Free acceptance

According to Goff and Jones (at 18):

> a defendant, who is not contractually bound, may have benefited from services rendered in circumstances in which the court holds him liable to pay for them. Such will be case if he *freely accepts* the services. In our view, he will be held to have benefited from services rendered if he, as a reasonable man, should have known that the plaintiff who rendered the services expected to be paid for them, and yet he did not take a reasonable opportunity open to him to reject the proffered services.

The same principle applies in respect of goods: Goff and Jones, 26. Similarly, Professor Birks states (at 114–15) the principle of free acceptance as a test of enrichment in a form which seems sympathetic to the people who clean motorists' windscreens uninvited at traffic lights:

> We have seen that free acceptance constitutes a ground for restitution, going to the word 'unjust'. For when a defendant has passed up an opportunity to reject a benefit knowing that it was not offered gratuitously he has only himself to blame for the resulting situation. But free acceptance also goes to the issue of enrichment. For it defeats the possibility of subjective devaluation. If I have stood by watching you clean my car knowing that you did not intend a gift, I cannot easily appeal to my right of free choice. For I made my choice when I had the opportunity to reject. If I did not want the car cleaned, I should have said so. A free acceptance therefore disables recourse to the argument from subjective devaluation.

This approach to the issue of enrichment has caused disquiet amongst some scholars. The onus is placed upon the defendant actively to refuse a benefit in such circumstances. Both Goff and Jones and Professor Birks believe that free acceptance satisfies both the enrichment and the ground for restitution stages of the enquiry. The latter question will be dealt with below in Chapter 15. Beatson has argued that pure services which result in no easily marketable end-product cannot properly be characterised as beneficial. Beatson instead proposes an 'exchange value test' of enrichment. In Beatson's view the adoption of the test of free acceptance leads to an 'over-inclusive concept of enrichment': Beatson, 'Benefit, Reliance and the Structure of Unjust Enrichment' (1987) 40 CLP 71; also in Beatson, 21–44. Burrows attacks the concept of free acceptance as establishing enrichment as a matter of principle. In his view the neglect of an opportunity to reject demonstrates no more than indifference to the benefit being proffered: Burrows, 'Free Acceptance and the Law of Restitution' (1988) 104 LQR 576, at 580; also in Burrows (1998), 72, at 77. Burrows argues instead for a 'bargained-for' principle of benefit. Birks has responded to his critics, defending free acceptance as an argument for resisting subjective devaluation: Birks, 'In Defence of Free Acceptance' in Burrows (1991), 105, at 127–43. To date free acceptance has not received explicit judicial recognition. It does, however, command the support of the two leading treatises. As a practical matter, Goff and Jones's advocacy of free acceptance as a test of enrichment should be immediately contrasted with its recognition of officiousness as a factor negativing the right to restitution: Goff and Jones, 63–65. Contrast Birks, who is sceptical as to whether there is any need for a limiting principle of officiousness in the law of restitution: Birks, 102–3.

1.4.3 Incontrovertible benefit

According to Goff and Jones (at 22):

> There is much to be said for the view that a person has been incontrovertibly benefited if a reasonable person would conclude that he has been saved an expense which he otherwise would necessarily have incurred or where he has made, in consequence of the plaintiff's acts, a realisable financial gain.

Birks similarly adopts the concept of incontrovertible benefit, proposing the test that no reasonable man would attempt recourse to the argument from subjective devaluation on the facts: Birks, 116–21. Birks, prefers a *realised* in money test to Goff and Jones's *realisable* test: Birks, 121–24.

It might be thought that the argument of incontrovertible benefit would be equally as controversial as the test of free acceptance. The latter at least looks at the conduct, or absence of conduct, of the defendant to justify overriding subjective devaluations. In contrast, incontrovertible benefit adopts a more direct objective approach. This is said to be justified in two cases. First, the saving of a necessary expense. Secondly, the retention by the defendant of a realised or realisable financial benefit. These instances of enrichment appear to be generally accepted. In addition, they appear to be the only explanation of a number of leading cases in the law of restitution. For example, the purchaser of a stolen car who carried out improvements in the mistaken, but honest, belief that he was the owner was held to be entitled to an award in respect of the work done (*Greenwood* v *Bennett* [1973] QB 195: see 3.11.2 below). This now has partial statutory recognition under s. 6 of the Torts (Interference with Goods) Act 1977. Similarly, a plaintiff who supposed himself to be managing director of a company, but whose underlying contract of employment was void, was entitled to reasonable remuneration for services rendered (*Craven-Ellis* v *Canons Ltd* [1936] 2 KB 403: see 12.3 below). In *China Pacific SA* v *Food Corporation of India, The Winson* [1982] AC 939, salvors were held entitled to reimbursement from the cargo owners for expenses incurred in preserving the cargo (see Chapter 9).

In *Proctor & Gamble Philippine Manufacturing Corp.* v *Peter Cremer GmbH & Co., The Manila* [1988] 3 All ER 834, Hirst J accepted in principle the test of incontrovertible benefit as advocated by Goff and Jones, although he further held that the facts did not justify a finding of enrichment. Buyers under an international sales contract had paid additional sums to ensure the shipment of a cargo from the Philippines to Rotterdam, after the shipowner had become insolvent. Subsequently, when the vessel arrived in Rotterdam the buyers rejected the cargo and terminated the contract. The sellers were held liable to refund the buyers the price of the goods, but were not liable to reimburse the buyers for the additional freight paid to the shipowner. Hirst J rejected an argument that the sellers were saved the expense of shipping the cargo to Europe where it was more saleable than at the port of embarkation.

1.4.4 Positive and negative benefits

The first limb of incontrovertible benefit, the saving of necessary expense, demonstrates that restitution encompasses negative benefits as well as positive accretions to the defendant's wealth. The Court of Appeal case of *Phillips* v *Homfray* (1883) 24 Ch D 439 was once understood to deny that restitution could extend to negative benefits: Birks, 129. However, the better view is that the court in *Phillips* v *Homfray* was not concerned with the general question of whether enrichment extended to both positive and negative benefits, but was concerned with the narrower (and now obsolete) question of what types of action could survive against the estate of a deceased person during the currency of the old *actio personalis moritur cum persona* rule: Meagher, in Finn, at 60–67; Birks, 'Civil Wrongs — A New World', *Butterworths Lectures 1990–1991* (1992), at 64–67. For detailed discussion see Chapter 25. In any event the cases where the enrichment takes the form of the discharge of a debt (see 1.4.5) or other obligation of the defendant clearly exemplify that restitution can extend to negative as well as positive benefits. The existence of negative enrichments also seems to have been assumed in the recent decision of the House of Lords in *Banque Financière de la Cité* v *Parc (Battersea) Ltd* [1999] 1 AC 221.

1.4.5 Discharge of debt

A defendant can be enriched by the discharge of a debt or other obligation which he owes to a third party, by a payment or other performance by the claimant; but discharge does not follow automatically. According to Goff and Jones (at 16–17):

> The defendant may also benefit if money is paid not to him but to a third party, to his use. But at common law he will only benefit if the plaintiff's payment discharges the debt which he owes to a third party. It is not easy to discharge another's debt in English law. This will occur only if the debtor authorised, or

subsequently ratified, the payments. There are few exceptions to this principle, which appears to be of little merit now that debts are freely assignable.

The general rule is that a payment by the claimant operates to discharge the defendant's indebtedness, and accordingly enrich the defendant, only if the payment is made by the claimant with the actual or apparent authority of the defendant, or if the defendant subsequently ratifies the payment. Therefore, a bank which mistakenly paid money to an apparent creditor of one of its customers, ignoring its customer's instructions to the contrary, did not discharge its customer's indebtedness to a third party (*Barclays Bank Ltd* v *W. J. Simms, Son & Cooke (Southern) Ltd* [1980] QB 677). In contrast, where a bank mistakenly makes a payment with the actual or apparent authority of the customer, the indebtedness of the customer is discharged (*Lloyds Bank plc* v *Independent Insurance Co. Ltd* [1999] 2 WLR 986). The case of *B. Liggett (Liverpool) Ltd* v *Barclays Bank Ltd* [1928] 1 KB 48, which appears to assume automatic discharge in the situation, must be wrong.

There are only a few exceptions to the need to demonstrate authority or subsequent ratification. These include payments made under legal compulsion or in circumstances of necessity, which have also been held effective to discharge the debt (*Owen* v *Tate* [1976] QB 402). For a sophisticated analysis, see Birks and Beatson, 'Unrequested Payment of Another's Debt' (1976) 92 LQR 188; also in Beatson, 177–205. It has been argued that the authorities and principle favour a rule of automatic discharge: Friedmann, 'Payment of Another's Debt' (1983) 99 LQR 534; Burrows, 222–30. However, as positive law currently stands, a debt can only be said to be discharged in five situations:

(a)   a payment with actual or apparent authority;

(b)   subsequent ratification by the debtor;

(c)   in circumstances where the claimant is legally compellable in addition to the defendant to pay the debt;

(d)   where the payment was reasonably necessary for the benefit of the defendant; and

(e)   where there is some community of interest between the claimant and the defendant in respect of property.

For further discussion see Chapter 20.

1.4.6   Profiting from wrongdoing

In the 'restitution for wrongs' branch of restitution, the enrichment consists of profits from wrongdoing. To date, there is still little sophisticated discussion or analysis of this in either the case law or the juristic writings. As a matter of principle, it seems clear that the following must be demonstrated:

(a)   the defendant has committed a wrong, in a sense of a breach of a primary legal duty owed to the claimant;

(b) the defendant has profited as a result of his breach of duty owed to the claimant.

It is in this way that the claimant demonstrates that the enrichment has been received at his expense, in the sense of by a wrong done to him.

It can be easily envisaged that demonstrating a sufficient causal link between the breach of duty and the resulting benefit may be controversial in some cases. The majority of the case law to date concerns defendants in a fiduciary or confidential relationship, and it has been rather readily assumed that the breach of duty was the occasion for profiting. In some cases, the apparent harshness of this has been mitigated by the provision of an equitable allowance for the skill and effort of the fiduciary in making the profit for which he has to account over to the claimant (*Boardman* v *Phipps* [1967] 2 AC 46; *O'Sullivan* v *Management Agency and Music Ltd* [1985] QB 428). This approach overlaps with the principle of no restitution without counter-restitution (see 1.3.3 above). For discussion, see Goff and Jones, 33–36. The causation issue may arise with greater poignancy if there is an expansion of the availability of restitutionary damages for breach of contract. It may be asked whether a more stringent causal test should be applied where the defendant is in neither a fiduciary nor a confidential relationship. In addition to the threshold causation question, Birks has stated that 'there is a need, as yet unsatisfied, for rules of remoteness of gain' (at 351). While the principles are immature, it can be concluded that there are three factors which potentially limit the enrichment received by a wrongdoer:

(a) it may be impossible to demonstrate a sufficient causal link;

(b) by analogy with the remoteness test in the tort of negligence, it may be thought that certain gains are too remote from the initial breach of duty; and

(c) where the defendant is not guilty of fraud or bad faith, the court may make an allowance for his work and skill in creating the profits.

For discussion see Birks, 351–55.

It should also be observed in the light of *Ministry of Defence* v *Thompson* [1993] 2 EGLR 107 that the argument from subjective devaluation may be relied upon by a non-cynical wrongdoer to diminish the amount of a claim for restitutionary damages arising from wrongdoing. See below at 25.4.

FURTHER READING

Asterisks indicate especially useful works.

The principle of unjust enrichment

*Goff and Jones, 11–15
*Birks, 1–27

American Law Institute, *Restatement of the Law of Restitution: Quasi-Contracts and Constructive Trusts* (St Paul, 1937)

Winfield, 116–89

Lord Wright (1937) 51 Harv LR 383

Seavey and Scott, 'Restitution' (1938) 54 LQR 29

P. Winfield, 'The American Restatement of the Law of Restitution' (1938) 45 LQR 529

W. Holdsworth, 'Unjustifiable Enrichment' (1939) 55 LQR 37

R. Goff, 'Reform of the Law of Restitution' (1961) 24 MLR 85

A. Burrows, 'Contract, Tort and Restitution — A Satisfactory Division or Not?' (1983) 99 LQR 217

S. Hedley, 'Unjust Enrichment as the basis of Restitution — An overworked concept' (1985) 5 *Legal Studies* 57

P. Birks, 'Unjust Enrichment — A Reply to Mr Hedley' (1985) 5 *Legal Studies* 67

G. Jones, 'A Topography of the Law of Restitution' in Finn, 1

L. Smith, 'The Province of the Law of Restitution' [1992] Can Bar Rev 673

S. Hedley, 'Unjust Enrichment' [1995] CLJ 578

S. Hedley, 'Restitution: Contract's Twin?' in Rose (1997), 247–74

A. Burrows, 'Understanding the Law of Restitution: A Map Through the Thicket' (1995) 18 UQLJ 149; also in Burrows (1998), 45–71

A. Burrows, 'Restitution: Where do We Go From Here?' in Burrows (1998), 99–119

*P. Birks, 'Misnomer' in Cornish, 1–29

G. Virgo, 'What is the Law of Restitution About?' in Cornish, 305–29

W. Swadling, 'What is the Law of Restitution About?: Four Categorical Errors' in Cornish, 331–37

Enrichment

*Goff and Jones, 16–36

*Birks, 108–32

*J. Beatson, 'Benefit, Reliance and the Structure of Unjust Enrichment' (1987) 40 CLP 71; also in Beatson, 21–44

*A. Burrows, 'Free Acceptance and the Law of Restitution' (1988) 104 LQR 576; also in Burrows (1998), 72–98

M. Garner, 'The role of subjective benefit in the law of unjust enrichment' (1990) 10 OJLS 42

*P. Birks, 'In defence of free acceptance' in Burrows (1991), 105, 127–46

A. Simester, 'Unjust free acceptance' [1997] LMCLQ 103

S. Stoljar, 'Unjust enrichment and unjust sacrifice' (1987) 15 MLR 603

D. Byrne, 'Benefits for services rendered' in McInnes, 87

At the expense of

Goff and Jones, 37–41

Birks, 132–39

L. Smith, 'Three-party restitution: a critique of Birks's theory of interceptive subtraction' (1991) 11 OJLS 481

A. Tettenborn, 'Lawful Receipt — A Justifying Factor?' [1997] RLR 1–12

Grounds for restitution

Goff and Jones, 41–46, 73–75

P. Birks, 'The independence of restitutionary causes of action' (1990) 16 UQLJ 1

*P. Birks, 'The Law of Restitution at the End of an Epoch' (1999) 28 W Ans L Rev 13

Defences and limits upon restitutionary claims

Goff and Jones, 46–72

Birks (1992), 123–47

P. Birks in Birks (1995), 322–48

2 The Legacy of History: Restitutionary Techniques at Common Law and in Equity

2.1 THEORETICAL FOUNDATIONS

The underlying principle of the law of restitution is that a person who has been unjustly enriched at the expense of another is required to restore the value of the benefit received to the other (compare *Restatement of the Law of Restitution: Quasi Contracts and Constructive Trusts*, American Law Institute (1937), §1). In respect of the branch of the subject which concerns restitution in response to wrongdoing, a second principle underlies recovery, namely that a person is not permitted to profit by his own wrong at the expense of another (compare *Restatement*, §3). These principles clearly have their roots in moral philosophy. This does not detract from their usefulness as organising principles for instances of recovery in the law of restitution. The principles are no more vague than the injunction that bargains should be upheld, which underpins the law of contract, or the neighbour principle in the tort of negligence. The principles afford no licence to a judge to follow his own moral convictions or to attempt to achieve natural justice. They are fleshed out by the instances of recovery in the decided cases. The principle of unjust enrichment has been entrenched as the general theory since *Lipkin Gorman* v *Karpnale Ltd* [1991] 2 AC 548, but it has not always held sway. In the eighteenth century Lord Mansfield had recognised a principle akin to unjust enrichment as underpinning the action for money had and received. In *Moses* v *Macferlan* (1760) 2 Burr 1005, at 1012, 97 ER 676, he famously observed: 'In one word, the gist of this kind of action is, that the defendant, upon the circumstances of the case is, obliged by the ties of natural justice and equity to refund money.'

Such 'generalities' attracted the scorn of early twentieth-century judges such as Hamilton LJ in *Baylis* v *Bishop of London* [1913] 1 Ch 127 and Scrutton LJ in *Holt* v *Markham* [1923] 1 KB 504. The latter scornfully observed (at 513): 'the whole history of this particular form of action has been what I may call a history of well-meaning sloppiness of thought.' Perhaps fearing that too large a generalisation would upset settled law, such judges clung to the notion that the basis of the obligation in restitution was implied contract or implied promise. Such was the emphatic opinion of Lord Sumner (as Hamilton LJ became) in *Sinclair v Brougham* [1914] AC 389, the leading early twentieth-century House of Lords case which stunted the development of a coherent law of restitution for the next 50 years. The implied contract fallacy, which necessitated the bizarre pretence that the thief of money impliedly promised to repay it, had apparently deep roots in Roman Law and the old system of pleading.

Only in *Westdeutsche Landesbank Girozentrale* v *Islington London Borough Council* [1996] AC 669 was the fiction eventually rejected. Lord Browne-Wilkinson asserted (at 710):

> Subsequent developments in the law of restitution demonstrate that this reasoning is no longer sound. The common law restitutionary claim is based not on implied contract but on unjust enrichment: in the circumstances the law imposes an obligation to repay rather than implying an entirely fictitious agreement to repay.... In my judgment, your Lordships should now unequivocally and finally reject the concept that the claim for moneys had and received is based on an implied contract. I would overrule *Sinclair v Brougham* on this point.

Nevertheless, given the abstraction of the underlying principle, Lord Wright's comment on Lord Mansfield's statement of principle is instructive: 'Like all large generalizations, it has needed and received qualification in practice' (*Fibrosa Spolka Akcyjna* v *Fairbairn Lawson Combe Barbour Ltd* [1943] AC 32, at 62). In some respects the cautious conclusion of Lord Diplock in *Orakpo* v *Manson Investments Ltd* [1978] AC 95, at 104, still represents an accurate statement of English law: 'there is no general doctrine of unjust enrichment recognised in English law. What it does is to provide specific remedies in particular cases of what might be classified as unjust enrichment in a legal system that is based upon the civil law.'

Contrast the view of the High Court of Australia, where unjust enrichment was described by Deane J in *Pavey & Matthews Pty Ltd* v *Paul* (1987) 162 CLR 221 as follows (at 256–57):

> It constitutes a unifying legal concept which explains what the law recognizes, in a variety of distinct categories of case, an obligation on the part of a defendant to make fair and just restitution for a benefit derived at the expense of the plaintiff and which assists in the determination, by the ordinary processes of legal reasoning, of the question whether the law should, in justice, recognize such an obligation in a new or developing category of case.

The implied contract fiction has now been jettisoned in England. Accordingly, restitution is now capable of developing and adapting to meet new situations and new modes of transacting. As Sir Donald Nicholls V-C observed in *CTN Cash and Carry*

Ltd v *Gallaher* [1994] 4 All ER 714, at 720, 'The categories of unjust enrichment are not closed'. (See Goff and Jones, 5–11.)

Sometimes it is suggested that English law should recognise a generalised right to restitution. It is not always easy to discern what this call involves, although it appears to be a suggestion that once a defendant has been enriched at the expense of the claimant, there must presumptively be restitution unless the defendant can affirmatively prove some legal justification for retaining the benefit. Such is the approach of some civil law systems. However, it is submitted that it is still necessary and desirable for the claimant affirmatively to prove some unjust factor or ground for restitution which entitles him to relief. It is a general rule of English law that he who asserts must prove. A presumption in favour of restitution would be detrimental to the public interest in the stability of transactions and the security of receipt. It would encourage speculative and wasteful litigation.

2.2   HISTORICAL FOUNDATIONS

In *Moses* v *Macferlan* (1760) 2 Burr 1005, at 1012, 97 ER 676, Lord Mansfield, the Chief Justice of the King's Bench, describing the action for money had and received, stated:

> it lies for money paid by mistake; or upon a consideration which happens to fail; or for money got through imposition (express or implied); or extortion; or oppression; or an undue advantage taken of the plaintiff's situation, contrary to laws made for the protection of persons under those circumstances.

This taxonomy is substantially similar to any modern list of grounds for restitution. Therefore by the mid-eighteenth century much of the modern law of restitution was already in place, in the form of a body of common law doctrine usually termed quasi-contract. This name, and the implied contract theory upon which it was supposedly based, owes much to the circumstance that after *Slade's Case* (1602) 4 Coke 92 b, 76 ER 1074 actions in what we would now describe as contract and restitution, were both brought utilising the form of action called *assumpsit*. The forms of action were the nominate sequence of writs which entitled the plaintiff to a remedy if he could bring his case within the parameters of a particular form. This old-fashioned system of pleading was abolished by the Common Law Procedure Act 1852. However, this primitive system of pleading had formed the organising categories in legal thought for centuries. As Birks has recently written (in Cornish, 2–3):

> When the scaffolding provided by the forms of action was knocked away in the nineteenth century, the common law had not yet prepared the rational structures necessary for stability. Much as some crabs scuttle into a crevice while a new shell hardens, it found temporary security in tighter respect for precedent.

As regards the new intellectual framework for organising the disparate body of legal material, some subjects faired better than others. For example, it was contemporaneous with Victorian procedural reforms that the first modern treatises on the law of contract began to be written and the subject was taught in the emerging university law schools. It was at this stage that quasi-contract, with its common procedural heritage and fictional promises and requests, was hived off as an appendix to the law of genuinely consensual transactions. It was not until the 1930s with the publication of Winfield's *The Province of Law of Tort* (1931), especially at 116–89, and the *Restatement of the Law of Restitution: Quasi Contracts and Constructive Trusts* (1937) by the American Law Institute that modern discussion of the subject began. As far as English law is concerned, the two landmarks of the second half of the twentieth century were the publication of Goff and Jones's magisterial account of precedent, *The Law of Restitution* (1966), and of Peter Birks's classic of analytical jurisprudence, *An Introduction to the Law of Restitution* (1985). On the judicial front, in the 1990s doctrine came full circle with the acceptance of the principle of unjust enrichment in *Lipkin Gorman* v *Karpnale Ltd* [1991] 2 AC 548 and the rejection of the implied contract heresy in *Westdeutsche Landesbank Girozentrale* v *Islington London Borough Council* [1996] AC 669.

2.3   *IN PERSONAM* AND *IN REM*

A foundational distinction in civil law is between *obligation* and *ownership*. An obligation or right *in personam* is a claim against a person. In contrast, a claim to ownership or a right *in rem* is a claim to an interest in a thing, which depends upon the continued existence of that thing. Therefore if A agrees to buy B's car for £1,000 we can distinguish between A's claim against B for compensation for non-delivery of the car which is a *personal* right, and a claim by A against B for delivery of the car, which is a *real* claim. Claims for the return of property which has been lost or stolen are not within the province of the law of restitution. Such claims are analytically within the law of property, although traditionally handled by English law via tortious remedies for interference with rights. In contrast, most claims in the law of restitution are personal claims. Usually property has passed in the money or property which has been transferred to the defendant. The claim is a personal one which, if successful, results in judgment in debt correlating to the value by which the defendant has been unjustly enriched.

However, the law has occasionally permitted restitutionary proprietary claims, whereby the claimant succeeds in demonstrating that not only has the defendant been unjustly enriched at his expense, but that the defendant remains unjustly enriched at his expense through the retention of money or other property which represents the value subtracted from him. The advantage of pursuing an *in rem* claim of this nature, is potentially two-fold. First, the claimant will be a secured creditor in the event of the defendant's insolvency. Secondly, in some circumstances, the asset in question may have increased in value. A restitutionary proprietary claim results in the judgment granting an interest in an asset or assets of the claimant usually by way of trust or charge. The basis for permitting and recognising such *restitutionary proprietary claims* remains controversial. They are, however, to be distinguished from *pure proprietary claims* which belong with the law of property and are outside the boundaries of the law of unjust enrichment. A defendant is not enriched by receiving or retaining property which the law recognises as belonging to the claimant. A claim for its return is purely proprietary.

2.4   COMMON LAW AND EQUITY

The component of the law of restitution traditionally known as quasi-contract, which developed at common law, constitutes the foundations of most of the modern law. However, techniques also developed in equity for reversing unjust enrichment; but it was not until the publication of the *Restatement* in the United States or of *Goff and Jones* in England that the two components of the modern law were systematically analysed alongside each other. The situation was neatly encapsulated by Lord Wright in *Fibrosa Spolka Akcyjna* v *Fairbairn Lawson Combe Barbour Ltd* [1943] AC 32, where he said (at 64): 'In fact, the common law still employs the action for money had and received as a practical and useful, if not complete or ideally perfect, instrument to prevent unjust enrichment, aided by the various methods of technical equity which are also available.'

Despite the passing of the Judicature Act 1873, fusing the administration of law and equity, restitution has been hampered by continuing asymmetry between the differing approaches of common law and equity to particular problems. For historical reasons, equitable techniques have been more commonly employed where wealth has gone astray at the instance of a recalcitrant fiduciary, such as a trustee or company director, or where trust funds or corporate assets have been dissipated. The tension between competing strategies and the possibility of inconsistent results is one of the major problems faced by the modern law: see Beatson, 244–58. It is still necessary to introduce separately the common law forms of action and the devices of technical equity which are still employed either directly or by analogy in modern case law.

2.5   QUASI-CONTRACT

First, this has nothing to do with the law of genuinely consensual bargains. It was at one stage fashionable to distinguish between 'implied contracts in facts' and 'implied contracts in law'. The former encompassed situations where the courts, employing the objective approach, discerned a genuinely consensual contract in the acts or performance of the parties, without any explicit contractual intention being voiced. Such cases belong in the province of the law of contract. For a recent example consider *G. Percy Trentham Ltd* v *Architral Luxfer Ltd* [1993] 1 Lloyd's Rep 25. The latter category, of implied contracts in law, involved cases where the promise was entirely fictional. These are now the common law components of the law of restitution. Historically they utilised the same form of action as genuinely consensual contracts, namely *assumpsit* ('he undertook') and in particular the writ of *indebitatus assumpsit* ('having become indebited he promised to pay'). In *Fibrosa* v *Fairbairn* [1943] AC 32, Lord Wright stated (at 63):

> The writ of *indebitatus assumpsit* involved at least two averments, the debt or obligation and the assumpsit. The former was the basis of the claim and was the real cause of action. The latter was merely fictitious and could not be traversed, but was necessary to enable the convenient and liberal form of action to be used in such cases. This fictitious assumpsit or promise was wiped out by the Common Law Procedure Act 1852.

Therefore in quasi-contractual cases the plea of the promise was entirely fictional and could not be denied by the defendant. Four sub-categories of *indebitatus assumpsit* were employed in situations we would now classify as being concerned with reversing unjust enrichment:

    (a)   the action for money had and received;
    (b)   the action for money paid;
    (c)   *quantum meruit*; and
    (d)   *quantum valebat*.

In respect of the last two, these species of *indebitatus assumpsit* replaced earlier nominate writs of *quantum meruit* and *quantum valebat*.

2.5.1   Action for money had and received

This was the core of quasi-contract, being a common law, personal action which lay only to recover money (*Nightingal* v *Devisme* (1770) 5 Burr 2589, 98 ER 361). As such it forms the core of the modern law of restitution and is the branch where the courts have been most explicit about the unjust factor or ground for restitution. The five principal situations in which action for money had and received was employed were:

    (a)   money paid under a mistake;
    (b)   money paid under compulsion;
    (c)   money paid where there was a failure of consideration;
    (d)   in situations where the plaintiff was permitted to employ the device of waiver of tort, whereby he could recover the benefits received by a tortfeasor, rather than claim compensation for loss; and
    (e)   where the plaintiff could trace money at common law into the hands of the defendant, usually an indirect recipient.

Since the Victorian procedural reforms there is no need to plead the fictional promise. Further, the ancient restriction to money would no longer apply today and, as long as problems of enrichment were overcome, an action for restitution would apply in respect of the non-money benefits by analogy with the old action for money had and received.

2.5.2   Action for money paid

This was a common law, personal form of action. It lay where a plaintiff paid money to a third party resulting in the defendant's benefiting because his debt to that third party was discharged by the payment. It lay only where the plaintiff and defendant were liable to a common claimant, in circumstances where the defendant was primarily liable for the debt. Therefore it was a pre-condition of recovery that the plaintiff was legally compellable to make the payment and that the payment had the effect of discharging the defendant's debt. The action was thus concerned with enrichment in the shape of discharge of another's liability. The restriction to money paid to a third party could not be maintained in principle today. Further, it is an open question whether the right to recover should be extended to circumstances where a claimant pays or transfers benefits, not because of any legal compulsion, but as a result of reasonably necessary intervention in the defendant's affairs. Before the Victorian procedural reforms, it was necessary to plead a request to make the payment by the defendant, but this was obviously fictional.

2.5.3   *Quantum meruit*

This was a common law, personal claim, meaning 'as much as he deserved', or, in modern parlance, 'reasonable remuneration'. The enrichment took the form of services rendered. It had both contractual and restitutionary manifestations. In *British Steel Corporation* v *Cleveland Bridge & Engineering Co.* [1984] 1 All ER 504 Robert Goff J said (at 509):

> A *quantum meruit* claim (like the old actions for money had and received and for money paid) straddles the boundaries of what we now call contract and restitution, so the mere framing of a claim as a *quantum meruit*, or a claim for a reasonable sum, does not assist in classifying the claim as contractual or quasi-contractual.

Contractual claims are now embodied in statute. If there is an otherwise complete express contract for services but no price is specified, a reasonable charge is payable (Supply of Goods and Services Act 1982, s. 15). As with the action for money paid, before the Victorian procedural reforms it was necessary to plead a request by the defendant. Claims in restitution for services rendered faced difficulties in establishing enrichment. Usually this could be demonstrated where the services were requested, freely accepted or incontrovertibly beneficial. The courts have been less explicit with regard to grounds for restitution in respect of claims for services rendered. However, there are instances of *quantum meruit* recovery which can be categorised as arising from mistake (*Craven-Ellis* v *Canons Ltd* [1936] 2 KB 403), necessity (*Rogers* v *Price* (1829) 3 Y & J 28, 148 ER 1080) and failure of consideration (*Rover International Ltd* v *Cannon Film Sales Ltd* [1989] 1 WLR 912).

2.5.4. *Quantum valebat*

This was a common law, personal form of action meaning 'as much as it was worth', or, in modern parlance, 'a reasonable price'. This is the appropriate form where the enrichment received is in the form of tangible personal property. It is less commonly encountered because *quantum meruit* is often used compendiously in respect of claims for work and materials (in this context often described as the common counts for work and materials). Similarly, the action 'straddles' contract and restitution. In an express contract for the sale of goods, if the price is not determined by the parties, a reasonable price is payable (Sale of Goods Act 1979, s. 8). Historically, a request had to be pleaded, but this was clearly fictional. There appear to have been quasi-contractual instances of recovery (e.g., *Sumpter* v *Hedges* [1898] 1 QB 673, in respect to the claim for the chattels). There is little explicit discussion in the case law of issues of enrichment and grounds for restitution. As with *quantum meruit* claims, enrichment will be established by demonstrating that goods were requested, freely accepted or incontrovertibly enriching. With regard to grounds for restitution, these should be symmetrical with the unjust factors developed in relation to money claims.

2.6 RESCISSION

Rescission is the process of setting aside and unwinding a contract or other transaction, where the integrity of the transferor's intent has been vitiated. It constitutes the paradigm restitutionary response to benefits transferred under apparently binding contracts, where the transferor's consent to the transaction is defective. It developed both at common law and in equity. Before the Judicature Act, for example, rescission was available at common law for misrepresentation, but only where there was proof of fraud. After the Victorian reforms it was the more liberal rules and flexible machinery of the courts of equity which were adopted and rescission is now available for a negligent or even wholly innocent misrepresentation (*Erlanger* v *New Sombrero Phosphate Co.* (1878) 3 App Cas 1218, *per* Lord Blackburn). The right to rescind or avoid a contract now extends to cases of duress, undue influence and mistake.

Where the transaction is wholly executory, rescission extinguishes the obligations which the parties have assumed. However, where there has been some performance of the transaction, rescission operates as a *restitutionary proprietary claim* under which there is mutual restitution of all the species of benefits: money, goods, land, and intangibles (including the rights of action created by the transaction itself). In *Newbigging* v *Adam* (1886) 34 Ch D 582, Bowen LJ stated (at 595):

> There ought, as it appears to me, to be a giving back and a taking back on both sides, including the giving back and taking back of the obligations which the

contract has created, as well as a giving back and the taking back of the advantages.

Therefore in relation to both executory and partly-executed or fully-executed transactions rescission is restitutionary in effect. In *Whittaker* v *Campbell* [1983] 3 All ER 582, Robert Goff LJ stated (at 586):

> Looked at realistically, a misrepresentation, whether fraudulent or innocent, induces a party to enter into a contract in circumstances where it may be unjust that the representor should be permitted to retain the benefit (the chose in action) so acquired by him. The remedy of rescission, by which the unjust enrichment of the representor is prevented, though for historical and practical reasons treated in books on the law of contract, is a straightforward remedy in restitution subject to limits which are characteristic of that branch of the law.

Rescission is, at least in theory, available as a self-help remedy, but ultimately it may require the support of a judicial order.

Rescission which operates retrospectively, by restoring benefits which have been transferred, is sometimes termed rescission *ab initio*, although it may not perfectly restore parties to their pre-transaction position. It should therefore be contrasted with termination in response to a breach of contract and discharge by frustration which operate prospectively only. Different considerations apply to restitution of benefits in respect of broken and frustrated contracts.

Traditionally there was some insistence that the restitution of benefits should be of precisely the same benefits as were originally transferred. It was said that there should be *restitutio in integrum*. That is, there was a rule that rescission would be allowed only where precise counter-restitution was possible. However, the courts were astute to do what was 'practically just' (*Erlanger* v *New Sombrero Phosphate Co.* (1878) 3 App Cas 1218, at 1279) and were particularly robust on the plaintiff's behalf where he was the victim of fraud (*Spence* v *Crawford* [1939] 3 All ER 271). There was even House of Lords authority suggesting that services could never be restored (*Boyd & Forrest* v *Glasgow & South-Western Railway Company* [1915] SC (HL) 20). More recently, both juristic writings and the courts have insisted upon the flexible nature of the remedy of rescission and there are suggestions that precise counter-restitution will not be insisted upon, but that there may be substitutionary counter-restitution (*O'Sullivan* v *Management Agency and Music Ltd* [1985] QB 428; *Smith New Court Securities Ltd* v *Citibank NA* [1997] AC 254, at 262 *per* Lord Browne-Wilkinson).

2.7   TRACING AND CLAIMING

The majority of restitution claims concern direct recipients of subtracted benefits or profiteering wrongdoers. In such cases the 'enrichment' and 'at the expense of' stages of the enquiry are satisfied by applying common-sense rules on benefit and causation. More complicated cases occur where the claimant's wealth passes through several hands, or the value subtracted from him is now to be found in a new form. Claims against remoter recipients or to a new repository of the claimant's wealth are often made and a sophisticated regime obtains in respect of them. Both juristic and judicial authority now insist on sharply distinguishing *tracing* and *claiming*.

First, it is necessary to distinguish pure proprietary claims, where the claimant seeks to recover an asset belonging to him which still exists in its original form. These are part of the law of property, although usually they don tortious garments in the English courts. Thus, if I locate my stolen bicycle, my claim to be entitled to it is proprietary in nature. This is described as *following* in the terminology of Smith (at 6–10). In contrast, *tracing* is the process whereby the restitutionary claimant may identify wealth subtracted from him even though the original property has been exchanged with other assets. The essential concern is with substitutions. The reach of restitution is extended by recognising, somewhat artificially, that value derived from the claimant inheres in the product of the exchanges. Therefore, if the thief exchanges my stolen bicycle for £100 or for a video recorder, the law may regard the substituted asset as traceably derived from my wealth. Despite the artifice, tracing through substitutions of assets is permitted.

Sophisticated and (perhaps over-) technical rules and presumptions have been developed to identify value subtracted from a claimant in the hands of a potential defendant. Differing approaches were observable at common law and in equity, although the latter's approach was more liberal to claimants and tended to supersede the former in practice. However, tracing was neither a right, nor a remedy. It satisfied the identification threshold set by the 'enrichment' and 'at the expense of' inquiries. It could also identify the quantum of relief, whether value received or value surviving. It did not, however, complete the investigation. *Claiming* required a ground for restitution, and ultimately an election as to the measure and nature of relief. Tracing could support a *personal* claim either at law (money had and received) or in equity (so-called knowing receipt). More commonly the motive for tracing was to lay the foundation for a restitutionary *proprietary* claim, especially where the defendant was insolvent (in the shape of a constructive trust or equitable lien or charge). Therefore tracing assists the restitutionary claimant in more complicated cases to identify what has become of his assets in order ultimately to lay claim to them. For the distinction between tracing and claiming, see Smith (at 10–14).

In the leading judicial discussion of the distinction in *Boscawen v Bajwa* [1996] 1 WLR 328, Millett LJ observed (at 334–35):

> Tracing properly so-called, however, is neither a claim nor a remedy but a process. Moreover, it is not confined to the case where the plaintiff seeks a proprietary remedy; it is equally necessary where he seeks a personal remedy against the knowing recipient or knowing assistant. It is a process by which the plaintiff traces what has happened to his property, identifies the persons who have handled or received it, and justifies his claim that the money which they handled or received (and, if necessary, which they still retain) can properly be regarded as representing

his property. He needs to do this because his claim is based on retention by him of a beneficial interest in the property which the defendant handled or received. Unless he can prove this he cannot (in the traditional language of equity) raise an equity against the defendant or (in the modern language of restitution) show that the defendant's unjust enrichment was at his expense.... The plaintiff will generally be entitled to a personal remedy; if he seeks a proprietary remedy he must usually prove that the property to which he lays claim is still in the ownership of the defendant. If he succeeds in doing this the court will treat the defendant as holding the property on a constructive trust for the plaintiff and will order the defendant to transfer it in specie to the plaintiff.

Therefore in a *personal* claim for money received, the cause of action is constituted once the defendant receives the property. In contrast, where a restitutionary *proprietary* claim is made, the claimant must reach beyond the veil of receipt and demonstrate that the defendant remains enriched at his expense: that is, there is some identifiable asset in which value subtracted from him still inheres. The divergent common law and equitable techniques for tracing and claiming will now be considered.

2.7.1 Tracing and claiming at common law

Where money could be traced from the plaintiff into the hands of either a direct or indirect recipient who was not a bona fide purchaser for value, the plaintiff had a quasi-contractual, personal claim to recover in the form of an action for money had and received. The cause of action was constituted when it was demonstrated that money had reached the hands of the recipient. It did not have to be shown that money remained in the hands of the recipient. Where the recipient was a good faith purchaser the money passed into currency (*Miller* v *Race* (1758) 1 Burr 452, 97 ER 398). For a recent successful claim see *Lipkin Gorman* v *Karpnale Ltd* [1991] 2 AC 548. It is traditionally stated that the common law power to trace is defeated if the money was mixed with other money en route to the defendant recipient. However, it was possible at common law to trace value through a substitution of money for other assets (*Taylor* v *Plumer* (1815) 3 M & S 562, 105 ER 721). For a recent application see *Trustee of the Property of F. C. Jones & Sons Ltd* v *Jones* [1997] Ch 159. In practice tracing at common law is not often relied on, because of the more sophisticated approach of equity. The only claim available at common law was a personal judgment for money had and received. See Chapter 27.

2.7.2 Tracing in equity

The power to trace in equity aided a plaintiff in identifying benefits which had been subtracted from his assets into the hands of direct and indirect recipients. The plaintiff was entitled to trace through mixtures and substitutions, and sophisticated rules and presumptions were developed governing how the interests of competing claims to combined assets should be adjudicated. There were two essential pre-conditions before this power could be exercised:

(a)   the wealth must have been subtracted in circumstances which involved a breach of trust or other fiduciary relationship;
(b)   the plaintiff must have been able to establish a proprietary base.

In *Borden (UK) Ltd* v *Scottish Timber Products Ltd* [1981] Ch 25, Buckley LJ stated (at 46): 'It is a fundamental feature of the doctrine of tracing that the property to be traced can be identified at every stage of its journey through life.' According to Birks (at 379): 'If [the plaintiff] wishes to assert a right *in rem* to the surviving enrichment, the plaintiff must show that at the beginning of the story he had a proprietary right in the subject-matter, and that nothing other than substitutions or intermixtures happened to deprive him of that right *in rem*.'

It must be stressed that tracing is a power or technique, and not a cause of action in itself. Tracing may lead to a *personal* claim in equity, termed knowing receipt (although the need for knowledge is controversial), where the cause of action is complete once the value reaches the hands of the defendant recipient. Alternatively, where an asset can still be identified as representing the claimant's wealth, in the defendant's hands, a restitutionary *proprietary* claim may be sought. See generally Chapters 28 to 30.

2.7.3.   Constructive trust

By all odds the most important contribution of equity to the remedies for prevention of enrichment is the device we all know as the constructive trust. For the device Lord Mansfield deserves neither credit nor blame. It emerged from the fog of eighteenth-century equity and in its modern applications is much more recent than the remedy of quasi-contract. (Dawson, 26)

Dawson further identified the two different spheres in which constructive trusts have been recognised (at 32–33):

It should nevertheless be clear by now that the constructive trust in its modern form is a purely remedial device, aiming principally at the prevention of unjust enrichment. It has taken a place beside quasi-contract as a generalised remedy, giving specific rather than money restitution. It has contributed to the efficient and ingenious techniques reaching particular assets. It has contributed also an additional motive for prevention of enrichment, the motive compelling restitution of profit as a means of deterring wrongdoing.

Within *subtractive unjust enrichment* the constructive trust functions as a restitutionary *proprietary* claim which can be the result of a successful tracing exercise. In this context the English courts are moving towards the American position, voiced by Dawson, that the device is remedial rather than institutional: 'Where a person holding title to property is subject to an equitable duty to convey it to another on the ground that he would be unjustly enriched if he were permitted to retain it, a constructive trust arises.' (See *Restatement*, §160.) The recognition of a constructive trust with the claimant as beneficiary has two keys advantages: first, the claimant obtains priority over unsecured creditors in the event of the defendant's insolvency; secondly, if the trust property has increased in value the claimant is entitled to the profits. Further, within *restitution for wrongs*, constructive trusts are imposed for prophylactic reasons to force wrongdoers to disgorge their ill-gotten gains (*Attorney-General for Hong Kong* v *Reid* [1994] 1 AC 324). In this latter context the cause of action does not depend upon tracing, but breach of a legal duty arising in another category, usually fiduciary duty. See Chapter 30.

2.7.4   Equitable lien or charge

> The modern equitable lien as a device for accomplishing restitution is for the most part an off-shoot of the constructive trust. In its modern applications it is the end result of tracing. (Dawson, 34)

Whereas a consensual lien or charge is the right of a creditor to have a particular asset appropriated to the discharge of his debt, the equitable lien or charge identifies an asset in the hands of the defendant to which value belonging to the plaintiff has been contributed. The claimant is held entitled to a quantified interest or part-share of the assets. The remedy is more proportionate to the enrichment received by the defendant. Accordingly an equitable lien or charge is a restitutionary *proprietary* claim which entitles a restitutionary claimant to priority over unsecured creditors. Where the lien takes the form of a quantified interest it seems that the claimant will not be entitled to profits, but where the lien takes the form of a proportionate share in an unidentified asset, it seems the claimant is entitled to a proportionate share of any profits. The greater sensitivity or proportionality of the equitable lien has led to it being favoured in some recent authorities: for example, *Lord Napier and Ettrick* v *Hunter* [1993] AC 713. See Chapters 28 and 30.

2.7.5   Subrogation

Subrogation means substitution, or, using the favoured metaphor, stepping into the shoes of another. It is the transfer of a right of action from one party to another by operation of law. Whereas 'assignment' is the technique by which a right of action is transferred consensually, where the transfer results by operation of law it is termed 'subrogation'. The entitlement of the restitutionary claimant to enforce the right of action vested in him as a result of subrogation constitutes a restitutionary *proprietary* claim. For example, in indemnity insurance, where an insurer pays the insured following the occurrence of an insured event, the insurer is entitled to be subrogated to the position of the insured with respect to any claim the insured may have against any wrongdoer in respect of the event. Subrogation typically arises in respect of insurance, guarantees and invalid loans. See Chapter 22.

2.7.6   Resulting trusts

This is potentially an equitable restitutionary *proprietary* claim in the context of *substractive* unjust enrichment. Resulting trusts arise in many contexts, but there have been attempts in juristic writings to explain resulting trusts on unjust enrichments grounds: Birks, 57–64; Birks, 'Restitution and Resulting Trusts' in Goldstein (ed.), *Equity and Contemporary Legal Developments* (1992), at 335–73; compare Swadling, 'A New Role for Resulting Trusts' (1996) 16 *Legal Studies* 110. The potential for resulting trusts as a vehicle for restitution in response to unjust enrichment has been curtailed by the decision in *Westdeutsche Landesbank Girozentrale* v *Islington London Borough Council* [1996] AC 669. See Chapter 16.

2.8   CONCLUSION

> When we take all these remedies together the main source of our present difficulties becomes quite evident. It is the multiplicity of our procedural resources for prevention of unjust enrichment, a multiplicity which greatly exceeds those in any other legal system. But the multiplicity of remedies is complicated further by diversity of origins. Each remedy has come to us from a separate source, with its own mode of tradition. Each function is somewhat different and prevents enrichment by different means. (Dawson, 38–39.)

This embarrassment with remedial riches complicates claims of the modern law of restitution. Successful actions must be argued by reference to, and by analogy from, historically derived principles and techniques. However, it is likely that future years will see some rationalisation of the techniques needed. First, there is likely to be an elimination of inconsistency and overlap between the approaches of common law and equity, especially in the field of tracing. Secondly, the recognition that tracing is a process or means of identification should simplify the debate as to when it is appropriate, if ever, to award a restitutionary proprietary remedy. Thirdly, where possible antiquated and easily misunderstood language should be jettisoned in favour of the more analytically exact language of juristic writings and more recent judicial pronouncements.

FURTHER READING

Historical foundations

J. Baker, *An Introduction to English Legal History* 3rd edn (1990), 409–26
A. W. B. Simpson, *A History of the Common Law of Contract* (1987), 489–565
P. Atiyah, *The Rise and Fall of Freedom of Contract* (1979), 764–70

P. Birks, 'English and Roman Learning in *Moses* v *Macferlan*' (1984) 37 CLP 1

D. Ibbetson, *A Historical Introduction to the Law of Obligations* (1999), 263–293

Philosophical foundations

S. Hedley, 'Unjust Enrichment as the basis of Restitution — an overworked concept' (1985) 5 LS 56

K. Barker, 'Unjust Enrichment: Containing the Beast' (1995) 15 OJLS 457

N. McBride and P. McGrath, 'The Nature of Restitution' (1995) 15 OJLS 33

L. Ho, 'The Nature of Restitution — A Reply' (1996) 16 OJLS 517

Forms of action

J. Baker, *An Introduction to English Legal History*, 63–83

Birks, 29–39, 111–13

Birks (1992), 87–91

Winfield, 'The Province of the Law of Tort' (1931), 116–89

D. Ibbetson, 'Implied Contracts and Restitution: History in the High Court of Australia' (1988) 8 OJLS 312

Law and equity

J. Beatson, 'Unfinished Business: Integrating Equity' in Beatson, 244–58

P. Birks, 'Equity in the Modern Law: An Exercise in Taxonomy' (1996) 26 W Aus L Rev 1, esp. 1–25; 66–99

P. Birks, 'Equity, Conscience and Unjust Enrichment' (1999) 23 Melb Univ L Rev 1

Equitable techniques

Birks, 83–85, 90–91, 93–98, 171–73, 191–92, 389–93

G. Elias, *Explaining Constructive Trusts* (1990)

C. Mitchell, *The Law of Subrogation* (1994)

L. Smith, *The Law of Tracing* (1997)

R. Chambers, *Resulting Trusts* (1997)

Comparative law

B. Markesinis, W. Lorenz and G. Dannemann, *The German Law of Obligations — Volume I, The Law of Contracts and Restitution: A Comparative Introduction* (1997), 43–45, 710–816

Dawson, *Unjust Enrichment — A Comparative Analysis* (1951)

K. Zweigert and H. Kötz, *An Introduction to Comparative Law,* 3rd edn (1998), translated by T. Weir, 537–94

R. Zimmermann, *The Law of Obligations — Roman Foundations of the Civilian Tradition* (1996) 834–901

PART B

DEFECTIVE TRANSFERS

3 Mistake

3.1 THEORETICAL FOUNDATIONS

A person who transfers wealth to another because he is labouring under a mistake can argue that the other has been unjustly enriched at his expense. The rationale for recovery is that the transferor's apparent intention to benefit the other was defective because he was not apprised of all the material facts. He would not have made the transfer had he been aware of the true state of affairs. According to Birks, mistake belongs within non-voluntary transfer, as an example of vitiated intention (Birks, 146–73).

There have been attempts to assimilate mistake with the ground of recovery termed failure of consideration. See Matthews (1980) 130 NLJ 587–89; and Butler, in Finn, 87–124, 131–37. The former argues that in the majority of cases supposed contractual liability is the motive for payment, and when it transpires there is no such liability the consideration for the payment wholly fails. The latter argues that the basic principle for the recovery of mistaken payments is failure of the purpose for which the payment is made. This is to be judged by an objective assessment of the purposefulness or intentionality of the payment.

These arguments are, however, flawed, resulting in oversimplification. Sometimes recovery will be possible on either ground, especially where there is partial performance of void contracts. However, though they may overlap, often they do not. It is central to Birks's scheme that mistake involves *vitiation* of intention, whereas failure of consideration involves *qualification* of intention. A misprediction is not a qualifying mistake. If I pay money to a charity hoping that my good works will receive recognition, perhaps a knighthood, I cannot recover when my uncommunicated intentions are frustrated. However, if I specify the terms of my payment, perhaps my name on a new hospital wing, and those are accepted by the recipient, there is a conditional (and potentially reversible) transaction. Birks insightfully observes ((1990) 2 JCL 227, at 235): 'The typical claim for failure of consideration is … a misprediction with the element of risk-taking eliminated by the recipient's having accepted the basis of the transfer and hence its conditionality.'

Cases concerning mistaken payments of money constitute a significant concern of the law of restitution. Instances of recovery in cases of non-monetary benefits are more rare, and difficulties in satisfying the tests for enrichment require their separate treatment. A number of issues need to separated out. First, it is necessary to consider briefly recent arguments about the existence of a distinct cause of action in unjust enrichment termed 'ignorance'. Secondly, it is necessary to distinguish the wholly distinct regime where the mistaken transfer takes place pursuant to an apparently binding contract or similar dispositive act, which will be considered in the next chapter. Thirdly, for two centuries English law drew a significant distinction between mistakes of fact and mistakes of law. The former rendered a payment recoverable; the latter did not. That bifurcation has now been rejected in a landmark House of Lords case. However, mistakes of law still demonstrate some peculiar difficulties of their own. Lastly, given the liberality of the regime of recovery in respect of extra-contractual transfers, attention is necessarily shifted to the work of defences such as good faith purchase and change of position which protect security of receipt, and mitigate what might otherwise be a peril to the stability of transactions.

The leading academic discussion of the need to balance the definition of the underlying cause of action with appropriately drawn defences to provide for the social cost of mistakes employs a 'law and economics' methodology. Beatson and Bishop argue in 'Mistaken Payments in the Law of Restitution' (1987) 37 U of Toronto LJ 149–85 (also in Beatson 137–73), that an efficient test would be one that encouraged cost-effective precautions. Sutton agrees with Beatson and Bishop's conclusion but questions their methodology in 'Mistaken Payments: An Inner Logic Infringed?' (1987) 37 U of Toronto LJ 389–412. Sutton criticises the economic approach, and asserts the primacy of traditional legal scholarship. For Beatson's response see Beatson, 173–76.

3.2   MISTAKE AND IGNORANCE

Is recovery on the ground of mistake confined to situations where the transferor actively considered the factual and legal matrix surrounding the proposed transfer but reached the wrong conclusion, or does it extend to situations where no thought is given to the issue? The dictionary meaning of 'mistake' seems to encompass the wider view, including 'an error or blunder in action, opinion or judgment', 'a misconception or misunderstanding' and also 'to choose badly or incorrectly'. Consider two slightly different hypothetical examples. First, a clerk feeds incorrect information into a computer upon which basis payments are made. Secondly, a computer responsible for effecting payments is programmed correctly, but because of a malfunction makes incorrect distributions, of which its operators are blithely unaware.

Birks characterises mistake as limited to situations where some responsible human agent commits an error of deliberation in some active reasoning process. He therefore suggests that recovery on the ground of mistake should be supplemented by a cause of action which he terms 'ignorance', where the transferor is unaware that wealth is haemorrhaging from his assets: Birks 140–46 and [1989] LMCLQ 296. Mistake is an example of vitiated voluntary intent. In contrast, ignorance of the transfer evidences the *absence* of any transmissive consent. Birks accordingly argues that recovery on the ground of ignorance is *a fortiori* recovery based on mistake. This argument will be considered in Chapter 5. Further, it will recur and its impact will need to be considered elsewhere, in particular with regard to tracing cases and indirect recipients (see Chapters 27–29).

However, the need for a distinct category of ignorance has been doubted and the prevailing judicial view appears to be that mistake as recognised in the case law encompasses the wider common-sense view covering both instances of ignorance and of mistake (*David Securities Pty Ltd* v *Commonwealth Bank of Australia* (1992) 175 CLR 353, at 369, 374). In the leading House of Lords case on mistaken payments, *Kleinwort Benson Ltd* v *Lincoln City Council* [1999] 2 AC 349, Lord Hope of Craighead, citing *David Securities*, insisted (at 410): 'the concept of mistake includes cases of sheer ignorance as well as positive but incorrect belief.' Goff and Jones also reject the need for a separate category of ignorance: Goff and Jones, 175–77.

3.3 FACT AND LAW

3.3.1 Origins of the distinction

Until 1998 the law governing the recoverability of mistaken payments was dominated by the distinction between mistakes of fact, which prima facie grounded recovery, and mistakes of law, which did not. The line between the two was difficult to draw, proved malleable in practice and was finally abrogated by the House of Lords in the landmark case of *Kleinwort Benson Ltd* v *Lincoln City Council* [1999] 2 AC 349. The plaintiff bank and the defendant local authority entered into an interest rate swap agreement. Subsequently, in another case it was decided that such contracts were *ultra vires* and beyond the capacity of local authorities, and accordingly void. The transaction was fully performed. The bank sought restitution of the net sums paid under the transaction on the basis of a mistake, and sought to rely on s. 32(1)(c) of the Limitation Act 1980. Langley J held that he was bound by Court of Appeal authority to hold the mistake was one of law and accordingly irrecoverable. A leap-frog appeal was allowed to the House of Lords under s. 12 of the Administration of Justice Act 1969. The House of Lords by a majority held that the plaintiff could recover, although the mistake was one of law, abrogating the common law mistake of law bar. It made no difference that the transaction was fully performed, as opposed to partially performed. Accordingly the bank could rely on s. 32(1)(c) of the Limitation Act 1980. Time began to run once the bank discovered its mistake, which was not until the decision of the courts holding that such transactions were *ultra vires* and void.

There is now a unitary law of mistaken payments which can be shortly stated: a mistake which causes a transferor to make a payment is prima facie recoverable. The consequence is that much of the attention has switched to defences. However, before turning to the modern law the reasons for abrogating the traditional distinction between facts or law should be briefly examined. Evidence of the arbitrariness of the distinction is often sought by contrasting the decisions in the two leading early nineteenth-century authorities. In *Kelly* v *Solari* (1841) 9 M & W 54, 152 ER 24, an insurer paid out on a life policy overlooking the fact the policy had lapsed by reason of non-payment of a premium. The insurer was held entitled to restitution on the basis of mistake of fact. Compare *Bilbie* v *Lumley* (1802) 2 East 469, 102 ER 448, where an insurer met a claim on a marine policy, apparently unaware that the policy was voidable for the non-disclosure of a material letter relating to the time of the sailing of the vessel. The letter was in fact disclosed before the payment was made. The insurer claimed to recover the money on the express basis of mistake of law, namely that he was not aware at the time of payment that he had a complete defence of non-disclosure. The claim was summarily rejected.

The policy reasons for the old mistake of law bar were eloquently set out by Gibbs CJ in *Brisbane* v *Dacres* (1830) 5 Taunt 143, 128 ER 641. They are three-fold. First, floodgate fears that such a claim would be urged in every case ('there are many doubtful questions of law'; at 152). Secondly, the principle of finality which applies where the party has the choice to litigate the question or to submit to the demand. Accordingly any payment made in such circumstances operates to close the transaction between the parties. Thirdly, the interest in security of receipts, and in particular a desire to protect defendants who have changed their position upon the faith of a payment.

These are powerful arguments. However, they were ultimately rejected by the Law Commission (*Restitution: Mistakes of Law and Ultra Vires Public Authority Receipts and Payments*, Law Com. No. 227, 1994) and the House of Lords on the grounds of principle. First, the principle of unjust enrichment requires that where payment was made as a result of the payer's mistake, the money should be prima facie recoverable unless there were special circumstances to justify retention. Secondly, the distinction between fact and law was 'capricious'. Thirdly, this led to the development of numerous exceptions and qualifications which undermined the generality of the non-recovery rule. As a result of the difficulty of stating the law and the heterogeneous exceptions, the area of law was ripe for judicial manipulation to achieve practical justice, which had resulted in uncertainty and unpredictability for the application of the rule (*Kleinwort Benson Ltd* v *Lincoln City Council* [1999] 2 AC 349, at 370–72 *per* Lord Goff). The distinction between fact and law had been rejected in other jurisdictions (*Air Canada* v *British Colombia* (1989) 59 DLR (4th) 161 (Canada); *David Securities Pty Ltd* v *Commonwealth Bank of Australia* (1992) 175 CLR 353 (Australia) and *Morgan Guaranty Trust of New York* v *Lothian Mutual Council* [1995] SLT 299 (Scotland)) and its rejection in English law was long overdue. However, the facts and decision of the majority in the *Kleinwort Benson* case create particular difficulties concerning what constitutes a mistake of law, and these will need to be returned to below.

3.3.2 The former exceptions to the mistake of law rule

It is necessary briefly to review the former exceptions to the mistake of law rule. The abrogation of the rule may not be as significant in practice as some had anticipated, because of the large number of exceptions where recovery was allowed, before *Kleinwort Benson*.

First, it did not apply to payments made to or made by an officer of the court, such as a liquidator or a trustee in bankruptcy (*Ex parte James* (1874) LR 9 Ch App 609). Secondly, it did not apply to claims made by the beneficiaries after payments had been made by personal representatives or trustees under a mistake of law (*Re Diplock* [1948] Ch 465; [1951] AC 251). Thirdly, mistakes of foreign law were treated as mistakes of fact (*Lazard Brothers & Co. v Midland Bank Ltd* [1933] AC 289). Fourthly, the mistake of law rule was never stringently applied in equity (*Cooper v Phibbs* (1867) LR 2 HL 149; *Gibbon v Mitchell* [1990] 3 All ER 338). Fifthly, the courts were reluctant to categorise mistakes as being ones of law. For example, in *Cooper v Phibbs* (above), where the plaintiff mistakenly bought property which he already owned, the House of Lords granted restitution. They distinguished the general law and private rights of ownership. The latter were categorised as matters of fact. Sixthly, the mistake of law rule did not operate as a bar to recovery, but simply did not ground recovery. Accordingly, if a separate unjust factor could be established such as duress, recovery would follow despite the mistake of law (*Maskell v Horner* [1915] 3 KB 106; *Westdeutsche Landesbank Girozentrale v Islington London Borough Council* [1994] 4 All ER 890, at 933 *per* Hobhouse J). Seventhly, public authorities were not entitled to take advantage of the mistake of rule law when exercising a statutory discretion to award restitution (*R v Tower Hamlets London Borough Council ex parte Chetnik Developments Ltd* [1988] AC 858). Eighthly, the mistake of rule law did not apply where there was an unequal relationship between the parties, such that the plaintiff was not *in pari delicto* (*Kiriri Cotton Co. Ltd v Dewani* [1960] AC 192). For a full list of exceptions see Law Commission, *Restitution: Mistakes of Law and Ultra Vires Public Authority Receipts and Payments* (Law Com. No. 227, 1994), paras 2.5 to 2.15. As Lord Goff observed in *Kleinwort Benson Ltd v Lincoln City Council* [1999] 2 AC 349 (at 372): 'these exceptions and qualifications are heterogeneous and in truth betray an anxiety to escape from the confines of a rule perceived to be capable of injustice.'

It seems safe to say that all these exceptions to the former rule of irrecoverability now constitute examples of the new general principle of recoverability. There is one problem case, however, namely the *Re Diplock* claim. In such a case the mistake of law is not that of the claimants, but of the executors. It remains unclear, in the wake of *Kleinwort Benson*, whether the traditional restrictions upon the *Diplock* action still persist. The restitutionary claim of the unpaid beneficiary is limited by a requirement that the next of kin's remedies must have been exhausted against the executors (*In re Diplock* [1948] Ch 465, 503–504; [1951] AC 251, at 267–68). It is unclear whether this restriction survives the decision in *Kleinwort Benson*. For earlier criticism see Goff and Jones, 113–14, 702; Birks, 442; and contrast Smith (1991) 11 OJLS 481, 497–500.

See further, Lord Nicholls in Cornish, 231, 239–41, rejecting the bar on restitution until the remedies against the personal representatives are exhausted. Another view is that a *Diplock* claim is best characterised as arising from ignorance (of the claimants) rather than depending on the mistake of law (by the executors): Birks, 143–45. See 5.1 below.

3.4 THE GROUND FOR RESTITUTION

Leaving aside particular difficulties thrown up by the *Kleinwort Benson* decision, the law governing mistaken payments, whether of fact or law, can be concisely stated. We are concerned with payments not made pursuant to an apparently binding contractual arrangement. Where it is the case that a payment is made which is expressly or impliedly governed by an apparently binding contract, but that contract was entered into as a result of a mistake, the principles differ. This is in accordance with the contractual or transactional matrix question and the associated principle of the primacy of contract. As Robert Goff J observed in *Barclays Bank Ltd v W. J. Simms, Son & Cooke (Southern) Ltd* [1980] QB 677, at 695: 'if the money was due under a contract between the payer and payee, there can be no recovery on this ground unless the contract itself is held void for mistake ... or is rescinded by the plaintiff.' The principles and authorities are discussed in Chapter 4. In contrast, the paradigm instances of autonomous restitutionary recovery are situations where a party makes a payment supposing himself to be under a contractual or other legal liability to pay, when in fact there is no such liability. Restitution was first authoritatively granted in respect of such mistakes as to liability (*Kelly v Solari* (1841) 9 M & W 54, 58, 152 ER 24 *per* Parke B; *Aiken v Short* (1856) 1 H & N 210, 215, 156 ER 1180 *per* Bramwell B). However, the notion of a liability mistake was extended to cases where the liability was to a third party (*R. E. Jones Ltd v Waring & Gillow Ltd* [1926] AC 670), where the liability was anticipated rather than actual (*Kerrison v Glyn, Mills, Currie & Co.* (1911) 81 LJKB 465), and even where the liability arose under a moral obligation rather than legal one (*Larner v London County Council* [1949] 2 KB 683). In the first half of the twentieth century it was proposed that the ground of recovery should be limited to cases of 'fundamental' mistake (*Norwich Union Fire Insurance Society Ltd v W. H. Price Ltd* [1934] AC 455; *Morgan v Ashcroft* [1938] 1 KB 49). However, the leading discussion rejects the test of fundamentality and instead substitutes a simple causation-based strategy.

The seminal first instance decision of Robert Goff J in *Barclays Bank Ltd v W. J. Simms, Son & Cooke (Southern) Ltd* [1980] QB 677 established the causal approach. The defendant entered into a written building contract with a housing association. The housing association drew a cheque for £24,000 upon the plaintiff bank, in favour of the defendant. The next day the defendant was placed in receivership. The housing association, learning of this, instructed the bank not to pay the cheque when presented, in the belief that it was entitled to do so under the building contract. The receivers, who did not know of the stop instruction, presented the cheque at the company's bank for special clearance. An employee of Barclays overlooked the stop instruction and paid the cheque. Barclays, learning of its error, sought restitution from the company or the receiver on the basis of a mistake of fact. It was held that they were entitled to recover, and there were no applicable defences. Robert Goff J stated the law in two propositions: one establishing the principle of recovery; the other elaborating exceptions. The first proposition (at 695) provides that: 'If a person pays money to another under a mistake of fact which causes him to make the payment, he is prima facie entitled to recover it as money paid under a mistake of fact.' It is not necessary to show that the mistake was 'as between' payer and payee, or that it was shared by both (*Jones Ltd* v *Waring & Gillow Ltd* [1926] AC 670; *Barclays Bank Ltd* v *W. J. Simms* [1980] QB 677, at 894). Contrast *Nurdin & Peacock plc* v *D. B. Ramsden & Co. Ltd* [1999] 1 All ER 941, where Neuberger J suggested that the mistake must be directly connected to the payment or else connected to the relationship between payer and payee (at 963).

The *Barclays Bank* v *Simms* approach has been held to be appropriate for cases of mistake of law, as well as mistake of fact, by the High Court of Australia in *David Securities Pty Ltd* v *Commonwealth Bank of Australia* (1992) 175 CLR 353. This approach is likely to be followed by the English courts, despite the curious failure of the House of Lords to do little more than allude to the applicable test of recovery in the *Kleinwort Benson* case. The causation-based strategy is assumed by the second question in Lord Hope's three-stage test for mistaken payments ([1999] 2 AC 349, at 407). Confirmation that this is likely to be the approach of the English courts is provided by *Nurdin & Peacock plc* v *D. B. Ramsden & Co. Ltd* [1999] 1 All ER 941, where Neuberger J concluded (at 964):

> whether one looks at it as a matter of logic, as a matter of authority, or as a matter of common sense, it seems to me that the test propounded by Robert Goff J in the *Barclays Bank* case should apply equally to a case where the money was paid under a mistake of law.

3.5 RESTRICTIONS ON RECOVERY

Such a liberal regime of restitution must necessarily be curtailed by appropriate defences which are characteristic of restitutionary recovery. The second proposition of law in *Barclays Bank* v *Simms* (see 3.4) establishes three key limitations on recovery in mistake cases. Robert Goff J (at 695) stated that a claim may fail where:

> (a) the payer intends that the payee shall have the money at all events, whether the fact be true or false, or is deemed in law so to intend; or (b) the payment is made for good consideration, in particular if the money is paid to discharge, and does discharge, a debt owed to the payee (or a principal on whose behalf he is authorised to receive the payment) by the payer or by a third party by whom he is authorised to discharge the debt; or (c) the payee has changed his position in good faith, or is deemed in law to have done so.

These defences will now be considered individually.

3.5.1 Proposition (2)(a): submission to an honest claim

The liberalisation of the ground for recovery by the House of Lords in *Kleinwort Benson Ltd* v *Lincoln City Council* [1999] 2 AC 349, appeared to some commentators to constitute too great an interference with the stability of transactions. However, it is submitted that this is not necessarily the case. It clear from a close reading of the speeches of the majority of the House of Lords that the intention of their Lordships was to switch attention from unprincipled restrictions on the cause of action to a more sensitive regime of appropriate defences. What will prove crucial in the context of claims for the return of money paid under a mistake, especially one of law, is the policy upholding compromises entered into in good faith and payments made in submission to an honest claim. The concept of the settlement of or submission to an honest claim has been prominent in the work of Goff and Jones in establishing restrictions on the reach of restitution. In particular, Goff and Jones have consistently argued that the cases on payment under a mistake of law should be reinterpreted on the basis that the courts were upholding payments made in submission to a honest claim. Goff and Jones states (at 214):

> In so far as the rule in *Bilbie* v *Lumley* [(1802) 2 East 469, 102 ER 448] lays down that a payment made to close a transaction in settlement of an honest claim is irrecoverable, it embodies a sound rule of policy. Such settlements should not be lightly set aside. The payer has had his opportunity to dispute legal liability in court and has chosen to forego it.

Goff and Jones suggest (at 215) that the only practical consequence of the distinction between facts and law is the greater likelihood of the payer under a mistake of law assuming the risk that he is mistaken, whereas this is uncommon in relation to mistakes of fact. The principle is well established. Robert Goff J explicitly based his proposition 2(a) in *Barclays Bank* v *Simms* upon the *dictum* of Parke B in *Kelly* v *Solari* (1841) 9 M & W 54, 152 ER 25. There, the learned Baron suggested the following limit on recovery for a mistake of fact (at 59):

> If, indeed, the money is intentionally paid, without reference to the truth or falsehood of the fact, the plaintiff meaning to waive all enquiry into it, and that the person receiving shall have the money at all events, whether the fact be true or false, the latter is certainly entitled to retain it.

The practical problem remains that while it appears that the law now recognises the defence of submission to an honest claim, it has never been explicitly applied in the cases. Therefore it is hard to state with certainty the circumstances in which it will be established. Goff and Jones are agnostic whether submission to an honest claim is properly described as a defence or a limit upon the availability of restitution: Goff and Jones, 234. It is submitted on the basis of the ordinary principle that he who asserts must prove, that it is best recognised as a defence. Accordingly the burden of proof for establishing a binding settlement on payment and submission to an honest claim is upon the recipient. This would also be consistent with Robert Goff J's classification of submission to an honest claim alongside the defences of good faith purchase and change of position in *Barclays Bank* v *Simms*. If it were considered that the security of transactions requires more protection, the courts could adopt the position that good faith is presumed in the absence of evidence to the contrary. These matters could not yet be said to be settled.

It is clear in any event that the risk-taking payer will be precluded from recovering money. The leading speech of Lord Goff of Chieveley in *Kleinwort Benson Ltd* v *Lincoln City Council* [1999] 2 AC 349 states (at 382):

> Of course, I recognise that the law of restitution must embody specific defences which are concerned to protect the stability of closed transactions. The defence of change of position is one such defence; the defences of compromise, and settlement of an honest claim (the scope of which is a matter of debate), are others. It is possible that others may be developed from judicial decisions in the future.

Lord Hoffmann also seemed to envisage (at 401) that a risk-taker would not recover, without explicitly referring to compromise or submission to an honest claim:

> I should say in conclusion that your Lordships' decision leaves open what may be difficult evidential questions over whether a person making a payment has made a mistake or not. There may be cases in which banks which have entered into certain kinds of transactions prefer not to raise the question of whether they involve any legal risk. They may hope that if nothing is said, their counter-parties will honour their obligations and all will be well, whereas any suggestion of a legal risk attaching to the instruments they hold might affect their credit ratings. There is room for a spectrum of states of mind between genuine belief in validity, founding a claim based on mistake, and a clear acceptance of the risk that they are not.

However, it may be that Lord Hoffmann's formulation goes to the question of what is an operative mistake, rather than envisaging a distinct defence of submission to a honest claim.

The third member of the majority in *Kleinwort Benson* identified three distinct restrictions on recovery which are relevant here. Lord Hope of Craighead stated (at 412) that 'A payment made in the knowledge that there was a ground to contest liability will be irrecoverable'. This formulation was explicitly based upon the judgment of Lord Abinger CB in *Kelly* v *Solari* (1841) 9 M & W 54, 152 ER 24: 'There may also be cases in which, although he might by investigation learn the state of facts more accurately, he declines to do so, and chooses to pay the money notwithstanding'. Lord Hope treated this restriction as an additional ingredient of the cause of action. Subsequently, Lord Hope identified several defences of general application. Leaving aside estoppel and change of position, his Lordship clearly accepted that 'there is the defence that the money was paid as, or as part of, a compromise' (at 412). This can be explained as a matter of a principle, the payment resulted in a binding contract supported by consideration (accord and satisfaction) which could not be easily re-opened (as explained by Brennan J in *David Securities Pty Ltd* v *Commonwealth Bank of Australia* (1992) 175 CLR 353, at 395). Alternatively the defence could be explained as a matter of policy, promoting the validity of freely entered into compromises (as explained by Dickson J in *Hydro Electric Commission of Township of Nepean* v *Ontaria Hydro* (1982) 132 DLR (3d) 193, at 218). In addition Lord Hope acknowledged Goff and Jones's suggestion that settlement of an honest claim should be a defence. Its existence had been acknowledged by the Supreme Court of Canada by Dickson J in the *Ontario Hydro* case (at 206) and by Le Forest J in *Air Canada* v *British Columbia* (1989) 59 DLR (4th) 161, 191, and by the High Court of Australia in the *David Securities* case (1992) 178 CLR 353, at 373–74 *per* Mason CJ. Returning to the facts of *Kleinwort Benson*, Lord Hope gave the most detailed guidance of any of the members of the court as follows (at 413):

> In the *Westdeutsche* case [1994] 4 All ER 890, 934 Hobhouse J said that the principle of voluntary payments could not be applied unless there was a conscious appreciation by the payer that the contracts were or might be void, and that on the evidence in the *Islington* case there clearly was no voluntary assumption of risk in any respect that was relevant. It is not clear, as there has been no evidence, whether there was a voluntary assumption of risk in any of the cases which are before us in these appeals. So I would not be prepared to say that it was a defence which in these cases was available. It is sufficient for my purpose that, while the precise limits of it have still to be clarified, it is a defence which applies generally irrespective of the nature of the mistake.

Accordingly it is for the recipient who seeks to rely upon the principle of submission to an honest claim to plead and lead evidence of the nature of the risk which would materialise if it transpired that the payer was mistaken, and that the payer nevertheless made the payment with a conscious appreciation of that risk. It may be that such evidence is difficult to garner. It is likely that a judge will have to take a common-sense view of the nature of the transaction, how parties in that context understood it and the relative sophistication of the players. The kind of documents which might support such an allegation may occasionally turn up upon disclosure, but it seems more likely than not that any such explicit discussion of the risk in a mistaken payments case would be found in documents with the benefit of legal professional privilege. For further discussion of compromise and submission to an honest claim as defences, see Chapter 33.

3.5.2 Proposition 2(b): good faith purchase

Robert Goff J's second proposed defence reflects the primacy of contractual reasoning in determining whether a payment was properly made. It was explicitly based upon the decision in the difficult case of *Aiken* v *Short* (1856) 1 H & N 210, 156 ER 1180, the facts of the case have a passing resemblance to Victorian melodrama, centring on the discovery of a later will. George Carter, who was not a party to the action, owed money to Short. Carter acknowledged his debt under a bond and further mortgaged his interest in property, which he believed he was entitled to receive under the will of his brother, Edwin Carter, to secure the debt. Subsequently the same interest was mortgaged to the plaintiff bank as second mortgagee. When Short's widow and executrix applied to George Carter for payment, he suggested she approach the bank. The bank, supposing itself to be the second mortgagee, paid the executrix in order to improve the quality of its security. Only then was a later will of Edwin Carter discovered, under which it transpired that George Carter had no substantial interest under the will. The plaintiff bank sought to recover the money from the executrix on the basis of mistake of fact.

Bramwell B stressed that the bank had the option to pay, and would have limited the ground of recovery to mistakes as to liability. This is no longer a reason which would preclude restitution today given the liberalisation of the ground for recovery. More significantly, Pollock CB and Platt B stressed that the defendant had a valid debt and a clear right to the money as against Carter. Given that the defendant had approached Carter first and he had referred her to the bank, Pollock CB concluded: 'The money was, in fact, paid by the Bank, as the agents of Carter' (at 214). Pollock CB stressed that the defendant had not contributed to the plaintiff's mistake. The plaintiff was itself at fault in paying the money without more careful investigation. On the latter point, it would not in view of *Kelly* v *Solari* be correct to suggest that contributory negligence would bar a claim to recover money now on the grounds of mistake of fact. Pollock CB sketched the following hypothetical which clearly illustrates the operation of good faith purchase in this context. The learned Chief Baron asked rhetorically (at 214):

> Suppose it was announced that there was to be a dividend on the estate of a trader, and persons to whom he was indebted went to an office and received instalments of the debts due to them, could the party paying recover back the money if it turned out that he was wrong in supposing that he had funds in hand?

Goff and Jones, who in earlier editions had accepted the characterisation of this defence as good faith purchase, now treat *Aiken* v *Short* as an example of change of position: Goff and Jones, 204–205. The concern appears to be that the ground of restitution is mistake, not a claim based on title. The strict view is taken that good faith purchase should be a defence only where a claim is based upon title either at common law or in equity. This reasoning should not be accepted. First, it is clear from *Aiken* v *Short* and dicta in the subsequent House of Lords case of *Kerrison* v *Glyn, Mills, Currie & Co.* (1911) 81 LJKB 465, at 470 *per* Lord Atkinson, at 472 *per* Lord Mersey, that good faith purchase is an autonomous defence here. Secondly, good faith purchase extinguishes a restitutionary claim in full, and not merely *pro tanto* as is the case with change of position. Thirdly, and most crucially, payment in such circumstances amounts to a valid accord and satisfaction, which can be set aside only in accordance with the rules of contract law. The primacy of contract ousts the possibility of restitutionary recovery here, unless the contractual matrix can be set aside. As Robert Goff J said in *Barclays Bank* v *Simms* [1980] QB 677, at 695:

> However, even if the payee has given consideration for the payment, for example, by accepting the payment in discharge of a debt owed to him by a third party on whose behalf the payer is authorised to discharge it, that transaction may itself be set aside (and so provide no defence to the claim), if the payer's mistake is induced by the payee, or possibly even where the payee, being aware of the payer's mistake, did not receive the money in good faith.

This suggests that the contractual matrix could be side-stepped in at least two cases. First, where it can be rescinded because of a misrepresentation by the payee. Secondly, where there is no contract in accordance with the objective principle of construction of contract formation. As a matter of principle, other contractual vitiating factors could equally result in the contract being set aside.

Returning to the facts of *Barclays Bank* v *Simms*, the crucial question was whether the bank had acted with authority in making the payments. If it had the recipient could rely upon the defence of good faith purchase. Robert Goff J held that where a bank overlooks a countermand and pays a cheque it acts outside its mandate or authority. Accordingly it is not entitled to debit its customer's account and the debt owed to the payee is accordingly not discharged. It will be recalled from the discussions of the general principles of enrichment in 1.4.5 that a debt is not validly discharged unless payment emanates from the debtor or a person with authority to act on his behalf.

Robert Goff J's reasoning in *Barclays Banks* v *Simms* has been criticised by Goode (1981) 97 LQR 254, at 258–9. He states that it concentrates too much upon the *actual* authority of the bank, and neglects to consider the *apparent* authority of the bank. In the law of agency, authority is either actual (whether express or implied) or apparent. In the former category the principal manifests his consent to the agent acting on his behalf to the agent. In the latter species of authority the principal manifests his consent that the agent represent him, directly to the third party who deals with the agent. The principal represents that the agent is empowered to act on his behalf, or in the usual parlance 'holds out' the agent as his representative, and the third party relies upon that manifestation of consent by entering into the transaction proposed by the agent. Goode argues that the consequence of the reasoning is that ordinary transactions would be upset by allowing the bank to recover in such circumstances. Suppose a customer pays for goods with a cheque, and despite the goods being wholly satisfactory, subsequently instructs his bank to stop the cheque. If the bank overlooks the countermand and pays, why should it be entitled to recover from the seller?

The view of Robert Goff J was that by granting restitution to the bank, the result was that the parties could concentrate on the proper dispute between debtor and creditor. It is not clear what the true dispute here was. The bank's customer appeared concerned that its creditor had been placed in receivership. It should be noted that in any dispute between the customer and the defendant, the defendant may be able to rely upon the 'cheque rule' by which payment under a bill of exchange constitutes a specially insulated payment upon which summary judgment can be readily obtained. There are only limited defences including fraud and total failure of consideration: Andrews, paras 6-016 and 6-019. The power to award summary judgment is now contained in CPR Part 24. It seems that matters of practice, such as the cheque rule, survive in the new regime. See 39.3. On this basis it seems difficult to see what defence the bank's customer would have to a claim upon the cheque, unless there was a total failure of consideration. For example, if there had been no work done in respect of the payment. This appears unlikely on the facts, as the payment was pursuant to an interim certificate issued by the architect. However, the availability of the cheque rule in this context has been doubted by Goode (1981) 97 LQR 254, at 259–60. If so, the payee can plead change of position.

It is a further curious feature of *Barclays Bank* v *Simms* that the insolvency of the defendant company did not appear to be a problem. The receiver had requested special clearance for the cheque, although it was not suggested that this indicated he was aware of the stop instruction. The bank soon demanded return of the money, and brought its claim against the company and/or the receiver, who from the date of the writ kept the £24,000 in dispute in a separate account pending the outcome of the proceedings (at 685). Presumably the receiver having notice of the dispute over the £24,000 was unable to use the money validly to discharge obligations of his appointing bank.

A restrictive approach to the question of the bank's authority could work injustice where the bank's customer became insolvent and a defendant recipient was made to disgorge money to the bank, with little prospect of ever recovering from the now insolvent customer. This was the situation in *Lloyds Bank plc* v *Independent Insurance Co. Ltd* [1999] 2 WLR 986. Insurance agents owed some £162,387.90 of premium income to the defendant insurance company. The agents had cashflow problems. A director of the insurance agents paid cheques into its bank account, including one for £168,000, and these were credited to the agents' account with the plaintiff as uncleared effects. The director informed the bank manager that he would like payment to be made to the defendant insurance company of the debt as soon as possible. The payment was to be made by a CHAPS transfer which is an irrevocable instantaneous electronic inter-bank payment. The manager informed the director that payment would take place once the cheques had cleared. However, two of the bank's other employees, mistakenly believing that the state of the account represented cleared funds, made the payment. Subsequently the cheque for £168,000 was dishonoured pushing the agents' account into overdraft.

The Court of Appeal held that although the money was prima facie recoverable by the bank as paid under a mistake of fact, here the money was paid for good consideration and was accordingly irrecoverable. The payment had discharged a debt owed to the payee. The payment by the bank, made with the actual authority to do so on behalf of its customer, was effective to discharge the debt. The crucial fact was the director of the agents' insistence on speedy payment to the defendant. When the bank manager had told the agents' director that payment would not be made until the cheques had cleared, this was simply the bank manager telling the customer that it was not obliged to make the CHAPS transfer until it was satisfied as to its own receipt. It could not be said that the insurance agents had qualified the bank's authority by insisting it did not make the payment until the funds had cleared. Accordingly, though it was not obliged to do so, the bank was entitled to make the payment within the scope of its actual authority.

Curiously the Court of Appeal did not accept in the alternative that the bank had apparent authority to make the payment. It seems there was no holding out by the agent of its bank in relation to this particular transaction. Further, the Court of Appeal found it difficult to identify any reliance by the defendants upon such holding out or representation. It may seem curious, at first sight, that the courts are reluctant to recognise apparent authority in this context. The reason appears to be that if it were held that the bank had no actual authority, but only apparent authority, the payee would be entitled to keep the money. In this situation the bank, having acted outside its mandate, would not be entitled to debit its customer's account. Accordingly the bank would be the loser and its customer would have its debt paid off without having to make any contribution. It is the perceived unfairness of this which makes the courts unwilling to recognise apparent authority, in the absence of underlying actual authority. On the particular facts of the *Lloyds Bank* case the holding that the bank paid with actual authority appears to be correct. However, given the insolvency of the customer and the fact that the bouncing cheque pushed the account massively into overdraft, the bank was the eventual loser in this scenario. Lastly, in *Lloyds Bank plc* v *Independent Insurance Co. Ltd*, Peter Gibson LJ stated (at 1005): 'I cannot accept that the defence of bona fide purchase has been overtaken by or subsumed in the defence of change of position. Both defences may co-exist.'

For general discussion of good faith purchase, and in particular the position of banks, see Goff and Jones, 204–12. It seems the autonomy of good faith purchase in the mistaken payments context is now entrenched, given it forms the ratio of a modern Court of Appeal decision. For general consideration of good faith purchase, see Chapter 31.

3.5.3   Proposition 2(c): change of position

Robert Goff J's proposed defence of change of position in *Barclays Bank* v *Simms* was technically premature. The decisions of the House of Lords in *R. E. Jones Ltd* v *Waring & Gillow Ltd* [1926] AC 670 and *Ministry of Health* v *Simpson* [1951] AC 251 were obstacles in favour of the recognition of change of position. *Lipkin Gorman* v *Karpnale Ltd* [1991] 2 AC 548 retrospectively legitimates this first instance discussion of principle. Change of position existed in prototype form under the guise of estoppel. The defence succeeded in *Holt* v *Markham* [1923] 1 KB 504, where a First World War RAF officer was overpaid a gratuity upon demobilisation. It was held that he was misled into believing he was entitled to the money, which he had subsequently invested in a company which went into liquidation. Estoppel was also successful in extinguishing the claim of a local authority which had overpaid sick pay to a teacher in *Avon County Council* v *Howlett* [1983] 1 WLR 605, even though the reliance expenditure was only half the value of the sums received.

However, estoppel had two key disadvantages. First, it required a breach of duty by the payer or a representation by him that the payment was a proper one. Secondly, it appeared to be an all-or-nothing defence, rather than operating proportionately to the expenditure incurred in reliance upon a payment. *Lipkin Gorman* removes these obstacles. Estoppel was most prominent in the case law on mistaken payments, and it seems that in the future change of position will be most prominent in the same context.

The principles and case law are reviewed in Chapter 32. It is clear that change of position is equally applicable to mistakes of law as to mistakes of fact (*Kleinwort Benson Ltd* v *Lincoln City Council* [1999] 2 AC 349, at 382 *per* Lord Goff of Chieveley, at 401 *per* Lord Hoffmann and at 412 *per* Lord Hope of Craighead; *Nurdin & Peacock plc* v *D. B. Ramsden & Co. Ltd* [1999] 1 All ER 941, at 956–7 *per* Neuberger J).

3.6 SPECIAL PROBLEMS OF MISTAKE OF LAW

3.6.1 What constitutes a mistake of law?

Relief for payments made under a mistake of law give rise to some particular problems of their own. We have already considered the importance of submission to an honest claim (see 3.5.1) which appears to have more potential application as a defence in respect of payments made under a mistaken understanding of the law rather than of the factual context. In addition there are intractable problems in determining what amounts to a mistake of law. This is an issue on which a number of widely different opinions are held, as is evidenced by the split in the Judicial Committee of the House of Lords in the *Kleinwort Benson* case. The Law Commission, in proposing the statutory abrogation of the mistake of law rule, considered that the characterisation of a mistake as one of law of itself should not make any difference to whether a claim to restitution should succeed. However, they considered the difficult problem of how the courts should deal with a judicial change in the law. According to the declaratory theory of common law, an authoritative statement of the law is deemed always to be the law. This potential retrospective effect was viewed as having implications for the security of transactions. Accordingly the Law Commission proposed a special provision for this in its draft Restitution (Mistakes of Law) Bill in cl. 3:

(1) An act done in accordance with a settled view of the law shall not be regarded as founding a mistake claim by reason only that a subsequent decision of a court or tribunal departs from that view.

(2)   A view of the law may be regarded for the purpose of this section as having been settled at any time notwithstanding that it was not held unanimously or had not been the subject of a decision by a court or tribunal.

See generally Law Commission, *Restitution — Mistakes of Law and Ultra Vires Public Authority Receipts and Payments* (Law Com. No. 227, 1994), and in particular on the settled understanding of the law restriction see paras 5.2 to 5.13. Goff and Jones, in the current edition and before the decision of the House of Lords in *Kleinwort Benson*, concluded (at 238) that a claim to recover:

should fail if made in reliance on a judicial decision subsequently over-ruled in independent litigation. It is unlikely that an English court will conclude that a payer was mistaken on such facts. The declaratory theory of judicial law-making is surely dead.

3.6.2   The *Kleinwort Benson* case

To the surprise of much of the legal community, the majority of the House of Lords in *Kleinwort Benson Ltd* v *Lincoln City Council* [1999] 2 AC 349 took the opposite view. The House of Lords was expressly asked to rule on the question of whether a payment made under a settled understanding of the law was irrecoverable. Lord Goff of Chieveley in the leading speech considered the declaratory theory of judicial decision at length. His Lordship concluded (at 378–79):

The historical theory of judicial decision, though it may in the past have served its purpose, was indeed a fiction. But it does mean that, when judges state what the law is, their decisions do, in the sense I have described, have a retrospective effect. That is, I believe, inevitable. It is inevitable in relation to the particular case before the court, in which events must have occurred some time, perhaps some years, before the judge's decision is made. But it is also inevitable in relation to other cases in which the law as so stated will in future fall to be applied. I must confess that I cannot imagine how a common law system, or indeed any legal system, can operate otherwise if the law is to be applied equally to all and yet be capable of organic change.

In Lord Goff's view it was not appropriate to hold that the settled understanding of the law of defence formed part of the common law. The supposed defence was not a true defence, but rather reflected a theoretical view that a payment made in such circumstances was not made under an operative mistake at all (at 382). Lord Goff was emphatic that the mistake in the swaps cases was plainly a mistake of law. When the money was paid, it was the belief of the payer that he was under a legal obligation to do so. Once the true legal position was declared by the Divisional Court and subsequently by the House of Lords in *Hazell* v *Hammersmith and Fulham London Borough Council* [1992] 2 AC 1, the payer discovered that, under the law now held to be applicable at the date of the payment, there was no such obligation. If one accepts Lord Goff's premise as to the impact of the declaratory theory of common law, the conclusion that the money is prima facie recoverable does inevitably follow.

Lord Goff's view should be immediately contrasted with the leading minority speech of Lord Browne-Wilkinson that 'the moneys are not recoverable since, at the time of payment, the payer was not labouring under any mistake'. His Lordship concluded (at 358):

> although the decision in *Hazell* is retrospective in its effect, retrospection cannot falsify history: if at the date of each payment it was settled law that local authorities had capacity to enter into swaps contracts, the bank were not labouring under any mistake of law at that date. The subsequent decision in *Hazell* could not create a mistake where no mistake existed at the time.

Lord Browne-Wilkinson essayed a hypothetical example whereby a single decision of the Court of Appeal in 1930 established a legal rule. In 1990 a payment was made on the basis of the rule in that case. The payer received advice that the decision was good law. In 1997 the House of Lords overruled the 1930 case. Would the payer be entitled to recover the money? Lord Browne-Wilkinson adverted to the rule that the cause of action in restitution vests when the mistake payment is made: *Baker* v *Courage & Co.* [1910] 1 KB 56. However, under the hypothetical there would be no cause of action at the date of payment. On the majority view the money would, however, be recoverable, although the majority did not explicitly discuss when the cause of action arose. Lord Browne-Wilkinson found this too fanciful (at 359):

> It would not have been possible to issue a writ claiming restitution on the grounds of mistake of law until the 1997 decision had overruled the 1930 Court of Appeal decision. Therefore a payment which, when made, and for several years thereafter, was entirely valid and irrecoverable would subsequently become recoverable. This result would be subversive of the great public interest in the security of receipts and the closure of transactions.

In Lord Browne-Wilkinson's view the money was irrecoverable whether the payment was made where law had been established by a previous judicial decision which was subsequently overruled, or where there is settled law in the absence of a judicial decision. There was simply no mistake (at 363):

What constitutes the unjust factor is the mistake made by the payer at the date of payment. If, at the date of payment, it was settled law that payment was legally due, I can see nothing unjust in permitting the payee to retain moneys he received at a time when all lawyers skilled in the field would have advised that he was entitled to receive them and the payer was bound to pay them. Again it is critical to establish the position at the time of payment: if, at that date, there was nothing unjust or unmeritorious in the receipt or retention of moneys by the payee in my judgment it was not an unjust enrichment for him subsequently to retain the moneys just because the law was, in one sense, subsequently changed.

Accordingly Lord Browne-Wilkinson would have recognised the defence where there was a decision which was subsequently overruled, and where there was settled law in the absence of a judicial decision (such as textbook law). Given these complications, Lord Browne-Wilkinson preferred to wait for statutory reform of the rule pursuant to the Law Commission's proposal. His Lordship suggested that any new law should also regulate the appropriate limitation period of this type of action.

Lord Lloyd of Berwick agreed, stating that 'for your Lordships to accept half the package proposed by the Law Commission and reject the other half, would cause me some disquiet' (at 392). Lord Lloyd considered cl. 3 of the Law Commission's proposal to be a definitional clause, clarifying and limiting what is meant by a mistake in this context (at 393). Lord Lloyd also clearly articulated one policy and one moral reason for this conclusion. First, the policy favouring finality in transactions, especially in the commercial context. Secondly, Lord Lloyd could see no moral reason why the payee should be obliged to make restitution in such circumstances: 'Where is the unjust factor?' (at 395).

Lord Hoffmann's speech proved crucial, not least because his Lordship candidly acknowledged that he had changed his mind. Lord Hoffmann's first thoughts were that not only would a payment on a settled view of the law lead to the conclusion that there was no operative mistake, but also a payment on the basis of a tenable view of the law. In the context of the retrospectivity of judicial decisions, the state of mind of the payer should be characterised as a misprediction, rather than a mistake. However, Lord Hoffmann's ultimate view was in accord with Lord Goff's view. His Lordship considered it important to place the right to recover mistaken payments in its wider context of the law of unjust enrichment. It did not matter where there was a mistake of fact whether or not the payer could have discovered the true state of affairs. Money paid under a mistake of fact was recoverable because the payer would not have paid if he had known the true state of affairs. The only oddity about mistake of law was that the true state of affairs could not be discerned at the time of payment. Lord Hoffmann concluded (at 400): 'Retention is prima facie unjust if he paid because he thought he was obliged to do so and it subsequently turns out that he was not.'

Lord Hoffmann accepted that there was an alternative reason for recognising the settled understanding of the law of defence. However, in reasoning suffused with the theory of judicial decision-making of the legal philosopher Ronald Dworkin, his

Lordship decided that such a policy-motivated defence was not a matter for the judiciary (at 401):

> the adoption of the 'settled view' rule would be founded purely upon policy; upon a utilitarian assessment of the advantages of preserving the security of transactions against the inevitable anomalies, injustices and difficulties of interpretation which such a rule would create. That is not a course which I think your Lordships should take.
>
> I accept that allowing recovery for mistake of law without qualification, even taking into account the defence of change of position, may be thought to tilt the balance too far against the public interest in the security of transactions.

While acknowledging strong arguments in favour of leaving the whole matter for Parliament, Lord Hoffmann ultimately sided with the majority, urging Parliament to take action over the difficult question of limitation. One view of Lord Hoffmann's speech is that it is the furthest that English law has gone towards the civil law position of presuming that restitution should be awarded where a transfer has taken place and it turns that there is no legal justification for the transfer. Such an approach would dispense with the need for the claimant affirmatively to prove a ground for restitution or just factor. On Lord Hoffmann's view it seems sufficient that as it turned out the payment was unnecessary. It is hard to see how this counters the view of the minority that in such circumstances it is difficult to identify the moral reason why the payee should refund the money. It is submitted that the potential wider interpretation of and implications of Lord Hoffmann's speech should not be the future path of English law. It should always be for the claimant to establish a reason why money should be returned. The principle of the finality of transactions and in favour of the security of receipt demands this.

The final speech of the majority, that of Lord Hope of Craighead, has also provoked debate. Lord Hope explicitly adverted to the difference of approach between the common law, which demands an unjust factor, and civil law systems which look for the absence of the legal justification for the enrichment. Lord Hope was clear (at 407) that under English law a payer had to address three questions: '(1) Was there a mistake? (2) Did the mistake cause a payment? And (3) did the payee have a right to receive the sum which was paid to him?' Only the first question was in dispute in the present case. Lord Hope would have liked to have known more about the circumstances of the mistake, and bemoaned the sparseness of the pleadings in the absence of a request for further and better particulars. Lord Hope spends more time than any of the other judges addressing the question of whether there was a mistake of law on the facts of *Kleinwort Benson*. His Lordship stated (at 411, emphasis added):

> On the whole it seems to me to be preferable to avoid being drawn into a discussion as to whether a particular decision changed the law or whether it was merely declaratory. It would not possible to lay down any hard and fast rules on

this point. Each case would have to be decided on what may in the end be a matter of opinion, about which there may be room for a good deal of dispute. It is better to face up to the fact that every decision as to the law by a judge operates retrospectively, and to concentrate instead on the question — which I would regard as the critical question — whether the payer would have made the payment if he had known what he is now being told was the law. *It is the state of the law at the time of the payment which will determine whether or not the payment was or was not legally due to be paid, and it is the state of mind of the payer at the time of the payment which will determine whether he paid under a mistake.* But there seems to be no reason in principle why the law of unjust enrichment should insist that that mistake must be capable of being demonstrated at the same time as the time when the payment was made. A mistake of fact may take some time to discover. If there is a dispute about this, the question of whether there was a mistake may remain in doubt until the issue has been resolved by a judge. Why should this not be so where the mistake is one of law?

It appears that this passage is internally contradictory. Whereas the general thrust of the argument supports the majority view point, the italicised words appear to support the minority view. If the state of law at the time of payment governs whether it is legally due, surely the money is irrecoverable and the subsequent decision must be overlooked. This contradicts the general tenor of Lord Hope's speech. The only way to resolve the conundrum is to read the italicised words as implicitly qualified by the declaratory theory. That is, the state of law at the time of the payment is only established later, but with retrospective effect. Lord Hope, drawing upon the judgment of Hobhouse J in *Westdeutsche Landesbank Girozentrale* v *Islington London Borough Council* [1994] 4 All ER 890, at 931, decided explicitly that there was an operative mistake here. Lord Hope had earlier said that mistake extended to cases of ignorance. This seems to be Lord Hope's view of the state of mind of market participants in relation to swaps when the transactions were entered into and payments were made. Such parties were blissfully unaware of the legal risk posed by the provisions of the Local Government Act 1972 and the subsequent stringent interpretation applied to them by the Audit Commission, the Divisional Court and ultimately the House of Lords. This clearly demonstrates the repudiation of the reasoning of *Bilbie* v *Lumley* (1802) 2 East 469, 102 ER 448, in which the mistake of law bar was explicitly based upon the maxim that ignorance of the law is no excuse.

The italicised passage in the above extract from Lord Hope's speech is relied upon by Hedley in the *Cambridge Law Journal* in contradicting the head-note writers of both the *Weekly Law Reports* ([1998] 3 WLR 1095) and the *All England Law Reports* ([1998] 4 All ER 513). Hedley asserts that Lord Hope agrees with the majority only once it has been established there is an actionable mistake. In Hedley's view, Lord Hope would not allow for the retroactive effect of judicial overruling. Hedley concludes that a true picture of the ratio of *Kleinwort Benson* is more complicated than the over-simplified account of the head-note writers. Hedley argues ([1999] CLJ 21, at 22–23):

So it appears that Lord Hope *would* deny liability in a case where 'settled law' was later overturned; but he denied there was any 'settled law' here. For Lords Browne-Wilkinson and Lloyd, by contrast, whether a particular rule was 'settled' was a more open-ended question, which they preferred to remit to a lower court. This creates a ticklish situation in the law of precedent. A majority held that 'settled law' defeats liability, *and* a majority held that it did not do so here, Lord Hope forming part of both majorities. As it is, the proposition stated in both head-notes, that a plea of 'settled law' *never* defeats liability, is one which two Lords supported but three denied. What proposition of law will ultimately be regarded as the ratio of the case remains to be seen.

Hedley's reading of the case must prove somewhat controversial. It appears to concentrate on the italicised passage, but to ignore the context in which that passage occurs (especially the immediately preceding and subsequent sentences).

Hedley's argument is right to this limited extent. Lord Hope devoted more consideration than Lords Goff or Hoffmann to the question of whether there was an operative mistake on the facts of *Kleinwort Benson*. However, Lord Hope went on to reject the introduction of a settled law defence by judicial development. Lord Hope cited the consultation paper published by the Scottish Law Commission in the wake of *Morgan Guaranty Trust Co.* v *Lothian Regional Council* 1995 SLT 299, entitled *Judicial Abolition of the Error of Law Rule and Its Aftermath* (Scot Law Com. Discussion Paper, No. 95) (1996). Lord Hope listed three reasons against judicial recognition of the proposed defence. First, the difficulties of precisely defining the defence and the evidential difficulties of establishing a basis for such a defence. Secondly (at 414–15):

a payment made on a settled view of the law is more likely to be excusable, and thus to be one where restitution would more obviously be justified, than a payment made as a result of one man's mistake or ignorance.

Thirdly, even if the policy of finality in transactions were favoured, it was not appropriate for the judges to rule upon this important question of public policy, when the Scottish Law Commission had demonstrated a need for caution. Accordingly Lord Hope answered the questions posed for the Appellate Committee in the same terms of Lord Goff of Chieveley (at 418), which included the statement (at 389):

There is no principle of English law that payments made under a settled understanding of the law which is subsequently departed from by judicial decision shall not be recoverable in restitution on the ground of mistake of law.

Accordingly the safer view is that Lord Hope was of one mind with Lords Goff and Hoffmann. The head-note writers can be exonerated. His Lordship did not require it to be demonstrated that a mistake of law had to be discoverable at the time of payment. Indeed his Lordship states in the last-quoted passage that someone who pays in accordance with a settled view of the law has a greater moral claim for restitution than somebody who pays as result of a sloppy mistake of fact. Accordingly it is wrong to read Lord Hope's speech in the way which Hedley proposes.

3.6.3   An appraisal of the decision in *Kleinwort Benson*

Obviously the decision of the House of Lords in *Kleinwort Benson Ltd* v *Lincoln City Council* will provoke debate for many years to come. Two contrasting case notes in the *Law Quarterly Review* and the *Cambridge Law Journal* demonstrate two opposed views. Hedley, whose views have already been discussed in detail at 3.6.2 above, is sceptical of the reasoning and censorious about what he sees as a botched piece of judicial law-making: [1999] CLJ 21. In contrast, in a more theoretical discussion John Finnis applauds the decision of the majority: (1999) 115 LQR 170.

A number of points can be made. First, the decision is to be welcomed for its approximation of mistakes of fact and mistake of law. The distinction between them was capricious and inconsistent with principle. Secondly, the case is to be welcomed for its apparent acceptance that mistake embraces ignorance. It is not necessary to demonstrate an active but flawed reasoning process. Payments and transfers made while blissfully unaware of the true factual or legal context will lead to restitution. Thirdly, the result of the case is that attention is switched to important defences such as change of position, good faith purchase, and most crucially, where the mistake is one as to law, compromise and submission to an honest claim. It is submitted that contractual compromise and non-contractual submission to an honest claim will bar recovery in most of those situations where it has been feared the impact of *Kleinwort Benson* would be to upset the finality of transactions.

The existence of compromise and submission to an honest claim (although the latter is still difficult to define and discern) will protect the security of receipt and will promote the finality of transactions. Consider the following hypothetical. Several hundred cases are pending before the courts on the question of whether an obligation to pay exists in particular circumstances. One lead case is selected and the Court of Appeal rules that there is a legal obligation to make the payments. In the lead case the reluctant payer becomes a judgment debtor. Where that judgment is complied with, it is clear that the law of unjust enrichment will not reopen that transaction. This is the principle of *res judicata* (*Kleinwort Benson Ltd* v *Lincoln City Council* [1999] 2 AC 349, at 410 *per* Lord Hope). In all the other cases the decision of the Court of Appeal is accepted and compromises entered into and acted upon, yet the matter never proceeds to judgment. Such cases will be governed by the principle of compromise or submission to an honest claim. Those transactions should not be reopened even if the House of Lords subsequently overruled the decision of the Court of Appeal, whether one year later or 10 years later.

Despite the protection given by these defences, the decision of the majority can still be called into question. Given the central importance of the finality of transactions and the security of receipts, the approach to the unjust factor or ground for restitution remains unsatisfactory. Therefore the final comment on *Kleinwort Benson* is a criticism of the majority's definition of an operative mistake of law. The view of the minority has much to commend to it. This was indeed the view of the Law Commission and is a view that has won favour in other jurisdictions. However, the settled view of the law of defence has its own problems. There may be difficult evidential questions as to whether a settled view of the law existed. This seems to require in some cases expert evidence as to what a particular view of the law, probably among specialist practitioners, was at some date in the past. Whether the expert evidence is properly given by academic lawyers or practitioners, or a mixture of both, is itself a contentious question. Accordingly, it is submitted that the better view is that the stronger version of the defence adverted to by Lord Hoffmann is to be preferred. Lord Hoffmann's first thoughts were that money paid on the basis of a tenable view of what the law was, should be irrecoverable. Indeed, as Lord Hoffmann said, in such circumstances it cannot be said that there was any mistake at all. A person who investigates the legal context and pays upon a tenable view of it has taken the risk that his understanding may turn out to be mistaken. In such circumstances there is no unjust factor or ground for restitution. Equally it could be said that even if the money were prima facie recoverable, there is a defence of submission to an honest claim. The public policy in favour of the finality of transactions and compromise requires that it should be recognised that there is both no operative mistake in such cases and that in any event there is a submission to an honest claim. Accordingly Lord Hoffmann's first view is preferred to his ultimate position.

3.6.4 The aftermath

One decided case since *Kleinwort Benson* has had to consider its implications. In *Nurdin & Peacock plc* v *D. B. Ramsden & Co. Ltd* [1999] 1 All ER 941, a commercial lease contained provision for quarterly payments of £207,683, but in the fourth and fifth years of the term these were increased by some £59,338, before reverting again to the usual level at the end of the five-year cycle. However, when the time came the landlord continued to demand the higher figure. The plaintiff, an assignee, paid these sums without protest, until having had the opportunity to examine the lease it announced it would only pay the lower figure, and would set off overpayments against the rent. However, it was advised soon after by its lawyers to keep paying the higher sum until the dispute was settled by arbitration or litigation. It was further advised that such overpayments would be recoverable if the claim was successful. This advice, prior to *Kleinwort Benson*, was wrong.

Neuberger J held that in relation to the overpayments before the examination of the lease, the plaintiff company was mistaken in failing to ensure that the level of payments was varied, or that they forgot that a lesser sum was now payable. In contrast, as regards the later overpayments, these were caused by the advice that if they were successful in proceedings the money would be recoverable. In relation to the former category of payments, these were mistakes of fact, indeed liability mistakes which had always grounded recovery. In respect of most of the remaining overpayments, Neuberger J held that there was an agreement on the correspondence to repay if the tenants were successful in their contention. However, this left one overpayment, paid prior to the agreement. This was recoverable on the basis of a mistake of law. Namely that the payer had mistakenly believed that the money would be readily recoverable if it were not due. This was not true at the time of payment because of the currency of the mistake of law rule. Accordingly the money was recoverable as paid under a mistake of law! Neuberger J accepted that a certain degree of circularity and illogicality underlay the argument. If the money was recoverable now there was no mistake. Conversely, if there was no mistake, the money could not be recovered. Neuberger J cut the Gordian knot by insisting that at the time of payment there was a mistake of law (at 964–5). Presumably one ignores the retrospective effect of judicial decisions where it stands in the way of restitution.

3.7 CONTRIBUTORY NEGLIGENCE

A mistaken payment is recoverable however negligent the payer may have been. This is established by the leading case of *Kelly* v *Solari* (1841) 9 M & W 54, 152 ER 24, which held that it was no defence that the plaintiff had the means of knowledge of the truth within its own records. Lord Abinger CB stated (at 58): 'I think the knowledge of the fact which disentitles the party from recovering, must mean a knowledge existing in the mind at the time of the payment.' Therefore careless forgetfulness was no bar to recovery. This principle has been affirmed in *Rover International Ltd* v *Cannon Film Sales Ltd* [1989] 1 WLR 912, where Kerr LJ stated that 'a genuine mistake is not vitiated by carelessness' (at 922). Most recently, in *Banque Financière de la Cité* v *Parc (Battersea) Ltd* [1999] 1 AC 221, Lord Steyn referred to the failure of the bank to take elementary precautions to protect its position (which had persuaded Morritt LJ in the Court of Appeal to decline restitution). Lord Steyn stressed that restitution was not fault-based and there was no need to prove any misrepresentation. The negligence of the bank was 'akin to the carelessness of a mistaken payer: it does not by itself undermine the ground of restitution' (at 227).

3.8 NON-MONEY BENEFITS

There is a paucity of authority here. Two factors account for this. First, the comparative immaturity of the law of restitution. Secondly, even under the modern law, it will be difficult to satisfy the test of enrichment in relation to non-money benefits. Even so, there is some modern authority, and indeed partial statutory recognition of a role for unjust enrichment reasoning here. There are cases both at common law and in equity.

3.8.1 Common law

In the rather unsatisfactory, war-time case of *Upton-on-Severn Rural District Council* v *Powell* [1942] 1 All ER 220, Powell's Dutch barn caught fire. He telephoned his local police station at Upton to ask for 'the fire brigade to be sent'. The police sent for the Upton fire brigade who came and dealt with the fire. All the parties were unaware that although the barn was in the Upton police district, it was in the Pershore, not the Upton, fire district. Powell would have been entitled to the services of Pershore fire brigade for free, whereas the Upton fire brigade was entitled to make contracts and charge for services performed outside its area. The Court of Appeal held that the Upton fire brigade was entitled to remuneration for the services performed for Powell upon the basis of an 'implied promise'.

First, the case is irreconcilable with ordinary contractual principles. As was argued in vain, by counsel for Powell, neither party had any relevant contractual intention. The Upton fire brigade thought it was rendering gratuitous services in the normal course of its duty. Powell thought he was receiving the services of the appropriate fire brigade without charge. Secondly, despite the reference in the brief judgment of Lord Greene MR to an implied promise, the case is also difficult to reconcile with unjust enrichment principles. Powell did not request or accept services which he knew he would be expected to pay for. Goff and Jones think it unlikely that Powell was incontrovertibly benefited since he was entitled to the Pershore fire brigade services for free: Goff and Jones, 252. The better view is that Pershore fire brigade was the party enriched by Upton's mistaken discharge of its (Pershore's) duty to extinguish Powell's fire. Accordingly, the wrong person was made liable in this case.

A more promising authority is *Gebhardt* v *Saunders* [1892] 2 QB 452, in which the plaintiff tenant discharged the statutory obligation of the landlord to abate a nuisance under s. 4 of the Public Health (London) Act 1891. It was impossible to tell at the time when the work was done whether the nuisance was caused by a structural defect and accordingly the defendant landlord's responsibility, or by improper use by the tenant and accordingly his liability. It turned out to be the former. While the case is commonly discussed in chapters on legal compulsion (see 20.6 below), it seems preferable to characterise the unjust factor as mistake: Birks, 191. That mistake was the appropriate ground for restitution appears faintly in the judgment of Day J (at 457):

> If two people are required to do certain work under a penalty in case of disobedience, and one does the work, and it turns out afterwards that the other ought to have done it, the expenses are properly money paid at the request of the person who was primarily liable, but who neglected to do the work.

3.8.2 The leading case

Perhaps the most interesting common law authority is *Greenwood* v *Bennett* [1973] QB 195. Bennett, who managed a garage, required some repairs to be done to a Jaguar car before selling it in the course of trade. The car was worth between £400 and £500. Bennett entrusted the car to Searle to do the necessary repairs at a cost of £85. Searle, while driving the car on a frolic of his own, crashed it and decided to sell it in its unrepaired state. Harper bought the car from him for £75, which was a fair price in its damaged stated. Harper made good the damage to the tune of £226 in labour and materials. He subsequently sold the car to Prattle for £450. Later, the police took possession of the car and Searle was convicted of theft. The chief constable brought an interpleader summons to determine title to the car. The county court judge ordered the car to be returned to Bennett who then sold it for £400. It was accepted on appeal that Bennett's garage owned the car, but Harper claimed £226 from Bennett for the improvements to the car. Lord Denning MR considered the case as if it had been brought as a claim for specific delivery. In such a case his Lordship was of the view that a court of equity would order the return of the vehicle only upon condition that payment was made to Harper for the work done. The car having been already returned here, it was necessary to order the plaintiffs to pay Mr Harper the £226. Lord Denning referred to the individualistic dictum of Pollock CB in *Taylor v Laird* (1856) 35 LJ Ex 329, at 332: 'One cleans another's shoes; what can the other do but put them on?' Lord Denning MR distinguished that case (at 202, emphasis added):

> That is undoubtedly the law when the person who does the work knows, or ought to know, that the property does not belong to him. He takes the risk of not being paid for his work on it. But it is very different when he honestly believes himself to be the owner of the property and does the work in that belief ... Here we have an innocent purchaser who bought the car in good faith and without notice of any defect in the title to it. He did work on it to the value of £226. The law is hard enough on him when it makes him give up the car itself. It would be most unjust if the company could not only take the car from him, but also the value of the improvements he has done to it — without paying for them. There is a principle at hand to meet the case. It derives from the law of restitution. The plaintiffs should not be allowed unjustly to enrich themselves at his expense. The court will order the plaintiffs, if they recover the car, or its improved value, to recompense the innocent purchaser for the work he has done on it. *No matter whether the plaintiffs recover it with the aid of the courts, or without it, the innocent purchaser will recover the value of the improvements he has done to it.*

Lord Denning MR accordingly (in the italicised words) countenanced the possibility not just of a passive claim (as a defence and counterclaim where the true owner sought specific delivery), but also an active claim which could be advanced by the improver as claimant. Phillimore and Cairns LJJ agreed that at least the passive claim was available. Further, it was appropriate on the instant facts to order the plaintiffs to pay for the value of the work done. There was little explicit discussion of the issue of enrichment. However, Phillimore LJ said that it was 'not seriously disputed in this case that the £226 had improved the value of the car, making its value far above what it was' (at 202). There was no possibility of free acceptance or request on the facts of this case. Accordingly, *Greenwood v Bennett* constitutes one of the leading examples of the recognition of incontrovertible benefit in the English law of unjust enrichment. It is further clear that the ultimate beneficiary of the mistaken improvement is the true owner. The appropriate ground for restitution is mistake. In the modern law, it seems clear that both an active as well as a passive claim will be available. However, for the contrary view see Weir [1973] CLJ 23.

3.8.3 Statutory recognition

The power of the court to grant an allowance to the improver of personal property as a condition for an order of the delivery of the goods is now recognised by s. 3(7) and s. 6 of the Torts (Interference with Goods) Act 1977. The Act is confined to the passive claim which was recognised in *Greenwood* v *Bennett*, and does not explicitly advert to the active claim. Section 6 of the 1977 Act explicitly recognises a significant counterclaim where the owner claims his property or its value, based upon the principle of unjust enrichment. By s. 6:

(1) If in proceedings for wrongful interference against a person (the 'improver') who has improved the goods, it is shown that the improver acted in the mistaken but honest belief that he had good title to them, an allowance shall be made for the extent to which, at the time as at which the goods fall to be valued in assessing damages, the value of the goods is attributable to the improvement.

(2) If, in proceedings for wrongful interference against a person (the 'purchaser') who has purported to purchase the goods—

    (a)   from the improver, or

    (b)   where after such a purported sale the goods passed by a further purported sale on one or more occasions, on any such occasion,

it is shown that the purchaser acted in good faith, an allowance shall be made on the principle set out in subsection (1).

For example, where a person in good faith buys a stolen car from the improver and is sued in conversion by the true owner the damages may be reduced to reflect the improvement, but if the person who bought the stolen car from the improver sues the improver for failure of consideration, and the improver acted in good faith, subsection (3) below will ordinarily make a comparable reduction in the damages he recovers from the improver.

(3) If in a case within subsection (2) the person purporting to sell the goods acted in good faith, then in proceedings by the purchaser for recovery of the purchase price because of failure of consideration, or in any other proceedings founded on that failure of consideration, an allowance shall, where appropriate, be made on the principle set out in subsection (1).

By s. 6(4) the principle also applies to contracts of hire purchase and other purported bailments of personal property.

3.8.4 Other authority

In *Rover International Ltd* v *Cannon Film Sales Ltd* [1989] 1 WLR 912, valuable work was carried out on behalf of Rover in respect of films belonging to Canon. The work was done in the mistaken belief that there was a contractual obligation to do the work and a contractual right to reimbursement in the shape of a portion of the profits from distributing the films. In fact, the underlying purported contract turned out to be void because of the incapacity of Rover at the relevant time. It was conceded on appeal that Rover was entitled to a *quantum meruit* in respect of the work done. The case is considered in more detail at 12.2. For discussion see Birks (1992), 86–96.

Lastly, brief mention should be made of the counterclaim by the defendant Ward in the case of *Guinness plc* v *Saunders* [1990] 2 AC 663. A director of the plaintiff company had been paid £5.2 million in connection with services rendered during a takeover bid. However, the underlying contract turned out to be void for want of authority. Ward claimed to be entitled to retain the money either on a *quantum meruit* basis, or as an equitable allowance. The claim must evidently have been based upon mistake or failure of consideration. The House of Lords gave short shrift to the counterclaim. Briefly, an award to a director in such a case would contradict the policy governing fiduciaries, their remuneration and the obligation to avoid a conflict between duty and interest. For more detailed discussion see 12.2 and Birks [1990] LMCLQ 330.

3.8.5 Equity

Similar principles have developed in equity in relation to the mistaken improvements of land. The seminal statement is in the speech of Lord Cranworth LC in *Ramsden* v *Dyson* (1866) LR 1 HL 129. A tenant took leases over two plots of land in Huddersfield and Bolton, spending in excess of £1,800. The tenant knew he had only a tenancy from year to year, or a tenancy at will, but believed that by building he became entitled to call for a 60-year lease. The landlord's successor sought to eject the tenant. The House of Lords held that on the evidence there was no encouragement or conduct on the part of the landlord which would justify equitable intervention, either to resist the ejection or to compensate the tenant for his improvement. The case is perhaps better known for its recognition of the doctrine of proprietary estoppel in the speech of Lord Kingsdown, dissenting. In contrast, the statement of principle by Lord Cranworth LC is more akin to unjust enrichment reasoning (at 140–41):

> If a stranger begins to build on my land supposing it to be his own, and I, perceiving his mistake, abstain from setting him right, and leave him to persevere in his error, a court of equity will not allow me afterwards to assert my title to the land on which he had expended money on the supposition that the land was his own. It considers that, when I saw the mistake into which he had fallen, it was my duty to be active and state my adverse title; and that it would be dishonest in me to remain wilfully passive on such an occasion, in order afterwards to profit by the mistake which I might have prevented.

This statement of principle clearly establishes two restitutionary principles. First, a defendant may be enriched where he freely accepts a benefit, knowing that he has the opportunity to reject it. Secondly, the benefit is an unjust one, either on the basis of the mistake by the improver, or again on the basis of free acceptance. In the instant case, the tenant made no mistake as to his present rights but was simply in error about the future conduct of a landlord. Accordingly it was only a misprediction rather than a mistake: Birks, 277–79.

This doctrine of acquiescence was restated by Fry J in *Willmott v Barber* (1880) 15 Ch D 96. Fry J enunciated his famous five probanda (at 105–106):

> In the first place the plaintiff must have made a mistake as to his legal rights. Secondly, the plaintiff must have expended some money or must have done some act (not necessarily upon the defendant's land) on the faith of his mistaken belief. Thirdly, the defendant, the possessor of the legal right, must know of the existence of his own right which is inconsistent with the right claimed by the plaintiff. . . . Fourthly, the defendant, the possessor of the legal right, must know of the plaintiff's mistaken belief of his rights. If he does not, there is nothing which calls upon him to assert his own rights. Lastly, the defendant, the possessor of the legal right, must have encouraged the plaintiff in his expenditure of money or in other acts which he has done, either directly or by abstaining from asserting his legal right.

Fry J, consistently with the principle as it has developed in relation to mistaken payments, held the contributory negligence by the mistaken improvement would not preclude recovery. Fry J commented: 'when the plaintiff is seeking relief, not on a contract, but on the footing of a mistake of fact, the mistake is not the less a ground for relief because he had the means of knowledge' (at 106).

Despite these seminal statements of principle, there has to date been little evidence of successful recovery by mistaken improvers of land. The subsequent history of proprietary estoppel has been more concerned with the doctrine of encouragement, as recognised by Lord Kingsdown in his dissenting speech in *Ramsden v Dyson*, rather than the doctrine of acquiescence as recognised by Lord Cranworth LC in the same case. The former doctrine appears to have more to do with perfection of expectations, rather than the reversal of unjust enrichment. For consideration of proprietary estoppel, see *Amalgamated Investment & Property Co. Ltd v Texas Commerce International Bank Ltd* [1982] QB 84 and *Taylor's Fashions Ltd v Liverpool Victoria Trustees Co. Ltd* [1982] QB 133.

3.9 PRACTICAL ISSUES

The burden of proof rests upon the payer or transferor to prove both the mistake and the causal efficacy of the error. There is no authoritative guidance in this context as yet as to whether the latter enquiry is satisfied where it is shown that the mistake was *a* cause, or whether it needs to be a significant cause. It is submitted that the former should suffice. As explained in 3.7 above, it is no bar to recovery that one factor in making the payment was the payer's own carelessness. As a matter of principle, and given the modern emphasis upon defences, it seems that where the 'but for' test of causation is satisfied, the claimant can succeed. Authority seems to support the wide formulation of mistake to include cases of what has been termed ignorance.

Does the payer need to give evidence that the person responsible for making the payment (if any such person exists or can be identified) did in fact make a mistake? In *Avon County Council* v *Howlett* [1983] 1 WLR 605, the defendant teacher was overpaid by the council while absent from work through sickness. There was no evidence from the relevant pay clerk(s), but the Court of Appeal inferred that the plaintiff council continued to pay the defendant at a full rate because the pay clerks concerned were unaware or had forgotten that the defendant had been sick and absent for more than six months. It was held that human error gave rise to the mistakes because the incorrect information had been fed into the computer. The Court of Appeal pointed out that the plaintiffs had not been able to identify the individual person or persons who were responsible for the errors. However, the Court suggested that in similar cases the responsible individuals should be identified and called as witnesses. Slade LJ stated (at 620): 'Employers who pay their employees under a computerised system should not in my opinion assume from the decision of this court in the present case that, if they overpay their employees through some kind of mistake, they are entitled to recover it simply for the asking.'

It is submitted that this stringent approach to the question of evidence may not be good law now. One fact weighing on the Court's mind in the *Avon County Council* case was the distinction between mistakes of fact and mistakes of law. Given the liberal approach of cases such as *Barclays Bank* and *Kleinwort Benson*, it is unlikely that the defence will have much to gain from insisting upon evidence as to the nature and quality of the mistake involved. It has been submitted that ignorance of a transfer will qualify as an operative mistake, as well as an active but erroneous decision-making process. In modern conditions there is little need for detailed probing of the actual conditions which generated the mistake.

FURTHER READING

Asterisks indicate especially useful works.

Cause of action

Goff and Jones, 177–202, 213–34, 236–39
Birks, 146–73
*J. Beatson and W. Bishop, 'Mistaken Payments in the Law of Restitution' (1986) 36 U of Toronto LJ 149–85 (also in Beatson, 137–76)
R. Sutton, 'Mistaken Payments: An Inner Logic Infringed?' (1987) 37 U of Toronto LJ 389

On defences

*R. Goode, 'The Bank's Right to Recover Money Paid on a Stopped Cheque' (1981) 97 LQR 254
P. Matthews, 'Stopped Cheques and Restitution' [1982] JBL 281

For the argument for mistake cases to be classified on the basis of failure of consideration

P. Matthews, 'Money Paid Under Mistake of Fact' (1980) 130 NLJ 587

P. Butler, 'Mistaken Payments, Change of Position and Restitution' in Finn, 87–137

On Kleinwort Benson

S. Hedley, 'Restitution — Mistake of Law — Reform in Haste, Repent at Leisure' [1999] CLJ 21

J. Finnis, 'The Fairy Tale's Moral' (1999) 115 LQR 170 (philosophical)

L. Smith, 'Restitution for Mistake of Law' [1999] *Restitution Law Review* 148

P. Birks, 'The Law of Restitution at the End of an Epoch' (1999) 28 W Aus L Rev 13, 30–49

On non-money benefits

T. Weir, 'Doing Good by Mistake — Restitution and Remedies' [1973] CLJ 23

P. Matthews, 'Freedom, Unrequested Improvements and Lord Denning' [1981] CLJ 340

E. McKendrick, 'Restitution and the mis-use of chattels — the need for a principled approach' in N. Palmer and E. McKendrick (eds), *Interests in Goods*, 2nd edn (1998), 897–917

4 Rescission for Misrepresentation and Mistake

4.1 INTRODUCTION

An important theme of this text is English law's respect for the security of transactions, recognised in the importance of the third question in the unjust enrichment enquiry (see 1.2). Where the alleged operative mistake takes place in the context of an apparently binding contractual arrangement, a distinct regime applies. There is a stark asymmetry between the treatment of spontaneous mistakes which result in binding contractual arrangements, where relief is rare, and spontaneous mistakes which result in extra-contractual payments or other transfers, where (as we saw in Chapter 3) a liberal regime of recovery obtains. Turning to contractual mistake, it is necessary to distinguish between a mistake which is induced by a misrepresentation by the transferee, and one which was spontaneously entertained by the transferor (Birks, 146–47). Since the Judicature Acts English courts have followed the liberal regime of the old Courts of Equity, in prima facie granting relief where contracts are entered as a result of misrepresentation, whether fraudulent, negligent or innocent. This leaves little room for the autonomous doctrine of mistake in the contractual context. Relief in response to a spontaneous mistake is rare. The remedy for an actionable misrepresentation is rescission, a cause of action in unjust enrichment.

Its juridical nature was examined by Robert Goff LJ in *Whittaker v Campbell* [1983] 3 All ER 582, at 586:

> Looked at realistically, a misrepresentation, whether fraudulent or innocent, induces a party to enter into a contract in circumstances where it may be unjust that the representor should be permitted to retain the benefit (the chose in action) so acquired by him. The remedy of rescission by which the unjust enrichment of the representor is prevented, though for historical and practical reasons treated in

books on the law of contract, is a straightforward remedy in restitution subject to limits which are characteristic of that branch of the law.

Nineteenth-century decisions on misrepresentation and non-disclosure by company directors and promoters provide a rich seam of case law, yielding sophisticated mechanisms for effecting mutual restitution under tainted transactions. The detail of the law can be found in the contractual texts (although the best account is by Goff and Jones, 257–88) and it is proposed here to consider only briefly conditions for the availability of rescission and the limits upon its availability.

4.2 WHAT IS AN ACTIONABLE MISREPRESENTATION?

First, it is traditionally stated that there must be a representation of fact, although to the extent that this formulation excludes representations of law it must be regarded with suspicion in the wake of *Kleinwort Benson Ltd* v *Lincoln City Council* [1999] 2 AC 349. There remain difficulties over whether a non-expert opinion can ground relief (see Goff and Jones, 261–63). As Lord Campbell LC famously stated, a representation can extend to a 'nod or a wink, or a shake of a head or a smile' (*Walters* v *Morgan* (1861) 3 De GF & J 718–24. However, where the transaction is not one of insurance, nor the representor a fiduciary, English law does not grant relief for non-disclosure.

The representation must be false and causally efficacious. The deceit case of *Edgington* v *Fitzmaurice* (1885) 29 Ch D 459, suggests that it is sufficient if the representation was *a* cause and not necessarily *the* cause of the representee entering into the transaction. Where the representation was material, in a sense of being capable of inducing a reasonable person to enter into the transaction, the burden of proving that the actual representee was not so induced shifts to the representor (*Redgrave* v *Hurd* (1881) 20 Ch D 1, at 21; *Smith* v *Chadwick* (1884) 9 App Cas 187, at 196). Alternatively, even where the representation was not material, the representee will succeed if he can demonstrate that it was calculated to induce him to enter into the transaction, and that he was so induced. Where the conditions are fulfilled a prima facie right to rescind obtains.

Where the transaction is executory, rescission simply takes the form of setting aside the otherwise binding obligations which the parties have assumed. Further, even where the transaction is partly or fully executed (Misrepresentation Act 1967, s. 1) the setting aside of extant obligations can be supplemented by an order that there be mutual restitution of benefits transferred under the contract, including money, land and personal property.

4.3 RESCISSION AND INDEMNITY

Claims for rescission for misrepresentation have been less common in the last three decades. Prior to the 1960s, compensatory damages for misstatements had been confined to cases where fraud could be proved. However, in the wake of s. 2(1) of the Misrepresentation Act 1967 and the common law developments since *Hedley Byrne & Co. Ltd* v *Heller & Partners Ltd* [1964] AC 465, there has been greater focus on compensatory options. Due to this shift of emphasis, it can be forgotten that rescission can encompass the grant of an indemnity against potential future liabilities.

In *Newbigging* v *Adam* (1886) 34 Ch D 582, the plaintiff was induced to enter into a partnership on the basis of misrepresentations as to the state of the business. Rescission was ordered comprising the return of the net sums which had been contributed to the business, together with an indemnity from the remaining partner against partnership debts and liabilities which he might be liable to pay. Bowen LJ observed (at 595):

> There ought, as it appears to me, to be a giving back and a taking back on both sides, including the giving back and taking back of the obligations which the contract has created, as well as the giving back and the taking back of the advantages.

Bowen LJ would confine the indemnity to obligations *created* by the contract. Cotton LJ held that the plaintiff was entitled to be 'relieved from the consequences and obligations which are the result of the contract which is set aside' (at 589); Fry LJ held (at 596): 'the plantiff is entitled to an indemnity in respect of all obligations entered into under the contract when those obligations are within the necessary or reasonable expectation of both the contracting parties at the time of the contract.' However, even on the wider formulations of Cotton LJ and Fry LJ the entitlement is not equivalent to a right to compensation. The question of the indemnity was no longer a live issue before the House of Lords, where it was accepted that there were no outstanding liabilities ((1888) 13 App Cas 398).

In *Whittington* v *Seale-Hayne* (1900) 82 LT 49, the plaintiff entered into a lease of premises for the purpose of poultry breeding. There were misrepresentations as to the sanitary conditions of the premises. It was held that the indemnity did not extend to the value of lost poultry, lost profits and other expenses. However, given the wide availability of damages for misrepresentation, the issue is one of pedagogical interest rather than practical importance. For discussion see Goff and Jones, 256–58.

4.4   LIMITS TO THE RIGHT TO RESCIND

By its very nature rescission is a drastic and stringent remedy the availability of which is circumscribed by a number of bars. It was at one time thought that the remedy was unavailable where a contract was fully executed, but such doubts have been removed by s. 1 of the Misrepresentation Act 1967. More significantly, rescission has often been perceived to be confined to the realm of the tangible. The aim of the courts, according to Lord Blackburn, 'has always been ... to give this relief whenever, by the exercise of its powers, it can do what is practically just, though it cannot restore the parties precisely to the state they were in before the contract' (*Erlanger* v *New Sombrero Phosphate Co.* (1878) 3 App Cas 1218, 1278–79). However, there has been insistence that mutual restitution be possible. Therefore, unless the party seeking relief can himself provide counter-restitution (*restitutio in integrum*) rescission will not be available. Birks has written of the courts regarding the impossibility of counter-restitution as being a defence in the law of restitution (Birks, 415–24, 475–76).

Certain benefits have been perceived by their very nature to be incapable of being restored, for example, services. In *Boyd & Forrest* v *Glasgow & South-Western Railway Company* [1915] SC (HL) 20, the House of Lords would have denied rescission of a railway construction contract on this ground. Lord Shaw of Dumfermline stated (at 36):

> The railway is there, the bridges are built, the excavations are made, the rails are laid, and the railway itself was in complete working two years before this action was brought. Accounts cannot obliterate it, and unless the railway is obliterated *restitutio in integrum* is impossible.

Similarly, a transferee cannot eat a cake and restore it. In contrast, it was possible in the sale of a business for the court to order an account of profits and make allowances for the deterioration in the subject-matter transferred (*Lagunas Nitrate Co.* v *Lagunas Syndicate* [1899] 2 Ch 392). The fact that the transferee can escape a bad bargain, for example, where the value of shares had dropped astronomically between the date of purchase and rescission, does not bar relief (*Armstrong* v *Jackson* [1917] 2 KB 822). Conversely, where the representee had sold shares to the representor following fraudulent misrepresentations as to the company's profitability, and the value of the shares had increased in the intervening period, the seller was entitled to the recovery of the shares (*Spence* v *Crawford* [1939] 3 All ER 271). Lord Wright stressed (at 288–89) that the court would be more drastic in exercising its powers in a case of fraud than in a case of innocent misrepresentation: 'Though the defendant has been fraudulent, he must not be robbed, nor must the plaintiff be unjustly enriched, as he would be if he both got back what he had parted with and kept what he received in return.' In that case the seller had to give credit for the purchase moneys received, but the buyer had to give up dividends received while off-setting subsequent losses.

The approach of the older cases could be utilised in support of the modern imperative to disregard difficulties of precise counter-restitution, and rather insist on mutual restitution, if necessary by valuing benefits transferred, and allowing substitutionary counter-restitution in money. The leading twentieth-century authorities concern undue influence. See 1.3.3, 2.6 and 32.4. However, in a case concerning the tort of deceit, the House of Lords has signalled its preference for the flexible approach. In *Smith New Court Securities Ltd* v *Citibank NA* [1997] AC 254, Lord Browne-Wilkinson was sceptical of a concession that a share purchase contract could not be rescinded simply because the stock that had been disposed of (at 262):

if the current law in fact provides (as the Court of Appeal thought) that there is no right to rescind the contract for sale of quoted shares once the specific shares purchased have been sold, the law will need to be closely looked at hereafter. Since, in such a case, identical shares can be purchased on the market, the defrauded purchaser can offer substantial *restitutio in integrum* which is normally sufficient.

A particular incidence of the counter-restitution obstacle, which is stated as a separate bar to rescission, is where a third party has acquired rights to the subject-matter of the original contract. In addition the remedy must be sought promptly (in practice meaning within weeks and months, rather than years) and the party seeking relief must unequivocally evince an intention no longer to treat the contract as binding, otherwise the right to rescind will be lost on the grounds of lapse of time or affirmation.

4.5   SECTION 2(2) OF THE MISREPRESENTATION ACT 1967

The stringency of full restitution as a response to what might be a comparatively minor or trivial misrepresentation prompted the legislature to give the courts an unparalleled discretion in s. 2(2) of the 1967 Act to disallow restitutionary relief and instead substitute compensation. Section 2(2) counter-balances the liberating influence of s. 1 which removed bars to rescission. It applies only in cases of non-fraudulent misrepresentation. Fraud unravels all.

Given what little authority there has been on rescission in the last three decades, there is accordingly even less on this subsection. The discretion is explicitly stated to be equitable. The court must have regard to:

(a)   the nature of the misrepresentation;
(b)   the loss that would be caused by it if the contract were upheld; and
(c)   the loss that rescission would cause to the representor.

Section 2(3) seems to anticipate that damages under s. 2(2) would be in a lesser amount than damages under s. 2(1). In *William Sindall plc* v *Cambridgeshire County Council* [1994] 1 WLR 1016, it was alleged that a valuable piece of land had been purchased as a result of misrepresentation concerning the non-existence of a sewer crossing the property. The allegation was not made out, but Hoffmann LJ indicated that if it had, he would have exercised the discretion under s. 2(2). In valuable guidance Hoffmann LJ stated that the measure of recovery under the subsection could never exceed recovery for damages for breach of warranty. Ordinarily the measure would be the difference between the property as it was represented to be and the property as it actually was. It will not encompass consequential losses (*Thomas Witter Ltd* v *TBP Industries Ltd* [1996] 2 All ER 573 at 588–91).

4.6 RESCISSION FOR MISTAKE

4.6.1 Common law mistake

The wide scope of the English jurisdiction to relieve against even innocent misrepresentations leaves little room for relief for mistake. It appears inapt to speak of two streams of case law where there has been only a trickle of authority, but what little there is suggests a different approach at common law to that which obtains in equity.

The leading common law case is *Bell* v *Lever Brothers Ltd* [1932] AC 161, supplemented by the influential discussion of Steyn J in *Associated Japanese Bank (International)* v *Credit du Nord SA* [1989] 1 WLR 255. Where a contract governs the transfer of benefits there is no room for the operation of the law of unjust enrichment, but where the contract is held to be void relief may be available. In *Bell*, Lever Brothers sought restitution of generous golden handshakes paid to the plaintiffs who were the management team of one of its subsidiary companies. The plaintiffs cooperated in the merger of this subsidiary company with its nearest rival and had given up valuable service contracts. However, Lever Brothers subsequently discovered that earlier, in breach of duty, the plaintiffs had made small profits on their own account by speculating on the cocoa market. Lever Brothers failed to establish fraud or non-disclosure. The House of Lords held that the contract would have been void where both parties were labouring under a mistake, and the subject-matter of the contract was essentially different to that which the parties assumed it to be. However, by a majority, it was held that the mistake was not of that magnitude.

The case is authority for a narrow doctrine of mistake at common law. A contract will be held to be void at common law if the subject-matter no longer exists (*res extincta*) or where the subject-matter already belongs to the purchaser (*res sua*). Where the mistake is only as to a quality of the subject-matter of the contract it will be void only where, first, the mistake is common to both parties, secondly, the difference renders the subject-matter essentially and radically different from what both parties thought it to be, and thirdly, there were reasonable grounds for that belief (*Associated Japanese Bank (International)* v *Credit du Nord SA* [1989] 1 WLR 255). In that case an accessory guarantee contract for the obligations under a sale-and-leaseback transaction in respect of non-existent engineering machines, was held to be void as closely analogous to the *res extincta* cases. Once the contract is void, in accordance with the third question, the contractual matrix is inapplicable, and claims may be brought for restitution of any money or property transferred. It was assumed in *Bell* that had the contract been void for mistake, the £50,000 golden handshakes would be recoverable, presumably on the ground of mistake or total failure of consideration.

4.6.2 Equitable mistake

There was some authority for equitable relief on the grounds of mistake in contract before the Judicature Acts (for example, *Cooper* v *Phibbs* (1867) LR 2 HL 149, a *res sua* case), but there was little authority for a coherent doctrine of equitable mistake until the bold synthesis of Denning LJ in *Solle* v *Butcher* [1950] 1 KB 671. It seems that mistake in equity does not render a contract void, but the court may set aside the contract where, first, the mistake is common, secondly, the subject-matter is rendered fundamentally different to what the parties supposed it to be, and thirdly, the party seeking relief is not himself at fault. *Solle* and *McGee* v *Pennine Insurance Co. Ltd* [1969] 2 QB 507 suggest that the test of fundamentality is less stringent than the common law test of 'essentially and radically different'. More recently, however, the Court of Appeal has signalled a return to the principle of sanctity of bargain, marginalising cases such as *Grist* v *Bailey* [1967] Ch 532 and *Laurence* v *Lexcourt Holdings Ltd* [1978] 1 WLR 1128 which followed the equitable route, by insisting on greater respect for the contractual allocation of risks in assessing allegations of mistake (*William Sindall plc* v *Cambridgeshire County Council* [1994] 1 WLR 1016). What is clear about the equitable doctrine is that the relief available to the court goes beyond simply awarding restitution, but can encompass setting aside contractual obligations and imposing new terms upon the parties. Therefore these cases are of only marginal significance to the law of restitution.

FURTHER READING

Asterisks indicate especially useful works.

Anson, 248–55, 327–32
*Goff and Jones, 257–98
Birks, 159–64
J. Cartwright, *Unequal Bargaining — A Study of the Vitiating Factor in the Formation of Contracts*, (1991), 61–148
N. Nahan, 'Rescission: A Case for Rejecting the Classical Model' (1997) 27 W Aus L Rev 66

5 *Ignorance*

5.1 THEORETICAL FOUNDATIONS

'Ignorance' is here used to mean lack of knowledge. Ignorance accordingly encompasses both the individual person who is unaware that her purse is being taken out of her bag, and the large corporation whose wealth is haemorrhaging away as the result of a dishonest scheme by a trusted employee.

Nothing was heard of ignorance as a ground for restitution until 1985 and the publication of Professor Birks's seminal work. Birks argued that cases of ignorance presented a stronger claim to restitution than those involving the most fundamental mistake. A claimant who was unaware of the transfer of wealth could in no way have consented to it. It was the paradigm instance of non-voluntary transfer. The argument is only sketched out in the *Introduction*. Ignorance is used to explain simple two-party cases of taking or finding another person's money (*Neate* v *Harding* (1851) 6 Ex 349, 155 ER 577 and *Moffatt* v *Kazana* [1969] 2 QB 152). Further, it was argued that ignorance was the true ground for restitution in *In re Diplock* [1948] Ch 465. Whereas that case is ordinarily classified as one based upon the mistake of law by the executors, the actual claimants were the next of kin. They were not the victims of any mistake. Rather the money was paid away without their consent by the executors. Lastly, ignorance could operate in respect of non-money benefits such as the claim by the owner of the horse for a *quantum valebat* against the person who 'borrows' the animal without consent, as contemplated by Lord Mansfield in *Hambly* v *Trott* (1776) 1 Cowp 371, at 375; 98 ER 1136. See for the argument Birks, 140–46.

An explosion of reported litigation over the succeeding 10 years concerning the dissipation of corporate assets and disputes over laundered moneys propelled this theoretical proposition to the centre-stage. In 1989, Peter Birks published his magisterial essay 'Misdirected Funds: Restitution for the Recipient' [1989] LMCLQ 296, which contained the full length version of the thesis. The proposed ground for restitution of ignorance became a battle ground for the future of the subject. Should the law be concerned with the integrity of the transferor's decision-making process? Or rather should the law be concerned with the conduct and state of mind of the defendant recipient? How should two seemingly irreconcilable streams of case law be rationalised? Common law authority appeared to favour strict liability of the recipient. In contrast, cases argued upon equitable principles (which predominated) appear to favour liability based on fault. Further, should the same restitutionary principles apply equally to simple two-party subtraction cases and more complex cases of indirect receipt? The debate has continued to rage in the journals, and to date ignorance has not been recognised as a ground for restitution in any reported case. The ultimate resolution of this debate will have profound implications for the structure of the law of unjust enrichment. The thesis and its detractors will now be reviewed.

5.2   BIRKS'S THESIS: IGNORANCE AS A GROUND FOR RESTITUTION

There are a number of essential steps in the argument. First, the legal responsibility of the recipient of misdirected funds is based on a regime of strict liability, subject to his being able to establish a restitutionary defence which would extinguish or diminish that prima facie liability. Liability in restitution is generally not based on fault. Secondly, the regime of strict liability obtains both for comparatively simple two-party situations, and for where money is misdirected through numerous hands before reaching the defendant. There is no difference in principle between two-party and multi-party configurations. Thirdly, the cause of action or ground for restitution is usually ignorance, meaning that the transferor did not know about the movement of wealth, and accordingly gave no consent to it. If the mistaken payer is entitled to restitution, it necessarily follows that the person whose money is siphoned off without his knowledge is equally entitled. Fourthly, the state of mind of the defendant recipient is not irrelevant; it is simply irrelevant to establishing the cause of action. The defendant's conduct and knowledge is highly relevant to whether he can avail himself of any of the appropriate restitutionary defences: mainly, good faith purchase, ministerial receipt, or good faith change of position.

Birks accordingly reviews the authorities and analyses them in terms of strict or fault-based liability. Those supporting strict liability include the cases commonly treated as examples of tracing at common law such as *Clarke* v *Shee and Johnson* (1774) 1 Cowp 197, 98 ER 1041 and *Banque Belge pour L'Etranger* v *Hambrouck* [1921] 1 KB 321. In addition, the crucial case favouring strict liability is *In re Diplock* [1948] Ch 458. It is important that this case was decided on equitable principles, and in many ways it forms the crux of Birks's argument. In contrast are a number of cases decided explicitly on the basis of fault. These cases are usually classified under the label of knowing receipt in equity. Despite the fact that it is a personal claim, knowing receipt is often stated to render the recipient accountable as a constructive trustee. Examples include *Carl Zeiss Stiftung* v *Herbert Smith & Co. (No. 2)* [1969] 2 Ch 276 and, favouring a high degree of fault, *In re Montagu's*

Settlement Trusts [1987] Ch 264. These authorities insist on want of probity. Elsewhere, equitable authorities require at least constructive knowledge to ground liability. Birks argues that the equity cases contradict the policy of strict liability for personal restitutionary claims which is already well established at common law. Birks emphatically favours the maintenance of the strict liability orientation of the law of restitution, subject to appropriate defences. He concludes ([1989] LMCLQ 296, at 341):

> The personal liability of the recipient of misdirected funds is a strict restitutionary liability. It is based on the proposition that the defendant (the recipient) has been enriched at the expense (in the subtraction sense) of the plaintiff, in circumstances in which that enrichment is unjust by reason of the plaintiff's not having consented to it. The 'unjust' factor can be named 'ignorance', signifying that the plaintiff, at the time of the enrichment, was absolutely unaware of the transfer from himself to the defendant. 'Ignorance' is similar to but, as a factor calling for restitution, stronger than mistake, for in cases of mistake the plaintiff's decision is impaired but in cases of 'ignorance' impairment is an understatement: there is no decision at all.... The strict quality of the recipient's liability does not exclude the possibility that some recipients may be able to take advantage of special defences.

The 1989 essay is an extraordinary work of synthesis. It draws upon disparate streams of poorly understood doctrine and neglected case law, such as tracing at common law, tracing in equity and knowing receipt. It creatively reinterprets those authorities in a rational and intelligible manner, which is consistent with the structure and policies of the modern law of unjust enrichment. It was written when *Agip (Africa) Ltd* v *Jackson* [1990] Ch 265, [1991] Ch 547 had just been decided at first instance and *Lipkin Gorman* v *Karpnale Ltd* [1989] 1 WLR 1340, [1991] 2 AC 548 had progressed as far as the Court of Appeal. A not uncharacteristic reaction was that of Charles Harpum, who in Birks (ed.), *The Frontiers of Liability* (1994), vol. 1, 9, described it as 'an important article, more notable for the excellence of its ideas than for its use of precedent' and stated that Birks's 'argument was untenable on the authorities as they stood prior to *Lipkin Gorman* [in the House of Lords]' (at 24). Birks discusses the decision of the House of Lords in *Lipkin Gorman* in Birks, 'The English Recognition of Unjust Enrichment' [1991] LMCLQ 473, where he laments the House of Lords' characterisation of the cause of action as being a proprietary one, and insists it should properly be classified as arising in 'ignorance'. Birks returned to the theme of the tension between strict and fault liability in Birks, 'Persistent Problems in Misdirected Moneys: A Quintet' [1993] LMCLQ 218. This essay also deals more explicitly with problems thrown up by the technique of tracing in the misdirected funds cases.

5.3 SUPPORTERS AND DETRACTORS

In an equally magisterial, but more orthodox, account preceding Birks's 1989 article, Charles Harpum surveyed the equitable authority: Harpum, 'The Stranger as

Constructive Trustee' (1986) 102 LQR 114, 267. Harpum argued that the accountability of the recipient and that of the assistant should be sharply distinguished. Whereas constructive knowledge was sufficient to make the former liable, the latter should be liable only in the event of dishonesty or want of probity. Harpum's arguments are updated in more concise form in Harpum, 'The Basis of Equitable Liability' in Birks (ed.), *The Frontiers of Liability* (1994), vol. 1, at 9–25. Harpum argues in the wake of *Lipkin Gorman* v *Karpnale Ltd* [1991] 2 AC 548 and the recognition of the defence of change of position, that liability in equity for the recipient should be strict, subject to defences. While it can be observed that in the result, the position reached by Harpum is similar to that of Birks, the two differ as to the relationship between law and equity. Birks favours fusion between the components of the modern law. Harpum is content to restate equitable principles as a supplement to the common law. A similar position was taken by Sir Peter Millett in 'Tracing the Proceeds of Fraud' (1991) 107 LQR 71. The learned judge, who had had by that time considerable experience of money laundering litigation, argued (at 71):

> in all but the simplest cases recourse to the common law should be abandoned, that attempts to rationalise and develop the common law rules are unlikely to succeed and should no longer be pursued, and that attempts should be made instead to develop a unified restitutionary remedy based on equitable principles.

Sir Peter Millett also took the view that the liability of the recipient should be strict, whether or not he had parted with the money, but subject to change of position.

The most direct challenges to ignorance as a cause of action come from Swadling and Virgo. In Swadling, 'A claim in restitution?' [1996] LMCLQ 63, a comment upon *Macmillan Inc.* v *Bishopsgate Investment Trust plc (No. 3)* [1996] 1 WLR 387, it is said of Birks's advocacy of a cause of action termed ignorance (at 64): 'though the logic of the argument is compelling, it is ultimately flawed, for it takes no account of the effects the different vitiating factors have on the passing of property between plaintiff and defendant.' Swadling argues that ordinarily the property will pass in money where there has been a mistaken payment. Only if there has been a fundamental mistake (e.g., as to the identity of the payee) will property remain with the transferor. In a case of wealth subtracted from a person who is ignorant of the transfer, no property passes because there was no consent whatsoever to the transaction. Accordingly, the transferor's claim is one for the vindication of property rights. Swadling goes on to argue that a restitutionary claim is unavailable in these circumstances, because a claimant cannot show that the defendant has been enriched at his expense. Even when the claimant's title is erased by mixing or by an exception to *nemo dat*, according to Swadling there still no transfer or conveyance of a proprietary interest from claimant to defendant. What the defendant has is a new title. Accordingly *Macmillan* was a proprietary claim. Swadling is even sceptical as to whether *Lipkin Gorman* is a restitutionary, rather than a proprietary, claim.

It should be observed that the argument proceeds on the basis of authority, rather than principle. It must also be observed that the authority which exists originates largely from a criminal context: *Moynes* v *Cooper* [1956] 1 QB 439; *Ilich* v *R* (1987) 162 CLR 110, at 140–41; Williams [1977] CLJ 62. The argument appears to rest upon a technical view of the passing of title. It assumes narrow interpretations of both the 'enrichment' test and the 'at the expense of' test. It is assumed that the defendant is not enriched unless he has indefeasible legal title to the money. Secondly, it is assumed that 'at the expense of' is confined to a direct conveyance from claimant to defendant. Both limited conceptions can themselves be questioned. It is submitted that the courts are more likely to take a common-sense view as to the satisfaction of the requirement of the defendant being enriched at the expense of the claimant. What is crucial is that the defendant has been enriched in fact, and identifiably so by value ultimately derived from the claimant. In most misdirected funds cases, title, at least in the common law sense, will have been readily erased on the way to the defendant. Where a tracing exercise is necessary, it is artificial to speak of the claimant vindicating his proprietary rights, as Swadling himself concedes in respect of *Lipkin Gorman*.

Even more emphatic is Virgo, who in 'Reconstructing the Law of Restitution' (1996) 10 TLI 20, another discussion of *Macmillan*, argues (at 24):

> The conclusion from this interpretation of *Macmillan* and its implications for the explanation of *Lipkin Gorman* is ironic and surprising. *Lipkin Gorman* v *Karpnale*, the leading case in the law of restitution, which recognised that there is an independent body of law based on the principle of reversing unjust enrichment, should not be regarded as having anything to do with unjust enrichment at all. The cause of action should have been treated as proprietary with restitutionary remedies being awarded to vindicate the plaintiff's continuing proprietary interest, an interest which continued beyond the point when the defendant received the money from the thief.

Swadling's arguments are questioned by Grantham and Rickett in 'Restitution, Property and Ignorance — A Reply to Mr Swadling' [1996] LMCLQ 463, who argue that the focus of restitution is upon value and benefit. While accepting that in many cases ignorance will not pass any title to the defendant, the authors do not accept that this should preclude a restitutionary claim. Grantham and Rickett are unsure as to whether a transferor who has lost his title would in any event have a proprietary claim. Swadling's arguments are adopted and developed by Bant, ' "Ignorance" as a Ground of Restitution — Can It Survive?' [1998] LMCLQ 18. Lord Millett, in contrast, appears to accept a restitutionary cause of action in the situations discussed by Birks, but prefers the nomenclature of 'want of title' to 'ignorance': Sir Peter Millett, in Cornish, 199, at 209. Similarly Lord Nicholls favours a rationalisation of knowing receipt, switching to a restitutionary regime based on strict liability, but subject to change of position. The argument makes much use of *Re Diplock*: Lord Nicholls in Cornish, at 231–45.

5.4 CONCLUSIONS

Birks has consistently and persuasively argued for a separate category of non-voluntary transfer termed ignorance. However, even Birks admits that the line between ignorance and mistake may be hard to draw in practice: Birks, 142. It may have been that the advocacy of ignorance was influenced by a desire to escape now-discarded restrictions upon recovery of the mistaken payments, such as that only a fundamental mistake or liability mistake engendered recovery and that a mistake of law did not. A narrow view of mistake is no longer a concern.

Burrows accepts Birks's argument about ignorance: Burrows, 139–60. However, it is difficult to reconcile this with Burrows's flawed insistence upon a privity restriction in the law of unjust enrichment: Burrows, 44–54. Ignorance as a ground of restitution is also accepted by McKendrick, 'Tracing Misdirected Funds' [1991] LMCLQ 378 and McKendrick, 'Restitution, Misdirected Funds and Change of Position' (1992) 55 MLR 377.

In opposition to the recognition of ignorance, are the arguments of Swadling, Virgo and Bant, who appear to prefer a greater role for pure proprietary claims at the expense of restitutionary claims in respect of misdirected funds. Also ranged against Professor Birks's elegant arguments are the following. First, as a matter of positive law, no English case explicitly acknowledges ignorance as ground for restitution. Secondly, Goff and Jones reject ignorance as a separate ground of restitution to mistake: Goff and Jones, 175–77. Thirdly, mistake has been defined by appellate courts to include cases of ignorance (*David Securities Pty Ltd v Commonwealth Bank of Australia* (1992) 175 CLR 353, at 369–74 and *Kleinwort Benson Ltd v Lincoln City Council* [1999] 2 AC 349, at 410). See 3.2 above. Fourthly, Goff and Jones also conclude that ignorance may prevent legal title to property passing, and accordingly classify *Lipkin Gorman* as a claim based upon the fact that the defendant received the claimant's property: Goff and Jones, 177. Fifthly, with respect to claims for knowing receipt, recent case law still insists upon knowledge or fault on behalf of the defendant, and often a high degree of fault before awarding restitution (*In re Montagu's Settlement Trusts* [1987] Ch 264 and *Eagle Trust plc v SBC Securities Ltd* [1995] BCC 231).

FURTHER READING

Asterisks indicate especially useful works.

Birks, 140–46
Goff and Jones, 175–77
*C Harpum, 'The Stranger as Constructive Trustee' (1986) 102 LQR 114, 267
*P. Birks, 'Misdirected Funds: Restitution from the Recipient' [1989] LMCLQ 296
P. Birks, 'Misdirected Funds' (1989) 105 LQR 352
P. Birks, 'Misdirected Funds Again' (1989) 105 LQR 528
A. Burrows, 'Misdirected Funds — A Reply' (1990) 106 LQR 20

*Sir Peter Millett, 'Tracing the Proceeds of Fraud' (1991) 107 LQR 71

P. Birks, 'The English Recognition of Unjust Enrichment' [1991] LMCLQ 473, 473–97

*P. Birks, 'Persistent Problems in Misdirected Money: A Quintet' [1993] LMCLQ 218

*C. Harpum, 'The Basis of Equitable Liability' in Birks (ed.), *The Frontiers of Liability* (1994), vol. 1, 9–25

S. Gardner, 'Knowing Assistance and Knowing Receipt: Taking Stock' (1996) 112 LQR 56

*W. Swadling, 'A Claim in Restitution?' [1996] LMCLQ 63

G. Virgo, 'Reconstructing the Law of Restitution' (1996) 10 *Trusts Law International* 20

R. Grantham and C. Rickett, 'Restitution, property and ignorance — a reply to Mr Swadling' [1996] LMCLQ 463

E. Bant, ' ''Ignorance'' as a ground for restitution — can it survive?' [1998] LMCLQ 18

Sir Peter Millett, 'Restitution and Constructive Trusts', in Cornish, 199–207

*Lord Nicholls, 'Knowing Receipt: The Need for a New Landmark', in Cornish, 231–45

C. Harpum, 'Knowing Receipt: Some Reflections', in Cornish, 247–50

6 Duress

6.1 THEORETICAL FOUNDATIONS

An individual's right to a free and fair choice in the disposal of his wealth necessitates the law's protection where a party is coerced into a transaction as the result of a threat to his interests. Historically, the common law protected a person's interest in bodily integrity and, in a more limited way, in his proprietary interests. More recently the law has been generalised to encompass non-proprietary economic interests, most commonly entitlement to contractual performance. This rationalisation was prompted by an influential article by Beatson which concluded that 'in a modern society there is no justification for the assumption that physical coercion is more potent than economic coercion': 'Duress as a Vitiating Factor in Contract' [1974] CLJ 97. The ingredients of the cause of action were identified by Lord Diplock in *Universe Tankships Inc. of Monrovia* v *International Transport Workers' Federation, The Universe Sentinel* [1983] 1 AC 366, at 384:

> The rationale is that his apparent consent was induced by pressure exercised upon him by that other party which the law does not regard as legitimate, with the consequence that the consent is treated in law as revocable unless approbated either expressly or by implication after the illegitimate pressure has ceased to operate on his mind.

It is appropriate to consider three factors. First, the ingredients for a plea of duress, namely causally efficient illegitimate pressure. Secondly, the nature of the interests protected. Thirdly, restrictions on the availability of relief where a prima facie case has been made out. The law has developed briskly over recent decades, as was noticed in *Woolwich Equitable Building Society* v *Inland Revenue Commissioners* [1993] AC 70, where Lord Goff observed (at 165): 'I would not think it right, especially bearing in mind the development of the concept of economic duress, to regard the categories of compulsion for present purposes as closed.'

6.2 THE INGREDIENTS OF DURESS

6.2.1 Pressure

This encompasses threats, both explicit and implicit. A threat is an insistent 'unless' statement which specifies adverse consequences if the recipient does not undertake the demanded course of conduct. For example, 'If you do not do the washing-up, I will leave you'. The courts will review the whole of the evidence and may identify a veiled threat although there is no specific demand (*B & S Contracts and Designs Ltd v Victor Green Publications Ltd* [1984] ICR 419). In that case an implicit threat not to provide urgently needed services unless an extra payment was made was held to be an implicit threat. There may be difficult cases where the parties are already in a contractual relationship, but where one laconically announces that he cannot continue to perform. Falling on the other side of the line was *Williams v Roffey Brothers & Nicholls (Contractors) Ltd* [1991] 1 QB 1, where the Court of Appeal upheld a good faith renegotiation of a construction sub-contract where the initiative for the promise to pay more to secure completion of the work came from the main contractor. In the view of Russell LJ, there was 'no hint' of duress by the sub-contractor on the pleaded facts (at 17). That case is also authority for the proposition that in the context of commercial renegotiations the defence of duress has replaced the contractual doctrine of consideration as the conceptual vehicle of determining whether the new arrangements should be upheld (see also *Vantage Navigation Corp. v Suhail and Saud Bahwan Buildings Materials LLC, The Alev* [1989] 1 Lloyd's Rep 138, at 147).

6.2.2 Illegitimacy

The touchstone of illegitimacy can be traced back to *The Universe Sentinel* [1983] 1 AC 366 and appears to have been deliberately chosen as broader than 'unlawful'. That case concerned the long-running campaign by the ITF to 'black' ships sailing under 'flags of convenience' in order to improve the employment condition of crews on board. The conduct of the trade union, though prima facie unlawful and tortious, was legitimated by statute. This immunity in respect of tortious causes of action was held by the majority of the House of Lords not necessarily to extend to a cause of action in restitution, which was not dependent upon the breach of a primary duty imposed by law. Lord Diplock observed (at 385):

> The use of economic duress to induce another person to part with property or money is not a tort *per se*; the form that the duress takes may, or may not, be tortious. The remedy to which economic duress gives rise is not an action for damages but an action for restitution of property or money exacted under such duress and the avoidance of any contract that had been induced by it.

Despite this recognition that the threatened course of conduct need not necessarily be a breach of a legal duty, the vast majority of the decided cases do concern threats of tortious conduct, or threats to break contractual undertakings. The limits were tested in *CTN Cash and Carry Ltd* v *Gallaher Ltd* [1994] 4 All ER 714, where a long-running dispute between a wholesale supplier and a retailer over which was responsible for a stolen consignment of cigarettes was resolved by the supplier demanding full payment, stating that otherwise it would not in the future grant credit facilities to the retailer. The retailer paid. Subsequently the wholesaler accepted that the cigarettes had been its responsibility. The Court of Appeal held that the wholesaler was fully entitled to refuse to enter into any future contracts with the retailer, or to enter into future contracts on similar terms to those which had previously obtained with them. Steyn LJ accepted that the fact that the wholesaler had 'used lawful means does not by itself remove the case from the scope of the doctrine of economic duress' (at 718). It was accepted that in a number of cases threats of lawful acts had engendered restitutionary claims, but it was suggested that the category of lawful act duress was small.

6.2.3 Inducement

The most difficult question in many duress claims is whether the requirement of causation is satisfied. In the leading case of *Barton* v *Armstrong* [1976] AC 104, the Privy Council divided on the question of whether threats of violence were influential, when there were commercial factors inducing the recipient of the threats to sign an agreement. One difficulty is that the causal requirement appears to be more stringent in respect of threats to economic interests. For the purpose of duress to the person, *Barton* v *Armstrong* establishes that it is sufficient that threats of violence were *a* reason for entering transaction as opposed to *the* reason, or predominate reason or clinching reason. Further, it was held, apparently by analogy with fraudulent misrepresentation, that the burden of proof on causation was reversed. It was for the party making the threats to demonstrate that they contributed nothing to the other party's decision to transact.

This victim-friendly approach to causation is not replicated when we turn to the cases where economic interests have been threatened. It was suggested in the earlier cases, somewhat cryptically, that the pressure must have overborne the victim's will or must amount to a 'coercion of the will so as to vitiate consent' (*Occidental Worldwide Investment Corp.* v *Skibs A/S Avanti, The Siboen and The Sibotre* [1976] 1 Lloyd's Rep 293, at 336; *Pau On* v *Lau Yiu Long* [1980] AC 614). One interpretation of these phrases is that it required the pressure to be not simply *a* cause but *the* cause or the dominant cause. However, in the most recent discussion in the House of Lords, Lord Goff considered this test inappropriate and instead suggested that 'it is now accepted that economic pressure may be sufficient to amount to duress for this purpose, provided at least that the economic pressure may be categorised as illegitimate and has constituted a significant cause inducing the plaintiff to enter into the relevant contract' (*Dimskal Shipping Co. SA* v *International*

Transport Workers' Federation, The Evia Luck (No. 2) [1992] 2 AC 152, at 165; compare *Crescendo Management Pty Ltd* v *Westpac Banking Corp.* (1988) 19 NSWLR 40, at 45–46 which applied the *Barton* v *Armstrong* test of *a* cause and the reversal of the burden of proof to a case of economic duress).

More helpfully, the courts have consistently identified four factors going to the question as to whether the threats were a cause or a significant cause:

    (a)   Was there any protest?

    (b)   Did the victim have any reasonable alternative course of action, including the availability of adequate legal remedies?

    (c)   Did the victim receive independent advice?

    (d)   What subsequent steps were taken to avoid the contract?

See *Pau On* v *Lau Yiu Long* [1980] AC 614, at 635. Further, it has been suggested by Kerr LJ that the consequences of a refusal to cooperate by the victim must be 'serious and immediate' (*B & S Contracts and Designs Ltd* v *Victor Green Publications Ltd* [1984] ICR 419, at 428). The importance of protest has been stressed in a number of cases (*Maskell* v *Horner* [1915] 3 KB 106, *The Siboen and The Sibotre* [1976] 1 Lloyd's Rep 293 and *North Ocean Shipping Co. Ltd* v *Hyundai Construction Co Ltd, The Atlantic Baron* [1979] QB 705). The perceived adequacy and ready availability of an alternative legal remedy, such as delivery up for wrongful interference of goods or an injunction compelling contractual performance, were factors in *Astley* v *Reynolds* (1731) 2 Str 915, 93 ER 939 and *Pau On* v *Lau Yiu Long* [1980] AC 614. All these factors can be summed up in the question: did the victim have any reasonable alternative course of action? However, the victim need not be helpless or lacking in options. Rather, as Justice Holmes observed in *Union Pacific RR* v *Public Commission of Missouri* 248 US 67, at 70: 'It always is for the interest of the party under duress to choose the lesser of two evils. But the fact that a choice was made according to interest does not exclude duress. It is the characteristic of duress properly so called.'

6.3 THE TRADITIONAL CATEGORIES

6.3.1 Duress to the person

This encompasses threats of violence to an individual or his immediate family. The leading case is *Barton* v *Armstrong* [1976] AC 104, which, as described in 6.2.3 above, adopts a causal test which is very favourable to the recipient of the threat. A struggle for control of a development company led to Barton agreeing to buy out Armstrong's interest. Subsequently Barton sought to have the agreement set aside on the basis of threats of violence, mostly consisting of late-night, heavy-breathing phone calls. The trial judge refused relief, holding that commercial necessity was the predominant motive for Barton's entering the contract. The Privy Council (by a majority) disagreed with this holding of fact, stating that the threats were at least *a* reason for entering the contract, and that was sufficient.

6.3.2   Duress of goods

In *Maskell* v *Horner* [1915] 3 KB 106, Lord Reading CJ stated (at 118): 'If a person pays money, which he is not bound to pay, under the compulsion of an urgent and pressing necessity or of seizure, actual or threatened, of his goods he can recover it as money had and received.'

It was once thought that there was a significant distinction between payments and agreements to pay. A payment made as a result of duress of goods was recoverable in restitution (*Astley* v *Reynolds* (1731) 2 Str 915, 93 ER 939). In contrast, if a party promised money under an agreement resulting from duress of goods, that contract was valid (*Skeate* v *Beale* (1841) 11 Ad & E 983, 113 ER 688). One consequence of the recognition of duress in the commercial context is that this anomaly has been discarded (*The Evia Luck (No. 2)* [1992] 2 AC 152). The classic case is that of a bailee, often a carrier, who refuses to return the goods of the bailor unless an additional uncontracted for benefit is provided. In *Astley* v *Reynolds*, a pawnbroker claimed interest over the maximum permitted amount, and refused to deliver up the pledgor's goods unless it was paid. It was held (at 916):

> this is a payment by compulsion; the plaintiff might have such an immediate want of his goods, that an action of trover [wrongful interference with goods] would not do his business . . . we must take it that he paid money relying on his legal remedy to get it back.

The older cases concern carriers, often the new-fangled railway companies. Consider, for example, *Great Western Railway Co.* v *Sutton* (1869) LR 4 HL 226, in which Willes J stated (at 249):

> when a man pays more than he is bound to do by law for the performance of a duty which the law says is owed to him for nothing, or for less than he has paid, there is a compulsion or concussion in respect of which he is entitled to recover the excess by *condictio indebiti*, or action for money had and received. This is every day's practice as to excess freight.

For a recent example in the context of carriage of goods by sea, consider *The Alev* [1989] 1 Lloyd's Rep 438.

Even when the mistake of law bar was extant, while not providing a cause of action itself, it did not prohibit recovery on the alternative basis of duress of goods. Often the payment, while made under protest, would be made under a mistaken understanding of the law (*Maskell* v *Horner* [1915] 3 KB 106).

6.4   THE RECOGNITION OF ECONOMIC DURESS

Birks has suggested that it may be necessary to use a test of bad faith in the context of economic duress. In this context bad faith is described as pressure 'intended to exploit the plaintiff's weakness rather than to solve financial or other problems of the defendant': Birks, 183. This suggestion was made to deal with the problem of policing renegotiations of contracts. With some prescience Birks employs an example from the building contract context (at 182–83), which posed the problem eventually faced by the Court of Appeal in *Williams* v *Roffey Brothers & Nicholls (Contractors) Ltd* [1991] 1 QB 1. The difficulty in this context is in mediating between two conflicting policies, one favouring accommodation between the parties, the other fostering responsibility and realism in the context of renegotiations and in the bidding and tendering process. The liberal approach to consideration taken by the Court of Appeal in that case leaves it to the doctrine of economic duress to establish the boundaries of reasonable renegotiation. It may be that bad faith itself is not the touchstone; rather, what is required is the deliberate exploitation of the victim's perceived weakness. A threat not to supply goods or services may leave a victim little practical choice but to comply with the oppressor's demands where, for example, the victim has in turn obligations to third parties to render performance, and those goods or services are not readily available elsewhere. Many of the cases emphasize that a finding of duress is a matter of fact for the first instance judge (*Hennessy* v *Craigmyle & Co. Ltd* [1986] ICR 461, at 469 *per* Sir John Donaldson MR).

An early case featuring deliberate exploitation is *D & C Builders* v *Rees* [1966] 2 QB 617. The defendant owed a firm of jobbing builders the sum of £480. The builders were in dire financial straits. While the defendant was incapacitated by flu, his wife offered the builders £300 on an 'all-or-nothing' basis. Fearing bankruptcy, they accepted. When the firm sued for the balance, the Court of Appeal found for it, applying the rule in *Foakes* v *Beer* (1884) 9 App Cas 605 that part payment of a debt does not discharge the debt. Lord Denning MR's judgment (at 625) contains an early account of economic duress as an alternative ratio:

> The debtor's wife held the creditor to ransom. The creditor was in need of money to meet his own commitments, and she knew it . . . she was putting undue pressure on the creditor. She was making a threat to break the contract (by paying nothing) and she was doing it so as to compel the creditor to do what he was unwilling to do (to accept £300 in settlement): and she succeeded. He complied with her demands. That was on recent authority a case of intimidation.

In *Occidental Worldwide Investment Corp.* v *Skibs A/S Avanti, The Siboen and The Sibotre* [1976] 1 Lloyd's Rep 293, Kerr J was prepared to accept that economic duress may vitiate a contract, but rejected as 'much too wide' the submission that duress is made out 'whenever one party to a contract threatens to commit a breach of it and the other party agrees to vary or cancel the contract under this threat because it has no effective legal remedy in respect of the threatened breach and has in this sense been compelled to agree' (at 334–35). The facts fell a long way short of duress. A charterers' representative had failed to protest in time at a threatened withdrawal of vessels unless more hire was paid. Further, it was held, he regarded the renegotiation as a binding compromise and had sought to uphold it in a subsequent arbitration. Therefore, although acting under great pressure, it was commercial pressure only (at 336).

In *North Ocean Shipping Co. Ltd* v *Hyundai Construction Co. Ltd, The Atlantic Baron* [1979] QB 705, a shipbuilding contract had a price payable in instalments in US dollars. After the first instalment the dollar was devalued by 10 per cent, and the yard demanded a corresponding increase in the value of the remaining instalments, making it clear that otherwise the ship would not be completed. The case was a borderline one, but ultimately Mocatta J decided that although a prima facie case of economic duress was made out, the variation had subsequently been affirmed by the buyers. There had been no effective protest by the buyers and they had in turn received consideration in the form of a corresponding increase in the letter of credit in their favour which acted as security against default by the shipbuilders. In support of the finding of duress there was the fact that the buyers submitted because they had agreed to a lucrative three-year time charter of the vessel with Shell beginning on completion, but the shipbuilders were unaware of this fixture. It should be noted that the buyers did not allege that the shipbuilders' proposals were made in bad faith. However, Mocatta J did 'not consider the Yard's ignorance of the Shell charter material. It may well be that had they known of it they would have been even more exigent' (at 719). While failing on the facts, these cases provided the first explicit support in English law for the recognition of economic duress.

Subsequent cases yield clear findings of the application of economic duress. In *B & S Contracts and Designs Ltd* v *Victor Green Publications Ltd* [1984] ICR 419, the plaintiffs agreed to erect stands for the defendants for an exhibition at Olympia from 23 April to 27 April 1979. The plaintiffs were embroiled in an industrial dispute with their employees. The defendants were prepared to advance part of the contract price to the plaintiffs, whose employees were refusing to do the contract work, knowing that the plaintiffs were having cash-flow problems. However, the plaintiffs made it plain that they would not complete their obligations unless they received a further sum in excess of the contract price. As at 17 April the situation was summed up by a director of the defendants: 'Well, you have me over a barrel' (at 422). The money was paid, but later deducted from the balance of the contract price. The defendants later successfully resisted a claim for the extra sum on the ground of duress. As Griffiths LJ made clear (at 426), in view of the timescale a refusal to comply would have meant the defendants would not have been able 'to erect the stands ... which would have dearly caused grave damge to their reputation and I would have thought might have exposed them to very heavy claims from the exhibitors who had leased space from them.' These third-party consequences were obvious to the plaintiffs.

Similarly in *Vantage Navigation Corp.* v *Suhail and Saud Bahwan Building Materials LLC, The Alev* [1989] 1 Lloyd's Rep 138, shipowners refused to release steel transported under 'freight prepaid' bills of lading to the defendant cargo-owners in Muscat. The time charterers had become insolvent owing the shipowners substantial sums in unpaid hire, so the shipowners insisted on the cargo-owners paying port expenses and discharging costs. The cargo-owners signed agreements under protest, which they subsequently repudiated. The delay in delivering steel would have seriously dislocated the defendants' business, which included supplying the steel for sub-buyers in the building trade in Muscat. There was only limited scope for obtaining alternative supplies, and that would involve financial penalties. The cargo-owners therefore urgently needed the steel. Hobhouse J had little reluctance in holding that it was a case of economic duress or duress of goods. Significantly he observed (at 145): 'The plaintiffs did make a threat which was illegitimate, and, if it be relevant, they knew it to be illegitimate'.

In *Atlas Express Ltd* v *Kafco (Importers and Distributors) Ltd* [1989] QB 833, Kafco had secured a large contract to supply basketware for Woolworths. Atlas agreed to deliver the goods at a rate of £1.10 per carton. Subsequently, it was discovered that Atlas had overestimated the number of cartons they could carry and the agreed price was therefore uneconomic. Atlas wanted to escape this bad bargain. They sent a lorry to Kafco's premises with new terms specifying a minimum price of £440 per trailer. The driver was instructed to drive away if the new terms were not signed. Kafco's director signed but felt 'over a barrel'. Tucker J held that the new terms were procured by duress. The deliveries were crucial to Kafco's commercial survival. This was obvious to Atlas's manager and 'was known by him' (at 837). It would have been difficult, if not impossible, to find alternative carriers able to meet the delivery dates at that time. Furthermore, if goods were not supplied Woolworths would have sued Kafco for lost profits and would have ceased trading with them. This was also 'well-known' by Atlas's directors (at 838). The cases in which economic duress has been proved appear to require the deliberate exploitation of a position of advantage, that is knowing of the victim's circumstances, or where the consequences for the victim are entirely obvious.

Lastly, it is necessary to consider the well-known case of *Williams* v *Roffey Brothers & Nicholls (Contractors) Ltd* [1991] 1 QB 1, where duress was not pleaded. It is essential to ascertain why not. Sub-contractors tendered too low, and got into financial difficulties. The main contractors, in view of a penalty clause in the main contract, agreed to pay extra to the sub-contractors to secure timeous completion. The Court of Appeal held that the renegotiation was supported by consideration. Russell LJ said there was 'no hint' of duress in the pleaded defence (at 17). Purchas LJ said, 'In the present case the question of duress does not arise' (at 21). He concluded that it was 'open to the plaintiff [sub-contractors] to be in deliberate breach of the contract in order to "cut his losses" commercially' (at 23). So what takes this case outside the realm of compulsion? It appears that the initiative for the renegotiation came from the main contractors. Therefore, it seems, no pressure or threat was applied by the sub-contractors. There was simply a laconic 'I cannot go on'. An important factual finding was that the main contractors seemed to have realised all along that the tender price was too low. Renegotiation was probably inevitable and they had brought it upon themselves. Therefore bargaining power, as well as the presence or absence of bad faith, is an important factor. A party in a weaker bargaining position is unlikely to be found guilty of duress. For discussion, see Birks [1990] LMCLQ 342, at 344–47 and Beatson, 126–29.

6.5   LAWFUL ACT DURESS

The recent case of *CTN Cash and Carry Ltd* v *Gallaher Ltd* [1994] 4 All ER 714 suggests that a party will hardly ever succeed in establishing duress where the threatened course of conduct is lawful. If the category of 'lawful act' duress is to have any content, the most obvious candidates for inclusion are cases usually categorised as being examples of actual undue influence. The cases concern threats made to prosecute a person, usually a close relation of the victim, unless the victim complies with certain demands.

In *Williams* v *Bayley* (1866) LR 1 HL 200, the son forged endorsements, apparently of his father's, on promissory notes. The bankers insisted that the father settle the liabilities of some £6,000 or £7,000. The father stated that he was an old man, and did not wish to beggar himself, but could assist in reason. The bankers said they did not wish to place any pressure upon him. At the crucial meeting the father's solicitor helpfully added that it was 'a case of transportation for life' (at 202), and refused to be a part of the subsequent agreement under which the father agreed to accept liability for the whole amount and to mortgage his colliery business to the bankers to secure that sum. The House of Lords held unanimously that, although there was no direct threat of prosecution by the bankers, the agreement was invalid and the charge could be set aside on the grounds of undue influence. It appears to have been held that there was at least an implicit threat to prosecute the son. Lord Cranworth LC said a fair inference from the events was that the bankers were intimating: '"Give us security to the amount of these notes, and they shall all be delivered up to you; or do not give us security, and then we tell you we do not mean to compound a felony; in other words, we mean to prosecute"' (at 212). Lord Westbury made clear the principle underlying the decision (at 220): 'you shall not make a trade of a felony. If you are aware that a crime has been committed, you shall not convert that crime into a source of profit or benefit to yourself'. For an even earlier example, see *Collins* v *Hare* (1828) 1 Dow & Cl 139, 6 ER 476.

In similar circumstances a guarantee was set aside in *Mutual Finance Ltd* v *John Wetton & Sons Ltd* [1937] 2 KB 389. Obviously threats to prosecute the criminally culpable are not unlawful, but the coupling of the threat with a demand for benefits renders it illegitimate. Porter J in *Mutual Finance* decided unhesitatingly that the facts did not fall within the category of common law duress (at 395). That certainty has since been doubted by academic writers in the light of the recent expansion of the scope of duress: Birks, 185; Burrows, 185–88.

What seems to matter, where the pressure is not to threaten to commit a tort or a breach of contract, is the combination of a threat to do something lawful, with a demand for money or other benefits. The analogy with blackmail is striking. As Lord Atkin stated in *Thorne* v *Motor Trade Associations* [1937] AC 797, at 806–807:

The ordinary blackmailer normally threatens to do what he has a perfect right to do — namely communicate some compromising conduct to a person whose knowledge is likely to affect the person threatened. Often indeed he has not only the right but also the duty to make the disclosure, as of a felony, to the competent authorities. What he has to justify is not the threat, but the demand of money.

It is important here to record Lord Scarman's analysis in *The Universe Sentinel* [1983] 1 AC 366, at 401:

> In determining what is legitimate two matters may have to be considered. The first is as to the nature of the pressure. In many cases this will be decisive, though not in every case. And so the second question may have to be considered, namely the nature of the demand which the pressure is applied to support.
> The origin of the doctrine of duress in threats to life or limb, or to property suggests strongly that the law regards the threat of unlawful action as illegitimate, whatever the demand. Duress can, of course, exist even if the threat is one of lawful action: whether it does so depends upon the nature of the demand.

The equity cases on threats to prosecute can be rationalised on the basis that the party exerting pressure cannot justify his demand for benefits because of the public policy insisting on the disclosure of information of suspected criminal activity, and against attempts to enrich oneself by exploiting the possession of such information. It may be that the category is slightly wider, along the lines as suggested by Lord Atkin, in the criminal context, in *Thorne*. That is, it concerns communicating some compromising conduct to a person whose knowledge is likely to affect the person threatened. In *Barton* v *Armstrong* [1976] AC 104, Barton, the company managing director, agreed to buy out the holding of Armstrong, the company chairman, in the company after threats of violence from Armstrong. Suppose the threat had instead been to reveal to Barton's wife that her husband was having an affair with his secretary, or was a practising homosexual, and it was that which caused Barton to enter into the contract. Could such a contract stand? In principle it seems not. For discussion, see Beatson, 129–37 and Birks, 177–79, 184–85.

6.6 SUBMISSION TO AN HONEST CLAIM

Where a person with full knowledge of the facts pays money which he is not in law bound to pay, and it is clear he is paying it voluntarily to close the transaction, it cannot be recovered in restitution (*Maskell* v *Horner* [1915] 3 KB 106). It may well be that the recognition of submission to an honest claim in the context of duress claims is simply another way of describing the requirement which appears to be implicit in economic duress cases, that the oppressor must have deliberately exploited a position of advantage. However, it is submitted that the two concepts are different. What the victim needs to prove affirmatively is illegitimate pressure which caused him to enter into the transaction. Deliberate exploitation of advantage may be an element of this, but this appears to be tested objectively. Even where there is objectively determined deliberate exploitation, it remains open to the alleged oppressor to demonstrate that subjectively he acted in complete good faith. It is submitted that this is the best explanation of *CTN Cash and Carry Ltd* v *Gallaher Ltd* [1994] 4 All ER 714 (see 6.2.2). The fact that the claim by the supplier of cigarettes was made in good faith appears to have weighed heavily with the Court of Appeal in determining that there was no duress. If the claim had been made by the supplier, realising that it had no case in law for recovery of the money, it seems the claim for restitution would have succeeded.

6.7   NATURE AND LIMITS OF RELIEF

Some cases have suggested that a transaction tainted by duress is void, although the statements were made in the context of the effect only as between the immediate parties (*Barton* v *Armstrong* [1976] AC 104 and *The Siboen and The Sibotre* [1976] 1 Lloyd's Rep 293). The better view is that a transaction clouded by duress is voidable at the election of the victim (*The Atlantic Baron* [1979] QB 705; *The Universe Sentinel* [1983] 1 AC 366). The latter case states that any resulting contract may be avoided, and consequently any money and property paid under it may be recovered in restitution. See also *The Evia Luck (No. 2)* [1992] 2 AC 152.

One consequence of the voidability rule is that bars similar to those which apply in respect of rescission for misrepresentation apply by analogy to duress claims (see 4.4). First, affirmation. For example, in *The Atlantic Baron* it was held that the subsequent conduct of the victim amounted to an affirmation of the agreement which was prima facie tainted by duress. Secondly, lapse of time will bar a claim to avoid for duress. Protests must registered timeously and as soon as the illegitimate pressure is relaxed. Thirdly, third parties' intervening rights would preclude avoidance, leaving only the faint possibility of a claim in damages under the economic torts. Fourthly, counter-restitution difficulties may also frustrate a claim, although it is likely that the courts will strive to unwind the contract against the oppressor, as against a deceitful party.

FURTHER READING

Asterisks indicate especially useful works.

Goff and Jones, 307–55
*Birks, 174–85
*Beatson, 95–136
Anson, 270–77
J. Dawson, 'Economic Duress — an Essay in Perspective' (1947) 45 Mich LR 253
Atiyah, 'Economic Duress and the "Overborne Will"' (1982) 98 LQR 197
E. Macdonald, 'Duress by Threatened Breach of Contract' [1989] JBL 460

P. Birks 'The Travails of Duress' [1990] LMCLQ 342

T. Honoré, 'A Theory of Coercion' (1990) 10 OJLS 94

R. Halson, 'Opportunism, Economic Duress and Contractual Modifications' (1991) 107 LQR 649

J. Carter and G. Tolhurst, 'Restitution for Duress' (1996) 9 JCL 220

7 Undue Influence

7.1 THEORETICAL FOUNDATIONS

The equitable jurisdiction to grant relief in respect of transactions tainted by undue influence operates as a supplement to the common law of duress. Its concern is with more subtle forms of exploitation and victimisation. The recent expansion of common law duress to encompass illegitimate pressure in general, and in particular economic duress, has not lessened the need for, nor recourse to the equitable principles. The two sets of principles operate in different spheres. The rules on duress mark the boundaries of legitimate market behaviour for commercial parties of relatively equal bargaining power. Undue influence is concerned with closer relationships, and situations of dependency (physical, emotional and sexual).

Identification of the essence of undue influence has proved controversial. One academic view stresses that undue influence is concerned with 'excessively impaired consent', emphasising the right to a free and fair consent, being a claimant-sided ground of restitution: Birks and Chin, 'On the Nature of Undue Influence' in Beatson and Friedmann (eds), *Good Faith and Fault in Contract Law* (1995), 57. Another juristic view is that it concerns wicked exploitation, or wrongdoing by the defendant and that this is the core of the cause of action: Bigwood, 'Undue Influence: ''Impaired Consent'' or ''Wicked Exploitation''?' (1996) 16 OJLS 503. The leading Victorian case stresses victimisation (*Allcard* v *Skinner* (1887) 36 Ch D 145, at 182 *per* Lindley LJ). The Court of Appeal has recently entered into this controversy stating in the leading modern case of *Royal Bank of Scotland* v *Etridge (No. 2)* [1998] 4 All ER 705 that it 'is not confined to cases of abuse of trust and confidence; it is also concerned to protect the vulnerable from exploitation' (at 712). This sits on the fence between the two opposed positions.

The more pressing practical concern is to identify how equity deploys evidential presumptions to put at risk any transaction entered into with or procured by a person's loved ones. This is the field of defective transaction, in which the rights of third parties derived from relationships tainted by an operative vitiating factor have been put most searchingly under the spotlight. It is first necessary to consider the relationship between influencer and victim, before turning to more modern authority on the rights of third parties which may be infected by a defect in such relationships.

7.2 THE CATEGORIES OF UNDUE INFLUENCE

The distinction between actual and presumed undue influence dates back at least to *Allcard* v *Skinner* (1887) 36 Ch D 145 and the judgment of Cotton LJ (at 171):

> The first class of cases may be considered as depending on the principle that no one shall be allowed to retain any benefit arising from his own fraud or wrongful act. In the second class of cases the Court interferes, not on the ground that any wrongful act has in fact been committed by the donee, but on the grounds of public policy, and to prevent the relations which existed between the parties and the influence arising therefrom being abused.

A more refined categorisation has been employed since *Bank of Credit and Commerce International SA* v *Aboody* [1990] 1 QB 923, at 953, which was adopted in the leading House of Lords case of *Barclays Bank plc* v *O'Brien* [1994] 1 AC 180, at 189–90. This divides the cases into three classes:

(a)   actual undue influence (class 1);
(b)   classes of presumed undue influence, sub-divided into:
    (i)   cases where the presumption arises by operation of law (class 2A), and
    (ii) cases where the presumption arises because of the particular relationship of the influencer and claimant (class 2B).

7.2.1   Class 1: Actual undue influence

In such a case the complainant proves affirmatively by evidence that actual or express undue influence was used to procure the transaction. Examples include a bullying housekeeper who dominated an elderly employer who had become dependent upon her, and who showered her with gifts (*In re Craig (deceased)* [1971] Ch 95); and the wife by an arranged marriage who was bullied into putting up the matrimonial home, which was in her name alone, as security for her husband's ailing business (*Bank of Credit and Commerce International SA* v *Aboody* [1990] 1 QB 923).

7.2.2   Class 2A: Presumed undue influence by operation of law

In certain cases the presumption arises by operation of law where a certain relationship or status is established. For example:

(a)   solicitor and client (*Wright* v *Carter* [1903] 1 Ch 27);
(b)   trustee and beneficiary (*Plowright* v *Lambert* (1885) 52 LT 646);

(c)   guardian and ward (*Hatch* v *Hatch* (1804) 9 Ves 292, 32 ER 615: 'if the Court does not watch these transactions with a jealousy almost invincible, in a great majority of cases it will lend its assistance to fraud' (*per* Lord Eldon LC, at 297));

(d)   parent and infant child (*Bainbrigge* v *Browne* (1881) 18 Ch D 188; *Re Pauling's Settlement Trust* [1964] Ch 303, at 336).

These categories could not be said to be closed. Of more practical concern is the fact that two key relationships do not fall into this category of legally presumed undue influence. First, the relationship between spouses, such as a domineering husband over his wife. Secondly, the relationship between an adult child and an elderly parent. These two form the main concern of the next category.

7.2.3   Class 2B: Relational presumed undue influence

If the relationship falls outside class 2A, the claimant is still entitled to lead evidence of the *de facto* existence of a relationship under which he generally reposed trust and confidence in the influencer. It was settled in *Bank of Montreal* v *Stuart* [1911] AC 120 and confirmed by the House of Lords in *Barclays Bank plc* v *O'Brien* [1994] 1 AC 180, that the relationship of husband and wife does not fall within class 2A, but belongs in class 2B.

The following relationships on the particular facts have been held to give rise to a presumption of undue influence:

(a)   husband and wife (*Royal Bank of Scotland* v *Etridge (No. 2)* [1998] 4 All ER 705);

(b)   the relationship between adult son and elderly parents (*Avon Finance Co. Ltd* v *Bridger* [1985] 2 All ER 281);

(c)   employer and young inexperienced employee (*Credit Lyonnais Bank Nederland NV* v *Burch* [1997] 1 All ER 144);

(d)   experienced manager and young pop musician (*O'Sullivan* v *Management Agency and Music Ltd* [1985] QB 428);

(e)   great-nephew and elderly great-uncle (*Cheese* v *Thomas* [1994] 1 WLR 129; although it appears to have been conceded); and

(f)   most exceptionally, bank manager and elderly customer (*Lloyds Bank Ltd* v *Bundy* [1975] 1 QB 326 (although it is submitted that that case would be pleaded, argued and decided differently today — the son would be the alleged influencer, and the bank would be alleged to have constructive notice of that influence).

7.3   THE IMPACT OF UNDUE INFLUENCE UPON A TRANSACTION

Where class 1 actual or express undue influence is demonstrated, the transaction will be set aside as between influencer and claimant and there must be restitution of any benefits rendered. In class 2 cases, where a legal or factual presumption of undue influence arises, the burden of proof shifts to the influencer to prove that the complainant entered into the transaction with 'full, free and informed thought' (*Zamet* v *Hyman* [1952] 1 WLR 1442, at 1445 *per* Lord Evershed MR). If the influencer cannot discharge this onus of proof, rescission follows.

7.4   MANIFEST DISADVANTAGE

In cases of *presumed* undue influence, as between influencer and claimant, there is a requirement that the transaction complained of be shown to be manifestly disadvantageous (*National Westminster Bank plc v Morgan* [1985] AC 686). It was at one stage thought that such a requirement extended to all cases of undue influence, but the House of Lords clarified that it was unnecessary where actual undue influence was established (*CIBC Mortgages plc v Pitt* [1994] 1 AC 200, overruling *Bank of Credit and Commerce International SA v Aboody* [1990] 1 QB 923 on this point). Even as regards presumed undue influence there has been criticism of the requirement of a manifestly disadvantageous transaction, essentially on the grounds that it confuses substantive unfairness with procedural unfairness. The House of Lords has suggested that the requirement may need to revisited, but it is currently binding on all courts (*CIBC Mortgages plc v Pitt* [1994] 1 AC 200, at 209).

Whatever the merits in regarding manifest disadvantage as an affirmative factor to be approved by the claimant in raising the presumption of undue influence, it is clear that in any event it would be treated as a powerful evidential factor giving rise to the presumption. Further, the fact of the manifest disadvantage is also relevant to the impact of the transaction upon the rights of third parties. This will be returned to at 7.6 below. Where there is severe manifest disadvantage, or indeed the transaction is financially inexplicable, there may be an overlap between the protection of presumed undue influence and the court's jurisdiction to set aside unconscionable bargains (*Credit Lyonnais Bank Nederland NV v Burch* [1997] 1 All ER 144; *Royal Bank of Scotland v Etridge (No. 2)* [1998] 4 All ER 705, at 713). In Australia, recourse is had more readily to the unconscionability jurisdiction in situations which English lawyers would channel into undue influence (*Commercial Bank of Australia Ltd v Amadio* (1983) 151 CLR 447; and see *Garcia v National Australia Bank Ltd* (1998) 155 ALR 614).

What amounts to undue influence or gives rise to the presumption? Acts or conduct may not be necessary. The relationship may be one either of trust and confidence, or of ascendency and dependency. Sometimes the concept of domination is used, but it is not necessary to show a dominating influence to give rise to the presumption of undue influence (*Goldsworthy v Brickell* [1987] Ch 378). Unlike common law duress, no pressure need be exerted, because none may be needed (*Bank of Montreal v Stuart* [1911] AC 120, at 136: 'She was ready to sign anything that her husband asked her to sign and do anything he told her to do'). In contrast, the allegation of undue influence failed in *Barclays Bank plc v O'Brien* itself where heavy family pressure was brought to bear upon the wife, but she was not overborne by her husband ([1993] QB 109, at 141–42).

7.5   REBUTTING THE PRESUMPTION

'The wrongdoer must prove that the complainant entered into the transaction as a result of the free exercise of her independent will' (*Royal Bank of Scotland v Etridge*

(No. 2) [1998] 4 All ER 705, at 714). The solution usually adopted is to demonstrate that there has been independent advice for the claimant, most notably independent legal advice. This was the strategy of the House of Lords in *Barclays Bank plc v O'Brien* [1994] 1 AC 180, in order to protect wives who had stood surety for their husbands' obligations to banks, and this leads into the question of the rights of third parties. However, as the Court of Appeal commented in *Royal Bank of Scotland v Etridge (No. 2)* [1998] 4 All ER 705, at 711:

> Unfortunately, as the number of cases which have come before the court since *O'Brien's* case demonstrates, the protection which ought to be afforded to the wife by the provision of independent legal advice has in many cases proved illusory. The advice which the wife has received has often been perfunctory, limited to an explanation of the documents and yet inadequate to dispel her misunderstanding of the real extent and liability which she was undertaking, and not directed to ensure that she was entering into the transaction of her own free will rather than as the result of illegitimate pressure from her husband or blind trust in him.

Detailed guidance upon the form and content of such independent legal advice is given by the Court of Appeal in *Etridge* ([1998] 4 All ER 705, at 715–17; 719–22).

7.6   THIRD PARTY RIGHTS

Over the last decade there has been an explosion of cases brought particularly by wives, who have claimed undue influence by their husbands resulting in them entering into obligations with a bank in order to provide security for the husbands' ailing businesses. It must be observed that banks cannot escape criticism for the widespread (but now discontinued) practice of seeking all-moneys guarantees encompassing the matrimonial home, in return for what was often only short-term additional finance for businesses whose prospects were not good. However, the bank is not the influencer and stands in the position of a third party to the relationship between influencer and claimant. For its rights to be affected by a defect in that relationship something more must be shown. The balancing policy factors were clearly exposed by the House of Lords in *Barclays Bank plc v O'Brien* [1994] 1 AC 180, in the speech of Lord Browne-Wilkinson (at 188):

> In a substantial proportion of marriages it is still the husband who has the business experience and the wife is willing to follow his advice without bringing a truly independent mind and will to bear on financial decisions. The number of recent cases in this field shows that in practice many wives are still subjected to, and yield to, undue influence by their husband. Such wives can reasonably look to the law for some protection when their husbands have abused the trust and confidence reposed in them.
>
> On the other hand, it is important to keep a sense of balance in approaching these cases. It is easy to allow sympathy for the wife who is threatened with the

loss of her home at the suit of a rich bank to obscure an important public interest viz, the need to ensure that the wealth currently tied up in the matrimonial home does not become economically sterile. If the rights secured to wives by the law renders vulnerable loans granted on the security of matrimonial homes, institutions will be unwilling to accept such security, thereby reducing the flow of loan capital to business enterprises. It is therefore essential that a law designed to protect the vulnerable does not render the matrimonial home unacceptable as security to financial institutions.

The House of Lords in *O'Brien* rejected two theories as a basis for impugning third party rights. First, one based on agency; and, secondly, an 'invalidating tendency' or special equity for wives. The basis for impugning such transactions is now held to be notice. As the Court of Appeal stated in *Royal Bank of Scotland v Etridge (No. 2)* [1998] 4 All ER 705, at 717:

> a person who has been induced to enter into a transaction by undue influence, misrepresentation or some other vitiating factor has an equity to have the transaction set aside, and the equity is enforceable against third parties, including third parties who have given value, with notice, actual constructive or imputed, of the equity: see *Bainbrigge v Browne* (1881) 18 Ch D 188.

This was held not to be a defence of bona fide purchase but was much the same in effect. There are two ways of analysing the role played by notice in claims by the victim against third parties. First, the relationship between the claimant and the defendant is governed by a binding contractual matrix, and that will be displaced only if the bank has notice that the claimant's consent was impaired. Secondly, the bank is entitled to plead good faith purchase as a defence, although it will not succeed if it is on notice. For a defence of the bona fide purchase analysis see O'Dell [1997] CLJ 71. At one time it was thought that the burden of proof was upon the bank or other third party to show that it was not put upon notice (*Barclays Bank plc v Boulter* [1997] 2 All ER 102 and *Royal Bank of Scotland v Etridge* [1998] 4 All ER 705, at 718 (criticised by Barker 'O'Brien, Notice and the Onus of Proof' in Rose (1998), 78–88). However, the House of Lords has now emphatically held that the onus of proving notice (actual or constructive) is upon the claimant seeking to implicate the third party in the circumstances which constitute the undue influence or other vitiating factor (see *Barclays Bank plc v Boulter* [1999] 4 All ER 513). This holding supports the first explanation of the role of notice. It is an ingredient in the cause of action against the third party that must be affirmatively proven by the claimant in order to displace the direct contractual matrix between them.

Actual notice is unproblematic and existed on the facts of *Bank of Credit and Commerce International SA v Aboody* [1990] 1 QB 923. Imputed notice is concerned with notice derived from an agent's knowledge. Section 199(1)(ii)(b) of the Law of Property Act 1925 governs. Therefore, if a solicitor is engaged to give independent advice, the bank is not affected by notice of anything which he discovers, unless he was acting as a bank's solicitor at the time when he discovered it (*Halifax Mortgage Services Ltd v Stepsky* [1996] Ch 207). Most cases will concern constructive notice. The Court of Appeal in *Etridge* summarised the effect of the decision in *O'Brien's* case as follows (at 719):

> even so, the bank is put on enquiry by a combination of two factors: (a) the transaction is not on its face to the financial advantage of the wife; and (b) there is a substantial risk that, in procuring his wife to guarantee or provide collateral security for his debts, the husband has acted improperly.

The same principles apply as a result of these cases where the bank is aware that the parties are cohabiting, whether married or unmarried, and whether heterosexual or homosexual. In order to avoid being fixed with constructive notice, the authorities require the bank to ensure that the claimant receives independent legal advice. This is relevant both to the question of whether the wife can set aside the transaction as against the husband and as to whether the bank had constructive notice of the wife's equity. The Court of Appeal in *Etridge* summed up the situation in which the bank can protect its interest by urging wives to obtain independent legal advice before entering into the transaction. The effect of the previous authority is summarised at [1998] 4 All ER 705, at 721–22. In effect the decision casts the responsibility for explaining the transaction and its implications upon solicitors, and expressly holds that a duty of care is owed by the solicitor to the wife (and also possibly to the bank) in the course of discharging this duty. The practical effect seems to be to redirect many complaints in future from the conduct of the bank to the conduct of the solicitor. At the time of writing, *Etridge* is on appeal to the House of Lords.

7.7   CONSEQUENCES

The consequence of undue influence is that the transaction is voidable, and may be rescinded at the election of the claimant against the influencer or any party who has notice of the transaction, actual or constructive. The usual bars to rescission apply: affirmation, counter-restitution impossible, third party rights intervening and lapse of time. Affirmation and laches barred relief in the case of *Allcard v Skinner* (1887) 36 Ch D 145.

FURTHER READING

Asterisks indicate especially useful works.

Goff and Jones, 356–75
Anson, 277–87
*P. Birks and C. Chin, 'On the Nature of Undue Influence' in J. Beatson and D. Friedmann (eds), *Good Faith and Fault in Contract Law* (1995), 57–97
R. Bigwood, 'Undue Influence: "Impaired Consent" or "Wicked Exploitation"?' (1996) 16 OJLS 503 (theoretical)

S. Cretney, 'Mere Puppets, Folly and Imprudence: Undue Influence for the Twenty First Century' [1994] *Restitution Law Review* 3

R. Hooley, 'Taking security after *O'Brien*' [1995] LMCLQ 346 (practical)

M. Chen Wishart, 'The *O'Brien* Principle and Substantive Unfairness' [1997] CLJ 60

E. O'Dell, 'Restitution, Coercion by a Third Party, and the Proper Role of Notice' [1997] CLJ 71

*K. Barker, '*O'Brien*, Notice and the Onus of Proof', in Rose (1998), 78–88

*J. Cartwright, 'Taking Stock of *O'Brien*' [1999] *Restitution Law Review* 1

8 Inequality and Unconscionability

8.1 THEORETICAL FOUNDATIONS

Beyond the realms of compulsion and exploitation (which are the concerns of duress and undue influence) there exists a vigorous debate as to whether there is any residual jurisdiction to grant relief where a transaction is a result of unfair use of bargaining power or is manifestly substantively unfair. The starting point is the general principle of party autonomy, or more classically 'freedom of contract'. In *Printing & Numerical Registering Co.* v *Sampson* (1875) LR 19 Eq 462, Sir George Jessel MR proclaimed (at 465):

> if there is one thing which more than another public policy requires, it is that men of full age and understanding shall have the utmost liberty of contracting, and that their contracts when entered into freely and voluntarily, shall be held sacred and shall be enforced by Courts of justice.

Where an apparently defective transaction cannot be shown to be tainted by duress or undue influence, and where no statutory relief is available, unconscionability is a legal last-chance saloon. Accordingly, there have been only sporadic examples of transactions being unwound on this ground in recent decades. The jurisdiction is sometimes invoked in modern times, most commonly in obiter dicta. In *Alec Lobb Ltd* v *Total Oil GB Ltd* [1983] 1 WLR 87, Peter Millett QC, sitting as a deputy judge concluded (at 94–95) that:

> It is probably not possible to reconcile all the authorities, some of which are of great antiquity, on this head of equitable relief, which came into greater prominence with the repeal of the usury laws in the nineteenth century. But if the cases are examined, it will be seen that three elements have almost invariably been present before the court has interfered. First, one party has been at a serious

disadvantage to the other, whether through poverty, or ignorance, or lack of advice, or otherwise, so that circumstances existed of which unfair advantage could be taken.... Secondly, this weakness of the one party has been exploited by the other in some morally culpable manner ... and thirdly, the resulting transaction has been, not merely hard or improvident, but overreaching and oppressive.

First it is necessary to consider the rejection by the English courts of a general principle of inequality of bargaining power. Secondly, the traditional categories of unconscionable bargains (expectant heirs and poor and ignorant persons) are introduced. Thirdly, the difficult issue of mental disadvantage will be addressed. Commonwealth authorities suggest there is potential for a wider jurisdiction. For discussion, see Bamforth [1995] LMCLQ 538.

8.2 INEQUALITY OF BARGAINING POWER?

In *Lloyds Bank Ltd* v *Bundy* [1975] 1 QB 326, the Court of Appeal reached the startling conclusion that an elderly farmer who had mortgaged away his property in an attempt to salvage his son's ailing business, did so as a result of undue influence by the bank manager. Lord Denning MR was prepared to go further, creating a new super-category of judicial intervention termed 'inequality of bargaining power', utilising precedents involving duress, undue influence, unconscionable transactions and salvage agreements. The Master of the Rolls stated (at 339) that:

English law gives relief to one who, without independent advice, enters into a contract upon terms which are very unfair or transfers property for a consideration which is grossly inadequate, when his bargaining power is grievously impaired by reason of his own needs or desires, or by his own ignorance or infirmity, coupled with undue influences or pressures brought to bear on him by or for the benefit of the other.

The test proposed appeared to include both a requirement of manifest disadvantage and some morally culpable conduct on the part of the transferee or those acting for him. It therefore combined elements of substantive and procedural unfairness. However, the House of Lords rejected the need to erect any general principle against the inequality of bargaining power in *National Westminster Bank plc* v *Morgan* [1985] AC 686. Lord Scarman intimated that the task was best left to Parliament (at 708). Similarly, in *Hart* v *O'Connor* [1985] AC 1000, the Privy Council insisted on drawing a sharp line between cases of 'procedural unfairness' and those of 'contractual imbalance'. Lord Brightman categorised undue influence as a species of the former and continued (at 1018):

The two concepts may overlap. Contractual imbalance may be so extreme as to raise a presumption of procedural unfairness, such as undue influence or some other form of victimisation. Equity will relieve a party from the contract which he has been induced to make as a result of victimisation. Equity will not relieve a party from a contract on the ground only that there is contractual imbalance not amounting to unconscionable dealing.

The modern English view is that the law does not intervene solely on the grounds of substantive unfairness. What must be shown is a deliberate abuse of the other party's special disadvantage, amounting to morally culpable behaviour on the part of the stronger party. Sometimes this may be inferred by the coincidence of three factors: (1) special disadvantage, (2) unfair terms and (3) the absence of independent advice.

8.3   EXPECTANT HEIRS

The case law on unconscionable bargains has taken on a somewhat archaic flavour in a less class-conscious age. The two traditional categories concern 'expectant heirs' and the 'poor and ignorant'. With regard to the former group, the jurisdiction to relieve them of their folly in selling reversionary interests was skilfully curtailed by a majority of the House of Lords in *O'Rorke* v *Bolingbroke* (1877) 2 App Cas 814. Here a son sold his expectancy to his father's estate in order to undertake study in medicine. He was unaware of his father's state of health, and when his father died soon afterwards 'probably from drink' (at 828) he sought to escape the bargain. The price was appropriate if the father's health was good, but it turned out to be a bad bargain given his actual state of health. The deal had been negotiated by the father on behalf of the son, and it seems the father had even boasted to the son of his good health. The law was taken to have been authoritatively stated by Lord Selborne in *Aylesford* v *Morris* (1873) LR 8 Ch App 484, as involving weakness on one side and usury, extortion or advantage taken on the other side of the transactions. The court's intervention required (at 491):

> an unconscientious use of the power arising out of these circumstances and conditions; and when the relative position of the parties is such as prima facie to raise this presumption, the transaction cannot stand unless the person claiming the benefit of it is able to repel the presumption by contrary evidence, proving it to have been in point of fact fair, just and reasonable.

Therefore the rule operates analogously to presumed undue influence. Where the requisite conditions are shown to exist, the burden of proof is reversed and the transferee must convince the court of the absence of anything unconscionable in his behaviour. On the facts of *O'Rorke* v *Bolingbroke*, given the knowledge of transferor and transferee, it was held that this burden was discharged. The majority of the House of Lords took the view that it was perfectly sensible for a young man to acquire a profession in order to provide for himself.

This jurisdiction, which appears not to have been invoked in the courts in modern times, is further curtailed by s. 174 of the Law of Property Act 1925, whereby a bargain with an expectant heir which is made in good faith is not to be set aside merely because it is at an undervalue.

8.4   POOR AND IGNORANT PERSONS

In *Fry* v *Lane* (1888) 40 Ch D 312, two brothers sold their interests in a farm and other property in Bristol, at what appeared to be a considerable undervalue. Kay J stated that they were both poor and ignorant men, to whom the temptation of the immediate possession of £100 would be too great. He held (at 322):

> The result of the decisions is that where a purchase is made from a poor and ignorant man at a considerable undervalue, the vendor having no independent advice, a Court of Equity would set aside the transaction. This will be done even in the case of property in possession, and *a fortiori* if the interest be reversionary.

Where the transaction is questioned, the burden of proof was upon the transferee to show that the purchase was fair, just and reasonable. Interestingly, while setting the transaction aside the judge refused to award costs to the two brothers.

This quaint ground of relief was briefly resuscitated in 1968 in *Cresswell* v *Potter* [1978] 1 WLR 255, where Megarry J substituted for the traditional test the proto-politically correct language of 'a member of the lower income group' and 'less highly educated' (at 257). See also *Backhouse* v *Backhouse* [1978] 1 WLR 243.

However, there is little evidence of any vigorous application of such principles in modern times. The high watermark of judicial enunciation of an unconscionability jurisdiction comes in the recent Court of Appeal case of *Credit Lyonnais Bank Nederland NV* v *Burch* [1997] 1 All ER 144, where a guarantee given by a junior employee to a bank in respect of her employer's obligation was described as one which no respectable lending institution could enter into. The case was pleaded, argued and finally disposed of on the more familiar ground of presumed undue influence, but Millett and Nourse LJJ were equally content to stigmatise the transaction as unconscionable as between the employee and the bank (apparently without the need to invoke the concept of constructive notice). Ultimately it was the lack of independent advice coupled with the apparently inexplicable basis of the transaction which prompted such judicial censure. Compare the approach of the High Court of Australia in *Commercial Bank of Australia Ltd* v *Amadio* (1983) 151 CLR 447.

Commonwealth cases have gone further and have developed a broad approach to the question of what amounts to a special disadvantage. In *Louth* v *Diprose* (1992) 175 CLR 621, a lovesick solicitor was held to be entitled to the restitution of gifts which he had showered upon the cynical recipient of his unrequited adoration. See also *Nichols* v *Jessup* [1986] 1 NZLR 226. For discussion, see Bamforth [1995] LMCLQ 538.

8.5   MENTAL DISADVANTAGE

The context in which the unconscionability jurisdiction shows most potential for growth, given an increasingly ageing population, is in respect of transactions entered into with those at a mental disadvantage. The Privy Council has restated the law in modern times in terms of the traditional test in *Hart* v *O'Connor* [1985] AC 1000. An elderly farmer sold his property to a neighbour, although at the time the former was held to lack sufficient mental capacity to enter into such an agreement. However this was not known to the transferee. It was held that the bargain was unimpeachable in the absence of any evidence that the transferee knew or ought to have known about the absence of mental capacity. In the absence of any evidence of unconscionable conduct by the transferee, the courts uphold the objective appearance of consent even though one party was in a state of advanced senile dementia. This can be explained either on the basis of the objective principle in respect of contract formation, or on the basis that the purchaser acted in good faith. Notice would preclude reliance on the governing contractual matrix or the availability of bona fide purchase.

Perhaps the furthest the English judges have gone is the decision of the Privy Council in *Boustany* v *Pigott* (1993) 69 P&CR 298. The court set aside a lease granted by a 70-year-old woman on unfavourable terms and without the benefit of her usual advisers. It was satisfied that the circumstances evidenced morally reprehensible behaviour on the part of the tenant (at 303).

8.6   CONSEQUENCES AND PRACTICAL ISSUES

Of more practical significance than the judge-made jurisdiction are the statutory powers under s. 137–140 of the Consumer Credit Act 1974, as to which see Goff and Jones, 381–83.

Where relief on the grounds of unconscionability can be established the main practical implication is that the burden of proof is reversed. The transferee must satisfy the court that the transaction was a free and fair one. The evidential factors which the courts consider in giving rise to the presumption include the following:

(a)   lack of independent advice;

(b)   the resulting transaction appears manifestly disadvantageous to the transferor or there is a gross disparity between the consideration provided and the property transferred;

(c)   the social and intellectual status of the transferor, including relative youth and inexperience or age and infirmity;

(d)   any evidence of improper or overreaching behaviour by the transferee in procuring the bargain, even though it falls short of legally culpable behaviour.

If the presumption cannot be rebutted by evidence that the transaction was a free and fair one, the claimant may rescind the transaction against the oppressor or any other party with notice of the circumstances. The usual bars to rescission apply: affirmation, counter-restitution impossible, lapse of time, third party rights intervening.

Where the conduct of the oppressor cannot be stigmatised as morally culpable, the courts may make no order as to costs (*Fry* v *Lane* (1888) 40 Ch D 312, at 324–25). Alternatively the court may award costs to the defendant: Goff and Jones, 381.

FURTHER READING

Asterisks indicate especially useful works.

Goff and Jones, 376–88.

Birks (1991), 50–52

J. Beatson, 'Unconscionability: Placebo or Pill?' (1981) 1 OJLS 426

H. Beale, 'Inequality of Bargaining Power' (1986) 6 OJLS 123

J. Barton, 'The Enforcement of Hard Bargains' (1987) 103 LQR 118 (historical)

*N. Bamforth, 'Unconscionability as a vitiating factor' [1995] LMCLQ 538

S. Thal, The Inequality of Bargaining Power Doctrine: The Problem of Defining Contractual Unfairness' (1988) 8 OJLS 17

*M. Chen Wishart, 'The *O'Brien* Principle and Substantive Unfairness' [1997] CLJ 60

D. Capper, 'Undue influence and unconscionability: a rationalisation' (1998) 114 LQR 479

9 *Necessitous Intervention*

9.1 THEORETICAL FOUNDATIONS

In contrast to civil law systems, there is no general principle of English law that those who render necessary services, or confer other necessary benefits in an emergency or other necessitous circumstances to the advantage of another, have a right to reimbursement for their efforts. However, there are pockets of case law from disparate contexts — maritime salvage, burial of the dead, care of the mentally incompetent and agency of necessity — where something akin to restitution has been awarded. Scholars have sought to generalise these single instances, but the current law forms an uneven patchwork. Often-cited judicial dicta express the robust individualism of the common law. Most famously, Bowen LJ stated in *Falcke* v *Scottish Imperial Insurance Co.* (1886) 34 Ch D 234, at 248:

> The general principle is, beyond all question, that work and labour done or money expended by one man to preserve or benefit the property of another do not according to English law create any lien upon the property saved or benefited, nor, even if standing alone, create any obligation to repay the expenditure. Liabilities are not to be forced upon people behind their backs any more than you can confer a benefit upon a man against his will.

In *Falcke* the owner of the equity of redemption in a life insurance policy paid a premium in order to ensure the policy did not lapse. His claim for a lien against the mortgagee of the policy failed. There was no evidence of any request or free acceptance of his intervention. Further, it could be observed there was no necessity, and that he acted out of self-interest. For further discussion of *Falcke*, see 15.2.4. More recently, Lord Diplock in *China Pacific SA* v *Food Corporation of India, The Winson* [1982] AC 939, commented (at 961): 'It is, of course, true that in English law a mere stranger cannot compel an owner of goods to pay for a benefit bestowed upon him against his will.'

There are twin concerns. First, the characteristic difficulties of establishing enrichment where the intervention takes the form of transferring property or rendering services. Recourse to an objective measure of benefit will be possible only where the conditions for free acceptance or incontrovertible benefit can be satisfied, although the latter test would appear more appropriate in such circumstances. It is interesting to speculate whether such an argument would now succeed on the facts of the *Falcke* case. Secondly, prior to the development of the modern law of restitution there was no explicit recognition of an unjust factor or ground for restitution based upon necessitous intervention, outside of the maritime context. The thrust of modern scholarship promotes such development. For the future, a party wishing to argue for wider relief on the grounds of necessity may find comparative material of more assistance than domestic developments to date.

9.2 MARITIME SALVAGE

The details of the law of maritime salvage are beyond the scope of this book. Its concerns are rewarding necessitous interventions at sea where they preserve life and property. It has been rationalised as being concerned with the reversal of unjust enrichment: Birks, 304 – 308. However, the calculation of salvage awards in practice reflects more diverse policies. For a useful survey from a restitution perspective, see Goff and Jones, 483 – 98.

The courts have had the opportunity of extending the principles of salvage, but to date have confined it within its original context. In *Nicholson* v *Chapman* (1793) 2 H Bl 254, 126 ER 536, a quantity of timber was secured in a dock by the Thames, but broke loose from its ropes and was carried by the tide to Putney where it was left at low water upon a towpath. Chapman carried the timber to a nearby place of safety beyond the reach of the tide. He then refused to deliver the timber to Nicholson, its owner, unless he was remunerated for his efforts. It was held that Chapman had no lien and was guilty of wrongful interference with Nicholson's goods. Eyre CJ stated that the question was whether this could be equated with salvage. He concluded (at 257):

> Goods carried by sea are necessarily and unavoidably exposed to the perils which storms, tempest and accidents (far beyond the reach of human foresight to prevent) are hourly creating, and against which, it too often happens that the greatest diligence and the most strenuous exertions of the mariner cannot protect them. When goods are thus in imminent danger of being lost, it is most frequently to the hazard of the lives of those who save them, that they are saved. Principles of public policy dictate to civilised and commercial countries, not only the propriety, and even the absolute necessity of establishing a liberal recompense for the encouragement of those who engage in so dangerous a service.

The Court of Common Pleas held that property going astray on a navigable river far from the sea did not fall within the scope of this policy. In dicta the court suggested that it might uphold a claim for recompense by the finder and preserver of another's property if it was brought as a personal claim. However, the claim to a lien (a proprietary remedy), which is available in true maritime salvage, was not available in land-based cases (*Binstead* v *Buck* (1777) 2 W Bl 1117, 96 ER 660). The court further adumbrated two public policy reasons why a lien should be denied the land-based finder and preserver of property. First, concern about the 'wilful attempts of ill-designing people to turn their floats and vessels adrift, in order that they might be paid for finding them' (at 259). That is, the existence of a proprietary remedy might endanger as much as preserve property in the long run. Secondly, if a lien was available there was a danger that the owner of property would always pay too much in order to secure its release.

The boundaries of maritime salvage were preserved by the House of Lords in *The Goring* [1988] AC 831, where classic salvage services were performed again on the Thames near Reading Bridge for the eponymous vessel. Lord Brandon held that the salvage jurisdiction did not extend to non-tidal inland waters. Further, he rejected the suggested extension by way of analogy and for reasons of public policy put forward by Sheen J and Sir John Donaldson MR in the lower courts ([1987] QB 687, at 693 and 706–707 respectively). For criticism, see Rose (1989) 9 OJLS 167. In *Falcke* v *Scottish Imperial Insurance Co.* (1886) 34 Ch D 234, Bowen LJ observed of the doctrine of maritime salvage (at 249): 'No similar doctrine applies to things lost upon land, nor to anything except ships or goods in peril at sea.'

9.3   AGENCY OF NECESSITY

The principles of agency of necessity originated in the law merchant in two particular situations. First, the power of the master of a vessel in an emergency to dispose of the cargo and perform other necessary actions. Secondly, the right of reimbursement of the acceptor of a bill of exchange for the honour of the drawer. There is respectable authority that the principle is confined to such exceptional cases (*Hawtayne* v *Bourne* (1841) 7 M & W 595, at 599, 151 ER 905 *per* Parke B; *Gwilliam* v *Twist* [1895] 2 QB 84, at 87 *per* Lord Esher MR and *Jebara* v *Ottoman Bank* [1927] 2 QB 254, at 270–71 *per* Scrutton LJ). In contrast, in cases where there is a pre-existing relationship between the parties, commonly bailment, there has been some judicial support for an expansion of doctrine. In *Prager* v *Blatspiel, Stamp and Heacock Ltd* [1924] 1 KB 566, McCardie J stated that agency of necessity would arise if three conditions were satisfied:

(a)   the agent must be unable to communicate with the principal in order to obtain instructions as to what to do to safeguard the latter's interests;
(b)   the action taken must be commercially necessary;
(c)   the agent must act bona fide and in the best interests of the principal.

It is controversial whether there is anything particularly agency-orientated about many of the authorities where agency of necessity is adverted to. It is necessary to distinguish two distinct situations. In *China Pacific SA* v *Food Corporation of India, The Winson* [1982] AC 939, Lord Diplock observed (at 958):

> Whether one person is entitled to act as agent of necessity for another person is relevant to the question whether circumstances exist which in law have the effect of conferring on him authority to create contractual rights and obligations between that other person and a third party that are directly enforceable by each against the other. It would, I think, be an aid to clarity of legal thinking if the use of the expression 'agent of necessity' were confined to contexts in which this was the question to be determined and not extended, as it often is, to cases where the only relevant question is whether a person who without obtaining instructions from the owner of goods incurs expense in taking steps that are reasonably necessary for their preservation is in law entitled to recover from the owner of the goods the reasonable expenses incurred by him in taking those steps.

Only the former, triangular configuration raises agency issues. The latter, linear configuration raises no issues of legal representation, but only of a direct right to restitution. The facts of *The Winson* involved a linear claim. Salvors off-loaded wheat from a stranded vessel and arranged and paid for its storage pending collection by the cargo-owners. They were held entitled to reimbursement. Lord Diplock stated that, as regards two-party cases, impossibility of communication with the owner was not a condition precedent to the claim. The owner's failure to give instructions when apprised of the situation sufficed. Note that the triangular situation would have arisen with a variation of the facts if the warehouses in which the cargo was stored had sued the owner directly on a contract purportedly made upon the owner's behalf by the salvor. The determination of this question was expressly left open. In obiter dicta in *In re F (Mental Patient: Sterilisation)*[1990] 2 AC 1, Lord Goff of Chieveley stated that the intervener must act prudently, and must not be acting officiously (at 74–76). Lastly, it is worth citing Lord Diplock's observation in *The Winson* that 'English law is economical in recognising situations that give rise to agency of necessity' (at 962).

9.4 BAILMENT

The linear restitutionary claim traditionally discussed in terms of agency of necessity most commonly involves a pre-existing bailment. Bailment involves the transfer of possession of tangible personal property. In *Prager* v *Blatspiel, Stamp and Heacock Ltd* [1924] 1 KB 566, London fur merchants acted on behalf of a Bucharest furrier in buying and dressing skins. World War I intervened. After Romania was invaded by Germany, the London agents sold skins belonging to the Bucharest furrier on their own account. A plea of agency of necessity was rejected as a defence to a claim for wrongful interference with goods when the war was over. There was no factual necessity: dressed furs were not perishable goods and the sellers, who had sold the skins after a great increase in value, had not acted bona fide.

The clearest authority granting restitution in a case of pre-existing bailment is *Great Northern Railway Co.* v *Swaffield* (1874) LR 9 Ex 132. The railway company carried a horse on behalf of the defendant to a station, but the horse was not collected from the station. The company accordingly arranged for this horse to be looked after by a stable. The defendant refused to pay for the charges incurred, and eventually the plaintiffs met the sum themselves, delivered the horse, and made a personal claim for the stabling charges. The Court of Exchequer held that they were entitled to reimbursement. Pollock B stressed that the railway company as a carrier had a duty to take reasonable care of the horse such as a man who would take reasonable care of his goods. By analogy with maritime authority (*Notara* v *Henderson* (1872) LR 7 QB 225 and *Gaudet* v *Brown, Cargo Ex Argos* (1873) LR 5 PC 134), it was held that there was a correlative right to reimbursement for necessary expenses incurred. This is consistent with the dicta in *Nicholson* v *Chapman* (1793) 2 H Bl 254, 126 ER 536, favouring a personal claim, but rejecting a proprietary claim in the form of a lien. Further, the House of Lords in *China Pacific SA* v *Food Corporation of India, The Winson* [1982] AC 939 stressed the relationship between the salvors and the cargo-owners gave rise to a direct relationship of bailment. Salvage services required the off-loading of the cargo and its conveyance to a place of safety. Thereafter, according to Lord Diplock (at 960):

> the bailment which up to the conclusion of salvage services had been a bailment for valuable consideration became a gratuitous bailment; and so long as that relationship of bailor and bailee continued to subsist the salvors, under the ordinary principles of the law of bailment too well known and too well-established to call for any citation of authority, owed a duty of care to the cargo owner to take such measures to preserve the salved wheat from deterioration by exposure to the elements as a man of ordinary prudence would take for the preservation of his own property. For any breach of such duty the bailee is liable to his bailor in damages for any diminution of the value of the goods consequent upon his failure to take such measures; and if he fulfils that duty he has, in my view, a correlative right to charge the owner of the goods with the expenses reasonably incurred in doing so.

9.5 BURIAL CASES

Burial of the dead provides another pocket of case law from which the inchoate general principle of relief for necessitous intervention might be developed. In *Jenkins* v *Tucker* (1788) 1 H Bl 90, 126 ER 55, a father paid the funeral expenses of his married daughter while her husband, who was primarily liable for the expense, was abroad on his estate. The Court of Common Pleas allowed the father, as a proper person to interfere, to recover his expenses in an action of money paid. This supports the requirement that the intervention should not be officious. The style of funeral should be suitable to the standing of the person. Similarly in *Rogers* v *Price* (1829) 3 Y & J 28, 148 ER 1080 the plaintiff undertaker who was called to attend the deceased, who had died at his brother's house, succeeded in *quantum meruit* against the estate of the deceased. It was admitted that the funeral was suitable to the degree of the deceased. The policy underlying recovery was stated by Garrow B (at 34):

> Suppose a person to be killed by accident at a distance from his home; what, in such a case ought to be done? The common principles of decency and humanity, the common impulses of our nature, would direct every one as a preliminary step, to provide a decent funeral, at the expense of the estate; and to do that which is immediately necessary upon the subject, in order to avoid what, if not provided against, may become an inconvenience to the public.

This case appears to allow any appropriate person to make a claim (including professional undertakers) provided the action was not officious.

9.6   CARE FOR THE MENTALLY INCOMPETENT

In *In re Rhodes* (1890) 44 ChD 94 the Court of Appeal held that a brother who had provided for his sister's confinement in a private asylum was prima facie entitled to reimbursement for the expenses incurred. It was held that the mental incompetent's estate was liable. The court emphatically enunciated that the obligation was one imposed by law, and rejected an earlier Court of Appeal's reliance on the implied contract fallacy (*cf In re Weaver* (1882) 21 ChD 615). However, the decision is marred by an additional requirement that money must have been paid with intention on the part of the intervener that it should be repaid. There being little evidence of this, the claim was rejected. For criticism of this requirement see Birks, 199.

9.7   EQUITABLE ANALOGIES

The equity jurisdiction of the High Court promotes and supervises the proper administration of trusts and estates. This has been held in recent cases to justify claims for reimbursement or increased reimbursement for trustees and insolvency practitioners. In *In re Duke of Norfolk's Settlement Trusts* [1982] Ch 61, the Court of Appeal allowed the trustees' claim to increased remuneration on the ground that it was beneficial to the administration of the trust. The case law describes the jurisdiction as 'closely analogous to "salvage" ' (*In re Duke of Norfolk's Settlement Trusts* [1979] Ch 37, at 59 *per* Walton J). That case was relied upon in *In Re Berkeley Applegate (Investment Consultants) Ltd (in liquidation)* [1989] Ch 32, where an investment company was placed in voluntary liquidation. The costs were likely to be considerable and to exceed the company's free assets. It was held that pursuant to this inherent jurisdiction the liquidator could claim out of the trust assets managed by the company. Edward Nugee QC (sitting as deputy High Court judge) held that this included not simply reimbursement, but a right to reasonable remuneration. He distinguished the *Falcke* case (at 50):

> As a condition of giving effect to [the investors'] equitable rights, the court has in my judgment a discretion to ensure that a proper allowance is made to the

liquidators ... [I]f the liquidator had not done this work, it is inevitable that the work, or at all events a great deal of it, would have had to be done by someone else, and on an application to the court a receiver would have been appointed whose expenses and fees would necessarily have had to be borne by the trust assets.... The allowance of fair compensation to the liquidator is in my judgment a proper application of the rule that he who seeks equity must do equity.

While these cases cannot properly be described as an emergency as in the classic salvage cases, it is necessary in commercial terms to ensure that assets are realised in such circumstances, and this may well require skilled intervention by an appropriate person. Clearly the court has control over and jealously guards the work of fiduciaries and insolvency practitioners.

FURTHER READING

Asterisks indicate especially useful works.

Goff and Jones, 461–82 (general); 483–98 (maritime salvage)
J. Dawson, '*Negotiorum Gestio*: The Altruistic Intermeddler' (1960–61) 74 Harv LR 817–65, 1073–1129 (comparative)
S. Stoljar, '*Negotiorum Gestio*' in *International Encyclopaedia of Comparative Law* (1984), vol X, chap. 17 (comparative)
*Birks, '*Negotiorum Gestio* and the common law' [1971] CLP 110
*Rose, 'Restitution for the Rescuer' (1989) 9 OJLS 167

PART C

INEFFECTIVE TRANSACTIONS

10 Contracts Discharged by Termination for Breach

10.1 THEORETICAL FOUNDATIONS

This area sees a sensitive interplay between contractual remedies and claims in restitution. It is axiomatic that each and every breach of contract entitles the victim to claim damages, and that those damages are normally assessed by reference to what the victim would have gained had the contract been properly performed. In many cases, damages for breach would be the exclusive remedy. Additionally, in some cases the victim may be entitled to terminate the contract if the breach is a very serious one, or if it is a breach of a fundamental term of the contract. This contractual scheme does not wholly exclude the operation of the law of restitution. However, fundamental limitations still apply: where a benefit is transferred from one party to another and its transfer is provided for by the express or implied terms of a valid or subsisting contract, there can be no recourse to the law of restitution.

Nevertheless, where two preconditions are fulfilled, restitutionary relief may be available. First, the contract must be legitimately terminated. Secondly, where the claimant makes an advance payment, and the other party's breach is so serious that no resulting benefit was conferred upon him, the claimant is entitled to recover the payment on the ground of total failure of consideration. The majority of the cases have been concerned with claims by the innocent party and claims for money. However, there have been some cases concerned with non-money benefits and claims by the party in breach. It seems that all these cases are referable back to the idea of a failure of consideration. The benefit was conferred on a conditional basis, and where that condition fails, it is prima facie recoverable. For reasons of language the cause of action has been perceived as one which operates exclusively in the contractual context. For example, in *Westdeutsche Landesbank Girozentrale* v *Islington London Borough Council* [1994] 4 All ER 891, Hobhouse J stated (at 924):

The phrase 'failure of consideration' is one which in its terminology presupposes that there has been at some stage a valid contract which has been partially performed by one party. It is essentially a concept for use of the law of contract and provides a common law remedy governed by rigid rules granted as of right when the contract becomes ineffective through breach or otherwise.

However, it is a mistake to link failure of consideration with the doctrine of consideration which supplies one of the requirements for a binding contract. The leading guidance is provided by Viscount Simon LC in *Fibrosa Spolka Akcyjna* v *Fairbairn Lawson Combe Barbour Ltd* [1943] AC 32, at 48:

> when one is considering the law of failure of consideration and of the quasi-contractual right to recover money on that ground, it is, generally speaking, not the promise which is referred to as the consideration, but the performance of the promise.

That case conclusively established that the right to recover money on the ground of failure of consideration was a claim which lay outside or dehors the contract. In the view of Lord Wright such a claim was designed to remedy unjust enrichment or unjust benefit. The effect of the totality requirement and the requirement of discharge was to permit recourse to the law of restitution only where a party had got nothing in return for his performance. As Lord Wright observed (at 72):

> the English rule of recovering payment the consideration for which has failed works a rough justice. It was adopted in more primitive times and was based on the simple theory that a man who was paid in advance for something which he has never got ought to have his money back. It is further imperfect because it depends on an entire consideration and a total failure.

Nowadays the totality requirement is seen as working injustice and is often circumvented. To date, in the context of contracts terminated for breach, it remains a precondition of recovery. The criticisms of the totality rule, and the possibilities of reform or judicial development, will be considered below. The requirement of termination has rarely suffered similar criticisms and this follows from it being derived from the fundamental principle that a contractual regime excludes the operation of restitution (although the need for termination has been overlooked on at least one occasion in the House of Lords: *Miles* v *Wakefield Metropolitan District Council* [1987] AC 539). For the contrary view, that unjust enrichment should be available even though the contract is undischarged, see Smith (1999) 115 LQR 245. Even if the House of Lords were to revisit the requirement of totality, it is submitted that termination should still be a precondition of restitutionary relief and that continuing regard will have to be had to the terms of the contract which has been terminated in judging the appropriateness or otherwise of imposing a restitutionary solution.

10.2 THE NATURE OF TERMINATION FOR BREACH

The most sophisticated account of termination for breach in English law is the classic speech of Lord Diplock in *Photo Productions Ltd* v *Securicor Ltd* [1980] AC 827, at 848–50. A number of fundamental propositions can be derived from this judgment. A valid and effective contract consists of *primary* obligations, which are ascertained by the courts by the techniques of construction and implication. For example, one party agrees to render goods and services and the other party agrees to pay the price. With regard to remedies, the courts commonly enforce the primary obligations as a matter of right where it is a obligation to pay money via the action of debt, and can as a matter of discretion, where it is appropriate to do so, compel specific performance of other primary obligations such as the transfer of property. However, a contract also consists of *secondary* obligations, which operate upon breach or default by one or other party. Two secondary obligations are imposed by law. First, the general secondary obligation, which is to pay damages for any losses resulting from a breach of contract. Secondly, the anticipatory secondary obligation, more commonly known as the right to elect for termination.

In modern contract law termination for breach is available by two routes. First, the court characterises the parties' obligations. Some terms, either as a matter of positive law (because classified as such by statute, most famously in the Sale of Goods Act 1979, or by previous judicial exegesis) or as a matter of construction of the particular contract, are characterised as fundamental terms or conditions. Any breach of such term gives rise to the right to terminate, whether or not the breach has serious consequences. If this process does not resolve the question of whether the innocent party can quit, the second stage is to examine the nature, seriousness and consequences of the breach. If the failure in performance is so serious that it deprives the innocent party of 'substantially the whole benefit which it was the intention of the parties that was expressed in the contract that he shall obtain as consideration' for his own performance, he is entitled to terminate (*Hong Kong Fir Shipping Ltd* v *Kawasaki Kishen Kaisha* [1962] 2 QB 26, at 66 *per* Diplock LJ, as explained in *Bunge Corp. New York* v *Tradax Export SA Panama* [1981] 1 WLR 711). However, in addition the parties may agree their own secondary obligations, and the court must determine what these are by construction. Such provisions include express termination, liquidated damages, retention of title and *force majeure* clauses.

In this context the nature of the termination becomes easier to discern. It is clear that termination in response to breach is prospective only (*Photo Production Ltd* v *Securicor Ltd* [1980] AC 827; *Johnson* v *Agnew* [1980] AC 362, 392–93 *per* Lord Wilberforce and *Hyundai Heavy Industries Co. Ltd* v *Papadopoulos* [1980] 1 WLR 1129 (the last two cases relying on the classic analysis of Dixon J in the High Court of Australia in *Macdonald* v *Denys Lascelles Ltd* (1933) 48 CLR 457)). It is to be contrasted with rescission in response to misrepresentation or undue influence, where the process of rescission unwinds prior performance by the parties on unjust enrichment principles. Such cases are concerned with the defective *formation* of contracts, whereas we are now concerned with the defective *performance* of contracts. For Birks there is a critical distinction in the law of restitution, between cases where the intention to transfer is vitiated (such as by mistake or misrepresentation) and cases where the intention to contract is qualified or conditional: Birks, 219. Some of the older cases make the mistake of confusing these two grounds of ineffectiveness of contracts and suggest that before there can be a restitutionary solution the whole contract must be rescinded and the parties returned to *status quo* (e.g., *Hunt* v *Silk* (1804) 5 East 449, 102 ER 1142). This is no longer good law. However, the rule that termination is prospective simply means that future unperformed obligations are discharged. Partial performance by one or both parties prior to termination may well result in a benefit to the other party which can legitimately be the concern of an autonomous claim in unjust enrichment, or which might be taken into account in valuing damages where an innocent party sues for breach. The underlying policy must be sensitivity to the contractual regime. Restitution must be not be allowed to redistribute a consensual allocation of risk.

Returning to the analysis of Lord Diplock in *Photo Productions Ltd* v *Securicor Ltd* [1980] AC 827, where a contract remains undischarged the sole remedy is damages. Indeed the basic measure of damages is the difference between the performance promised and the performance actually received, which will involve taking into account net benefits received by the innocent party as a result of performance. A similar approach would be appropriate where a contract has been terminated following breach and a claim is made to contractual damages. However, it seems that the innocent party may have a free election between claiming contractual damages and suing in restitution. A sensitive question is whether recourse to restitution should be allowed to subvert the contractual allocation of risks and allow the innocent party to escape a bad bargain. Damages in contract are primarily measured by the deficiencies in performance of the primary obligations of the party in breach, less net benefits received. However, in addition, the parties may have agreed their own secondary obligations which would control the transfer of benefits even after the contract is terminated. The parties may have provided for the return or retention of particular benefits. Therefore an advance payment by the party in breach might be construed as being a deposit, and therefore forfeit if the primary obligations are broken. This illustrates the essential nature of termination. The contract does not come to an end for all purposes. Instead the regime of primary obligations which apply while the contract is valid and binding is, upon termination, replaced by a new regime of secondary obligations. The secondary obligations, as has been said, include the general secondary obligation to pay damages for losses resulting from breach and any secondary obligations agreed upon by the parties themselves, which may include the modification or exclusion of the general secondary obligation to pay damages. Therefore, in considering the possibility of restitutionary relief, the courts will first have to decide as a matter of construction whether the parties have provided for the re-transfer or retention of benefits conferred by either party prior to termination.

10.3   CONTRACTUAL RIGHTS TO REPAYMENT

Contracts will often contain the machinery for the repayment of sums overpaid by one party in respect of performance not received, resulting in a contractual obligation to make restitution. Such provisions, which are ascertained by the techniques of construction or implication, belong properly within the province of the law of contract, but are illuminating from the perspective of restitution as well. Such provisions will make recourse to the law of restitution not only pointless but also inappropriate. The example of time charterparties is instructive. In *Pan Ocean Shipping Co. Ltd* v *Creditcorp Ltd, The Trident Beauty* [1994] 1 WLR 161, Pan Ocean chartered the eponymous vessel from Trident at an agreed daily hire rate of US$6,400 per day payable 15 days in advance. Advance payments were made, but for the relevant period the vessel was rendered off-hire because she was undergoing repairs. Accordingly Pan Ocean got nothing in return for its money. As between the charterer and the shipowner the time charterparty was the governing contractual matrix. Where a vessel is rendered off-hire pursuant to the contractual definition of such circumstances, it becomes inevitable that there will be adjustments in the hire paid. Where the relationship is ongoing the usual practice is that deductions are made when the next instalment of hire costs is due. The contract provided by clause 18 that 'any overpaid hire ... [is] to be returned at once'. If hire was overpaid a contractual debt pursuant to that clause arose. However, Lord Goff of Chieveley observed (at 164):

> even in the absence of any such express contractual provision, advance hire which proves to have been paid in respect of a period during which the vessel was rendered off-hire under a term of the contract must ordinarily be repaid, and if necessary a term will be implied into the contract to that effect ... [A]s between shipowner and charterer, there is a contractual regime which legislates for the recovery of overpaid hire. It follows that, as a general rule, the law of restitution has no part to play in the matter; the existence of the agreed regime renders the imposition by the law of a remedy in restitution both unnecessary and inappropriate.

That this was a contractual, rather than a quasi-contractual means of recovery was reinforced by the fact that recovery could effectively be obtained where there was a partial failure, and not just a total failure in respect of any advance payments of hire. This illustrates the greater sensitivity of an agreed contractual regime of repayment. It is significant that such a regime may exist not simply pursuant to express terms, but may be the result of implication of terms. It may be thought that there is a danger of returning to the implied contract fallacy by such an approach. However, if the implication satisfies the contractual tests of necessity or business efficacy it is submitted that there will be no tension between contract and restitution. Indeed, as regards cases of partial failure, an implied contractual regime will avoid current uncertainties about the restitutionary right to recovery in cases of partial failure.

A further illustration of an implied contractual right to recover money paid arises in the context of performance bonds. In *Cargill International* v *Bangladesh Sugar & Food* [1996] 4 All ER 563 (QBD), [1998] 1 WLR 461 (CA), the Court of Appeal upheld Morison J's decision that where a performance bond was issued by a seller in an international sale as security for performance of its undertakings, the buyer was entitled to demand the full amount under the bond upon default, although ultimately there would be 'accounting' between the parties. The buyer would be entitled to retain only the amount of any loss suffered as a result of the seller's breach, and must refund any balance. The case concerned an agreement to sell to sugar c.&.f. (c.) Chittagong. The buyer rejected the goods because of alleged late arrival and the age of the vessel. The market price of sugar had fallen and the buyer had suffered no loss as a result of the breach. It was held that the bond was a guarantee of performance, not a penalty. Symmetry prevailed: if the buyer's loss exceeded the amount of the bond (here 10 per cent of the c.&.f. price), the buyer could sue for the balance; conversely, if the bond were called upon and the loss was less than that amount, there must be repayment of the excess. The juridical basis relied upon by the judge was an implied term, with the judge expressly concluding that the basis of recovery was 'contractual rather than quasi-contractual' ([1996] 4 All ER 563, at 573). The judge's ruling as a matter of general principle was approved of by the Court of Appeal in *Comdel Commodities Ltd.* v *Siporex Trade S.N.* [1997] 1 Lloyd's Rep 424, in the context of a performance bond entered into by a *buyer* as security for his promise to supply a letter of credit timeously. On appeal in *Cargill*, Morison J's elucidation of the general principle was not challenged. Rather it was argued that the contractual words excluded the general rule. This was not accepted. In such cases, the principle of subsidiarity applies, and the contract displaces restitution. The only escape route would be through the jurisdiction over penalties (see 10.8.2) and relief against forfeiture (see 10.8.5).

10.4 RECOVERY AGAINST A NON-PARTY?

The main question which arose in *Pan Ocean Shipping Co. Ltd* v *Creditcorp Ltd, The Trident Beauty* [1994] 1 WLR 161, was the possibility of recovery against a third party. Trident, the shipper, was in financial difficulties, and in order to finance its operation it had arranged credit facilities with Creditcorp. As part of this arrangement Trident had assigned its right to hire from the vessel to Creditcorp. By notice two days after the time charter was signed, Trident informed Pan Ocean that all hire payments should be made directly to Creditcorp. An advance payment due from Pan Ocean of US $93,600 was accordingly paid to Creditcorp. As was stated above, because the vessel was rendered off-hire during this period Pan Ocean got nothing in return for its money. The vessel was subsequently withdrawn and Pan Ocean was held entitled to terminate the charterparty accepting Trident's conduct as repudiatory. Trident was insolvent so Pan Ocean sought restitution of the US $93,600 from Creditcorp on the ground of total failure of consideration. Note that the requirements of termination and total failure were met. However, the House of Lords refused the claim against Creditcorp as assignee. Lord Goff stressed the importance of the contractual regime between Pan Ocean as charterer and Trident as shipowner for the relationship between charterer and Creditcorp as assignee. Whereas the benefit of the debt had been assigned to Creditcorp, the burden of performing the contract remained on Trident. Lord Goff insisted that Pan Ocean had no remedy against Trident in restitution on the ground of failure of consideration, its only remedy being its contractual right to recover against Trident (although now obviously worthless given Trident's financial circumstances). Lord Goff foresaw 'serious difficulties . . . if the law seeks to expand the law of restitution to redistribute risks for which provision has been made under an applicable contract' (at 166). This is a clear application of the principle of primacy of contract.

It is submitted that the decision can be analysed either from the point of view of the ground for restitution, or with regard to applicable defences. There was no unjust factor or ground for restitution here. There was no failure of the bargained for counter-performance. The contractual regime between charterer and shipowner meant that the charterer was entitled to the use of the vessel, or, in the event of that primary obligation not being performed, an express secondary obligation upon the shipowner to return overpaid hire. This express secondary obligation had accrued as a contractual debt before the contract was terminated. Therefore there was no failure of consideration in that Pan Ocean had got exactly what it bargained for under the contractual secondary regime. The fact that the value of the secondary obligation of the shipowner was rendered worthless by reason of its financial circumstances did not cause a failure of the bargained for counter-performance. Equally the law of restitution was ousted by the second contract between the shipowner Trident and Creditcorp, the financiers. Under that contract Creditcorp had provided facilities to Trident in return for its covenant to repay and the assignment of hire such as that payable by Pan Ocean. Lord Goff observed (at 166): 'Creditcorp, is not the mere recipient of a windfall but is an assignee who has purchased from Trident the right to receive the contractual debt.' The contractual matrix, including both the time charterparty and the financing contract, never contemplated an obligation on the assignee to refund overpaid hire. Rather it explicitly imposed the obligation of repayment upon the shipowner. This can be explained by reference to primacy of contract, effectively ousting the operation of restitution both as regards direct and indirect parties. Alternatively it can be rationalised in a way which appealed to Neill LJ in the Court of Appeal, that 'Creditcorp were in a position analogous to that of a bona fide purchaser for value' ([1993] 1 Lloyd's Rep 443, at 449, which also appealed to Lord Goff [1994] 1 WLR 161, at 166). Lord Woolf in addition stressed that the assignee should have no obligation to repay because he had no responsibility for the non-performance of the primary obligations by the shipowners.

It is worth considering briefly whether Creditcorp could have maintained a cause of action if advance hire had been payable but had not been paid in the same circumstances. Prima facie Pan Ocean appear liable to pay, but it is arguable that as assignee Creditcorp would have been subject to all the equities that the debtor could raise *vis-à-vis* the assignor. In which case the fact that the vessel was rendered off-hire and that Pan Ocean received nothing in return may have precluded a cause of action. This illustrates how the law attaches importance to the sanctity of receipt, where moneys may be retained in circumstances in which they could no longer be actively claimed. *The Trident Beauty* neatly illustrates that the contractual regime may oust restitutionary recovery not only against the immediate party but also against third party beneficiaries, where the matrix of rights and obligations does not contemplate recovery from such a third party.

However, the case is thoroughly criticised by Barker ([1994] LMCLQ 305) who attacks, first, the fallacy of dependency, whereby it is assumed that rights against the assignee must be parasitic upon rights against the original contracting party. Secondly, the fallacy of fault, which it is argued is not relevant as an ingredient of the cause of action for failure of consideration. Thirdly, the House of Lords is criticised for vagueness on the issue of bona fide purchase and the issue of the security of receipt. Lastly, with regard to risk allocation, Barker poses the question of whether there was any implied contractual provision for the events which happened: 'Certainly, [Pan Ocean] contracted into a regime of recoupment with the client, but does this really mean that they were thereby abandoning all of the rights provided by the law of unjust enrichment?' (at 310). Further, the case leads 'to damaging presumptions: that if one specifies contractual rights, one is confined to them; and that if the plaintiffs want restitution from a third party, they must bargain for it'. For the reasons advanced above, and for the reason that contractual silence upon a question may be as evocative as contractual express provision, it is suggested that Barker's criticisms are ill-founded. The House of Lords was correct to pay attention to both operative contracts and the scheme of protection they provided by their express and implied terms.

For the related problem of whether a sub-contractor can short-circuit the contract structure to sue the employer where the main contractor is insolvent, see Watts, 'Does a subcontractor have restitutionary rights against the employer?' [1995] LMCLQ 398. In the light of *The Trident Beauty* it is suggested the answer is generally 'No'.

10.5   THE REQUIREMENT OF TOTAL FAILURE

10.5.1   Criticisms of the totality requirement

Total failure of consideration requires, at least notionally, that the claimant has received none of the benefits which the claimant bargained for under the contract. There are three broad criticisms.

First, there is the argument of principle. The recipient of a benefit under a now discharged contract is unjustly enriched not just in cases of total failure of consideration, but also where the consideration has partially failed. This can be illustrated by the old case of *Hunt* v *Silk* (1804) 5 East 449, 102 ER 1142, where Hunt took immediate possession of premises prior to the execution of a lease and paid £10 on the understanding that the landlord would carry out necessary repairs within 10 days. This was not done, and some days after the 10-day deadline elapsed, Hunt left the premises and claimed back £10. The Court of King's Bench held that the intermediate occupation, which could only be referred to the contract, meant there could be no recovery in an action for money had and received. The result appears to be somewhat harsh at the expense of the tenant.

Secondly, it is argued that the machinery of the modern law of unjust enrichment is now able to deal better with situations where each side has conferred a benefit upon the other, by insisting that restitution be accompanied by counter-restitution. It seems the courts now contemplate readily the possibility of substitutionary counter-restitution in money. Compare developments in relation to contracts rescinded for undue influence (*O'Sullivan* v *Management Agency and Music Ltd* [1985] QB 428 (see 1.3.3)) and in respect of breach of fiduciary duty (*Boardman* v *Phipps* [1967] 2 AC 46 (see 1.4.6 and Birks, 475–76)).

Thirdly, the stringency of the totality requirement is undermined by the development of exceptions and by judicial manipulation of the test to achieve a just result. For example, in *Rowland* v *Divall* [1923] 2 KB 500, the court disregarded the intermediate use of a car which had been supplied by a non-owner, in awarding the purchaser the return of the full purchase price paid. The common law's rejection of apportionment was regretted by Goff, nearly 40 years ago: Goff (1961) 24 MLR 85, at 89–92. It was accepted that where the payee was in breach, the rule caused no problems in practice, as the payer could recoup benefits in the claim for damages for breach. However, where the payer was in breach, and there had been partial performance by both parties, the payer had no cause of action in contract (as the party in breach) and no claim in restitution, because there had been no total failure of consideration. Goff advocated (at 90): 'The simple solution appears to be to grant a general right of recovery to the extent that the consideration for the payment has partially failed, subject always to the payee's right to recover damages in respect of any breach of which the payer has been guilty.' The author then drew attention to the limited statutory reforms of the Apportionment Act 1870 (see Goff and Jones, 548) and the Law Reform (Frustrated Contracts) Act 1943.

Subsequently, the same author, as Lord Goff of Chieveley, observed in *Westdeutsche Landesbank Girozentrale* v *Islington London Borough Council* [1996] AC 669, at 682:

There has long been a desire among restitutionary lawyers to escape from the unfortunate effects of the so-called rule that money is only recoverable at common law on the ground of failure of consideration where the failure is total, by reformulating the rule upon a more principled basis; and signs that this will in due course be done are appearing in judgments throughout the common law world, as appropriate cases arise for decision.

That case concerned a void contract, which raises different issues to cases of contracts terminated for breach. It is interesting to note that whereas Lord Goff thought the ground of recovery was probably *partial* failure of consideration (at 683), Lord Browne-Wilkinson was insistent there was a *total* failure. Payments were made on the basis that the other party was subject to legal obligations. It was not, because of the voidness of the transaction. Accordingly there was total failure (at 710–11).

10.5.2   Arguments for the totality requirement

First, there is a species of argument from contractual primacy, that by partial performance a party becomes ineluctably bound up by the contractual regime. In its extreme form this argument suggests that where there has been any performance the parties can never be returned to the *status quo* and therefore restitution is not possible. This appears to confuse termination for breach, which is prospective in effect, with rescission for some operative vitiating factor, which acts retrospectively. Such confusion about the nature of termination is manifest in the judgments in *Hunt* v *Silk* (see 10.5.1) and seriously undermines the reasoning deployed. The argument for contractual primacy, while appropriate for undischarged contracts, loses much of its force where the contractual regime of primary obligations comes to an end as a result of a valid termination. It is clear that any restitutionary recovery in this context must be sensitive to the contractual regime, but that does not appear to require a mechanical insistence that the consideration should have wholly failed.

Secondly, there is a respectable argument that the contract price or rate of remuneration should provide a ceiling of recovery in unjust enrichment. This is based on a policy that recovery in restitution should not allow a party to escape from the consequences of a bad bargain. This argument has not yet prevailed in England, and in any event does not appear to necessitate the totality requirement but rather a regime which allows recovery for partial failure but capped by reference to the contractual rate.

The best defence of the requirement of total failure is that it demonstrates the common law courts instinctively addressing the tension between the contractual regime and restitutionary recovery, and allowing the latter only where one party has not received any of the benefits for which he bargained. This was the explanation of Lord Wright in *Fibrosa Spolka Akcyjna* v *Fairbairn Lawson Combe Barbour Ltd* [1943] AC 32, at 72, where he said 'The English rule of recovering payment the consideration for which has failed worked rough justice . . . in more primitive times'. Lord Wright went on to speak favourably of the development by the Court of Equity of a more sensitive system of apportionment in cases where a premium was paid for a partnership which ended prematurely (contained in s. 40 of the Partnership Act 1890).

The limitations and weaknesses of these arguments, academic criticisms and recent judicial evasion, suggest that the requirement of totality is on the wane. However, the removal of this artificial bar should not mean that the courts can relax their vigilance against restitution being allowed to subvert a contractual allocation of risk. For fuller discussion, see McKendrick, 'Total Failure of Consideration and Counter-Restitution: Two Issues or One?' in Birks (1995), 217, and Birks, 'Failure of Consideration' in Rose (1996), 179.

10.5.3   Recent judicial development

Recent judicial criticism of the totality rule is generally found in obiter dicta at the highest appellate level. For example, in *David Securities Pty Ltd* v *Commonwealth*

Bank of Australia (1992) 175 CLR 353, the leading judgment of Mason CJ and brethren commented (at 383): 'In cases where consideration can be apportioned or where counter-restitution is relatively simple, insistence on total failure of consideration can be misleading or confusing.' That case was concerned with abrogating the Australian mistake of law rule, and the point did not arise for decision.

More significantly, a recent decision of a strong committee of the Privy Council took a decisive step towards apportionment. In *Goss* v *Chilcott* [1996] AC 788, the plaintiff company lent money to the defendants secured by a mortgage. However, the contract and security were rendered unenforceable because the contract was altered by an agent of the plaintiff without the defendants' authority, under the rule in *Pigot's Case* (1614) 11 Co Rep 26b, 77 ER 1177. The defendants had paid two instalments of interest, but had repaid none of the principal sum before this was discovered. The Privy Council held that the principal was recoverable in restitution on the ground of failure of consideration. There was no illegality and no suggestion of a policy precluding restitution. The payment of two instalments did not preclude recovery on the basis that the failure was not total. It was legitimate to treat interest and principal separately. However, it was clear that the Board would have been willing to go further. Lord Goff of Chieveley, delivering the advice and relying on *David Securities*, observed (at 798):

> In the present case, since no part of the capital sum had been repaid, the failure of consideration for the capital sum would plainly have been total. But even if part of the capital sum had been repaid, the law would not hesitate to hold that the balance of the loan outstanding would be recoverable on the ground of failure of consideration; for at least in those cases where apportionment can be carried out without difficulty, the law will allow partial recovery on this ground.

It should noted that this authority concerned an unenforceable contract, not one terminated for breach.

A rather unsatisfactory authority at Court of Appeal level in a case of termination for breach suggests recovery was permitted on the basis of partial failure of consideration, although the judges treated the claim as one based on a total failure. In *D. O. Ferguson & Associates* v *Sohl* (1992) 62 Build LR 95, the plaintiff builder abandoned a site leaving the work uncompleted. The price was £32,194.15, and the defendant employer had paid some £26,738.75. The judge rejected the plaintiff's claim for the balance of the price, holding that he had committed the repudiatory breach of contract. The defendant's claim for breach yielded only nominal damages, as he had had the work completed at less than the balance due. However, the judge held that the defendant was entitled to recover some £4,673 which represented the amount overpaid, given that the value of the work done by the P was worth only £22,065.76. This award was upheld by the Court of Appeal on the basis either that there was a total failure of consideration, or no consideration for the amount once paid. The case can only be explained as recovery on the basis of partial failure, or perhaps mistake, if the defendant wrongly believed that the value of the work at the time of payment equalled the amount paid. However, it illustrates increasing judicial impatience with the traditional insistence on totality. For discussion see Skelton, 1–8, 20–33, 101–103.

10.6 RECOVERY OF MONEY BY THE INNOCENT PARTY

Money is recoverable where the contract is terminated and there has been a total failure of consideration. The latter requirement proves more problematic and is capable of manipulation. Has the payer received anything in return for his money? Has the payee done anything to justify the retention of the money? That the test is a stringent one has been confirmed recently by the House of Lords in *Stocznia Gdanska SA* v *Latvian Shipping Co.* [1998] 1 WLR 574 (albeit in the context of a claim by the party in breach). Lord Goff stated (at 588): 'In truth, the test is not whether the promisee has received a specific benefit, but rather whether the promisor has performed any part of the contractual duties in respect of which the payment is due.' Therefore where there is defective performance which nevertheless results in something of value to the claimant, restitution is not possible. Accordingly, in *Linz* v *Electric Wire Company of Palestine Ltd* [1948] AC 371, Linz bought preference shares which subsequently turned out to be invalid. In the meantime Linz had sold the shares to a third party, although for substantially less than she had paid. The Privy Council held that she had got exactly what she had bargained for, having been registered as shareholder and having received value from a subsequent transferee. In *Baltic Shipping Co.* v *Dillon, The Mikhail Lermontov* (1993) 111 ALR 289, a 14-day cruise was rudely interrupted by the sinking of the vessel on the tenth day. The High Court of Australia rejected arguments that the provision of the cruise was an entire obligation, or that the consideration for the trip was entirely nullified by the disaster which had occurred. Mason CJ concluded (at 295): 'The consequence of the respondent's enjoyment of the benefits provided under the contract during the first eight full days of the cruise is that the failure of consideration was partial, not total.' It should be noted that the cruise company had voluntarily refunded the portion of the contract price relating to the remainder of the holiday. However, the respondent was not entitled in law to recover the balance.

The artificiality and inconsistency produced by the totality requirement are neatly illustrated by the results in cases involving the sale of goods, both domestic and international.

10.6.1 Domestic sales

Section 12 of the Sale of Goods 1979 requires that the seller has a right to sell the goods. Section 14 (as amended) provides that the goods should be of satisfactory (previously merchantable) quality. Both terms are explicitly conditions, any breach of which entitles the buyer to reject the goods, i.e., a right to terminate the contract. The buyer will lose the right to terminate and to reject the goods where he accepts them, or is deemed to have accepted them under s. 35. The Act is evasive on the right to recover the purchase price, simply stating by s. 54 that 'Nothing in this Act affects the right of the buyer or the seller . . . to recover money paid where the consideration for the payment of it has failed'. Note that the statute does not expressly refer to the totality requirement. The Act only explicitly provides rights of termination and to damages. Restitution of the price is left to the common law.

In *Rowland* v *Divall* [1923] 2 KB 500, Divall sold a car to Rowland, a car dealer, for £334. Subsequently, Rowland repainted the car and in turn sold it to a customer. However, the car turned out to be stolen and it was repossessed by the police. Rowland refunded the customer's money and in turn sought restitution of £334 from Divall. The first instance judge held that because of intermediate use of the car for a period of four months there had been no total failure, and that Rowland was confined to his remedy in damages. The Court of Appeal disagreed. While accepting as a general rule that a buyer could not terminate the contract of sale and claim restitution of the price unless he could restore the goods, the Court held it would be absurd to insist on such a precondition in this case. Atkin LJ stated (at 507): 'In fact the buyer has not received any part of that which he contracted to receive — namely, the property and the right of possession and, that being so, there has been a total failure of consideration.' The same result follows where the hire-purchaser of a car purports to sell it to another, in breach of his obligation in the hire-purchase agreement (*Warman* v *Southern Counties Car Finance Corporation* [1949] 2 KB 576; *Butterworth* v *Kingsway Motors* [1954] 1 WLR 1286 and *Barber* v *NWS Bank plc* [1996] 1 All ER 906).

It seems somewhat artificial in these cases to talk about a total failure of consideration, given the extensive intermediate use enjoyed in some of them. However, the courts clearly regard as fundamental the entitlement to rights of ownership and legal possession, rather than simple physical enjoyment. The result in practice of the restitutionary rights enjoyed by buyers and sub-buyers is to pass the burden back up a chain of sales to the party who wrongfully sold the car in the first instance, or more commonly in the case of stolen goods, to the party dealing with the thief. As a matter of principle, the courts' disregard of benefits derived from intermediate enjoyment can be defended on the basis that such benefits were enjoyed not at the expense of the immediate seller (for example, Divall in *Rowland* v *Divall*), but at the expense of the true owner of the goods. The owner, it seems on principle, would be entitled to claim in respect of those benefits from the person enjoying intermediate use. The problem generally arises in practice nowadays only in the context of stolen goods. A private purchaser of a motor car which is still subject to a hire-purchase agreement obtains good title if he is the first private purchaser in good faith under Part III of the Hire Purchase Act 1964. Such a buyer may in the alternative still rely upon restitutionary rights (*Barber* v *NWS Bank plc* [1996] 1 All ER 906). In addition, some protection is now provided for the buyer of stolen goods who carries out improvements on them (see s. 3(7) and s. 6 of the Torts (Interference with Goods) Act 1977 (discussed in 3.8.3).

With regard to s. 14, the critical thing in practice is whether the buyer is sufficiently prompt in exercising his right to reject the goods for breach of the quality obligation. If he is held to have accepted or is deemed to have accepted under s. 35 (as amended in 1994), restitutionary recovery is not possible and he is confined to his right to damages for breach of warranty of quality, under s. 53, which is prima facie the difference between the value of the goods delivered and the goods as they were promised to be: (s. 53(3)). Accordingly, in *Yeoman Credit Ltd* v *Apps* [1962] 2 QB 508, Apps was held to have accepted an 'unusable, unroadworthy and unsafe' vehicle because he made no serious effort to return the car. Instead he kept it for nearly six months and paid three instalments of the price, thereby affirming the contract. Similarly in *Bernstein* v *Pamson Motors (Golders Green) Ltd* [1987] 2 All ER 220, a purchaser was held to have accepted a car which as supplied was dangerously unsafe, after only a few weeks and very little driving. However, where a purchaser is held entitled to reject the car for a breach of s. 14, he is entitled to recover the full purchase price upon a total failure of consideration together with damages for any consequential loss flowing from the breach of contract. In the leading case of *Rogers* v *Parish (Scarborough) Ltd* [1987] 2 All ER 232, the Court of Appeal held that a purchaser was entitled to reject a brand new Range Rover, costing £16,000, which proved unsatisfactory due to faulty oil seals, engine, gearbox and bodywork defects. Rejection was legitimate and restitution followed even though the car had been driven 5,500 miles and had been used over a period of months. The purchaser recovered the money paid for the vehicle, together with the value of a vehicle traded-in in part exchange, and damages for breach of contract. The case sharply illustrates the practical relevance of acceptance. The retailer had failed to plead that the plaintiff was precluded from rejecting the car by reason of acceptance. It was held too late to raise this argument for the first time in the Court of Appeal.

Sections 34 and 35 of the Sale of Goods Act 1979 have been amended by the Sale and Supply of Goods Act 1994 since the cases of *Rogers* and *Bernstein*, clarifying the situation in which the buyer accepts or is deemed to accept. However, the cases remain useful illustrations of the interplay of contractual and restitutionary remedies where defective goods are supplied. In particular, it is clear that whereas it is for the buyer to prove a breach of s. 14, and that he has a prima facie right to reject the goods, it is for the seller to plead and prove that the contract remains alive, and that the buyer is confined to a remedy in damages because the doctrine of acceptance under s. 35.

10.6.2 International sales

In *Comptoir d'Achat et de Vente du Boerebond Belge SA* v *Luis de Ridder Ltd, The Julia* [1949] AC 293, a Belgian buyer purchased rye on terms explicitly labelled 'c.i.f. Antwerp'. The buyer paid the price against shipping documents, including a delivery order. However, the ship never reached Antwerp following the German invasion of Belgium. Instead the goods were unloaded at Lisbon. The buyer claimed restitution of the price upon a total failure of consideration, and the seller countered that delivery of the shipping documents was sufficient part-performance to exclude such rights. The House of Lords held, somewhat artificially, that the agreement was not a true c.i.f. contract under which a seller performs his obligations by tendering a bill of lading and other shipping documents, but was rather an 'arrival' contract. The substitution of a delivery order for a bill of lading was clearly influential. Lord Porter observed (at 310): 'The taking of steps towards performance is not necessarily a part performance of a contract. The question is whether the purchaser has got what he is entitled to in return for the price.' The rye was apparently part of a bulk cargo, and therefore at that time the buyer could obtain neither property nor possession until physical delivery of the goods at Antwerp. Accordingly it was more in the nature of advance payment, rather than payment in return for property in the goods which would ordinarily pass if there was payment against a bill of lading and the goods were not part of a bulk.

Nowadays, following the passing of the Sale of Goods (Amendment) Act 1995, which inserted a new s. 20A into the 1979 Act, it is possible for a buyer to obtain property in goods which are shipped in bulk and where payment has occurred. Further, the Carriage of Goods by Sea Act 1992 now covers a wider variety of shipping documents, including delivery orders. In conclusion it must be said that the reasoning of the House of Lords in *The Julia* was somewhat artificial, and appears to be motivated by a desire to allow the buyer to recoup the price for goods which were never physically delivered.

The analysis in *Kwei Tek Chao v British Traders & Shippers Ltd* [1954] 2 QB 459 is to be preferred. Hong Kong buyers purchased a chemical commodity, 'Rongalite C', c.i.f. Hong Kong. The buyer paid the price against shipping documents, including the bill of lading, which it subsequently turned out falsely stated the shipment date of the cargo. This would have entitled the buyer to reject the documents as being non-genuine and the goods as non-conforming with their description under s. 13. However, ultimately the buyer was held to have accepted the goods under s. 35. The buyer claimed to recover the purchase price upon a total failure of consideration and damages for breach of contract. Devlin J held that the restitutionary claim failed. It had been advanced on the basis that the bill of lading was a forgery, because of the mis-dating, which therefore meant that the buyer had not got what it had bargained for. This was rejected by Devlin J, who held that despite the inaccuracies in the bill of lading it was still a valid receipt for the goods, effective as a document of title and constituted evidence of a valid contract for carriage of goods by sea. Therefore it could not be said that the buyer had not got what it had bargained for, and accordingly it was confined to its remedy in damages. The position might be different if no goods were shipped and the bill could properly be described as completely legally ineffective or a nullity.

10.6.3   Restitution and damages?

In English law it seems clear that the victim of a breach who elects to terminate the contract is entitled to damages for any proveable loss, and in addition where the consideration has totally failed to the return of the price or any part of the price which has been paid. A clear example in the consumer sales context is *Rogers v Parish (Scarborough) Ltd* [1987] 2 All ER 232. In the commercial context, in *Millar's*

Machinery Co. Ltd v *David Way and Son* (1935) 40 Com Cas 204, a defective gravel-washing machine was supplied but eventually rejected by the buyer. The seller claimed a £350 balance on the price of the machine, claiming that it had not been validly rejected. The buyer counter-claimed for the return of a £350 advance payment and damages for wasted expenditure incurred in obtaining replacement machinery. The buyer was held to have validly rejected and was entitled to recover its £350 and damages. Branson J said (at 209):

> I think it a fair estimate to say that the defendants [the buyer] are out of pocket to the extent of £426 in respect of the machinery. If the defendants get that, and the £350 which they have paid, they will be as nearly as I can estimate in the position in which they would have been had there been no breach of the plaintiffs' contract.

The Court of Appeal dismissed an appeal.

Outside of the context of sale of goods the same approach is supported in influential dicta of Lord Denning MR in *Heywood* v *Wellers* [1976] QB 446. A solicitor (or more accurately an unqualified clerk) negligently handled a woman's complaint about harassment. She was held entitled to damages to include costs thrown away in the defective proceedings for an injunction which were brought on her behalf. £175 had been paid on account of costs. Lord Denning MR stated (at 458):

> So the solicitors were entitled to nothing for costs: and Mrs Heywood could recover the £175 money paid on a consideration which had wholly failed. She was, therefore, entitled to recover it as of right. And she is entitled to recover as well damages for negligence. Take this instance. If you engage a driver to take you to the station to catch a train for a day-trip to the sea, you pay him £2 — and then the car breaks down owing to his negligence. So that you miss your holiday. In that case you can recover not only your £2 back but also damages for the disappointment, upset and mental distress which you suffered.

10.6.4   *The Mikhail Lermontov*

In contrast to the position in English law, the High Court of Australia in *Baltic Shipping Co.* v *Dillon, The Mikhail Lermontov* (1993) 111 ALR 289, held that to combine restitution and damages in this way was logically inconsistent. Mrs Dillon booked a 14-day cruise in the South Pacific and paid AU$2,205 in advance. On the tenth day the vessel struck a rock off New Zealand, was holed and sank. Mrs Dillon lost some of her possessions and suffered personal injury. The shipping company voluntarily repaid part of the advance payment (representing the lost days). In the Admiralty Division of the Supreme Court and in the Court of Appeal of New South Wales, Mrs Dillon was held entitled to recover both the remainder of the fare and damages for breach of contract, including damages for mental distress. The High Court of Australia agreed with the award of damages, but held that she was not entitled to restitution of the fare. Mason CJ concluded (at 300):

First, restitution of the contractual consideration removes, at least notionally, the basis on which the plaintiff is entitled to call on the defendant to perform his or her contractual obligations. More particularly, the continued retention by the defendant is regarded, in the language of Lord Mansfield, as 'against conscience' or, in the modern terminology, as an unjust enrichment of the defendant because the condition upon which is it was paid, namely, performance by the defendant may not have occurred. But, equally that performance, for deficiencies in which damages are sought, was conditional on payment by the plaintiff. Recovery of the money paid destroys performance of that condition. Secondly, the plaintiff will almost always be protected by an award of damages for breach of contract, which in appropriate cases will include an amount for substitute performance or an amount representing the plaintiff's reliance.

This conclusion requires careful handling. It is cogently criticised by Barker [1993] LMCLQ 291 on three grounds. First, people bargain for primary obligations (here a cruise) not secondary obligations (damages). Secondly, the suggestion that restitutionary recovery extinguishes a cause of action 'plays tricks with time'. The recovery of a trivial bus-fare would not automatically preclude a passenger suing in contract for spinal injuries caused by the driver's negligence. Thirdly, the notion that contract damages, which aim to take the plaintiff forward in time, are inconsistent with restitutionary remedies, which are backward-looking, is based on woolly thinking. Barker concludes (at 295–96):

> So the appropriate principles to compare, when deciding upon the logical compatibility of damages and the action for money had and received, are not the principles of 'enforcement' and 'rescission' (whatever these may mean) but those of 'compensation' and 'restitution'; the rectification of unjust losses and restoration of unjust gains. Once this is realized, and the misleading imagery of a plaintiff's moving forwards and backwards in time is removed, it becomes apparent that the two actions are not incompatible at all. It is quite feasible, on one set of facts, both to eradicate a loss and to restore a gain, though one must always be careful that, in so doing, the plaintiff is not compensated twice.

Barker is correct to stigmatise the implications of some of the dicta in *The Mikhail Lermontov*. However, it must be remembered that the company had already refunded that part of the purchase price which related to lost days. It seems clear that the High Court regarded that as appropriate. If it had not been refunded voluntarily, a proportionate part of the purchase price would have been a head of loss recoverable as damages for substitute performance. All *The Mikhail Lermontov* seems to decide is that the finding of constructive total failure by the lower courts, based on the premise that the accident negated the whole benefit to be derived from the holiday, was not sound. Sometimes it might be arguable that the whole holiday was ruined: for example, if the accident had happened in the first couple of days of the cruise, before the benefits of a holiday have truly materialised. The case further illustrates

that in practice, as far as the innocent party is concerned, the requirement of total
failure works no injustice. It is clear that the courts will refund to the innocent party
the whole or part of any advance payment, where the innocent party has received
nothing in return. In practice this is more commonly done in a claim for substituted
performance as a head of loss within damages for breach of contract, rather than
being conceptualised as quasi-contractual recovery on the ground of failure of
consideration, whether total or partial. It is submitted that it is within the reach of
judicial development of law, explicitly to acknowledge that in a claim arising out of
a breach of contract, the innocent party can both, in Barker's phrase, recover
compensation for unjust losses and recoup for unjust benefits where he has received
nothing in return for his advance payment. The courts must remain astute as to the
possibility of double recovery or over-compensation.

10.6.5   Contractual ceilings

If the development described in 10.6.4 occurs, attention will move away from the
primitive totality bar towards the more appropriate question of contractual ceilings
on recovery. A consistent theme of the modern law of restitution is the need for
non-contractual recovery not to subvert a contractually agreed allocation of risk. It
can be argued that even an innocent party should not be allowed to escape a bad
bargain by claiming in restitution rather than claiming damages for breach of
contract. In the law of contractual remedies, a party may prima facie elect between
an *expectation* measure of recovery (which may include lost profits), where the aim
is to look towards a notional post-performance position of the innocent party, or a
reliance measure of recovery (usually encompassing wasted expenditure), which
seeks to compensate the claimant by returning him to the position he would have
been in if he had never acted upon the other's promise. The Court of Appeal has
recently held that the expectation measure forms the ceiling of recovery in contract
damages. A claimant is entitled to be put in the position he would have been in if a
contract had been performed, but is not entitled by way of damages to be put in a
better position than he would have been in if the contract had been performed.
Therefore a licensee of a garage who spent considerable sums improving the
premises which were the subject of the licence, and from which he was subsequently
wrongfully evicted, was entitled only to nominal damages. His claim for wasted
expenditure in improving the garage was disallowed as it resulted in fixtures which
would have to be left behind at the end of the licence period. He was permitted by
his local authority to continue his business from home and therefore was in a better
position than he would have been in if the contract had been properly performed (*C
& P Haulage* v *Middleton* [1983] 1 WLR 1461).

   Claimants often switch to the wasted expenditure measure because it can be easier
to calculate than the lost profits measure. Where profits are difficult to calculate, it
may still be attractive to claim the reliance measure. Whereas the claimant must
prove his wasted expenditure, it is for the defendant to plead and prove the value of
any contractual ceiling (*CCC Films (London) Ltd* v *Impact Quadrant Films Ltd*

[1985] QB 16). It is submitted, although the point has not arisen in English law, that the courts will find that contractual ceilings are relevant where money is claimed upon a total or partial failure of consideration. In contrast, some American authorities suggest there is no such ceiling. In *Bush v Canfield* Conn 495 (1818), the plaintiff escaped a bad bargain. Canfield agreed to sell Bush 2,000 barrels of wheat flour at US$7 a barrel by a contract made in February, delivery to be on or before 1 May. Bush paid a $5,000 deposit. Canfield failed to deliver, even though the market price of wheat flour had fallen to $5.50 on 1 May. Bush was held entitled to restitution of the full $5,000. The main argument against contractual ceilings is that it is unattractive for the defendant to rely upon the terms of the contract which he has broken to reduce or extinguish the amount of the claimant's recovery. This can be countered by saying that this may ascribe too much moral condemnation to a contract breaker. *Bush v Canfield* involved a futures contract where the market price is everything. It is submitted that in English law, arguments supporting contract ceilings should be taken seriously, especially in the commercial context. By analogy with the principle that a claimant cannot escape a bad bargain by electing to sue for reliance damages rather than expectation damages, it should follow that a claimant should not be able to escape the expectation measure ceiling by attempting to switch to a claim in restitution. Contrast Birks, in Rose (1996), 179, at 187–93, and Skelton, 24–42.

10.7 NON-MONEY CLAIMS BY AN INNOCENT PARTY

10.7.1 Non-money claims and enrichment

Characteristically, non-money claims in this context are dogged by conceptual under-development and paucity of authority. Where the innocent party confers a non-money benefit upon the party in breach, in principle the same issues should arise as regards money payments, subject only to the difficulty of establishing enrichment.

First, it should be recalled that the innocent party has contractual remedies. If there is an agreed price and the innocent party has performed the whole of his side of the bargain, he may elect not to treat the other's breach as repudiatory and terminate the contract, but instead claim for the price of the goods or services. If the contract did not stipulate a price but was one for the supply of goods, a reasonable price is payable in the form of a contractual *quantum valebat* (Sale of Goods Act 1979, s.8). Where the contract is for the provision of services and no price is specified, a reasonable charge is payable in the form of a contractual *quantum meruit* (Supply of Goods and Services Act 1982, s. 15). Further, if the innocent party does elect to terminate the contract he may well claim as a head of loss damages for the value of any performance rendered prior to termination. Therefore the contractual matrix does not necessarily drop out of the picture. The paucity of authority on restitutionary claims by the innocent party in respect of non-money benefits suggests that contractual actions in debt and damages are currently doing much of the work.

Secondly, if a restitutionary claim is brought for non-money benefits the ground for restitution or unjust factor must be the same as in money claims, namely failure of consideration. The requirement of totality has never been explicitly required in respect of non-money claims by the innocent party. Therefore it appears as a matter of principle that recovery may be allowed upon a total or partial failure of consideration.

Thirdly, it should be remembered that it is not necessary that the defendant contract-breaker should actually have received a valuable benefit; it is sufficient that the claimant had undertaken some part at least of the requested contractual performance. Problems of enrichment will be overcome by the fact that the defendant contract-breaker requested the performance. If it is argued that the defendant did not want partial-performance, it can be countered that it is unattractive for him to say so when he is himself in breach of contract. Alternatively, enrichment difficulties may be overcome by the application of the principles of free acceptance or incontrovertible benefit.

The last point is illustrated by the leading case of *Planché* v *Colburn* (1831) 8 Bing 14, 131 ER 305. The defendants planned to publish a periodical series entitled *The Juvenile Library* and commissioned Planché to write a volume on costume and ancient armour for the series for £100. Planché did a considerable amount of the work, including making one journey to inspect a collection of ancient armour and making some drawings of the collection. The author was ready and willing to complete and tender the manuscript, but the defendants refused to publish it. The earlier volumes of the library had not been successful and the project had been abandoned. It was argued on behalf of the defendants that Planché could not recover in contract because he had neither tendered nor delivered the work in accordance with its terms. Further, it was argued he could not recover under the common counts for work and labour while he was bound by the special contract to deliver the work. However, the Court of Common Pleas upheld a finding by the jury that the defendants having abandoned the contract must pay Planché £50. Tindal CJ stressed that the defendants were in breach and the contract had been terminated. He said (at 16):

> I agree that, when a special contract is in existence and open, the Plaintiff cannot sue on a quantum meruit: part of the question here, therefore, was, whether the contract did exist or not. It distinctly appeared that the work was finally abandoned .... Under these circumstances the plaintiff ought not to lose the fruit of his labour.

The case has proved controversial. Birks regards it as awarding restitution on the ground of failure of consideration: Birks, 126–27, 232, 286–87. In contrast Burrows rationalises it as an award of damages for breach of contract in either the expectation or reliance measure: Burrows, 8–9, 267. Further, Beatson explains the case on a principle of injurious reliance, which appears to be analogous to promissory estoppel: Beatson, 35.

It must be stressed that the case was explicitly decided on the basis of a *quantum meruit* claim. It is proposed that the best rationalisation is as follows. First, it was shown that the innocent party was the victim of a breach which entitled him to treat the contract as at an end. This seems clear from the fact that Planché did not feel obliged to tender the work. Secondly, where a contract is legitimately terminated the innocent party has a free election between claiming damages for breach of contract in either the expectation or reliance measure, or claiming in restitution for any performance undertaken pursuant to the contractual terms, recoverable as a *quantum meruit*. The fact that the service was requested overcomes enrichment difficulties. It is not necessary that the defendant should receive any valuable benefit as a result of the performance. There is no insistence that there should be any total failure of consideration to ground recovery. In practice there usually is as the contract-breaker refuses to pay for any of the benefits received.

This appears to be confirmed in *De Bernardy v Harding* (1853) 8 Ex 822, 155 ER 1586. Harding erected seats for spectators to view the funeral procession of the Duke of Wellington. He engaged De Bernardy as a foreign agent to promote the event and sell tickets abroad. It was agreed that De Bernardy would be remunerated by a percentage share of the tickets he sold. De Bernardy expended money on advertising, accommodation and clerks, but before he had sold any tickets, Harding told him not to do so as he would sell all the tickets on the spot. De Bernardy accordingly sent all applicants to Harding and after the funeral submitted a bill to Harding for his work and expenses. Harding himself paid the printers and others employed by De Bernardy, but refused him any remuneration for his work. At the trial it was held that De Bernardy could not recover on a *quantum meruit* but ought to have sued for damages for breach of contract. However, this was reversed by the Court of Exchequer Chamber which ordered a retrial, where it was left to the jury to decide whether the original contract had been terminated. Alderson B stated (at 824):

> Where one party has absolutely refused to perform, or has rendered himself incapable of performing, his part of the contract, he puts it in the power of the other party either to sue for a breach of it, or to rescind the contract and sue on a *quantum meruit* for the work actually done.

10.7.2 Contractual ceilings

As described above, where the contract is terminated, it appears that the innocent party can either sue for damages for breach of contract, or can claim reasonable remuneration for work actually done on a *quantum meruit* basis. However, consistently with the arguments made above in relation to money claims, it is submitted that it is open to the defendant to argue that the contractual rate of remuneration should provide a ceiling for such a *quantum meruit* claim. No such problem arose in *Planché v Colburn* (see 10.7.1) where the *quantum meruit* recovery was equivalent to half of the contract price. Interestingly, in *De Bernardy v Harding* it was explicitly argued on behalf of the plaintiff that where a contract is terminated, the work done under it must be paid for according to its actual value, the contractual rate of remuneration being rendered inapplicable by the defendant's conduct. However, while it is plausible to say that it is not appropriate for a defendant contract-breaker to rely upon the terms of the contract which he has refused to perform or performed badly, the innocent party should not as a matter of principle be entitled to throw off the contractual price structure and effectively escape a bad bargain.

What authority there currently is does in fact support the free election of the innocent party between damages and *quantum meruit*, the latter not being subject to any contractual ceiling. In *Lodder* v *Slowey* [1904] AC 442, the plaintiff agreed to build a tunnel under the property of a local authority. The council subsequently wrongly excluded the contractor from the property and prevented him from completing the work in breach of contract. The council also seized the works and plant of the plaintiff. The plaintiff claimed on a *quantum meruit* basis the value of the works done by him. The first instance judge held that the plaintiff was entitled only to nominal damages because he had not produced evidence to show that he could have made a profit if he had been allowed to finish the work. The Court of Appeal of New Zealand and the Privy Council disagreed, holding that where a contractor was wrongfully excluded from the site after part-performance, and is thereby precluded from completing the contract, he is entitled to treat the contract as terminated and claim on a *quantum meruit* basis for the work done and the materials supplied prior to termination, being some £1,015. It was said to be immaterial whether the contractor would have made a profit or loss if he had been allowed to complete. Lord Davey, delivering the advice of the Privy Council, concluded (at 453):

> Their Lordships also agree with the learned judges as to the proper measure of damages, or (more accurately) as to the right of the respondent to treat the contract as at an end and sue for work and labour done instead of suing for damages for breach of the contract.

It does not seem to have been argued on behalf of the defendants that a contractual ceiling would apply, and counsel for the plaintiff was not called upon to argue as to whether the correct measure of relief had been adopted. Therefore while contractual ceilings were not explicitly argued for, the Privy Council appeared emphatic that such an argument was not appropriate.

The same result was reached after more explicit consideration in the United States in *Boomer* v *Muir*, 24 P 2d 570 (1933). Muir was the main contractor for a large hydro-electric project, and in May 1926 he appointed Boomer as sub-contractor for construction of a dam. Work was to be completed by 1 December 1927. Boomer was to receive monthly progress payments based on 90 per cent of the value of work done in the previous months. Disputes arose between the parties almost as soon as the work began. In December 1927, Boomer eventually left the site leaving the work unfinished, though near completion. The evidence suggested that Muir had not supplied materials quickly enough, thus slowing Boomer's progress and increasing his costs. Boomer was held by the District Court of Appeal of California to be entitled to quit the job because of the main contractor's failure to furnish materials timeously. He was further entitled to recover the reasonable value of the work done under the contract on a *quantum meruit*, even though such recovery would exceed the contract price. Boomer accordingly recovered over $250,000 on a *quantum meruit* basis, whereas only $20,000 remained due and owing under the contract. Dooling J stated:

> To hold that the payments under the contract may limit recovery where the contract is afterwards rescinded through the defendant's fault seems to us to involve a confusion of thought. A rescinded contract ceases to exist for all purposes. How can it then be looked to for one purpose, the purpose of fixing the amount of the recovery? . . . [T]he defendant by his own wrong having put an end to the contract, cannot insist on its terms to limit the recovery, even though part payments have been made for part performance.

With respect, it is submitted that the approach of the Californian court itself rests upon a confusion of thought, depending upon a drastic view of termination for breach which renders the contract ineffective for all future purposes. The preferable view, as outlined above in 10.2, is that, in English law, termination operates prospectively, and the secondary regime which operates when the primary obligations come to an end may still as a matter of construction be affected by the original terms of the contract. It is submitted that in appropriate cases the courts will be sensitive to an argument that the valuation of non-money benefits rendered by the innocent party should capped by reference to the contractual rate of remuneration. This can either be a contractual ceiling argument based upon the policy of primacy of contract (and operating at the third stage of enquiry), or a valuation ceiling which looks to the contract rate of remuneration to see what value the defendant requested or accepted, to satisfy the test of enrichment (at the first stage of the enquiry). *Boomer* v *Muir* and *Lodder* v *Slowey* should be rationalised as cases involving damages for breach of contract. It was clearly arguable that the contractors in the two cases did in fact suffer losses which were caused by the non-cooperation of the other party, such losses being ones which naturally flowed from the breach of contract.

For discussion see Skelton, 43–85.

10.8   RECOVERY OF MONEY BY THE PARTY IN BREACH

It is sometimes tempting to see the right of the innocent party to recover in restitution, where a contract is discharged following the other party's breach, as an aspect of that party's claim for a remedy flowing from the breach. However, it is misconceived to view such claims in this way. The claim does not flow from the other party's wrongdoing in not performing the contract; it simply follows from the fact that the innocent party has paid money, conferred some valuable benefit or carried out some requested performance and has received nothing in return for it. The cause of action is grounded on principles of unjust enrichment, and is not in any way dependent upon the other's wrongdoing. The availability of claims arising from wrongdoing admittedly complicates the picture and requires a certain degree of sensitivity in ensuring that unjust benefits are not reversed twice: once using restitutionary techniques and also under the guise of a head of loss compensated by damages. Therefore the autonomous nature of the cause of action in unjust enrichment means that as a matter of principle such a claim is also available where the party in breach has paid money, conferred a valuable benefit or carried out some requested performance for the innocent party. However, successful claims by the party in breach have been sporadic and have not historically been understood to be grounded upon the same principle as recovery by the innocent party, namely failure of consideration.

Modern analysis suggests that the party in breach may too have a remedy in restitution. Here the picture is not complicated by the cumulative availability of a remedy for breach of contract. It seems clear as a precondition to recovery, on general principles, that the contract should have been terminated. If the contract is kept alive at the option of the innocent party, it is difficult to see how the party in breach can claim in restitution when a valid contract still governs both any part-performance and any as yet unperformed obligations. Secondly, there has recently been some insistence that any failure of consideration must be *total* by analogy with claims to recover money by the innocent party. Previously, with the basis of the claim being one for failure of consideration not even appreciated, it was not explicitly adverted too. Traditionally the question whether the transfer of value by the party in breach was conditional or unconditional has been dealt with by characterising payments as deposits, instalments or advance payments. For discussion of the impact of contract ceiling arguments upon money claims by the party in breach, see Skelton, 86–92.

10.8.1   Deposits and contracts for the sale of land

In the classic case of *Howe* v *Smith* (1884) 27 Ch D 89, the Court of Appeal provided guidance on the meaning and nature of deposits at common law. In a contract for the sale of land the purchaser paid £500 of a total purchase price of £12,500 in advance. The sale did not go ahead due to a delay on the part of the purchaser, who, having been refused a decree of specific performance, sought restitution of the £500. The purchaser's delay was held to amount to a breach of contract, which presumably entitled the vendor to regard the contract as at an end. The advance payment was held to be a deposit and therefore irrecoverable. Cotton LJ treated the matter as one of precedent, which laid down that a deposit was a guarantee for a contract to be performed. If the contract is terminated as a result of a breach by the payer, he has no right to recover the money. Bowen LJ's judgment treated the matter more as one of construction or interpretation. He said (at 98):

> We have therefore to consider what in ordinary parlance, and as used in an ordinary contract of sale, is the meaning which business persons would attach to the term 'deposit'. Without going at length into the history, or accepting all that has been said or will be said by other members of the Court on that point, it comes

shortly to this, that a deposit, if nothing more is said about it, is, according to the ordinary interpretation of business men, a security for the completion of the purchase. But in what sense is it a security for the completion of the purchase? It is quite certain that the purchaser cannot insist on abandoning his contract and yet recover the deposit, because that would enable him to take advantage of his own wrong.

Similarly, Fry LJ treated the status of the money deposited as depending upon the express or implied terms of the contract. He suggested an implied term that in the event of the contract being performed the money should be brought into account, but where it is not performed the money would remain the property of the payee. It is submitted that the approach of Bowen and Fry LJJ is to be preferred. It is a question of construction whether an advance payment is a deposit or earnest, intended to provide the payer with a motive for performing the contract and providing the payee with security in the event of the other's breach. The use of the word 'deposit', while persuasive, should not ultimately be determinative of the status of such a payment on ordinary principles of construction and characterisation. The use of deposits is familiar in contracts for the sale of land, contracts for the hire of venues and contracts for the provision of holidays. Many modern contracts explicitly provide for a deposit to be paid, and for it, or a proportion of it, to be forfeited in the event of the payer unjustifiably withdrawing from the contract.

10.8.2 Unreasonable deposits

In *Workers Trust & Merchant Bank Ltd* v *Dojap Investments Ltd* [1993] AC 573, the Privy Council held that the payer of an unreasonable deposit was entitled to restitution of it. The bank sold land to Dojap at auction for a price of Jamaican $11.5 million. A 25 per cent deposit was payable under the contract, and accordingly Dojap paid $2,875,000. The contract further provided that the balance was to be paid within 14 days, that time was of the essence and that if the buyer defaulted the deposit was forfeit. Dojap tendered the necessary cheque seven days late. This was returned, the bank terminated the contract and purported to forfeit the deposit. The Privy Council held that in order to be reasonable the true deposit must be objectively operating as earnest money, and not as a disguised penalty. While admitting there was nothing logical about the customary deposit of 10 per cent, the Privy Council held that any departure from such a figure must be justified by special circumstances. Lord Browne-Wilkinson stressed the exceptional nature of deposits (at 578–79):

> In general, a contractual provision which requires one party in the event of his breach of the contract to pay or forfeit a sum of money to the other party is unlawful as being a penalty, unless such provision can be justified as being a payment of liquidated damages being a genuine pre-estimate of the loss which the innocent party will incur by reason of the breach. One exception to this general rule is the provision for payment of a deposit by the purchaser on a contract for the

sale of land.... Ever since the decision in *Howe* v *Smith*, the nature of such a deposit has been settled in English law. Even in the absence of express contractual provision, it is an earnest for the performance of the contract: in the event of completion of the contract, the deposit is applicable towards payment of the purchase price; in the event of the purchaser's failure to complete in accordance with the terms of the contract, the deposit is forfeit, equity having no power to relieve against such forfeiture.

However, the parties were not entitled to abuse the special position of deposits by attaching the label 'deposit' to a penalty. The Privy Council relied upon the judgment of Denning LJ in *Stockloser* v *Johnson* [1954] 1 QB 476, explicitly drawing the analogy with equity's power to relieve against forfeiture and the common law prohibition of penalty clauses (see 10.8.5). The court accordingly had jurisdiction to relieve against forfeiture and order restitution of the whole deposit, although the payee would have been entitled to set-off any loss he had actually suffered as a result of the payer's breach. Note that the whole 25 per cent was recoverable, and the party insisting upon an unreasonable deposit was not entitled to keep 10 per cent of the purchase price.

While the Privy Council was not explicit on the question, it is submitted that the cause of action was grounded upon failure of consideration, or alternatively it is a species of policy-motivated restitution analogous to the general jurisdiction to relieve against forfeiture. *Dojap* can be contrasted with *Union Eagle Ltd* v *Golden Achievements Ltd* [1997] 2 All ER 215, in which a 10 per cent deposit was paid for the purchase of real property. The time of completion was to be of the essence. The purchaser tendered the balance of the purchase money 10 minutes too late and the vendor terminated. The Privy Council refused relief against forfeiture, either by granting extra time, or by awarding restitution of the deposit. Lord Hoffmann's advice is suffused with the need for certainty. In relation to contracts for the sale of interests in land, there is a statutory jurisdiction to order restitution of deposits under s. 49(2) and (3) of the Law of Property Act 1925. For discussion see Beale, (1993) 109 LQR 524–30.

10.8.3   Advance payments and sale of goods

In contracts for the sale of goods the characteristic performance of the seller is the transfer of title in tangible personal property to the buyer. Where the buyer makes an advance payment, but does not complete the contract in breach of contract, he may still be held entitled to recover the advance sum. In *Dies* v *British and International Mining and Finance Corporation Ltd* [1939] 1 KB 724, the buyer agreed to buy rifles and ammunition at a total cost of £270,000. The buyer paid £100,000 in advance, but subsequently, in breach of contract, failed to accept delivery of the goods. This seller then treated the contract as terminated. The buyer was held prima facie entitled to restitution of £100,000, subject to the seller being entitled to set-off damages for breach of contract. Stable J observed that 'neither by the use of the word "deposit" or otherwise, is there anything to indicate the payment of £100,000 was intended or was believed by either party to be in the nature of a guarantee or earnest for the due performance of the contract' (at 742). By explicit description and as a matter of law it was held to be a part-payment. Stable J held (at 743):

> the general rule is that the law confers on the purchaser the right to recover his money, and that to enable the seller to keep it he must be able to point to some language in the contract from which the inference to be drawn is the parties intended and agreed that he should.

Stable J attributed the cause of action to a right arising out of the terms of the contract, and rejected the argument that recovery was based upon a total failure of consideration. He held that there was neither a total nor a partial failure of consideration. Stable J's reluctance to base recovery explicitly on the ground of failure of consideration is probably due to the currency at the time of the rule in *Chandler* v *Webster* [1904] 1 KB 493, which seemed to deny the parties any possibility of recovery on the ground of failure of consideration (for discussion see 11.2). Such reticence would now be unnecessary: Birks, 236–37.

10.8.4 Shipbuilding contracts

In *Hyundai Heavy Industries Co. Ltd* v *Papadopoulos* [1980] 1 WLR 1129, Hyundai agreed to 'build, launch, equip and complete' a vessel and 'to deliver and sail' her to the buyer. The contract price included 'all costs and expenses for designing and supplying all necessary drawings of the vessel'. The vessel was a multi-purpose cargo ship and a price of US$14.3 million was payable in five instalments, the first two each being 2.5 per cent of the total price ($357,500). The first instalment was paid but the second instalment was not paid in accordance with the timetable set out in the contract. Hyundai elected under an express termination clause to cancel the contract. Hyundai sought to recover the second instalment from guarantors of the buyer's obligations. The House of Lords upheld summary judgment in favour of Hyundai on the ground that the guarantors were liable, because under the contract between the buyer and Hyundai, cancellation did not affect the accrued right to payment of the second instalment (Lord Russell and Lord Keith *dubitante* on this point). Viscount Dilhorne stressed that the contract was not simply one of sale, but more resembled a building contract. Lord Fraser of Tullybelton stressed the underlying economics and the pricing structure (at 1148):

> It seems very likely that the increasing proportions of the contract price represented by the five instalments bore some relation to the anticipated rate of expenditure, though we have no information on which to make any nice comparison between the amount of expenses that the builder would have to bear from time to time, and the amounts of the instalments payable by the buyer. I do not think that such comparisons are necessary. It is enough that the builder was

bound to incur considerable expense in carrying out his part of the contract long
before the actual sale could take place.

The contract price was not simply the purchase price. It has been suggested that the
approach is best explained as one which rests primarily upon the construction of the
contract. Reliance expenditure by the payee will be protected, albeit in a rough and
ready fashion, by holding that where expenditure was envisaged as part of the
contract price, any advance payment is irrecoverable in restitution or remains due in
contract. The construction approach can be supplemented by restitutionary principles which can make sure that the party incurring expenditure does not thereby
receive a windfall: Beatson, 45–77.

The House of Lords revisited the issue on virtually identical facts in *Stocznia
Gdanska SA* v *Latvian Shipping Co.* [1998] 1 WLR 574, where a Polish shipyard
undertook to 'design, build, complete and deliver' two refrigerated vessels.
Correspondingly, Latvian buyers undertook to pay in four instalments. The second
instalment of 20 per cent was payable within five banking days of the yard giving
notice of keel-laying. Proper notice was given but the instalment was not
forthcoming. The trial judge and the House of Lords awarded the shipyard summary
judgment in respect of the second instalment, expressly applying *Hyundai*. The Court
of Appeal had been attracted to an argument that the contract by its express terms
entitled the seller, in the event of termination, to retain and apply instalments already
paid by the purchaser in order to recoup wasted expenditure. Accordingly any
common law rights were displaced by the self-imposed contract regime.

In contrast the House of Lords applied the presumption of construction that a
contracting party does not intend to abandon any remedies for breach of contract
arising by operation of law. The question was approached as one involving total
failure of consideration: the money was payable unless it could be shown that the
buyer obtained nothing in return for the payment. The crucial question was one of
characterisation. What species of contract was the court dealing with? What was the
characteristic performance of the yard? As in *Hyundai* these were not simple sales,
but contracts for work and materials. This was a logically prior question to any
discussion of failure of consideration. Lord Goff was clear that 'payment of
instalments for the price was geared to progress in the construction of the vessel' (at
588). Having thus identified the contract as one for work and materials with the
geared level of instalments to compensate the yard for any reliance losses, the
restitutionary notion of failure of consideration was inapplicable. See further [1998]
LMCLQ 308. *Hyundai* was also followed, outside the shipbuilding context, by the
Court of Appeal in *Rover International Ltd* v *Cannon Film Sales Ltd* [1989] 1 WLR
912, in relation to the Proper Film appeal.

10.8.5   Relief against forfeiture

In *Stockloser* v *Johnson* [1954] 1 QB 476, the existence of an equitable power to
relieve against forfeiture of advance payments provoked disagreement in the Court

of Appeal. A buyer purchased plant and machinery for use in a lime quarry. The price was payable in instalments, and the contract provided that if the buyer should fail to pay any instalment within 28 days of its formal due date, the seller could retake possession of the machinery and that instalments already paid were forfeit. Bad weather made the enterprise less profitable than the buyer anticipated and he was soon in default. The seller repossessed the machinery and terminated the contract. The buyer claimed restitution of instalments already paid. The Court of Appeal held that no relief was available on these facts. Denning LJ distinguished the case from one where a seller seeks to enforce a penalty clause. Here money had been handed over in part-payment of the purchase price, and property had passed to the seller once it was paid. It was not obtained by extortion or oppression. Denning LJ summarised the law as follows (at 489–90):

(1) *When there is no forfeiture clause.* If money is handed over in part payment of the purchase price, and then the buyer makes default as to the balance, then, so long as the seller keeps the contract open and available for performance, the buyer cannot recover the money; but once the seller rescinds the contract or treats it as at an end owing to the buyer's default, then the buyer is entitled to recover his money by action at law, subject to a cross-claim by the seller of goods for damages ...

(2) *But when there is a forfeiture clause or the money is expressly paid as a deposit (which is equivalent to a forfeiture clause)*, then the buyer who is in default cannot recover the money at law at all. He may, however, have a remedy in equity, for despite the express stipulation of the contract, equity can relieve the buyer from forfeiture of the money and order the seller to repay it on such terms as the court thinks fit.

The equity to relieve against forfeiture is clearly discretionary and two preconditions are necessary. First, the forfeiture clause must be of a penal nature, in that it is out of all proportion to any damage suffered by the seller. Secondly, it must be unconscionable for the seller to retain the instalments, and this is judged not at the time of the contract, but by the circumstances existing when the jurisdiction is invoked. Therefore if a buyer contracts to pay for a necklace in instalments, if he defaults after paying 10 per cent of the price in instalments, the seller will be entitled to retain the instalments paid and reclaim the necklace. However, if 90 per cent of the instalments have been paid, and the seller reclaims the necklace after the buyer defaults, equity would relieve against forfeiture. Somervell LJ broadly agreed. In contrast Romer LJ, in a judgment suffused with respect for the principle of sanctity of contract, held that there was no such equity of restitution. He further suggested that it was unlikely that the problems envisaged by the majority, such as the necklace example, would arise in practice. Someone who had raised nine-tenths of the agreed price would have little difficulty in borrowing the remaining 10 per cent on the security of his interest.

The division in the Court of Appeal was adverted to in the later case of *Workers Trust & Merchant Bank Ltd* v *Dojap Investments Ltd* [1993] AC 573, where the Privy

Council did not feel it necessary to decide between the two different views as to the existence of the jurisdiction to relieve against forfeiture, although it appeared that their sympathy lay more with Somervell and Denning LJJ. For discussion of relief as an example of restitution for inequality or a policy-motivated species of restitution, see Birks, 211–16. See further Anson, 608–10.

10.9   RECOVERY OF NON-MONEY BENEFITS BY THE PARTY IN BREACH

Given the combination of the less sympathetic treatment of a party in breach and enrichment difficulties arising from non-monetary claims, it is unsurprising that there is a dearth of authority on this point. As a matter of principle, if the party in breach has performed part of his contractual obligation and this has resulted in a valuable benefit in the hands of the innocent party, he should be able to recover a reasonable price for the work done on the ground of failure of consideration. If enrichment difficulties can be overcome by the application of the tests of request, free acceptance or incontrovertible benefit, the party in breach is entitled to say that he has had nothing in return for the benefit he has conferred.

Two cases illustrate the point. In *Sumpter* v *Hedges* [1898] 1 QB 673, a builder contracted to erect two houses and stables upon the defendant's land for £565. The builder did work worth £333 and received part of the price, but then announced that he had no money and could not complete. The contract was held to have been abandoned as a result of the builder's breach. The defendant finished the work himself, using materials that the builder had left behind. The builder claimed in respect of the work done and materials provided in the common counts. He succeeded in respect of the materials on a *quantum valebat* basis, but was unable to recover in respect of the work done on a *quantum meruit* basis. The reasoning of the Court of Appeal is suffused within implied contractual reasoning. In the absence of anything from which a new contract to pay for the work done could be inferred, they were unwilling to allow recovery upon a *quantum meruit*. The judgment of Collins LJ, while open to criticism upon modern analysis in many ways, suggests that in some circumstances the party in breach may be able to recover on the ground of failure of consideration, or possibly free acceptance (at 676):

> There are cases in which, though the plaintiff has abandoned the performance of a contract, it is possible for him to raise the inference of a new contract to pay for the work done on a *quantum meruit* from the defendant's having taken the benefit of that work, but, in order that that may be done, the circumstances must be such as to give an option to the defendant to take or not to take the benefit of the work done. It is only where the circumstances are such as to give that option that there is any evidence on which to ground the inference of a new contract.

Here the employer had no choice but to accept the work already done, but did not need to use the materials left on the site by the contractor. Accordingly he had to pay for the materials. The position of the party in breach who has substantially performed is that he is able to bring a claim in debt for the agreed sum, or a contractual *quantum meruit*, subject to a cross-claim for damages for breach by the employer: compare *Hoenig* v *Isaacs* [1952] 2 All ER 176 with *Bolton* v *Mahadeva* [1972] 1 WLR 1009. See, for general discussion of the contractual rules of the entire obligation rule and the doctrine of substantial performance, Anson, 484–89. The Law Commission in *Pecuniary Restitution on Breach of Contract* (Law Com No. 121 (1983)) made recommendations for reform, to allow the party in breach to recover up to the value of the contractual ceiling, the value of the work done and subject to a cross-claim in damages. These were not accepted by the Government, and have not been implemented. For discussion see Birks, 259–64 and Burrows (1984) 47 MLR 76.

Hain Steamship Co. Ltd v *Tate & Lyle Ltd* [1936] 2 All ER 597 turned on the anomalous rule in carriage of goods by sea that a deviation by the carrier under a charterparty is a breach of contract which automatically discharges the contract without any need for an election to terminate by the innocent party. Where contractual freight (remuneration) is payable at the end of the voyage, it seems that where the contract remains discharged there is no obligation on the charterer to pay in contract. Accordingly the carrier might render to the cargo-owner the benefit of valuable services without any express contractual obligation upon the cargo-owner to pay for them. The House of Lords rejected the view of Scrutton LJ that a consignee of a cargo, whether the holder of a bill of lading or not, would not be liable to pay remuneration to the carrier after a deviation, despite benefiting by the receipt of valuable services to his goods. Scrutton LJ had said (at 611):

The fact that a volunteer without authority renders services to another man's property does not give him a right to remuneration, or a right to keep the property unless he gets remuneration. There is no authority on the question; but as a matter of logic, I think the claim for freight fails.

In contrast the members of the House of Lords were sympathetic in dicta to the restitutionary claim. Lord Wright MR sketched the following example (at 612):

A steamer carrying a cargo of frozen meat from Australia to England deviates by calling at a port outside the usual permitted route: it is only the matter of a few hours extra steaming: no trouble ensues except the delay in time. The cargo is duly delivered in England at the agreed port. The goods owner has had for all practical purposes the benefit of all that his contract required; he has had the advantages, of the use of a valuable ship, her crew, fuel, refrigeration and appliances, canal dues, port charges, stevedoring. The shipowner may be technically a wrongdoer in the sense that he has once deviated, but otherwise over a long period he has been performing the exacting and costly duties of a carrier at sea. I cannot help thinking that epithets like 'unlawful' and 'unauthorised' are not apt to describe such services; it may be that by the maritime law the relationship of carrier and goods owner still continues despite the deviation, though subject to the modifications consequent upon the deviation. Nor can I help feeling that the court would not be slow to infer an obligation when the goods are received at the destination to pay, not indeed the contract freight, but a reasonable remuneration.

The cause of action appears to be for failure of consideration: the carrier has received nothing in return for valuable services. Enrichment can be overcome by application of the principle of free acceptance, or more likely incontrovertible benefit. Scrutton LJ appears to be correct to suggest that the carrier would have no lien to support his claim to reasonable remuneration. A simple personal claim to recover on a *quantum meruit* basis would suffice in appropriate cases. *Hain* v *Tate & Lyle* neatly illustrates that a breach of contract may only be a matter of technicality, and should not shut a party out of recovery of restitution as a matter of course. In contrast, industrial action short of a strike causes problems for remuneration under contracts of employment. Some members of the House of Lords in *Miles* v *Wakefield Metropolitan District Council* [1987] AC 539 (at 553 *per* Lord Brightman; at 561 *per* Lord Templeman) suggested that a *quantum meruit* may be payable. This does not accord with restitutionary principles as the contracts were not terminated. See Sales (1988) 8 OJLS 301–11. Contrast *Wiluszynski* v *Tower Hamlets London Borough Council* [1989] ICR 493; noted Mead (1990) 106 LQR 192.

For discussion of non-money claims by the party in breach and contract ceilings see Skelton, 92–100.

10.10   THE FUTURE?

It seems likely that the traditional but sporadic insistence upon totality will be repudiated by the judiciary when the appropriate case arises. It is clearly the case that there is no longer any such requirement in respect of void contracts (see *Westdeutsche Landesbank Girozentrale* v *Islington London Borough Council* [1996] AC 609 and 12.2.1), if indeed it could be said with certainty that such a requirement ever applied in those contexts. The totality requirement has been excised in relation to frustrated contracts by statute (see below, Chapter 11). The fictional nature of many findings of totality, as in *Rowland* v *Divall*, *The Julia*, and *D. O. Ferguson* v *Sohl*, suggests that the rule is ripe for judicial reinterpretation. Once recovery for partial failure is allowed, the claims by the party in breach and non-money claims by either party are likely to achieve greater prominence. There is likely to be more explicit consideration whether the courts are compensating unjust losses or reversing unjust gains in the wake of a broken contract. The consistent theme of this chapter is that arguments about the primacy of the contractual regime will then come into sharper focus. It may well be that English courts will be sympathetic to arguments for contractual ceilings and valuation ceilings where a contract is discharged by termination for breach. Compare Birks in Rose (1996), 179, at 187–93, and Skelton, *Restitution and Contract* (1998).

FURTHER READING

Asterisks indicate especially useful works.

Goff and Jones, 510–17; 523–55

Birks, 219–48, 258–64

Anson, 604–14

S. Stoljar, 'The Doctrine of Failure of Consideration' (1959) 75 LQR 53 (historical)

G. Palmer, 'The Contract Price as a Limit on Restitution for Defendant's Breach' (1959) 20 Ohio State LJ 264

J. Dawson, 'Restitution without Enrichment' (1981) 61 Boston ULR 565, 576–605

*J. Beatson, 'Discharge for Breach: Instalments, Deposits and Other Payments Due Before Completion' (1981) 97 LQR 389; also in Beatson, 45–77.

E. McKendrick, 'Total Failure of Consideration and Counter-restitution: Two Issues or One?' in Birks (1995), 217

*P. Birks, 'Failure of Consideration', in Rose (1996), 179–202

G. McMeel, 'Failure of Consideration and Construction — The Primacy of Contract' [1998] LMCLQ 308

A. Skelton, *Restitution and Contract* (1998)

S. Smith, 'Concurrent Liability in Contract and Unjust Enrichment: The Fundamental Breach Requirement' (1999) 115 LQR 245

Deposits and relief against forfeiture

H. Beale, 'Unreasonable Deposits' (1983) 109 LQR 524

11 Contracts Discharged by Frustration

11.1 THEORETICAL FOUNDATIONS

The grounds for relieving parties from their contractual obligations by reason of frustration or other supervening events lie squarely in the province of contract law. The limits of the force of contractual obligation where there has been a material change of circumstances are necessarily informed by principles other than unjust enrichment. Contract law further provides the main consequence of frustration, namely, discharge. Both parties are from the date of the frustrating event relieved from future obligations. In addition, a party may have partially performed its obligations, prior to the frustrating event, perhaps resulting in a benefit to the other party. Here restitution performs its characteristic function of mopping up in the wake of failed contracts.

However, it is important when considering restitutionary solutions to have regard to the underlying reason(s) why contract law treats both parties as discharged. The doctrine granting relief where there has been an exceptional change of circumstances was initially characterised as one resulting from the application of those most characteristically contractual techniques, construction or interpretation and the implication of terms. Later in its development judges became more self-confident and were happier to ascribe the doctrine to rules of law created by judicial intervention, circumscribing the limits of sanctity of contract. This approach has been recently summarised by Bingham LJ in *J. Lauritzen AS* v *Wijsmuller BV, The Super Servant Two* [1990] 1 Lloyd's Rep 1, at 8:

> The doctrine of frustration was evolved to mitigate the rigour of the common law's insistence on literal performance of absolute promises.... The object of the doctrine was to give effect to the demands of justice, to achieve a just and reasonable result, to do what is reasonable and fair, as an expedient to escape from injustice where such would result from enforcement of a contract in its literal terms after a significant change in circumstances.

Where a contract is discharged automatically by operation of the doctrine, it will commonly be the case that one or both parties will have engaged in acts of part-performance. The parties may themselves have provided for discharge or suspension of performance under a *force majeure* clause, and for the consequences of ineffectiveness. However, where the parties have not made such provision and the contract is discharged at common law, it is primarily to techniques of restitution to which they must turn. The common law quasi-contractual response has been superseded by a statutory regime under the Law Reform (Frustrated Contracts) Act 1943 in relation to benefits conferred before the time of discharge. The crucial fact that neither party is at fault for the circumstances giving rise to the discharge should be the governing concern when the court exercises the discretions available to it under terms of the statute. The common law still has a potential for operation where further benefits are transferred after the time of discharge and for certain contracts which are not governed by the Act.

11.2 INADEQUACIES OF THE COMMON LAW

First, in the context of frustration the quasi-contractual claim for money received on the ground of a total failure of consideration provided an obvious cause of action. However, case law confused the ground of total failure of consideration, a restitutionary cause of action, with the contractual conception of consideration (*Chandler* v *Webster* [1904] 1 KB 493). It was there held that since discharge was prospective only, each party had the benefit of the other's obligations in the meantime, and accordingly there could never be a *total* failure of consideration. This was the first and major defect of the common law. This error was exposed in *Fibrosa Spolka Akcyjna* v *Fairbairn Lawson Combe Barbour Ltd* [1943] AC 32 and the *Chandler* v *Webster* fallacy was repudiated. Viscount Simon LC authoritatively stated (at 48):

> In English law, an enforceable contract may be formed by an exchange of a promise for a promise, or by the exchange of a promise for an act — I am excluding contracts under seal — and thus, in law relating to the formation of contract, the promise to do a thing may often be the consideration, but when one is considering the law of failure of consideration and of the quasi-contractual right to recover money on that ground, it is, generally speaking, not the promise which is referred as the consideration, but the performance of the promise. The money was paid to secure performance and, if performance fails the inducement which brought about the payment is not fulfilled.

Therefore English sellers who had agreed to supply machinery to Polish buyers under a contract subsequently discharged by supervening illegality (namely, the German occupation of Poland during the Second World War), were held liable to refund the £1,000 advance payment on the ground of total failure of consideration. The fact that the contract was valid prior to discharge, and that accordingly the Polish buyers had the benefit of an executory agreement to perform, was not apt to exclude the right to recover money on the ground of total failure of consideration. The case, however, highlighted two further defects in the common law which were thought to merit statutory reform. The second defect was the requirement of total failure itself, which was regarded as being an inappropriate restriction on relief when neither party was at fault. See for example, *Whincup* v *Hughes* (1871) LR 6 CP 78. In *Fibrosa*, the House of Lords overlooked preparatory work done by the English sellers in reliance upon the contract which might have militated against the finding of total failure. This was done by characterising the contract as a simple sale, rather than one for manufacture and supply. It was assumed that the common law could do nothing to relieve against partial failure. This dovetails with the third defect, namely the perceived inability of the common law to make an allowance for partial performance and to permit that to be set off against the money claim by way of counter-restitution.

The above three defects concerned money claims. They were matched by defects in respect of claims for property and services. First there was the doctrine of the entire obligations, where a party rendering services or supplying goods and services was held not to be entitled either to a portion of a stipulated contract price, or to a quasi-contractual *quantum meruit* where supervening events prevented further performance. Therefore the widow of a seaman who died some six weeks into a nine-week voyage was unable to recover in contract or quasi-contract because he had contracted for payment only upon working to the port of destination (*Cutter* v *Powell* (1795) 6 Term Rep 320, 101 ER 573). Further, engineers who had agreed to install and erect machinery on the defendant's premises were unable to recover upon a *quantum meruit* basis when an accidental fire destroyed both the premises and some of the machinery while work was in progress. They were held to have contracted not to be able to recover anything until the work was completed (*Appleby* v *Myers* (1867) LR 2 CP 651). This was part of a wider defect. The courts had perhaps too much regard to the supposed continuing effect of the now discharged contract. The second major defect was conceptual under-development. *Quantum meruit* lacked the structure to deal with problems such as valuation of benefit until the underlying principle of unjust enrichment was perceived as the foundation of such a claim. Therefore in *Appleby* v *Myers* the court would have permitted relief only if there was 'something to justify the conclusion that the parties have entered into a fresh contract' (at 661). The fictional request underlying *quantum meruit* was doing harm in that it could always be argued that the defendant had not requested merely partial performance.

11.3   THE SCOPE OF THE 1943 ACT AND THE PRIMACY OF CONTRACT

The Law Reform (Frustrated Contracts) Act 1943 applies where two conditions are satisfied under s. 1(1): (i) where the contract has become 'impossible of performance or been otherwise frustrated'; (ii) where it is governed by English law. There are a number of excepted contracts under s. 2(5): voyage charterparties, bills of lading, insurance contracts and contracts for the sale of specific goods, where the perishing of the goods leads to frustration. The sale of specific goods is governed by s. 7 of the Sale of Goods Act 1979. The remainder are governed by the common law. Further, party autonomy is preserved under s. 2(3), whereby continuing respect is to be shown for any contractual provision which was intended to operate in the event of frustration:

> (3)   Where any contract to which this Act applies contains any provision which, upon the true construction of the contract, is intended to have effect in the event of circumstances arising which operate, or would but for the said provision operate, to frustrate the contract, or is intended to have effect whether such circumstances arise or not, the court shall given effect to the said provision and shall only give effect to the foregoing section of this Act to such extent, if any, as appears to the court to be consistent with the said provision.

Therefore it is envisaged that by express or implied terms the parties may contract out of the Act either completely or partially. In the leading case on the Act, Robert Goff J rejected a submission that s. 2(3) applied only where the relevant contractual provision was *clearly* intended to have effect in the event of frustration. The operation of the subsection was to be determined by ordinary principles of construction (*BP Exploration (Libya) Ltd* v *Hunt (No. 2)* [1979] 1 WLR 783, at 806). The subsection formed the principal ground of appeal in the House of Lords in the same case where it was held that nothing in the contract provided for the consequences of the political risk which eventuated there ([1983] 2 AC 353).

11.4   MONEY CLAIMS UNDER THE 1943 ACT

11.4.1   The main claim

Section 1(2) of the Law Reform (Frustrated Contracts) Act 1943 provides:

> (2)   All sums paid or payable to any party in pursuance of the contract before the time when the parties were so discharged (in this Act referred to as 'the time of discharge') shall, in the case of sums so paid, be recoverable from him as money received by him for the use of the party by whom the sums were paid, and, in the case of sums so payable, cease to be so payable. ...

Money obligations after the time of discharge no longer exist as a matter of common law. The Act provides in relation to such obligations accruing before the time of discharge that where unpaid, they cease to be due, and that where paid they are prima facie recoverable. The main claim is effectively a statutory action for money had and received and, like its common law predecessor, is available as a matter of right. The court has no discretion with respect to the main claim. The crucial departure from the common law is that it 'is not necessary that the consideration for the payment should have wholly failed' (*BP* v *Hunt* [1979] 1 WLR 783, at 800). Accordingly, in *Gamerco SA* v *ICM/Fair Warning (Agency) Ltd* [1995] 1 WLR 1226, pop promoters who had paid $412,500 to the group Guns 'n' Roses as an advance for a pop concert subsequently frustrated because of problems with the venue, were held entitled to recover that money as of right. Similarly, advance payments or farm-in contributions made by BP under a frustrated joint venture were recoverable under s. 1(2) in *BP* v *Hunt* [1981] 1 WLR 232, at 240.

11.4.2   Cross-claim for expenditure incurred

The 1943 Act provides two mechanisms for circumstances where one of the parties has incurred expenditure. First, under the proviso to s. 1(2), an action can be brought or an allowance can be made for such expenditure. Secondly, if the expenditure results in a valuable benefit to the other party an active claim may be made under s. 1(3). The proviso to s. 1(2) is intended to balance the abolition of the totality requirement for the main claim. As Robert Goff J said in *BP* v *Hunt* [1979] 1 WLR 783, at 800: 'claims under section 1(2) are not limited to cases of total failure of consideration, and cases of partial failure of consideration can be catered for by a cross-claim by the defendant under section 1(2) or section 1(3) or both.'

The proviso to s. 1(2) states:

> Provided that, if the party to whom the sums were so paid or payable incurred expenses before the time of discharge in, or for the purpose of, the performance of the contract, the court may, if it considers it just to do so having regard to all the circumstances of the case, allow him to retain or, as the case may be, recover the whole or any part of the sums so paid or payable, not being an amount in excess of the expenses so incurred.

Note that the section provides for alternatively a passive claim or allowance where money has already been transferred, or an active claim for reliance expenditure incurred where money was payable but not forthcoming. Curiously the legislature has regard to the original contract to provide a ceiling for claims for expenditure under the proviso. The maximum value of any such allowance or award would be determined by what sums were due under the contract before the time of discharge. This at first sight may seem to be a rather artificial limitation, but can perhaps be rationalised on the basis of an analogy with commercial practice. Instalments payable often reflect a rough and ready assessment of the amount of work which it is anticipated will be done by the time of payment. Whereas it might be possible for the transferor of money to escape a bad bargain by operation of the main claim under s. 1(2), it will not be possible under the proviso for the party incurring expense similarly to evade a bad bargain.

One interpretation of the cause of action under the proviso, is that it is analogous to the restitutionary cause of action underlying the main claim, namely failure of consideration. The expenditure would cover benefits in the form of goods and services as well as payment of money to third parties. Therefore it would have the same scope as the old claims for *quantum meruit, quantum valebat* and money paid. Enrichment difficulties would be overcome by the fact that the main claimant requested the things done; or if it is suggested that the main claimant only requested full performance, incontrovertible benefit may be employed. However, the proviso goes further than this and does not require any valuable benefit actually to be conferred upon the main claimant. The preferable analysis is that the proviso is a statutory claim analogous to promissory estoppel which can be both raised as a shield where there is a main claim, or indeed utilised as a sword where there is no main claim, but where money was payable. A third analysis which works only with respect to the passive claim is that of Robert Goff J in *BP v Hunt* [1979] 1 WLR 783, at 800:

> The allowance for expenses is probably best rationalised as a statutory recognition of the defence of change of position. True, the expenses need not have been incurred by reason of the plaintiff's payment; but they must have been incurred in, or for the purpose of performance of the contract under which the plaintiff's payment has been made, and for the reason it is just that they should be brought into account.

Whichever of these latter two views is preferred, it seems more correct to categorise the proviso as concerned with protecting wasted expenditure under the principle of injurious reliance rather than with reversing unjust benefits.

It must be stressed that the proviso provides a discretion, not a right. The exercise of the discretion is structured into a two-stage process. First, the party incurring expenditure, whether as a claimant or cross-claimant, has the burden of establishing that he has incurred expenses before the time of discharge, and that the expenditure was for the purpose of or in performance of the contract. Problems of enrichment or valuation will need to be overcome, usually by reference to the overall request. Note that the expenses incurred operate as a ceiling to any award or allowance under the proviso. The second stage is for the court to award a just sum not exceeding the value of the expenses so incurred. Garland J stressed that the burden of proof is upon the party claiming the allowance or award and emphasised the discretionary nature of the assessment of the just sum in the recent case of *Gamerco SA v ICM/Fair Warning (Agency) Ltd* [1995] 1 WLR 1226.

A hypothetical example may assist in assessing how this discretion may be exercised. Suppose B contracts for S to manufacture and supply a machine. Subsequently, and after S has incurred expenditure, the use of the machine is prohibited by environmental legislation and the contract is discharged. What would the award be if the contract price was £100,000 (£50,000 payable with the order and £50,000 upon delivery), where S has incurred expenditure of some £25,000? One view is that S is entitled to an allowance or award for the full value of the expenditure incurred. This is the approach of Robert Goff J consistent with his rationalisation of the proviso as being based upon change of position (*BP v Hunt* [1979] 1 WLR 783, at 800). However, this approach did not persuade Garland J in *Gamerco SA* v *ICM/Fair Warning (Agency) Ltd.* A second (and it is submitted preferable) view is that the court should apportion the expenditure between the parties on an equal basis. Therefore, an award or allowance of £12,500 in our hypothetical example would ensure that S and B equally share the loss resulting from a discharge of the contract. This is preferable having regard to the fact that neither party is at fault for the failure of the contract. However, where the contract is more in the nature of a joint venture with each party incurring expenditure, a third and broader approach may be necessary. This was so in *Gamerco SA* v *ICM/Fair Warning (Agency) Ltd*, where it was held that Guns 'n' Roses had incurred expenses roughly totalling $50,000, but equally the pop promoters who had made the advance payment had themselves incurred expenses totalling some $450,000. Neither parties' expenditure resulted in a valuable benefit to the other. Having particular regard to the promoters' loss, Garland J decided that justice was better done by making no deduction from the main claim under the proviso. The case neatly illustrates that the valuation of the expenses incurred operates only as a ceiling and that the distinct stage of awarding a just sum may be anything from nil to the limit of the ceiling.

Gamerco was essentially a replay of the classic case of *Taylor* v *Caldwell* (1863) 3 B & S 826, 122 ER 309, in which fire destroyed a music-hall where a series of concerts had been arranged. The impressario had sought to recover his wasted expenditure in an action for breach of contract. It seems that *Taylor* v *Caldwell* would be decided the same way today, because the jurisdiction under s. 1(2) is artificially confined to situations where sums are paid or payable in accordance with the contractual terms before the time of discharge. No advance payment was paid or payable. The Act does not give the court a wide discretion to assess and apportion the losses of the parties. To this extent there have been calls in the academic literature for a wider discretion than currently provided under s. 1 of the 1943 Act.

11.5 NON-MONEY CLAIMS UNDER THE 1943 ACT

11.5.1 Court's discretion under s. 1(3)

The difficulties posed by enrichment other than in the form of money could not be better illustrated than by the elaborate provision made by the legislature for non-money benefits conferred pursuant to subsequently frustrated contracts. Whereas money paid is recoverable as of right, only a discretion exists in relation to non-money benefits under s. 1(3). Further, the contestable nature of enrichment is illustrated by the legislature's curious two-stage test for an award. Section 1(3) provides:

> (3)   Where any party to the contract has, by reason of anything done by any other party thereto in, or for the purpose of, the performance of the contract, obtained a valuable benefit (other than a payment of money to which the last foregoing subsection applies) before the time of discharge there shall be

recoverable from him by the said other party such sum (if any), not exceeding the value of the said benefit to the party obtaining it, as the court considers just, having regard to all the circumstances of the case and, in particular, —

(a)   the amount of any expenses incurred before the time of discharge by the benefited party in, or for the purpose of, the performance of the contract, including any sums paid or payable by him to any other party in pursuance of the contract and retained or recoverable by that party under the last foregoing subsection, and

(b)   the effect, in relation to the said benefit, of the circumstances giving rise to the frustration of the contract.

First, therefore, the court must assess a valuable benefit which was actually obtained by the other party. This is not the award itself but, like the expenses assessed under the proviso of s. 1(2), forms a ceiling of any award. Secondly, the court then has the discretion to award a just sum not exceeding the valuable benefit. At the first stage of assessing the valuable benefit the court under s. 1(3)(b) has to have regard to the effect upon the benefit of the circumstances giving rise to frustration. This may create problems which will be reverted to. Further, by s. 1(3)(a), the court may make an allowance for any expenditure incurred by the recipient of the valuable benefit in or for the purpose of performance of the contract. It is submitted that this factor in the court's discretion is analogous to the proviso to s. 1(2), in that it aims to protect the injurious reliance of the transferee which may not necessarily have resulted in any benefit. In contrast, Robert Goff J in *BP* v *Hunt* [1979] 1 WLR 783, suggested (at 804) that:

the allowance for expenses is a statutory recognition of the defence of change of position. Only to the extent that the position of the defendant has so changed that it would be unjust to award restitution, should the court make an allowance for expenses. . . . The question whether the defendant has suffered a change of position has to be judged in the light of all the circumstances of the case.

It should be observed that the statutory discretion differs from the common law defence of change of position in that the common law defence is available as of right where relevant expenditure is incurred upon the faith of the payment by a bona fide transferee. The discretionary nature of s. 1(3) should not be underplayed. In *BP* v *Hunt*, Robert Goff J was prepared to accept that s. 1(2) effectively awarded restitution of net benefits (consistent with his view that the transferee was entitled to retain the value of expenditure incurred), whereas such a conclusion could not be reached on the operation of s. 1(3) under which the net benefit only provided a ceiling of an award. While Robert Goff J was not explicit about the ground for restitution under s. 1(3), it appears by analogy with s. 1(2) that the cause of action is one for failure of consideration. The subsection has been considered in detail in only one reported case, namely the great case of *BP* v *Hunt*.

11.5.2   *BP* v *Hunt*: The factual matrix

In *BP Exploration (Libya)* v *Hunt (No. 2)* [1979] 1 WLR 783 (QBD), [1981] 1 WLR
232 (CA), [1983] 2 AC 352 (HL) (all three stages are reported in [1982] 1 All ER
925), Hunt, a Texan oil man, was granted a concession to develop a potential oil field
in the Libyan desert. However, he lacked the resources and experience to explore and
develop the field. Consequently he entered into a joint venture agreement with BP.
Under the agreement Hunt agreed to transfer half his interest in the field to BP, and
in return BP undertook to explore and develop the field using its own resources.
Further, it agreed to make advance transfers to Hunt of cash and oil, termed 'farm-in
contributions'. BP had no right to claim any contribution from Hunt for development
costs unless and until oil came 'on stream', that is, was being extracted in
commercially worthwhile quantities. Thereafter the oil was to be shared equally by
BP and Hunt. However, BP would be entitled to recoup Hunt's half-share of the
development costs (which ran into many millions of dollars) by deducting
three-eighths of Hunt's half-share of the oil until it had recouped 125 per cent of his
share of development costs and the advance 'farm-in contributions'. Once the
field came on stream, operating and further development costs would be borne
equally. Therefore the risk of not finding oil in commercially worthwhile quantities
was on BP.

Drilling was successful and the oil field came into production in January 1967.
However, following a revolution in Libya, the new regime of Colonel Gaddafi
expropriated or 'nationalised' BP's interest in the field. In December 1971, BP's
employees were excluded from the facility. Hunt attempted to carry on operations
but in a position of increasing difficulty, and eventually his share of the concession
was also expropriated in June 1973. At the time of expropriation of its interest, BP
had received a substantial amount (some two-thirds) but not the whole of the
reimbursement oil to which it was entitled under the contract. BP accordingly
brought a claim under s. 1(3) of the Law Reform (Frustrated Contracts) Act 1943. It
was held that the contract was governed by English law and became frustrated upon
the expropriation of BP's interest in December 1971.

The judgment of Robert Goff J, which was substantially upheld on appeal, contains
a characteristically valuable contribution on construction of the 1943 Act and its
operation in relation to the circumstances in *BP* v *Hunt* itself, and also many
hypothetical examples canvassed in argument. Further, it constitutes a substantial
contribution to restitution scholarship in general. Valuable guidance is provided on
the exercise of the discretion entrusted to judges under the proviso of s. 1(2) and under
s. 1(3). Robert Goff J firmly located the Act within the English law of restitution and
asserted that the underlying principle of recovery was the prevention of the unjust
enrichment of either party to the contract at the other's expense. The Act was not
designed to apportion the loss between the parties. In contrast, in dicta, the Court of
Appeal got 'no help from the use of words which are not in the statute' ([1981] 1 WLR
232, at 243). However, in the wake of the subsequent development of the law of
restitution it seems likely that Robert Goff J's view would be preferred nowadays.

11.5.3 *BP* v *Hunt*: Identifying and valuing the benefit

As a matter of statutory construction, Robert Goff J held that in appropriate cases the valuable benefit should be identified as the end-product of services. Thus, in the case of prospecting for minerals, the value of any minerals discovered, if any, would be the valuable benefit under the 1943 Act. However, where services have no end-product, such as surveying or transporting goods, the value of the services themselves will be the valuable benefit. This conclusion was compelled by two factors in the Act. First, s. 1(3) draws a clear line between the benefit to the defendant and the actual performance by the plaintiff. Secondly, s. 1(3)(b) clearly envisages the court having regard to the product of the plaintiff's performance.

In assessing the ceiling of any award Robert Goff J distinguished three stages: first, the identification of the defendant's benefit; secondly, apportionment of the said benefit; and, thirdly, valuation of the said benefit. Having identified the valuable benefit as being the end-product of services in appropriate cases, Robert Goff J went on to say that where the valuable benefit was the result of contributions by both plaintiff and defendant, the court would have to apportion each parties' contribution to the benefit. With regard to the final stage of valuation, the court must not be distracted by the fact that a relatively simple service may give rise to a very valuable benefit, such as in the prospecting for minerals example where a major find might result from little effort. Conversely, substantial work may result in no or even negative benefit, such as where a room in good decorative order is redecorated in execrable taste. Further, the appropriate time of valuation is the time when the benefits are received.

11.5.4 *BP* v *Hunt*: Assessing the just sum

Moving on to the next stage required under s. 1(3), namely the assessment of a just sum, Robert Goff J decided (at 805) that in most cases the statutory discretion should be exercised so as to award the equivalent of a *quantum meruit*, subject to the valuable benefit ceiling:

> where (as in the case of a benefit conferred under a contract thereafter frustrated) the benefit has been requested by the defendant, the basic measure of recovery in restitution is the reasonable value of the plaintiff's performance — in the case of services, a *quantum meruit* or reasonable remuneration, and in the case of goods, a quantum valebat or reasonable price.

Robert Goff J stated that the 1943 Act was surprisingly silent on the question of the continuing relevance of consideration in the terms of the contract. However, he held it to be relevant for three purposes. First in determining the full scope of the work to be done. It may be the case that the plaintiff contracted to recover only if the work was completed (this appears to be a survival of the entire obligation rule). Secondly, 'the contract consideration is always relevant as providing some evidence of what will be a reasonable sum to be awarded in respect of the plaintiff's work'. Thirdly, 'the contract consideration, or a rateable part of it, may provide a limit to the sum to be awarded' (at 805–806). These results flowed either from the general principles of the law of restitution, or could be said to operate by virtue of s. 2(3). The result is the survival in appropriate cases of the entire obligation rule. Robert Goff J concluded (at 807): 'only if upon a true construction of the contract the plaintiff has contracted on the terms that he is to receive no payment in the event which has occurred, will the fact that the contract is "entire" have the effect of precluding an award under the Act.' Further, the learned judge recognised the contract price as forming a contractual ceiling or valuation ceiling upon recovery.

11.5.5   *BP* v *Hunt*: **Application to the facts**

Robert Goff J accordingly first *identified* Hunt's benefit as prima face the transformation of a bare concession of unknown potential into a giant oil field in production, in which he had a half interest. However, Hunt's benefit was greatly reduced by the circumstances giving rise to the frustration and was limited to the oil he had received and the value of the settlement Hunt had obtained from the Libyan government, in accordance with s. 1(3)(b). Secondly, the judge had regard to *apportionment*, and on the basis of a concession by counsel held that one half of that benefit was attributable to BP's efforts and one half was attributable to Hunt's own contribution to the joint venture, namely the oil concession itself. Thirdly, Robert Goff J *valued the benefit* to Hunt (taking into account both his expenses, under s. 1(3)(a), and circumstances giving rise to the frustration of the contract, under s. 1(3)(b)) at US$84,951,000. Robert Goff J held that BP was not entitled to the restitution of benefits received by Hunt, rather the relevance of the benefit under s. 1(3) was to provide a ceiling for the sum to be awarded.

Turning to the *calculation of the just sum*, the judge held that the contractual consideration for BP's services in exploring and developing the field provided the best evidence of a reasonable remuneration to be awarded in the circumstances. The contractual consideration contemplated for BP's performance was the transfer of a half interest in the concession and the receipt of reimbursement oil. Therefore if BP had received the whole of the reimbursement oil, in addition to its half share in the concession, no sum would have been awarded under the Act. Here the just sum consisted of the value of BP's expenditure on Hunt's account in exploring and developing the field, but limited to only 100 per cent of that cost, not 125 per cent (as contemplated by the contract), the value of the 'farm-in contributions' and BP's expenditure in operating the field on Hunt's account after the oil came on stream. All items were valued at the date that they were incurred or received. From this sum of US$98,105,146 was to be deducted the value of the reimbursement oil already received, some $62,702,000. The total sum was $35,403,146, so there was no need to reduce the award, because the benefit ceiling was greater than the just sum.

The judgment was upheld in the Court of Appeal, except that the farm-in contributions of money were held to be properly recoverable under s. 1(2) not s. 1(3).

The Court of Appeal stressed the discretionary nature of the exercise, and therefore appeals will be unusual unless the judge makes an error of law in exercising his discretion. The Court of Appeal laconically announced: 'What is just is what the trial judge thinks is just.' ([1981] 1 WLR 232, at 238). The appeal to the House of Lords was primarily concerned with s. 2(3). Despite the Court of Appeal's broad statement, it is submitted that the principled structure provided for the exercise at the discretion by Robert Goff J will be appropriate in all future cases.

11.6   POST-DISCHARGE EVENTS

The Act applies to benefits transferred or expenditure incurred only up to the time of discharge. Where parties continue performance in ignorance of the fact that the contractual framework has been discharged, the position is still regulated by common law. It seems that the ground for restitution of benefits will be either mistake or failure of consideration. Mistaken transfer is appropriate where one or both parties mistakenly believe they are still under a contractual liability to transfer benefits. Alternatively, failure of consideration can explain the ground for recovery. The basis upon which a transfer is made, namely the existence of a valid and binding contract, has fallen away.

There is only one authority in this area, the assistance of which is questionable as it was subsequently overruled, albeit on a different ground. In *Société Franco Tunisienne d'Armement* v *Sidermar SPA, The Massalia* [1961] 2 QB 278, it was held that a voyage charterparty for the carriage of iron ore from India to Genoa was frustrated by closure of the Suez canal. The vessel had instead proceeded via the Cape of Good Hope, twice the distance of the trip via Suez. This finding of frustration was subsequently overruled by the Court of Appeal in *Ocean Tramp Tankers Corp.* v *V/O Sovfracht, The Eugenia* [1964] 2 QB 226, which held that there was no frustration in such circumstances. However, in *The Massalia* the shipowners had claimed for a *quantum meruit*. The services were apparently rendered after the frustrating event, but in any event voyage charterparties are an excepted contract

The courts have been sensitive in developing the doctrine of frustration not to allow parties to escape a bad bargain where the change in circumstances is no more than increased costs due to, for example, labour shortages or difficulties obtaining materials. In the leading case of *Davis Contractors Ltd* v *Fareham UDC* [1956] AC 696, contractors sought to escape a fixed-price building contract in such circumstances, and to claim upon a quasi-contractual *quantum meruit*. They failed. Where a contract is frustrated the common law appears to permit a party to escape a bad bargain in this way. Neither party is at fault, and it seems difficult to mount an argument based upon a contractual ceiling. The problem is analogous to that which has arisen in contracts discharged by breach, as seen in the American case of *Boomer* v *Muir*, 24 P 2d 570 (1933) (discussed above at 10.7.2). It may still be arguable that the common law doctrine of entire obligation means that a quasi-contractual recovery in such circumstances may never exceed the contractual price or a rateable proportion thereof.

under s. 2(5) of the 1943 Act. Pearson J, discussing *Craven-Ellis* v *Canons Ltd* [1936] 2 KB 403 (see 12.3) and the dicta of Lords Atkin, Wright and Maugham in *Hain Steamship Co. Ltd* v *Tate & Lyle Ltd* [1936] 2 All ER 597 (see 10.9), held the present claim was *a fortiori* from those statements of principle. Pearson J held the shipowners carried the goods 'for the charterers' benefit and with the consent of the charterers. In my view, the law implies or imposes an obligation for the charterers to pay reasonable freight' (at 314).

11.7 PRACTICAL ISSUES

Nearly 40 years ago Robert Goff observed that the main defect in the 1943 Act was that 'it has vested in the courts a discretion so wide as to render it very difficult for a lawyer to give firm advice to his clients on the prospect of a claim under the Act' ((1961) 24 MLR 85). Accordingly the best advice in most cases for those drafting contracts is to exclude its operation under the contracting out provisions of s. 2(3) (Stewart and Carter [1992] CLJ 66, at 122). The paucity of reported cases may be misleading, as the Act may often be invoked behind closed doors in arbitration.

Where the Act applies the following should be noted. The onus of proof under the 1943 Act is clearly upon the party claiming or cross-claiming. Therefore, under s. 1(2) the transferor of money has the onus of proof where money has been transferred, but the transferee has the onus of proof with regard to an allowance or an award under the proviso (*Gamerco SA* v *ICM/Fair Warning (Agency) Ltd* [1995] 1 WLR 1226). Similarly, under s. 1(3) the onus of proof is upon a claimant who has conferred a valuable benefit upon a transferee to establish the valuable benefit and to lead evidence as to what a just sum should be, namely in many cases what the reasonable value of goods and services provided was. Conversely, under s. 1(3)(a), it is submitted that the transferee has the onus of establishing any expenditure incurred in or for the performance of the contract, to be taken into account as a factor in the judicial exercise of discretion. Robert Goff J decided in *BP* v *Hunt* [1979] 1 WLR 783, at 800, 803–804, that all benefits and expenditure should be assessed and valued at the time they were received or incurred, and that therefore the Act made no allowance for the time-value of money in respect of the valuation of expenses under the proviso of s. 1(2), or the award of a just sum under s. 1(3). However, the statutory power to award interest provided some relief in these circumstances once the judgment was obtained upon a main claim (see 38.3).

FURTHER READING

Asterisks indicate especially useful works.

Goff and Jones, 510–15; 555–77
Birks, 249–58
Anson, 526–34
*G. Treitel, *Frustration and Force Majeure* (1994), 537–69

A. Haycroft and D. Waksman, 'Frustration and Restitution' [1984] JBL 207

J. Barton, 'Contract and *Quantum Meruit*: the Antecedents of *Cutter* v *Powell*' (1987) 8 J Legal History 48 (historical)

*E. McKendrick, 'Frustration, Restitution and Loss Apportionment' in Burrows (1991), 147–70

E. McKendrick, 'The Consequences of Frustration — The Law Reform (Frustrated Contracts) Act', in E. McKendrick (ed.), *Force Majeure and Frustration of Contract*, 2nd edn (1995), 223–44

A. Stewart and J. Carter, 'Frustrated Contracts and Statutory Adjustment: The Case for a Reappraisal' [1992] CLJ 66

12 Void and Unenforceable Contracts

12.1 THEORETICAL FOUNDATIONS

It should be the first duty of a court to uphold, rather than to invalidate, an apparently binding promise or agreement. The positive requirements for a binding contract are concerned with identifying the necessary contractual intention and a good reason to reinforce the moral sanctions for breach of faith with legal obligations. Hence the doctrines of offer, acceptance, consideration and the various remedies for compensating induced but misplaced reliance on the words or conduct of others.

In contrast, an apparent agreement may be tainted by a number of factors. First, failure of offer and acceptance to correspond, suggesting the parties were at cross-purposes. Secondly, the substance of the intended contractual performance may involve illegal or immoral conduct, or be contrary to public policy so as to offend the conscience of the court. Thirdly, statute may provide for essential formalities before a contract will be enforced, or even before it is recognised as such. Fourthly, one of the parties may be affected by initial incapacity. Lastly, a common mistake may make the subject-matter of the contract essentially and radically different from what the parties believed it to be.

The ground of invalidity may be relevant to the proper operation of restitutionary principles where a contract is held to be void. Voidness entails that the law never recognised any obligations arising from the transaction. Obviously where a void contract remains wholly executory there is no need for the deployment of the principle against unjust enrichment. In contrast, where there has been partial, or even full, performance of the supposed obligations of the parties, restitutionary techniques are often utilised in their characteristic function of mopping up in the wake of ineffective transfers. Contracts are sometimes said, with heavy-handed and unnecessary emphasis, to be 'null and void', or to be wholly without legal effect. As an elementary proposition this is true, but it may rather oversimplify the legal scene.

Void contracts are properly to be contrasted with voidable contracts, where an operating vitiating factor clouds the intention of at least one of the parties. A voidable contract is subsisting until a party entitled to rescind or set it aside elects to do so. In the meantime, money and other property which passed under the contract were effectively transferred (although they may be restored by the machinery of rescission). The transferee of chattels has a voidable title and is able to pass good title to a third party purchasing in good faith without notice (Sale of Goods Act 1979, s. 23; *Lewis* v *Averay* [1972] 1 QB 198). In contrast, no obligations arise under a void contract, and there is no need for either party to take any action to render the contract ineffective. Money and other property transferred thereunder moves without any effective legal basis. The result of the rules of common law tracing and currency (see Chapter 27) is that money which is paid soon ceases to be traceable and passes into currency. Accordingly the legal property in money passes to the transferee in most cases, even though the contract is void.

With respect to goods transferred under a void contract, it is necessary to distinguish the parties' intention to contract and the transferor's intention to pass property. The voidness of the contract necessitates no more than that no obligations, including the obligation to transfer property, ever existed. There is no clear authority on whether property can pass in goods where a contract is void though not illegal. Where a contract is both void and illegal it has been held that property can pass the transferee (*Singh* v *Ali* [1960] AC 167; *Belvoir Finance Co. Ltd* v *Stapleton* [1971] 1 QB 210; and Birks (1993) 23 W Aus L Rev 194, at 197). As a matter of principle, it can be argued that property passes because it was intended to pass in property, regardless of the underlying voidness of the transaction. However, this is qualified by cases where the intention to pass property (in addition to the contractual intention) is vitiated by a fundamental mistake by the transferor (usually as to the identity of the transferee). This is perhaps the best explanation of *Cundy* v *Lindsay* (1878) 3 App Cas 459. Where the benefit to the defendant consists of money paid to a third party which validly discharges an obligation of the defendant or takes the shape of services rendered, it is clear that there can never be restoration *in specie* of the benefit received. It remains necessary to be sensitive to the differences between different types of enrichment in this context. The rules of contract, property law and tracing form the necessary background to any consideration of the role of unjust enrichment. With regard to both money claims and claims in respect of non-money benefits, there has been controversy about the appropriate ground for restitution.

The first portion of this chapter considers contracts which are held to be void but not illegal. Recent developments in the law of restitution, generated by the 'swaps' fiasco, have greatly clarified the law regarding money claims. The law governing non-money claims remains less developed. This chapter then goes on to consider cases where statute renders the performance of one or both parties unenforceable. This raises similar problems to void contracts. The additional difficulties caused where a contract is held to be tainted with illegality are postponed until Chapter 13. The cases involving local authorities entering into interest rate swap transactions which were beyond their capacity and authorities on unauthorised insurance business merit separate consideration.

12.2   VOID CONTRACTS AND MONEY CLAIMS

12.2.1   The ground for restitution

It would be perfectly easy to envisage a legal rule whereby money and other benefits transferred under a void contract were subjected to a simple scheme of mutual restitution. Accordingly, where both parties have performed some or all of their respective obligations, the court would simply assess the value of the benefit conferred by each and award restitution of the net sum outstanding to the party who had contributed more to the supposed bargain. Indeed such a regime obtains in civil law systems where the voidness of the contract entails the enrichment of each without legal cause. See Zweigert and Kötz, *An Introduction to Comparative Law* (3rd edn, 1998) at 537–51. This strategy, though simple and apparently attractive, is not (as yet) the approach of English law. As a matter of principle, English law requires that the claimant identify, plead and prove a ground for restitution or unjust factor. 'Voidness of contract' is not such a ground for restitution. The voidness of the contract does entail, in accordance with the third question in our enquiry, that there is no binding contractual matrix to which the court must have regard (see 1.2). This follows from contract law's own insistence that no obligations were ever created by the void transaction. At the fourth stage of our enquiry, the claimant must establish a reason why the enrichment must be reversed. The usual nominate grounds of restitution which are pertinent in this context are mistake and failure of consideration.

The swaps cases have caused a legal revolution in our understanding of money claims. With regard to claims to recover money on the ground of mistake, before 1998 there was always the possibility that a transferor would be met with a plea that his mistake was one of law. It was in the context of a void swaps contract that the House of Lords decided in *Kleinwort Benson Ltd* v *Lincoln City Council* [1999] 2 AC 349 that the money was recoverable even though the mistake was one of law. Had this case been decided earlier in the decade, matters may have progressed more smoothly with regard to the mopping up of the swaps transaction. However, many of the earlier swaps cases were argued in terms of failure of consideration. That, at least, appears to be the result of the other leading House of Lords judgment in a swaps case, namely *Westdeutsche Landesbank Girozentrale* v *Islington London Borough Council* [1996] AC 669. The matter is not free from doubt, however, because the House of Lords was not concerned in that appeal with the ground for restitution. Accordingly the views expressed at first instance and in the Court of Appeal retain some authority. The judges there preferred not to rest recovery upon failure of consideration, but rather to synthesise a new ground for restitution, termed 'no consideration' or 'absence of consideration'. At first instance in *Westdeutsche*, Hobhouse J expressed the premiss for his argument ([1994] 4 All ER 891, at 924):

> The phrase 'failure of consideration' is one which in its terminology presupposes that there has been at some stage a valid contract which has been partially

performed by one party. It is essentially a concept for use in the law of contract and provides a common law remedy governed by rigid rules granted as of right where the contract becomes ineffective through breach or otherwise.... In the case of *ultra vires* transactions such as those with which I am concerned where there is not and never has been any contract, I prefer to use the phrase 'absence of consideration'.

In the view of Hobhouse J, where both parties had performed at least some of their respective obligations, it was impossible to say there had been a total failure of consideration (at 929): 'In my judgment, the correct analysis is that any payments made under a contract which is void *ab initio*, in the way that an *ultra vires* contract is void, are not contractual payments at all.' Hence Hobhouse J preferred 'absence of consideration' to 'failure of consideration'. This was based on a number of late eighteenth- and early nineteenth-century authorities on void annuities. In the Court of Appeal, Dillon LJ used the language of 'no consideration' and 'total failure of consideration' as though they were interchangeable. In the view of Leggatt LJ ([1994] 1 WLR 938, at 953): 'There was no total failure of consideration, only partial.... There can have been no consideration under a contract void *ab initio*. So it is fallacious to speak of the failure of consideration having been partial.'

These passages are instructive because they indicate the reason why Hobhouse J and Leggatt LJ preferred to eschew failure of consideration as the cause of action. The learned judges believed that, short of the House of Lords, it was not possible to allow recovery in restitution unless there was a total failure of consideration. Where there was both performance and counter-performance there could be no such total failure of consideration. However, the annuities cases provided clear authority for relief in the context of void contracts, where in some cases both parties had performed. These were pressed into service, together with selective quotes from more recent authority, to support a new unjust factor termed 'absence of consideration' or 'no consideration'.

This project, while worthy in its motives, was misguided for a number of reasons. First, Hobhouse J, and to a lesser extent the Court of Appeal, came close to flirting with the fallacy in *Chandler* v *Webster* [1904] 1 KB 493, which was overruled by the House of Lords in *Fibrosa Spolcka Akcyjna* v *Fairbairn Lawson Combe Barbour Ltd* [1943] AC 32. The error in the earlier case was to equate the quasi-contractual doctrine of total failure of consideration with the doctrine of consideration in respect of contractual formation. It is certainly true to say that in the majority of cases where there is held to be failure of consideration, there is a failure of a specified contractual counter-performance. Further, it is true to say that the vast majority of cases in which the language of failure of consideration is explicitly used are cases concerning contracts which are at least initially valid. However, failure of consideration properly understood means failure of the basis of transfer or failure of condition: Birks, 222–26; Birks (1993) 23 U W Aus L Rev 195, at 208–14. Accordingly failure of consideration is the unjust factor where an intending house buyer, keen to complete, pays the would-be vendor a deposit, as a token of good faith, and the negotiations which have been conducted 'subject to contract' fall through (*Chillingworth* v *Esche* [1924] 1 Ch 97). Secondly, it is hard to see why the judges at the earlier stages of *Westdeutsche* were concerned about the totality requirement. The essence of the *Chandler* v *Webster* fallacy concerned the prospective nature of discharge for breach or frustration. The contract was held to have existed for at least a short period of time, and accordingly each party had the benefit of those obligations whilst extant; consequently there could never be a total failure. In contrast, where the underlying contract is void *ab initio* the claimant received no such bargained-for benefit. The payer performed on the basis that he would have the benefit in return for binding legal obligations. This has not turned out to be the case and accordingly it is possible to speak of total failure. Alternatively, it can be argued that it is wrong in principle to transpose the requirement of *total* failure of consideration from the context of contracts discharged by termination for breach, where it originated, to the different context of void contracts. The requirement of total failure may be defensible, or at least explicable, in relation to the breach cases (see 10.5.2). However, it is hard to see any basis either in principle or on authority for the totality requirement in relation to void contracts. Before *Westdeutsche* there was little in the way of explicit discussion of the ground for recovery where a contract was void. It was far from clear that there was any requirement of a total failure of consideration in the authorities. As a matter of principle there is no reason why moneys paid under a void contract should not be recovered, whether the failure of consideration was total or partial.

The reasoning of Hobhouse J and the Court of Appeal in *Westdeutsche* attracted considerable academic criticism: Birks (1993) 23 U W Aus L Rev 195; Swadling [1994] RLR 73 and Burrows [1995] RLR 15. The appeal to the House of Lords in *Westdeutsche* was notionally concerned only with the question of interest. In dicta, Lord Goff of Chieveley expressed his tentative agreement with the academic criticism of 'absence of consideration'. Lord Goff dissented on the main question of interest. However, it is submitted that this does not detract from the authority of these particular observations. Lord Goff opined ([1996] AC 669, at 683):

> the concept of failure of consideration need not be so narrowly confined. In particular it appears from the annuity cases themselves that the courts regarded them as cases of failure of consideration; and concern has been expressed by a number of restitution lawyers that the approach of Hobhouse J is contrary to principle and could, if accepted, lead to undesirable consequences ... [His Lordship cited the works of Birks, Swadling and Burrows above.] However since there is before your Lordships no appeal from the decision that the bank was entitled to recover the balance of the payments so made in a personal claim in restitution, the precise identification of the ground of recovery was not explored in argument before the Appellate Committee. It would therefore be inappropriate to express any concluded view upon it. Even so, I think it right to record that there appears to me to be considerable force in the criticisms which have been expressed; and I shall, when considering the issues on this appeal, bear in mind the possibility that it may be right to regard the ground of recovery as failure of consideration.

A more emphatic vindication of the traditional failure of consideration approach is to be found in the leading speech of the majority by Lord Browne-Wilkinson. His Lordship, however, does not expressly differ from the views expressed by the judges in the lower courts. Lord Browne-Wilkinson decided that *Sinclair* v *Brougham* [1914] AC 398 should be overruled. His Lordship continued (at 710–11):

> It follows that in *Sinclair* v *Brougham* the depositors should have had a personal claim to recover the moneys at law based on a total failure of consideration. The failure of consideration was *not* partial: the depositors had paid over their money in consideration of a promise to repay. That promise was *ultra vires* and void; therefore the consideration for the payment of the money wholly failed. So in the present swaps case (though the point is not one under appeal) I think the Court of Appeal were right to hold that the swap moneys were paid on a consideration that wholly failed. The essence of the swap agreement is that, over the whole term of the agreement, each party thinks he will come out best: the consideration for one party making a payment is an obligation on the other party to make counter-payments over the whole term of the agreement.

Like many recent pronouncements of the House of Lords, it is difficult to weigh the precise effect of dicta such as these. The opinions of their Lordships were reached without the benefit of argument. However, together with the academic opinions, the views must be regarded as authoritative.

In *Guinness Mahon & Co. Ltd* v *Kensington & Chelsea Royal London Borough Council* [1999] QB 215, the Court of Appeal further considered the question of the unjust factor in respect of a completed swap transaction. It was held there was no distinction in principle between a fully-performed and partially-performed *ultra vires* swap transaction. Both would be unwound. The bargained-for benefit was a reciprocal contractual obligation, which neither party obtained. Morritt LJ regarded the cause of action as total failure of consideration, and treated the decision of Hobhouse J and the Court of Appeal in *Westdeutsche* as proceeding on the same basis (as Lord Browne-Wilkinson had done). Waller LJ engaged with the ongoing debate (at 231): 'There is in my view great force in the argument that 'absence' of consideration as opposed to 'failure' of consideration should not by itself be a ground for restitution.' Further, Waller LJ sounded a note of caution about whether restitution would be automatic simply because of the voidness of the underlying obligations: 'I have serious doubts as to whether simply because a party can show that a contract between them duly completed was void for whatever reason, that should automatically lead to the court being prepared simply to unravel the contract.' Waller LJ reminded himself that the decision of the Court of Appeal in *Westdeutsche* remained binding, despite the dicta in the House of Lords. Ultimately his Lordship was convinced that the true reason for recovery (following a suggestion of Birks) was policy-motivated. The factor which tipped the balance in the swaps cases was the *ultra vires* principle, and the need to protect the public from what Leggatt LJ in *Westdeutsche* had termed the council's 'ill-considered financial dispositions' ([1994] 1 WLR 935, at 951). Robert Walker LJ stated that the phrase 'failure of consideration' in this context may be 'confusing' ([1999] QB 215, at 236). His Lordship appeared to be agnostic on the true unjust factor (at 239–40):

> Either there was a total failure of consideration, in that neither side to the supposed contract undertook any valid obligation, or there was, in Hobhouse J's preferred expression, absence of consideration. The choice between the two expressions may be no more than a matter of which is the apter terminology.

This does not seem to advance the debate much further, except to continue the uncertainty. Waller LJ's reminder that *Westdeutsche* in the Court of Appeal has binding force on the lower courts may be the most significant observation in *Guinness Mahon*.

Some tentative conclusions can be advanced. First, representatives of both the majority and the minority in the House of Lords in *Westdeutsche* preferred the traditional language of failure of consideration, to the newly-coined grounds for restitution preferred by the lower courts. Accordingly, it is not safe to regard absence of consideration or no consideration as distinct unjust factors. In strict theory it must be observed that the Court of Appeal's decision on the ground for restitution is the binding one. However, the point in rebuttal is that it is seriously arguable that the unjust factor has been 'reinterpreted' in the House of Lords and by the Court of Appeal itself in *Guinness Mahon*. Secondly, while still employing the language of *totality*, both Lord Goff and Lord Browne-Wilkinson saw the existence of payments and counter-payments under a void contract as not inconsistent with a finding of total failure. Neither party had received the bargained-for benefit, namely, a valid contractual obligation on the other party. It may have been more honest to admit that this was a case of recovery on the basis of partial failure. There is no need for the totality requirement to be transplanted from the realm of contracts discharged by termination for breach into the wholly different field of void contracts. There was never any question of a valid contractual matrix governing the rights and responsibilities of the parties. The imperative behind the totality requirement, which appears to limit recourse to restitution, where there has been a valid bargain, has no application where the contract is wholly void. The recognition of recovery on the basis of mistake of law in *Kleinwort Benson* v *Lincoln City Council* and the broad approach to recovery on the basis of failure of consideration expressed in dicta by the House of Lords in *Westdeutsche* means that in practice money is easily recoverable where it has been paid under a contract which is void. It may even be thought that the reality of the situation is that the voidness of the contract is sufficient to engender restitution. However, Waller LJ's suggestion that the swaps cases are distinct from void contracts in general because of the policy of *ultra vires* is an astute one. It remains important to identify the underlying reason for voidness.

As a matter of formal law it is still necessary to plead either mistake or failure of consideration or both. The plea of mistake and failure of consideration in the alternative is illustrated by a case pre-dating the recent House of Lords' excursions on this topic. In *Rover International Ltd* v *Cannon Film Sales Ltd* [1989] 1 WLR 912, the parties bargained for a joint venture for the distribution of films in the Italian cinema. Rover and Thorn EMI (who were subsequently taken over by Cannon) entered into a purported agreement providing for the dubbing into Italian and distribution of the latter's films, including the well-known movie 'Highlander'. The agreement provided for gross receipts to be split between the parties in agreed proportions. Rover were to pay an advance of $1.5 million in instalments. Rover was a special project vehicle incorporated in Jersey for the purpose. The purported contract was dated 5 December 1985. However, Rover was not incorporated (and therefore had no legal existence) until 6 February 1986. Rover had paid some five instalments totalling $312,500 before a dispute arose. It was then discovered that the underlying contract was void *ab initio* due to Rover's incapacity at the relevant time. Rover being a Jersey company, s. 36C of the Companies Act 1985 had no application. Rover claimed restitution of the instalments on the ground of mistake of fact or failure of consideration. Kerr LJ rejected a submission that there was little evidence that there was an operative mistake. In his Lordship's view the facts spoke for themselves. The money had been paid under a belief that there was a valid and binding contract between the parties and (this then being a relevant holding) the mistake was one of fact, not of law. Dillon LJ was content to allow recovery alternatively on the ground of mistake of fact or as money paid for a consideration that has wholly failed. Kerr LJ considered the question of total failure of consideration in some detail. His Lordship stated the test (at 923):

The question whether there has been a total failure of consideration is not answered by considering whether there was any consideration sufficient to support a contract or purported contract. The test is whether or not the party claiming total failure of consideration has in fact received any part of the benefit bargained for under the contract or purported contract.

In the view of Kerr LJ, Rover had bargained for the opportunity to participate in the profits from the film's release. The invalidity of the contract meant that it got nothing for which it had bargained. The intermediate possession of the film for the purpose of dubbing and preparation was a mere incident of the purported agreement, which was onerous rather than beneficial. This illustrates that the insistence on *totality* is easily satisfied on the facts where the underlying contract is void *ab initio*. In any event, the supposed need for totality in relation to void contracts does not rest upon firm foundations.

In *Guinness plc* v *Saunders* [1990] 2 AC 663, Guinness sought recovery of £5.2 million paid to Ward, an American attorney and former director of the company, which was made at the time of the controversial bid by Guinness to take over Distillers. Ward, together with the then Chief Executive, Saunders, and another director, Roux, formed a take-over sub-committee of the Board. That sub-committee agreed to pay Ward 0.2 per cent of the ultimate value of the bid, if successful, for his services in connection with the bid. This came to £5.2 million, which was paid via a

Jersey company which Ward controlled. The House of Lords awarded Guinness restitution of the full £5.2 million on a summary judgment application under old RSC Ord. 14. Under Guinness's articles of association, only the board of directors had the necessary authority to authorise remuneration of a director in such circumstances. Lord Templeman observed (at 693): 'The fact is that Guinness never did contract to pay anything to Mr Ward. The contract on which Mr Ward relies is not voidable but non-existent.' However, as Birks comments: '"Void contract" or "non-existent contract" is not in itself a ground for restitution' (Birks [1990] LMCLQ 330, at 332). Lord Goff of Chieveley, on the basis that the contract was void for want of authority, opined (at 698) that: 'Guinness was therefore entitled to recover from Mr Ward the money paid under it on the ground of total failure of consideration, or alternatively on the basis that he had received the money as constructive trustee.'

Nevertheless, it must be observed that it is difficult to speak of a total failure of consideration, in that it does appear that Mr Ward had performed the specified services. (For discussion of the counterclaim, see 12.3.) This may be circumvented by saying that Guinness did not get the intended bargained-for benefit, namely a contractual right to the services which were provided. In that somewhat artificial way, the case can be approximated to one of total failure of consideration. It is awkward in that Guinness, or rather those empowered to act on its behalf (the board), did not bargain for anything. Alternatively, it could be argued that the requirement of totality is inappropriate in the context of void contracts. Birks rejects failure of consideration because of the work done under the purported contract, and instead suggests that the appropriate cause of action is mistake: Birks [1990] LMCLQ 330, at 331–33. In summary, the case can be defended on the basis of an unjust factor, which was either mistake or possibly failure of consideration.

12.2.2   Fully- and partially-performed void contracts

Does it make a difference that the void contract is fully performed, rather than partially performed? In the context of the void interest rate swap cases the answer has been consistently 'No'. It is difficult to say with certainty whether this will be a general rule for void contracts, or whether the solution is informed by the reason for invalidity: namely, the *ultra vires* doctrine and the control of public finances. In the first lead case, *Westdeutsche Landesbank Girozentrale* v *Islington London Borough Council*; *Kleinwort Benson* v *Sandwell Borough Council* [1994] 4 All ER 890 (see 12.4.3), Hobhouse J held that the cause of action of absence of consideration arose whether the contract was partly performed (an 'open' swap), or fully performed (a 'closed' swap), as in the case of the first Sandwell swap (at 930). Birks (in (1993) 23 UW Aus LR 195) criticised this conclusion where the appropriate cause of action was failure of consideration (which he preferred to no consideration) (at 228). However, if mistake were relied upon instead, Birks saw the difficulty in insisting upon a rule excluding fully-executed transactions from the restitutionary regime. A rule excluding such transactions *per se* would be unprincipled, but Birks suggested that it could be argued that when the deal was complete, the force of the mistake was spent, in that once the counter-performance was obtained no prejudice could result from the mistake (at 230–31). Burrows was of the view that only mistake of law could justify restitution where the transaction was fully executed: [1995] RLR 15, at 18–19. He rejected Birks's attempt to exclude fully-performed contracts, because it runs counter to principle and precedent which establish mistake as sufficient to ground recovery, without the need for any separate enquiry into prejudice.

In *Kleinwort Benson Ltd v Lincoln City Council* [1999] 2 AC 349, where the cause of action was explicitly mistake of law, the majority favoured Burrows's view (at 385–87 *per* Lord Goff; at 415–16 *per* Lord Hope). The former observed that Birks's thesis required the final payment to wipe out previously accrued claims resulting from earlier performance. Further, *Hazell v Hammersmith and Fulham London Borough Council* [1992] 2 AC 1 entailed that all swaps, whether open or closed, were *ultra vires* the local authority: 'the *ultra vires* rule is not optional' (at 387). Lord Hope agreed with the Court of Appeal in *Guinness Mahon & Co. Ltd v Kensington & Chelsea Royal London Borough Council* [1999] QB 215, which had been decided on the basis of failure of consideration or no consideration. Lord Hope pointed out that the mistake was that the payment was believed legally due, not as to whether the other party would perform. In *Guinness Mahon* the Court of Appeal could see no valid reason why the fact that a swap was fully performed ('closed') should preclude restitution, rejecting arguments of Birks. Morritt LJ said recovery was 'a necessary corollary of the principle of *ultra vires* and the purpose for which it exists' (at 230). Robert Walker LJ concluded: 'the injustice of the council's enrichment does not vanish because the term of the void contract ran its course' (at 240). It remains to be seen whether the reasoning of the case is confined to cases of *ultra vires*, or whether it will be applied to all void contracts. *Guinness plc v Saunders* [1990] 2 AC 663 may suggest full performance is an irrelevant consideration for void contracts in general.

12.3   VOID CONTRACTS AND NON-MONEY CLAIMS

Two problems bedevil the consideration of non-money benefits transferred under void contracts. First, the difficulty of establishing enrichment. Secondly, the authorities to date have not been explicit about the ground for restitution. With respect to the former problem, older authorities have been reinterpreted in the light of the new juristic tests of free acceptance and incontrovertible benefits. With regard to the latter problem, Birks has argued for the need for symmetry in respect of unjust factors. Problems of enrichment apart, the same grounds for restitution should apply in respect of money and non-money benefits: Birks (1992), 86–87. See 1.3.2. Accordingly, in line with the money cases, the grounds for restitution will usually be mistake, or failure of consideration or both.

The leading pre-war case is *Craven-Ellis v Canons Ltd* [1936] 2 KB 403, in which the plaintiff, Craven-Ellis, was engaged by the defendant company, initially in the capacity as a valuer and estate agent. From 1928 to 1931 he worked for the company without a formal contract. Then in April 1931 a formal agreement was executed with the company's seal setting out the terms from which Craven-Ellis was to act as the company's managing director. However, none of the directors, including Craven-Ellis, was capable of making such an agreement as none of them held the necessary qualification shares as required under the articles of association. Accordingly the agreement was void *ab initio*. The Court of Appeal held that he was entitled to recover on an *quantum meruit* basis in respect of the services rendered. For the first period of employment it would now seem appropriate to characterise this as a contractual example of *quantum meruit*. However, for the second period of employment as managing director, the claim must arise in unjust enrichment. This is borne out by the judgment of Greer LJ (at 412):

> In my judgment, the obligation to pay reasonable remuneration for the work done when there is no binding contract between the parties is imposed by a rule of law, and not by an inference of fact arising from the acceptance of services or goods. It is one of the cases referred to in books on contracts as obligations arising *quasi ex contractu*, of which a well-known incident is a claim based on money had and received.

First, with regard to enrichment, the first edition of Goff and Jones classified *Craven-Ellis* as a case involving the free acceptance of services (at 31, 278). However, Birks argued that if a company was incapable of contracting for the services of Craven-Ellis, it was equally incapable of accepting them. Accordingly the case could be explained only on the basis of incontrovertible benefit: Birks [1971] CLP 110, at 120–22. This explanation is now accepted by Goff and Jones, 587–89. Secondly, with regard to the unjust factor, this can now be characterised as either mistake as to the validity of the underlying contract, or upon the basis of a consideration which has wholly failed: Craven-Ellis received nothing in return for his services rendered.

Craven-Ellis v *Canons Ltd* is often compared with the subsequent decision of the Court of Appeal in *In re Cleadon Trust Ltd* [1939] 1 Ch 286, in which a company director expended over £53,000 paying debts owed by the company at the request of its managing director, in the expectation that he would repaid. A resolution of the board of directors purported to ratify the payments, but this was invalid because the meeting was inquorate. On the company's liquidation the director sought restitution. The majority of the Court of Appeal held that the company was under no obligation either at common law or in equity to reimburse him. The case is a difficult one to reconcile with the modern approach. The enrichment was in the form of a discharge of the company's obligations under guarantees which it had signed. Birks regrets that a crucial question was not posed: were the company's debts discharged by the payment by the director, or by the subsequent decision of the liquidator to treat the obligations as extinguished: Birks, 289–90. Burrows treats the case as one which supports a rule of automatic discharge of debts: Burrows, 229–30. This is not necessarily correct, as a director of the company, with the concurrence of the managing director, would have sufficient apparent authority to discharge the company's obligations. What is clear is that the company was enriched either at the time of the original payment, or by the subsequent ratification of the liquidator in treating the obligations as discharged. Attention is therefore focussed on the unjust factor question. Birks contrasts *Craven-Ellis* v *Canons Ltd* as a case where the unjust factor was mistake as to a present fact, with *In re Cleadon Trust Ltd* in which there was simply a misprediction: the director confidently expected to be repaid. See Birks, 147 and 167. Birks accordingly considers that the case could only have succeeded on the grounds of free acceptance, but only if the liability was discharged by the subsequent approbation of the liquidator: Birks, 289–90. It may in addition be arguable that the case should have been decided on the basis of total failure of consideration: namely, that the director received nothing in return for his expenditure. However, the director had not bargained for anything in return or specified the basis on which he was making the transfer, and was in effect a risk-taker: Birks, 278. This appears to be supported by the reasoning of the majority of the Court of Appeal. Scott LJ (at 311–12) referred to:

> two fundamental conclusions of fact to be drawn from the evidence: (1) that the company as a juridical persona took no action whatsoever; it could take none and was therefore wholly impassive; and (2) the appellant's advances so far as the company was concerned were purely voluntary and gratuitous.

Sir Wilfred Greene MR dissented, allowing the claim in equity, by analogy with the cases on subrogation: see Goff and Jones, 153–56; Mitchell, 162–64. For an early discussion of the two cases, see Denning, '*Quantum Meruit*: The Case of *Craven-Ellis* v *Canons Ltd*' (1939) 55 LQR 54.

More recently, the case of *Rover International Ltd* v *Cannon Film Sales Ltd* [1989] 1 WLR 912 demonstrates the operation of *quantum meruit* in relation to void contracts. Rover's claim for the repayment of instalments of money has already been discussed in 12.2.1 above. In addition, as part of the joint venture arrangement under the void contract, it was agreed that Rover would arrange for the dubbing of the films into Italian, related artwork and other expenses. The films remained the property of Cannon at all times. The work done in respect of the films was to be taken into account in apportioning the profits under the terms of the purported agreement. The underlying contract being void for Rover's incapacity, a claim was made for the valuable services done by it and its sister company in respect of the films. By the appeal stage it was common ground, in the words of Kerr LJ (at 922) that:

> Rover's claim for something by way of a *quantum meruit* was irresistible in principle. In the face of the common mistaken belief held by both parties until about 25 July 1986 that the agreement was binding ... the task of the court — to put it broadly for the moment — was clearly to carry out a process of equitable restitution.

The concession was said to be rightly made. The *quantum meruit* would include an element of reasonable remuneration (presumably an element of profit over and above time and money expended). The ground for restitution was accordingly mistake, or possibly failure of consideration. Accordingly the unjust factor was the same for the money and the non-money claims. See on the issue of symmetry, Birks (1990) 2 JCL 227, at 229–30.

Having conceded the existence of a right to a *quantum meruit*, the defendants sought to undermine it by arguing for a contractual ceiling. This argument was misconceived. The argument sought to vivify the terms of the void contract to limit the recovery of Rover. Crucial to the argument, however, was that Rover should be limited to the benefits to which it would have been entitled up to date of the termination of the purported agreement by Cannon pursuant to an express termination clause. This would have rendered the quantum of recovery derisory. Kerr LJ regarded the reliance upon the voidness of the contract and the assertion of the contractual ceiling as an impermissible attempt to have 'the best of both worlds' (at 927). The contractual ceiling argument was flawed because in principle such an argument is based upon the assumption of risk by a party under a once valid and binding transaction. The argument is inapplicable to contracts which are void *ab initio* where the risk has never been run. The rejection of the inappropriate and exceptionally stringent contractual ceiling in *Rover* v *Cannon* does not undermine arguments in favour of contractual ceilings in their appropriate context, where a contract has been discharged by termination for breach. In addition, the case cannot be taken as a rejection of the concept of a valuation ceiling relevant only to the enrichment question, whereby a *quantum meruit* is calculated by reference to a contractual rate of remuneration. Here, a valuation ceiling may be appropriate because the contractual rate of remuneration establishes the subjective valuation of the recipient of the benefit received. For discussion see Birks (1990) 2 JCL 227, at 231–33; Beatson (1989) 105 LQR 179.

A *quantum meruit* claim was also advanced in *Guinness plc* v *Saunders* [1990] 2 AC 662. It will be recalled that the House of Lords ordered restitution of money paid by Guinness to one of its former directors under a contract which was void for want of authority. Mr Ward, the former director, sought to resist summary judgment by advancing a counterclaim for the value of the services rendered under the purported contract. This was unanimously rejected by the House of Lords. Lord Templeman's speech is unfortunate in that it is infected by traces of the implied contract heresy. Indeed his Lordship anachronistically sought to explain *Craven-Ellis* v *Canons Ltd* on the basis of an implied contract (at 693). This would appear to be a more archaic approach than was actually adopted by the Court of Appeal in that 1930s case. Lord Templeman thought it was sufficient to observe that the plaintiff in *Craven-Ellis* was not a director, and accordingly there was no obstacle to a claim for a *quantum meruit*. Lord Templeman was, however, emphatic that where the articles entrusted the power of remuneration to the board of directors, the court would not intervene to short-circuit that aspect of the corporate constitution. Mr Ward was in any event bound as a member of the board of directors to carry out the services which he had rendered. The claim was put forward alternatively on the basis of a common law *quantum meruit* or an equitable allowance for a fiduciary. Lord Templeman gave short shrift to the latter way of putting the case, by insisting that a trustee must not profit from the trust, except as provided by the trust deed, or in this case the articles of association. Lord Goff considered either basis of claim to be inconsistent with the principle that a fiduciary must not place himself in a position of conflict of interest, and accordingly is not allowed to seek remuneration except as expressly provided for by the trust deed (or in this case, articles of association). While an equitable allowance had been allowed in *Boardman* v *Phipps* [1967] 2 AC 46, that jurisdiction would not be awarded in every case. Lord Goff observed (at 701):

> It seems to me therefore that it can only be reconciled with [the no conflict rule] to the extent that the exercise of the equitable jurisdiction does not conflict with the policy underlying the rule. And, as I see it, such a conflict will only be avoided if the exercise of the jurisdiction is restricted to those cases where it cannot have the effect of encouraging trustees in any way to put themselves in a position where their interests conflict with their duties as trustees.

The circumstances of Mr Ward were very different from those in *Boardman* v *Phipps*. Lord Goff was reluctant to decide whether the jurisdiction could extend to company directors, as well as trustees. His Lordship concluded (at 701–702):

> The simple fact remains that, by agreeing to provide his services in return for a substantial fee the size of which was to be dependent upon the amount of a successful bid by Guinness, Mr Ward was most plainly putting himself in a position in which his interests were in stark conflict with his duty as a director.

Accordingly, even where the contract was void, the award of a *quantum meruit* for services rendered under the ineffective contract may still be displaced by other operative rules of law. Here, the policy of deterring fiduciaries from placing themselves in a position of conflict of interest precluded the award of any *quantum meruit* on the facts of this case. For discussion, see Birks, 'Restitution without Counter-Restitution' [1990] LMCLQ 330, and Beatson and Prentice (1990) 106 LQR 365. Note that the transaction would now be governed by s. 35A and s. 322A of the Companies Act 1985 (as amended). See Birks [1990] LMCLQ 330, at 337–38. It seems unlikely that an insider such as Mr Ward would be able to enforce such a transaction as a company director.

12.4 THE 'SWAPS' LITIGATION

In a judgment delivered in January 1991 the House of Lords decided that local authorities lacked the capacity to enter into interest rate swap transactions. Thousands of such transactions had been entered into by local authorities before concern became widespread that they lacked the power to do so. The consequence of the public law decision was a decade of private law wrangling as those contracts were unwound. Indeed, it can be said that the litigation arising out of the swaps fiasco succeeded in propelling the arcane English law of restitution from its Victorian stultification into a principled regime fit for the twenty-first century.

Swaps have reached the House of Lords on three occasions. The most significant holding is the abrogation of the mistake of law rule. In addition, there have been rulings on ancillary practical matters such as the conflict of laws and interest. Swaps are properly considered alongside other void contracts. However, the reason for voidness, namely the incapacity of the local authorities, may be significant in the regime which the courts have adopted. The public policy underlying *ultra vires* is said to be the protection of the public and, in particular in this context, those who contribute to local government finances. The background to the swaps cases can be found in what remains a very informative contemporaneous discussion by Loughlin, 'Innovative Financing in Local Government: The Limits of Legal Instrumentalism' Part I in [1990] PL 372, especially at 388–406 and Part II in [1991] PL 568, especially at 568–82. A valuable recent survey with a restitutionary angle is McKendrick, 'Local Authorities and Swaps: Undermining the Market?' in R. Cranston (ed.), *Making Commercial Law — Essays in Honour of Roy Goode* (1997), 201.

12.4.1   What is a swap?

Interest rate swaps are an off-shoot of the Eurobond market and are a species of financial derivative. The principle underlying the transaction is explained by Loughlin [1990] PL 372, at 388:

> Two borrowers enter into an agreement to exchange interest rate payments on their debts. Party A has a debt at a floating rate of interest. He believes that interests rates are about to rise and therefore would like it fixed at the current market rate. Party B (known as a counterparty) is someone with a fixed-rate debt who thinks that interest rates are about to fall. She would therefore prefer to have a floating rate debt. The swaps market facilitates the exchange of risk on these debts. Party A, with a floating rate debt, pays fixed rate payments to his counterparty; in exchange Party B pays him at the floating rate.

These financial devices can be useful for many purposes. First, the management of commercial risk. Secondly, tax planning. Thirdly, and increasingly commonly, speculation. The Divisional Court's description of the mechanics of a swaps contract in *Hazell v Hammersmith and Fulham London Borough Council* [1992] 2 AC 1 was accepted by Lord Templeman (at 24):

> an agreement between two parties by which each agrees to pay the other on a specified date or dates an amount calculated by a reference to the interest which would have accrued over a given period on the same notional principal sum assuming different rates of interest are payable in each case. For example, one rate may be fixed at 10 per cent and the other may be equivalent to the six month

London Inter-bank Offered Rate ('LIBOR'). It the LIBOR rate over the period of the swap is higher than 10 per cent then the party agreeing to receive 'interest' in accordance with LIBOR will receive more than the party entitled to receive 10 per cent. Normally neither party will in fact pay the sums which it has agreed to pay over the period of the swap but instead will make a settlement on a 'net payment basis' under which the party owing the greater amount on any day simply pays the difference between the two amounts due to the other.

12.4.2   The *ultra vires* holding

By the end of the 1980s nearly 100 British local authorities had participated in the swaps market. Many had used it for sensible debt management, but increasingly it was seen as a way of generating additional income, especially by the use of front-end premiums (which allowed local authorities to circumvent central government restrictions upon their borrowing). However, some local authorities appeared to be indulging in speculation. Pre-eminent was the Hammersmith and Fulham London Borough Council, which entered into a total of 592 transactions involving a total notional value of £6 billion. At the height of its activity, Hammersmith had cornered 0.5 per cent of the world's swaps market. By the late 1980s concern was expressed by the Audit Commission for Local Authorities in England and Wales about the legality of these contracts. The local authority's powers were provided by s. 111(1) of the Local Government Act 1972:

> Without prejudice to any powers exercisable apart from this section but subject to the provisions of this Act and any other enactment passed before this Act, a local authority shall have power to do anything (whether or not involving expenditure, borrowing or lending of money or the acquisition of disposal of any property or rights) which is calculated to facilitate, or is conducive or incidental to, the discharge of any of their functions.

The Divisional Court and ultimately the House of Lords held, adopting a strict construction of the statute, that the transactions were *ultra vires* (*Hazell* v *Hammersmith and Fulham London Borough Council* [1990] 2 QB 697, [1992] 2 AC 1). In addition, the House of Lords was impressed by the fact that Parliament had granted building societies only limited statutory power to enter the swaps market (Building Societies Act 1986, s. 23; Building Societies (Prescribed Contracts) Order 1986 (SI 1986 No. 2098)). In the absence of an express power to enter into this market, the courts were not willing to imply such a power. Lord Ackner emphasised the policy of protecting the public from 'unlimited resort to the swap market' (at 46). The House of Lords in *Hazell* gave little guidance on the implication of its ruling for the many transactions which had been declared void at a stroke. Lord Templeman laconically stated (at 36): 'The consequences of any *ultra vires* transaction may depend on the facts of each case.'

In *Westdeutsche Landesbank Girozentrale* v *Islington London Borough Council* [1996] AC 669, Lord Goff of Chieveley commented upon the *Hazell* decision (at 680):

> I wish to record that it caused grave concern among financial institutions, and especially foreign banks, which had entered into such transactions with local authorities in good faith, with no idea that a rule as technical as the *ultra vires* doctrine might undermine what they saw as a perfectly legitimate commercial transaction.

Indeed his Lordship may have understated the level of concern, or rather consternation, amongst the commercial community. The decision in *Hazell* ran directly counter to the general trend of authority in the twentieth century of wherever possible avoiding the consequence of stigmatising a contract as void. *Hazell* was probably the worst decision for English commercial law during the twentieth century and is characteristic of the poor quality of judgments which emanated from the House of Lords in the late 1980s. The failure of the House of Lords to come to terms with the sophisticated practices of the swaps market and the realities of local authority funding are exposed by Loughlin [1991] PL 568, at 590–95. However, the Government refused to enact retrospective legislation to solve the difficulties. Accordingly, it was left to the immature law of restitution to pick up the pieces.

Before turning to the question of how the law developed to accommodate these transactions, it is worth noting Loughlin's doubts about the appropriateness of the principle of unjust enrichment in this context. First, ordering restitution would penalise local authorities which had used swaps for prudent debt management, but would benefit those like Hammersmith which had indulged in speculation. Secondly, attempting to return the parties to the *status quo* is both inappropriate and arguably impossible. In the sophisticated market of derivatives, where transactions are often linked together as part of a portfolio, it is simply not possible to undo the transaction and its consequences: 'The impact of full restitution of payment would be essentially arbitrary' ([1991] PL 568, at 575). However, that is a solution which the courts have adopted. The law was developed to order restitution of net benefits received. Arguments relying upon linked transactions have been rejected. So too have arguments against restitution where the transactions have been completed. English law has treated each individual swap agreement as though it were a discrete arrangement, rather than part of an overall risk-management strategy.

12.4.3   The lead cases

Nearly 200 writs were issued in the wake of *Hazell*. The Commercial Court, in a decisive piece of active case management, encouraged all the parties to cooperate to avoid any unnecessary duplication of issues. This was done by the selection of lead cases. In fact, many cases settled rather quickly. Burrows presciently pinpointed the reason for this ([1995] RLR 15):

The high rate of out-of-court settlements reflects a widely-shared view at the Bar, as I perceive it, that whichever party makes a gain from a void swap contract at the expense of the other party is, subject to defences, unjustly enriched and should make restitution; and that any barriers which the present law puts against that conclusion would be removed, if a case gets there, by the House of Lords.

Eventually, in early 1993, Hobhouse J tried two lead cases: *Westdeutsche Landesbank Girozentrale* v *Islington London Borough Council*; *Kleinwort Benson* v *Sandwell Borough Council* [1994] 4 All ER 890 (Hobhouse J and CA) (also known as *Swaps 1*) and *Kleinwort Benson Ltd* v *South Tyneside Metropolitan Borough Council* [1994] 4 All ER 972 (also known as *Swaps 2*). The *Westdeutsche* case eventually reached the House of Lords in an appeal confined to the question of interest ([1996] AC 669), in which Hobhouse J's first instance judgment was described as 'masterly' (at 682, *per* Lord Goff). Hobhouse J's judgment is indeed a remarkable achievement, spanning many questions in the law of restitution. It repays close study. The main finding which caused controversy, was that the ground for restitution in respect of void contracts was either 'no consideration' or 'absence of consideration' (see 12.2.1). It was common ground in the case that no illegality was involved. Hobhouse J identified the rationale of the *ultra vires* rule ([1994] 4 All ER 890, at 915): 'In the case of local authorities, it exists for the better regulation of local authorities in the public interest and, in relation to their revenue-raising powers, for the protection of their ratepayers (or charge payers).'

In addition to holding that absence of consideration was the unjust factor, Hobhouse J held (as the authorities then stood) that any mistake was a mistake of law and that the money could not be recovered on that basis (at 931). Hobhouse J rejected any suggestion that there was a voluntary assumption of risk that the transaction was invalid (which appears to be the same as a submission to an honest claim). See 33.1. In addition to the common law claim based on absence of consideration, Hobhouse J held that the plaintiffs were entitled to trace their money and to a proprietary claim in equity. This aspect of the case, while winning approval in the Court of Appeal did not survive examination in the House of Lords. See 30.7.3. Lastly, *Westdeutsche* includes seminal discussions of change of position (see 32.3), limitation (see 36.2) and interest (see 38.2). Further, Hobhouse J and the Court of Appeal held that there was no difference in principle between an open and closed swap. Net restitution was ordered, even though the supposed transaction had been fully performed. (See 12.2.2.) Subsequently, in *Kleinwort Benson Ltd* v *South Tyneside Metropolitan Borough Council* [1994] 4 All ER 972, Hobhouse J rejected a passing on defence (see 34.3).

12.4.4 The annuities cases

A remarkable feature of the swaps litigation was the rediscovery of a forgotten line of cases concerned with failure to comply with the terms of the Grants of Life Annuities Act 1777. Failure to register an annuity with the Court of Chancery within

20 days of execution rendered the arrangement null and void. However, the courts treated void as being voidable after the decision in *Davis* v *Bryan* (1827) 6 B & C 651, 108 ER 591. Crucial to Hobhouse J's reasoning was the fact that there were payments on both sides in the annuities contract. The beneficiary of the annuity could recover the premium paid, even though he had received instalments under the supposed contract. Such payments were held to be recoverable by both parties as money had and received (*Shove* v *Webb* (1787) 1 Term Rep 732, 99 ER 1348; *Hicks* v *Hicks* (1802) 3 East 16, 102 ER 502). The Court of Chancery reached the same position by granting a remedy of account (*Byne* v *Vivian* (1800) 5 Ves Jun 604, 31 ER 762; *Hoffman* v *Cooke* (1801) Ves Jun 623, 31 ER 772 and *Bromley* v *Holland* (1802) Coop G 9, 35 ER 458). Hobhouse J stressed that these cases were not based upon mistake of fact. Rather, *Hicks* v *Hicks* clearly established that restitution must be mutual. The parties must be returned to their original position. It was also urged upon Hobhouse J that the cases drew a distinction between partly- and fully-performed transactions. However, Hobhouse J rejected this. The resurrection of these archaic annuities cases was brief and is of little practical interest in the wake of the House of Lords decisions in the swaps cases.

12.4.5   The ground for restitution

This proved to be one of the most contentious issues in the swaps cases. Two particular problems arose. First, what was the correct characterisation of the personal obligation to make restitution at common law? Secondly, in addition to the common law claim, was any additional equitable relief available? The second problem gave rise to issues concerning both the unjust factor (the fourth question) and the nature of relief: whether personal or proprietary (the sixth question in the restitutionary enquiry). The resolution of these questions has proved central in the law of restitution as a whole. Accordingly it is discussed in detail elsewhere.

Briefly, in relation to the first issue, Hobhouse J and the Court of Appeal in *Westdeutsche* favoured a new unjust factor termed 'absence of consideration' or 'no consideration'. This attracted considerable academic criticism and accordingly the House of Lords in *Westdeutsche* reformulated the claim as one arising on the more traditional basis of a total failure of consideration ([1996] AC 669). The decision of the Court of Appeal in *Guinness Mahon & Co. Ltd* v *Kensington & Chelsea Royal London Borough Council* [1999] QB 215 demonstrates considerable continuing uncertainty on this question. See 12.2.1 above.

With regard to the second issue, both Hobhouse J and the Court of Appeal held that Westdeutsche was entitled to trace its money into the local authority's funds and to an equitable charge over those funds to secure the claim. As Hobhouse J pointed out, there was no question of the insolvency of the council. Accordingly, given that no problem of insolvency arose, and that there was no claim to any greater sum than the value received (leaving aside the question of interest), it is difficulty to see the need for a proprietary claim. The proprietary remedy was awarded by applying a very relaxed version of tracing and an instrumental implementation of the fiduciary relationship precondition. In contrast, the House of Lords emphatically and unanimously rejected the proprietary claim analysis. For discussion see 30.7.3.

Returning finally to the first problem, of the correct characterisation of the common law claim, the decision of the House of Lords in *Kleinwort Benson Ltd v Lincoln City Council* [1999] 2 AC 349 abrogated the mistake of law rule in respect of claims for restitution. At bottom, all the swaps cases turned upon the misconstruction of a particular statute, namely s. 111 of the Local Government Act 1972. More accurately, the ground for restitution can be stated to be ignorance of the law, rather than the mistake of law. Prior to the decision in *Hazell* there had been no authoritative ruling upon the capacity of local authorities in this context. For a full consideration of mistake of law and the swaps cases, see 3.5. In conclusion, mistake (or ignorance) of the law yielding a common law personal claim appears to be the most apt characterisation of the cause of action in the swaps cases. The argument that the mistake claim should be reinforced by a proprietary claim has not yet been advanced, but appears unlikely to succeed in view of the decision of the House of Lords in *Westdeutsche*.

12.4.6 Other Issues

The issue which concerned the House of Lords in *Westdeutsche* [1996] AC 669 was the availability of interest. Hobhouse J and the Court of Appeal, having concluded that an equitable proprietary claim was also available, held that they had the jurisdiction to grant compound, rather than simple, interest. In contrast, the House of Lords unanimously rejected the existence of an equitable proprietary claim. The majority held that in the result compound interest could not be awarded. Lords Goff and Woolf dissented, arguing that the courts should develop the power to grant compound interest in respect of all restitution claims. See 38.2.

On another ancillary matter, another House of Lords decision in *Kleinwort Benson Ltd v Glasgow City Council* [1999] 1 AC 153 provided an important ruling on the conflict of laws aspect of restitution. In particular, it provided guidance on the construction of Sch. 4 of the Civil Jurisdiction and Judgments Act 1982, which in a modified version of the Brussels Convention allocates jurisdiction between constituent parts on the United Kingdom. See 37.4.

A further decision of Hobhouse J, in *Morgan Grenfell & Co. Ltd v Welwyn Hatfield District Council* [1995] 1 All ER 1, addressed the question of the whether the swaps agreement were wagering contracts under the Gaming Act. Section 18 of the Gaming Act 1845 provides that agreements 'by way of gaming or wagering' are null and void. Hobhouse J neatly sidestepped Lord Templeman's observation that Hammersmith's activities in *Hazell* were 'more akin to gambling than insurance' ([1992] 2 AC 1, at 35). Hobhouse J decided that the purpose of the council was debt management, and any speculative dimension was only a subordinate element of the arrangement. In any event, the contracts were rescued by the provision in s. 63 of the Financial Services Act 1986 because they were entered into 'by way of business'.

In *TSB Bank of Scotland plc v Hatfield and Welwyn District Council* [1993] 2 Bank LR 267, Hobhouse J decided that a claim in restitution sounded in debt, rather than damages.

South Tyneside Metropolitan Borough Council v *Svenska International plc* [1995] 1 All ER 545, is an important case on change of position. Clarke J laid down a general rule that the change of position must be based upon an actual, not an anticipatory, receipt. See 32.3.

Lastly, *Kleinwort Benson Ltd* v *Birmingham City Council* [1997] QB 380 is a significant case where the courts have rejected the defence of passing on in respect of private transactions. See 34.3.

It can be seen that the issues covered in the swaps cases have made a wide-ranging contribution to the development of the law of restitution. However, one can hardly be sanguine about this given the immense amount of public money which must have been spent extricating the local authorities from the difficulties which they had partly brought upon themselves and were partly forced on them by the decision of the House of Lords in *Hazell*.

12.5   UNENFORCEABLE CONTRACTS

Sometimes legislation renders a contract unenforceable by one or both parties. What happens where a party, who is subject to a statutory preclusion of enforceability, confers a benefit upon the other? English law previously rendered unenforceable a large number of contracts under the Statute of Frauds 1677 and s. 40 of the Law of Property Act 1925 where there was insufficient compliance with specified formalities. The Statute of Frauds has now been largely abolished, except in respect of particular forms of guarantee. Similarly s. 40 of the Law of Property Act 1925 has been superseded by s. 2 of the Law of Property (Miscellaneous Provisions) Act 1989, which provides more starkly that there is no contract unless the requisite formalities are complied with. The Law Commission in recommending this change clearly contemplated that restitution would be available in appropriate cases where there was a supposed contract to dispose of an interest in land: *The Transfer of Land: Formalities and Contracts for Sale or other Dispositions of an Interest in Land* (Law Com. No. 164, 1987). See *Yaxley* v *Gotts* [1999] *The Times*, 8 July.

There is little modern authority on benefits transferred pursuant to unenforceable contracts. In line with general theory, the ground for restitution would appear to be failure of consideration, or possibly mistake. Failure of consideration would appear to be the basis of the claim for the return of a deposit paid by a would-be purchaser of land under an agreement expressly 'subject to contract', where the vendor was unwilling to complete (*Chillingworth* v *Esche* [1924] 1 Ch 97). In addition to demonstrating a failure of consideration, there is also first instance authority that the claimant must demonstrate that the recipient of the benefit was not ready, able or willing to perform his side of the unenforceable contract. In *Thomas* v *Brown* (1876) 1 QBD 714, the plaintiff entered into a contract to buy a leasehold interest in a shop from the defendant. She paid a deposit of £70. The purchaser had second thoughts about the transaction, because the vendor's name was not disclosed, and sought to repudiate it. She claimed the return of her deposit. The court held that it did not need to decide whether the agreement was unenforceable for insufficient compliance with the Statute of Frauds. Quain J refused the claim for restitution (at 723): 'Now where, upon a verbal contract for the sale of land, the purchaser pays the deposit and the vendor is always ready and willing to complete, I know of no authority to support the purchaser in bringing an action to recover back the money.' See Goff and Jones, 503. Burrows erects the ready-and-willing principle of *Thomas* v *Brown* into a general rule in respect of ineffective contracts, although there appears to be little necessity for this as a matter of principle: Burrows, 257–8.

Where money is paid under a contract which is rendered unenforceable by statute, or simply has no existence as under s. 2 of the Law of Property (Miscellaneous Provisions) Act 1989, the appropriate ground for recovery may be mistake or failure of consideration. The liberalisation of mistake, to include mistake of law (and sheer ignorance of law) in *Kleinwort Benson Ltd* v *Lincoln City Council* [1999] 2 AC 349, should ensure that money claims give rise to few problems in practice. More problematical are claims for non-money benefits, such as services rendered under unenforceable contracts. The leading authority is a discussion by the High Court of Australia.

In *Pavey & Matthews Pty Ltd* v *Paul* (1987) 162 CLR 221, the High Court of Australia recognised the autonomy of the law of restitution and unjust enrichment as the 'unifying legal concept' which provided the subject's deeper structure (at 256, *per* Deane J). The plaintiff company was a licensed builder which had renovated a cottage for Ms Paul under an oral contract. Section 45 of the Builders Licensing Act 1971 (New South Wales) provided:

A contract ... under which the holder of a licence undertakes to carry out ... any building work ... specified in a building contract is not enforceable against the other party to the contract unless the contract is in writing signed by each of the parties ... and sufficiently describes the building work the subject of the contract.

The work was done, and there was no allegation of defective performance. Ms Paul refused to pay. The builders sued for a *quantum meruit*. The High of Court of Australia, Brennan J dissenting, held that the section did not prevent a licensed builder from recovering upon a *quantum meruit* basis for the work done and materials supplied under an oral building contract. Mason, Wilson and Deane JJ explicitly described the right to recover as one based upon unjust enrichment, rather than an implied contract. The judgment of the High Court deployed impressive historical learning. Deane J delivered the leading judgment. Deane J stated that the old form of action accommodated two distinct categories of claim: first, the recovery of the debt under a genuinely consensually agreement; secondly, the recovery of a debt where the law itself imposes an obligation to pay for a benefit accepted (at 255). Deane J criticised older English authority such as *Scott* v *Pattison* [1923] 2 KB 723, which treated claims to recover a benefit conferred under a fully executed but unenforceable contract as belonging within the first category. In an important passage Deane J stated (at 256):

It follows from what has been said above that the cases in which a claimant has been held entitled to recover in respect of an executed consideration under an agreement upon which the Statute of Frauds precluded the bringing of an action should be seen as falling within the second and not the first category. In that second category of case, the tendency of common lawyers to speak in terms of implied contract, rather than in terms of obligation imposed by law ... should be recognized as but a reflection of the influence of discarded fictions, buried forms of action and the conventional conviction that, if the common law claim could not properly be framed in tort, it must necessarily be dressed in the language of contract. That tendency should not be allowed to conceal the fact that, in that category of case, the action was not based upon a genuine agreement at all. Indeed, if there was a valid and enforceable agreement governing the claimant's right to compensation, there would be neither occasion nor legal justification for the law to superimpose or impute an obligation or promise to pay a reasonable remuneration. The quasi-contractual obligation to pay fair and just compensation for a benefit which has been accepted will only arise in a case where there is no applicable genuine agreement or where such an agreement is frustrated, avoided or unenforceable. In such a case, it is the very fact that there is no genuine agreement or that the genuine agreement is frustrated, avoided or unenforceable that provides the occasion for (and part of the circumstances giving rise to) the imposition of the obligation to make restitution.

A number of points must be made. First, Deane J asserts that recovery of an executed consideration under an unenforceable contract sounds in quasi-contract or restitution, not contract. Secondly, it is clear that Deane J is explicitly considering the contractual matrix question here. If there were a genuine and effective consensual agreement, there could be no right to recourse to the law of restitution, in accordance with the principle of subsidiarity or the primacy of contract. Thirdly, Deane J held that the unenforceable contract was not irrelevant, but could constitute evidence of what work was requested and accepted under the transaction. Fourthly, where the unenforceable contract has not been rescinded or terminated, the *Thomas* v *Brown* requirement applied. The claimant must demonstrate that the defendant is not ready and willing to perform the obligations under the arrangement. Lastly, the unenforceable contract may be referred to for the purposes of a contractual, or more properly a valuation, ceiling (at 257):

> The defendant will also be entitled to rely on the unenforceable contract, if it has been executed but not rescinded, to limit the amount recoverable by the plaintiff the contractual amount in a case where that amount is less than what would constitute fair and reasonable remuneration.

In contrast, Dawson J took the view that the claim sounded in contract, rather than restitution. However, in his Honour's view the claim was enforceable because it was a case involving an executed consideration. The oral agreement in *Pavey* was one to pay a reasonable remuneration. Accordingly, whether one sees a claim as arising in contract or in unjust enrichment, the quantum of recovery would be the same. The issue which divided the majority of the High Court of Australia from Brennan J was whether the public policy underlying the New South Wales legislation precluded not just a claim in contract, but the distinct claim in unjust enrichment. Brennan J concluded (at 244): 'In my opinion, s. 45 precludes the arising of an enforceable debt. The contractual promise to pay is clearly unenforceable and there is no room, while the unenforceable contract is subsisting, for a quasi-contractual claim.' This appears, with respect to his Honour, to give too much emphasis to the terms of the unenforceable contract. The reasoning appears to rest upon an extreme version of the primacy of contract or subsidiary principle. However, the third question in the restitutionary enquiry does not preclude recourse to the law of unjust enrichment where the supposed contract is ineffective, because it is discharged by reason of breach or frustration, or is otherwise void or unenforceable. Accordingly, on this point the view of Deane J is to be preferred. However, to the extent to which Brennan J's reasoning rests upon the fact that to allow a claim in quasi-contract or unjust enrichment would frustrate the policy of the statute, it is submitted that his reasoning is to be preferred to that of the majority. On this point the reasoning of the majority is less convincing. Deane J observed (at 262):

> It may be that the bringing of an action as on a common indebitatus count would conflict with the apparent legislative policy underlying s. 45 if the claimant in such an action were entitled as of right to recover the amount which the building owner had agreed to pay under the unenforceable agreement.

This did not apply where the claim entitled the builder only to reasonable remuneration for work actually done. However, it must be observed that in *Pavey*, Ms Paul did end up having to pay the amounts stipulated under the oral contract, which is the very thing the statute rendered unenforceable by the builder.

A different view, following an extremely valuable review of the historical background, is that of Ibbetson who concludes ((1988) 8 OJLS 312, at 326):

> Despite the lengthy consideration of the possibility of the existence of a restitutionary remedy in this context, we should not lose sight of the fact that it still has to be established that the restitutionary remedy should be available in any particular case. In some situations, perhaps, the statutory language will be such as to indicate that it should not be. *Pavey* v *Paul* is close to the borderline and there is a superficial attraction in the argument that the allowance of the plaintiff's *quantum meruit* claim amounts in reality to enforcement of the contract, the very result which the Builders Licencing Act outlaw. This argument is adequately countered by Mason, Wilson and Deane JJ. Although the *quantum meruit* recovered by Pavey is in fact identical to what had been promised in the contract, this is wholly coincidental and completely independent of the parties' agreement. If he had been promised a determinate sum, still his recovery would only have been on a *quantum meruit*.

Ibbetson concludes that the appropriate unjust factor was free acceptance. For further consideration as to whether free acceptance or failure of consideration is the appropriate unjust factor, see 15.2. For further consideration of the question of whether public policy should have precluded a restitutionary claim in this context, see 35.5.

12.6   UNAUTHORISED CONDUCT OF INSURANCE BUSINESS

Section 2 of the Insurance Companies Act 1974, which was superseded by s. 2 of the Insurance Companies Act 1982, prohibited the carrying on of insurance business in the UK by unauthorised persons. The unenforceability of contracts entered into in breach of s. 2 is now provided for in s. 132 of the Financial Services Act 1986, which has effectively been held to have retrospective effect in respect of all business conducted in breach of both the 1974 and the 1982 Acts.

The case law both prior to and subsequent to the passing of the 1986 Act illustrates the considerable difficulties which statutory prohibition creates both in respect of the enforceability of contracts and the availability of restitution in respect of such arrangements. It is worth briefly reviewing the jurisprudence. Before the passing of the 1986 Act this topic would have been included under illegal contracts in Chapter 13. In *Bedford Insurance Co. Ltd* v *Instituto de Resseguros Do Brasil* [1985] QB 966, Parker J held that reinsurance contracts entered into in breach of s. 2 of the Insurance Companies Act 1974 were void *ab initio*. The interpretation section of the Act defined insurance business as 'effecting and carrying out contracts of insurance' (s. 83). Accordingly the performance of the contract by the reinsurers fell within the mischief of the Act. Those obligations were unenforceable. Subsequently, in *Stewart* v *Oriental Fire and Marine Insurance Co. Ltd* [1985] QB 988, Leggatt J reached the opposite conclusion. The court enforced a reinsurance contract entered into in breach of the 1974 Act at the suit of the reinsured. Leggatt J referred to the 'widespread consternation' caused by the earlier decision in *Bedford* (at 997) and accepted a submission that it was wrong. Leggatt J cited with approval the decision of the High Court of Australia in *Yango Pastoral Co. Pty Ltd* v *First Chicago Australia Ltd* (1978) 139 CLR 410, which permitted an unauthorised banking business to enforce mortgages and guarantees. Leggatt J did not accept Parker J's view that the statute expressly prohibited the formation or the performance of contract. Leggatt J stated (at 1009):

It is not the intention of the statute to leave a person uninsured who has entered into an apparently valid contract of insurance of a relevant class with an insurer who turns out, unbeknown to the person seeking insurance, to have effected it without authorisation and to be similarly without authorisation to carry it out.

Further, he concluded (at 1011):

To render individual contracts of insurance void would indeed be not merely inconsistent with the policy of the Act of 1974 but would be repugnant to it. Public policy requires the protection, rather than the prejudice, of insured persons, and at the very least should avoid an offending insurer being able to resist the payment of claims.

The leading case prior to the passing of the 1986 Act, which sought to resolve this controversy, was *Phoenix General Insurance Co. of Greece SA* v *Halvanon Insurance Co. Ltd* [1988] QB 216. At first instance Hobhouse J struck an intermediate position. The general purpose of the 1974 Act was to protect potential insured parties. Hobhouse J observed (at 230): 'The Act therefore does not make the transaction of insurance *per se* objectionable or illegal; it merely prohibits one party from engaging in it, unless he has first obtained the requisite authorisation.' Further, rejecting the approach of both *Bedford* and *Stewart* Hobhouse J concluded (at 232): 'The illegality does affect the whole of the transaction but only the part of the plaintiffs in them.' It was necessary to separate two questions of enforceability: (i) enforceability by the innocent insured party; (ii) enforceability by the guilty insurance company.

The Court of Appeal in *Phoenix* was able to hold that the particular transactions were saved by the transitional provisions pursuant to the insurance legislation. However, in influential dicta the Court of Appeal preferred the view reached by Parker J in *Bedford* and overruled the decision of Leggatt J in *Stewart*. Kerr LJ stated (at 268): 'any contract which is prohibited by statute, either expressly or by implication, is illegal and void.' Kerr LJ acknowledged that to construe the legislation prohibiting the contract would 'prevent the insured from claiming under the contract and would merely leave him with the doubtful remedy of seeking to recover his premium as money had and received' (at 273). While acknowledging that statute could impose either a bilateral or a unilateral prohibition upon a contract, Kerr LJ held he was bound by the language of s. 83 of the 1974 Act to hold that the obligations of both parties were prohibited by necessary implication. Subsequently in *Re Cavalier Insurance Co. Ltd* [1989] 2 Lloyd's Rep 430, an insured party to an unenforceable contract was held to be entitled to restitution of the premium on the grounds of total failure of consideration, in circumstances where the parties were not *in pari delicto*. In contrast, where claims had been made and paid there was no total failure.

However, this convoluted common law tale is confined to legal history in the light of the passing of s. 132 of the Financial Services Act 1986 and its subsequent interpretation by the Court of Appeal. The authorities do, however, illustrate divergent judicial attitudes to statutory prohibition and the problem of the enforceability of contacts made in breach of statute. It is submitted that the approach of Hobhouse J in *Phoenix* was more consistent with the policy of the Act. The Court of Appeal in *Hughes* v *Asset Management plc* [1993] 3 All ER 669 was able to hold that the prohibition of unauthorised persons from dealing in securities under the (now repealed) Prevention of Fraud (Investments) Act 1958 did not render resulting contracts unenforceable. Nothing in this statute compelled this result. The Court followed the reasoning, but not the result, in *Phoenix*.

The drafting of s. 132 of the Financial Services Act 1986 is not entirely happy. The material parts provide:

(1)   Subject to subsection (3) below, a contract of insurance ... which is entered into by a person in the course of carrying on insurance business in contravention of section 2 of the Insurance Companies Act 1982 shall be unenforceable against the other party; and that party shall be entitled to recover any money or other property paid or transferred by him under the contract, together with compensation for any loss sustained by him as a result of having parted with it.
. . .
(3)   A court may allow a contract to which subsection (1) above applies to be enforced or money or property paid or transferred under it to be retained if it is satisfied—
(a)   that the person carrying on insurance business reasonably believed that his entering into the contract did not constitute a contravention of section 2 of the said Act of 1982; and
(b)   that it is just and equitable for the contract to be enforced or, as the case may be, for the money or property paid or transferred under it to be retained.
(4)   Where a person elects not to perform a contract which by virtue of this section is unenforceable against him or by virtue of this section recovers money or property paid or transferred under a contract he shall not be entitled to any benefits under the contract and shall repay any money and return any other property received by him under the contract.
. . .
(6)   A contravention of section 2 of the said Act of 1982 shall not make a contract of insurance illegal or invalid to any greater extent than is provided in this section; and a contravention of that section in respect of any contract of insurance shall not affect the validity of any reinsurance contract entered into in respect of that contract.

This is as tangled a provision as it may be possible to envisage. The 1986 Act, and s. 132 in particular, received its Royal Assent some 29 days after the decision of the Court of Appeal in *Phoenix*.

A number of points may be made about the provisions of the Act. First, the intention appears to be to render unauthorised contracts of insurance unenforceable by the insurer, but enforceable by the insured: s. 132(1). Secondly, the unauthorised contract of insurance is not illegal or invalid beyond the basic provision in s. 132(1) that it is unenforceable by the insurer: s. 132(6). Thirdly, the court is given a discretion in appropriate circumstances to allow the contract to be enforced by the insurer: s. 132(3). Fourthly, and of significance to the law of restitution, s. 132(1) entitles the insured to recover any money or other property transferred under the contract, and in addition compensation. However, the insured must elect between enforceability and rescission. The two are not cumulative: s. 132(4). Presumably an insured can wait and see whether the risk eventuates, during the currency of the partially unenforceable contract. If it does not, the insured could perhaps choose to rescind on the last day of the risk. If the risk eventuates, the insured will elect to enforce. This appears to be the purport of the section. Alternatively, it might be argued that once the insured discovers that the insurer is unauthorised he must elect whether to keep the arrangement open or to rescind and seek an authorised insurer elsewhere.

The leading discussion on the meaning of s. 132 is *Group Josi Re (formerly Groupe Josi Réassurance SA) v Walbrook Insurance Co. Ltd* [1996] 1 WLR 1152. Staughton LJ observed that the timing and 'questionable drafting' of the provision would suggest it was an ill-thought out response, aimed at reversing the decision of the Court of Appeal in *Phoenix*. However, it seems that the provision featured in the original version of the Bill, predating that decision. More likely, it seems that the provision was a response to the confusion caused by the earlier *Bedford* and *Stewart* cases. Saville LJ, in contrast, was emphatic that the provision was 'clearly designed to reverse the conclusion reached in the *Phoenix General Insurance* case'. Saville LJ helpfully summarised the effect of the legislation (at 1173):

> The central provision of the section is s. 132(1). To my mind this makes clear that the effect of the prohibition is only to make the contract of insurance unenforceable on the part of the insurers (subject to the saving in s. 132(3)), leaving it not only enforceable on the part of the insured, but also giving the insured the additional (and by s. 132(4) alternative) rights specified at the end of the subsection. In short s. 132 enables the insured to enforce the carrying out of the contract on the part of the insurers.

In addition, the Court of Appeal in *Group Josi Re* reached a startling conclusion that the 1986 Act had retrospective effect. Earlier in *D. R. Insurance Co. v Seguros American Banamex* [1993] 1 Lloyd's Rep 120, Mr Adrian Hamilton QC, sitting as Deputy Judge, held that the section did not have retrospective effect. That was rejected by Gatehouse J in *Bates v Barrow Ltd* [1995] 1 Lloyd's Rep 680. Staughton LJ preferred the latter view. His Lordship preferred a purposive interpretation of s. 132 in order to prevent insurance companies refusing to pay claims on the basis that they were unauthorised. *Group Josi Re* concerned business carried on between 1974 and 1976 by a Belgian reinsurance company in breach of the 1974 Act. This did not pose a problem. In the view of Saville LJ, the only statute rendering unauthorised insurance illegal, void or unenforceable at the relevant time was the 1982 Act. Saville LJ was emphatic that the 1986 Act had retrospective effect at least in respect of contracts governed by s. 2 of the 1982 Act. In addition, on the facts of the present case the performance of the contract in question was to take place after the coming into force of s. 132. The practical effect in *Group Josi Re* is that s. 132 has retrospective effect. Whereas the reasons advanced may not be compelling, one can applaud the Court of Appeal for extending the protective effect of the section. In the result, it provides a protected class of persons with the unilateral right to enforce a contract, together with the additional right of rescission and restitution if they so elect.

FURTHER READING

Asterisks indicate especially useful works.

Void contracts

Goff and Jones, 499–509, 578–606; 652–62

P. Birks, 'Restitution for services' [1974] CLP 13

A. Denning, '*Quantum Meruit*: The Case of *Craven-Ellis* v *Canons Ltd*' (1939) 55 LQR 54

*P. Birks, 'Restitution after ineffective contracts: Issues for the 1990s' (1990) 2 JCL 227

J. Carter, 'Services rendered under ineffective contracts' [1990] LMCLQ 495, 506–509

*P. Birks, 'Restitution without counter-restitution' [1990] LMCLQ 330

S. Arrowsmith, 'Ineffective transactions and unjust enrichment: A framework for analysis' (1989) 9 LS 121

S. Arrowsmith, 'Ineffective transactions, unjust enrichment and problems of policy' (1989) 9 LS 307

On the swaps cases

D. Cowan 'Banks, Swaps, Restitution and Equity' [1993] LMCLQ 300

*P. Birks, 'No consideration: Restitution after void contracts' (1993) U W Aus L Rev 195

A. Burrows, 'Swaps and the friction between common law and equity' [1995] RLR 15

*E. McKendrick, 'Local Authorities and Swaps: Undermining the Market' in R. Cranston (ed.), *Making Commercial Law — Essays in Honour of Roy Goode* (1997), 201–37 (a valuable survey of the background and main issues in the swaps cases)

A. Hudson, *Swaps, Trusts and Restitution* (1999)

P. Birks and F. Rose (eds.), *Lessons from the Swaps Litigation* (2000)

Unenforceable contracts

A. Denning, '*Quantum Meruit* and the Statute of Frauds' (1925) 41 LQR 79

*D. Ibbetson, 'Implied Contracts and Restitution: History in the High Court of Australia' (1988) 8 OJLS 312

J. Beatson, 'Unjust Enrichment in the High Court of Australia' (1988) 104 LQR 13

Unauthorised insurance contracts

M. Clarke, 'Illegal Insurance' [1987] LMCLQ 201

13 Illegality and Public Policy as Grounds for Restitution

13.1 THEORETICAL FOUNDATIONS

The starting-point is the proposition that modern legal systems generally promote the freedom to transact. Accordingly, freedom of contract and the right to dispose of one's wealth as one sees fit constitute part of the deeper structure of our civil law. This commitment to individual autonomy rests upon a policy choice. However, public policy may also identify countervailing reasons why a prima facie enforceable transaction should not be accompanied by legal obligations. The topic of illegality cuts across the provinces of contract, property, trusts and restitution. Our concern is obviously primarily the last. However, the necessary starting-point is the general principles as they developed in relation to contractual cases. As is often the case, where common lawyers lack surefootedness, they resort to Latin maxims. There are two time-honoured principles. First, *ex turpi causa non oritur actio*, or in the vernacular 'no right of action arises out of a shameful cause'. Secondly, *in pari delicto potior est conditio defendentis*, or in the vernacular, 'where both are guilty of wrongdoing, the position of the defendant is stronger'.

The main source of public policy precluding the enforcement of obligations is statutory prohibition. In addition, the courts have enumerated their own common law heads of public policy. Two major problems have blighted English law under this heading. First, the courts have not always been sensitive in the exercise of statutory construction in ascertaining the public policy underlying the statute. In the result, often the very party which the statute intended to protect has suffered as a result of a blunt application of the illegality rule. Secondly, having regard to express or implied statutory prohibitions may have been less problematical in the pre-industrial age. However, in the modern regulatory state the proliferation of regulatory Acts and delegated legislation has posed problems for this topic, which the judiciary has not always been able to cope with successfully. In the post-war period a new approach was developed, eventually yielding the 'public conscience' test which in effect gave the judges a discretion in considering whether or not to deny enforceability of obligations. That development was repudiated by the House of Lords in the early 1990s, signalling a return to the traditional rules (although these are often difficult to discern and apply). Any rationalisation of this topic now requires legislative action, and the Law Commission has recently published a consultation paper: *Illegal Transactions: The Effect of Illegality on Contracts and Trusts* (LCCP, No. 154, 1998).

With respect to illegality in the law of restitution, it is necessary to draw a distinction between causes of action and defences (although this is not easy to do). Illegality *per se* is obviously not a restitutionary cause of action. However, within this context there are arguably two distinct grounds for restitution. First, the unjust factor of 'repentance' or repudiation of an illegal transaction (usually identified by the Latin tag, *locus poenitentiae*, or 'time for penitence'), which despite its theological-sounding name appears to rest upon a public policy of encouraging withdrawal from illegal enterprises. However, its scope is something of a matter for debate. Secondly, where the parties are not equally steeped in wrongdoing (*non in pari delicto*) the more innocent party, or a member of a protected class, may be entitled to restitution to escape from the transaction. This latter topic overlaps with the question of defences. Where a contract or other transaction is unenforceable by reason of illegality, the obligations will be unenforceable, and further illegality will operate as a defence to any attempt to seek the recovery of benefits transferred. The exception for parties who are not *in pari delicto* can be seen as an exception to that general rule of illegality operating to preclude a restitutionary claim. Alternatively, it may be categorised as a special class of case for a particular instance of transactional inequality. The main discussion of illegality precluding restitutionary claims is postponed to Chapter 35. Lastly, it should be noted that the phrase 'illegality' tends to be used without any degree of precision. It may be preferable to use the term 'public policy' as either grounding or precluding a restitutionary claim. However, restitutionary texts identify public policy as a separate topic from illegality which may ground or preclude restitutionary claims. These will also need to be considered briefly. However, it can be difficult to draw a line with any precision between the traditional cases of illegality and the more modern analysis in terms of public policy.

13.2   THE CONTRACTUAL RULES

The seminal statement of principle was by Lord Mansfield in *Holman* v *Johnson* (1775) 1 Cowp 341 at 343, 98 ER 1120:

> The objection, that a contract is immoral or illegal as between plaintiff and defendant, sounds at all times very ill in the mouth of the defendant. It is not for his sake, however, that the objection is ever allowed; but it is founded on general principles of policy, which the defendant has the advantage of, contrary to the real justice, as between him and the plaintiff, by accident, if I may say so. The principle

of public policy is this; *ex dolo malo non oritor actio*. No Court will lend its aid to a man who founds his cause of action upon an immoral or illegal act. If, from the plaintiff's own stating or otherwise, the cause of action appears to arise *ex turpi causa* or the transgression of a positive law of this country, there the court says he has no right to be assisted. It is upon that ground that the Court goes; not for the sake of the defendant, but because they will not lend their aid to such a plaintiff. If the plaintiff and the defendant were to change sides and the defendant was to be bring his action against the plaintiff, the latter would then have the advantage of it; where both are equally at fault, *potior est conditio defendentis*.

In contrast, the post-war period saw the development of a 'public conscience' test which appears to have been founded in part upon seminal discussions by Devlin J in *St John Shipping Corp.* v *Joseph Rank Ltd* [1957] 1 QB 267 and by Diplock LJ in *Hardy* v *Motor Insurers' Bureau* [1964] 2 QB 745. However, the new test went further than these authoritative discussions. A sequence of cases in the late 1980s articulated the so-called public conscience test: *Thackwell* v *Barclays Bank plc* [1986] 1 All ER 676, *Saunders* v *Edwards* [1987] 1 WLR 1116, *Euro-Diam Ltd* v *Bathurst* [1990] 1 QB 1 and *Howard* v *Shirlstar Container Transport Ltd* [1990] 1 WLR 1292. The approach was best summarised by Nicholls LJ in the Court of Appeal in *Tinsley* v *Milligan* [1992] Ch 310, at 319:

> the underlying principle is the so-called public conscience test. The court must weigh, or balance, the adverse consequences of granting relief against the adverse consequences of refusing relief. The ultimate decision calls for a value judgment.

This more flexible approach was rejected by both the minority and the majority in the House of Lords in *Tinsley* v *Milligan* [1994] 1 AC 340. Lord Goff of Chieveley, of the minority, stressed that the statement of principle by Lord Mansfield in *Holman* v *Johnson* was not a principle of justice, but rather a principle of policy which led to indiscriminate and unfair consequences. The established rules allowed no room for any discretion. Lord Goff accordingly rejected the balancing operation enunciated in the Court of Appeal which would have revolutionised legal rules which had been established for 200 years. His Lordship thought reform of the rules was better left to the Law Commission and the legislature. Lord Goff concluded (at 362): 'As I read the authorities, they reveal a consistent application of the principle [of illegality], subject only to the recognition of a *locus poenitentiae* for the claimant where the illegal purpose has not been carried into effect.' Lord Browne-Wilkinson, on behalf of the majority, agreed with Lord Goff's rejection of the public conscience test. More recently, the High Court of Australia in *Nelson* v *Nelson* (1995) 184 CLR 538 has not spoken with a single voice on this question. Toohey J, dissenting in part, appeared to apply the public conscience test (at 595–7), whereas McHugh J explicitly rejected the unstructured discretion which the test conferred, preferring the greater certainty of clearly expressed principles (at 611–14). For discussion see LCCP, No. 154, paras 4.1 to 4.5.

13.3   REPENTANCE AS A GROUND FOR RESTITUTION

For Birks, this is a species of policy-motivated restitution, aimed at discouraging the perpetration of illegal conduct: Birks, 299–303. Two difficult questions arise. First, when can a claimant successfully repudiate an illegal transaction and claim restitution? How late can he leave it? The courts have show greater and lesser degrees of indulgence on this point. Secondly, does the claimant need to be genuinely penitent, or does timeous withdrawal, for whatever reason, suffice?

In *Taylor* v *Bowers* (1876) 1 QBD 291, the plaintiff had transferred his stock-in-trade to his nephew with a view to deceiving his creditors. Before there was any agreement with the creditors, the nephew transferred the goods (apparently without the consent of the plaintiff) to the defendant who was one of the plaintiff's creditors. At first instance Cockburn CJ stressed that other than transferring the goods to the nephew, nothing more had been done to further the fraudulent scheme before the plaintiff repudiated the transaction. Cockburn CJ concluded (at 295):

Under these circumstances, we think that the plaintiff is entitled to recover back his property from the defendant. The action is not founded upon the illegal agreement, nor brought to enforce it, but, on the contrary, the plaintiff has repudiated the agreement, and his action is found on that repudiation.

The Court of Appeal agreed.

A note of caution was struck in *Kearley* v *Thomson* (1890) 24 QBD 742, in which the plaintiff bribed the defendant solicitors not to appear at the public examination of his bankrupt friend. The defendants took the money and did not appear. Before the plaintiff's friend was discharged from bankruptcy, the plaintiff claimed restitution for the £40 he had paid to the defendants. It was held, in the light of the part-performance, that it was too late to succeed on the grounds of repentance. Fry LJ was sceptical about the statement of principle in *Taylor* v *Bowers*, and suggested re-examination. It any event, it would not apply in the case of part-performance. Fry LJ illustrated this with an example (at 747):

Let me put an illustration of the doctrine contended for, which was that partial performance did not prevent the recovery of the money. Suppose a payment of £100 by A to B on a contract that the latter shall murder C and D. He has murdered C, but not D. Can the money be recovered back? In my opinion it cannot be.

The leading modern authority on the contractual rules insists on genuine repentance and may render this cause of action of little practical significance. In *Bigos* v *Bousted* [1951] 1 All ER 92, the claimant had entered into a scheme to circumvent exchange controls in order to ensure a sufficient supply of Italian currency for his wife and daughter during a stay in Italy. The claimant transferred a share certificate as security for this arrangement. The transferee did not perform, and in any event the claimant's wife and daughter returned home earlier than intended. The claimant sought the return of the share certificate from the transferee. Pritchard J reviewed the authorities and concluded (at 100) that they demonstrated that:

> there is a distinction between what may, for convenience, be called the repentance cases, on the one hand, and the frustration cases, on the other hand. If a particular case may be held to fall within the category of repentance cases, I think the law is that the court will help a person who repents, provided his repentance comes before the illegal purposes has been substantially performed.

Whereas the judge was willing to hold that there had been no part-performance to exclude the claimant from the remedy, he was not prepared to hold that this was a genuine case of repentance. Rather, the premature return of his family was the true occasion for his withdrawal from the illegal transaction.

In contrast, in a leading modern case on illegality and trusts, the Court of Appeal has taken the opposite view. In *Tribe v Tribe* [1996] Ch 107, Millett LJ observed (at 135):

> It is impossible to reconcile all the authorities in the circumstances in which a party to an illegal contract is permitted to withdraw from it. At one time he was allowed to withdraw so long as the contract had not been completely performed; but later it was held that recovery was barred once it had been partly performed: see *Kearley v Thomson* (1890) 24 QBD 742. It is clear that he must withdraw voluntarily, and that it is not sufficient that he is forced to do so because his plan has been discovered. In *Bigos v Bousted* [1951] 1 All ER 92 this was, perhaps dubiously, extended to prevent withdrawal where the scheme has been frustrated by the refusal of the other party to carry out his part.
>
> I would hold that genuine repentance is not required. Justice is not a reward for merit; restitution should not be confined to the penitent. I would also hold that voluntary withdrawal from an illegal transaction when it is ceased to be needed is sufficient.

It is submitted that this approach is correct, and that this should be applied as it was clearly intended to, to all illegal transactions, including contracts and trusts. It is misconceived to attempt to strike a high moral tone in respect of transactions where inevitably neither parties' hands are clean. If repentance, or rather repudiation of an illegal transaction, is to remain a distinct unjust factor, the following preconditions should be sufficient. First, there must be a voluntary withdrawal from the illegal transaction. Secondly, the transaction must be executory, or alternatively there must have been no significant part-performance. It may be that this latter requirement may be superseded by a regime which allows for recovery in cases of part-performance, but subject to a requirement of counter-restitution.

13.4   WHERE THE PARTIES ARE NOT EQUALLY RESPONSIBLE FOR THE ILLEGALITY

There is an overlap here with the former rule of common law that payments pursuant to a mistake of law were irrecoverable. The decision of the House of Lords in *Kleinwort Benson Ltd* v *Lincoln City Council* [1999] 2 AC 349 abrogated the mistake of law rule. Previously an exception had developed to the rule of irrecoverability where the parties were not equally to blame for the illegality of the transaction. The seminal discussion, as often, is by Lord Mansfield in *Browning* v *Morris* (1778) 2 Cowp 790 at 792, 98 ER 1364:

> where contracts or transactions are prohibited by positive statutes, for the sake of protecting one set of men from another set of men; the one, from their situation and condition, being liable to be oppressed or imposed upon by the other; there the parties are not *in pari delicto*; and in furtherance of these statutes, the person injured, after the transaction is finished and completed, may bring his action and defeat the contract.

The leading case is *Kiriri Cotton Co. Ltd* v *Dewani* [1960] AC 192, in which a landlord required a tenant to pay a premium or 'key money' as a precondition of being granted the lease. Such premiums were prohibited by the Ugandan Rent Restriction Ordinance. Neither party appreciated this. The tenant sought restitution of the money paid. Here both parties were mistaken as to the law and it was a prohibited transaction. Lord Denning, delivering the advice of the Privy Council, stated (at 204) that 'if as between the two of them the duty of observing the law is placed on the shoulders of the one, rather than the other — it being imposed on him specially for the protection of the other — then they are not *in pari delicto* and the money can be recovered back'.

It might be thought in the wake of *Kleinwort Benson* that the best approach to these cases is to reclassify them on the basis of there being examples of recoverability on the grounds of mistake of law. However, the authorities still require separate treatment, in that the mistake of law overlaps with the entering into of a prohibited transaction. In that situation the claimant is prima facie precluded from seeking any relief in respect of the transaction, unless he can establish something more. That something more, as Lord Denning points out in *Kiriri*, is that the statute is aimed at protecting a class of persons to which the claimant belongs. *Kiriri Cotton* can be contrasted with the somewhat questionable earlier authority of *Green* v *Portsmouth Stadium Ltd* [1953] 2 QB 190. It was there held that the Betting and Lotteries Act 1934 was not passed for the protection of bookmakers. Denning LJ's *ex tempore* dictum in that case, that the existence of the right to restitution depended solely upon statutory interpretation (at 196), should be treated with caution.

The problem has been common in the field of insurance, where certain transactions are prohibited, presumably for the protection of the public. The position of the insured is strong where a mistake of law is caused by the fraud of the insurer. In

Hughes v *Liverpool Victoria Legal Friendly Society* [1916] 2 KB 482, the plaintiff entered into a life insurance contract which was illegal and void under the Life Assurance Act 1774. However, the defendant fraudulently misrepresented that the transaction was lawful. The plaintiff was held entitled to recover the premiums paid. The decision should be contrasted with the earlier unsatisfactory case of *Harse* v *Pearl Life Assurance Co.* [1904] 1 KB 558, where the misrepresentation was innocent rather than fraudulent. The Court of Appeal held the *non in pari delicto* exception did not apply. This case can no longer be regarded as good law after *Kleinwort Benson Ltd* v *Lincoln City Council* [1999] 2 AC 349. More recently, in the case of unauthorised insurance under s. 2 of the Insurance Companies Act 1974, the decision in *Re Cavalier Insurance Co. Ltd* [1989] 2 Lloyd's Rep 430 followed *Kiriri Cotton*. The insured was held to be not *in pari delicto* with the unauthorised insurer. The duty was firmly upon the insurer to comply with the statutory duty. Accordingly the insured was held entitled to recover premiums paid. In contrast, where claims have been met the premiums could not be recovered because there was no total failure of consideration. While this is a sound example of common law principle, the case must now be regarded as wrongly decided for failing to take into account the retrospective effect of s. 132 of the Financial Services Act 1986. See the discussion of *Group Josi Re* v *Walbrook Insurance Co. Ltd* [1996] 1 WLR 1152 in 12.6.

13.5   POLICY-MOTIVATED RESTITUTION

So far this chapter has been concerned with restitutionary circumventions of the general rule prohibiting the enforcement of, or other relief in respect of, illegal transactions. At bottom, the illegality rule stems from a public policy as to the proper role of the court in respect of contracts or other transactions which offend an express or implied statutory prohibition, or otherwise are in breach of a head of public policy recognised at common law. The exceptions recognised to the general prohibition of relief, namely the *locus poenitentiae* and *non in pari delicto* cases, can also be explained on the basis that they rest upon the public policy favouring restitution. In addition, where the underlying transaction is not tainted by illegality the leading restitutionary texts recognise that public policy may found a restitutionary claim. Of course, at root all restitution claims are founded upon the public policy encapsulated in the principle against unjust enrichment. What we are concerned with here, briefly, are cases which cannot be explained on the basis of non-voluntary transfer, free acceptance or some other established ground for restitution. Birks, therefore, argues that policy-motivated restitution is the best explanation for otherwise disparate streams of case law: Birks, 294–312.

Birks's sample of cases resting on public policy include the following. First, the duty of public authorities to return money exacted without any lawful authority. This is now recognised in *Woolwich Equitable Building Society* v *Inland Revenue Commissioners* [1993] AC 70 (see 17.1). Secondly, the *locus poenitentiae* or withdrawal from an illegal transaction ground for restitution discussed in this chapter. Thirdly, the jurisdiction to award maritime salvage. Goff and Jones also see public policy as a ground for restitution in appropriate cases such as maritime salvage, *Woolwich* and the strict prophylactic rule forcing fiduciaries to disgorge gains made from their position: Goff and Jones, 45. By analogy, public policy may also preclude a restitutionary claim, and this will be dealt with below in Chapter 35.

FURTHER READING

Goff and Jones, 607–35
Birks, 424–32
Anson, 381–98
Law Commission, *Illegal Transactions: The Effect of Illegality on Contracts and Trusts* (Consultation Paper, No. 154, 1998)
F. Rose, 'Restitutionary and Proprietary Consequences of Illegality', in Rose (1996), 203–34

Repentance

J. Grodecki, 'In Pari Delicto Potior est Conditio Defendentis' (1955) 71 LQR 254
J. Beatson, 'Repudiation of Illegal Purpose as a Grounds for Restitution' (1975) 91 LQR 313
R. Merkin, 'Restitution by Withdrawal from Executory Illegal Contracts' (1981) 97 LQR 420
Law Commission Consultation Paper No. 154, paras 2.49 to 2.56

Public policy

Birks, 294–312
Goff and Jones, 45, 67–72

14 Anticipated Contracts That Do Not Materialise

14.1 THEORETICAL FOUNDATIONS

English law, like other legal systems, insists on clearly defined requirements being satisfied for a binding contract. First, that both parties have the necessary contractual capacity. The consequences of incapacity in the swaps cases were considered in 12.4. Secondly, performance should not involve illegal conduct or offend public policy. The consequences of illegality and breach of public policy were considered in Chapter 13. Thirdly, that each party should manifest the necessary contractual intention, which is usually demonstrated by the identification of a proposal or an offer which is accepted or assented to by the recipient. Fourthly, as a matter of authority rather than principle, English law still insists upon compliance with the doctrine of consideration. The promise or performance must be given in exchange for some requested counter-performance. There must be an element of reciprocity in the rights and obligations which are engendered. Fifthly, some types of contract must be in a particular form before they will be enforced. Non-compliance with formality requirements was considered in Chapter 12. Sixthly, the obligations to be enforced must be sufficiently certain. Vague or ambiguous provisions may render a contract unenforceable.

This chapter is concerned with contracts that fail to crystallise because of the absence of correspondence between offer and acceptance. In such cases it is either impossible to conclude that the necessary mutual contractual intention existed, or it may be said that the apparent intention was too vague or ambiguous to constitute a binding legal instrument. English law possesses a very black-and-white conception of contractual responsibility, with its simple concepts of offer, acceptance and counter-offer. This often entails that anticipated transactions never come to fruition in negotiations for large-sale contracts, such as in the construction industry. Similarly, in the ordinary high-street context of the sale of an interest in real property the parties, by the use of the words 'subject to contract', may postpone the moment when negotiations crystallise into bargain almost indefinitely. Often, especially in the construction industry, valuable work is done on the project either before a contract is signed, or even where no contract is eventually signed. English contract law recognises no general doctrine of good faith in contract negotiations or any similar conceptual vehicle for compensating such extra-contractual performance. Accordingly, parties look outside the resources of the law of contract, and principles from the law of tort, estoppel and restitution have been utilised to ground pre-contractual responsibility.

Where a restitutionary solution is sought two key difficulties must be overcome. First, has the defendant been enriched by the claimant's pre-contractual perform-ance? If so, secondly, is there an operative ground for restitution in the circumstan-ces? The identification of an appropriate unjust factor has proved controversial. The two prime candidates are free acceptance and failure of consideration. Two factors which have influenced the courts in cases where restitutionary solutions can be identified are (i) the fact that one party was 'responsible' for the breakdown in negotiations; and (ii) the fact that the claimant's expenditure was much greater than that which would be normally risked at the pre-contractual stage. Beatson has criticised the deployment of restitutionary techniques here as inappropriate. Unjust enrichment reasoning is distorted by employing an 'over-inclusive test of benefit'. Beatson argues that what is being protected here is the claimant's injurious reliance upon the other. This suggests that the cases are more akin to those on promissory estoppel (albeit employed as a cause of action) than they are to mainstream restitution cases: Beatson, 5–8, 21, 31–9. See also Jones, 'Claims Arising Out of Anticipated Contracts which do not Materialize' (1980) 18 UW Ontario L Rev 447.

14.2 THE NEGOTIATION PROCESS

The leading English authority of *British Steel Corporation* v *Cleveland Bridge and Engineering Co. Ltd* [1984] 1 All ER 504 provides model guidance to the role of unjust enrichment claims in this context. It clearly establishes the subsidiarity of restitution and the primacy of contract. The facts resemble the 'battle of the forms' cases familiar from contract formation. CBE was involved with the construction of a bank building in Saudi Arabia. The building was to be of an unusual construction, with the main body suspended from four columns, with a steel lattice-work frame. CBE approached BSC with a view to the latter manufacturing the cast-steel nodes for use at the centre of the lattice-work. CBE sent to BSC a 'letter of intent' stating that it was its intention to enter into a sub-contract for the manufacture of the nodes and requesting BSC to commence work immediately pending preparation of a formal contract. BSC commenced manufacture. In the meantime various draft contracts passed backwards and forwards but no agreement could be reached on the final terms of the proposed formal contract. The first nodes which were cast were unsatisfactory and various alterations in the original specification were agreed. It was only after the first nodes were manufactured that CBE made it clear that it required delivery of the nodes in a particular sequence. All the nodes were eventually delivered, but without the signing of a formal contract. BSC claimed £222,843.70 as the price of 137 cast-steel nodes as either goods sold and delivered (that is, a contractual claim) or upon a *quantum meruit* basis. CBE admitted that the goods were sold and delivered, but counter-claimed some £867,735.68 on the basis of late delivery of nodes and delivery out of sequence.

At the hearing BSC put its case firmly on a quasi-contractual footing. The first issue accordingly was whether there was ever any binding contract. Robert Goff J held that this was primarily a question of construction. His three-stage approach demonstrates the primacy of contractual reasoning. The first question for the court was whether there was any ordinary 'executory contract', or a bilateral contract under which the parties had assumed mutual rights and obligations. This required consideration of whether the documents complied with the mirror-image rule of offer and acceptance. Secondly, if no executory contract could be discerned, was there an 'if' or unilateral contract. In such an arrangement A requests B to do something, and promises B that if he so performs he will receive something in return. The contract is unilateral in character because only A ever undertakes an obligation.

On a close examination of the evidence Robert Goff J rejected the view that the negotiations, and in particular the 'letter of intent', ever crystallised into either a binding bilateral contract or a unilateral contract. Only if these questions are answered in the negative is it permissible to go onto the next stage. No contract having been identified, the principle of subsidiarity had no role to play. Robert Goff J decided there was liability in restitution (at 511):

> Both parties confidently expected a formal contract to eventuate. In these circumstances, to expedite performance under that anticipated contract, one requested the other to commence the contract work, and the other complied with that request. If thereafter, as anticipated, a contract was entered into, the work done as requested will be treated as having been performed under that contract; if, contrary to their expectation, no contract was entered into, then the performance of the work is not referable to any contract the terms of which can be ascertained, and the law simply imposes an obligation on the party who made the request to pay a reasonable sum for such work as has been done pursuant to that request, such an obligation sounding in quasi contract or, as we now say, in restitution.

Robert Goff J accordingly dismissed the counter-claim and allowed the claim.

It should immediately be noted that the result is somewhat asymmetrical in that only the party rendering goods and services has a claim. The claim for late delivery lacked a contractual vehicle and therefore disclosed no cause of action. This harsh conclusion was mitigated on the facts of the case, by Robert Goff J's finding that, in any event, BSC was not in breach of any of the alleged contractual obligations. It can be seen that restitution cannot provide a universal solvent to the problem of contracts which do not fully crystallise. One only needs to vary the facts to consider what would have happened if the nodes had been defectively manufactured, causing the bank building to collapse. Surely a court would strive to find a binding contract?

A more robust approach to the issue of contract formation was taken by the Court of Appeal in *G. Percy Trentham Ltd* v *Archital Luxfer Ltd* [1993] 1 Lloyd's Rep 25. The main contractor of a building project requested the defendant to carry out the work of installing aluminum doors and windows in the building. The work was completed and the defendant was paid. Subsequently it turned out that there were problems with the windows and doors. The building owner complained to the main contractor, who in turn complained to the defendant. As in *British Steel*, there had been protracted negotiations which had not crystallised into a formal contract. The defendant, somewhat unmeritoriously, took the point that no contract had ever come into being. The first instance judge struggled, but eventually discerned a sufficiently corresponding offer and acceptance. The Court of Appeal agreed, in the result, but used different reasoning. Steyn LJ sympathised with the judge's attempt to piece together a binding contract from the correspondence. However, Steyn LJ preferred to say that a contract had come into being by way of mutual performance, stressing the objective theory of formation. This common-sense approach to the problems of contract formation may well reduce the need for recourse to the law of restitution in this context.

The approach of Steyn LJ is reminiscent of the classic judgment on the battle of the forms of Lord Denning MR in *Butler Machine Tool Co. Ltd* v *Ex-Cell-O Corp. (England) Ltd* [1979] 1 All ER 965. The Master of the Rolls discussed situations in which parties would succeed in relying upon their standard terms. Where two commercial actors were vying to bargain on their own terms and conditions, the courts would generally favour the party who fired the 'last shot', namely the one whose terms and conditions were last on the table, before the contract was formed. However, in some cases this would not yield a result. Accordingly, in appropriate cases the courts would consider both parties' proposed terms (at 968):

> The terms and conditions of both parties are to be construed together. If they can be reconciled so as to give a harmonious result, all well and good. If differences are irreconcilable, so that they are mutually contradictory, then the conflicting terms may have to be scrapped and replaced by a reasonable implication.

14.3   RISK ANALYSIS

It is often necessary to commit oneself to expenditure in the hope of obtaining a contract. A person may invest in a brand new suit and an expensive train fare in order to attend a job interview, in which he may not be successful. The risks may be greater in tendering for a role in a major construction project, or the provision of goods or services to a public authority. As Bingham LJ observed in *Blackpool and Fylde Aero Club Ltd* v *Blackpool Borough Council* [1990] 1 WLR 1195, at 1201–02, the position of the bidder in such a process can be an unenviable one. The seminal case of *William Lacey (Hounslow) Ltd* v *Davis* [1957] 1 WLR 932 demonstrates that there are often three stages in such a tendering process. First, the initial tendering phase, in which work undertaken by bidders is done entirely at their own risk and can never be recouped (if no contract results). Secondly, a more advanced stage of the bidding process in which a party is selected and encouraged to carry out expenditure greater than that which would normally take place at the pre-contractual stage. Such expenditure may be recouped in restitution if no contract eventuates. Thirdly, if a contract does eventuate the contractual matrix governs, and it is up to the bidder to have bargained to cover his pre-contractual costs when stipulating his price.

In *William Lacey*, the defendant owned war-damaged premises which he wished to redevelop. The plaintiff building company submitted the lowest tender for reconstruction work, and were led to believe that they would receive the contract. Subsequently, at the request of the defendant, they prepared further estimates for the purposes of obtaining necessary licences, for negotiations for a claim to the War Damage Commission, and further, to make alterations to the design for the redeveloped premises. Later the defendant sold the premises, no formal contract having ever been entered into. Barry J rejected the contractual claim, but then considered a claim for a *quantum meruit*. Barry J found as a fact that the additional work carried out fell outside the realm of that normally carried out gratuitously in the tendering process. It was strenuously argued for the defendant that work was done in the expectation that it would be recouped under any eventual contract. Effectively the plaintiffs took a gamble. Barry J decided that the modern view of the scope of *quantum meruit* was best illustrated by *Craven-Ellis v Canons Ltd* [1936] 2 KB 403 (see 12.3) and *Upton-on-Severn Rural District Council* v *Powell* [1942] 1 All ER 220 (see 3.8.1). Barry J continued (at 939):

> I am unable to see any valid distinction between work done which has to be paid for under the terms of a contract erroneously believed to be in existence and work done which has to be paid for out of the proceeds of a contract which both parties erroneously believed was about to be made. In neither case was the work to be done gratuitously, and in both cases the parties from whom payment was sought requested the work and obtained the benefit of it. In neither case did the parties actually intend to pay for the work otherwise than under the supposed contract, or as part of the total price which would become payable when the expected contract was made. In both cases, when the beliefs of the parties were falsified, the law implied an obligation — and, in this case, I think the law should imply an obligation — to pay a reasonable price for services which had been obtained.

It should be observed that there is a distinction between *Craven-Ellis* and *Upton-on-Severn Rural District Council* and the instant case. Both those cases concerned the rendering of benefit under an operative mistake. The facts of *William Lacey* disclosed not a mistake, but rather a misprediction (see Birks, 147). It will be necessary to come back to this case when considering the appropriate ground for restitution. See 14.6.

William Lacey should be contrasted with the facts of the more recent case of *Regalian Properties plc* v *London Docklands Development Corp.* [1995] 1 WLR 212. A development company tendered in 1986 for the residential development of land in London's Docklands. LDDC accepted their tender 'subject to contract' and other conditions. Negotiations dragged on over two years, delays being caused both by LDDC's difficulties in obtaining vacant possession of part of the site, and also by disagreements over the eventual price caused by fluctuations in the property market, which initially spiralled and then fell away in 1988. No formal contract ever materialised. The plaintiffs sought restitution of some £3 million representing fees paid to various professional firms in respect of the proposed development and in preparation for the proposed contract. Rattee J attempted to marginalise *William Lacey* by suggesting that the work done in the earlier case was purely for an extraneous purpose, namely, for the purpose of negotiations with the War Damage Commission. In contrast, in *Regalian* all the expenditure was for the purpose of enabling the development company to obtain and perform the proposed contracts. Rattee J stressed the importance of the words 'subject to contract', and appeared to construe that phrase as meaning that there should be no obligations (and presumably not just no contractual obligations) in the absence of the formal contract. Rattee J was explicit in the significance of these key words and their relationship to the allocation of risk (at 231):

> Each party to such negotiations must be taken to know (as in my judgment Regalian did in the present case) that pending the conclusion of a binding contract any cost incurred by him in preparation for the intended contract will be incurred at his own risk, in the sense that he will have no recompense for those costs if no contract results. ... by deliberate use of the words 'subject to contract' with the admitted intention that they should have their usual effect, LDDC and Regalian each accepted that in the event of no contract being entered into any resultant loss should lie where it fell.

14.4   ENRICHMENT

Sometimes where an anticipated contract fails to materialise, enrichment poses no problems because it is in the form of money, which is incontrovertibly enriching. For example, where an intending purchaser of land pays a deposit to the would-be vendor while negotiations are 'subject to contract' and the deal fails to crystallise, the payer is entitled to restitution of the money (*Chillingworth v Esche* [1924] 1 Ch 97).

However, most of the case law concerns enrichment in the form of goods supplied, services rendered and money paid to third parties. In the leading case of *British Steel Corporation v Cleveland Bridge and Engineering Co.* [1984] 1 All ER 504, specialist nodes were made to the defendants' order and were accepted by the defendants. While there were complaints about late delivery and delivery out of sequence, there was no suggestion that the nodes had not been put to use in the building project. Here there was a clear tangible benefit. It should be noted, however, that Robert Goff J considered it sufficient to overcome problems of enrichment that there had been a request for work to be done, under the terms of the 'letter of intent'. Request is *a fortiori* from free acceptance, and overcomes the problem of subjective devaluation. In any event, there was no debate in that case as to whether the goods were enriching or not; rather, attention was focussed on alleged contractual counter-claim.

In contrast, in *William Lacey* [1957] 1 WLR 932 there appears to have been no tangible benefit moving from the plaintiff to the defendant. As in *British Steel*, there was a request that the additional work should be undertaken by the plaintiff. Further, Barry J relied upon the earlier case of *Craven-Ellis* v *Canons Ltd* [1936] 2 KB 403, which has since been categorised as a leading example of incontrovertible benefit.

On the similar facts of *Regalian Properties plc* v *London Dockland Development Corp.* [1995] 1 WLR 212, restitution was sought in respect of the money paid to various professionals, such as architects, regarding the project. It was contended by the plaintiffs that the resulting designs and the obtaining of detailed planning permission were of benefit to the defendant, in that they enhanced the value of its property. Rattee J was 'not satisfied that any such or any other ascertainable benefit accrued to LDDC' (at 225). The judge also alluded to the fact that the subsequent property crash meant that nobody would wish to develop the site in the way envisaged by the plaintiffs. It is hard to see the relevance of this factor, if it could have been shown that the work was requested or freely accepted by the defendant. Overall, the issue received scant attention given Rattee J's firm view that the words 'subject to contract' ousted any possibility of legal liability.

Brewer Street Investments Ltd v *Barclays Woollen Co. Ltd* [1954] 1 QB 428 is a further illustration of the request principle in the context of leasehold property. The plaintiff landlords owned premises in the West End of London, and the defendants were prospective tenants. The essential terms of a 21-year lease were agreed between them, including the rent, subject to contract. Negotiations continued, and both parties confidently expected the lease to eventuate. The defendants, anxious to enter as soon as possible, desired certain alterations to be made to the premises. In correspondence they agreed to be responsible for the cost of these. However, negotiations broke down and the alterations, which had progressed considerably, were halted. The plaintiffs paid off the contractors and claimed reimbursement from the defendants. The Court of Appeal upheld the finding that they were entitled to be reimbursed. Denning LJ pointed out that the claim was to one for money paid. Significantly, the request by the prospective tenants indicated a willingness to pay upon completion of the work, not for uncompleted work. Denning LJ explicitly considered it as a matter of risk allocation. Denning LJ concluded (at 437):

> In my opinion the prospective tenants ought to pay all the costs thrown away. The work was done to meet their special requirements and was prima facie for their benefit and not for the benefit of the landlords. If and in so far as the work is shown to have been of benefit to the landlords, credit should be given in such sum as may be just. Subject to such credit, the prospective tenants ought to pay the cost of the work, because they in the first place agreed to take responsibility for it; and when the matter goes off without the default of either side, they should pay the costs thrown away. There is no finding here that the work was of any benefit to the

landlords, and in the circumstances the prospective tenants should, I think, pay the amount claimed.

Here the prospective tenants obtained no tangible benefit. Indeed the benefit, if any, was in the hands of the landlord. The Court of Appeal also indicated *arguendo* that in the analogous scenario, in which landlords allow prospective tenants on to the property to carry out improvements in anticipation of the lease, if the landlords subsequently broke off negotiations for no reason, the prospective tenants could recover the value of work done in restitution (at 431).

14.5   FAULT

The question has sometimes been addressed in the case law whether one party is at fault for a breakdown in negotiations. This factor has not proved crucial, and is in any event difficult to reconcile with the decision of the House of Lords in *Walford* v *Miles* [1992] 2 AC 128 that English law does not recognise an agreement to negotiate, nor any duty to negotiate, in good faith. Such an obligation is regarded as unworkable in practice and inconsistent with the adversarial stance of the parties. However, in *Brewer Street* v *Barclays Woollens* [1954] 1 QB 428, the first instance judge did consider it to be crucial which of the parties was responsible for the breakdown in negotiations. If it were the landlords, the judge would have held that they had no right to reimbursement. Somervell LJ agreed with his conclusion that it was the prospective tenants who had caused the deadlock by insisting on an option to purchase. Denning LJ thought that neither party was at fault. The disagreement was on a point which had not been part of their agreement in principle. Denning LJ realistically thought that it was hard to impugn the negotiating strategy of either party. In contrast, Romer LJ placed the blame for the breakdown of negotiations squarely upon the shoulders of the defendants. However, both Somervell LJ and Denning LJ were prepared to hold on the assumption that neither party was at fault, that the defendant prospective tenants should still pay for the work which they had insisted on. The decision in *Regalian* does not sit comfortably with this Court of Appeal authority, which decided that even though arrangements were 'subject to contract' there could be an action in restitution for preparatory work. The case was not discussed by Rattee J, but was cited in argument. It is submitted that as a matter of principle and authority the earlier decision of the Court of Appeal should be preferred.

Overall it seems that fault is not a factor which is explicitly considered relevant in the English authorities. This can be contrasted with the decision of the Supreme Court of New South Wales in *Sabemo Pty Ltd* v *North Sydney Municipal Council* [1977] 2 NSWLR 880. In a similar fact configuration to *Regalian* the plaintiff successfully tendered for a building lease of land belonging to the defendant local authority. Sheppard J allowed the plaintiff's claim for Aus$426,000 in respect of work done before the defendant council deliberately decided to drop the proposal. The judge recognised that by allocating fault in this way, he was adopting a somewhat novel approach, but based his conclusion upon the remarks of Somervell and Romer LJJ in *Brewer Street* v *Barclays Woollens* [1954] 1 QB 428, although noting that Denning LJ did not proceed on that basis. Sheppard J concluded (at 901): 'the defendant's decision to drop the proposal is the determining factor.' In *Regalian*, Rattee J did not think the decision in *Sabemo* represented English law. In any event, the reason for the breakdown in relationship for the parties in *Regalian* was their inability to agree the key term, namely the price of the development. It seems neither party was at fault. Similarly, it can be said that in the cases of *British Steel* and *William Lacey* there was no explicit discussion of fault. As English law currently stands, it is hard to see how fault can be a relevant factor. It should be borne in mind, though, that that may change if English law moves towards an explicit recognition of an obligation to observe good faith in the conduct of negotiations.

14.6   THE GROUND FOR RESTITUTION

It can be observed that the above statements of principle in the leading cases of *British Steel* and *William Lacey* do not disclose any unjust factor resembling the usual grounds of recovery in restitution. Robert Goff J in *British Steel* appears to treat the request contained in the defendant's 'letter of intent' as determinative both of the issue of enrichment and injustice.

One view is that of Beatson and Jones, referred to above (see 14.1), that the cases do not belong within the province of restitution at all, but are rather concerned with protecting injurious reliance. This theory would favour the development of promissory estoppel and related doctrines to provide recompense for misplaced reliance on the statements or conduct of others. The broadest statements in English law on promissory or equitable estoppel are to be found in *Amalgamated Investment & Property Co. Ltd* v *Texas Commerce International Bank Ltd* [1982] QB 84, in the judgments of Robert Goff J at first instance and Lord Denning MR and Brandon LJ in the Court of Appeal. The High Court of Australia has gone one step further in explicitly recognising promissory estoppel as a cause of action in the seminal case of *Walton Stores (Interstate) Ltd* v *Maher* (1989) 164 CLR 387. English law still has further to go along this road.

In contrast, the approach of Birks is to see cases involving contracts which do not come to fruition as being central to his conception of free acceptance as a ground for restitution: see Birks, 265–93. In response, Burrows has criticised Birks's reliance upon free acceptance as an unjust factor (and also as a test for enrichment). Burrows argues that the majority of the cases relied upon by Birks can be explained on other, less controversial grounds. Most significantly, with regard to ineffective contracts such as those which never materialise, it is argued that the ground for restitution is usually 'failure of consideration': Burrows, 'Free Acceptance in the Law of Restitution' (1988) 104 LQR 576; and see Burrows, 315–20. Birks in reply has accepted many of these points but still insists on a now more limited role for the concept of free acceptance: Birks, 'In Defence of Free Acceptance' in Burrows (1991) 105, at 109–27. See Chapter 15 below.

It must be observed that it is ahistorical to utilise the concept of failure of consideration in respect of services rendered and other non-money benefits. The concept of total failure of consideration originated in respect of money claims, where a contract had been discharged by termination for breach or frustration. However, as a matter of principle, there should be symmetry between different types of enrichment: the unjust factors or grounds for restitution should be the same for each. Here we are concerned with the conditional transfer of wealth, in anticipation of remuneration under a binding contract. The condition is that the transferor anticipates he will be remunerated under the contract which he hopes will eventuate. Recovery will follow if the recipient can be shown to have accepted the condition attached to the transfer. Otherwise the benefits were conferred at the transferor's own risk. Accordingly, the unjust factor is either free acceptance (or request), or possibly failure of consideration.

FURTHER READING

Asterisks indicate especially useful works.

Goff and Jones, 663–75

*G. Jones, 'Claims Arising Out of Anticipated Contracts which fail to Materialize' (1980) 18 UW Ontario L Rev 447

Beatson, 5–8, 21, 31–39

E. Farnsworth, 'Pre-Contractual Liability and Preliminary Agreements, Fair Dealing and Failed Negotiations' (1987) 87 Col L Rev 217

E. McKendrick, 'The Battle of the Forms and the Law of Restitution' (1988) 8 OJLS 197

J. Carter, 'Services Rendered Under Ineffective Contracts' [1990] LMCLQ 495, 499–506

Birks, 265–93

A. Burrows, 'Free Acceptance and the Law of Restitution' (1988) 104 LQR 576; also in Burrows (1998), 72–98

P. Birks, 'In Defence of Free Acceptance' in (1991), 105, 109–27

J. Carter and M. Furmston, 'Good Faith and Fairness in the Negotiation of Contracts' (1994–5) 8 JCL 1–15, 93–119

*E. McKendrick, 'Work Done in Anticipation of a Contract which does not Materialise', in Cornish, 163–94

*S. Hedley, in Cornish, 195–98

15 Free Acceptance

15.1 THEORETICAL FOUNDATIONS

The life of free acceptance has to date been largely confined to the academic texts and journals. In the leading works of Goff and Jones and Professor Birks, the doctrine of free acceptance has a unique and significant dual role in that it can both satisfy the test of enrichment and establish a ground for restitution or unjust factor. The test is concerned exclusively, it seems, with the enrichment in the form of goods and services, and perhaps money paid to third parties. Accordingly, as a ground for restitution it appears unique in that it applies only to these types of benefit. Goff and Jones argue (at 18):

> In our view, [the defendant] will be held to have benefited from the services rendered if he, as a reasonable man, should have known that the plaintiff who rendered the services expected to be paid for them, and yet he did not take a reasonable opportunity open to him to reject the proffered services. Moreover, in such a case, he cannot deny that he has been *unjustly* enriched.

The same argument is made in relation to goods: Goff and Jones, 26.

Birks based his argument upon the following notorious hypothetical example (at 265):

> Suppose that I see a window-cleaner beginning to clean the windows of my house. I know that he will expect to be paid. So I hang back unseen until he has finished the job; then I emerge and maintain that I will not pay for work which I never ordered. It is too late, I have freely accepted the service. I had my opportunity to send him away. I chose instead to let him go on. I must pay the reasonable value of his work.

The argument was developed at some length: Birks, 265–93. The key elements of free acceptance are said to be:

(a)   the defendant's knowledge of the claimant's non-gratuitous intent; and
(b)   the defendant's neglect of an opportunity to reject the goods or services.

The approach of Birks has been criticised by Burrows who rejects free acceptance as an unjust factor. Burrows advances the important insight that most of the cases relied upon by Goff and Jones and Birks in support of free acceptance can be explained on other, less controversial grounds. Most importantly, with regard to authorities on ineffective contracts, whether discharged by breach or frustration, or whether void or incomplete, Burrows argued that the ground of restitution is usually 'failure of consideration': Burrows (1988) 104 LQR 576. In response, Birks has accepted many of the points made by Burrows, but still insists on a now more limited role for the concept: Birks, in Burrows (1991), 105, 109–27. To date, this debate has been of little practical significance; however, it is proposed to examine briefly the authorities which are relied upon in support of free acceptance as a ground for restitution. It can be observed at the outset that most of the authority is found in obiter dicta, rather than forming the basis of any binding decision.

15.2   THE PRINCIPLES AND THE AUTHORITIES

15.2.1   Birks's original thesis

Birks's argument for free acceptance was intended to reinterpret a body of case law involving ineffective contracts, and authorities imposing legal responsibility in situations where a genuinely consensual contract could not be identified. Free acceptance was therefore proffered as the explanation of cases where a party was held responsible for expenditure incurred, on the assumption that a contract would eventuate (*William Lacey (Hounslow) Ltd* v *Davis* [1957] 1 WLR 932; *Sabemo Pty Ltd* v *North Sydney Municipal Council* [1977] 2 NSWLR 880; *British Steel Corporation* v *Cleveland Bridge & Engineering Bridge Co. Ltd* [1984] 1 All ER 504). See the discussion of these cases in Chapter 14. Similarly, free acceptance was said to explain older cases such as *Wetherby* v *Banham* (1832) 5 C & P 228, 172 ER 950 and *Lamb* v *Bunce* (1850) 4 M & S 275, 105 ER 836. Birks also argued that the doctrine of acquiescence espoused in *Ramsden* v *Dyson* (1866) LR 1 HL 129 and *Willmott* v *Barber* (1880) 15 Ch D 96 constitutes a sister doctrine in equity. For the full argument see Birks, 265–93. It can be observed that none of the authorities mentioned is explicitly in terms of free acceptance. Birks also employs a concept of limited acceptance to explain the award of restitution in some cases where there has been part performance of ineffective contracts: Birks, 126–27, 232, 238–41, 250–51. This is used to explain the claim in cases such as *Planché* v *Colburn* (1831) 8 Bing 14, 131 ER 305, in which an innocent party who had performed under a contract subsequently terminated in response to the other party's breach, could claim a reasonable sum for work done. Limited acceptance would also underlie a claim by the party in breach for work done under a contract subsequently terminated, as discussed in *Sumpter* v *Hedges* [1898] 1 QB 673 and *Hain Steamship Co. Ltd* v *Tate & Lyle Ltd* [1936] 2 All ER 597. While limited acceptance is utilised as a test for enrichment, Birks concedes that the appropriate ground of restitution is failure of consideration. Similarly, limited acceptance would be the test of enrichment under s. 1(3) of the Law Reform (Frustrated Contracts) Act 1943.

15.2.2 Beatson's rejection of free acceptance

Birks's reliance upon free acceptance, especially in relation to the pre-contractual liability cases, is criticised by Beatson. Beatson is sceptical as to whether pure services can ever be enriching, and proposes an exchange-value test of enrichment, in preference to one based on free acceptance. Beatson also seems to be sceptical of its explanatory force as a ground for restitution. On the cases concerned with anticipated contracts which never materialise, Beatson comments ((1987) 40 CLP 71, at 79): 'These cases are concerned with "consent", "acquiescence", "reliance", "fault" and "risk" rather than "enrichment" or "benefit".' Beatson is also concerned that the expansive approach to free acceptance neglects the objective principle of construction of contract. See generally Beatson (1987) 40 CLP 71; also in Beatson, 21–44. Beatson explains *Planché* v *Colburn* on the basis of compensation for injurious reliance, rather than free acceptance. This is consistent with his thesis that pure services do not constitute a relevant benefit within the law of restitution: Beatson (1987) 40 CLP 71, at 79.

15.2.3 Burrows's rejection of free acceptance

Burrows thoroughly criticises free acceptance both as a ground for restitution and as a test of enrichment. He rejects Birks's use of the authorities and proposes his own reinterpretation of earlier case law: (1988) 104 LQR 577; also Burrows (1998), 72–98. In regard to the cases concerning the mistaken improvement of land, Burrows insists on the importance of mistake as articulated by the courts in *Ramsden* v *Dyson* and *Willmott* v *Barber* (above). With respect to services rendered or goods supplied under a contract discharged by breach or frustration, Burrows argues that the appropriate unjust factor is failure of consideration. That is, the claimant has not received what he had bargained for in return for supplying the benefit to the defendant. This, it is argued, is the best explanation of cases such as *De Bernardy* v *Harding* (1853) 8 Ex 822, 155 ER 1586, *Lodder* v *Slowey* [1904] AC 442 and *Boomer* v *Muir*, 24 P 2d 570 (1933). Burrows would exclude *Planché* v *Colburn* from the law of restitution, arguing that the case is best explained as one awarding contractual damages. Similarly, *Sumpter* v *Hedges* is outside the law of unjust enrichment. The court simply awarded damages for the tort of wrongful interference with goods. In relation to contracts discharged by frustration, again the relevant unjust factor is failure of consideration coupled with Burrows's own preferred bargained-for test of enrichment. With regard to services rendered or goods supplied under void, unenforceable and anticipated contracts, Burrows also argues that the unjust factor is failure of consideration. Burrows believes that by excising free acceptance as a ground for restitution the coherence and elegance of the law is improved. In essence, the argument advanced is one based on symmetry. Burrows concludes ((1988) 104 LQR 576, at 598): 'while Birks rightly explains that it must be correct for failure of consideration to be as applicable to non-money benefits as it is to money, he does not consistently carry through that approach.'

15.2.4 Birks's refined thesis

Birks has responded to these criticisms, adopting some of the arguments made, while restating the main thesis in Birks, 'In Defence of Free Acceptance' in Burrows (1991), 105–46, especially at 105–27. In the original argument Birks had acknowledged that the authorities prior to 1957 (the date of the *William Lacey* case) had a contractual flavour. Birks argued that the post-war period saw an emancipation from the contractual roots. However, in seeking to defend the doctrine Birks relies upon some earlier formulations as the best statements of free acceptance. In *Leigh* v *Dickeson* (1884) 15 QBD 60, the Court of Appeal refused a counterclaim by a tenant and part-owner for money paid to the benefit of the landlord in respect of appropriate repairs and improvements to their property. Brett MR emphasised an important distinction (at 64–65):

> Voluntary payments may be divided into two classes. Sometimes money has been expended for the benefit of another person under such circumstances that an option is allowed to him to adopt or decline the benefit: in this case, if he exercises his option to adopt the benefit, he will be liable to repay the money expended; but if he declines the benefit he will not be liable. But sometimes the money is expended for the benefit of another person under such circumstances, that he cannot help accepting the benefit, in fact that he is bound to accept it: in this case he has no opportunity of exercising any option and he will come under no liability.

The judgment of Bowen LJ in *Falcke* v *Scottish Imperial Insurance Co.* (1886) 34 Ch D 234 is relied upon by Birks in support of free acceptance, even though the authority is more commonly relied upon as one which is hostile to the recognition of claims in respect of non-money benefits (see 9.1). Emanuel was the ultimate owner of the equity of redemption in a life insurance policy, which was subject to several prior mortgages. In 1883, Emanuel paid the annual premium of £1,212 in the belief that if it was not paid the policy would lapse. Emanuel's claim to a lien to secure his share over the policy proceeds was rejected by the Court of Appeal. Bowen LJ, in rejecting the claim for reimbursement or a lien, did suggest that recovery might be possible in some circumstances (at 249):

With regard to ordinary goods upon which labour or money is expended with a view of saving them or benefiting the owner, there can, as it seems to me, according to the common law be only one principle upon which a claim for repayment can be based, and that is where you can find facts from which the law will imply a contract to repay or to give a lien. It is perfectly true that the inference of an understanding between the parties — which you may translate into other language by calling it an implied contract — is an inference which will unhesitatingly be drawn in cases where the circumstances plainly lead to the conclusion that owner of the saved property knew that the other party was laying out his money in the expectation of being repaid. In other words, you must have circumstances from which the proper inference is that there was a request to perform the service.

Bowen LJ concluded there was no adoption or ratification of Emmanuel's expenditure to save the policy by the mortgagee. Nor was there any acquiescence in the payment by Emanuel such as to give rise to an obligation as recognised in equity.

To these two examples cited by Birks we may add a third. In *Sumpter* v *Hedges* [1898] 1 QB 673, a builder had abandoned a contract to build houses when the work was incomplete. The owner of the land accepted this repudiatory breach and completed the work himself using some materials left behind by the builder. The claim of the builder for the materials succeeded, but the Court of Appeal held that the builder was entitled to nothing in respect of work done prior to termination. Collins LJ stressed that the contract had been abandoned and observed (at 676):

There are cases in which, though the plaintiff has abandoned the performance of a contract, it is possible for him to raise the inference of a new contract to pay for the work done on a *quantum meruit* from the defendant's having taken the benefit of that work, but, in order that that may be done, the circumstances must be such as to give an option to the defendant to take or not to take the benefit of the work done. It is only where the circumstances are such as to give that option that there is any evidence on which to ground the inference of a new contract.

Accordingly, where the work was already incorporated on land belonging to the defendant, there was no such opportunity to reject.

The principle espoused in these three cases was distilled by the authors of *Smith's Leading Cases* in the notes on *Lampleigh* v *Braithwaite* (1616) Hobart 105, 80 ER 255, as follows (at I, 156):

If a person knows that the consideration is being rendered for his benefit with an expectation that he will pay for it, then if he acquiesces in its being done, taking the benefit of it when done, he will be taken impliedly to request it being done: and that will import a promise to pay for it.

This principle was relied upon by those acting for the risk-taking director who had discharged the company's debts in *In re Cleadon Trust Ltd* [1939] 1 Ch 286. However, the Court of Appeal unanimously held that there was no basis to support its application on the facts. See 12.3.

Birks is now convinced that free acceptance cannot explain the ground for restitution in cases such as *Pavey & Matthews Pty Ltd* v *Paul* (1987) 162 CLR 221, even though that authority was decided explicitly on the basis of acceptance of work done. Birks accepts the distinction drawn by Garner ((1990) 10 OJLS 42, at 48) between initial unconscionability and supervening unconscionability. It is only initial unconscientiousness on the part of the recipient which entitles a risk-taker to a right to reimbursement. Rarely does such initial unconscientiousness exist where a contract proves to be ineffective. Accordingly, Birks accepts Burrows's thesis that the unjust factor in such cases is failure of consideration: 'That brilliant and indubitably correct insight both reinstates an unjust factor in *Pavey* and achieves a major advance in the intellectual coherence of the law of restitution' (Birks, in Burrows (1991), 105, 111). Birks accordingly accepts failure of consideration as the unjust factor in respect of contracts discharged by breach or frustration, void and unenforceable contracts, and cases where liability has been imposed in pre-contractual activities. To this extent Birks accepts the Burrows thesis, but the remainder of the argument departs from Burrows, and in particular the requirement of a bargained-for benefit. Birks refines the test for failure of consideration considerably. He argues (at 115–16):

> There is a difference between, on the one hand, transferring value in the mere hope that a particular state of affairs will eventuate but taking the risk that it may not, and, on the other, transferring value on the basis that that state of affairs must eventuate. In what does that difference consist?... The minimum conditions... are that the intervener tell the recipient his terms in circumstances in which the latter has an opportunity to repudiate, or that with the like opportunity the recipient know those terms and the intervener know that the recipient knows. Insufficient is the case in which the recipient secretly knows.

It seems that *Re Cleadon Trust Ltd* must be explained on the basis that the director had not made sufficient communication of his intention to be repaid, thereby providing the company with an opportunity to reject. Birks now accepts that the window-cleaner example was not appropriate. Employing a new hypothetical, the 'mean bystander' at a street performance at the Edinburgh Festival, Birks accepts that certain risk-takers would not act differently if they were aware of the state of mind of potential defendants: Birks, in Burrows (1991), 107, 121.

15.3   FREE ACCEPTANCE AND UNCONSCIENTIOUS RECEIPT

Free acceptance was incongruous in the Birks schema because it was based upon the conduct of the defendant rather than concern with the integrity of the transferor's decision. Liability to make restitution where there has been vitiated or qualified intention is generally strict. There is no enquiry into the state of mind of the defendant. If free acceptance is to be accepted as a defendant-sided ground for restitution, it should be treated alongside other examples of unjust enrichment by reason of unconscientious receipt. This is indeed acknowledged by Birks, who adopted another suggestion of Burrows ((1988) 104 LQR 576, at 599) that fault-based restitution should play a restricted role. Birks (in Burrows ((1991), 107) states (at 144–45): 'Free acceptance, and indeed fault-based restitution generally, should be regarded as a long-stop, not to be called upon until the enquiry into plaintiff-sided factors has produced a negative result.'

Other examples of fault-based restitution arise in equity, such as the claim to recover misdirected funds on the grounds of so-called knowing receipt: see Chapter 29. It is difficult to see how this suggestion can be put into practice, short of a ruling by a superior court that defendant-sided factors calling for restitution occupy a subsidiary position to claimant-sided grounds for restitution. Where a claimant's advisers believe the defendant-sided factors are stronger, they will inevitably pursue that cause of action in preference to one based on non-voluntary transfer.

In conclusion, it is worthwhile to repeat the observation that free acceptance has to date excited more attention in the academic community than in the courts. Two practical factors may account for this. First, while one can identify judicial statements of free acceptance as a ground for restitution, there has rarely been a case in which such a claim has succeeded. Secondly, as a practical matter, it must be difficult to garner evidence of the availability of, and the neglect of, an opportunity to reject the proffered goods and services.

FURTHER READING

Asterisks indicate especially useful works.

Birks, 99, 104, 114–16, 126–27, 232, 238–41, 250–51, 265–93

S. Stoljar, 'Unjust Enrichment and Unjust Sacrifice' (1987) 50 MLR 603

*J. Beatson, 'Benefit, Reliance and the Structure of Unjust Enrichment' (1987) 40 CLP 71; also in Beatson, 21–44

*A. Burrows, 'Free Acceptance and the Law of Restitution' (1988) 104 LQR 576; also in Burrows (1998), 72–98

G. Mead, 'Free Acceptance: Some Further Considerations' (1989) 105 LQR 460

M. Garner, 'The role of subjective benefit in the law of unjust enrichment' (1990) 10 OJLS 42

*P. Birks, 'In Defence of Free Acceptance' in Burrows (1991), 105–46, especially at 105–27

A. Simester, 'Unjust Free Acceptance' [1997] LMCLQ 103

16   Resulting Trusts

16.1   THEORETICAL FOUNDATIONS

It has been argued that the resulting trust has the potential to develop as the main restitutionary *proprietary* claim in the context of subtractive unjust enrichment. Its potential area of application overlaps with claims which at common law would generally be classified as depending upon 'failure of consideration' as a ground for restitution. The recognition of resulting trusts as vehicles for restitutionary recovery is currently hampered by the decision of the House of Lords in *Westdeutsche Landesbank Girozentrale* v *Islington London Borough Council* [1996] AC 669 (see 16.2). The leading proponents of the resulting trust as a manifestation of restitutionary doctrine are Professor Birks, Dr Chambers and Lord Millett. The argument that the resulting trust belongs within the law of restitution was first advanced by Birks, 60–64. The argument was developed in a longer discussion by Birks, 'Restitution and Resulting Trusts' in Goldstein (ed.), *Equity and Contemporary Legal Developments* (1992), 335–73. Birks argued (at 338): 'The resulting trust, properly understood, has a much larger role in the law of restitution than is usually thought, as great a role or greater than the constructive trust.' Such resulting trusts apply in two cases. First, apparent gifts to a transferee who cannot rebut the presumption of a resulting trust or cannot rely upon the presumption of advancement. Secondly, situations in which a transferee receives property on trust but the trust fails to exhaust the entire beneficial interest. Birks concluded (at 368–69):

> The proposition at the heart of this paper is that, within the field of subtractive unjust enrichment, if and so far as personal restitutionary claims — viewed from the other side, restitutionary obligations — are backed by equitable proprietary claims, we should learn to attribute those proprietary rights to the resulting trust, not the constructive trust.

The position advanced was avowedly experimental and tentative. In response, Swadling, in 'A New Role for Resulting Trusts?' (1996) 16 LS 110, rejects the position adopted by Birks. The result of Birks's arguments appears to be that in all cases of vitiated voluntariness, mistake, compulsion, etc., and in many of cases of non-contractual failure of consideration, or qualified intention, in addition to a common law claim for money had and received, the claimant would also be entitled to a restitutionary proprietary claim based upon a resulting trust. In the absence of evidence that there was a intention to make a gift, the presumption of resulting trust in all these cases remains unrebutted. Swadling observes that it is only with some 'artificiality' that contractual examples of qualified intention, or failure of consideration are excluded from this conclusion. Swadling argues (at 111–12):

> the resulting trust has little or no part to play in the law of restitution. Essentially, the argument which will be put is that Birks is wrong to admit of only one type of evidence which will rebut the presumption of resulting trust which arises in the case of a gratuitous transfer, *viz* positive evidence of a donative intent. An examination of the historical origins of the resulting trust reveals that *any* evidence which is inconsistent with the presumption that the transferee is to be a trustee will suffice. And proof that the payment was made by mistake or for some other reason which makes its receipt unjust will always contradict that presumption of trust. In other words, proof of the unjust factor will itself be the evidence which rebuts the presumption of resulting trust.

Swadling distinguishes between *automatic* resulting trusts and *presumed* resulting trusts following Megarry J in *In Re Vandervell's Trusts (No. 2)* [1974] Ch 269, at 289. Swadling argues that the latter should more accurately be described as a 'presumed *intention* resulting trust'. At its heart the presumption merely shifts the burden of disproving the trust onto the transferee. Any trust which is created is based upon what the parties actually intended. Accordingly, where there is a mistaken gift, it cannot be said that either of the parties had any intention to create a trust. Lastly, Swadling advances three reasons to treat Birks's thesis with caution. First, and of most practical significance, is that it would promote the majority of restitutionary claims to a proprietary rather than a personal claim. Secondly, it would contradict and undermine much of the definition and precision achieved by the existing law. Thirdly, in effect it would recognise no consideration as a ground for restitution, which would be inconsistent with Birks's arguments elsewhere: see Birks, 'No Consideration: Restitution after Void Contracts' (1993) 23 W Aus LR 195. It is submitted that the arguments of Swadling are to be preferred to those of Birks. The resulting trust argument is further rejected by Burrows [1995] RLR 15, at 25–29. The arguments of Burrows and Swadling were accepted in *Westdeutsche* by Lord Goff of the minority (at 689–90) and Lord Browne-Wilkinson of the majority (at 708–709). However, the debate cannot be said to be over because there remains one judicial proponent of the resulting trust in the shape of Lord Millett.

16.2   ORTHODOX RESULTING TRUST ANALYSIS

In *Westdeutsche Landesbank Girozentrale* v *Islington London Borough Council* [1996] AC 669, Lord Browne-Wilkinson stated (at 708):

Under existing law a resulting trust arises in the two sets of circumstances: (A) where A makes a voluntary payment to B or pays (wholly or in part) for the purchase of property which is vested either in B alone or, in the joint names of A and B, there is a presumption that A did not intend to make a gift to B: the money or property is held on trust for A (if he is the sole provider of the money) or in the case of joint purchase by A and B in shares proportionate to their contributions . . . (B) where A transfers property to B *on express trusts*, but the trusts declared do not exhaust the beneficial interest.

Therefore, on orthodox analysis there are two distinct species of resulting trusts. First, the *presumed* resulting trust, or in Swadling's terminology, the *presumed intention* resulting trust. This arises where A pays money or transfers property to B for no consideration, or makes a financial contribution (either in full or in part) to the purchase of property which is in the name of B alone or in the names or A and B. Here equity raises a presumption that A did not intend to make a gift to B. The money or property is held on trust for A if he is the sole provider of funding, or in the case where both have provided money for the purchase in proportionate shares. At bottom, this is simply an evidential rule. Equity does not presume that people readily make gifts. It places the burden of proving that the transaction was a gift upon the transferee. There is a counter-presumption of advancement where the transferor is a father and the transferee is a child, and where the transferor is the husband and the transferee is a wife. Here the burden of proving that the transaction was not intended to operate as a gift lies with the transferor. The leading authorities are *Vandervell* v *Inland Revenue Commissioners* [1967] 2 AC 291 and *In re Vandervell's Trusts (No. 2)* [1974] Ch 269. The presumption of resulting trust and the presumption of advancement were also at issue in two leading cases on illegality: *Tinsley* v *Milligan* [1994] 1 AC 340 and *Tribe* v *Tribe* [1996] Ch 107, discussed at 35.4.

The second species of resulting trust was labelled the *automatic* resulting trust by Megarry J in *In re Vandervell's Trusts (No. 2)* [1974] Ch 269, at 294:

The resulting trust here does not depend on any intentions or presumptions, but is the automatic consequence of A's failure to dispose of what is vested in him. Since *ex hypothesi* the transfer is on trust, the resulting trust does not establish the trust, but merely carries back to A the beneficial interest that has not been disposed of. Such resulting trust has not established a trust but merely carries back to A the beneficial interest that has not been disposed of. Such resulting trusts may be called 'automatic resulting trusts'.

It is crucial here that A has transferred property by way of an express trust. For some reason the beneficial interest is not exhausted. In these circumstances, where the basis of the transfer collapses, the property is then held in resulting trust for A. See for example: *In re the Trusts of the Abbott Fund* [1900] 2 Ch 326; *In re Ames' Settlement* [1946] Ch 217; and *In re West Sussex Constabulary's Widows, Children and Benevolent (1930) Fund Trusts* [1971] Ch 1. In *Westdeutsche Landesbank Girozentrale v Islington London Borough Council* [1996] AC 669, Lord Browne-Wilkinson cast doubt upon the terminology of automatic resulting trusts. In his Lordship's view (at 708): 'Both types of resulting trust are traditionally regarded as examples of trusts giving effect to the common intention of the parties. A resulting trust is not imposed by law against the intentions of the trustee (as in a constructive trust) but gives effect to his presumed intention.'

It is submitted that even in the wake of the rejection of Birks's thesis by the House of Lords in *Westdeutsche*, both species of resulting trusts are explicable on the basis of the principle against unjust enrichment. First, with respect to the presumed intention resulting trust, these do appear to be based upon non-voluntary transfer, and in particular vitiated intent. The presumption leads to many unintended transfers being reversed. Where the presumption of advancement does not operate, it places the burden upon the alleged donee to demonstrate that it was a gift. However, as Swadling has argued, where the transferor is mistaken or transfers as a result of some other unjust factor, the presumption is displaced. Secondly, the automatic resulting trust is a particular doctrine applicable where express trusts have failed. It operates analogously to failure of consideration in respect of contractual claims. At its broadest it belongs within non-voluntary transfer, in particular qualified intention.

It is worth briefly considering the fate of the resulting trust argument in *Universe Tankships Inc. of Monrovia v International Transport Workers' Federation, The Universe Sentinel* [1983] 1 AC 366. It will be recalled that the shipowners sought restitution of a payment made to the ITF's welfare fund. A common law claim for money had and received succeeded. See 6.2. An alternative argument that it was held upon resulting trust succeeded before Parker J in the Commercial Court ([1981] ICR 129). It was argued that the contribution to the fund was void because the fund was a non-charitable purpose trust. The House of Lords unanimously rejected this argument, holding that the fund was governed by contract (the rules of the ITF) and had not been constituted by means of the trust. Accordingly, the underlying transaction not being an express trust, there was no room for the doctrine of resulting trust.

16.3 LORD MILLETT AND RESULTING TRUSTS

Sir Peter Millett, writing extrajudicially in 'Tracing the Proceeds of Fraud' (1991) 107 LQR 71, suggested that the resulting trust may come to the assistance of a party whose money has been stolen by a thief. This proposition appears to be an attempt to circumvent the fiduciary relationship requirement which is seen as a precondition to a successful proprietary claim as a result of a tracing exercise. Subsequently, Millett J in *El Ajou v Dollar Land Holdings plc* [1993] 3 All ER 717 considered the position of the victims of a massive fraud who could not satisfy the breach of fiduciary obligation requirement — 'They were simply swindled'. Millett J suggested that they were able to rescind the transaction which had been induced by false and fraudulent misrepresentations and to revest the equitable title to the purchase money in themselves. This was sufficient to support an equitable tracing claim. Millett J then suggested (at 734): 'if this is correct, as I think it is, then the trust which is operating in these cases is not some new model remedial constructive trust, but an old-fashioned institutional resulting trust.'

In a more recent extrajudicial contribution, Sir Peter Millett in 'Restitution and Constructive Trusts' in Cornish, 199–217 argues that constructive trusts respond only to equitable wrongdoing, such as breach of fiduciary duty. Accordingly they belong within restitution for wrongs. In contrast, accepting the argument of Chambers, *Resulting Trusts* (1997), the learned judge argues that a resulting trust arises 'whenever the legal title has been transferred to another and the person who provided it did not intend to pass the whole beneficial interest to the recipient' (at 201). Accordingly, resulting trusts belong in autonomous unjust enrichment. Sir Peter Millett accepts Swadling's argument that the presumption of resulting trust can be rebutted by any evidence which is inconsistent with the trust, except for evidence that there was an ineffective attempt to create a trust. The learned judge continues (at 202): 'The classic resulting trust arises when a settlor fails to dispose of his entire beneficial interest. This, coupled with evidence that it did not intend to benefit the trustee, creates a resulting trust in favour of the settlor.' Sir Peter Millett accepts the argument of Chambers that there is no distinction in principle between a so-called automatic resulting trust and the presumed resulting trust: Chambers, 40*ff*. At the heart of Sir Peter Millett's article lies a fundamental disagreement with the approach to resulting trusts of Lord Browne-Wilkinson in the *Westdeutsche* case. These are based upon 'unorthodox' views as to the nature of the resulting trust and of the role of equity acts on conscience. Preferring the analysis of Chambers, Sir Peter Millett concludes (at 210): 'I do not see how we can develop a coherent doctrine of proprietary restitution for subtractive unjust enrichment unless it is based on the resulting trust as traditionally understood.'

16.4   THE CHAMBERS THESIS

In his 1997 book entitled *Resulting Trusts*, Chambers argues that the so-called presumed resulting trust and automatic resulting trust rest on the same principles, and that the traditional distinction between the two is illusory. The trust, like its cousin the constructive trust, arises by operation of law. However, unlike the latter, it gives effect to intention. It is argued that a resulting trust arises whenever property is transferred to another, and the transferor (or the person whose wealth provided the property) does not intend to transfer the whole of the beneficial interest in the asset to the transferee. In the words of Lord Millett ([1998] RLR 283):

> What Dr Chambers articulates with great clarity is that the resulting trust responds to the absence of an intention on the part of the transferor to pass the beneficial interest, not a positive intention to retain it.

In the result, if Chambers's views are accepted, the resulting trust should become the mainstay of restitutionary proprietary claims in response to subtractive unjust enrichment.

FURTHER READING

Asterisks indicate especially useful works.

Birks, 57–64, 156

Sir Peter Millett, 'Tracing the Proceeds the Fraud' (1991) 107 LQR 71

*P. Birks, 'Restitution and Resulting Trusts' in Goldstein (ed.), *Equity and Contemporary Legal Developments* (1992), 335–73

*W. Swadling, 'A New Role for Resulting Trusts?' (1996) 16 LS 110

*R. Chambers, *Resulting Trusts* (1997); reviewed by Lord Millett [1998] *Restitution Law Review* 283

Sir Peter Millett, 'Restitution and Constructive Trusts' in Cornish (1998), 199–217

PART D

RESTITUTION AND PUBLIC AUTHORITIES

17 Claims Against Public Authorities: The Woolwich Principle

17.1 THEORETICAL FOUNDATIONS

Article 4 of Bill of Rights 1689 proclaims:

> That levying money for or to the use of the Crowne by pretense of prerogative without grant of Parlyament for longer time or in other manner than the same is or shall be granted is illegal.

What then, if a purported tax is demanded and paid, when in fact the tax was not lawfully due, either because the taxing regulations were *ultra vires* the empowering Act, or the statute or regulations were misconstrued, or for some other reason? Can the taxpayer claim his money back?

Two factors suggest that restitution should be as of right. First, the unique authority and coercive powers of the State. Secondly, the imperative of the principle of legality or, in the traditional phrase, respect for the Rule of Law. Prior to the 1990s, claims by citizens against the State for restitution in such circumstances were litigated in terms of more orthodox grounds for restitution. Often the claims were brought under the heading of mistake. However, the mistake of law bar which was not abrogated until 1998 proved an obstacle to many claims. Similarly, many citizens were not mistaken but paid up under protest and sought to contest liability later. Some claims were therefore brought by way of duress and a particular expansion of it in this context, termed the *colore officii* principle: see Goff and Jones, 323–27.

Academic writers sought to generalise from these particular instances a distinct principle of recovery in claims brought against public authorities. Professor Cornish (1987) 14 *J Malaysian and Comparative Law* 41 and Professor Birks in Finn, 164, advocated the recognition of a new ground for restitution based on the fact that a *ultra vires* demand had been made, without the need for the claimant to prove mistake or duress. These arguments were accepted by the House of Lords in the *Woolwich* case. This chapter focuses on the common law right. On statutory rights of recovery, see Law Com. No. 227 (1994), Parts VII to XVI.

17.2   THE *WOOLWICH* CASE

The background to *Woolwich Equitable Building Society* v *Inland Revenue Commissioners* [1993] AC 70 was that the Inland Revenue had decided that the way building societies paid the sums representing income tax on the interest payable to their depositors should be brought into line with the scheme of payment by banks. Parliament gave its authority by s. 40 of the Finance Act 1984, which empowered the Inland Revenue to make appropriate secondary legislation. The resulting Income Tax (Building Societies) Regulations 1986 (SI 1986 No. 482) included transitional provisions. These transitional arrangements were objected to by Woolwich, who claimed that they involved an element of double taxation. Woolwich launched a judicial review of the regulations. In the meantime, fearing adverse publicity, Woolwich paid the sums claimed, but expressly under protest and without prejudice to their rights. The sums paid totalled some £57 million. Woolwich then issued a writ of summons claiming restitution of the money and interest thereon. On 31 July 1987, Nolan J decided the regulations were *ultra vires* as alleged (*R* v *Inland Revenue Commissioners, ex parte Woolwich Equitable Building Society* [1987] STC 654), which was eventually affirmed in the House of Lords ([1990] 1 WLR 1400).

The Inland Revenue repaid the money with interest from 31 July 1987. It refused to pay interest for the period prior to Nolan J's judgment. Woolwich's claim to interest for the earlier period under s. 35A of the Supreme Court Act 1981, amounted to some £6.73 million. The recovery of such interest depended upon the question whether they had a cause of action to recover the money as a debt from the date at which it was received by the Revenue. The claim for interest was also heard before Nolan J who rejected it ([1989] 1 WLR 137). However, both the Court of Appeal, by a majority, and the House of Lords, by a majority, held that Woolwich were entitled to restitution, and therefore interest, as a right.

In a magisterial leading speech, Lord Goff of Chieveley characterised the issue as 'whether money exacted as taxes from a citizen by the Revenue *ultra vires* is recoverable by the citizen as of right' (at 163). Lord Goff observed that as the law then stood, money was recoverable only if paid under a mistake of fact or compulsion. Two particular species of compulsion were common in such claims. First (at 164):

Money paid to a person in a public or quasi-public position to obtain the performance by him of a duty which he is bound to perform for nothing or for less than the sum demanded by him is recoverable to the extent that he is not entitled to it. Such payments are often described as having been demanded *colore officii*.

Secondly (at 165):

Money paid to a person for the performance of a statutory duty, which he is bound to perform for a sum less than that charged by him, is also recoverable to the extent to the overcharge. A leading example of such a case is *Great Western Railway Co. v Sutton* (1869) LR 4 HL 226.

Lord Goff considered the academic authorities and prior case law. His Lordship concluded (at 171–72):

Take any tax or duty paid by the citizen pursuant to an unlawful demand. Common justice seems to require that tax to be repaid, unless special circumstances or some principle of policy require otherwise; prima facie, the taxpayer should be entitled to repayment as a right.

Lord Goff concluded that the money demand by a public authority would be prima facie recoverable where it was demanded *ultra vires*, and in other situations, such as where the authority misconstrued the relevant statute or regulations.

Lord Browne-Wilkinson agreed, stating (at 197) that 'this is the paradigm of a case of unjust enrichment'. Lord Browne-Wilkinson adverted to the recovery of money on the basis that it had been paid 'without consideration', suggesting: 'There is in my view a close analogy to the right to recover money paid under a contract the consideration for which has wholly failed' (at 197). Lord Slynn made up the majority. His Lordship observed (at 200):

If the legislature finds that limitations on the common law principle are needed for reasons of policy or good administration then they can be adopted by legislation, e.g. by a short limitation period, presumptions as to validity, even (which I mention but do not necessarily think appropriate since the matter has not been discussed) a power in the courts to limit the effects of any order for recovery comparable to that conferred on the European Court of Justice by Article 174 [now 231] of the EEC Treaty.

Lord Keith of Kinkel and Lord Jauncey of Tullichettle dissented, the former explicitly on the basis of the limits of judicial law making (at 161): 'To give effect to Woolwich's proposition would, in my opinion, amount to a very far reaching exercise of judicial legislation.' Accordingly, Woolwich recovered the interest.

17.3   LIMITATIONS ON THE *WOOLWICH* PRINCIPLE

First, against which bodies should the *Woolwich* principle be available? Secondly, are there are any special defences which are relevant to this context? Thirdly, are there any procedural difficulties in pursuing restitution against public bodies?

With regard to the first question, *Woolwich* itself was a claim against an organ of central government performing that most characteristic of executive functions, tax-gathering. Their Lordships were reluctant to say too much about the scope of the principle. Beatson, in (1993) 109 LQR 401, at 409, identifies five grounds in Lord Goff's speech, with which Lord Browne-Wilkinson agreed, for recognising the new restitutionary right:

(a)   the principle of legality;
(b)   the unusual coercive powers of the State;
(c)   the absence of a right of recovery would penalise the good citizen who trusts the State and pays;
(d)   the Crown has the right to recover payments made out of the Consolidated Fund without authority as a matter of right (*Auckland Harbour Board* v *The Crown* [1924] AC 318);
(e)   the right to repayment recognised in respect of sums claimed by public bodies under European Community Law (*Amministrazione delle Finanze dello Stato* v *SpA San Giorgio* [1983] ECR 359).

Beatson observes that the first and fourth factors apply only to the Crown. In contrast, Beatson notes (at 410):

> The second, third and fifth are, however, wider; the first two extending to local government and the last to all public bodies and possibly to other bodies, such as utilities, not traditionally thought of as within the public sphere, but which are subject to a measure of state control.

It seems clear that local government and other public bodies are within the scope of the principle. The utilities pose the poignant question: Given the fondness of recent governments for privatisation, will utility companies providing gas, electricity and telecommunications fall within or without the *Woolwich* principle? Beatson regards this as less problematical than is commonly thought. The crucial factor in respect of heavily regulated utilities is that their only authority for exacting payment is under the statute which grants them their monopoly or other special rights. Accordingly, in Beatson's view the *Woolwich* principle 'should apply to other public bodies whose authority to charge is subject to and limited by public law principles, and to other bodies whose authority to charge is solely the product of statute, and thus limited' (at 417–18).

Turning to the second main limitation — defences — it seems unlikely that the usual restitutionary defences of good faith purchase and change of position will have a role to play in the public law context. It seems unlikely that a governmental body can realistically allege change of position. See *Rural Municipality of Shorthoaks* v *Mobil Oil of Canada* (1975) 55 DLR (3d) 1. More significant in practice are likely to be two more controversial defences. First, the submission to an honest claim. Lord Goff certainly adverted to this possibility in his assessment of the current law, before his reformulation of principle in *Woolwich*. Lord Goff stated (at 165) that a payment was voluntary and accordingly irrecoverable where:

The payer has the opportunity of contesting his liability in proceedings, but instead gives way and pays. . . . So where the money has been paid under pressure of actual or threatened legal proceedings for its recovery, the payer cannot say that for that reason the money has been paid under compulsion and is therefore recoverable by him. If he chooses to give way and pay, rather than obtain the decision of the court on the question whether the money is due, his payment is regarded as voluntary and so is not recoverable.

Lord Goff interpreted the earlier authority of *William Whiteley Ltd* v *The King* (1909) 101 LT 741 as an example of this principle. Similarly, Lord Goff held that the money would irrecoverable where:

The money has otherwise been paid in such circumstances that the payment was made to close the transaction. Such would obviously be so in the case of a binding compromise; but even where there is no consideration for the payment, it may have been made to close the transaction and so be irrecoverable.

Maskell v *Horner* [1915] 3 KB 106 was cited as authority for this proposition. Lord Slynn also treated *William Whiteley* and *Twyford* v *Manchester Corporation* [1946] Ch 236 as examples of payments made to close transactions, or alternatively wrongly decided (at 204). It is submitted that short of actual contractual compromise, the courts would be reluctant to hold that a citizen has submitted to an honest claim by a public authority. There would need to be clear evidence of a decision not to pursue an opportunity of challenging the basis of the claim. The difficulty is that the concept of submission to an honest claim comes close here to contradicting the principle underlying recovery. If there is a desire to encourage administrative legality, that policy will be frustrated by readily allowing public bodies recourse to a defence of submission to an honest claim. For submission to an honest claim generally, see 33.1.

The other defence which may be of significance in this context is the controversial issue of passing on. The premise is that the payer has suffered no unjust loss, as the burden has been borne by its customer. Lord Goff adverted to the defence at the conclusion of his speech in *Woolwich*, but saw it as properly a matter for the Law Commission (at 177–78). The defence won favour with the majority of the Supreme Court of Canada in *Air Canada* v *British Columbia* (1989) 59 DLR (4th) 161, especially at 193–94 *per* La Forest J. However, it has been rejected by the High Court of Australia in *Commissioner of State Revenue (Vic)* v *Royal Insurance Australia Ltd* (1994) 182 CLR 51 and in respect of private transactions in recent English law (see 34.1). Passing on is questionable in principle. Further, even if it were recognised, it poses insuperable evidential and mathematical difficulties. The better view, in the absence of statutory provision, is that English common law does not recognise the defence of passing on.

The third limitation concerns procedural questions. In *Woolwich* itself, the building society issued separate proceedings in the public law and private law arenas.

It seems clear that even though a claim for restitution might raise issues of *ultra vires*, there is no need for claimants to pursue an application for judicial review as a precondition to recovery. This avoids the discretions and stringent time limits under CPR Sch. 1, RSC Ord. 53. Given that there is a private law cause of action (which is in effect what *Woolwich* decided), the case falls within *Roy* v *Kensington and Chelsea and Westminster Family Practitioner Committee* [1992] 1 AC 624, rather than within the exclusivity principle of *O'Reilly* v *Mackman* [1983] 2 AC 236. This wins support in Lord Slynn's speech (at 200): 'If a claim lies for money had and received, judicial review adds nothing.' This was accepted by the Court of Appeal in *British Steel plc* v *Customs and Excise Commissioners* [1997] 2 All ER 366. See Beatson (1993) 109 LQR 1, at 4–5.

17.4   THE GROUND FOR RESTITUTION

Birks, in arguing for a special right to restitution against public authorities, categorises recovery as an example of policy-motivated restitution: Birks, 294–99. Birks, while always stressing the importance of the Rule of Law, has suggested that in broad terms the cause of action can be seen as arising in transactional inequality: Birks, in Finn, 164 at 175–76. In assessing the decision of the House of Lords, Birks again asks what was the unjust factor ([1992] PL 580 at 587):

> The most obvious answer in this case, and probably the right one, would be to say that the reason why the enrichment had to be given back lay in the necessity of confining public bodies within their lawful powers or, in other words, in the need to insist on the principle of legality.

Beatson sees the right to recover as a restitutionary analogue to the tort of misfeasance in a public office. It is an obligation shaped by its operation in the context of public law. For Beatson, the crucial aspect of the right to recovery is focussed upon preventing public bodies from acting outside their powers. Beatson concludes ((1993) 109 LQR 401 at 417):

> To sum up, the *Woolwich* principle clearly applies to taxes and duties levied by governmental bodies which are *ultra vires* because of the invalidity of the relevant subordinate legislation. It almost certainly applies where the *ultra vires* nature of the levy stems from an error of law or an abuse of discretion. The position of levies vitiated by procedural unfairness is less clear but, in principle, should not differ.

Both Birks and Beatson note Lord Browne-Wilkinson's wider justification for recovery, namely that the money has been 'paid without consideration' (at 197). This, together with an *en passant* comment of Lord Goff's (at 166, discussing *Campbell* v *Hall* (1774) 1 Cowp 204, 98 ER 1045: 'the simple fact remains that recovery was stated to be founded upon the absence of consideration for the payment'), was relied upon in the swaps cases as embodying a new unjust factor, termed 'no consideration' or 'absence of consideration'. This appears to bring English law closer to the civilian idea of enrichment without cause. Birks doubts the utility of such a wide principle: [1992] PL 580, 587–88. In any event, in the swaps litigation the courts appear to have rejected no consideration in favour of the more traditional term of failure of consideration. See 12.4.

FURTHER READING

Asterisks indicate especially useful works.

Goff and Jones, 676–86

P. Birks, 'Restitution from Public Authorities' [1980] CLP 191

W. Cornish, 'Colour of Office, Restitutionary Redress Against Public Authority' (1987) 14 *J Malaysian & Comparative Law* 41

*P. Birks, 'Restitution from the Executive: A Tercentenary Footnote to the Bill of Rights', in Finn, 164–205

A. Burrows, 'Public Authorities, *Ultra Vires* and Restitution', in Burrows (1991), 39–69

P. Birks, ' "When Money is Paid in Pursuance of a Void Authority...." A duty to repay?' [1992] PL 580

*J. Beatson, 'Restitution of Taxes, Levies and Other Imposts: Defining the Extent of the *Woolwich* Principle' (1993) 109 LQR 401

E. McKendrick, 'Restitution of unlawfully demanded tax' [1993] LMCLQ 88

*Law Commission, *Restitution: Mistakes of Law and Ultra Vires Public Authority Receipts and Payments* (Law Com. No. 227) 1994, Parts VI to XVII

J. Beatson [1995] RLR 280, 286–88

N. Bamforth, 'Restitution and the scope of judicial review' [1997] PL 603

R. White, 'Restitution and the doctrine of *ultra vires*' (1999) 115 LQR 380

18   Restitution Claims by Public Authorities

As a matter of principle, it might be thought that a public authority seeking recourse against a citizen would be required to establish an appropriate ground for restitution or unjust factor, as would be the case in a transaction between private citizens. Accordingly, it would have to prove mistake, failure of consideration or some other factor. If there is any imbalance in the relationship, it is likely that the public authority is in the superior position. However, this is not the law. The leading authority is *Auckland Harbour Board* v *The Crown* [1924] AC 318, a decision of the Privy Council. Viscount Haldane enunciated the rule (at 327) that:

> Any payment out of the consolidated fund made without Parliamentary Authority, is simply illegal and *ultra vires*, and may be recovered by the Government if it can, as here, be traced. ... to invoke analogies of what might be held in a question between subject and subject is hardly relevant.

This was followed in the unsatisfactory Supreme Court of Victoria case of *Commonwealth of Australia* v *Burns* [1971] VR 825. In *Burns*, the government paid the defendant a pension to which she was not entitled. There was clearly a mistake, and it is difficult to see why the case was not decided on that basis. However, Newton J followed *Auckland Harbour Board*. His Honour interpreted Viscount Haldane's reference to tracing as not referring to the process in equity, but rather simply to tracing the identity of the recipient of the money. This, it is submitted, was correct. The case is unsatisfactory, however, in that the defendant, who had been assured that the money was due, was denied recourse to estoppel because there was no lawful authority for the payments in the first place. This is unconvincing. It is submitted that a payee in the position of the defendant in *Burns* would nowadays be entitled to a generous application of the defence of change of position (see Chapter 32).

The *Auckland Harbour Board* case was relied upon by Lord Goff of Chieveley in *Woolwich Equitable Building Society* v *Inland Revenue Commissioners* [1993] AC

70 as a reason in favour of the development of a principle that public authorities were under duty to return money which had been demanded on an *ultra vires* basis. It should be noted that Lord Goff interpreted the claim in *Auckland Harbour Board* as being 'proprietary in nature' (at 177). The proprietary explanation appears to be misconceived, because the language of tracing does not appear to have been used with any precision by Viscount Haldane.

It is an open question whether the principle enunciated in these cases is confined to payments out of the consolidated fund, or extends to all payment by central government, or indeed other public authorities. It is perhaps surprising that this cause of action was not utilised in the swaps cases, although the simple answer may be that the authorities were the net beneficiaries in the majority of reported cases. Whether local authorities can claim the benefit of the *Auckland Harbour Board* right is an open question: Burrows [1995] RLR 15, at 19. It seems to have been assumed that the local authorities could rely upon *ultra vires* as a cause of action by Lord Hope in *Kleinwort Benson Ltd* v *Lincoln City Council* [1999] 2 AC 349. His Lordship rejected an argument that a *bank* could not recover simply because the transaction was fully performed, observing (at 416):

The authorities, unlike the bank, can say that the transactions which they entered into were beyond their capacity. As their accounts must be rectified the transactions, although closed, must be reopened to enable them to recover the money which they had no power to pay out. In a case where the bank was the net beneficiary it cannot retain the net benefit which it received in the form of *ultra vires* payments from the local authorities. It would be unjust if the bank were not able to recover its net loss in those cases where the balance lies the other way.

The Law Commission considered reform of this peculiar unjust factor, but has not recommended any. See Law Com. No. 227, Part XVII.

FURTHER READING

Law Commission, *Mistakes of Law and Ultra Vires Public Authority Receipts and Payments* (Law Com. No. 227), 1994, Part XVII
Goff and Jones, 231
R. White, 'Restitution and the doctrine of *ultra vires*' (1999) 115 LQR 380

PART E

COMPLEX ENTITLEMENTS
AND LIABILITIES

19   Complex Entitlements

19.1   THEORETICAL FOUNDATIONS

The division of the modern law of restitution into two super-categories of (a) subtractive or autonomous unjust enrichment and (b) restitution for wrongs, is most prominent in Birks's writings: Birks, 6–7, 39–44, 99, 313. This bifurcation is winning acceptance in the cases. For a recent example see *Banque Financière de la Cité* v *Parc (Battersea) Ltd* [1999] 1 AC 221, at 226 *per* Lord Steyn. However, it is submitted that this simple two-fold division is insufficient to account for all the authorities. In particular, whereas the two Birksian categories are capable of explaining most bipartite cases, they are less successful at accommodating situations where more than two parties are involved.

Restitutionary techniques are prominent in adjusting and apportioning what are here termed complex entitlements and complex liabilities. Beatson has observed: 'restitution is a method of short circuiting complex multi-party liabilities, as where the liability of one has been borne by another [and] in contribution cases' (Beatson, 244). The case law traditionally organised under the heading 'legal compulsion' and the doctrine of contribution ascertain and adjust responsibilities of multiple co-obligers. These doctrines are appropriate where a claimant has the option of suing more than one defendant in a cause of action based upon a wrong (including breach of contract). Restitution has no role to play in that main action, but is responsible for adjusting the outcome as between the potential defendants. Accordingly the action for money paid shifts responsibility to the party primarily liable. Similarly, the doctrine of contribution adjusts and apportions responsibility where it is shared between multiple potential defendants.

Whereas those principles adjust complex liabilities on the defendant (or wrong-doer) side of the forensic equation, doctrines have also developed to ascertain and apportion complex entitlements on the potential claimants' side. There is a large body of cases from disparate, (usually) commercial contexts, which do not fit into the traditional bifurcated scheme of analysis. Restitution cannot be seen here as autonomous. Nor is it parasitic upon breach of duty by the defendant. Rather, the award of restitution is parasitic upon recovery by or upon the award of a remedy to a claimant who successfully recovers in respect of a wrong (including breach of contract).

Many of the cases are by-products of the now discarded contractual doctrine of privity. Even in the wake of the Contract (Rights of Third Parties) Act 1999, these cases still have an independent life. First, the cases are not confined to situations involving breach of contract. Secondly, as the Law Commission itself acknowledged when recommending the new legislation, its proposals do not touch upon this branch of the common law, which will be left for judicial development: Law Commission, *Privity of Contract: Contracts for the Benefit of Third Parties* (Law Com. No. 242, 1996, paras 2.36 to 2.46, 5.12 to 5.18 and 11.16 to 11.22, especially at para. 5.15). The central issue is whether, in awarding a wrong-based remedy to a claimant, the court will compensate not just the immediate claimant, but other parties who are also interested in performance by the defendant of his primary obligation.

A simple but controversial example is provided by *Jackson* v *Horizon Holidays Ltd* [1975] 1 WLR 1468. Mr Jackson booked a family holiday in Ceylon with Horizon Holidays at a price of £1,200. The hotel fell short of the quality of accommodation which he had been promised. Horizon conceded liability. The Court of Appeal held that Mr Jackson could recover not only in respect of his own mental distress, but also in respect of that suffered by his wife and twin infant children. Lord Denning MR delivered the only substantive judgment. His Lordship refused to categorise the interests of the other members of the family as based upon trust or agency. While conceding that only the father could bring the cause of action, Lord Denning MR denied that the father was limited to recovering his own loss. He could recover on behalf of the other members of the family too. Lord Denning MR concluded (at 1473): 'Once recovered, it will be money had and received for their use.' While some doubt was cast upon the reasoning in the *Jackson* case by dicta in the House of Lords in *Woodar Investment Development Ltd* v *Wimpey Construction UK Ltd* [1980] 1 WLR 277, no doubt was cast upon the result. However, it is submitted that in the light of more recent House of Lords authority the approach of Lord Denning in the *Jackson* case would now be seen as orthodox.

The existence of several pockets of case law where the English courts award compensation in excess of the interest of the claimant, which the claimant is under a duty to account for to his co-entitled parties, was acknowledged in the speech of Lord Diplock in *The Albazero* [1977] AC 774 at 846:

Nevertheless, although it is exceptional at common law that a plaintiff in an action for breach of contract, although he himself has not suffered any loss, should be entitled to recover damages on behalf of some third person who is not a party to the action for a loss which that third person has sustained, the notion that there may be circumstances in which he is entitled to do so was not entirely unfamiliar to the common law and particularly to that part of it which, under the influence of Lord

Mansfield and his successors, Lord Ellenborough and Lord Tenterden, had been appropriated from the law merchant.

I have already mentioned the right of the bailee, which has been recognised from the earliest period of our law, to sue in detinue or trespass for loss or damage to his bailor's goods although he cannot be compelled by his bailor to do so and is not himself liable to the bailor for loss or damage: *The Winkfield* [1902] P 42. Nevertheless, he becomes accountable to his bailor for the proceeds of the judgment in an action by his bailor for money had and received. So too the doctrine of subrogation the case of insurers, which was adopted from the law merchant by the common law in the eighteenth century, involved the concept of the nominal party to an action at common law suing for a loss which he had not himself sustained and being accountable to his insurer for the proceeds to the extent that he had been indemnified against the loss by the insurer. In this instance of a plaintiff being able to recover as damages for breach of contract for the benefit of a third person, a loss which that person had sustained and he had not, the insurer is entitled to compel an assured to whom he has paid a total or partial indemnity to bring the action. A third example, once again in the field of mercantile law, is the right of an assured to recover in an action on a policy of insurance upon goods the full amount of loss or damage to them, on behalf of anyone who may be entitled to an interest in goods at the time when the loss or damage occurs, provided that it appears from the terms of the policy that he intended to cover their interests. This rule was established as applicable to all forms of insurance upon property by the middle of the nineteenth century (*Waters* v *Monarch Fire and Life Insurance Co.* (1856) 5 E & B 870, 119 ER 705) and, as respects marine insurance, is now incorporated in section 26(3) of the Marine Insurance Act 1906.

In addition to Lord Diplock's three examples, it is necessary to consider the carriage of goods example which was at issue in *The Albazero*, and more recent authority on the employer's right of recovery in a construction contract in respect of defective work. First, though, it is necessary to distinguish the different questions which arise in such cases.

19.2 SIX QUESTIONS DISTINGUISHED

First, the parties must be introduced. There is a wrongdoer who has broken some primary obligation, whether imposed by law or whether assumed under a contract. The wrongdoer would be the defendant in the main claim and can be designated as 'X'. The claimant in the main claim has the right to vindicate a cause of action against X, and this usually takes the form of a secondary obligation on X to pay compensatory damages. The claimant or rightholder in the main claim can be designated as 'RH'. The claimant whose name appears on the face of the record of the main claim may have only a limited or nominal interest in the performance of X's duty. In these cases there is a third person who is also interested in securing the performance of X's primary and secondary obligations. Sometimes, especially in contractual cases, this third person has no direct right of legal recourse against X. Nor is it a case that RH has contracted on behalf of the third person as his agent. This third person we can designate as 'TP'. Most typically the reason why both RH and TP are interested in securing due performance by X of his legal obligations or reparation for a breach of X's duty, is that they are either concurrently or successively interested in the same property.

19.2.1   The reparation question

Where the claimant (RH) seeks compensation in event of a breach by the wrongdoer (X) of his obligations, can RH's measure of recovery encompass not just his own interest, but also the interest of the co-entitled third person (TP)? This question arises outside the law of unjust enrichment. It is properly regarded as the province of the remedies for torts and breaches of contract.

19.2.2   The restitution question

Where the reparation question is answered affirmatively, what relationship obtains between the claimant, RH, and the third person, TP? Has TP a legal claim against RH for a share of the proceeds reflecting his interests in that which has been recovered from X? In effect, has TP any ground for restitution?

19.2.3   The proprietary claim question

This question should be kept distinct from the preceding question. Where TP has a claim against RH, is the right a personal claim or a proprietary claim? This will obviously be of significance if RH is insolvent, if the fund increases or deceases in value. This is analogous to the nature of relief question, which arises in respect of claims in autonomous unjust enrichment and restitution for wrongs.

19.2.4   The compulsion question

Where TP suffers loss and RH suffers little or no loss, but only RH has a claim in law for the loss caused by X, can TP compel RH to bring a claim against X for his benefit? The only possible basis for this appears to be a contractual or consensual agreement that TP should have such a right.

19.2.5   The direct recourse question

In cases where TP has a direct claim, either by contractual or by other legal duty of X, what effect does this have? Does the existence of a direct claim preclude RH from claiming both in respect of his and his co-entitled party's interest in performance of the duty?

19.2.6   The satisfaction question

Where both RH and TP have a claim against X, does recovery in respect of both parties' interests, by either RH or TP, bar the other from proceeding against X? Is one co-entitled party thereby confined to a restitutionary claim against the other entitled party?

19.2.7   Summary

Obviously these questions overlap and have not always been clearly distinguished in the authorities. However, they illustrate that the unjust enrichment principle is playing a subsidiary and corrective role here. The role of restitution must remain sensitive to principles and policies of contract and tort which supply the main claims.

19.3   THE BAILEE'S RIGHT OF ACTION

Bailment is the relationship where the possession of tangible personal property is transferred from the owner (bailor) to another who has custody of the goods (bailee). The bailee's possessory interest in the chattel which is the subject-matter of the bailment is a proprietary interest. It has always entitled him to a cause of action against a person who wrongfully interfered with the goods. This right of reparation has long been held to encompass not just the bailee's own limited interest in the chattel, but the full value of the goods reflected in the interests of both bailor and bailee (*Wilbraham* v *Snow* (1540) 2 Wm Saunds 47, 85 ER 624; *Sutton* v *Buck* (1810) 2 Taunt 302, 127 ER 1094; *Burton* v *Hughes* (1824) 2 Bing 173, 130 ER 272; *Turner* v *Hardcastle* (1862) 11 CB (NS) 653, 142 ER 964; *Swire* v *Leach* (1865) 18 CB (NS) 479, 144 ER 531; *Jeffries* v *Great Western Railway Co.* (1856) 5 E & B 802, 119 ER 680; *Meux* v *Great Eastern Railway Co.* [1895] 2 QB 387, and *The Winkfield* [1902] P 42).

   With regard to the issue of restitution, it is well established that the bailee, having subtracted from any compensation recovered sums in respect of his own interest (any charges or expenses), must account over to the bailor for the balance of the proceeds. This was traditionally done by way of action for money had and received (*Turner* v *Hardcastle*; *Swire* v *Leach* and *The Winkfield*). The proprietary claim question has never directly arisen. In modern times the bailor has generally been regarded as having a cause of action himself for wrongful interference with goods, usually pursuant to a collateral bailment where the wrongdoer is a sub-bailee (*Morris* v *C.W. Martin & Sons Ltd* [1966] 1 QB 716; *The Pioneer Container* [1994] 2 AC 324). This does not appear to preclude either party from suing and recovering in full, although such recovery by either bailor or bailee will preclude further recourse against the wrongdoer.

   The leading case of *The Winkfield* concerned the collision of two ships with the subsequent loss of one vessel carrying a cargo of mail. The Postmaster-General made a claim against the responsible shipowners. This comprised:

(a)   some £105 claimed by the Crown as its own property;

(b)   some £5,000 worth of mail in respect of which the parties interested had made claims from the Postmaster-General and had given him written authority to represent them in proceedings; and

(c)   some £1,700, being the estimated value of letters and parcels to which no claim had been made.

The Postmaster-General undertook to distribute to the owners any such sums received. The Court of Appeal allowed all three claims. It was not necessary that the bailee should in turn be liable to his bailor for breach of duty. Collins MR stated (at 54):

> The law is that in action against a stranger for loss of goods caused by his negligence the bailee in possession can recover the value of the goods although he would have had a good answer to an action by the bailor for damages for loss of a thing bailed.

The root principle is that as against a wrongdoer, possession is title. The wrongdoer may not take the point that the bailee has only a limited interest in the goods. However, full recovery by the bailee will preclude any action by the bailor against the wrongdoer (*Nicolls* v *Bastard* (1835) 2 Cr M&R 659, at 660, *per* Parke B *arguendo*: 'I think you will find the rule is, that either the bailor or bailee may sue, and whichever first obtains damages, it is a full satisfaction'; *The Winkfield* [1902] P 42, at 61).

Where the bailor and bailee cooperate it will still be possible to route the claim through one party. Sections 7 and 8 of the Torts (Interference with Goods) Act 1977 provide protection for the wrongdoer, by entitling him to question the interest asserted by a claimant in a claim for wrongful interference with goods, and to ensure that he is not exposed to double jeopardy. Despite dicta in *The Winkfield* concerning the satisfaction issue, s. 7 of the 1977 Act makes elaborate provision to protect the wrongdoer from the spectre of double recovery by those interested in the goods. It provides:

(1)   In this section 'double liability' means the double liability of the wrongdoer which can arise —

(a)   where one of two or more rights of action for wrongful interference is founded on a possessory title, or

(b)   where the measure of damages in an action for wrongful interference founded on a proprietary title is or includes the entire value of the goods, although the interest is one of two or more interests in the goods.

(2)   In proceedings to which any two or more claimants are parties, the relief shall be such as to avoid double liability of the wrongdoer as between those claimants.

(3)   On satisfaction, in whole or in part, of any claim for an amount exceeding that recoverable if subsection (2) applied, the claimant is liable to account over to

the other person having the right to claim to such extent as will avoid double liability.

(4) Where, as a result of enforcement of a double liability, any claimant is unjustly enriched to an extent, he shall be liable to reimburse the wrongdoer to that extent.

For example, if a converter of goods pays damages first to a finder of the goods and then to the true owner, the finder is unjustly enriched unless he accounts over to the true owner under subsection (3); and then the true owner is unjustly enriched and becomes liable to reimburse the converter of the goods.

Section 7(3) therefore provides an affirmative answer to the restitution question in the context of the personal property tort. The duty to account is now confirmed as a statutory cause of action. For the avoidance of doubt, s. 7(4) provides a safety-net, second statutory cause of action in unjust enrichment in what seems to be the unlikely event of double recovery by both bailor and bailee. Both statutory causes of action in unjust enrichment are concerned with preventing the possibility of over-compensation where there are multiple interests in chattels. Section 8(2) provides a framework mechanism for rules of court to protect the position of the wrongdoer when a claim is brought in wrongful interference with goods, where the wrongdoer suspects that there are other interested parties. Procedure and pleadings were provided for by RSC Ord. 15, r. 10A. This required full particulars of the different interests in goods by the claimant, and in the usual case required the claimant to have written authority on behalf of every other co-entitled party. These useful provisions appear not to have been re-enacted in the new Civil Procedure Rules. This is unfortunate, as they provide a model framework for identifying multiple interests on the claimant side of the forensic equation, and appropriate safeguards for defendants in such cases. Rather than being jettisoned, it is submitted that these rules should have been extended into other scenarios, usually contractual, where a claimant sues on behalf of multiple interested parties.

19.4 THE INSURED BAILEE

The relationship here between the rightholder, RH, and X is contractual. X has provided RH with indemnity insurance in respect of goods stored by RH. Where, as a matter of construction, the policy extends not just to goods owned by RH, but to the goods of which he is custodian, RH can recover in respect of the full value of the goods. With this positive answer to the reparation question, it follows that RH is then accountable to his bailor (TP) for the value of the goods having deducted his own interest (namely, charges and expenses).

In *Waters* v *Monarch Fire and Life Assurance Co.* (1856) 5 E & B 870, 119 ER 705, a wharfinger and warehouseman stored grain and flour belonging to his customers. His own interest in the goods was limited to a lien for cartage and warehouse rent. He insured the goods with the defendant company, including 'goods in trust or on commission therein'. No charge was levied on the customers for the insurance, neither were they informed of the policy. Further, the warehouseman had no express authority to effect insurance on the goods. When a fire occurred the Court of King's Bench held that the warehouseman was entitled to an indemnity, not limited to his own interest in the goods, but extending to the full value of his customers' goods entrusted to him. Lord Campbell CJ stated (at 871):

> What is meant in these policies by the words 'goods in trust'? I think that means goods with which the assured were entrusted; not goods held in trust in the strict technical sense ... but goods with which they were entrusted in the ordinary sense of the word. They were so entrusted with the goods deposited on their wharfs; I cannot doubt the policy was intended to protect such goods; and it would be very inconvenient if wharfingers could not protect such goods by a floating policy.

This case establishes that the bailee has an insurable interest as to the full value of the goods, not limited to his own rights. It was further suggested in dicta that the wharfinger would be a trustee for the owners as to the balance of the moneys recovered (at 879). A different result follows where as a matter of construction it is held that the bailee is only insured for an indemnity to cover his own losses. Accordingly, he could recover the full value of the goods only where he was himself in breach of duty to his bailor. In *North British and Mercantile Insurance Co. Ltd* v *Moffatt* (1871) LR 7 CP 25, this was held to be the case as a matter of construction where the policy covered 'goods in trust and on commission for which they [the bailees] are responsible'.

The leading case is the decision of the House of Lords in *Hepburn* v *A. Tomlinson (Hauliers) Ltd* [1966] AC 451. A road haulage firm insured 'goods in transit' with a Lloyd's underwriter. A cargo of cigarettes belonging to Imperial Tobacco was stolen from a warehouse. The House of Lords confirmed that a bailee had an insurable interest, not limited to his own loss or personal liability to the owner of goods, but up to the full value. Lord Reid observed (at 467–68):

> he can recover the value of the goods though he has suffered no personal loss at all. But in that case the law will require him to account to the owner of the goods who has suffered a loss, or as Lord Campbell says, he will be trustee for the owner. I need not consider whether this is a trust in the strict sense or precisely on what ground the owner can sue the bailee for money which he has recovered from the insurer. A similar situation would arise if the bailee sued a wrongdoer for the value of goods converted or destroyed by him: there is no doubt that such an action can succeed and equally I could think there is no doubt that the bailee must then account to the true owner.

The House of Lords was emphatic that there was a duty to account, while support for a proprietary claim, in the shape of a trust, was more muted.

In the subsequent first instance case of *Re E. Dibbens & Sons Ltd* [1990] BCLC 577, the proprietary claim question was starkly posed. A now insolvent furniture storage company had insured 'goods in trust'. A serious fire had occurred at one of its warehouses, which eventually led to its liquidation. The company had two classes of customer. First, those who had contracted with the company to store their goods, and who had in addition contracted for and paid for the company to insure their goods under an express term in the bailment contract. Secondly, a class of customers who had stored goods, but had not paid the company any sum in respect of insurance. Harman J found the proprietary claim point 'entirely uncovered by authority' (at 578). He observed (at 579):

> The claim arises because common law judges in the past have referred to claims on policies on insurance of goods in the hands of warehousemen as being moneys held in trust.... As so often when common law judges talk about trustees, who were the trustees, for what purpose were they trustees, and on what terms they held the trust fund was entirely unclear.

This case differed from earlier authorities in that the insured bailee was insolvent, and the dispute was between the bailee and the bailor, not the bailee and the insurance company. Harman J concluded that the rights of the second group of claimants, against the warehousemen had been exclusively contractual. They had no proprietary claim to the insurance money. In contrast, with respect to the first group of claimants, it was held that there was superimposed upon the contractual relationship a fiduciary obligation upon the warehousemen, upon receipt of the money, to arrange insurance accordingly. Harman J concluded (at 583):

> one does not have here a true trust relationship at all: one has a relationship of fiduciary obligation which can be satisfied out of the insurance fund available to pay those persons who contracted with the company to have those goods insured to the amount which they required to be insured if the fund will go so far.

While Harman J does not explicitly describe it as such, the effect of his judgment was to create an equitable lien over the fund in favour of the first claimants only. It can further be observed that the result was unfair to the second group of claimants. The true contest was between them and the warehouse's general creditors. The money was paid by the insurance company only with the intention that it would be paid on to the owners of the goods. It was never intended that this money would be available for the general creditors of the warehouse. The recognition of an equitable lien in respect of both groups of claimants would here ensure that the insured bailee was merely a convenient conduit pipe, regardless of its solvency or otherwise.

19.5 INDEMNITY INSURANCE: SUBROGATION AND RELATED ACTIONS

The principle of indemnity requires of a contract of indemnity insurance that the insured should be fully indemnified, but no more than fully indemnified. The insured should not profit by the occurrence of a risk. One technique by which the principle of indemnity is enforced, is by the doctrine of subrogation. Where the indemnity insurer pays the insured in respect of an insured loss, he is entitled to be substituted for the insured's right of action against the wrongdoer who caused the loss. This will be considered in more detail in Chapter 22. The claim is brought in the name of the insured, whether the insurer has chosen to be subrogated or not. Where an action is brought by an insured claimant, the wrongdoer cannot take the point against the insured that he has recovered, or may recover, upon a policy (*Yates* v *Whyte* (1838) 4 Bing (NC) 272, 132 ER 793). Insurance receipts do not preclude full recovery on the wrong-based cause of action. Where an insurer does not choose to exercise rights of subrogation, the insured is entitled to maintain the claim against the wrongdoer, and will often do so to recover sums which were not insured (for example, the policy excess and uninsured losses). In this action the insured may recover the full value of the losses: an affirmative answer to the reparation question. However, the insured is then under a duty to account for the sums which represent the interest of the insurer. That is, he must pay back to the insurer what has been paid to him. Accordingly, a duty to account is recognised: an affirmative answer to the restitution question.

It has recently been held by the House of Lords in *Lord Napier and Ettrick* v *Hunter* [1993] AC 713, that in addition there should be an affirmative answer to the proprietary claim question. Here investors, or 'names', in the Lloyd's insurance market suffered massive losses, but they were able to recover under stop-loss policies which they had entered into to spread the losses. The names were successful in litigation against their negligent managing agent. It was conceded that they had a duty to account to the stop-loss insurers for the sums which represented their interest in the sums recovered. The House of Lords held that, in addition, the settlement moneys in the hands of the names' solicitors were subject to an equitable lien in favour of the stop-loss insurers. The House of Lords was following an earlier line of authority which supported equitable intervention to reinforce the duty to account (*Randal* v *Cockran* (1748) 1 Ves Sen 98, 27 ER 916; *Blaauwpot* v *DaCosta* (1758) 1 Ed 130, 28 ER 633; *London Assurance Co.* v *Sainsbury* (1783) 3 Dougl 245, 99 ER 636; *White* v *Dobinson* (1844) 14 Sim 273, 60 ER 636, aff'd *sub nom White* v *Dobbinson* (1844) 166 LT (OS) 233; *Commercial Union Assurance Co.* v *Lister* (1874) LR 9 Ch App 483 and *King* v *Victoria Assurance Co. Ltd* [1896] AC 250). Lord Goff concluded (at 744):

> I have little doubt the distinguished judges who decided the cases in the line of equity authority to which I have referred must have considered that money received by an assured [RH] from a third party [X] in reduction of a loss paid by an insurer [TP] should not be treated as available for the assured's normal cashflow, and further that the rights of the insurer to such money was sufficiently strong to entitle the insurer to priority in the event of the assured's bankruptcy, as was indeed held by Wynn-Parry J in *Re Miller, Gibb & Co. Ltd* [1957] 1 WLR 703.

Lord Templeman agreeing stated that proprietary rights were essential otherwise 'the unsecured creditors of the insured will benefit by double payment' (at 737). The

House of Lords was emphatic that an equitable lien was the appropriate proprietary claim to impose. A constructive trust would pose significant practical difficulties. Lord Browne-Wilkinson concluded (at 752):

> this proprietary interest is adequately satisfied in the circumstances of subrogation under an insurance contract by granting the insurers a lien over the moneys recovered by the assured from the third party. This lien will be enforceable against the fund so long as it is traceable and has not been acquired by a bona fide purchaser for value without notice. In addition to the equitable lien, the insurer will have a personal right of action at law to recover the amount received by the assured as moneys had and received to the use of the insurer.

The proprietary claim aspect is further discussed at 22.4. For proprietary claims in general, see Chapter 30.

Where an indemnity insurer does exercise rights of subrogation by taking over the right of action of the insured, this can be seen to be an exercise in adjusting complex liabilities. The insured has a right of claim against both the wrongdoer and the insurance company. Where the insured decides to pursue the insurance company, the insurer is entitled to exercise rights of subrogation in order that it might pursue the person primarily liable, that is the wrongdoer. In contrast, where no rights of subrogation are exercised, the issue remains one of complex entitlements. The insured pursues a claim against the wrongdoer and recovers not only in respect of his own interest, but also in respect of the interest of the insurers. The duty to account is not subrogation properly so-called, but a cause of action of unjust enrichment to prevent the insured recovering in excess of its own interest. It should not be described as subrogation as it was by the House of Lords in *Napier* v *Hunter*: see Mitchell [1993] LMCLQ 192; Mitchell, 67–86. Similarly, where subrogation does take place and the insurer recovers in excess of its interest (for example, it recovers losses including the policy excess), it too must account over to the insured for the sums which represent the insured's interest. This also is an aspect of complex entitlements, not complex liabilities. In *Lonrho Exports Ltd* v *Export Credits Guarantee Department* [1999] Ch 158, 181–82, it was stated that the insured had a proprietary claim. As can be seen, the existence of indemnity insurance on the claimant side of the forensic equation requires a number of different causes of action in unjust enrichment to ensure that neither insurer nor insured recovers in excess of its own interest.

19.6 RIGHTS OF SUIT IN RESPECT OF GOODS CARRIED BY SEA

By analogy with the right of action of the bailee, the common law originally provided the consignor of goods carried by sea with a right of action against the carrier. This right of action extended to the full value of the goods, even where the consignor was no longer the owner of the goods. If he recovered in such circumstances he was accountable to the owner for the moneys received in respect of the owner's interest (*Joseph* v *Knox* (1830) 3 Camp 320, 170 ER 1397; *Dunlop* v *Lambert* (1839) 6 Cl & F 600, 7 ER 824). Similar results were reached in cases of carriage of goods by land

(*Davis* v *James* (1770) 5 Burr 2680, 98 ER 407; *Moore* v *Wilson* (1787) 1 Term Rep 659, 99 ER 1306).

With the development of documentary sales in respect of goods carried by sea, and in particular the recognition of the bill of lading as a document of title and as a transferable contract of carriage under the Bills of Lading Act 1855, the right of the consignor became anomalous and largely unnecessary in practice. It was revisited in modern times in *Albazero (Owners)* v *Albacruz (Cargo Owners), The Albazero* [1977] AC 774. Here charterers (RH) chartered a vessel from the shipowners (X) under a five-year time charter. Crude oil was shipped from Venezuela to Antwerp. The vessel and cargo became a total loss. Property in the cargo was no longer vested in the charterers at the time of loss, but in the indorsee of the bill of lading (TP), which was another member of the corporate group to which the charterers belonged. The cargo owners were time-barred because they had not brought an action within the one-year limitation period provided by the Hague Rules, Article III, rule 6, which governed the bill of lading. Accordingly, the charterers claimed for the arrived value of the goods lost. The House of Lords held that the charterers were not entitled to succeed. Lord Diplock, in a characteristically trenchant single speech, refused to overrule *Dunlop* v *Lambert* as an anomalous exception to the compensatory rule of damages. Rather, his Lordship sought to restate its rationale and to delimit the situations in which it would apply. While the utility of the rule in *Dunlop* v *Lambert* was undermined in the carriage by sea context by developments in relation to bills of lading, the rule still extended to other forms of carriage, including carriage by land and carriage by sea where no bill of lading had been issued. The rule was necessary only where there was no contractual relationship between the carrier and the person who sustained the actual loss (an affirmative answer to the direct recourse question: see 19.2.5). Lord Diplock concluded (at 847):

> The only way in which I find it possible to rationalise the rule *Dunlop* v *Lambert* so that it may fit into the pattern of the English law is to treat it as an application of the principle, accepted also in relation to policies of insurance upon goods, that in commercial contract concerning goods where it is in the contemplation of the parties that the proprietary interests in the goods may be transferred from one owner to another after the contract has been entered into and before the breach which causes loss or damage to the goods, an original party to the contract if such be the intention of both, is to be treated in law as having entered into the contract for the benefit of all persons who have or may acquire an interest in the goods before they are lost or damaged, and is entitled to recover by way of damages for breach of contract the actual loss sustained by those for whose benefit the contract is entered into.

Therefore the rule is of limited practical relevance in the modern context where goods are shipped in a chartered vessel and it is contemplated that the bill of lading is issued in respect of the goods, and the carrier therefore enters into separate contract of carriage with whoever becomes the owner of the goods. This is certainly the case in the wake of the repeal of the Bills of Lading Act 1855 and its replacement by the Carriage of Goods by Sea Act 1992.

However, the Carriage of Goods by Sea Act 1992 does utilise a similar principle to that which underlay *Dunlop* v *Lambert*. The Act now effects a more efficient transfer of the contractual rights incorporated in the bill of lading or other relevant shipping document. Section 2 provides that the contractual rights of suit are concentrated in the hands of the last lawful holder of the bill of lading or other document. Under s. 2(4):

Where, in the case of any document to which this Act applies—

(a)   a person with any interest or right in or in relation to goods to which the document relates sustains loss or damage in consequence of a breach of the contract of carriage; but

(b)   subsection (1) above operates in relation to that document so that rights of suit in respect of that breach are vested in another person,

the other person shall be entitled to exercise those rights for the benefit of the person who sustained the loss or damage to the same extent as they could have been exercised if they had been vested in the person for whose benefit they are exercised.

Accordingly an affirmative answer is given to our reparation question (see 19.2.1) where different successive interests in the goods have been harmed. The subsection was clearly inserted for the avoidance of doubt. However, it does not go on to provide that the bill of lading holder must account over to the earlier interested party in respect of compensation recovered for that co-entitled party's losses (if that earlier party still bears the loss). As a matter of principle, it is clear that such a restitutionary duty to account does exist.

19.7   EMPLOYERS' RIGHTS OF SUIT IN CONSTRUCTION CONTRACTS

On the developer's side of the contractual relations in a major construction project there may be many interested parties. The nominal employer may not be the building owner, but will often be a special project vehicle incorporated for the purpose. Motives of property speculation, fiscal advantage, and local government strategies to evade central government borrowing restrictions mean that the employer may not be the party who is ultimately interested in securing due contractual performance. The development site may change hands at some stage during the project, or it may be intended that a complex corporate framework remains in place.

The leading modern House of Lords case is *Linden Gardens Trust Ltd* v *Lenesta Sludge Disposals Ltd, St Martin's Property Corp. Ltd* v *Sir Robert McAlpine* [1994] 1 AC 85 which applied *The Albazero* principle ([1977] AC 774) to the construction context. In the second appeal in the *St Martin's* case, Corporation (RH), who were developing a site in Hammersmith, entered into a building contract in 1968 (containing an assignment-prohibition clause) with McAlpine (X). In 1976, RH assigned its interest in the development to Investments (TP), another company in the same group, and in the same document purported to assign the benefit of the building contract to TP. The contractor's consent had not been sought to the purported assignment of the benefit of the works contract. The House of Lords unanimously held that assignment-prohibition clauses were effective and not contrary to public policy. The assignment in the *St Martin's* case was defective and void. The question therefore arose in *St Martin's* as to whether RH, the assignor, was entitled to damages and in what amount? In the leading speech, Lord Browne-Wilkinson held that the assignor, RH, was entitled to substantial damages by analogy with *Dunlop* v *Lambert* (at 114–15):

> In my judgment the present case falls within the rationale of the exceptions to the general rule that a plaintiff can only recover damages for his own loss. The contract was for a large development of property which, to the knowledge of both Corporation [RH] and McAlpine [X], was going to be occupied, and possibly purchased, by third parties and not by Corporation itself. Therefore it could be foreseen that damage caused by a breach would cause loss to a later owner and not merely to the original contracting party, Corporation. As in contracts for the carriage of goods by land, there would be no automatic vesting in the occupier or owners of the property for the time being who sustained the loss of any right of suit against McAlpine. On the contrary, McAlpine had specifically contracted that the rights of action under the building contract could not without McAlpine's consent be transferred to third parties who became owners or occupiers and might suffer loss. In such a case, it seems to me proper, as in the case of carriage of goods by land, to treat the parties as having entered into the contract on the footing that Corporation would be entitled to enforce contractual rights for the benefit of those who suffered from defective performance but who, under the terms of the contract, could not acquire any right to hold McAlpine liable for breach.

Lord Griffiths was prepared to go further: the contractor was liable as a matter of principle for the normal measure of damages in works materials contracts, namely the cost of remedying the defect, irrespective of whether his employer had a proprietary interest in the subject-matter of the work or not (at 96–97). The other members of the House of Lords, while sympathetic to this broad approach, were not to prepared to endorse it without full argument. (Note that the narrower ratio of Lord Browne-Wilkinson limits the cause of action to cases where the third party has no direct right of action against the wrongdoer — an affirmative answer to the direct recourse question.)

Two significant Court of Appeal cases have developed and extended this principle. In *Darlington Borough Council* v *Wiltshier Northern Ltd* [1995] 1 WLR 68, the local authority (TP) wished to build a recreation centre on its land. The actual building contracts were entered into by a subsidiary of the bank, Morgan Grenfell, as employers (RH). By separate agreement between the financier and the council, the financier undertook at the end of the construction period to assign to the council the benefit of any right it had against the building contractor (X), including any cause of action. The council claimed that there were serious defects to the building which would cost £2 million to cure. The financier executed a deed of assignment transferring any rights or causes of action it might have against the contractor to the council. The measure of the council's damages as assignee depended on the damages which could have been claimed by the financier as assignor. The Court of Appeal unanimously held that in the circumstances the council was entitled to recover substantial damages for the defective performance of the building contracts where it was perceived that such defects would cause the council loss. Here it was known to all the parties that the building contracts was ultimately for the benefit of the council and the loss was eminently foreseeable. Dillon LJ held the case was *a fortiori* from the *St Martin's* case as there was no prohibition upon assignment in the building contract. Steyn LJ reached the same result relying both upon the speech of Lord Browne-Wilkinson and the view of Lord Griffiths, which his Lordship described as 'classic contractual theory' (at 80). Dillon LJ, with Waite LJ agreeing, was prepared also to hold that if the assignor had claimed damages before the assignment, it would hold such damages as constructive trustee for the council. Steyn LJ considered it unnecessary to consider the constructive trust question.

Most recently, in *Alfred McAlpine Construction Ltd* v *Panatown Ltd* (1998) 58 Con LR 56, Panatown (RH) were the developers and McAlpine (X) were the main contractors for the construction of an office building in Cambridge. The cost of the development was in excess of £10 million. Panatown were not the building owners, but were rather linked by a chain of contracts to the other members of the corporate group, namely UIP and ultimately UCL (who were the actual building owners). This deliberate contract structuring was a legitimate evasion of VAT. The employers argued that the building was fundamentally flawed and probably required demolition. A complicating factor was the existence of a collateral contractual undertaking by McAlpine to UIP (described as site-owner) termed the 'duty of care deed'. The first instance judge held that the direct contractual nexus between the contractors and UIP ousted the operation of the ratio in the *St Martin's* case, answering the direct recourse question in the affirmative. The learned judge was obviously concerned by the spectre of double recovery. The Court of Appeal, in a cogent single judgment delivered by Evans LJ, disagreed. Evans LJ treated UIP as owner (UCL was parent company of both UIP and Panatown) and Panatown as developers. The court posed a short question: does Panatown's claim for substantial damages fail because Panatown is not the owner of the property? Evans LJ in a bold synthesis suggested that the affirmative answer to the reparation question does not depend upon any so-called rule or exception to be discerned from earlier authority, but rather depends upon the intention of the parties. Therefore it is always a matter of construction or interpretation which determines whether or not contracting parties agree that one party may recover, not only on its own behalf, but also on behalf of other co-interested parties. Evans LJ concluded (at 93):

If this analysis is correct, then in our judgment *Dunlop* v *Lambert* establishes that the right to recover 'substantial damages', meaning the appropriate measure of damages, arises because the parties to the contract intended or contemplated that it should arise, their intention being ascertained from the terms of the contract and the circumstances in which it was made, in the usual way. This is, arguably, the 'classic contractual theory' to which Steyn LJ referred in the *Darlington BC* case. When the situation arises, the plaintiff recovers damages in respect of financial loss which in fact has been borne by another person, and he is liable to account to that other person accordingly. The rule therefore can be described as an 'exception' to the general rule that a plaintiff cannot recover damages in respect of another person's loss, but equally it is simply equivalent as saying that the general rule can be modified by agreement, express or implied, between the parties concerned.

In the view of Evans LJ, the so-called broader approach of Lord Griffiths in the *St Martin's* case was not an alternative route to the same conclusion, but rather espoused the underlying principle upon which the established (so-called) exceptions were based. Accordingly, applying this contract-based synthesis, the Court held that Panatown was prima facie entitled to recover substantial damages for defective work, notwithstanding that it was not the building owner.

Further, the existence of a duty of care deed between the contractor and UIP did not in itself exclude the operation of the underlying principle. As a matter of interpretation, the Court was clearly of the view that the existence of the deed did not preclude the employer's right to recover under the main contract. The answer to the direct recourse question was treated as being dependent on the construction of the relevant contracts. The duty of care deed was not inconsistent with allowing full recovery under the main building contract. Evans LJ did not envisage any problems with double recovery (at 100):

> The common law solution has been that the claimant who recovers damages in respect of a proprietary interest he does not own is liable to a claim by the owner for money had and received. It seems to me that there will be no risk of double recovery if damages are recovered by the employer 'on behalf of' the building owner, and that such damages would have to be taken into account if the building owner made a separate claim. The legal mechanisms would not be difficult to devise.

This recognises affirmative answers to both the restitution question and the satisfaction question. As has been suggested above, what is recognised is that an appropriate procedural mechanism could be developed whereby the claimant must disclose the differing interests in respect of which he seeks to recover. Such a procedural mechanism existed under the old RSC Ord. 15, r. 10A. It would certainly be possible to achieve the same result by a Practice Direction under the new Civil Procedure Rules. The Court of Appeal was clear that with regard to the reparation question, the developer could recover substantial (rather than the appropriate measure of) damages to cover not only his own interest, but also the interests of other co-entitled parties. Similarly, the Court of Appeal was emphatic that there was then a duty to account to the other interested parties. No question of insolvency arose, but Evans LJ did observe that it 'may be that "constructive trust" is a correct description of the same rules of law in an equitable guise, but it is unnecessary to say more' (at 100).

19.8 THE INSURED VENDOR OF REAL PROPERTY

A problem occurs where real property is damaged between contract and conveyance. In *Rayner* v *Preston* (1881) 18 Ch D 1, the purchaser completed and paid the full purchase price to the vendor even though the property was damaged by fire. The vendor had recovered a substantial indemnity from his insurers as well as the purchase price. The vendor refused to account to the purchaser with the insurance proceeds. The majority of the Court of Appeal could see no route for making him accountable for these insurance proceedings to the purchaser. In contrast, in a dissenting judgment James LJ proposed rendering the insured vendor accountable in equity. In a sequel, the vendor was made to refund the moneys to the insurance company (*Castellain* v *Preston* (1883) 11 QB 380). The problem is now governed by s. 47 of the Law of Property Act 1925, which adopts affirmative answers to both the reparation and the restitution questions. Section 47(1) provides:

> Where after the date of any contract of sale or exchange of property, money becomes payable under any policy of insurance maintained by the vendor in respect of any damage to or destruction of property included in the contract, the money shall, on completion of the contract, be held by or receivable by the vendor on behalf of the purchaser and paid by the vendor to the purchaser on completion of the sale or exchange, or as soon thereafter as the same shall be received by the vendor.

It should be noted that the statute gives no explicit answer to the availability of a proprietary claim.

19.9 CONCLUSION

With regard to our first question, namely the quantum of compensation recoverable where there are multiple interested parties on the claimant's side, there are now pockets of case law in which it is recognised that the claimant in the main action can recover in respect both of his own interests and the interests of other co-entitled parties. Such a right is recognised in respect of the personal property torts, and the role of restitution is codified by ss. 7 and 8 of the Torts (Interference with Goods) Act 1977. Further, in the contractual arena, there is increasing sensitivity to situations where one party contracts on his own behalf and also in effect on behalf of others concurrently or successively interested in the same property or subject-matter. The question is rightly treated as one of construction or interpretation.

Where the reparation question is answered in the affirmative, it never seems to have been doubted that the claimant to the main action has a duty to account over to the third person who is also interested in the money recovered. Sometimes the relationship will be governed by contract. However, sometimes it must arise in the law of unjust enrichment. The restitutionary solution is one which adjusts and apportions complex entitlements on the claimant side of the forensic equation. Therefore the rules which the courts have devised distinctly mirror those defendant-sided doctrines such as contribution and legal compulsion which ascertain and adjust complex legal liabilities of multiple wrongdoers.

The question of whether the claim of the interested third party should be a proprietary one has received mixed responses. However, in the leading case of *Lord Napier and Ettrick* v *Hunter*, the House of Lords conducted a most sophisticated discussion of proprietary claims in this area. The metaphor of the conduit pipe is difficult to resist. The moneys paid to the claimant of the main action were never paid to him beneficially.

Currently, with regard to the question of compulsion, this right appears to exist only in contracts of indemnity insurance. However, there is nothing to stop an interested third party bargaining for such a right in his relationship with the potential claimant in the main action. Such a clause could easily be envisaged in a contract between a bailor and a bailee.

The existence of a direct right of recourse by TP against X does not seem to preclude the recognition that RH can recover in full if he himself sues in the personal property tort cases. Some contractual cases have assumed that such a right would limit claimants to their own interests. The most recent authority in the contractual cases suggests that it is a matter of interpretation whether a direct right to recourse should preclude the right of one party to recover in full.

It is submitted that with respect to the satisfaction question, once one party has recovered in full, the cause of action against the wrongdoer is exhausted. The co-entitled party is confined to its restitutionary remedy against the other co-entitled party. It would be appropriate for rules of court to be drafted along the model of the personal property rules which were contained in RSC Ord. 15, r. 10A. However, these rules should be extended to contractual cases. Accordingly where a party suing in breach of contract intends to recover in respect not only of his own interest in the contractual performance, but also in respect of the interests of other parties, he should obtain the written consent of each co-entitled party. Further, or in the alternative, the respective interests of co-entitled parties must be specifically pleaded. This will avoid a multiplicity of claimants and unnecessary duplication of costs. Equally the wrongdoer X should be entitled to insist that any party whom he believes will benefit from recovery by RH should be brought before the court and added to the proceedings to ensure that he does not become liable to double jeopardy. In this way the fears about double recovery can be avoided. Even in the absence of rules of court, it is sound practical advice that those acting for claimants should plead the full interests in respect of which the claimants hope to succeed. Further, where multiple claimants are cooperating in channelling a claim through one party, written authority from each claimant to this course of action should be obtained.

FURTHER READING

Asterisks indicate especially useful works.

J. Cartwright, 'Damages, Third Parties and Common Sense' (1996) 10 JCL 244

*N. Palmer and G. Tolhurst, 'Compensatory and Extra-Compensatory Damages, the Role of the *"The Albazero"* in Modern Damages Claims' Part 1 (1997) 12 JCL 1 and Part 2 (1997) 12 JCL 97

N. Palmer, *Bailment*, 2nd edn (1991), 308–81

M. Clarke, *The Law of Insurance Contracts*, 3rd edn (1998), chap. 4

B. Coote, '*Dunlop v Lambert*: The Search for a Rationale' (1998) 13 JCL 91

N. Palmer and G. Tolhurst, 'Compensatory and Extra-Compensatory Damages, *Linden Gardens* and the "Lord Griffiths" Principle' (1998) 13 JCL 143

G. Treitel (1998) 114 LQR 527

I. Duncan Wallace QC, 'Third Party Damage: No Legal Black Hole?' (1999) 115 LQR 394

G. McMeel, 'Complex Entitlements: The *Albazero* Principle and Restitution' [1999] *Restitution Law Review* 21

20 Complex Liabilities: Recovery From a Party Primarily Liable

20.1 INTRODUCTION

The bipartite nature of much litigation may tend to conceal inherent complexity in many law suits. Suppose one car driver collides with another. Despite its apparent simplicity, even here insurance companies will be involved on both sides. In a shunting incident there may be a number of potential defendants and potential claimants. Similarly in commercial transactions, more than one party may be liable for a breach of a legal obligation, or be liable upon the same debt. Sometimes on the claimant side more than one person is concerned with the due performance of a legal obligation. The terminology of complex entitlements and complex liabilities is employed to demonstrate how the principle against unjust enrichment and restitutionary techniques are employed to mop up where there is a proliferation of interests on either side of the forensic equation. Complex entitlements were considered in Chapter 19. Now we turn to co-extensive liabilities. This chapter is concerned with cases where amongst a number of co-obligers one of them is adjudged to be primarily liable for the discharge of the legal duty. The next chapter considers the doctrine of contribution which ascertains and adjusts the liabilities of co-obligers where each is adjudged to have at least some share in the responsibility for a breach of legal duty.

20.2 LEGAL COMPULSION AND THE ACTION FOR MONEY PAID

The characteristic technique for a co-obliger to seek recovery from the person primarily liable is the old *action for money paid*. The case law is traditionally organised under the soubriquet of 'legal compulsion', and is aligned in a sequence with duress, undue influence and necessitous intervention. (See Birks, 173–203, especially 185–92 ; Goff and Jones, Part II B, especially 437–56.) However, it is submitted that its more natural home is in the context of the discussion of other doctrines which ascertain and apportion complex liabilities.

Legal compulsion is relevant in the limited sense that we are concerned with parties who are all liable to a common claimant. However, the gist of the action is that as between multiple obligers, one of them is the principal debtor, whereas the other's liability was only in an accessory capacity. Where it could be shown that one co-obliger is *primarily liable* the action for money paid would lie. As would be said nowadays, the party who is not primarily liable may recoup his expenditure from the principal debtor. The background is that a claimant faced with multiple obligers may pursue any one or more of them in respect of the obligation. Payments made by the claimant under the threat of or actual use of legal process are irrecoverable on public policy grounds. There is a limited exception where recourse to legal process is made in bad faith (*Duke De Cadaval v Collins* (1836) 4 Ad & E 858, 111 ER 1006; Goff and Jones, 312–16). So legal compulsion is not the gist of the action. Rather the crucial finding is that as between multiple co-obligers, one is primarily liable. The claimant in the main action is clearly entitled to his money, and to make legitimate use of the legal process (or the threat of it) to obtain it. Once successful, restitution plays a corrective function as between the co-obligers.

20.3 THE DISCHARGE OF DEBTS

A related principle which confirms that the law's concern is with complex *legal* liabilities is the rule that a debt can be validly discharged by a payment by a person other than the debtor only in very limited circumstances. This is an enrichment issue (see 1.4.5). If the claimant cannot satisfy the restrictive rules concerning when the debt of another is validly discharged, he will not be able to demonstrate that the defendant has been enriched.

There are two main exceptions to the 'no discharge by a stranger' rule. First, the debt will be discharged if the payment is by an authorised agent of the debtor, or is subsequently ratified and adopted by the debtor. Secondly, the payment will be effective to discharge the debt where the payer was acting under legal compulsion or was perhaps necessitously intervening on behalf of the debtor. See Birks and Beatson (1976) 92 LQR 188. Despite some academic advocacy of a principle of automatic discharge of debts, the rule is currently entrenched. The development or abrogation of this rule will be returned to below after considering the difficult leading case of *Owen v Tate* [1976] QB 402.

20.4 THE PRINCIPLE OF PRIMARY OR ULTIMATE LIABILITY

In *Exall v Partridge* (1799) 8 Term Rep 308, 101 ER 1405, Exall left his carriage at the premises of Partridge, a coach maker, where it was lawfully seized by Partridge's landlord as distress for rent arrears. Exall paid the rent arrears in order to redeem his carriage. He succeeded in an action for money paid against Partridge and his co-lessees. All the members of the court stressed that it was a case of compulsion, not a voluntary payment. Lawrence J stated (at 311): 'The justice of the case indeed is, that the one who must ultimately pay this money, should alone be answerable here.'

The underlying principle was stated in the first edition of *Leake on Contract* (at 41):

> Where the plaintiff has been compelled by law to pay, or, being compellable by law, has paid money which the defendant was ultimately liable to pay, so that the latter obtains the benefit of the payment by the discharge of his liability; under such circumstances the defendant is held indebted to the plaintiff in the amount.

This formulation was adopted and applied in the leading cases of *Moule* v *Garrett* (1872) LR 7 Ex 101, at 104 and *Brook's Wharf and Bull Wharf Ltd* v *Goodman Brothers* [1937] 1 KB 534, at 543–44. In the latter case the plaintiffs stored a consignment of animal skins in their warehouse on behalf of the defendant furriers who had imported them from Russia. The skins were stolen, but not due to any negligence on the part of the plaintiffs. The plaintiffs were personally liable to pay import duties upon the consignment under the relevant customs legislation. The Court of Appeal held that the defendant furriers were liable to reimburse the plaintiffs for the money they had been obliged to pay. Lord Wright MR both explicitly rested recovery upon the ground of unjust enrichment and drew an analogy with the law of guarantee in formulating the rule of recovery (at 544):

> The essence of the rule is that there is a liability for the same debt resting on the plaintiff and the defendant and the plaintiff has been legally compelled to pay, but the defendant gets the benefit of payment, because his debt is discharged either entirely or *pro tanto*, whereas the defendant is primarily liable to pay as between himself and the plaintiff. The case is analogous to that of a payment by surety which has the effect of discharging the principal's debt and which, therefore, gives a right of indemnity against the principal.

Indeed, the right of a surety who has been obliged to pay his principal's debt under the terms of a guarantee to reimbursement from his principal is the paradigm instance of this species of liability. The essential ingredient in the cause of action is that the clamant was liable only in an accessory capacity, whereas the defendant was primarily liable for the obligation which has been discharged by the claimant.

20.5   RECOUPMENT AND LEASEHOLD INTERESTS

In *Moule* v *Garrett* (1872) LR 7 Ex 101, the plaintiff was a tenant of premises which imposed upon the tenant an obligation to repair. The plaintiff assigned the lease to one Bartley, who in turn assigned to the defendant. Both assignments contained express covenants to indemnify the immediate assignor against any subsequent breaches of the repairing covenant. Dilapidations occurred during the defendant's possession, and the landlord recovered a sum in respect of this from the plaintiff. The Court of Exchequer Chamber held that the plaintiff was entitled to recoup that sum from the defendant. The defendant as ultimate assignee was the party by whose default the damage was occasioned and therefore was primarily liable.

Whereas the liability of an immediate assignee would be explicable on ordinary contractual principles, the liability of subsequent assignees is independent of contract (*Re Healing Research Trustee Co. Ltd* [1992] 2 All ER 481). However, where there was neither privity of contract nor privity of estate, there could be no liability at all (*Bonner v Tottenham and Edmonton Permanent Investment Building Society* [1899] 1 QB 161). In *Bonner* the plaintiff tenant had assigned the remainder of his lease to one Price, who in turn mortgaged his interest in the premises to the defendant building society by way of a sub-lease. The building society entered into possession but did not pay the rent due under the lease to the landlord. The plaintiff as the original tenant had to pay it, but was held not entitled to recoup it from the defendant building society. The plaintiff's contractual right of recourse against the immediate assignee was rendered valueless by the latter's insolvency. Here the plaintiff and the sub-lessee were not equally liable for the rent. The landlord had a direct right of recourse only against the plaintiff lessee. There was no community of interest between the original lessee and the building society. Even Vaughan Williams LJ, who was prepared to state a wider equitable principle of recovery, did not think the plaintiff entitled to succeed. The wider principle would apply where 'there is community of interest in the subject-matter to which the burden is attached, which has been enforced against the plaintiff alone, coupled with benefit to the defendant, even though there is no common liability to be sued' (at 174). However, here there was no commonality of interest: the obligation imposed upon the original lessee by the lease, occurred in a lease in which the sub-lessee had no interest. They were not common obligers.

For discussion of possible development based on Vaughan Williams LJ's wider principle, which is based upon an analogy with rights of contribution, see Goff and Jones, 391–93. The practical impact of these cases is now reduced by the Landlord and Tenant (Covenants) Act 1995.

20.6   OTHER ILLUSTRATIONS OF THE PRINCIPLE

In *Edmunds v Wallingford* (1885) 14 QBD 811, some of the stock-in-trade of two brothers was seized by a judgment creditor of the father while it was on the premises of the father. The father was primarily liable to the judgment creditor. He was held liable to repay his sons the value of the goods, even in the absence of any agreement to indemnify them. The earlier contrary case of *England v Marsden* (1866) LR 1 CP 529 was disapproved.

Similarly, in *Johnson v Royal Mail Steam Packet Co.* (1867) LR 3 CP 38, the mortgagees of two vessels who had paid the crews' past wages for which the defendant operators were primarily liable, were entitled to reimbursement from the latter. The payments had been made under the threat of the crews exercising their maritime lien. Willes J provided a homely example which neatly illustrates the operation of recoupment (at 45):

> A lends B his horse for a limited period, which would imply that he must pay for the expense of the horse's keep during the time he retains it. B goes to an inn and runs up a bill, which he does not pay, and the innkeeper detains the horse. In the meantime A has sold the horse out-and-out for its full price to C, and C is informed that the horse is at the inn, he proceeds there to take him away, but is told he cannot take him until the pays the bill, and he pays the bill accordingly and gets his horse; can C, who in order to get his horse is obliged to pay the debt of another, sue that other in action for money paid? We are clearly of the opinion that he could; and without heaping up authorities where it has been held, independent of contract, that a person occupying a property in respect of which there is a claim that ought to have been discharged by another, is entitled to reimbursement, we think that this is a case in which the mortgagees . . . are entitled to recover on the count for money paid.

The principle has also been applied in the context of the abatement of nuisances. In *Gebhardt* v *Saunders* [1892] 2 QB 452, the plaintiff tenant occupied a dwelling in which a public nuisance arose by reason of water and sewage collecting in a cellar due to a blockage in the drains. The statutory sanitary authority required the owner or occupier to resolve the situation. The tenant undertook the necessary work. The tenant would have been the responsible party if the nuisance was caused by improper use, but if the nuisance was due to a structural defect it was the landlord's responsibility. When it was discovered that the nuisance fell into the latter category it was held that the tenant was entitled to reimbursement for his expenditure from the landlord. Day J concluded (at 457):

> If two people are required to do certain work under a penalty in case of disobedience, and one does the work, and it turns out afterwards that the other ought to have done it, the expenses are properly money paid at the request of the person who was primarily liable, but who neglected to do the work.

Birks suggests that the unjust factor here is best characterised as mistake: Birks, 191. However, the underlying principle relied on by Day J was primary liability.

20.7   OFFICIOUSNESS AND *OWEN* v *TATE*

It is commonly said that where A is indebted to a friend, B, there can be no right to recoupment if C, an enemy of A, purports to pay off A's debt in order to convert himself into A's creditor (*Exall* v *Partridge* (1799) 8 Term Rep 308, at 310; 101 ER 1405 *per* Lord Kenyon CJ). So if Uriah Heep had paid money to Mr Micawber's creditors he would not thereby acquire any rights against Mr Micawber. There is clearly some discomfort with the idea that the new would-be creditor might be more exigent than the original creditor. However, this is hard to justify in the modern climate where debts are freely assignable. There are two ways of explaining the traditional approach, though. One is that the payment by the intervener is not effective to discharge the debt. It seems that the original debtor is still liable, and it is arguable that the creditor may be obliged to refund the money to the intervener on the ground of failure of consideration: Birks and Beatson (1976) 92 LQR 180, or Beatson, 177–205. Alternatively, it is said that the intervener is precluded if he officiously makes the payment or officiously exposes himself to liability for the debt: Goff and Jones, 444–49.

The leading case of *Owen v Tate* [1976] QB 402 illustrates the limits of the right to recoupment. The Tates had obtained a loan from a bank which was secured by a mortgage upon Ms Lightfoot's property. Subsequently, Ms Lightfoot sought help from her former employer, Mr Owen, who agreed to deposit money with the bank and sign and guarantee in respect of the money owed by the Tates, thereby substituting himself for Ms Lightfoot. This was done without consulting the Tates, and indeed they protested when they first heard that the mortgage over Ms Lightfoot's property was to be released. Subsequently, the Tates defaulted, and referred the bank to Owen. The bank enforced Mr Owen's guarantee. Owen claimed reimbursement from the Tates. The Court of Appeal refused the relief claimed. Scarman LJ stated (at 409–10):

It follows that the way in which the obligation came to be assumed is a relevant circumstance. If, for instance, the plaintiff has conferred a benefit upon the defendant behind his back in circumstances in which the beneficiary has no option but to accept the benefit, it is highly likely the courts will say that there is no right to indemnity or reimbursement. But (to take the other extreme) if the plaintiff has made a payment in a situation not of his own choosing, but where the law imposes an obligation upon him to make the payment on behalf of the principal debtor, then clearly the right of indemnity does arise. Not every case would be so clear-cut: the fundamental question is whether in the circumstances it was reasonably necessary in the interests of the volunteer or the person for whom the payment was made, or both, that the payment should made — whether in the circumstances it was 'just and reasonable' that a right of reimbursement should arise.

In his Lordship's view, Mr Owen 'was as absolute a volunteer as one could conceivably imagine anyone to be' (at 410). The result is rather unsatisfactory in that it is clear that if Ms Lightfoot had remained as surety for the Tates' obligations, she would have been entitled to the right to reimbursement if the bank had proceeded against her. The decision has attracted much academic criticism and comment: Birks, 189–92, 311–12; Mitchell, 166–67. The latter points out two key problems with the case. First, could it not be said that ultimately the Tates requested or accepted Owen's intervention when they encouraged the bank to have recourse against Owen, when they had defaulted. This would overcome the problem of establishing enrichment, and arguably supplies a ground for restitution. Secondly, the court overlooked s. 5 of the Mercantile Law Amendment Act 1856 (see 22.3) (which was not cited), which entitled Owen to a remedy on these facts. On that ground alone the case is *per incuriam*.

The reasonable necessity test devised by the Court of Appeal in *Owen* v *Tate* was applied subsequently in *The Zuhal K and the Selin* [1987] 1 Lloyd's Rep 151, in which a vessel was arrested. The shipowner asked its P & I Club to secure the release of the vessel, and therefore the club arranged for an insurance company to enter into a guarantee in respect of the shipowner's liability to the arresting cargo owner. The cargo owner claimed under the guarantee and the guarantor sought reimbursement from the shipowner. It was held that the P & I Club had actual, or at least ostensible, authority to arrange the guarantee from the insurance company. Further, Sheen J was under no doubt that it was reasonably necessary in the interest of the shipowner that the guarantee should be procured, and that in the circumstances it was just and reasonable that a right of reimbursement should arise. For discussion, see Watts [1989] LMCLQ.

20.8 COMMON INTEREST IN PROPERTY

The right to reimbursement has been further expanded by the Court of Appeal in *Kleinwort Benson Ltd* v *Vaughan* [1996] CLC 620. An employee of the bank purchased a property exclusively with money stolen from his employer. The house was in his and his wife's joint names (they were first and second defendants). The wife was innocent of any wrongdoing. The bank was held entitled to trace into the property in the defendants' names and lay claim to it. That property was subject to a prior legal charge, therefore the bank redeemed the charge in order to realise the value of the property. It was held that the defendants could not deny the bank's entitlement to a right of reimbursement against them. Such a payment could not be described as a voluntary one, even though there was no compulsion or necessity. Nourse LJ observed that the bank's interest in the property was encumbered by the prior charge. He concluded (at 624):

> It could not be realised to the best advantage while the charge remained in existence. So the redemption of the charge by the plaintiff was not a simple case of a volunteer paying off another's debt. It was the debt of those whose charge had partially defeated the plaintiff's right, as against them, to the beneficial interest in the property. The defendant cannot deny the plaintiff's entitlement to perfect that right.

Two points can be made. First, it was assumed that the defendants' obligations were discharged by the bank's payments even though there was no authority, compulsion or necessity. This appears to rest on a further exception to the rule that payments of another's debts do not discharge the obligation, i.e., where there is some common interest in property: Goff and Jones, 17–18; Mitchell, 167–71. As these writers acknowledge, this is difficult to reconcile with the well-known Court of Appeal authority of *Falcke* v *Scottish Imperial Insurance Co.* (1886) 34 Ch D 324, where a payment by the holder of the equity of redemption of a life insurance policy to save the policy was held not to entitle him to a lien (see 15.2.4). Secondly, what is the ground for restitution? This case goes further than the cases on co-obliged defendants. It appears to be a policy-motivated unjust factor based on the commonality of interest in property. For discussion of the relevant case law (which was not cited in *Vaughan*), see Sutton, in Burrows (1991), 71–104; Mitchell, 167–71.

20.9 THE DISCHARGE OF DEBTS REVISITED

A debt is clearly validly discharged when paid by the debtor as principal or by an agent of his either with prior authority, or by subsequent ratification. In addition, it has been held that a debt is validly discharged if paid by one under legal compulsion, or in circumstances where it is reasonably necessary for an intervener to pay in the interests of the debtor (*Owen* v *Tate* [1976] QB 402). Further, a party with a community of interest in property belonging to the defendant can make a payment to protect his own interest in the property, which has the effect of discharging the defendant's obligations (*Kleinwort Benson Ltd* v *Vaughan* [1996] CLC 620).

Outside of these circumstances the common law does not recognise the discharge of debts by interveners. Therefore it has been held that a mistaken payment does not usually discharge the debt of the third party (*Barclays Bank Ltd* v *W. J. Simms, Son & Cooke (Southern) Ltd* [1980] QB 677 (see 3.5.3), though compare *B. Liggett (Liverpool) Ltd* v *Barclays Bank Ltd* [1928] 1 KB 48, where a rule of automatic discharge appears to have been assumed (see 22.7)). Further, the restrictive rule of discharge of liability is supported by influential dicta in the House of Lords (*Esso Petroleum Co.* v *Hall, Russell & Co. Ltd, 'The Esso Bernicia'* [1989] AC 643, at 662–63 *per* Lord Goff of Chieveley). For discussion, see Beatson, 177–205. There is some academic advocacy of a rule of automatic discharge: Friedmann (1983) 99 LQR 534; Burrows, 222–30. However, the orthodox position is currently no discharge by a stranger, subject to the above exceptions.

FURTHER READING

Asterisks indicate especially useful works.

Goff and Jones, 16–18, 389–93, 437–56
Birks, 185–92
*Mitchell, 19–26, 162–71
*P. Birks and J. Beatson, 'Unrequested Payment of Another's Debt' (1976) 92 LQR 188; also in Beatson, 177–205
*D. Friedmann, 'Payment of Another's Debt' (1983) 99 LQR 534
R. Sutton, 'Payment of Debts Charged upon Property' in Burrows (1991), 71–104
*C. Mitchell, 'Distributing the Burden of Alternative Co-extensive Liabilities: Some Banking Cases Considered' in Rose (1998), 27–41

21 Complex Liabilities: Recovery from a Party with whom Liability is Shared

21.1 INTRODUCTION

Whereas the previous chapter was concerned with situations where one co-obliger was primarily liable for the discharge of an obligation, this chapter is concerned with situations where multiple obligors share a liability to a common claimant. The rules of contribution ascertain and adjust their mutual responsibilities. The foundation of the rights of co-obligers *inter se* is the principle of unjust enrichment. However, this is parasitic upon a prior determination as to their respective degrees of responsibility towards the claimant. The theoretical foundations were exposed by Eyre CB over 200 years ago in *Dering* v *Earl of Winchelsea* (1787) 1 Cox 318, at 321, 29 ER 1184:

> If we take a view of the cases both in law and equity, we shall find that contribution is bottomed and fixed on general principles of justice, and does not spring from contract; though contract may qualify it.

It is necessary to draw a distinction between debt and damages. Where there is a common liability in respect of the same debt, the common law still applies. In contrast, other claims for tort, breach of trust and actions in restitution are governed by the Civil Liability (Contribution) Act 1978. However, a recent decision of the Court of Appeal has placed a strain on this traditional distinction.

21.2 LIABILITY IN DEBT: THE CO-SURETY CASES

The leading early case of *Dering* v *Earl of Winchelsea* (1787) 1 Cox 318, 29 ER 1184 concerned joint sureties. The plaintiff and two others by three separate bonds became guarantors of the obligations of Thomas Dering to the Crown in respect of customs duties collected by him. He was the younger brother of the plaintiff. The younger

Dering became insolvent, apparently as a result of his gambling debts, and left the country and his debts behind. Judgment was obtained against the plaintiff in respect of those debts, and the plaintiff in turn sought contribution from his co-sureties. The Court of Exchequer repudiated an attempt to argue that the case was governed by contract, stating: 'It would be strange to imply any contract as among the sureties in this situation' (at 320). The obligation sprang from general principles of justice, or as we would say these days, unjust enrichment. However, the parties could contract around and exclude such rights to contribution. The fact that the parties entered into three separate bonds (at 322) rather than one made no difference. Eyre CB concluded (at 322):

> In all these cases the sureties have a common interest, and a common burthen; they are joined by the common end and purpose of their several obligations, as much as if they were joined in one instrument, with this difference only, that the penalties will ascertain the proportion in which they are to contribute, whereas if they had joined in one bond, it must have depended on other circumstances.

The court further drew an analogy with the principle of general average contribution in maritime law. General average contribution is explained on the basis of unjust enrichment by Goff and Jones, 427–36; compare Rose, 'General Average as Restitution' (1997) 113 LQR 569.

The principle which developed at common law and in equity was one which awarded contribution between co-sureties, indemnity insurers and mortgagors. What was required was that the parties should be liable to a common demand in respect of the same debt. Liability is shared equally, although this can be varied by contractual agreements. In *Stimpson* v *Smith* [1999] Ch 340, Peter Gibson LJ summarised the uncontroversial principles governing such relief (at 348):

> (1)   Where more than one person guarantee to the creditor the payment of the same debt, an equity arises such that if one of them pays more than his due proportion of the debt, he is entitled to a contribution from his co-guarantor or co-guarantors.
>
> (2)   It is immaterial whether the co-guarantors are bound jointly or severally, or jointly and severally, or by the same instrument, or by separate instruments, or in the same sum or in different sums, or at the same time, or different times, or whether the co-guarantor making the payment knows of the existence of the other co-guarantor or co-guarantors, as the right of contribution is not dependent upon agreement express or implied.
>
> (3)   Normally an action for contribution cannot be brought until payment has been made by a co-guarantor of more than his fair share of the common liability.

In exceptional circumstances, *quia timet* (or pre-emptive) relief can be sought, such as where judgment has been entered against one co-guarantor. In *Stimpson* v *Smith*, the Court of Appeal held that a stipulation in the guarantee that the creditor would give written notice of a demand was not a pre-condition to the right to relief against a co-surety. It could be waived by one co-guarantor as long as it was not officious to do so, and any payment made was not a voluntary payment. On contribution and co-sureties, see Goff and Jones, 399–409.

21.3   THE SCOPE OF THE 1978 ACT

At common law there was no right to contribution where multiple tortfeasors independently inflicted damage upon a victim. There was a partial reform in s. 5 of the Law Reform (Married Women and Tortfeasors) Act 1935, which has now been superseded by the Civil Liability (Contribution) Act 1978.

Section 1(1) of the Civil Liability (Contribution) Act 1978 provides:

> Subject to the following provisions of this section, any person liable in respect of any damage suffered by another person may recover contribution from any other person liable in respect of the same damage (whether jointly with him or otherwise).

The quantum of contribution is provided for by s. 2(1):

> in any proceedings for contribution under section 1 above the amount of the contribution recoverable from any person shall be such as may be found by the court to be just and equitable having regard to the extent of that person's responsibility for the damage in question.

The interpretation section, s. 6(1), provides:

> A person is liable in respect of any damage for the purposes of this Act if the person who suffered it . . . is entitled to recover compensation from him in respect of that damage (whatever the legal basis of his liability, whether tort, breach of contract, breach of trust or otherwise).

Lastly, s. 7(3) provides the following saving:

> The right to recover contribution in accordance with section 1 above supersedes any right, other than an express contractual right, to recover contribution (as distinct from indemnity) otherwise than under this Act in corresponding circumstances . . .

The scope of the operation of this Act and the extent to which it supersedes older authorities is a matter of some controversy since the expansive approach taken to the concept of 'damage' by the Court of Appeal in *Friends' Provident Life Office* v *Hillier Parker May & Rowden* [1997] QB 85. The plaintiffs were the employers under a contract for the construction of a shopping centre with the developers.

The plaintiffs engaged the defendant chartered surveyors who were responsible for ascertaining the correctness of claims by the developers and making recommendations of payment. The defendants verified claims by the developers including some £6,706,375 for notional interest. When the plaintiffs discovered that the interest should not have been charged, they initially sought recovery from the developers, but they were in financial difficulties. Accordingly the plaintiffs sued the defendants, claiming damages for negligence and breach of contract. The defendants issued third-party proceedings against the developers claiming contribution under the 1978 Act. The first instance judge struck out the third-party notice as disclosing no reasonable cause of action. Whereas it was arguable that the developers were liable in restitution to the plaintiffs, such restitutionary liability was outside the scope of the 1978 Act and did not constitute liability in respect of 'damage'. The Court of Appeal disagreed. Auld LJ characterised the claim against the developers as being one for money paid under a mistake or for no consideration (following the views of Hobhouse J and the Court of Appeal in *Westdeutsche Landesbank Girozentrale* v *Islington London Borough Council* [1994] 4 All ER 890; see 12.2). The Court was referred to a whole raft of authorities emphasising the autonomy of restitution and its foundations in reversing unjust enrichment, rather than imposing compensation for breach of a primary legal duty. However, Auld LJ concluded (at 102–103):

> In my judgment, despite the distinction between a claim for restitution and one for damages, each may be a claim for compensation for damage under sections 1(1) and 6(1) of the Act of 1978. The difference between asking for a particular sum of money back or for an equivalent sum of money for the damage suffered because of the withholding of it is immaterial in this statutory context, which is concerned with 'compensation' for 'damage'. The purpose and effect of the Act were to provide for contribution beyond that of joint tortfeasors for which section 6 of the Law Reform (Married Women and Tortfeasors) Act 1935 had previously provided. The contribution is asked to 'compensation' recoverable against a person in respect of 'any damage suffered by another' 'whatever the legal basis of his liability, whether tort, breach of contract, breach of trust or otherwise.' It is difficult to imagine a broader formulation of an entitlement contribution. It clearly spans a variety of causes of action, forms of damage in the sense of loss of some sort, and remedies, the last of which are gathered together under the umbrella of 'compensation'.

Further, the Court of Appeal also held, following the Court of Appeal in *Westdeutsche*, that it was arguable that the developers were liable for breach of trust. This now seems less secure in the light of the House of Lords decision in *Westdeutsche* [1996] AC 669. Accordingly the contribution claim was arguable in respect of a claim for breach of trust on the approach of the Court of Appeal.

There are difficulties with this in that most common law restitutionary claims such as the act for money had and received are seen as sounding in debt, rather than damages. The Law Commission Report on which the 1978 Act is based rejected a proposal that the new legislation should cover claims in debt: Law Commission, *Law of Contract, Report on Contribution* (Law Com. No. 79, 1977), paras 27 to 29. For criticism, see Goff and Jones, 395–97.

It is also hard to reconcile with the traditional approach which treats the liability of joint sureties and of indemnity insurers as being governed by the common law rather than the 1978 Act. This appears to have been assumed by the Court of Appeal in *Stimpson* v *Smith* [1999] Ch 340. Sometimes the liability of a guarantor is in respect of an obligation which sounds in damages, such as a construction company's obligations under a development contract, e.g., *Trafalgar House Construction (Regions) Ltd* v *General Surety & Guarantee Co. Ltd* [1996] AC 199. Similarly, it is traditionally asserted that the obligation under an indemnity insurance sounds in damages, not in debt (*Firma C-Trade SA* v *Newcastle Protection and Indemnity Association, The Fanti and the Padre Island* [1991] 2 AC 1, at 35–36 *per* Lord Goff of Chieveley; *Apostolos Konstantine Ventouris* v *Trevor Rex Mountain, The Italia Express (No. 2)* [1992] 2 Lloyd's Rep 281, at 285 *per* Hirst J). Accordingly it is difficult to see why such cases do not fall under the 1978 Act, although they are not usually treated as doing so: Mitchell [1997] RLR 27, at 29. It is submitted that, as far as the autonomous unjust enrichment claim in respect of the mistaken payment in the *Friends' Provident* case was concerned, the Court of Appeal was wrong as a matter of statutory construction to hold that it fell within the 1978 Act. Whether the 1978 Act, which makes no reference to unjust enrichment or restitution, should be amended in the light of developments in this area of law is a separate question.

21.4   CLAIMS UNDER THE 1978 ACT

It is not proposed to treat this question in detail. By far the best point of reference is Charles Mitchell, 'Civil Liability (Contribution) Act 1978' [1997] RLR 27; and see further Goff and Jones, 415–26. As has been observed above, the causes of action to which the Act applies received a very broad interpretation in the *Friends' Provident* case. A claim under the Act is an autonomous statutory cause of action. Mitchell states ([1997] RLR 27, at 28):

> Whilst it closely resembles the claims for contribution which lie at common law and in equity, for parties who pay more than their share of a jointly-owed debt, and is essentially restitutionary in nature, a claim for contribution under the 1978 Act is *sui generis*.

With regard to the apportionment of liability under the 1978 Act, the court must have regard to notions of what is just and equitable under s. 2(1). This is in contrast to the approach at common law and in equity where there is a common demand in respect of the same debt. There, in the absence of a contractual agreement to the contrary, liability is shared equally. Of the approach of the courts to these questions Mitchell, comments ([1997] RLR 27, at 34):

It is often said that when assessing the extent of a party's responsibility for damage under the Act the courts should take into account both the 'causative potency' and the 'blameworthiness' of the parties' actions, though it might be doubted whether these concepts are as well-adapted to assessing the relative liabilities of e.g., contract-breakers as they are to assessing the relative liabilities of tortfeasors: one breach of contract can be neither more nor less 'blameworthy' than another. It might also be questioned whether a useful conceptual distinction can always be drawn between the 'blameworthiness' and the 'causative potency' of the actions of parties who were liable for fault-based torts: since the criteria to which the courts refer when assessing the degree of such parties' blameworthiness can include the causative potency of their actions, the two can at times be inextricably intertwined.

21.5 DOUBLE INSURANCE AND CONTRIBUTION

The principle of indemnity requires that in a contract of indemnity insurance the insured must be indemnified, but never more than fully indemnified. Where the insured has more than one policy covering the same risk, the situation is described as double insurance. The insured, subject to contractual terms, may proceed against one insurer for the full amount. That insurer may then seek contribution against any other insurer. For example, in *American Surety Co. of New York* v *Wrightson* (1910) 103 LT 663, an American bank had a policy with the plaintiff insurer covering fraud of individual employees up to US$2,500. It had a further policy with the defendant underwriters at Lloyd's covering fraud and other losses up to £40,000. An employee caused the fraudulent loss of $2,680. The bank claimed $2,500 from the plaintiff and $180 from the defendant. The plaintiff insurer sought contribution. Hamilton J held that the defendant ought to pay the plaintiff a proportion of $2,680 in a ratio of 2,680:2,500. There was no authority on the question. Hamilton J caustically remarked (at 666–67): 'I am told it depends upon natural justice and upon principles of equity, and therefore I am driven to do the best with it I can.'

This area sees a sensitive interplay between the notion of contribution, which is founded upon general principles of justice and equity, and the impact of contractual terms in the underlying policies of insurance. In addition to common terms concerning the level of the excess and ceiling of any recovery, two other clauses have been considered in the case law. First, an exclusion clause under which the insurer will not pay if there is another insurance policy in respect of the same risk. Secondly, a rateable proportion clause, whereby if there is any other insurance covering the same risk or any part thereof, the insurer will not be liable for more than his rateable proportion thereof. The former type of clause has met with judicial hostility and has been construed out of existence (*Gale* v *Motor Union Insurance Co.* [1928] 1 KB 359; *Weddell* v *Road Transport and General Insurance Co. Ltd* [1932] 2 KB 563). With regard to the latter, what amounts to a rateable proportion is a difficult question.

In *Commercial Union Assurance Co. Ltd* v *Hayden* [1977] QB 804, the plaintiff company and the defendant underwriters had each entered into a policy with the insured in respect of public liability. The plaintiff's policy had a limit of £100,000 in respect of any one incident. The defendant's policy had a limit of £10,000 in respect of any one incident. Each policy contained a rateable proportion clause. A claim for some £4,425.45 was met by the plaintiff. In a claim for contribution, the plaintiff argued that the rateable proportion should be calculated on an 'independent liability' basis. Accordingly, where the claim was less than £10,000 it should be shared equally. However, if the claim was for £40,000, the independent liability of the plaintiff would be £40,000, and of the defendant £10,000. This would give a ratio of 4:1. In contrast, the defendant underwriters argued for a maximum liability basis. Therefore in every case, given the respective maximum liability of £100,000 and £10,000 respectively, each claim would be apportioned on a 10:1 basis. Cairns LJ observed that in property insurance the maximum liability basis was applied, except where there was a *pro rata* average clause (the use of which is widespread) when the independent liability basis is applied. In contrast, in the context of liability insurance the earlier case of *American Surety Co. of New York* v *Wrightson* had favoured the independent liability basis. However, Hamilton J's analogy in the earlier case between the case of co-insurers and co-sureties was relied upon by the defendant underwriters in *Hayden*. Cairns LJ rejected the analogies with property insurance or with the case of a co-surety. While accepting that the basis for apportionment between co-sureties was the maximum liability basis (although there was no binding decision to that effect), it was not appropriate in this situation. Cairns LJ was of the view that 'the independent liability basis is much more realistic in its results'. Further (at 816):

> The obvious purpose of having a limit of liability under an insurance policy is to protect the insurer from the effect of exceptionally large claims: it seems to me artificial to use the limits under two policies to adjust liability in respect of claims which are within the limits of either policy.

The Court took the view that the ways in which premiums were calculated in property and liability insurance are very different. The Court of Appeal was clearly of the view that to adopt the independent liability basis for liability insurance was more consistent with business expectations.

What is the effect if the insurer is entitled to escape liability because the insured is in breach of the claim's conditions under the policy? If the insured proceeds against the first insurer, he is unlikely to give the appropriate notice to the second insurer in respect of the loss. Does that failure deprive the first insurer (A) of any right to contribution against the second insurer (B)? The Court of Appeal in *Legal and General Assurance Society Ltd* v *Drake Insurance Co. Ltd* [1992] QB 887 held that the answer was 'No'. The appropriate date for assessing the existence of a right to contribution is the date of a loss. Lloyd LJ stated (at 893):

> there is a sharp distinction between the steps required to enforce a valid claim under a policy in force at the time of the loss, and a claim which never was valid, and never could be enforced. Thus if B has a good defence to the assured's claim

on the basis of misrepresentation or non-disclosure, there is no double insurance. Since the effect of the defence is that the contract was avoided *ab initio*, it is as if B had never been on risk at all. So also where the assured is in breach of condition, or has repudiated the contract *prior* to the loss, even if (though this is not so clear) the repudiation is only accepted thereafter. It may be said that the distinction between breach of condition prior to the loss and breach of condition subsequent to the loss is a narrow one. So it may be. But the difference is crucial. For it is at the date of the loss that a co-insurer's right to contribution, if any, accrues.

Ralph Gibson LJ dissented. For discussion, see Friedmann (1993) 109 LQR 51.

However, the conclusion reached in the *Legal and General* case was soon after doubted by the Privy Council in *Eagle Star Insurance Co. Ltd* v *Provincial Insurance plc* [1994] 1 AC 130. Lord Woolf, delivering the advice of the Privy Council, preferred the dissenting view of Ralph Gibson LJ in *Legal and General*. There was no justification for creating a special cut-off point for determining liability to make contributions. Here, both insurance companies were entitled to repudiate liability. One company had repudiated the policy before the accident occurred. The other was entitled to cancel because of non-compliance with the notice clause. Each should be treated the same way. In the event, contribution was ordered on a 50:50 basis because each insurer was under a statutory liability, irrespective of their contractual liability.

Despite this, the *Legal and General* case remains authoritative on a separate point. Both policies of insurance contained rateable proportion clauses. Therefore it was argued that when the first company paid the full amount in excess of the rateable proportion to the insured, it had made a voluntary payment which did not entitle it to contribution against the other insurer. The Court of Appeal accepted this argument despite s. 149 of the Road Traffic Act 1972 which imposes statutory liability upon the insurer to meet the third party's claim. This is because s. 149(4) of the Act entitled the insurer to recover the money from the insured. See now s. 151 of the Road Traffic Act 1988, and in particular s. 151(7). If this point had been taken in *Commercial Union* v *Hayden* [1977] QB 804, it seems that contribution would not have been ordered.

The *Legal and General* case does not assist us with the question whether these cases are now governed by the 1978 Act or are still governed by common law. The facts of the case pre-dated the coming into force of the 1978 Act. Given the broad approach to the word 'damage' in the *Friends' Provident* case and the traditional characterisation of insurance claims as sounding in damages, it seems possible that such cases are now governed by the statutory regime. See Goff and Jones, 409–13.

FURTHER READING

Asterisks indicate especially useful works.

Goff and Jones, 389–427
*C. Mitchell, 'The Civil Liability (Contribution) Act 1978' [1997] *Restitution Law Review* 27

D. Friedmann, 'Double Insurance and the Payment of Another's Debt' (1993) 109 LQR 51.

General average contribution

Goff and Jones, 427–36

F. Rose, 'General Average as Restitution' (1997) 113 LQR 569

22 Subrogation

22.1 THEORETICAL FOUNDATIONS

22.1.1 The nature of subrogation

The law of assignment is concerned with the transfer of interests in things. Leaving to one side the use of the terminology of assignment in respect of leasehold interests, the interests which are usually spoken of as being assigned are intangible ones. Whereas the language of sale is used in respect of tangible things such as land and goods, the language of assignment is used in respect of the transfer of an interest in a debt, other right of action or intellectual property rights. The starting-point for the recognition of a valid assignment is a consensual agreement between the transferor and the transferee. Any resulting assignment of an intangible interest may be outright, or by way of security. The common law's historic distrust of assignment has waned, and in the modern law, subject to some remaining restrictions and formalities, the statutory and equitable modes of assignment generally promote free transfer of intangible rights. Accordingly, the usual reason for the recognition of obligations and rights of assignor and assignee, and the reason for any change in proprietary entitlements, is grounded on the *consent* of the immediate parties to the transaction: transferor and transferee.

Contrast subrogation, which resembles assignment in that it concerns the transfer of rights and claims. Subrogation, which is an exclusively legal term of art, simply means substitution. Employing the favoured metaphor, a subrogated party steps into the shoes of another, for the purpose of maintaining a claim or right against a third person. It would be convenient if subrogation could be classified as quasi-assignment. That is, if one could say that whereas assignment arises by consent of the parties, subrogation arises by operation of law. However, in English law it is not possible to make such a tidy distinction. It is controversial whether one of the leading examples of subrogation rights, namely that of the indemnity insurer, arises consensually or by operation of law. Leaving aside examples of contractual subrogation, it is now widely recognised that the theoretical underpinnings of other instances of examples of subrogation is to be found in the principle of unjust enrichment.

22.1.2   Contractual and restitutionary explanations

Over 30 years ago in *Orakpo* v *Manson Investments Ltd* [1978] AC 95, Lord Diplock sought to identify this distinction within the subject (at 104):

> My Lords, there is no general doctrine of unjust enrichment recognised in English law. What it does is to provide specific remedies in particular cases of what might be classified as unjust enrichment in a legal system that is based upon the civil law. There are some such circumstances in which the remedy takes the form of 'subrogation,' but this expression embraces more than a single concept in English law. It is a convenient way of describing a transfer of rights from one person to another, without assignment or assent of the person for whom the rights are transferred and which takes place by operation of law in a whole variety of widely different circumstances. Some rights by subrogation are contractual in their origin, as in the case of contracts of insurance. Others, such as the right of an innocent lender to recover from a company moneys borrowed *ultra vires* to the extent that these have been expended on discharging in the company's lawful debts, are in no way based on contract and appear to defeat classification except as an empirical remedy to prevent a particular kind of unjust enrichment.
>
> This makes particularly perilous any attempt to rely upon analogy to justify applying to one set of circumstances which would otherwise result in unjust enrichment a remedy of subrogation which has been held to be available for that purpose in another and different set of circumstances.

Obviously Lord Diplock's mild restitution-scepticism, though evocative of the period, can now be treated with caution. His Lordship is correct to acknowledge that the technique has been employed in disparate and often factually complex situations. In addition to its two principal commercial manifestations, namely the right of the indemnity insurer and the right of the surety, subrogation is also deployed to redistribute rights and entitlements in the context of valid loans and invalid loans, amongst others.

More recently, the theoretical bases of subrogation have been revisited by the House of Lords. In *Banque Financière de la Cité* v *Parc (Battersea) Ltd* [1999] 1 AC 221, Lord Hoffmann bemoaned the fact (at 231) that:

> the subject of subrogation is bedevilled by problems of terminology and classification which are calculated to cause confusion. For example, it is often said that subrogation may arise either from the express or implied agreement of the parties or by operation of law in a number of different situations.

His Lordship then considered the difficulty of characterising the foundation of subrogation in indemnity insurance. Lord Hoffmann continued:

> Subrogation in this sense is a contractual arrangement for the transfer of rights against third parties and is founded upon the common intention of the parties. But the term is also used to described an equitable remedy to reverse or prevent unjust enrichment which is not based upon any agreement or common intention of the party enriched and the party deprived. The fact that contractual subrogation and subrogation to prevent unjust enrichment both involve transfers of rights or something resembling transfers of rights should not be allowed to obscure the fact that one is dealing with radically different institutions. One is part of the of the law of contract and the other part of the law of restitution. Unless this distinction is borne clearly in mind, there is a danger that the contractual requirement of mutual consent will be imported into the conditions for grant of the restitutionary remedy or that the absence of such a requirement will be disguised by references to a presumed intention which is wholly fictitious. There is an obvious parallel with the confusion by classifying certain restitutionary remedies as quasi-contractual and importing into them features of the law of contract.

22.1.3 Subrogation and the unjust enrichment enquiry

Another approach to subrogation is that of Birks, who in his seminal text, sought to marginalise the importance of subrogation (at 93): 'within the law of restitution it really adds nothing to the number of techniques already identified. It is in the nature of a metaphor which can be done without.' Birks emphasised that the apparent oddity of subrogation was that the benefit was of a negative character: Birks, 93–98.

Pursuing this insight further, it would be helpful to consider the difficulties raised by the technique of subrogation for our seven-stage enquiry into unjust enrichment (see 1.2). First, on the enrichment question, as Birks rightly points out, the enrichment is negative in character. Usually a payment is made in respect of a liability of the defendant, which sometimes has the result of discharging that liability. Here again, the rules on when a debt or other obligation are discharged by the actions of a party other than the debtor or obliger create difficulties which will be returned to. Secondly, with regard to the 'at the expense of' question, the factual configurations are always at least tripartite. It will necessary to demonstrate that the eventual enrichment received was at the expense of the claimant payer. This may sometimes require an exercise of identification or tracing. For example, in *Banque Financière de la Cité* v *Parc*, the plaintiff bank's money was routed through one Mr Herzig who was the general manager of the group of companies of which the defendant formed a part. Formally speaking there were two distinct contracts of loan. Lord Steyn was satisfied that the enrichment was at the expense of the plaintiff bank: 'To allow the interposition of Mr Herzig to alter the substance of the transaction would be pure formalism' (at 227).

With regard to the contractual matrix question, the principle of subsidiarity applies. This is seen most clearly in the context of insurance. Subrogation rights may be expressly bargained for. Equally, rights of subrogation may be contracted out of. The operation of the technique may be held to be inconsistent with the express or implied terms of the relevant contract (*Morris* v *Ford Motor Co. Ltd* [1973] QB 792 at 801–802 *per* Lord Denning MR and at 812–15 *per* James LJ). This issue has been of intense practical significance in relation to the emerging field of composite or co-insurance. Accordingly a sub-sub-contractor was held to be one of the insured parties under a contractors' all-risks policy, which are now common in the construction industry. The insurer could not pursue a claim by way of subrogation in respect of the sub-sub-contractor's alleged negligence because it was one of the insured, and not a third party (*Petrofina Ltd* v *Magnaload Ltd* [1984] QB 127). Similarly, fire insurance entered into by a landlord was construed as extending its scope of protection to the tenant who had negligently caused a fire (*Mark Rowlands Ltd* v *Berni Inns Ltd* [1986] QB 211). See also *Stone Vickers Ltd* v *Appledore Ferguson Shipbuilders Ltd* [1991] 2 Lloyd's Rep 288, reversed on other grounds [1992] 2 Lloyd's Rep 578; *National Oilwell Ltd* v *Davy Offshore Ltd* [1993] 2 Lloyd's Rep 582 and *Netherlands* v *Youell* [1997] CLC 738.

With regard to the fourth question, of the appropriate ground for restitution, it now appears to be commonly accepted that there is no single unjust factor in relation to cases with a technique of subrogation being deployed. Indeed, a number of different grounds for restitution, some of them innominate or hard to discern, appear to be in place.

On of the most poignant questions in relation to the technique of subrogation is the nature of relief. It seems that subrogation has operated to transfer both personal and proprietary rights. Accordingly it is capable of functioning as a restitutionary proprietary remedy and needs also to be considered alongside the constructive trust and equitable lien (with which it is sometimes deployed in tandem). It is here that Birks's metaphorical thesis sheds some insight. Where subrogation is confined solely to a personal claim, as a matter of analysis it would be preferable to say simply that there is a personal claim in restitution. Here what is being claimed is the value received by the defendant at the expense of the claimant in circumstances in which it is appropriate to order restitution. The language of substitutional subrogation adds little to this analysis. This appears to be implicitly accepted by Lord Steyn in *Banque Financière de la Cité* v *Parc (Battersea) Ltd* [1999] 1 AC 221, at 228:

> In my view, on an application of established principles of unjust enrichment [the plaintiffs] are entitled to succeed against [the defendant]. But, if it were necessary to do so, I would reach the same conclusion in terms of the principles of subrogation.

Given the recent recognition of unjust enrichment as a foundation for all non-contractual examples of subrogation, the earlier authorities must be treated necessarily with some circumspection. The important work on the area is the scholarship of Charles Mitchell, and in particular *The Law of Subrogation* (1994). It will be seen that his work and the earlier path-breaking efforts of Goff and Jones and

Professor Birks, have been influential in the recent authorities. Given the promiscuous use of the technique of subrogation in widely differing areas it is wise finally to recall the observation of Lord Edmund-Davies in *Orakpo v Manson Investments Ltd* [1978] AC 95, at 112:

> Apart from specific agreement and certain well-established cases it is conjectural how far the right of subrogation will be granted though in principle there is no reason why it should be confined to the hitherto-recognised categories.

22.2 THE DISTINCTION BETWEEN SIMPLE AND REVIVING SUBROGATION

Mitchell proposes a distinction between simple and reviving subrogation, which can be demonstrated by consideration of the two principal commercial manifestations of the doctrine.

In *simple* subrogation, one party owes an obligation to another, in contract or in tort, in respect of which he is primarily liable for the performance of that obligation: this party is designated PL. Correspondingly, the party to whom the obligation is owed is designated the rightholder, or RH. Another party makes a payment to RH in respect of the obligation owed by PL. Where the payment or transfer is *not* recognised as discharging the obligation of PL, no action for money paid is maintainable because PL has not been enriched by the discharge of his obligation. Accordingly the party making the payment may wish to be subrogated to or substituted for the position of RH. This party is designated by Mitchell as S.

The contract of indemnity insurance illustrates the technique of simple subrogation. Where an insurer (S) indemnifies its insured (RH) in respect of loss or damage covered by the policy, the payment does not have the effect in law of discharging the liability of or in any way exculpating a tortfeasor (PL) who was responsible for loss or damage. Accordingly it has been established for centuries that the insurer is entitled to take over any rights of action of the insured against the person primarily liable. In *Mason v Sainsbury* (1782) 3 Dougl 61, 99 ER 538, Lord Mansfield observed: 'Every day the insurer is put in the place of the insured.' As a matter of procedure, the action is brought in the name of the insured (RH) not the insurer (S) (*London Assurance Co. v Sainsbury* (1783) 3 Dougl 245, 99 ER 636).

As Mitchell notes, the effect of simple subrogation in this context is two-fold. First, it prevents the potential unjust enrichment of the primarily liable tortfeasor (PL) who might otherwise escape scot-free, where the insured (RH) has received a payment from the insurer (S). The effect of subrogation in practice, as utilised by the insurance industry, is to ensure that some wrongdoers remain responsible for the consequences of their actions. Secondly, the operation of simple subrogation in this context prevents the unjust enrichment of the insured (RH) who might otherwise be enriched by the receipt of moneys from the insurer (S) and the continued possession of a right of action which might yield recovery against the tortfeasor (PL). Thus the deployment of subrogation in the insurance context enforces the principle of indemnity, whereby the insured in a contract of indemnity insurance should be indemnified, but should never be more than fully indemnified (*Castellain* v *Preston* (1883) 11 QBD 380, at 386 *per* Brett LJ). Accordingly the insured is prevented from being unjustly enriched by double recovery in such situations.

In contrast, *reviving* subrogation operates where the payment to the rightholder (RH) in respect of the obligation owed to him by the person primarily liable (PL) operates to discharge the obligation of PL. Obviously the rules on the discharge of debts are significant here. Where the party making the payment (S) makes a payment directly, it will be effective to discharge the obligation if it is made with the actual or apparent authority of the party primarily liable. The payment need not be made by S directly to RH, but may be made directly or indirectly to PL who uses the value derived to pay off RH. What is important is that the assets are identifiably derived from S. Here there is an obvious overlap with the old action for money paid. In many cases S would have a claim in money paid. However, the courts have sometimes characterised the process as one whereby S takes over the rights of RH, which are fictionally revived for this purpose.

The law of guarantee provides the principal example. Where a surety (S) pays a creditor (RH) in respect of the debt which he has guaranteed, the payment operates to discharge the creditor's claim against the principal debtor (PL). Equally, any real security which the creditor held over the assets of the principal debtor will be discharged. Here, as between a surety (S) and the principal debtor (PL), the law fictionally revives the claims and securities to which RH was entitled and vests them in S. Under s. 5 of the Mercantile Law Amendment Act 1856, the guarantor is substituted for the position of the creditor against the principal debtor, irrespective of the fact that any such claims and securities may have been extinguished by the payment.

For discussion of simple and reviving subrogation see Mitchell, 1–15, especially at 5–11. For the reviving subrogation rights of sureties, see Mitchell, 54–60, and for the simple subrogation rights of the indemnity insurers see Mitchell, 67–86.

22.3   REVIVING SUBROGATION AND CLAIMS BY SURETIES

Security is a means of reinforcing an obligation. Where there is a loan, or where sale credit is provided, the creditor obviously has the benefit of the debtor's own personal obligation to pay the money due. In many situations, the creditor will seek to reinforce that underlying covenant with additional rights. Security takes two basic forms. First, under the law of guarantee the creditor may stipulate that an additional person undertakes to be responsible for the debt incurred by the person primarily liable. The surety accordingly adds his own personal obligation to answer for the obligations incurred by the primary debtor. Such guarantees constitute *personal* security. In addition, a creditor may seek security whereby the right to payment is reinforced by a proprietary entitlement over some asset of the debtor, usually by way of mortgage or charge. This is *real* security.

Where the creditor enforces the obligation against the surety, it is axiomatic that the surety would have the right to claim reimbursement from the party primarily liable. This could be maintained by way of the old action for money paid. However, as a matter of commercial reality the reason why the creditor has pursued the surety may make such a personal right of little economic value. The personal right arises under ordinary principles of unjust enrichment, with the unjust factor being traditionally described as being legal compulsion (see 20.2). However, the practical relevance of subrogation is that it may carry with it a proprietary entitlement for the party seeking subrogation to any real securities which the creditor (RH) had in respect of the obligations of the primary debtor (PL).

The position is governed by s. 5 of the Mercantile Law Amendment Act 1856, which provides:

> Every person who, being surety for the debt or duty of another, or being liable with another for any debt or duty, shall pay such debt or perform such duty, shall be entitled to have assigned to him, or to a trustee for him, every judgment, specialty, or other security which shall be held by the creditor in respect of such debt or duty, whether such judgment, specialty, or other security shall or shall not be deemed at law to have been satisfied by the payment of the debt or performance of the duty, and such person shall be entitled to stand in the place of the creditor, and to use all the remedies, and, if need be, and upon a proper indemnity, to use the name of the creditor, in any action or other proceeding, at law or in equity, in order to obtain from the principal debtor, or any co-surety, co-contractor, or co-debtor, as the case may be, indemnification for the advances made and loss sustained by the person who shall have so paid such debt or performed such duty, and such payment or performance so made by such surety shall not be pleadable in bar of any such action or other proceeding by him: Provided always, that no co-surety, co-contractor, or co-debtor shall be entitled to recover from any other co-surety, co-contractor, or co-debtor, by the means aforesaid, more than the just proportion to which, as between those parties themselves, such last-mentioned person shall be justly liable.

A number of points should be made about this somewhat long-winded provision. First, the surety as a matter of practice may either bring the action in his own name, or, pursuant to s. 5, may bring it in the name of the primary debtor. Secondly, the statute requires full satisfaction of the guaranteed debt. Thirdly, the statute entitles the surety to have the securities of the creditor assigned by him. It seems that this right is specifically enforceable. For discussion, see Mitchell, 54–60 and Goff Jones, 133–35.

22.4 SIMPLE SUBROGATION AND INDEMNITY INSURANCE

22.4.1 The principle of indemnity

The principle of indemnity requires of those contracts of insurance which are contracts of indemnity (for example, fire, marine, property and liability insurance, but not life and personal accident policies), that the insured should be fully indemnified but no more than fully indemnified. This principle was expressed in broad terms in the leading case of *Castellain* v *Preston* (1883) 11 QBD 380, at 388 by Brett LJ:

> as between the underwriter and the assured the underwriter is entitled to the advantage of every right of the assured, whether such right consists in contract, fulfilled or unfulfilled, or in remedy for tort capable of being insisted on or already insisted on, or in any other right, whether by way of condition or otherwise, legal or equitable, which can be, or has been exercised or has accrued, and whether such right could or could not be enforced by the insurer in the name of the assured by the exercise or acquiring of which right or condition the loss against which the assured is insured can be, or has been diminished.

Lord Templeman sketched an everyday example in *Lord Napier and Ettrick* v *Hunter* [1993] AC 713. Suppose a house is insured against fire for £100,000. The house is damaged by fire causing loss of £160,000. The insurers pay out £100,000. If the householder subsequently recovers £160,000 from a negligent builder who caused the fire, he must pay £100,000 to the insurers. The insured should not profit from the occurrence of the risk (at 728; Lord Templeman overlooks problems of under-insurance, and the principle of average might be raised by the insurer on these facts). As between the tortfeasor (PL) and the insured (RH), the tortfeasor cannot take the point that the insured has recovered, or may recover, upon an insurance policy to exculpate him from his responsibility (*Yates* v *Whyte* (1838) 4 Bing (NC) 272, 132 ER 793, *per* Park J: 'the wrongdoer should be ultimately liable notwithstanding a payment by the insurers'). Accordingly any insurance receipts do not preclude full recovery on RH's cause of action in tort.

22.4.2 Three district claims

There has been a tendency in the authorities to misdescribe some of the legal mechanisms employed to police the principle of indemnity as all being aspects of the doctrine of subrogation. This tendency is manifest in the leading discussion of *Castellain* v *Preston*, and more recently in the leading House of Lords case of *Lord Napier and Ettrick* v *Hunter*. The failure can be attributed to, in the terminology of this book, a failure to distinguish between complex entitlements and complex liabilities. Mitchell has convincingly argued that subrogation, strictly so-called, is one of three distinct remedies for giving effect to the underlying principle of indemnity: Mitchell, 'Subrogation and Insurance Law: Proprietary Claims and Excess Clauses' [1993] LMCLQ 192; and Mitchell, 67–86.

First, suppose a situation where the insured suffers a loss, and then unknown to the insurer he receives a payment from the tortfeasor who caused the loss. Subsequently the insurance company pays the insured. When the insurer learns of this error, it is clearly established that he can bring an action for money had and received from the ground of mistake of fact (*Stearns* v *Village Main Reef Gold Mining Co.* (1905) Com Cas 89; and see the discussion of Lord Browne-Wilkinson in *Lord Napier and Ettrick* v *Hunter* [1993] AC 713, at 751–52). This is a straightforward claim in autonomous unjust enrichment on the basis of mistake.

In a second scenario, the insurer pays the insured in respect of his loss first. The insurer is entitled to take over any right of action which the insured has against the wrongdoer who has caused the loss. It is this transfer of a cause of action, either by contractual agreement or by operation of law, which is subrogation properly so-called. As Lord Mansfield observed in *Mason* v *Sainsbury* (1782) 3 Dougl 61, at 64, 99 ER 538, at 540: 'every day the insurer is put in the place of the assured.' As a matter of practice, the action is brought in the name of the insured, not the insurer (*London Assurance Co.* v *Sainsbury* (1783) 3 Dougl 245, 99 ER 636). This is an example of simple subrogation which acts to prevent the potential unjust enrichment of both the insured and the wrongdoer. The cause of action was traditionally described as legal compulsion. However, in the analysis adopted in this book the ground of restitution is better identified as a species of policy-motivated restitution, which ascertains and apportions *complex liabilities* between multiple co-obligers. In the insurance context, both the insurer (S) and the tortfeasor (PL) are liable to the insured (RH) where an insured loss has been caused by the tortious conduct of PL. They are both potential defendants. Accordingly, by the deployment of both the no discharge rule and by entitling the insurer (S) to be subrogated to the position of RH, the law prevents the unjust enrichment of the tortfeasor. As between the two potential defendants subrogation ensures that the tortfeasor is ultimately liable. This is in accordance with the policy of making the tortfeasor pay, as advocated in *Yates* v *Whyte* over 150 years ago.

In the third scenario, the insurer pays the insured upon a loss, and subsequently the insured receives a payment from or recovers compensation from a wrongdoer in respect of the same loss. Here the principle of indemnity requires the insured to be subjected to a restitutionary obligation to account to the insurers in respect of those sums received in excess of the indemnity to which he was entitled. This was the factual situation in *Lord Napier and Ettrick* v *Hunter*, and although the obligation derives from the principle of indemnity, it is not technically subrogation. In the terminology of this book the cause of action arises out of the *complex entitlements* of the insured and the insurer as potential claimants in respect of a cause of action owed by the tortfeasor. The cause of action which is the legal response to the tortfeasor's conduct which has injured the insured, is axiomatically vested originally in the insured. However, given the existence of the indemnity insurance arrangement between the insured and the insurer, the insured is not the only party with an interest in the vindication of that right of action. Where the insurer chooses to exercise its right to simple subrogation, the cause of action will be vindicated in its name, although this may benefit ultimately both insurer and insured. For example, where there is a loss of £10,000 and a policy excess of £500, the insurer may pay out £9,500. If the insurer subsequently takes proceedings against the tortfeasor and recovers the full £10,000, the insurer must account to the insured for the £500 which represents the excess which the insured originally had to bear under the contract of indemnity. In dicta in *Lonrho Exports Ltd* v *Export Credits Guarantee Department* [1999] Ch 158, 181–82, this was said to be held on trust for the insured. In contrast, sometimes insurers do not choose to exercise their right to subrogation which remains vested in the insured who is at liberty to pursue those rights, subject to the duty to account. This was the situation in *Lord Napier and Ettrick* v *Hunter*.

22.4.3 The leading modern case

In *Lord Napier and Ettrick* v *Hunter* [1993] AC 713, 246 investors, or 'names', in the Outhwaite Syndicate 317/661 of the Lloyd's of London insurance market suffered massive personal losses because the managing agent of the syndicate underwrote large numbers of policies on their behalf in respect of asbestosis claims, without adequate re-insurance cover. The names had in turn insured their potential losses with stop-loss insurers, who agreed to insure a slice of the names' losses in excess of a certain amount, up to a fixed limit.

The litigation utilised a representative example, assuming a typical name's loss in the 1982 year of account. The hypothetical figures were a net underwriting loss of a £160,000. The excess of the stop-loss policy was £25,000 and the limit or ceiling was £100,000 above the excess. The stop-loss insurers paid out in full and accordingly the hypothetical name recovered £100,000 from them. Subsequently the names' negligence action against the syndicate's managing agents was settled in their favour. The settlement moneys were paid to the names' solicitors, Richards Butler, totalling some £160 million. Of that fund, some £130,000 was attributable to the £160,000 loss by the unfortunate imaginary name.

The first question considered by the House of Lords was the quantum of relief: how much were the stop-loss insurers entitled to recoup from the moneys paid to the names by the wrongdoing managing agent. How was the principle of indemnity to be given effect on the facts of this case? It was held that the effect of the excess clause and the limitation clause in the stop-loss policy was to create three layers or slices of risk. The hypothetical name was responsible for the first £25,000 of losses, the stop-loss insurers were responsible for the next £100,000 of losses in excess of £25,000, but up to a ceiling of £125,000. After that the name was again going to have to dig into his own pocket. In effect he was his own insurer in respect to the top and bottom slices of risk. The House of Lords held that the settlement moneys were to be applied from the top slice downwards: that is the first £35,000 would go to the name in respect of his losses in excess of the limit. The remaining £95,000 would be applied to the stop-loss insurers' middle layer of risk. Therefore the stop-loss insurers were entitled to £95,000, having originally paid £100,000. The initial £25,000 had to be borne by the name. The House of Lords rejected the names' contention that the settlement moneys should be applied in the first instance to the top and bottom slices of risks, so that they should be fully indemnified against all their losses. The commercial purpose of the excess clause was that the insured contracts to further risk of the first tranche of losses. Accordingly most of the settlement moneys in the hands of the names' solicitors were due to the stop-loss insurers.

This led to the second and main question in the appeal. Did the stop-loss insurers have a merely personal right against each name for money had and received, or did they have a proprietary interest in the fund held by Richards Butler? The House of Lords emphatically favoured a proprietary interest. Lord Templeman cited two factors in favour of a proprietary claim. First, it eliminated the need for 240 separate claims for money had and received against each individual name, many of whom were based overseas. The concern here was with an unnecessary multiplicity of actions. Secondly, his Lordship stressed that if a name went bankrupt it would make a 'mockery' of the insurer's rights: 'the unsecured creditors of the insured name will benefit by double payment' (at 737).

A further question therefore arose: what form should proprietary relief take? Proprietary relief had been rejected by the judges at first instance and in the Court of Appeal because of the perceived undesirability of introducing trust concepts into the commercial context of indemnity insurance. In the House of Lords, Lord Templeman acknowledged that the only possible equitable response was a constructive trust: 'the practical disadvantages would be fearsome' (at 738). The administrative and investment duties of a trustee were inappropriately burdensome. The solution favoured by the House of Lords was an equitable lien. Lord Browne-Wilkinson summed up the remedial position (at 752):

> this proprietary interest is adequately satisfied in the circumstances of subrogation under an insurance contract by granting the insurers a lien over the moneys recovered by the assured from the third party. This lien will be enforceable against the fund so long as it is traceable and has not been acquired by a bona fide purchaser for value without notice. In addition to the equitable lien the insurer will have personal right of action at law to recover the amount received by the assured as money had and received to the use of the insurer.

The proprietary analysis in the shape of an equitable lien here was not unattractive. First, the 'double payment' point is not unappealing. In the contractual scheme between the names as insured and the stop-loss insurers, it was never intended that the names should be entitled to more than the full indemnity. It should not make any difference whether the stop-loss insurers had formally exercised any right to subrogation proper. Secondly, the equitable lien ensured the avoidance of a multiplicity of unnecessary individual restitutionary proceedings. The main criticism to be levelled at the House of Lords' approach in *Napier* is the promiscuous use of the language of subrogation. It would have been better to speak about the principle of indemnity, and to identify distinctly each right granted to enforce a principle of indemnity. On this basis the right of simple subrogation is concerned with *complex liabilities* and redistributing the burden of obligations between multiple defendants. Conversely, where no rights of subrogation are exercised by an insurer, but the insured goes on to vindicate those rights of action, the duty to account enforces the principle of indemnity, and belongs within that part of the law of unjust enrichment which is concerned with redistributing the benefits obtained by vindicating rights of action between potential claimants. Accordingly cross-reference must be made to the chapter on *complex entitlements* (see 19.5).

It must be stressed that subrogation is a right which must be actually exercised by insurers. As has been seen, where the insurer does not invoke subrogation, the insured is free to pursue any cause of action in his own name and to control the proceedings. In practice the mechanism by which subrogation is achieved is usually to procure the signing of a letter of subrogation by the insured in return for payment of the indemnity money. This point is reinforced by Lord Templemen's second thoughts in *Napier* v *Hunter*. Originally his Lordship appeared prepared to make subrogation automatic: 'in my opinion the stop-loss insurers had an interest in the right of action possessed by the name against Outhwaite' ([1993] AC 713, at 738). Lords Goff and Browne-Wilkinson were more cautious, appreciating that the point did not arise for decision. On reflection, Lord Templeman agreed that the issue 'may require reconsideration in the light of further research' (at 740). These doubts were proper. Lord Browne-Wilkinson did not think that the recognition of a proprietary interest in the fund necessitated a pre-existing right over the cause of action. Where there is no claim by the insurer to simple subrogation, as a matter of first principle, the insured is entitled to vindicate the cause of action in his own name and without the interference of the insurance company. The insurance company is only entitled to subrogate upon payment of the indemnity. In return for the payment the insurer gets the benefit of the cause of action. The recognition of a proprietary interest in the cause of action, without the need for formal subrogation, might complicate proceedings. Could an insured compromise a claim without the consent of the insurer where such a proprietary interest was recognised? The correct position is that where there is a formal exercise of the rights of subrogation, the insurer does indeed have a proprietary interest in the cause of action. However, where there is no exercise of the right of subrogation, the insurer has no right, either personal or proprietary, unless or until the insured recovers moneys in respect of that cause of action in respect of the insurer's interest, for which he must then account over. The cause of action accrues once the insured is successful in vindicating the cause of action in his own name.

22.4.4   Subrogation and assignment

Lastly, a right akin to the indemnity insurer's right of subrogation may exist where a voluntary payment is made, and an effective assignment of a cause of action is taken in return. This procedure was not complied with in *Esso Petroleum Co.* v *Hall, Russell & Co. Ltd, 'The Esso Bernicia'* [1989] AC 643. The eponymous vessel was involved in an accident at Sullom Voe in the Shetland Islands, and as a result large quantities of bunker oil escaped, causing pollution. The owners, Esso, were a party to the Tanker Owners Voluntary Agreement Concerning Liability for Oil Pollution ('TOVALOP') and under the terms of this agreement paid over £500,000 to crofters in respect of damage to their sheep caused by oil on the foreshore. Subsequently, Esso sued Hall Russell, the builders of the tug involved in the accident, claiming that their negligence in designing and building the tug caused the accident. As one of the heads of loss, Esso claimed reimbursement of the sum paid to the crofters.

First, the House of Lords held under the tort of negligence that the payments to the crofters were voluntary and gratuitous and were therefore irrecoverable as they constituted pure economic loss. Secondly, the House of Lords denied the sums were recoverable in restitution, or by way of subrogation. Lord Goff stressed that the payments were not made pursuant to a contract of indemnity between Esso and the crofters. Accordingly, Esso's payment to the crofters did not discharge any obligation that Hall Russell may have owed to them in tort. His Lordship concluded (at 663):

> There can of course be no direct claim by Esso against Hall Russell in restitution, if only because Esso has not by its payment discharged the liability of Hall Russell, and so has not enriched Hall Russell; if anybody has been enriched, it is the crofters, to the extent that they have been indemnified by Esso and yet continue to have vested in them rights of action against Hall Russell in respect of the loss or damage which was the subject-matter of Esso's payment to them.

Lord Goff contrasted the position under the classic contract of indemnity insurance and gave a helpful account of the procedure in such cases (at 663):

> In normal cases, as for example under contracts of insurance, the insurer will on payment request the assured to sign a letter of subrogation, authorising the insurer to proceed in the name of the assured against any wrongdoer who has caused the relevant damage to the assured. If the assured refuses to give such authority, in theory the insurer can bring proceedings to compel him to do so. But nowadays the insurer can short-circuit this cumbrous process by bringing an action against both the assured and the third party, in which (1) he claims an order that the assured should authorise him to proceed against the third party in the name of the assured, and (2) he seeks to proceed (so authorised) against a third party. But it must not be thought that, because this convenient method of proceeding now exists, the insurer can without more proceed in his own name against a third party. He has no right to do so, so long as the right of action he is seeking to enforce is the right of action of the assured. Only if that right of action is assigned to him by the assured can he proceed directly against the third party in his own name (see e.g., *Compañia Columbiana de Seguros* v *Pacific Steam Navigation Co.* [1965] 1 QB 101). I have no doubt that the like principles apply in the present case.

See further *Lord Napier and Ettrick* v *Hunter* [1993] AC 713 and the discussion of Lord Hoffmann in *Banque Financière de la Cité* v *Parc (Battersea) Ltd* [1999] 1 AC 221, at 231. The fatal flaw in Esso's case was that it had not obtained a letter of assignment from the crofters in return for their payments. For discussion, see Weir [1989] LMCLQ 1. For discussion of indemnity insurance and subrogation generally, see Mitchell, 67–86 and Goff and Jones, 137–50.

22.4.5 Theoretical foundations

The theoretical foundations of subrogation in the insurance context should be alluded to. It seems to be impossible to deny that in many cases the availability of subrogation to the insurer will have a contractual flavour. Often it would be expressly provided for in the express terms of the policy. However, on an alternative analysis it can be readily explained in terms of the principle of unjust enrichment and the principle of indemnity. The possibility of alternative analysis has led to a (perhaps sterile) theoretical debate amongst the judiciary as to the theoretical and historical foundations of the doctrine.

Lord Diplock was a consistent and forceful advocate of the contractual theory. In *Yorkshire Insurance Co. Ltd* v *Nisbet Shipping Co. Ltd* [1962] 2 QB 330, Diplock J stated (at 339–40):

> The expression 'subrogation' in relation to a contract of marine insurance is thus no more than a convenient way of referring to those terms which are to be implied in the contract between the assured and the insurer to give business efficacy to an agreement whereby the assured in the case of a loss against which the policy has been made shall be fully indemnified, and never more than fully indemnified.

Lord Diplock reiterated his views in *Orakpo* v *Manson Investments Ltd* [1978] AC 95, at 105 and *Hobbs* v *Marlowe* [1978] AC 16, at 39.

In contrast, the House of Lords in *Lord Napier and Ettrick* v *Hunter* [1993] AC 713 was more cautious about the contractual designation and stressed the importance of the recognition of subrogation in equity as well as at common law. Lord Goff cautiously observed (at 743):

> Of course, it is proper to start with the contract of insurance, and to see how the common law courts have worked out the mutual rights and obligations in contractual terms with recourse to implied terms where appropriate. But, with all respect, I am unable to agree with Lord Diplock that subrogation is in this context concerned *solely* with the mutual rights and obligations of the parties under the contract.

The most recent discussion has stressed the central importance of a contract in determining the scope of subrogation where it arises pursuant to a contract of indemnity insurance. The practical significance of this is that the contract is the ultimate source of any rights of subrogation and determines the scope of such rights. In *Banque Financière de la Cité* v *Parc (Battersea) Ltd* [1999] 1 AC 221, Lord Hoffmann observed (at 231):

> Lord Diplock, for example, was of the view that the doctrine of subrogation in contracts of insurance operated entirely by virtue of an implied term of the contract of insurance (*Hobbs* v *Marlowe* [1978] AC 16, 39) and although in *Lord*

Napier and Ettrick v *Hunter* [1993] AC 713 your Lordships rejected the exclusivity of this claim for the common law and assigned a larger role to equitable principles, there was no dispute that the doctrine of subrogation in insurance rests upon the common intention of the parties and gives effect to the principle of indemnity embodied in the contract. Furthermore, your Lordships drew attention to the fact that it is customary for the assured, on payment of the loss, to provide the insurer with a letter of subrogation, being no more nor less than an express assignment of his rights of recovery against any third party. Subrogation in a sense is a contractual arrangement for the transfer of rights against third parties and is founded upon the common intention of the parties.

Accordingly the doctrine of subrogation in insurance contexts has been ascribed both to consent and to unjust enrichment. In accordance with the principle of subsidiarity, where there is a possibility of conflict between the contractual arrangements and the principles of unjust enrichment, the contractual matrix prevails.

22.5 VALID LOANS AND SUBROGATION

22.5.1 The earlier authorities

This is an example of reviving subrogation. Discussion of this topic is necessarily dominated now by the decision of the House of Lords in *Banque Financière de la Cité* v *Parc (Battersea) Ltd* [1999] 1 AC 221. The principle which the earlier cases had established was summarised by Lord Hutton (at 238):

> there is an equitable principle that where a lender advances a sum of money to another person intended to be a secured loan, and the money is used by that person to discharge a debt owed by him to a secured creditor, the lender is entitled to be subrogated to the charge of that creditor if his security proves to be defective.

In *Chetwynd* v *Allen* [1899] 1 Ch 353, a husband borrowed £2,000 which was secured upon two properties belonging to his wife. Subsequently the husband borrowed a further £1,200 from a second creditor, stating that he would pay off the debt on one of the properties and transfer that mortgage to the new creditor. The wife, who had consented to the original mortgages, knew nothing of the second transaction. The new lender was held entitled to step into the shoes of the first mortgagor whose charge was 'kept alive in equity' for his benefit (at 357). Similarly, in *Butler* v *Rice* [1910] 2 Ch 277, a wife owned properties in Bristol and Cardiff which were equitably mortgaged to a bank to secure a loan of £450. Her husband obtained a loan from Butler of £450 to pay off the mortgage over the Bristol property, failing to disclose the existence of the other property in Cardiff or the fact that both properties belonged to his wife. It was held that Butler was subrogated to the charge over the Bristol property.

In the Privy Council case of *Ghana Commercial Bank* v *Chandiram* [1960] AC 732, Lord Jenkins stated the beneficial presumption for the party wishing to be subrogated (at 745): 'It is not open to doubt that where a third party pays off a mortgage he is presumed, unless the contrary appears, to intend that the mortgage should be kept alive for his own benefit.' An important circumstance where this presumption will be displaced was identified by Oliver J in *Paul* v *Speirway Ltd* [1976] Ch 220, at 232:

> where on all the facts the court is satisfied that the true nature of the transaction between the payer of the money and the person at whose instigation it is paid is simply the creation of an unsecured loan, this in itself will be sufficient to dispose of any question of subrogation.

22.5.2 Tracing and subrogation

A more recent authority on subrogation in this context is *Boscawen* v *Bajwa* [1996] 1 WLR 328. Bajwa owned a house, which he had purchased with a loan from the Halifax Building Society. The outstanding loan was some £140,000 which was secured by a mortgage. Bajwa was in dire straits. He negotiated a sale of the property to purchasers who in turn arranged finance from the Abbey National. The Abbey National advanced £140,000 through the solicitors acting both for itself and the purchasers to Bajwa's solicitors, who in turn forwarded £140,000 to the Halifax. However, it seems that Abbey National's own solicitor was in equally straitened circumstances. His cheque bounced and he became bankrupt. In addition, the sale fell through. Neither vendor nor purchaser was contractually bound because there had not been compliance with the relevant formalities. Accordingly Mr Bajwa remained a legal owner of the property and the £1,000 or so outstanding to the Halifax was paid off by him. This action was brought by judgment creditors of Mr Bajwa to enforce a charging order against the property. It was common ground that a judgment creditor with a charging order could take only such interest as a debtor has in his property. The question was whether Mr Bajwa was the unencumbered owner of the property, or whether the Abbey National was entitled to be subrogated to the mortgage of the Halifax. The Court of Appeal held that the Abbey National was subrogated to the first charge of the Halifax. The effect of the premature payment of the Halifax by Bajwa's solicitors was that Abbey National's money was applied in breach of trust in partial discharge of Halifax's mortgage without obtaining completion of the sale and the execution of the new mortgage in favour of the Abbey National.

Millett LJ, in a 'valuable and illuminating analysis of the remedy of subrogation' (*Banque Financière de la Cité* v *Parc (Battersea) Ltd* [1999] 1 AC 221, at 233 *per* Lord Hoffmann), equated subrogation with the restitutionary proprietary remedies of the constructive trust and the equitable lien. Millett LJ concluded ([1996] 1 WLR 335, at 335):

if the plaintiff's money has been used to discharge a mortgage on the defendant's land, then the court may achieve a similar result by treating the land as subject to a charge by way of subrogation in favour of the plaintiff.

Subrogation, therefore, is a remedy, not a cause of action.... It is available in a wide variety of different factual situations in which it is required in order to reverse the defendant's unjust enrichment. Equity lawyers speak of a right of subrogation, or of an equity of subrogation, but this merely reflects the fact that it is not a remedy which the court has a general discretion to impose whenever it thinks it just to do so. The equity arises from the conduct of the parties on well settled principles and in defined circumstances which make it unconscionable for the defendant to deny the proprietary interest claimed by the plaintiff.

The Court of Appeal was accordingly of the view that it was legitimate to combine tracing and subrogation in arriving at the result. Tracing was the process whereby the Abbey National identified the money which originated from its funds which was eventually applied to discharge the Halifax's first legal mortgage. Subrogation was the remedial response which prevented the unjust enrichment of Mr Bajwa, which would result if the Abbey National were not entitled to step into the shoes of the Halifax. Millett LJ was less explicit about the relevant grounds for restitution. His Lordship took the view that subrogation was applicable even though it might be impossible to infer a common intention to keep alive a security. What was important was the intention of Mr Bajwa's solicitors, who must be regarded has having intended to keep the Halifax's mortgage alive for the benefit of the Abbey National pending completion. The *Paul* v *Speirway Ltd* restriction did not pose a problem: the Abbey National never intended to be an unsecured creditor. The facts were novel, but as a matter of justice the Court of Appeal took the view that subrogation should be granted (at 339–42).

The Court has been criticised for not being explicit about the relevant unjust factor. Mitchell has suggested that there was no mistake here, but rather a misprediction. The appropriate ground for restitution, he suggests, is failure of consideration by analogy with *Barclays Bank Ltd* v *Quistclose Investments Ltd* [1970] AC 567. That is, where money is advanced for a particular purpose, and that purpose fails, the payer is entitled to recovery of what was a conditional payment. See Mitchell [1995] LMCLQ 451.

22.5.3 The leading modern case

Turning to what is now the leading case of *Banque Financière de la Cité* v *Parc (Battersea) Ltd* [1999] 1 AC 221, which concerned the refinancing of a commercial property development at Battersea Wharf in London and a defective subordinated debt agreement. Parc was the owner of land in Battersea, and together with other companies, including one OOL, it constituted the Swiss-based Omni group. Mr Herzig was the chief financial officer of the parent company of the group, Omni Holdings. Parc had financed the purchase of the Battersea property with funding from Royal Trust Bank (RTB) which had a first charge, and from OOL which obtained a second charge. Banque Financière de la Cité (BFC) agreed to re-finance the RTB loan. In order to circumvent Swiss banking regulations the transaction was structured so that BFC would lend the money to Mr Herzig personally and he would in turn lend the money to Parc. BFC stipulated for the following protection. First, Parc would sign a promissory note to Herzig which he would in turn assign to BFC. Secondly, 35,000 bearer shares in Omni Holdings were pledged to BFC. Thirdly, BFC required a 'postponement letter' in respect of intra-group debts. This stated:

> This is to confirm that we and all companies of our group will not demand any repayment of loans granted to Parc (Battersea) Ltd, London, until the full repayment of your loan of DM 30m granted to Mr M Herzig, which is secured by a deep discount promissory note amounting to £10m issued by Parc (Battersea) Ltd.

This attempt to create a subordinated debt agreement, whereby BFC ranked above members of the group, was fatally flawed, because Mr Herzig lacked the necessary authority from OOL and other members of the group to sign the letter. The group collapsed. Mr Herzig was unable to repay the loan. BFC was able to recoup some DM 5m by enforcing its security in the pledged shares before they became wholly worthless. In the lower courts BFC claimed to be able to step into the shoes of RTB as first chargee. However, before the House of Lords a more limited proposition was advanced. BFC only claimed subrogation as against OOL. OOL should not be entitled to enforce its second charge so as to enrich itself at the expense of BFC. This claim was accepted by the House of Lords.

Lord Steyn believed it possible to award restitution without recourse to the technique of subrogation. In his Lordship's view (at 226): 'the important point is that BFC would not have lent had it not mistakenly believed that its priority in respect of intra-group indebtedness was secured effectively against subsidiaries of the group.' This was a straightforward case where the unjust factor was BFC's mistaken belief that it had a limited form of security against other members of the corporate group. Alternatively, Lord Steyn agreed that the same result could be reached by the route of subrogation, but limited to the taking over of rights *in personam* against other companies in the group. This was not a case of subrogation to proprietary rights.

Lord Hoffmann delivered the leading speech. The purported effect of the letter of postponement was that it was issued on behalf of all the group companies. Lord Hoffmann rejected the view that the remedy of subrogation required a common intention of the parties to keep the security alive. His Lordship distinguished the indemnity insurance cases which have a more contractual flavour. In contrast, Lord Hoffmann placed the current claim for subrogation firmly within the law of restitution. Five key authorities demonstrated that the alleged requirement of common intention had never formed part of the law: *Chetwynd v Allen* [1899] 1 Ch 353; *Butler v Rice* [1910] 2 Ch 277; *Ghana Commercial Bank v Chandiram* [1960] AC 732; *Paul v Speirway Ltd* [1976] Ch 220 and *Boscawen v Bajwa* [1996] 1 WLR 328. Lord Hoffmann concluded ([1999] 1 AC 221, at 234):

These cases seem to me to show that it is a mistake to regard the availability of subrogation as a remedy to prevent unjust enrichment as turning entirely upon the question of intention, whether common or unilateral. Such an analysis has inevitably to be propped up by presumptions which can verge upon outright fictions, more appropriate to a less developed legal system than we now have. I would venture to suggest that the reason why intention has played so prominent a part in the earlier cases is because of the influence of cases on contractual subrogation.

Mitchell has argued that the presumption of intention in cases such as *Ghana Commercial Bank* v *Chandiram* is unjustifiable both on authority and principle: Mitchell, 12–15. The tenor of Lord Hoffmann's remarks, as quoted above, might suggest concurrence with this view. However, his Lordship was more equivocal. Lord Hoffmann stated (at 234):

This does not of course mean that questions of intention may not be highly relevant to the question of whether or not enrichment has been unjust. I would certainly not wish to question the proposition of Oliver J in *Paul* v *Speirway Ltd* [1976] Ch 220 that, as against a borrower, subrogation to security will not be available where the transaction was intended merely to create an unsecured loan. I do not express a view on the question of where the burden or proof lies in these matters. ... However, if it is recognised that the use of the plaintiff's money to pay off a secured debt and the intentions of the parties about whether or not the plaintiff should have security are only materials upon a which a court may decide that the defendant's enrichment would be unjust, it could be argued that on general principles it is for the plaintiff to make out a case on unjust enrichment.

This equivocation as to the status of the presumption in the *Chandiram* case will not assist practitioners. It seems on balance that the House of Lords inclines to the view that it is for the claimant to prove affirmatively an unjust factor. Lord Hoffmann was also of the view that the appropriate ground for restitution in this case was the mistaken assumption of BFC that the postponement letter was binding on the companies in the group. As a result of that mistake money derived from BFC diminished the first charge held by RTB, which had the consequence of enriching OOL by improving the position of its second charge. Lord Hoffmann also accepted that the contributory negligence of the payer in not checking the authority of Mr Herzig did not defeat the claim. The fact that there was only a partial discharge of the first charge of RTB posed no problem to the award of subrogation in this case. Lastly, Lord Hoffmann acknowledged that the metaphor 'keeping the charge alive' required careful handling (following Birks, 93–97). What was required was that, as between the plaintiff and the defendant, matters are 'regulated *as if* the benefit of the charge had been assigned to [the plaintiff]' (at 236). Lords Clyde and Hutton delivered concurring speeches.

22.5.4   A critique of *Banque Financière* v *Parc*

This decision caused some dismay amongst practitioners and provoked varied academic comments. Professor Bridge is highly critical, arguing that the result of the decision is to expand the reach of restitution, neglecting traditional limitations, and that it undermines the principles and policies of insolvency law: Bridge, 'Failed Contracts, Subrogation and Unjust Enrichment: *Banque Financière de la Cité* v *Parc (Battersea) Ltd'* [1998] JBL 323. Theresa Villiers is more sympathetic. She argues that the unjust factor was mistake of fact. Although it was not a liability mistake, it would count as a causative mistake. Villiers considers the nature of the remedy imposed by the House of Lords and concludes: 'there is no simple dichotomy between personal and proprietary rights' (Villiers, 'A path through the subrogation jungle: whose right is it anyway?' [1999] LMCLQ 223, at 235). Villiers further argues that Lord Hoffmann's explicit reference to a public policy 'safety valve' upon the award of subrogation in particular, and unjust enrichment in general, 'may also signal the adoption of a novel and possibly wide ranging restriction on the application of unjust enrichment principles in new situations' (at 237).

Both academic and practitioner reactions suggest that there is something awry in the reasoning of the House of Lords in the *Parc* case. Whereas the general discussion of unjust enrichment principles and the principled analysis of subrogation are to be welcomed, the eventual result appears commercially undesirable. It is submitted that the reason for this is that the House of Lords did not have due regard to the principle of *subsidiarity*. The case demonstrates the importance of addressing all seven stages in the unjust enrichment enquiry identified in 1.2 of this work. Lord Steyn expressly discussed the enrichment, 'at the expense of', ground for restitution and defences questions. Similarly, Lord Hoffmann adverted to the enrichment question and the ground for restitution question. Further, his Lordship insisted upon a public policy bar which could still preclude restitution in all cases. However, none of their Lordships expressly considered the contractual matrix.

The fact that there were two contracts of loan in the case on differing terms was brushed aside as of little significance. It is submitted that the existence of two contracts of loan was crucial. First, BFC's main, bargained-for right was the personal covenant of Mr Herzig to repay his loan. This may have become worthless, but there is no suggestion that the contract was ever terminated for breach. As between BFC and Herzig, the borrower, this contract remained on foot and undischarged. Secondly, BFC also bargained for the security of a pledge of shares which was in fact realised. Thirdly, BFC bargained for the assignment of a promissory note, and accordingly an obligation to repay from Parc itself. In the circumstances this also turned out to be worthless, but it remained a valid obligation. Fourthly, BFC bargained for the postponement letter with Mr Herzig to be issued upon the behalf of all the members of the corporate group. However, it transpired that Mr Herzig lacked the necessary authority on behalf of other members of the corporate group. This was the fact which led the House of Lords to conclude that the appropriate ground for restitution was BFC's mistaken belief in the validity of the postponement letter. The difficulty with this, on first principles, is that it overlooks the fact that the transfer of the benefits (namely, the loan) remained regulated by the undischarged contracts of loan, under which there were still extant (though economically worthless) obligations upon Mr Herzig and Parc to make repayments. In addition, BFC had obtained and realised the security of the pledged shares in the holding company. Accordingly there had been some substantial performance of the loan and its accompanying securities, and there was no question of a total failure of consideration. The mistake relied upon by the House of Lords would have been sufficient if there had been no governing contractual matrix, or if that contractual matrix had been discharged in accordance with the rules of contract law. However, this was not done and BFC accordingly having made its contractual bed, should have been required to lie on it. The only consequence of Mr Herzig's want of authority was a further right of BFC against Mr Herzig personally to sue for breach of warranty of authority. Admittedly this was also worthless in economic terms, but it is the appropriate legal response to the facts as proved.

Other difficulties surround the remedy as granted by the House of Lords, and its appropriate characterisation as noted by Villiers. It is difficult to believe that even expressed as a subrogation claim *in personam* against OOL, this remedy did not have an impact upon the other unsecured creditors of Parc. It must be assumed that BFC was content with the form and order proposed and declared because it would be of some economic value to it.

In conclusion, therefore, *Parc* can be seen to be wrongly decided because the House of Lords neglected to address the essential third question as to whether the transfer of the benefits was regulated by an extant contract. The principle of subsidiarity was accordingly neglected. In this respect the decision in *Parc* is difficult to reconcile with other recent House of Lords' authorities such as *Pan Ocean Shipping Co. Ltd* v *Creditcorp Ltd, The Trident Beauty* [1994] 1 WLR 161 and *Stocznia Gdanska SA* v *Latvian Shipping Co.* [1998] 1 WLR 574. Where insolvency intervenes, it is tempting for claimants to hunt around for a deep-pocketed defendant who may have benefited from its contractual performance with the insolvent party. However, it is imperative that the courts do not override or ignore the deliberate transactional structuring to which the claimant assented. Regard must always been had to the primacy of contractual obligations.

22.6 INVALID LOANS AND SUBROGATION

22.6.1 The earlier authorities

Whereas the preceding section concerned valid loans, we now turn to the difficulties caused where the loan is invalid. Historically, this category yielded a rich seam of case law, much of which is difficult to reconcile. However, in modern times these authorities are of little practical significance. There are three main grounds of invalidity in the cases. First, a company may be held to lack capacity because the borrowing was not within the company's constitution and accordingly *ultra vires*.

Secondly, loans that were made to minors who lacked the capacity to enter into such contracts. Thirdly, loans that failed to comply with statutory formalities, usually for protection of debtors, and were accordingly void and/or unenforceable.

With regard to the first ground of invalidity, ss. 35 and 35A of the Companies Act 1985 (as amended in 1989) have effectively excised *ultra vires* from English corporate law, especially as regards third parties dealing with accompanying good faith. Secondly, the reduction in the age of the majority from 21 to 18 years and the stringent checks undertaken as a matter of routine by lenders in modern times result in few practical problems with minors' contracts. See also the Minors' Contracts Act 1987. The third category of unenforceable loans also raises few problems in modern times. The leading authorities concern the right of a lender, whose contract of loan is *ultra vires* the corporate borrower, to be subrogated to the rights of the company's creditors whose debts have been satisfied by money identifiably derived from the lender. The lender is entitled to be subrogated to both the personal and proprietary rights of those creditors. As such this is an example in Mitchell's terminology of reviving subrogation: Mitchell, 149–61.

In the leading case of *Blackburn Building Society* v *Cunliffe, Brooks & Co.* (1882) 22 Ch D 61, Lord Selborne LC observed (at 71):

> it is consistent with the general principle of equity that those who pay legitimate demands which they are bound in some way or other to meet, and have had the benefit of other people's money advanced to them for that purpose, shall not retain that benefit so as, in substance, to make those other people pay their debts.

The Court of Appeal in *Baroness Wenlock* v *The River Dee Company* (1887) 19 QBD 155, decided that subrogation was not confined to liabilities of the company existing at the time of the advance, but was capable of extending to debts and liabilities subsequently incurred which were identifiably paid out of the advance sum. The archaisms and fictions which riddle these authorities are especially manifest in the judgment of the Court delivered by Fry LJ (although one may suspect that his Lordship was employing a certain degree of irony; at 165):

> This equity is based on a fiction, which, like all legal fictions, has been invented with a view to the furtherance of justice. The Court closes its eyes to the true facts of the case, *viz*, an advance as a loan by the quasi-lender to the company, and a payment by the company to its creditors as out of its own moneys: and assumes on the contrary that the quasi-lender and the creditor of the company met together and that the former advanced to the latter the amount of his claim against the company and took an assignment of that claim for his own benefit. There is no reason that we can find for supposing that this imaginary transaction between the quasi-lender and the creditor was confined to the day and hour of the advance of the money to the company: in the coffers of the company the money really advanced as a loan is still thought of by the Court as the money of the quasi-lender: and the Court, as the author of the benevolent fiction on which its acts, can fix its own time and place

for the enactment of the supposed bargain between the two parties who have met and contracted together only in the imagination of the Court.

In the subsequent case of *In Re Wrexham, Mold and Connah's Quay Railway Co.* [1899] 1 Ch 440, a bank purported to lend money to a company to enable it to pay debenture holders. When the company became insolvent the bank sought to be subrogated to the position of the debenture holders, and in particular to the securities and priorities to which they were entitled. The Court of Appeal refused to allow subrogation to the secured rights of the debenture holders, stating that this was not the effect of the previous authority. To grant subrogation would turn an unsecured loan into a secured one. Indeed, the Court of Appeal doubted that the right recognised in the case had got anything to do with subrogation. Rigby LJ concluded (at 455):

> I think that the great preponderance of authority shews that the doctrine of subrogation has very little, if anything at all, to do with the equity really enforced in the cases and that there is, at any rate, no authority for any subrogation to the securities or priorities of the creditors paid off.... It seems to me that it would be unjust to other creditors that a fiction should be invented for the purpose of making an invalid loan more valuable than a valid one.

In contrast, the leading House of Lords case of *Nottingham Permanent Benefit Building Society* v *Thurstan* [1903] AC 6, appears to grant proprietary relief, with little reasoned discussion of the problem. A minor borrowed money from a building society in order to purchase property, and in turn purported to mortgage the property to the society as security for the advances. The mortgage was void for want of capacity under the Infants Relief Act 1874. The House of Lords held that the building society was subrogated to the rights of the vendor, to claim the purchase price and to obtain the benefit of the unpaid vendor's lien.

The position was not clarified by the subsequent and difficult decision of the House of Lords in *Sinclair* v *Brougham* [1914] AC 398, which concentrated upon tracing rather than subrogation. However, Lord Parker of Warrington did observe (at 440):

> it appears to be well settled that if the borrowed money be applied in paying off legitimate indebtedness of the company or association (whether the indebtedness be incurred before or after the money was borrowed), the lenders are entitled to rank as creditors of the company or association to the extent to which the money has been so applied. There appears to be some doubt as to whether this result is arrived at by treating the contract of loan as validated to the extent to which the borrowed money is so applied, on the ground that to this extent there is no increase in the indebtedness to the company or association, in which case, if the contract of loan involves a security for the money borrowed, the security would be validated to a like extent; or whether the better view is that the lenders are subrogated to the rights of the legitimate creditors who have been paid off.... It is still open to your

Lordship's House to adopt either view should the question actually come up for determination.

22.6.2   *Orakpo* and public policy

In modern times the main authority is *Orakpo* v *Manson Investments Ltd* [1978] AC 95, in which purported loans, which had been utilised for the purchase of commercial properties, were held to be unenforceable for non-compliance with the requisite formalities of s. 6 of the Moneylenders Act 1927. The lenders sought to be subrogated to the unpaid vendors' liens over the property. The House of Lords held, by a majority, that such a right would exist only if it had been the common intention of the parties that the moneys were so applied. Lord Diplock, favouring a contractual view of the right of subrogation, stated that the doctrine depended on the 'presumed mutual intentions' of the party wishing to be subrogated and the party borrowing the money. It was an implied term of the contract that the lender should be subrogated to the original creditors' security (at 104). In this case the contract was not void but unenforceable. Lord Diplock observed (at 106): 'Agreements or securities that are unenforceable are not devoid of all legal effect. Payments made voluntarily pursuant to their terms are not recoverable'. Lord Salmon held that to award subrogation would defeat the policy of the Act (at 111):

> It is true that because of the lender's breach of section 6 of the Moneylenders Act 1927 the legal charge, though valid, would be unenforceable. I cannot think however that it would proper to apply an equitable doctrine for the purpose of enabling a moneylender to escape from the consequences of his breach of the statute — particularly as to do so would also enable him to recover his money much earlier than he was entitled to do under the contract of loan.

In the words of Lord Edmund-Davies, to award subrogation would 'enable the court to express a policy of its own in regard to moneylending transactions which would be in direct conflict with the policy of the Act of 1927 itself' (at 115). A majority of the House of Lords further held that the proceedings were time-barred by the accelerated 12-month limitation period contained in s. 13 of the Moneylenders Act 1927.

The difficulties of reconciling the decisions in *Thurstan* and *Orakpo* are discussed by Mitchell, 158–61. In *Banque Financière de la Cité* v *Parc (Battersea) Ltd* [1999] 1 AC 221, Lord Hoffmann marginalised the significance of *Orakpo* by classifying it as a case where restitution would have been contrary to the public policy disclosed by the Moneylenders Acts (at 234). Accordingly *Orakpo* is practically irrelevant as a decision on a particular public policy yielded by a now obsolete statute.

22.6.3   Conclusion

To conclude, the streams of case law on subrogation and invalid loans are difficult to reconcile, and are in any event of little practical significance today.

First, it is difficult to see why the law of subrogation is utilised at all in the cases where there has been no claim to proprietary securities. As Birks has argued, it appears to be an unnecessary metaphor: Birks, 93-98. In the wake of developments elsewhere in the law of restitution, the need for recourse to the language of subrogation appears archaic and unnecessary.

The analogy with the swaps cases is striking. Where a loan is *ultra vires* and void the cause of action would now be seen to be, in the light of *Westdeutsche Landesbank Girozentrale v Islington London Borough Council* [1996] AC 669, failure of consideration (compare *In re Wrexham, Mold and Connah's Quay Railway Co.* [1899] 1 Ch 440, at 456 *per* Vaughan Williams LJ) or, in the light of *Kleinwort Benson Ltd v Lincoln City Council* [1999] 2 AC 349, mistake of law.

Secondly, where a claim is made to proprietary relief, subrogation may still be the appropriate technique for providing an appropriate remedy. However, the debate as to whether such proprietary relief should be granted should be conducted not by reference to authorities such as *Thurstan* and *Orakpo*, but rather in the light of the general principles and policies governing the award of restitutionary proprietary remedies in general, such as the constructive trust and equitable lien as discussed in authorities such as *Lord Napier and Ettrick v Hunter* [1993] AC 713, *Re Goldcorp Exchange Ltd* [1995] 1 AC 74, and *Westdeutsche* (see Chapter 30).

Thirdly, where the underlying contract is void or enforceable, usually by reason of statutory prohibition, the fundamental question remains whether the award of restitution, whether merely personal or in the shape of subrogation to an equitable lien, would offend the policy of the statute. This debate too would be better conducted by reference to more recent cases on public policy precluding a restitutionary claim, such as *Universe Tankships Inc. of Monrovia v International Transport Workers' Federation, The Universe Sentinel* [1983] 1 AC 366, *Dimskal Shipping Co. SA v International Transport Workers' Federation, The Evia Luck (No. 2)* [1992] 2 AC 152 and, on the issue of subrogation, *Banque Financière v Parc.* See Chapter 35.

22.7 BANKERS' RIGHTS OF SUBROGATION

There is little authority here save the controversial case of *B. Liggett (Liverpool) Ltd v Barclays Bank Ltd* [1928] 1 KB 48. The bank negligently, and in breach of its mandate, paid company cheques which had been signed by one director only. The cheques were payable to trade creditors who had supplied goods to the business. The company as plaintiff sought to recover the moneys paid by the bank as money had and received. Wright J held by analogy with the cases on unauthorised borrowings, that the bank was entitled to be subrogated to the position of the trade creditors. Wright J concluded (at 63–64):

In such a case there is obviously no conversion, but there is misapplication, under an honest mistake as to the validity of the authority, of the credits which constitute the medium of exchange in place of cash. Under these circumstances I think that the equity I have been referred to ought to be extended even in the case where a cheque which was paid out of the credit balance, and was not paid by way of overdraft, so that the bank will be entitled to the benefit of that payment if he could show that the payment went to discharge a legal liability of the customer. The customer in such a case is really no worse off, because the legal liability which has to be discharged is discharged, though it is discharged under circumstances which at common law would not entitle the bank to debit the customer.

This was, in the terminology of Mitchell, a case of reviving subrogation. However, the decision appears to assume that the debts of the trade creditors were automatically discharged by the bank's payment, although the bank was unauthorised to make those payments. This premise in the reasoning cannot stand in the light of the general rules on the discharge of debts in English law. See 1.4.5 and Chapter 20. *B. Liggett* was doubted by the Court of Appeal in *In re Cleadon Trust Ltd* [1939] 1 Ch 286 and is irreconcilable with the seminal decision of Robert Goff J in *Barclays Bank Ltd* v *W. J. Simms, Son & Cooke (Southern) Ltd* [1980] QB 677. The decision in *Liggett* appears to be wrong. For discussion see Mitchell, 126–30.

FURTHER READING

Asterisks indicate especially useful works.

*Goff and Jones, 120–69
  Birks, 93–98; 191–92; 189–93
*C. Mitchell, 'The Law of Subrogation' [1992] LMCLQ 483
*C. Mitchell, 'Subrogation and Insurance Law: Proprietary Claims and Excess Clauses' [1993] LMCLQ 192
*C. Mitchell, *The Law of Subrogation* (1994)
  C. Mitchell, 'Subrogation, Tracing and the *Quistclose* Principle' [1995] LMCLQ 451
  M. Bridge, 'Failed Contracts, Subrogation and Unjust Enrichment: *Banque Financière de la Cité* v *Parc (Battersea) Ltd* [1998] JBL 323
  T. Villiers, 'A path through the subrogation jungle: whose right is it anyway?' [1999] LMCLQ 223
  M. Clarke, *The Law of Insurance Contracts*, 3rd edn (1997), chap. 31

PART F

ENRICHMENT BY WRONGDOING

23 Breach of Fiduciary Duty

23.1 THEORETICAL FOUNDATIONS

A fiduciary is someone who has undertaken to act for or on behalf of another in a particular matter in circumstances which give rise to a relationship of trust and confidence. The distinguishing obligation of a fiduciary is the obligation of loyalty. The principal is entitled to a single-minded loyalty of his fiduciary.

(Bristol and West Building Society v Mothew
[1998] Ch 1, at 18 *per* Millett LJ)

The core idea of fiduciary duty is the assumption of responsibility for the property or affairs of others. Parallel developments at common law and in equity yielded the recognition of a duty of care of those in analogous positions of being entrusted with another's property or affairs, including bailees, carriers, trustees, directors and agents. The duty to take care of another's interests in such circumstances is clearly established, although the exact standard of liability may vary from case to case (*Henderson v Merrett Syndicates Ltd* [1995] 2 AC 145, at 205 *per* Lord Browne-Wilkinson; *Bristol and West Building Society v Mothew* [1998] Ch 1, at 16). The characteristic response is compensatory, although the remedies are respectively termed damages at common law and equitable compensation (*Target Holdings Ltd v Redferns* [1996] AC 421; *Bristol and West Building Society v Mothew* [1998] Ch 1, at 17). Breaches of this duty of care are not breaches of fiduciary duty: 'It is obvious that not every breach of duty by a fiduciary is a breach of fiduciary duty. . . . Breach of fiduciary obligation, therefore, connotes disloyalty or infidelity. Mere incompetence is not enough. A servant who loyally does his incompetent best for his master is not unfaithful and is not guilty of a breach of fiduciary duty.' (*Bristol and West Building Society v Mothew* [1998] Ch 1, at 16, 18 *per* Millett LJ).

It is with breaches of the obligation of loyalty with which we are now concerned. Where the money or property of another is entrusted to a person, equity has always been suspicious of the temptations which might thereby arise. A restitutionary response has therefore been recognised and is apt for two reasons. First, infidelity is likely to result in enriching behaviour for the person entrusted with the money or property of another. Secondly, the policy of deterrence or prophylaxis weighs heavily with the court. As Professor Jones argued in his seminal article, 'Unjust Enrichment and the Fiduciary's Duty of Loyalty' (1968) 84 LQR 472, at 474:

> The implications of equity's rule are far-reaching. Once a fiduciary is shown to be in breach of his duty of loyalty he must disgorge any benefit gained even though he acted honestly and in his principal's best interests, even though his principal benefited as well as he from his conduct, even though his principal could not otherwise have obtained the benefit, and even though the benefit was obtained through the use of the fiduciary's own assets and in consequence of his personal skill and judgment.

In a number of cases a too-mechanical application of these principles has led to unjust results.

23.2   WHO IS A FIDUCIARY?

It is submitted that the core ingredient of most instances of fiduciary responsibility is *consent*: the voluntary assumption of responsibility for the management of the property or affairs of another. There has traditionally been a reluctance to admit the consensual dimension of fiduciary duty. Perhaps the stringency of the law's response to lapses from duty, or perhaps a desire to keep the fiduciary label flexible for public policy reasons, has resulted in this underplay. However, the existence of the fiduciary regime is essential in any modern economic system. Contract law envisages parties dealing at arm's length. However, it is necessary and desirable for people to be able to entrust others with their affairs and to stipulate for loyal and disinterested management of their business. Most professions operate on this basis.

The core example of the disinterested management of the affairs of another is the prime example of fiduciary responsibility, namely that of the trustee. In addition, there are other status-based examples of the fiduciary regime: solicitors (*In re Hallett's Estate* (1880) 13 Ch D 696); company promoters (*Gluckstein v Barnes* [1900] AC 240); company directors (*Regal (Hastings) Ltd v Gulliver* [1942] 1 All ER 378); agents (*Logicrose Ltd v Southend United Football Club Ltd* [1988] 1 WLR 1256) and bailees, most recently in the context of recipients of goods supplied on retention of title terms (*Aluminum Industrie Vaassen BV v Romalpa Aluminum Ltd* [1976] 1 WLR 676). However, it would be wrong to confine the fiduciary label to particular examples of status or profession. In *English v Dedham Vale Properties Ltd* [1978] 1 WLR 93, at 110, Slade J stated:

> I do not think that the categories of fiduciary relationships which give rise to a constructive trusteeship should be regarded as falling into a limited number of

strait-jackets or as being necessarily closed. They are, after all, no more than formulae for equitable relief.

Nor should explicit or implicit consent necessarily be an exhaustive guide to fiduciary responsibility.

For example, in the leading case of *Boardman* v *Phipps* [1967] 2 AC 46, the solicitor to a will trust and a beneficiary under the trust staged a skilful takeover of an ailing textile company in which the trust held a minority shareholding. Using considerable business acumen the two men turned the fortunes of the company around. This was done with the acquiescence of the active trustees, although no formal consent was ever obtained (nor due to the incapacity of one of the trustees could it ever have been obtained). In a claim brought by one of the other beneficiaries, Wilberforce J labelled the two as 'self-appointed agents' for the trustees ([1964] 1 WLR 993, at 1007). The majority of the House of Lords agreed that the two were in a fiduciary position, and were in breach of it by using information and an opportunity which came to them by reason of their relationship with the trust. However, they did not approve of the appellation of 'self-appointed agents'. Lord Guest, for example, preferred to say that they 'placed themselves in a special position which was of a fiduciary character' ([1967] 2 AC 46, at 118). It is clear that the ascription of fiduciary responsibility is ultimately a matter for the courts. Regard is had to the underlying consensual relationship, including the terms of any contract between fiduciary and principal. This contractual matrix may exclude or modify the full rigour of the fiduciary regime (*Kelly* v *Cooper* [1993] AC 205). However, in the majority of cases the relationship is firmly bottomed on the consent or assumption of responsibility by the alleged fiduciary alone.

The recognition of fiduciary status does not conclude matters. In *SEC* v *Chenery Corp.* 318 US 80 (1943), Frankfurter J stated (at 85–86):

> To say that a man is a fiduciary only begins analysis; it gives direction to further enquiry. To whom is he a fiduciary? What obligations does he owe as a fiduciary? In what respect has he failed to discharge these obligations? And what are the consequences of his deviation from duty?

23.3 THE OBLIGATIONS OF THE FIDUCIARY

If the core obligation of the fiduciary is loyalty, the paradigm instance of breach of fiduciary duty is non-disclosure. The case law divides into two broad categories. First, transactions between the principal and fiduciary. Secondly, transactions or dealings by the fiduciary with third parties, whether purportedly done on behalf of the principal or not. As a general rule it may be stated that if the fiduciary makes full disclosure of all the circumstances to the principal and the principal gives informed consent to the dealings, the transaction will stand in either category. There is no room for a detailed survey of the case law and the content of the obligation here. Where the fiduciary deals directly with its principal, the burden of proof is upon the fiduciary to demonstrate affirmatively that the transaction was fair and that in the course of negotiations he made full disclosure of all the facts material to the transaction. Any non-disclosure by the fiduciary will entitle the principal to rescind the transaction. This is a leading exception to the general position in English law that non-disclosure does not vitiate transactions. If rescission is no longer possible, in the alternative the fiduciary will be liable to account for any benefits received as a result of the transaction, and the duty to account may in appropriate circumstances be reinforced by a proprietary restitutionary remedy. See Goff and Jones, 718–26.

A significant recent statement of authority came in *Guinness plc v Saunders* [1990] 2 AC 663. Guinness sought to recover £5.2 million paid to Ward, an American attorney and former director of the company, made at the time of the controversial bid by Guinness to take over Distillers. Ward together with the then chief executive, Saunders, and another director, Roux, formed a take-over sub-committee of the Board. That sub-committee agreed to pay Ward 0.2 per cent of the ultimate value of the bid if successful for his services in connection with the bid. This yielded £5.2 million. It was ultimately held by the House of Lords that Guinness's articles of association only empowered the board of directors to award such remuneration. Accordingly the contract was void for want of authority of the sub-committee. Lord Goff of Chievely stated (at 700):

> the directors of a company, like other fiduciaries, must not put themselves in a position where there is a conflict between their personal interests and their duties as fiduciaries, and are for that reason precluded from contracting with the company for their services except in circumstances authorised by the articles of association. Similarly, just as trustees are not entitled, in the absence of an appropriate provision in the trust deed, to remuneration for their services as trustees, so directors are not entitled to remuneration for their services as directors except as provided by the articles of association.

It was clear that in agreeing to provide his services in return for a substantial fee, the size of which was dependent upon the amount of the successful bid, Ward was blatantly in breach of his duty not to allow his own interests to conflict with his fiduciary responsibility.

The obligations of the fiduciary are multi-faceted, as recognised recently by Millett LJ in *Bristol and West Building Society v Mothew* [1998] Ch 1, at 18:

> This core liability has several facets. A fiduciary must act in good faith; he must not make a profit out of his trust; he must not place himself in a position where his duty and his interest may conflict; he may not act for his own benefit or the benefit of a third person without the informed consent of his principal. This is not intended to be an exhaustive list, but it is sufficient to indicate the nature of fiduciary obligations. They are the defining characteristics of the fiduciary.

23.4 REMEDIES FOR BREACH

The characteristic remedial response is that a fiduciary must disgorge the benefits derived from his breach of duty. Remedial flexibility is demonstrated by the two leading cases on the liability of company promoters.

In *Erlanger* v *New Sombrero Phosphate Co.* (1878) 3 App Cas 1218, a syndicate of promoters purchased the lease for a West Indian Island for £55,000. They promoted a company with the object of exploiting the island's phosphate reserve. Subsequently the syndicate sold the island to the company for £110,000. They failed to disclose the inflated price to the investor. The House of Lords unanimously held that the promoters stood in a fiduciary position towards the company and owed it a duty to make full disclosure of the circumstances of their acquisition of the property. The company was held entitled to rescind the contract and to restitution of the purchase price, conditional upon giving up possession of the island and paying over any profits made in the interim.

In *Gluckstein* v *Barnes* [1900] AC 240, a syndicate purchased the Olympia Exhibition Hall for £140,000. They subsequently promoted a company to which to sell the property for £180,000. The prospectus disclosed a profit of £40,000, but failed to disclose a further profit of £20,000 made in relation to the property. The House of Lords held one of the promoters accountable for his share of the secret profits. The House rejected an argument that the only remedy was rescission, relying upon the authority of *Hichens* v *Congreve* (1831) 4 Sim 420, 58 ER 157.

The claim to rescission in *Erlanger* can be rationalised either as based upon vitiated intent to transfer (arising from the non-disclosure), or alternatively as parasitic upon the wrong of breach of fiduciary duty. In contrast, the liability to account in *Gluckstein* is best classified as a claim based solely upon restitution of the wrongdoing. It would be artificial to describe it as a species of subtractive unjust enrichment. See Birks [1990] LMCLQ 330, at 331–32.

23.5 DIVERSION OF OPPORTUNITY

A common breach of duty is the diversion by the fiduciary of an opportunity which came to his knowledge in the course of acting on behalf of the principal. The seminal case is *Keech* v *Sanford* (1728) Sel Cas t King (Macnaughten) 175, 25 ER 223, in which a lease was managed by a trustee on behalf of an infant beneficiary. The landlord refused to renew for the infant. The trustee took the lease for his own benefit. It was held that he held the benefit of the lease on behalf of the infant, Lord King LC stating that 'the trustee is the only person of all mankind who might not have the lease' (at 62).

The principle has been rigorously applied. In *Regal (Hastings) Ltd* v *Gulliver* [1942] 1 All ER 378, [1967] 2 AC 134n, Regal formed a subsidiary for the purpose of acquiring the leases of two cinemas. The owners of the cinemas would agree to the leases only if the subsidiary company was fully capitalised. Regal could not afford to do this, so four of its directors each took a personal shareholding. Eventually the shares were sold at a considerable profit. Regal, under new management, claimed the profit from its former directors. It was held that Regal must succeed. Lord Russell of Killowen stated (at 144–45):

> The rule of equity which insists on those, who by use of a fiduciary position make a profit, being liable to account for that profit, in no way depends upon fraud, or absence of bona fides; or upon such questions or considerations as whether the profit would or should otherwise have gone to the plaintiff, or whether the profiteer was under a duty to obtain the source of the profit for the plaintiff, or whether he took a risk or acted as he did for the benefit of the plaintiff, or whether the plaintiff has in fact been damaged or benefited by his action. The liability arises from the mere fact of a profit having, in the stated circumstances, been made. The profiteer, however honest and well-intentioned, cannot escape the risk of being called upon to account.

It was clear that the directors could have protected themselves by a resolution of the Regal shareholders approving of their conduct. However, informed consent not having been obtained, they were liable to account.

This was the principle relied upon in *Boardman* v *Phipps* [1967] 2 AC 46, where the solicitor to a trust and a beneficiary were held liable to account for the profits made as a result of the successful take-over of a company in which the trust had a minority shareholding. It was sufficient that the two had obtained the information as a basis for the take-over and the opportunity of acquiring the shares as a result of acting on behalf of the trustee. It was stated that the transaction required the fully informed consent of both trustees and beneficiaries. These extreme applications of the principle are criticised in Jones, 'Unjust Enrichment in the Fiduciary's Duty of Loyalty' (1968) 84 LQR 472. See Goff and Jones, 729–34.

23.6   CORPORATE OPPORTUNITY DOCTRINE

The liability of directors and other senior employees of companies has spawned a particular contextual application of the diversion rules known as the 'corporate opportunity doctrine'.

In *Industrial Developments Consultants Ltd* v *Cooley* [1972] 1 WLR 443, the defendant was appointed managing director of the plaintiff company. The company offered construction and design services to large industrial enterprises, and the defendant was recruited for his expertise in the gas industry. The defendant on behalf of the company, entered into negotiations with the Eastern Gas Board with a view to the company designing and constructing new depots. These were unsuccessful. Subsequently the Gas Board approached the defendant with a view to him doing the work in his private capacity. The defendant falsely represented to the chairman of the group to which the company belonged, that he would have to resign on the grounds of ill-health. The defendant was held to be a constructive trustee of the benefits of the contract which he subsequently entered into with the Gas Board. Roskill J held that the defendant placed himself in a position where his own private interests and the interests of the company grievously conflicted. It was irrelevant whether or not the company would have obtained the benefit but for the breach of fiduciary duty.

In contrast, in *Island Export Finance Ltd* v *Umunna* [1986] BCLC 460, Umunna was appointed managing director of the defendant company which pursued business in West Africa. In 1976, Umunna secured a contract with the Cameroon postal authorities. Subsequently, in 1977 Umunna resigned as managing director due to his general dissatisfaction with the company. At the time the company was not actively seeking repeat or further orders from the Cameroon postal authorities. Umunna later obtained for his own company a similar contract from the Cameroon authorities. The defendant sought an account of profit. Hutchison J, relying on the Supreme Court of Canada authority of *Canadian Aero Service Ltd* v *O'Malley* (1973) 40 DLR (3d) 371, held that in the circumstances there was no duty to account. In particular the judge relied upon dicta of Laskin J in the *Canadian Aero* case (at 382):

> An examination of the case law in this Court and in the Courts of other like jurisdictions on the fiduciary duties of directors and senior officers shows the pervasiveness of a strict ethic in this area of the law. In my opinion, this ethic disqualifies a director or senior officer from usurping for himself or diverting to another person or company with whom or with which he is associated a maturing business opportunity which his company is actively pursuing; he is also precluded from so acting even after his resignation where the resignation may fairly be said to have been prompted or influenced by a wish to acquire for himself the opportunity sought by the company, or where it was his position with the company rather than a fresh initiative that led him to the opportunity which he later acquired.

Given that the new contract could not realistically be described as a maturing business opportunity and Mr Umunna's genuine reasons for resigning, the allegation of breach did not succeed.

For discussion of the question whether the remedy in this context should be a personal or proprietary one, see Goode, 'The Recovery of a Director's Improper Gains: Proprietary Remedies for the Infringement of Non-Proprietary Rights' in McKendrick (ed.), *Commercial Aspects of Trusts and Fiduciary Obligations* (1992), 137–48.

23.7 BRIBES AND SECRET COMMISSIONS

In *Boston Deep Sea Fishing & Ice Co.* v *Ansell* (1888) 39 Ch D 339, Ansell was the managing director of the plaintiff company. He entered into shipbuilding contracts on behalf of the company, but unknown to it took secret commissions from the shipbuilders. The Court of Appeal held that he was validly dismissed and was liable to account for the secret commissions received. The agent was liable to account to the principal either at common law in an action for money had and received, or under an equitable duty to account. In *Anangel Atlas Compania Naviera SA* v *Ishikawajima-Harima Heavy Industries Co. Ltd* [1990] 1 Lloyd's Rep 167, Leggatt J suggested (at 171): 'it may be said that the bribe consists in a commission or other inducement, which is given by a third party to an agent as such, and which is secret from its principal.' The motive of the fiduciary is irrelevant: it is conclusively presumed that he has acted corruptly. It would only be a defence for the fiduciary if it could be shown that the payment was made with the full, informed consent of the principal.

Where an agent does receive a bribe or secret commission, the principal has a large number of potential remedies. First, any contract of employment between principal and agent may be terminated. Secondly, both the fiduciary and the party paying the bribe are jointly liable for damages in the tort of deceit. Thirdly, the principal may rescind any contract which resulted between himself and the third party (*Logicrose Ltd* v *Southend United Football Club Ltd* [1988] 1 WLR 1256). Fourthly, within the law of unjust enrichment the principal may seek disgorgement of the amount of the bribe from the fiduciary, and also from the briber (*Arab Monetary Fund* v *Hashim* [1993] 1 Lloyd's Rep 543, at 564–65).

What has proved controversial is whether the restitutionary duty is personal or proprietary in nature. As has been observed above, the duty was recognised both at common law and in equity. The traditional English law view was enunciated in *Lister & Co.* v *Stubbs* (1890) 45 Ch D 1. The plaintiff company manufactured silk and Stubbs was their foreperson dyer responsible for purchasing the raw materials for dyeing. It seems that over a 10-year period he had received over £5,000 in secret commissions from Messrs Varley, a firm in Leeds, in relation to goods purchased on behalf of the plaintiff company. It was alleged that Stubbs had invested the money in land in Yorkshire and other investments. A strong Court of Appeal ruled that the obligation was personal only, Lindley LJ stating (at 15):

> The relation between them is that of debtor and creditor; it is not that of trustee and *cestui que trust*. We were asked to hold that it is — which would involve consequences which, I confess, startle me. One consequence, of course, would be that, if Stubbs were to become bankrupt, this property acquired by him with the money paid to him by Messrs Varley would be withdrawn from the mass of his creditors and handed over bodily to Lister & Co. Can that be right? Another consequence would be that, if the Appellants are right, Lister & Co. can compel Stubbs to account to them, not only for the money with interest, but for all the profits which he might have made by embarking in trade with it. Can that be right?

In Lindley LJ's view the argument was 'confounding ownership with obligation'.

However, the strict logic of this position has been rejected and the liability of the recalcitrant fiduciary made more stringent in an advice delivered by the Privy Council in *Attorney-General for Hong Kong* v *Reid* [1994] 1 AC 324. Reid was the acting Director of Public Prosecutions in the former colony, who had received bribes from Triad gangs (presumably to stifle prosecutions) before his corruption was exposed. The Privy Council held that property in New Zealand which Reid must have acquired with the proceeds of bribes was held on constructive trust for the Crown. In delivering the advice Lord Templeman declared (at 331):

> if the bribe consists of property which increases in value or if a cash bribe is invested advantageously, the false fiduciary will receive a benefit from his breach of duty unless he is accountable not only for the original amount or value of the bribe but also for the increased value of the property representing the bribe. As soon as the bribe was received it should have been paid or transferred instanter to the person who suffered from the breach of duty. Equity considers as done that which ought to have been done. As soon as bribe was received, whether in cash or in kind, the false fiduciary held the bribe on a constructive trust for the person injured.

The reference to the well-known equitable maxim is puzzling, as it has not previously been deployed in this context and seems to provide little logical support for a shift from a personal to a proprietary response. It derives from an extra-judicial discussion by Sir Peter Millett, 'Bribes and Secret Commissions' [1993] RLR 7.

It is submitted that the better view is that *Reid* is a decision based upon a public policy of deterrence or, more appropriately, punishment. Bribes and secret commissions are such a societal evil that a stringent proprietary remedy will be available in appropriate cases. This much is clear in an earlier statement of Lord Templeman (at 330–31) that: 'Bribery is an evil practice which threatens the foundations of any civilised society. In particular, bribery of policemen and prosecutors brings the administration of justice into disrepute.' However, it is submitted that the Privy Council has conflated two questions. First, when should a solvent fiduciary who has recently profited from the receipt of a bribe be entitled to retain the surplus? This is a value-received versus value-surviving question. Where the fiduciary is still solvent, prophylaxis favours stripping him of all the consequences of the bribe. In contrast, where he is insolvent, a claim should not exceed the actual value received, otherwise the general creditors will suffer a detriment, if the claim is a secured one. Secondly, there is the distinct question of whether the claim should be personal or proprietary, effectively securing the claim in the event of insolvency. As was suggested above, in an insolvent defendant case, the court should be more circumspect. If Reid had been insolvent, an equitable lien for the value received (and no more) would have been the most appropriate response, rather than a constructive trust. This case illustrates the danger of confounding the fifth and sixth questions in the restitutionary enquiry (see 1.2). For further discussion of the proprietary claim question, see 30.13.

Given the accumulation of remedies, the question arises which of them are alternative? As a matter of principle it is submitted that the principal must pursue either the fiduciary or the briber for the amount of the bribe, and cannot recover twice as much by suing both. Further, it has been held that as between the wrong-based claim to compensation in the tort of deceit and the restitutionary claim to the amount of the bribe, the principal must elect between these two alternative remedies before judgment (*Mahesan S/O Thambiah* v *Malaysia Government Officers' Co-operative Housing Society Ltd* [1979] AC 374, at 383 *per* Lord Diplock). Otherwise, it is clear that the principal may accumulate remedies. For example, he may recover the bribe from the fiduciary, terminate any contract of employment of the fiduciary, and rescind any contract made with a third-party briber. For discussion, see Jones [1989] CLJ 22.

23.8   PRACTICAL ISSUES

Once it is shown that a party is in a position of a fiduciary and is in breach of an obligation which is properly characterised as a fiduciary one, a number of important consequences flow.

First, the burden of proof will be upon the fiduciary to demonstrate that any transaction or dealings, whether with the principal or with a third party, could properly be entered into. In particular, the fiduciary will need to demonstrate that there has been disclosure by him to the principal of all material circumstances affecting the transaction. It will need to be shown further that the principal gave fully informed consent to any resulting transaction, or else ratified it subsequently having been apprised of all the material circumstances. The evidential onus is clearly upon the fiduciary and not the principal.

Secondly, the principal will be entitled to a full range of equitable remedies including rescission of any transaction entered into with the fiduciary itself, or any transaction with a third party who was privy to the breach of fiduciary duty (such as a briber who has paid a secret commission to an agent). The fiduciary will be liable to account for any benefits received, and may in appropriate circumstances be held to hold such benefits upon constructive trust for the principal. The liability is stringent. For example, there is no need to demonstrate lack of good faith where a fiduciary allows an actual conflict between his interest and his duty to his principal. Further, the recipient of a secret commission is conclusively presumed to have acted corruptly.

Thirdly, where there is a breach of fiduciary duty where money is paid in breach of fiduciary duty, the court in ordering repayment of the principal sum may award compound interest, rather than simple interest upon the debt (*Westdeutsche Landesbank Girozentrale* v *Islington London Borough Council* [1996] AC 669).

Fourthly, it may still be necessary to establish a payment in breach of trust or breach of fiduciary duty as a pre-condition to a successful tracing exercise in equity where recovery is sought against a recipient other than the fiduciary. This restriction has been much criticised (and sometimes evaded) but appears to remain intact after the decision of the House of Lords in *Westdeutsche*.

FURTHER READING

Asterisks indicate especially useful works.

Goff and Jones, 713–34; 738–42.
P. Finn, *Fiduciary Obligations* (1977)

*G. Jones, 'Unjust Enrichment and the Fiduciary's Duty of Loyalty' (1968) 84 LQR 472

Sir Peter Millett, 'Bribes and Secret Commissions' [1993] *Restitution Law Review* 7

R. Goode, 'The Recovery of a Director's Improper Gains: Proprietary Remedies for Infringement of Non-Proprietary Rights' in E. McKendrick (ed), *Commercial Aspects of Trusts and Fiduciary Obligations* (1992), 137–48

I. Jackman, 'Restitution for Wrongs' [1989] CLJ 302, at 311–14

24 Breach of Confidence

24.1 INTRODUCTION

The perceived need for protection of confidential information, whether government or trade secrets, or involving the intimate details of private relationships, has spawned a new civil wrong recognised in equity. The protection of confidential information has yielded obligations which are recognised in equity and for which disgorgement remedies are available. In *Seager* v *Copydex Ltd* [1967] 1 WLR 923, Lord Denning MR observed (at 931):

> The law on this subject does not depend on any implied contract. It depends on the broad principle of equity that he who has received information in confidence shall not take unfair advantage of it. He must not make use of it to the prejudice of him who gave it without obtaining his consent.

It is not appropriate to detail the law relating to the protection of confidential information. For an account, see Goff and Jones, 747–70. However, a good illustration of what amounted to protected trade secrets is provided by the recent case of *Universal Thermosensors Ltd* v *Hibben* [1992] 1 WLR 840, where former employees dishonestly took away with them their former employer's customer lists and pricing information. These were used in the course of operating a rival business. Sir Donald Nicholls V-C stated (at 850):

> What the defendants were not entitled to do was to steal documents belonging to the plaintiff, or to use for their own purposes information, which can sensibly be regarded as confidential information, contained in such documents regarding the plaintiff's customers or customer contacts or customer requirements or the prices charged. Nor were they entitled to copy such information onto scraps of paper and take these away and then use the information in their own business.

We shall briefly review some of the remedies for breach of confidence.

24.2 REMEDIES FOR BREACH OF CONFIDENCE

24.2.1 Restitutionary damages

In *Universal Thermosensors Ltd* v *Hibben* [1992] 1 WLR 840, the judge awarded damages on the basis that the plaintiff ought to be paid by the defendants for the use they made of the plaintiff's confidential information, even though the plaintiff suffered no loss of profits as a result (at 856). Sir Donald Nicholls V-C explicitly based the measure of damages on analogy with 'the user principle' (*Stoke-on-Trent City Council* v *W. & J. Wass Ltd* [1988] 1 WLR 1406, at 1416–18). See 25.2.

A similar award of damages was made in *Seager* v *Copydex Ltd* [1977] 1 WLR 923, where the defendants misused commercial information given to them in confidence in respect of a special type of carbon carpet grip. They were held to have acted in breach of confidence, even though it seemed that they made only unconscious use of the information they had received. The information provided a springboard for activity which was to the detriment of the confiders.

The appropriate measure of damages was further discussed in *Seager* v *Copydex Ltd (No. 2)* [1979] 1 WLR 809, where Lord Denning MR said that the damages should be measured by the price which a willing buyer, desirous of obtaining the information, would pay for it. This should be based upon a royalty which the seller of information could have stipulated for, and damages should be calculated by reference to a capitalisation of such a royalty. This amounted to an outright purchase of the confidential information, so that once the award of damages was satisfied the information would belong to the defendant.

These cases are concerned with what would now be called restitutionary damages for breach of confidence, where regard may be had to a suitable proportion of profits which must be disgorged in substitution for a compensatory measure.

24.2.2 Liability to account

In addition to damages, it has also been recognised that the misuser of confidential information may be liable to account, although this was refused in *Seager* v *Copydex* (apparently because the defendants were not conscious wrongdoers). The account is viewed as a more stringent remedy, stripping the wrongdoer of all the resulting profits.

In *Peter Pan Manufacturing Corp.* v *Corsets Silhouette Ltd* [1964] 1 WLR 96, the defendant was granted a licence to manufacture certain styles of brassiere in the UK and Eire by an American company. The company later showed new designs to the defendant. Subsequently the defendant manufactured two new styles of bra, based in part upon the new designs which had been seen by their designer and in part upon previous information given to them. The American company was given a perpetual injunction restraining the defendant from using such designs in breach of confidence in the future. At trial they elected for an account of profits rather than damages. Pennycuick J asked (at 108): 'What has the plaintiff expended on manufacturing these goods? What is the price which he has received on their sale? and the difference is profit.'

Similarly, in the well-known *Spycatcher* case, the *Sunday Times* had purchased the right to serialise a book written by a former member of the UK security service. The newspaper was held to have acted in breach of confidence (*Attorney-General* v *Guardian Newspapers Ltd (No. 2)* [1990] 1 AC 109). The House of Lords agreed that the *Sunday Times* should be liable for an account of profits flowing from its wrongdoing. Lord Keith of Kinkel expressly referred to the principle that no one should be permitted to gain from his own wrongdoing. This was of utility where confidential information was mis-used with a view to financial gain (at 262). In contrast, Lord Goff of Chieveley was sceptical of the usefulness of this generalisation in solving individual cases (at 286). The Crown was held entitled to an account of profits in respect of the publication in breach of confidence. The newspaper was not entitled to deduct any sums paid to the author of the book who had also clearly acted in breach of confidence. While no claim was advanced by the Crown to a constructive trust over the copyright of the book, Lord Keith (at 263) and Lord Griffiths (at 276) seemed sympathetic to the prospect of such a claim. For a full discussion, see Birks, 'A Lifelong Obligation of Confidence' (1989) 105 LQR 501.

24.2.3   Personal or proprietary relief?

The availability of proprietary relief was favoured by Lords Keith and Griffiths in the case of *Spycatcher* [1990] 1 AC 109, at 263 and 276. The Supreme Court of Canada awarded a constructive trust in response to a breach of confidence in *LAC Minerals Ltd* v *International Corona Resources Ltd* (1989) 61 DLR (4th) 14. This was welcomed by Davies ([1990] LMCLQ 4), but criticised as promoting remedial uncertainty by Birks ([1990] LMCLQ 460).

However, the recognition of a constructive trust over the fruit of bribes in *Attorney-General for Hong Kong* v *Reid* [1994] 1 AC 324, suggests that the English courts may favour proprietary relief in respect of enrichment by wrongdoing, at least where deterrence or punishment requires it. See 30.3. The constructive trust was favoured in dicta by Sir Richard Scott V-C at first instance in *Attorney-General* v *Blake* [1997] Ch 84, where he suggested that the treacherous defendant 'ought in equity to be required to hold the fruits of his wrongdoing for the person to whom the duty was owed' (at 96). However, notwithstanding *Reid*, the Vice-Chancellor thought that he was precluded from so holding by Court of Appeal authority: *Lister & Co.* v *Stubbs* (1890) 45 Ch D 1; *Halifax Building Society* v *Thomas* [1996] Ch 217. In contrast, the Court of Appeal in *Blake* [1998] Ch 439 would have preferred to award (presumably personal) damages for breach of contract, 'rather than distort the equitable concepts of fiduciary duty or constructive trust to achieve a just result' (at 459). At the time of writing, *Blake* is on appeal to the House of Lords.

FURTHER READING

Asterisks indicate especially useful works.

*Goff and Jones, 734–38; 747–70

F. Gurry, *Breach of Confidence* (1984)

*G. Jones, 'Restitution of Benefits Obtained in Breach of Another's Confidence' (1970) 86 LQR 463, especially at 483–91

Law Commission, *Breach of Confidence*, Law Com. No. 110 (1981)

G. Jones, 'Breach of Confidence — After *Spycatcher*' [1989] CLP 49

P. Birks, 'A Lifelong Obligation of Confidence' (1989) 105 LQR 501

I. Jackman, 'Restitution for Wrongs' [1989] CLJ 302, at 314–17

J. Davies, 'Duties of confidence and loyalty' [1990] LMCLQ 4

P. Birks, 'The remedies for abuse of confidential information' [1990] LMCLQ 460

R. Toulson and C. Phipps, *Confidentiality* (1996), 117–28

25 Restitutionary Damages for Tortious Wrongdoing

25.1 THEORETICAL FOUNDATIONS

'Tort' is the word which is still employed to denote those civil wrongs developed by the common law courts. Tortious (or wrongful) conduct characteristically consists of three elements. First, a breach of a primary legal obligation owed by the defendant to the claimant. Secondly, that breach injures or interferes with some legitimate interest of the claimant, whether in bodily integrity, reputation, property or economic assets. The coincidence of the breach of duty by the defendant with interference with the claimant's rights entitles the latter to seek redress in his own name. Thirdly, so far as the harm done is compensable, the legal response is the imposition of a secondary obligation on the defendant to pay to the claimant a sum of money, termed damages. Damages are conventionally measured by reference to the loss caused to the claimant. For a sophisticated account, arguing that other supposed ingredients of civil wrongs, such as harm and fault, are analytically inessential, see Birks, 'The Concept of a Civil Wrong' in Owen (ed.), *Philosophical Foundations of Tort Law* (1995), 31–51.

Non-compensatory awards such as exemplary damages were marginalised and confined to exceptional cases by the House of Lords in *Rookes* v *Barnard* [1964] AC 1129 and *Cassell & Co.* v *Broome* [1972] AC 1027. However, the perceived predominance of loss-based remedies fails to do justice to a variety of judicial techniques which strip tortfeasors of benefits derived from a breach of duty. The common law's supposed traditional 'hegemony of compensation' received a sustained critique in Birks, 'Civil Wrongs — A New World', *Butterworths Lectures 1990–1991* (1992). The primacy of a compensatory response also sat uncomfortably with the comparative willingness of the courts to award restitutionary responses to breaches of equitable duties, as we saw in the two preceding chapters. Recent case law and a Law Commission Report (*Aggravated, Exemplary and Restitutionary*

Damages, Law Com. No. 247, 1997) have signalled a greater role for remedies forcing wrongdoers to disgorge profits from wrongdoing at common law.

The threshold question is to identify cases for which a benefit-based measure of recovery is possible. One approach is to suggest that the courts should always have a discretion to award a benefit-based measure instead of a loss-based measure. A second approach is to confine the availability of disgorgement to particular species of tort. For example, traditionally a restitutionary approach has been available for various nominate torts, such as conversion and trespass. However, it has not been available in negligence. Modern theorists seeking to explain restitutionary awards incorporate one or more of three basic strategies. First, some theories consider the nature of the wrong committed or the interest which it seeks to protect. For example, a benefit-based measure might be considered to be confined to torts which protect proprietary (or analogous) interests. Such is the approach of Friedmann: 'Restitution of Benefits Obtained Through the Appropriation of Property or the Commission of a Wrong' (1980) 80 Col LR 504. In *Stoke-on-Trent City Council* v *W. & J. Wass Ltd* [1988] 1 WLR 1406, Nourse LJ suggested (at 1415):

It is possible that the English law of tort, more especially of the so-called 'proprietary torts', will in due course make a more deliberate move towards recovery based, not on loss suffered by the plaintiff, but on the unjust enrichment of the defendant.

Similarly, in an influential article Jackman has suggested that a restitutionary approach is apt for torts and other wrongs which protect 'facilitative institutions', that is legal powers such as property ownership, confidential and fiduciary relationships which require institutional protection: Jackman, 'Restitution for Wrongs' [1989] CLJ 302. Secondly, it may be asked whether a profit-stripping measure is appropriate on the basis of deterrence or as a prophylactic, to discourage such conduct in the future. Thirdly, the quality of the defendant's conduct may be a factor: was it intentional, cynical or exploitative? Any one or more of these factors may suggest a restitutionary response. However, the current positive law is not so tidy. For example, it is hard to understand why neither of the two last factors has led to the explicit pursuit of restitutionary measures for the tort of defamation.

25.2 FROM WAIVER OF TORT TO RESTITUTIONARY DAMAGES

There are a number of techniques whereby the law has regard to the benefit to the tortfeasor, rather than loss suffered by the claimant. The four main techniques are:

(a) waiver of tort;
(b) the 'user-principle';
(c) an account of profits; and
(d) an award of restitutionary damages (including by extension, mesne profits as damages for trespass, and, arguably, damages for use and occupation).

These may overlap. Indeed it may be preferable to regard the second as a justification for those cases in which restitutionary damages are more or less explicitly awarded. The modern view is that the term 'restitutionary damages' should be used as an umbrella phrase for all situations in which a defendant has been held to have benefitted by tortious conduct.

25.2.1   Waiver of tort

Waiver of tort is a quaint and inaccurate description of one way of forcing a tortfeasor to disgorge gains. It does not involve excusing the tortfeasor from the consequences of his breach of duty. In *United Australia Ltd* v *Barclays Bank Ltd* [1941] AC 1, Lord Atkin observed (at 28–29):

> the plaintiff never has the slightest intention of waiving, excusing or in any kind of way palliating the tort. If I find that a thief has stolen my securities and is in possession of the proceeds, when I sue him for them I am not excusing him. I am protesting violently that he is a thief and because of his theft I am suing him.

As was explained there, waiving the tort was a primitive tactic employed in times when it was not possible to combine two different forms of action in the same proceedings. A plaintiff was permitted to proceed in *assumpsit*, rather than pursue the form of action corresponding to the relevant nominate tort. This allowed the plaintiff to recover the value of that which was tortiously abstracted or utilised. There is a whiff of fiction here in that the defendant is considered to have impliedly promised that he would hand over the proceeds of his conduct. Historically the *assumpsit* form was attended by considerable procedural advantages over the tortious actions. These no longer apply, but for a succinct account see Beatson, 210–11. Traditionally the torts which could be waived have a proprietary flavour, such as conversion. However, the category was not so limited.

25.2.2   The 'user principle'

The old technique of waiving the tort had been circumvented in cases where the courts had more or less explicitly awarded a benefit-based measure in the guise of damages. Such restitutionary damages have recently been judicially explained on the basis of the 'user principle'. For example, in *Stoke-on-Trent City Council* v *W. & J. Wass Ltd* [1988] 1 WLR 1406, Nicholls LJ observed (at 1416):

> It is an established principle concerning the assessment of damages that a person who has wrongfully used another's property without causing the latter any pecuniary loss may still be liable to that other for more than nominal damages. In general, he is liable to pay, as damages, a reasonable sum for the wrongful use he has made of the other's property. The law has reached this conclusion by giving to the concept of loss or damage in such a case a wider meaning than merely

financial loss calculated by comparing the property owner's financial position after the wrongdoing with what it would have been had the wrongdoing never occurred.

There is a tendency, similar to that in relation to the old cases on waiver of tort, to invoke legal fiction, such as to dress up a benefit-based award as depending upon an extended view of loss. Such an approach has its academic defenders who have explained that the claimant does suffer a real loss, namely the opportunity to sell to the defendant the right to use the claimant's property: Sharpe and Waddams, 'Damages for Lost Opportunity to Bargain' (1982) 2 OJLS 290. There it is argued that such awards are based upon the reasonable licence fee which the claimant might have charged had his permission been asked for his property to be used. The better view is that it is preferable to avoid legal fiction, and accept that in appropriate cases, the courts are concerned to strip gains from wrongdoers.

25.2.3 Account of profits

The third technique is the account of profits, which originated in equity but which has been routinely used in respect of torts protecting intellectual property rights such as passing off. See, for example, *My Kinda Town Ltd* v *Soll* [1983] RPC 15, where Slade J stated (at 55): 'The purpose of ordering an account of profits in favour of a successful plaintiff in a passing off case is to prevent an unjust enrichment of the defendant by compelling him to surrender those profits.'

25.2.4 Synthesis: Restitutionary damages

The modern view is that each of these four techniques is ultimately analytically indistinguishable. All award restitution: that is, a measure of recovery based on the wrongdoer's gain. Therefore the Law Commission has recently exhorted practitioners and judges to use just one term, 'restitutionary damages': Law Com. No. 247, paras 3.82 to 3.84. That approach is favoured here, although it will be necessary on occasion for pedagogical purposes to disinter the origins of different streams of case law. One must be careful not to over-simplify, as the method of identifying the benefit differs between the different techniques. It is submitted that rationalisation would produce two possible measures of benefit. First, actual profits accruing to a wrongdoer (such as were the concern in cases of waiver of tort or where an account of profits has been awarded). Secondly, the reasonable price, hire or fee which the claimant could have obtained as the price of giving consent to the defendant's infringement of the claimant's rights. This may be regarded by some as bordering on fiction. However, it can also be explained on the basis of the expense saved by the defendant. This second measure does not require proof that the defendant has made a profit.

   Contrast Smith, who insists on the exclusive use of the term 'disgorgement' in preference to 'restitution' or 'restitutionary damages' in the context of restitution for wrongs: Smith, 19–21, 297–99; Smith (1992) 71 Can Bar Rev 672.

The following sections consider a number of nominate torts in which a restitutionary award has been made. The issues of procedural advantages and cumulative and alternative remedies will also be addressed. We are concerned here with restitution as a remedial response to a breach of duty arising in the law of torts. Therefore, for the detail of the ingredients of the causes of action, reference should be made to texts on tort. It is assumed in the following sections that the claimant can establish the necessary facts to entitle him to a cause of action. The only question which arises is whether he is entitled to elect for a restitutionary award. It now seems to be accepted that restitution here is parasitic upon a breach of duty arising in another legal category, namely tort. However, this may be unhistorical and a modern rationalisation. For the argument that the restitutionary cause of action is independent of the tort, and is generated by the receipt of a benefit not a breach of duty, see Beatson, 206–43 and Friedmann, in Cornish, 133.

25.3   WAIVER OF TORT — ADVANTAGES?

25.3.1   Historical foundations

A sensitive topic for discussion is the extent to which a claimant may, by switching to a restitutionary award, evade procedural disadvantages attendant upon pursuing a cause of action in tort. Given the modern understanding of restitution's role here as being confined to providing a further weapon in the judicial armoury against wrongdoing, as a matter of principle it should make little difference that a claimant opts for a restitutionary measure rather than a compensatory measure. However, that has not been the experience of the positive law. As Hedley points out, when considering pre-Common Law Procedure Act case law it is necessary to recall that the choice between suing, in tort or quasi-contract involved not only different substantive rules, but also different rules of procedure: (1984) 100 LQR 653, at 656. The background to many of the waiver of tort cases were attempts to circumvent the now defunct common law rule that a personal action in tort did not survive against a deceased person's estate (*actio personalis moritur cum persona*), whereas a contractual claim did. This rule was modified by the Law Reform (Miscellaneous Provisions) Act 1934, which substituted a régime of short limitation periods, and was eventually entirely abrogated by the Proceedings Against Estates Act 1970. However, while the rule was on foot it was advantageous to switch to the form of action of *assumpsit*, which was notionally contractual and was held to survive against the deceased's estate.

For example, *Hambly v Trott* (1776) 1 Cowp 371, 98 ER 1136 was a claim initially in trover and conversion (wrongful interference with goods) brought against the administrator of an estate in respect of sheep, goats, pigs, oats and cider converted by the deceased. Lord Mansfield (at 374) stated that: 'it seems unjust and inconvenient, that the testator's assets should not be liable for the value of what belonged to another man, which the testator had reaped the benefit of.' Therefore, while crimes and torts were buried with the offender, there was no objection to an action for money had and received being brought instead against a dead person's estate. This was permissible only where a gain was acquired by the wrongdoing and that benefit was recoverable from the executor. Difficulties arose with regard to which benefits could be recovered from an executor. Lord Mansfield had clearly envisaged that both positive accruals of wealth and negative benefits in the shape of a saving of expense were recoverable, essaying the following example (at 375): 'So if a man take a horse from another, and bring him back again; an action of trespass will not lie against his executor, though it would against him; but an action for the use and hire of the horse will lie against the executor.'

25.3.2   The controversial case of *Phillips v Homfray*

The broad approach of Lord Mansfield to the question of an enrichment by wrongdoing was not followed by the majority of the Court of Appeal in *Phillips* v *Homfray* (1871) LR 6 Ch App 770, (1883) 24 Ch D 439, where a judgment was obtained in 1871 against three defendants, Homfray, Forman and Fothergill, who had been secretly transporting coal and ironstone through passages beneath the plaintiff's farm. All three defendants (including the estate of Forman who had died in 1871) were ordered to account for the value of the minerals so abstracted. Further, enquiries were ordered as to the 'wayleave and royalty' which the two living defendants ought to pay to the plaintiff in respect of the use of the passages and as to any compensation for harm caused to the farm or the mineral deposits lying beneath it. In the meantime, however, Fothergill died and it was held that the enquiry as to 'wayleave and royalty' should not be pursued against him.

The Court of Appeal was unanimous in holding that because of the *actio personalis* rule, compensation could not be awarded against the deceased's estate. Further, Bowen and Cotton LJJ held that no wayleave and royalty award should be made, as only positive benefits were recoverable from an estate. They stated (at 454–55): 'it is not every wrongful act by which a wrongdoer indirectly benefits that falls under this head, if the benefit does not consist in the acquisition of property, or its proceeds or value.' Unfortunately, the joint judgment appears to be tainted by implied contractual reasoning. Bowen and Cotton LJJ continued (at 462–63): 'The circumstances under which he used the road appear to us to negative the idea that he meant to pay for it. Nor have the assets of the deceased defendant been necessarily swollen by what he has done. He saved his estate expense, but he did not bring into it any additional property or value belonging to another person.'

Baggallay LJ's dissenting judgment, suggesting that saving of expenditure was a recoverable benefit from the estate, has generally been preferred: see Goff and Jones, 776–78. However, the case is best interpreted as confined to delimiting the boundaries of the defunct *actio personalis* rule and therefore the debate is somewhat academic, given the abolition of the rule. Nevertheless, the case remains problematic if, as sometimes happens, it is interpreted as authority for wider propositions. First, it has been suggested that it supports the proposition that a restitutionary measure cannot be awarded in cases of wrongful occupation of land. Lloyd LJ appears to have assumed this in *Ministry of Defence* v *Ashman* [1993] 2 EGLR 102, at 106. Secondly, it is sometimes stated as authority for a proposition that enrichment by wrongdoing, either generally or in relation to trespass against land, is confined to positive not negative benefits. The better view is that the case does not support either wider proposition, but is concerned solely with the limits of the now discarded *actio personalis* rule. For discussion, see Law Com. No. 247, paras 3.14 to 3.16.

25.3.3   Limitation periods

It has already been noted that before the Victorian reforms, utilising the form of action of *assumpsit* had certain procedural advantages over the tortious actions: see Beatson, 210–11. However, these have now largely been swept away. There remain two areas — the defences of limitation and public policy precluding recovery (which it may be inapt to describe as procedural) — in which pursuing a disgorgement claim may appear superficially attractive. First, limitation of action, where the relevant periods often differ in contract and tort. For example, in *Chesworth* v *Farrar* [1967] 1 QB 407, a claim expressed to be one for money had and received, waiving the tort of conversion, was held to be governed by the contractual limitation period, which was at that time more attractive than the short limitation period against a deceased's estate in respect of tortious claims. In contrast, the bulk of the claim in relation to breach of a bailment was classified as tortious and was held to be barred. Edmund Davies J's reasoning is difficult to sustain, but he regarded himself as bound by the Court of Appeal in *In re Diplock* [1948] Ch 465, at 514, which classified restitutionary claims as contractual for the purposes of the Limitation Act 1939. (The current law on limitation is discussed in Chapter 36.) However, the preferable view is that both heads of claim which rested upon tortious causes of action should have been governed by the same limitation rules.

25.3.4   Public policy

The other area in which a restitutionary award might be thought to confer an advantage is with regard to issues of public policy, most significantly with statutory grants of immunity in respect of civil wrongs. Most typically these have arisen within the industrial relations context, where trade unions have been granted defences from certain sorts of tortious suit.

However, the leading case of *Universe Tankships Inc. of Monrovia* v *International Transport Workers' Federation, The Universe Sentinel* [1983] 1 AC 366 suggests that the courts would be sensitive in treating statutory immunity from suit in tort as a source of public policy governing the availability or otherwise of restitutionary awards. The ITF blacked the shipowner's vessel which sailed under a flag of convenience. The shipowner was held entitled to recover money paid to the ITF's welfare fund as money had and received on the ground of economic duress. Lord Diplock stressed that this was not a case of restitution for wrongs as economic duress was not necessarily tortious. He stated (at 385):

In extending into the field of industrial relations the common law concept of economic duress and the right to a restitutionary remedy for it which is currently in process of development by judicial decisions, this House would not, in my view, be exercising the restraint that is appropriate to such a process if it were so to develop the concept that, by the simple expedient of 'waiving the tort', a restitutionary remedy for money had and received is made enforceable in cases in which Parliament has, over so long a period of years, manifested its preference for a public policy that a particular kind of tortious act should be legitimised in the sense that I am using that expression.

It is clear from his Lordship's judgment that whether the restitutionary remedy lay in subtractive unjust enrichment or restitution for wrongs, the (then applicable) statutory immunity (Trade Union and Labour Relations Act 1974, ss. 13–14) was not directly applicable to a claim in restitution. However, it could provide a source of public policy to guide the courts as to what sort of conduct ought to be treated as legitimate. However, the majority of the House of Lords held that there was no public policy bar to recovery by analogy with the 1974 Act because on the facts the pressure complained of was insufficiently connected with the terms and conditions of the employment of the crew (under the definition of 'trade dispute' in s. 29).

In a subsequent case on similar facts, Lord Goff of Chieveley confirmed that the action need not be based on waiver of tort (*Dimskal Shipping Co. SA v International Transport Workers' Federation, The Evia Luck (No. 2)* [1992] 2 AC 152). These cases make clear that while it may appear superficially attractive and possible to circumvent bars imposed on tortious claims by statute, by switching to a restitutionary award, the courts will be sensitive to the fact that where the underlying cause of action is indistinguishable from the legitimised tort, restitution will not be allowed to frustrate the public policy underlying the statutory immunity. For further discussion, see 35.5.2.

To conclude, switching to a restitutionary measure is not likely to yield in the modern world any procedural advantages or to permit the evasion of tortious limitation periods or immunities. Rather, the obvious substantive advantage of switching to a benefit-based measure remains. In appropriate cases it will yield a greater award than a loss-based measure, especially when the loss-based measure would be nil.

25.4 TRESPASS TO LAND

25.4.1 The 'wayleave' cases

This tort, which protects the claimant's interest in the use and enjoyment of his real property, has often yielded a benefit-based measure of recovery, despite doubts cast by the case of *Phillips v Homfray* (1883) 24 Ch D 439. Other pre-Common Law Procedure Act cases demonstrated reluctance to allow issues of trespass and title to be aired in the relatively informal action of *assumpsit*, but such fears are now irrelevant. In contrast, in *Stoke-on-Trent City Council* v *W. & J. Wass Ltd* [1988] 1 WLR 1406, trespass to land was described by Nourse LJ as the 'first and best established exception' to the general rule that a plaintiff can only recover for actual loss suffered (at 1410). The Victorian age yielded a sequence of 'wayleave' cases which were the result of industrial expansion. In these cases defendants trespassed on others' property by transporting coals or other minerals through tunnels and passageways under others' land. Even if no deposits were taken from the plaintiff's land and no damage was inflicted, the courts awarded damages equivalent to the royalty which the plaintiff would have demanded for his permission to use his property (see *Martin* v *Porter* (1839) 5 M & W 351, 151 ER 149; *Jegon* v *Vivian* (1871) LR 6 Ch App 742 and *Phillips* v *Homfray* (1871) LR 6 Ch App 770). As was explained above, it is a mistake to regard *Phillips* v *Homfray* as being an authority hostile to restitution. It was concerned merely with the boundaries of the *actio personalis* principle. This emerges clearly if regard is had to the whole history of the litigation: (1871) LR 6 Ch App 770; (1883) 24 Ch D 439; (1890) 44 Ch D 694 and [1892] 1 Ch 465. For discussion, see Hedley (1984) 100 LQR 653; Meagher, 'Unjust Enrichment, Restitution and Proprietary Remedies' in Finn, 60–67 and Birks, *Butterworths Lectures 1990–1991* (1992), 64–67.

The approach of the wayleave cases was followed in *Whitwham* v *Westminster Brymbo Coal & Coke Co.* [1896] 2 Ch 538, where over many years the wrongdoer committed trespass by tipping the refuse from its colliery onto a portion of the plaintiff's land. The official referee assessed the diminution in the plaintiff's property at £200, but held that the reasonable value to the defendants of the land for tipping purposes was some £963. Chitty J and the Court of Appeal held that the higher sum was the appropriate measure of damages. This was applied in *Penarth Dock Engineering Co. Ltd* v *Pounds* [1963] 1 Ll L Rep 359, where the defendant purchased from the plaintiff a floating pontoon lying in a dock leased to the plaintiff. The defendant undertook to remove the pontoon as speedily as possible, but despite repeated requests the defendant did not remove the pontoon for some 18 months. Lord Denning MR (sitting as a first instance judge; at 362) stated that: 'The test of the measure of damages is not what the plaintiffs have lost, but what benefit the defendant obtained by having the use of the berth.' His Lordship awarded damages at a rate of £32 per week running from the time when the floating pontoon should have been removed from the berth onwards.

25.4.2   Mesne profits

An interesting sequence of cases has arisen where a tenant or licensee has remained upon real property after his entitlement has come to an end. Here a distinction is often drawn between mesne profits, which are damages for trespass recoverable from a tenant or other occupier who holds over after lawful termination of his tenancy or right to occupation without the consent of the owner, and an action for use and occupation, which is available against a tenant who holds over with the consent of the landlord. The latter has long been acknowledged to sound in quasi-contract (although it could be argued such a liability is genuinely consensual). The law has established that with regard to the former the landlord of residential property can recover damages from the trespasser who has wrongfully used his property whether or not he can show he would have let the property to anybody else, and whether or not he would have used the property himself (*Inverugie Investments Ltd* v *Hackett* [1995] 1 WLR 713). The seminal statement is that of Megaw LJ in *Swordheath Properties Ltd* v *Tabet* [1979] 1 WLR 285, at 288:

> It appears to me to be clear, both as a matter of principle and of authority, that in a case of this sort the plaintiff, when he has established that the defendant has remained on as a trespasser in a residential property, is entitled, without bringing evidence that he could or would have let the property to someone else in the absence of the trespassing defendant, to have as damages for the trespass the value of the property as it would fairly be calculated; and, in the absence of anything special in the particular case it would be the ordinary letting value of the property that would determine the amount of damages.

The principle was applied in a commercial context in *Inverugie Investments Ltd* v *Hackett*, where Hackett had purchased a long leasehold of 30 apartments in the Silver Sands Hotel in Grand Bahamas. The owners wrongfully ejected Mr Hackett in 1974, only giving up possession in 1990 after 15 ½ years of trespass. Hackett sought mesne profits in respect of that period during which the hotel had an occupancy rate of about 35 per cent and was at all times running at a loss. Lord Lloyd, delivering the advice of the Privy Council, stressed that because of the latter factor Hackett was not asking for an account of profits. Rather, following *Swordheath Properties Ltd* v *Tabet* and the discussion of principle by Nicholls LJ in *Stoke-on-Trent City Council* v *W. & J. Wass Ltd* (see 25.2.2), the Privy Council purported to apply the 'user principle'. The plaintiff need not have suffered any actual loss by being deprived of the use of his property. Correlatively, the trespasser need not have actually derived any benefit from the property. The trespasser must pay a reasonable rent for the use he has enjoyed. In the instant case the correct value was the reasonable rent for use of an apartment for 365 days of the year, despite the low occupancy rate. Their Lordships rejected an argument that the valuation should be based upon a chance of the trespasser making a profit from the letting of the apartments to tour operators: this would have involved a considerable discount because of the risk of low occupancy. The reasonable rent did not depend on whether there was one apartment or 30; rather the general principle applied.

25.4.3   The Ministry of Defence cases

The insensitive treatment by the Ministry of Defence of the deserted spouses of military personnel has given rise to unusual applications of the principle. In *Ministry of Defence* v *Ashman* [1993] 2 EGLR 102, Flight Sergeant Ashman occupied married quarters near RAF Halton with his spouse. He signed a certificate acknowledging that he was entitled to occupy the property only while he remained in the RAF and living with his spouse, and further acknowledged that he would be required to move his family from the accommodation if he ceased to live with his spouse. The charge was £95.41 per month. Somewhat ironically, Mr Ashman deserted his wife on 14 February 1991, and consequently on 14 March both husband and wife were given notice to vacate. Mrs Ashman and the children remained as they had nowhere else to go. She would not be entitled to local authority accommodation until the Ministry obtained a formal possession order, which it did on 17 December 1991. On 17 May 1991, Mrs Ashman had been served with further notice which asserted the Ministry's right to damages to trespass at a rate of £108.93 *per week* — that is, more than four times the concessionary rate. The Court of Appeal, in determining the quantum of mesne profits, rejected the asserted figures of the Ministry. Kennedy and Hoffmann LJJ held that the appropriate measure of damages was the figure that Mrs Ashman would have been required to pay for suitable local authority accommodation had it been available. Kennedy LJ acknowledged that in the usual case the appropriate measure would be 'the proper letting value of the property' (at 104). However, where the property was not normally let on the open market it was preferable to look at the benefit to Mrs Ashman of the use of the property, which should be obtained by looking at the alternative local authority rates rather than considering the evidence tendered by the Ministry as to the market rent. Hoffmann LJ stated that the plaintiff could elect between two alternative bases of recovery. First, the loss suffered as result of the trespass, being the normal measure of damages in tort. Secondly, the value of the benefit which the occupier has actually received. His Lordship continued (at 105):

> This is a claim for restitution. The two bases of claim are mutually exclusive and the plaintiff must elect before the judgment which of them he wishes to pursue. . . . It is true that in the earlier cases it has not been expressly stated that the claim for mesne profit for trespass can be a claim for restitution. Nowadays I do not see why we should not call a spade a spade.

Hoffmann LJ's approach to the valuation issue was both novel and lucid. Borrowing the concept of subjective devaluation from the writings of Birks (see Birks, 109–14), his Lordship observed that the benefit may not be worth as much to one defendant as to another. In particular, it may be less valuable to a defendant who was not free to reject it. The Ashmans would never have occupied the premises at the full market rate. Therefore the value to Mrs Ashman of the house was no more than she would have had to pay for suitable local authority housing, if she could have been immediately re-housed. Note that Hoffmann LJ develops the concept of subjective devaluation which had been utilised by Professor Birks to explain why objectively valuable benefits might be regarded by the law as worthless in the hands of particular plaintiffs. In *Ashman*, subjective devaluation was not used to wipe out completely the enrichment received, but rather to reduce *pro tanto* the quantum of benefit. The case neatly illustrates how the demands of adjudication can develop and expand the conceptual framework put forward by juristic writers. Lloyd LJ did not dissent, but would have preferred to decide the case on a different basis. It was for the plaintiff to prove its damages, and it had to show what rent it would have recovered had the property been let to another tenant. He was not satisfied that in practice the Ministry would have recovered any more than the artificially low level of rent which is charged to service personnel.

Ashman was followed in *Ministry of Defence v Thompson* [1993] 2 EGLR 107, in which Hoffmann LJ summarised the relevant principles. First, the owner of land which is occupied without his consent may elect to choose a loss-based measure, or restitution of the value of the benefit which the defendant has received. Secondly, the fact that the owner would have let the premises at a concessionary rate or not let them at all was irrelevant. Valuation depended on the benefit which the defendant actually received. Thirdly, a benefit may be less valuable to an involuntary recipient than to one who had a free choice as to whether to remain in occupation or go elsewhere. Fourthly (at 107):

> the value of the right of occupation to a former licensee who has occupied at a concessionary rent and who has remained in possession only because she could not be rehoused by the local authority until a possession has been made would ordinarily be whichever is the higher of the former concessionary rent and what she would have paid for local authority housing suitable for her needs, if she had been rehoused at the time when the notice expired.

The Court of Appeal upheld the judge's ruling that the previous concessionary rent was the appropriate measure of damages. For discussion, see Cooke, 'Trespass, Mesne Profits and Restitution' (1994) 110 LQR 420.

25.5 WRONGFUL INTERFERENCE WITH GOODS

Wrongful interference with goods is not strictly a tort, but rather a super-category of tortious actions which protect interests in tangible personal property. The phrase was introduced by the Torts (Interference with Goods) Act 1977 to encompass all wrongs in relation to chattels. These included trespass to goods, conversion, detinue (which was appropriate where a bailor sued a bailee; now abolished by s. 4 of the 1977 Act — fact situations which previously yielded a cause of action in detinue are now subsumed within conversion) and trover (which is the ancient name for the type of interference from which conversion developed). The 1977 Act is not a codification of the law on wrongful interference of goods, but constitutes a patchwork reform of this area. We are not in this text concerned with establishing the factual matters which must be pleaded in order to establish a cause of action for wrongful interference. Rather we assume that the cause of action has been made out, and the question arises whether a restitutionary measure is available in addition to the well-established right to compensatory damages. We saw in 25.3.1 that in *Hambly v Trott* (1776) 1 Cowp 371, 98 ER 1136, trover (now conversion) was held to survive against the estate of a deceased person if the plaintiff switched to money had and received and pursued the benefits which had been acquired by the testator. In addition to positive benefits such as the sheep, oats and pigs which were converted in that case, Lord Mansfield also suggested that a *quantum valebat* action would survive for wrongfully utilising the personal property of another (the 'horse' example). Therefore it was clearly envisaged that those torts which protect interests in personal property could be waived and the benefits received recoverable. *Chesworth* v *Farrar* [1967] 1 QB 407 provides modern confirmation that conversion is a tort which can be waived.

In a parallel development, a benefit-based measure has been awarded under the guise of compensatory damages. The leading case is *Strand Electric and Engineering Co. Ltd* v *Brisford Entertainments Ltd* [1952] 2 QB 246, where theatre owners hired theatrical equipment from the plaintiffs. At the end of the hire period the theatre owners refused to return the equipment, despite repeated requests by the plaintiffs. The plaintiffs successfully established detinue (now conversion) and obtained the return of their property. The Court of Appeal had to determine the correct measure of damages for the 43 weeks during which the equipment was wrongfully detained. The Court held that the plaintiffs were entitled to the reasonable rate of the hire of the goods for the period for which they were wrongfully detained. Somervell LJ held that the actual benefit obtained by the defendant was irrelevant. His Lordship continued (at 252): 'The nearest analogy is a claim for mesne profits. The measure there is a reasonable sum in the nature of rent for the user during the period of the defendant's trespass.' Romer LJ agreed in similar terms. Denning LJ agreed: 'The wrongdoer cannot be better off because he did not ask permission. He cannot be better off by doing wrong than he would be by doing right' (at 254). However, Denning LJ was more explicit than the others in describing the claim as restitutionary rather than compensatory. As the Earl of Halsbury LC pointed out in *Mediana (Owners of Steamship)* v *Comet (Owners of Lightship)* [1900] AC 113, at 117, it is no answer for a wrongdoer who has deprived a plaintiff of his chair to point out that he does not usually sit in it or that he has plenty of other chairs in the room. The plaintiffs were in the business of hiring out theatre equipment and were entitled to a reasonable hiring charge.

It is clear from these cases that the actual benefit of the chattel in the defendant's hands is not assessed. Alone of the three members of the Court of Appeal in *Strand Electric*, Denning LJ was prepared to say that in an appropriate case the owner might be entitled to an account of profits made by a wrongdoer resulting from the chattel. However, that was not the instant case.

As with trespass to land, the award of a reasonable rate of hire or rent as restitutionary damages does not depend upon whether the parties are in the business of hiring such property. In *Inverugie Investments Ltd* v *Hackett* [1995] 1 WLR 713, Lord Lloyd opined (at 718):

If a man hires a concrete mixer, he must pay the daily hire, even though he may not in the event have been able to use the mixer because of rain. So also must a trespasser who takes the mixer without the owner's consent. He must pay the going rate, even though in the event he has derived no benefit from the use of the mixer. It makes no difference whether the trespasser is a professional builder or a do-it-yourself enthusiast.

In addition to protecting interests in tangible personalty, it must also be recorded that actions for wrongful interference protect rights in what have been described as documentary intangibles, such as bills of exchange and bills of lading. These are defined by Professor Bridge in *Personal Property Law* (2nd edn, 1996), at 5–6, 62, as follows:

> Documentary intangibles are instruments or documents that are so much identified with the obligation embodied in them that the appropriate way to perform or transfer the obligation is through the medium of the document. The abstract and intangible right requires such a degree of concretised expression that it takes on some of the characteristics of a chattel.

A clear illustration of the use of wrongful interference with goods to protect documentary intangibles can be seen in *Lamine v Dorrell* (1705) 2 Ld Raym 1216, 92 ER 303, in which the defendant obtained possession of an intestate's debentures by wrongfully having administration granted to him, and thereby disposed of the debentures. The administration was subsequently repealed and the plaintiff granted administration, who then sought to recover the price for which the defendant had sold the debentures as money had been received. This action was allowed. Powell J commented (at 1216):

> It is clear that the plaintiff might have maintained detinue or trover for the debentures; but when the act that is done is in its nature tortious, it is hard to turn that into a contract, and against the reason of assumpsits. But the plaintiff may dispense with the wrong, and suppose the sale made by his consent, and bring an action for the money they were sold for, as money received to his use. It has been carried thus far already.

The use of conversion to protect rights in bills of exchange, in particular a cheque, was evidenced by *United Australia Ltd v Barclays Bank Ltd* [1941] AC 1, in which Barclays were sued alternatively for conversion of a cheque or for the face value of the cheque in an action for money had and received. As that case illustrates, the normal measure of damages for conversion of a documentary intangible is the value of the underlying obligation, not the nominal value of the paper which embodies it. *United Australia* was not strictly speaking a case of waiving of the tort of conversion as the plaintiffs were content with the compensatory measure of recovery. However, there appears to be no reason in principle why a claimant could not elect to choose the actual benefit derived by the wrongdoer from his act.

25.6 NUISANCE

Nuisance protects the claimant's interests in the use and enjoyment of his land. Correlatively, a defendant can clearly be enriched by committing an act of nuisance, such as operating a polluting business. However, there does appear to be any case in which a claimant has pursued a benefit-based measure of recovery as opposed to the traditional loss-based measures. One exception may be *Carr-Saunders* v *Dick McNeill Associates Ltd* [1986] 1 WLR 922, in which the appropriateness of a loss of bargaining position head of loss was recognised (at 931–32).

This can be contrasted with *Stoke-on-Trent City Council* v *W. & J. Wass Ltd* [1988] 1 WLR 1406, which concerned the tort of operating an unlawful rival market. The levying of an unlawful same day market within six and two-third miles of a franchise or statutory market is actionable at the suit of the market owner without proof of loss. The Court of Appeal in *Wass* stated that this particular tort can be characterised as a nuisance or a trespass, the better view being that it is nuisance. In that case the defendant began operating a Thursday market within the council's area without either a franchise or statutory authority. The council planned to operate its own Thursday market and warned the company that by continuing to operate the market it would be infringing the council's rights. The company continued to operate the market in defiance of the council and without planning permission. Peter Gibson J granted a permanent injunction restraining the company from holding the market. He further held that although the council's loss was nil, it was entitled to damages based on the licence fee it could have demanded from the company. The Court of Appeal disagreed on the measure of damages and awarded nominal damages only. Nourse LJ was not prepared to hold that the case constituted an exception to the general rule that in an action in tort the plaintiff recovers damages equivalent to the actual loss suffered. His Lordship was not prepared to extend the principle in cases such as *Swordheath Properties Ltd* v *Tabet* [1979] 1 WLR 285, *Strand Electric and Engineering Co. Ltd* v *Brisford Entertainments Ltd* [1952] 2 QB 246 and *Wrotham Park Estate Co. Ltd* v *Parkside Homes Ltd* [1974] 1 WLR 798 (a breach of covenant case) to the instant facts. Nicholls LJ had characterised those decisions as being based on the 'user principle'. In the view of Nourse LJ (at 1415):

> Although I would accept there may be a logical difficulty in making a distinction between the present case and the way-leave cases, I think that if the user principle were to be applied here there would be an equal difficulty in distinguishing other cases of more common occurrence, particularly in nuisance. Suppose a case where a right to light or right of way had been obstructed to the profit of the servient owner but at no loss to the dominant owner. It would be difficult, in the application of the user principle, to make a logical distinction between such an obstruction and the infringement of a right to hold a market. And yet the application of that principle to such cases would not only give a right to substantial damages where no loss had been suffered but would revolutionise the tort of nuisance by making it unnecessary to prove loss. Moreover, if the principle were to be applied in

nuisance, why not in other torts where the defendant's wrong can work to his own profit, for example in defamation?

This case evidenced a marked judicial reluctance to extend a benefit-based measure of recovery even into a context where a tort protects a proprietary interest and where the conduct of the defendant was in cynical disregard of the claimant's right. The explanation appears to be a policy fear that further extension of restitutionary reasoning here would mark a significant departure from the traditional compensatory approach of the common law. The Court of Appeal clearly thought that it would be trespassing on the domain of the most senior appellate court, if not that of the legislature. However, this timidity has not escaped criticism: see Birks, *Butterworths Lectures 1990–1991*, 57–59.

25.7   DECEIT, PASSING OFF AND INJURIOUS FALSEHOOD

In the view of Goff and Jones, deceit, and probably passing off and injurious falsehood, are all torts which can be waived: Goff and Jones, 780. However, this now needs to be treated with caution following *Halifax Building Society* v *Thomas* [1996] Ch 217. This was one of many mortgage fraud cases from the late 1980s. The defendant obtained mortgage finance by making fraudulent representations about his identity and creditworthiness. He soon fell into arrears and the building society obtained possession and enforced its security, selling the property to discharge the mortgage account. This left a surplus. The society claimed to be entitled to this surplus as against the defendant. In the meantime the defendant had been convicted of conspiracy. The Crown Prosecution Service also lay claim to the surplus pursuant to a confiscation order it had obtained. Under s. 105 of the Law Property Act 1925, the mortgagor (borrower) is entitled to any such surplus which prima facie belonged to the borrower on the sale of the mortgaged property. The Court of Appeal refused to hold that the society was entitled to disgorgement of the surplus either on the ground of waiving the tort, or upon the basis of a constructive trust. Peter Gibson LJ stressed that the society had elected to enforce the security, rather than rescind the voidable transaction on the basis of fraudulent misrepresentation. More significantly, the Court of Appeal was impressed by the fact that there was no danger of the fraudster being unjustly enriched in the circumstances. This was rather a case of competing claims between the society and the State to the proceeds of crime. Peter Gibson LJ commented (at 229):

In considering whether to extend the law of constructive trusts in order to prevent a fraudster benefiting from his wrong, it was also appropriate to bear in mind that Parliament has acted in recent years (notably in Part VI of the Criminal Justice Act 1988) on the footing that without statutory intervention the criminal might keep the benefit of his crime.

See also Hoffmann J in *Chief Constable of Leicestershire* v *M* [1989] 1 WLR 20, at 23. Therefore, given the statutory interventions, it is no longer safe to say that deceit is a tort which can be waived as a matter of course. However, where there is no confiscation order sought by the State, there remain equally good policy reasons for allowing individual plaintiffs to seek a disgorgement remedy against those who have profited by deceitful conduct at their expense. *Thomas* can be rationalised on the basis that 'privatised' disgorgement must yield to public confiscation, and where a wrongdoer has already been stripped of unjust gains, no further order is appropriate. See Law Com. No. 247, paras. 3.24 to 3.27.

25.8   ECONOMIC TORTS

A number of economic torts protect the claimant's interest in his entitlement to participate in the market, such as conspiracy, interference with trade and intimidation. These torts have had a somewhat chequered history, and it is not proposed to analyse the underlying necessary factual allegations required to establish whether a particular tort has been committed. Most typically, however, these torts involve deliberate conduct which may well result in the wrongdoer profiting at another's expense. The question therefore arises whether a restitutionary response is appropriate. There is some authority that interference with contractual relations may be a restitution-yielding wrong. As early as *Lightly* v *Clouston* (1808) 1 Taunt 112, 127 ER 774, such a principle appears to have been applied. The defendant enticed the plaintiff's apprentice away from a ship in Jamaica, and employed the boy upon his own ship to assist his voyage back to England. This amounted to the inaccurately (one hopes) named tort of seduction (which appears to be the model for the modern tort of interference in contractual relations). The plaintiff claimed in *quantum meruit* against the defendant for the value of the apprentice's labour. Sir James Mansfield CJ in the Court of Common Pleas reasoned by analogy with cases in which trover had been waived and converted into an action for money had and received. Here the master was entitled to waive the tort of seduction and his right to recover damages for the tort, and instead sue for the value of the labour of the apprentice. His Lordship commented (at 114): 'This case approaches as nearly as possible to the case where goods are sold, and the money has found its way into the pocket of the Defendant.' This should be contrasted with *Foster* v *Stewart* (1814) 3 N & S 191, 105 ER 582, in which Lord Ellenborough reluctantly followed *Lightly* v *Clouston*, considering the case had gone too far.

   In the leading modern authority, *Universe Tankships Inc. of Monrovia* v *International Transport Workers' Federation, The Universe Sentinel* [1983] 1 AC 366, it seems to have been accepted by the House of Lords that conduct which amounted to one of the economic torts may be waived. It will be recalled in that case that a donation to the ITF was held by the majority to be recoverable on the ground of economic duress. This appears to be a case of autonomous unjust enrichment. However, Lord Diplock's discussion also accepted that 'the form that the duress takes may, or may not, be tortious' (at 385). While it was not necessary to prove a tort in order to recover in the eyes of a majority, the facts as pleaded may have amounted to one of the economic torts. Two-party intimidation appears to be the most likely candidate. The dissenting judgment of Lord Scarman appeared to go further and treat all instances of economic duress as being examples of tortious conduct (at 400). The case provides limited support therefore for the 'waiver' of economic torts, although the House of Lords subsequently confirmed in *The Evia Luck (No. 2)* [1992] 2 AC 152 that such an approach was not necessary.

25.9 INTELLECTUAL PROPERTY TORTS

In the field of interference in intellectual property and passing off, it is well established that a plaintiff can choose to have either damages or an account of the profits made by the defendant by his wrongful acts (see *Lever* v *Goodwin* (1887) 36 Ch D 1, at 7 *per* Cotton LJ). A clear example of this principle is in the patent infringement case of *Watson Laidlaw & Co. Ltd* v *Pott Cassels and Williamson* [1914] RPC 104, in which a patentee elected to sue for damages rather than for an account of the profits. Part of the infringement had taken place in Java. Evidence suggested that the patentee could not have competed successfully on that island. The House of Lords rejected an argument that damages should not be awarded in respect of the Java infringement. Lord Shaw stated (at 119):

wherever an abstraction or invasion of property has occurred, then, unless such abstraction or invasion were to be sanctioned by law, the law ought to yield a recompense under the category or principle, as I say, either of price or of hire. If A, being a liveryman, keeps his horse standing idle in the stable, and B, against his wish or without his knowledge, rides or drives it out, it is no answer for B to say to A: 'Against what loss do you want to be restored? I restore the horse. There is no loss. The horse is none the worse; it is better for the exercise.' I confess to your Lordships that this seems to me to be precisely in principle the kind of question and retort which underlay the argument of the learned counsel for the appellants about the Java trade.

In that passage we see that even in the context of intellectual property a distinction is drawn between a strict account of profits and the application of restitutionary damages or the user principle.

The rationale of awarding an account of profits was considered in *My Kinda Town Ltd* v *Soll* [1983] RPC 15 (reversed on other grounds by the Court of Appeal [1983] RPC 407) by Slade J (at 55):

The purpose of ordering an account of profit in favour of a successful plaintiff in a passing off case is not to inflict punishment on the defendant. It is to prevent an unjust enrichment of the defendant by compelling him to surrender those profits, or those parts of the profits, actually made by him which were improperly made and nothing beyond this.

A taking of account of profits can be a difficult exercise. The case concerned two very similar pizza restaurants. Slade J acknowledged that in particular cases the whole of the relevant profits should be disgorged; however, in some cases only a part of the profits ought to be treated as having been improperly made by the defendant. Here the defendant's pizza restaurant was a thriving concern in its own right and a considerable part of the profits was held to owe nothing to the plaintiff's reputation. Slade J did not shrink from apportioning the profits and ordered an account only of those profits 'which are properly attributable to the use by the defendants of such name [a name similar to the plaintiff's] in the said business' (at 56). This appears to be an inchoate recognition of a limiting principle of 'remoteness of gain'. The supposed strict distinction between the account and damages based on the user principle has been rejected by the Law Commission, who consider that recent authority has reduced the supposedly technical nature of the former: Law Com. No. 247, para. 3.83.

25.10   MISCELLANEOUS TORTS

Defamation, which protects the claimant's interest in reputation, has already been alluded to in 25.1. It appears to be established that defamation is not a tort which can be waived. The fact that defamation is one of the few torts where jury trial is still permitted as a matter of course in a civil court means that the practical significance of this restriction may not be that great. It seems difficult to deny that, at least where the defendant is a newspaper or other journal, the jury's assessment of damages is on occasion coloured by the exceptional profits made as a result of defaming individuals. The view that the concept of waiving the tort cannot be pushed beyond certain limits found expression in some dicta by Viscount Simon LC, in *United Australia Ltd* v *Barclays Bank Ltd* [1941] AC 1, at 13 that 'it is clear that there are torts to which the process of waiver could not be applied; the tort of defamation, for example, or of assault, could not be dressed up into a claim in assumpsit'.

This seems to signal that just as reputation does not yield a restitutionary measure, neither should the claimant's interest in bodily integrity. One possible exception to this may be the early case of *Duke de Cadaval* v *Collins* (1836) 4 Ad & E 858, 111 ER 1006, in which a Portugese nobleman was arrested soon after arriving at Falmouth by one Collins. Collins claimed to be owed £16,200 by the Duke, which was untrue. The Duke understood little English, but signed an agreement agreeing to pay £500 pending a trial of the action in return for being released and free from future arrest. The Duke paid the £500 and was released. Collins's writ for supposed debt was set aside for irregularity, and subsequently the Duke in his action claimed the return of the £500. He succeeded. Lord Denman CJ stated (at 864): 'The arrest was fraudulent; and the money was parted with under the arrest, to get rid of the pressures.' As with *Barton* v *Armstrong* [1976] AC 104, this is generally analysed in terms of subtractive unjust enrichment on the grounds of duress. However, on an alternative analysis it could be regarded as disgorgement based upon the wrong of assault or false imprisonment. It seems safer to say that as the law currently stands those wrongs which protect bodily integrity and reputation do not yield benefit-based measures of recovery. This is in sharp contrast with the proprietary torts and may, as the law on this topic develops, become less and less defensible. A similar negative statement seems apt for the tort of negligence, which currently provides a régime of compensation (solely) for those injured by others whose conduct falls short of reasonable community standards. Lastly, of little practical relevance today are the old cases on usurpation of office in which many of the principles surrounding the waiver of tort were originally developed. Here it is clearly established that the usurper is liable to disgorge all the benefits received during the invasion of plaintiff's office. See *Arris* v *Stukeley* (1677) 2 Mod 260, 86 ER 260. Goff and Jones, 695–97.

25.11 ELECTION: CUMULATIVE AND ALTERNATIVE REMEDIES

25.11.1 Introduction

The modern orthodoxy is that a claim based upon the benefits received by a tortfeasor is an alternative claim to a remedy quantified by reference to the loss suffered by the claimant. Therefore it is clear as a matter of principle that the two claims cannot be combined. To this extent we can agree with Beatson that the old fashioned language of 'waiver of tort' at least had the advantage that it made it clear that claims are not cumulative: Beatson, 223–24. However, a note of caution should be sounded. It has already been noted that there are different streams of case law which quantify the measure of recovering with reference to the tortfeasor's gain. It is more accurate to say that, with reference to those cases built on the foundation of waiver of tort, the claims are alternative. The same appears to be the case where there is a choice between an account of profits and compensatory damages. In contrast, with regard to claims which have been conceptualised as damages and which are based upon a supposedly extended definition of loss, the courts have not necessarily been so scrupulous about the incompatibility of loss-based and benefit-based claims in one award.

25.11.2 Waiver of tort and account of profits

With regard to the waiver of tort stream of case law, the leading case is *United Australia Ltd* v *Barclays Bank Ltd* [1941] AC 1. Here United Australia had received a cheque for £1,900 from one of its debtors. United Australia's company secretary then indorsed the cheque to a company called MFG, without the authority of his principal. MFG deposited the cheque with Barclays. In 1935, United Australia sought to recover the money from MFG either on the basis that it was money lent, or as money had and received. However, before that case proceeded to judgment, MFG was wound up. During the course of the proceedings, United Australia discovered that the cheque had been accepted by Barclays; and therefore in 1937 it issued a fresh writ against Barclays claiming damages for £1,900 on the basis of either conversion, or negligence or as money had and received. The House of Lords gave judgment for

£1,900, and in doing so disapproved an earlier dictum of Bovill CJ in *Smith* v *Baker* (1873) LR 8 CP 350 that 'if an action for money had and received is so brought, that is in point of law a conclusive election to waive the tort' (at 355). The earlier proceedings did not preclude United Australia from maintaining a separate cause of action against a different defendant arising from the same facts. On the facts of the instant case the two acts of conversion were very different. MFG and the bank could not even be described as joint tortfeasors. While not necessary for the decision in the case, the very learned speeches in the House of Lords clarify that a plaintiff has an election between alternative remedies, and that there was no requirement to elect between a compensatory remedy and a restitutionary remedy until the final application for judgment. Viscount Simon LC cited with approval the earlier discussion in *Lamine* v *Dorrell* (1705) 2 Ld Raym 1216, 92 ER 303, which concerned wrongful interference with debentures. There Holt CJ stated (at 1217):

> if an action of trover should be brought by the plaintiff for these debentures after judgment in this *indebitatus assumpsit*, he may plead this recovery in bar of the action of trover, in the same manner as it would have been a good plea in bar for the defendant to have pleaded to the action in trover, that he sold the debentures, and paid to the plaintiff in satisfaction. But it may be a doubt if this recovery can be pleaded before execution.

Viscount Simon LC clearly stated the law as follows (at 19):

> The substance of the matter is that on certain facts he is claiming redress either in the form of compensation, i.e., damages as for a tort, or in the form of restitution of money to which he is entitled, but which the defendant has wrongfully received. The same set of facts entitles the plaintiff to claim either form of redress. At some stage of the proceedings the plaintiff must elect which remedy he will have. There is, however, no reason of principle or convenience why that stage should be deemed to be reached until the plaintiff applies for judgment.

Therefore it is clear that the election in these cases is between alternative remedies; and there is no binding election until judgment, or possibly execution. This should be contrasted with a distinct species of election, where there must be an election between inconsistent rights. For example, electing whether to rescind a contract as a result of misrepresentation, or alternatively deciding to keep the contract open and require performance of the other party. Similarly in the context of agency, there is doctrine of ratification, where an act is done on behalf of a principal but without authority. In such a case the principal can elect to ratify the act or not (*Verschures Creameries Ltd* v *Hull and Netherlands Steamship Co. Ltd* [1921] 2 KB 608).

The distinction between alternative and cumulative remedies was clarified in two Privy Council opinions not directly concerning restitutionary claims in respect of tortious conduct: *Mahesan S/O Thambiah* v *Malaysia Government Officers' Co-operative Housing Society Ltd* [1979] AC 374 and *Tang Man Sit* v *Capacious*

Investments Ltd [1996] 1 All ER 193. In the latter case Lord Nicholls of Birkenhead made it clear that where, for example, an account of profit and compensation for loss were available in respect of the same conduct, such remedies were inconsistent and alternative. There need be no election until judgment, and indeed the court may assist a plaintiff who does not know how much money a defendant has made from the unlawful use of his property by ordering discovery (now disclosure) and ancillary orders designed to give the plaintiff any information he needs in order to make up his mind: for example, *Island Records Ltd* v *Tring International plc* [1995] 3 All ER 444. In contrast, cumulative remedies do not force the plaintiff to make a choice. Where successive parties convert the same goods the plaintiff may proceed against either or both of them. The main limitation is that the plaintiff cannot recover from one or more of the defendants any amount in excess of his entitlement, whether measured by his loss or by the gain to the defendant(s). Only full satisfaction of the entitlement will preclude further suit in order to prevent double recovery. As his Lordship explained, this was the situation in *United Australia*, where the earlier proceedings against MFG, even if they had reached judgment, would not have barred United Australia from bringing fresh proceedings against the bank. Only if United Australia had recouped the whole of its entitlement in the earlier proceedings would it be precluded from taking further action.

25.11.3   'Wayleave' cases and the 'user' principle

Therefore it is clear that in the main stream of cases of restitutionary recovery for tortious conduct, the claimant must choose between a restitutionary measure and a compensation-based measure before proceeding to judgment. It is not possible to combine the two. In contrast, in the stream of authority which derives from the nineteenth-century 'wayleave' cases, such a clear distinction has not been drawn. It will be recalled that in these cases the courts proceeded upon the basis that the defendant tortfeasor must pay a reasonable rent or hire for the wrongful use of the plaintiff's property. In such cases the courts have also been prepared to combine such an award with a compensatory claim for any damage caused by the tortfeasor in addition to the reasonable rent or hire charge. For example, in *Phillips* v *Homfray* (1871) LR 6 Ch App 770, (1883) 24 Ch D 439, it will be recalled in the earlier proceedings in 1871 that it was decreed that there should be four enquiries:

(a)   as to the quantity of any minerals taken and their value;

(b)   the quantities of minerals transported under the plaintiff's land

(c)   the amount to be paid by the defendants to the plaintiff as 'wayleave and warranty' in respect of the use of the passages; and

(d)   whether the defendants' conduct had caused any damage to the farm or mineral deposits lying there under.

Note that the fourth and arguably the first enquiries are compensatory. In contrast, the second and third enquiries were those which would today be classified as restitutionary. None of the courts saw any inconsistency in combining these two heads of recovery. Similarly in *Strand Electric and Engineering Co. Ltd* v *Brisford Entertainments Ltd* [1952] 2 QB 246, the Court of Appeal was emphatic that it was not awarding an account of profits in respect of the wrongful interference with goods. In addition, Somervell LJ contemplated that any damages for depreciation in the chattels could be an item in a claim for special damage (at 252). Denning LJ stated that the reasonable hire the wrongdoer must pay would cover ordinary wear and tear, which would ordinarily be included in a hiring charge. However, if there was any further damage in addition to ordinary wear and tear, the wrongdoer must pay extra (at 254).

The result of these cases is that we need to be careful in laying down too general a rule as to which heads of loss cannot be combined in a single claim. Where the claimant effectively seeks account of profits made, that will ordinarily preclude him from claiming in respect of any additional damage. In contrast, in cases involving the wrongful detention of goods or the wrongful occupation of land, it seems to be possible to combine an entitlement to a reasonable rent or hire with damages in respect of any additional loss above ordinary wear and tear.

FURTHER READING

Asterisks indicate especially useful works.

Goff and Jones, 773–98

Birks, 313–33, 346–55

*J. Beatson, 'The Nature of Waiver of Tort' (1978–79) 17 UW Ont LR 1; also in Beatson, 206–43

*S. Hedley, 'The Myth of Waiver of Tort' (1984) 100 LQR 653

I. Jackman, 'Restitution for Wrongs' [1989] CLJ 303, at 305–11

*Birks, 'Civil Wrongs — A New World', *Butterworths Lectures 1990–1991* (1992), 55–112

*Law Commission, *Aggravated, Exemplary and Restitution Damages* (Law Com. No. 247, 1997), paras 3.1 to 3.84.

R. Sharpe and S. Waddams, 'Damages for lost opportunity to bargain' (1982) 2 OJLS 290

*D. Friedmann, 'Restitution for Wrongs: The Basis of Liability' in Cornish, 133–54

N. Andrews, 'Civil Disgorgement of Wrongdoer's Gains: The Temptation to do Justice' in Cornish, 155–62

26 Restitutionary Damages for Breach of Contract

26.1 THEORETICAL FOUNDATIONS

Judicial remedies for breach of contract sometimes enforce the primary obligations of one of the parties, by way of an action for an agreed sum or by a decree of specific performance in appropriate cases. Leaving to one side debt-enforcement actions, the primary remedy for breach of contract is damages. Such damages are traditionally compensatory. The aim of contractual damages is to place the claimant so far as money can do it in the position he or she would have been in had the contract been performed, or performed properly (*Robinson* v *Harman* (1848) 1 Ex 850, at 855; 154 ER 363, *per* Parke B). Such damages were described as protecting the *expectation* interest in the seminal discussion of Fuller and Perdue, 'The Reliance Interest in Contract Damages' (1936) 46 Yale LJ 52, at 373. Alternatively, the injured party may seek to recover for its wasted expenditure in reliance upon the other, termed the *reliance* interest by Fuller and Perdue. This is not a free election. Recent developments have reinforced the entrenched centrality of the expectation interest. Where the injured party has made a bad bargain and a claim for wasted expenditure would exceed lost profits, it has been held that the expectation measure forms a cap or ceiling upon the recoverable damages (*C & P Haulage* v *Middleton* [1983] 1 WLR 1461; *CCC Films (London) Ltd* v *Impact Quadrant Films Ltd* [1985] QB 16).

Until recently it was settled law that damages for breach of contract were compensatory in one of these two senses. This commitment to an exclusively compensatory approach was challenged in two seminal articles published in the 1980s. In Jones, 'Recovery of Benefits Gained from a Breach of Contract' (1983) 99 LQR 443, it was argued that there were sufficient authorities to enable a bold court to develop a general right to an account of profits for breach of contract which need not depend upon any accompanying right of property, breach of fiduciary duty, or the availability of specific performance. Alternatively, even if the broad right was not recognised a restitutionary claim should be available where a defendant has saved expense by failing to perform a collateral term of the contract. Further, it was argued that the conduct of the party in breach should be a factor for the court in determining whether to grant an account. In Birks, 'Restitutionary Damages for Breach of Contract: *Snepp* and the Fusion of Law and Equity' [1987] LMCLQ 421, it was argued that restitutionary damages should be awarded for breach of contract in appropriate cases, including at least 'the cynical exploitation of breach for the purpose of making a gain' (at 440). The difficultly with the formulations in these articles is the imprecision. The suggested greater remedial flexibility in respect of breach of contract may bring with it uncertainty. Perhaps in the light of this fear, there has been to date only a partial acceptance of the role for a benefit-based liability in respect of breach of contract. As Beatson has warned: 'This type of restitutionary relief has the capacity to revolutionize contract remedies and should be treated with great caution' (Beatson, 16).

26.2   ORTHODOXY AND ITS DEFENDERS

In *Tito* v *Waddell (No. 2)* [1977] Ch 106, Sir Robert Megarry VC stated (at 332):

> It is fundamental to all questions of damages that they are to compensate the plaintiff for his loss or injury by putting him as nearly as possible in the same position as he would have been in had he not suffered the wrong. The question is not one of making the defendant disgorge what he has saved by committing the wrong, but one of compensating the plaintiff.

Similarly in *Freeman* v *Niroomand* (1996) 52 Const LR 116, Millett LJ said (at 120): 'Damages for breach of contract are normally compensatory, not restitutionary. Generally they fall to be measured by the loss sustained by the injured party, not by the profit made or the expense saved by the contract-breaker.'

This principle has been consistently applied. In *Occidental Worldwide Investment Corp.* v *Skibs A/S Avanti, The Siboen and The Sibotre* [1976] 1 Lloyd's Rep 293, shipowners wrongfully withdrew ships in breach of the charterparties. The freight rate rose steeply and accordingly the owners made large profits from the ships for the remainder of the charter periods, amounting to some $3.2 million in excess of the original charter rates. The charterers claimed that they were entitled to an account of profits. Kerr J held that there was a wrongful repudiation, but that there was 'no basis' for an account of profits, although the charterers were entitled to damages on ordinary compensatory principles (at 337).

The most articulate defence of the traditional approach, identifying policy reasons why there should not be an expansion of restitutionary damages, is the judgment of Steyn LJ in *Surrey County Council* v *Bredero Homes Ltd* [1993] 1 WLR 1361. First, to investigate whether a breach of contract was deliberate or cynical was contrary to the general approach of the law of contract, in particular the principles governing the assessment of damages in which motive is generally irrelevant. Secondly, the introduction of restitutionary remedies would lead to more uncertainty in the assessment of damages in both commercial and consumer disputes. In contrast, predictability encouraged dispute resolution. Thirdly, in situations where the injured party has suffered no loss, it was not really justifiable to confer a windfall upon him or her. Fourthly, a recognition of restitutionary damages would have a tendency to discourage economic activity. Further, in the vast majority of cases any liability would be borne by insurance and consequently premiums would go up. In summary, adequate protection in the law of obligations did not require a general right to restitutionary damages, even in cases of cynical wrongdoing.

26.3 JUDICIAL RECOGNITION

Despite the doubts of Steyn LJ in the *Bredero* case, five years later in *Attorney-General* v *Blake* [1998] Ch 439 a differently constituted Court of Appeal (Lord Woolf MR, Millett and Mummery LJJ), albeit tentatively in obiter dicta and without the benefit of argument, stated (at 457):

> the law is now sufficiently mature to recognise a restitutionary claim for profits made from a breach of contract in appropriate circumstances. The difficult question is not whether restitutionary damages should ever be available for breach of contract, but in what circumstances they should be made available.

The Court went on to reject the view (prominent in the arguments of Jones and Birks) that the availability of restitutionary damages should depend upon the defendant's moral culpability. Further, the Court of Appeal stated that it would be insufficient that the party in breach was able to enter into a more profitable contract as a result of his breach. The House of Lords' refusal in a Scottish appeal to award substantial damages in the case of *Teacher* v *Calder* [1899] AC 451, in which a party in breach of contract refused to invest money in a timber merchants and instead invested it more profitability in a distillery, was described as sound law.

However, in *Blake* the Court of Appeal opined that restitutionary damages were appropriate in two situations where compensatory damages were inadequate (at 458). First, cases of 'skimped performance' or corner-cutting (see 26.6), in which the defendant does not provide the full benefits which he had contracted to provide. Their Lordships referred to the facts of the Louisiana case of *City of New Orleans* v *Fireman's Charitable Association* (1891) 9 So 486, where the firefighting service had not provided the contractually specified number of firefighters and had otherwise fallen short by way of performance. However, this had not led to any fires not being tackled effectively. The Court of Appeal in *Blake* agreed with Jones's view that a restitutionary measure was appropriate for such a case: (1983) 99 LQR 443, at 454–55. With respect to this example, it seems that the Court of Appeal accepted Professor Jones's narrower formulation that a restitutionary measure of damages is apt where there has been a saving of expense by the contract breaker. Secondly, in the view of the Court of Appeal restitutionary damages should be available 'where the defendant has obtained his profit by doing the very thing which he contracted not to do' (at 458, citing Birks [1987] LMCLQ 421, at 434). This formulation was held to be apt for the present case. Blake had broken his lifelong obligation of confidence owed to the Crown as an employee of the security services. However, despite an invitation by the Court of Appeal, the Crown advanced no claim to restitutionary damages, and the opinions expressed were clearly obiter dicta. At the time of writing, *Blake* is on appeal to the House of Lords, and the restitutionary damages point has been argued.

The second formulation, it is submitted, is too vague to be of practical utility. Is it not the case that every breach of contract involves the contract breaker doing what he has promised not to do, namely breaking the contract? The formulation was perhaps intended to cover only negative covenants, whereby somebody promises not to do something, and would not extend to cases of positive obligations. However, even this limitation appears insufficient to curtail the availability of restitutionary damages. It would mean that an employee who was subject to a restraint of trade provision following the termination of employment, which was held to be objectively reasonable, would be liable to account for profits made in breach of covenant in pursuing new avenues of employment. Currently such an employee would be liable only for losses suffered by the employer. Such a shift would offend the policy enunciated by Steyn LJ in *Bredero* of not structuring remedies so as to discourage economic activity. It seems clear that it is now wrong to treat the availability or otherwise of restitutionary damages for breach of contract as a monolithic question. Instead, particular species of breach should be considered to see whether principle or policy favours a restitutionary response.

26.4 BREACH OF FIDUCIARY DUTY

Where the breach of contract can also be stigmatised as a breach of fiduciary duty a disgorgement remedy has been awarded. In *Reading* v *Attorney-General* [1951] AC 507, Reading was an army sergeant stationed in Cairo who accepted nearly £20,000 in bribes to sit in his uniform on civilian lorries carrying illicit alcohol, in order to ensure that the vehicles were not searched by the police. The House of Lords held that he had been properly stripped of the bribes. Denning J had held that it was sufficient that a servant had unjustly enriched himself by virtue of his employment without the sanction of his employer ([1948] 2 KB 268, at 275). In his view there was no breach of fiduciary duty. In contrast the House of Lords held (agreeing with Asquith LJ in the Court of Appeal [1949] 2 KB 232, at 236) that 'the words "fiduciary relationship" in this setting are used in a wide and loose sense and include, *inter alia*, a case where the servant gains from his employment a position of authority which enables him to obtain the sum which he receives' ([1951] AC 507, at 516). This amorphous, and instrumental, use of the fiduciary label is severely criticised by Birks [1987] LMCLQ 421, at 436–40. There it is argued that the reasons for awarding restitution need to be more explicitly addressed. The dissenting reasoning of Deane J in the High Court of Australia in *Hospital Products Ltd* v *United States Surgical Corporation* (1984) 156 CLR 41, that breach of contract could be sufficient to give rise to a constructive trust, is cited approvingly, although Birks would prefer more direct recourse to restitutionary damages.

Similarly the fiduciary badge appears to underlie the rule in real property that where a party contracts to sell land to another, and before conveyance sells the same land to a third party, the vendor is held liable as a constructive trustee of any profit on the re-sale to the original purchaser (*Lake* v *Bayliss* [1974] 1 WLR 1073).

The Court of Appeal in *Attorney-General* v *Blake* [1998] Ch 439 appears to be moving in the direction favoured by Birks. It referred to the decision of the US Supreme Court in *Snepp* v *US* 444 US 507 (1980), in which that court imposed a constructive trust on the proceeds of a publication by a former security agent, and commented (at 459):

> We find the conclusion more attractive than the route by which it was reached. We would prefer to award restitutionary damages directly for breach of contract, rather then distort the equitable concepts of fiduciary duty or constructive trust in order to accommodate them.

26.5 PROPERTY AND DAMAGES IN LIEU OF AN INJUNCTION

A different strategy for expanding disgorgement remedies for breach of contract is to rely by analogy upon the protection of property given in the cases awarding restitutionary damages for tortious interference with property. This approach has an academic advocate in Friedmann, 'Restitution of Benefits Obtained Through the Appropriation of Property or the Commission of a Wrong' (1980) 80 Col LR 504. The coincidence of breach of contract and a proprietary interest is the background to what is viewed by some as a significant exception to the compensatory principle for contract damages. In *Wrotham Park Estate Co. Ltd* v *Parkside Homes Ltd* [1974] 1 WLR 798, developers purchased a parcel of land forming part of the estate and commenced the building of residential homes thereon, in a layout which constituted a breach of a restrictive covenant relating to the land. A claim to a mandatory injunction to demolish the homes was rejected as an 'unpardonable waste of much-needed homes'. However, Brightman J held that the estate was entitled to substantial damages against the developer under what is now s. 50 of the Supreme Court Act 1981 (originally Lord Cairns's Act 1858) which embodied the jurisdiction to award damages in lieu of specific performance or an injunction. Citing *Strand Electric and Engineering Co. Ltd* v *Brisford Entertainments Ltd* [1952] 2 QB 246 and *Penarth Dock Engineering Co. Ltd* v *Pounds* [1963] 1 Ll L Rep 359 (discussed in Chapter 25). Brightman J held (at 815): 'a just substitute for a mandatory injunction would be such a sum of money as might reasonably have been demanded by the plaintiffs from Parkside as a *quid pro quo* for relaxing the covenant.' The developers conceded that they had made some £50,000 in profits from the development. Brightman J envisaged that the estate could only have reasonably required a percentage of the anticipated profit as the price for the relaxation of the covenant. Accordingly he awarded the modest sum of £2,500 in substitution for the mandatory injunction.

The correct characterisation of this reasoning has proved controversial. For Sharpe and Waddams, 'Damages for Lost Opportunity to Bargain' (1982) 2 OJLS 290, it was an example of the court assessing a reasonable licence fee which the plaintiff might have charged for his consent to the defendant's action. Conversely, restitution scholars have rejected this artificiality and insisted that it was a straightforward disgorgement case. Steyn LJ accepted in *Surrey County Council v Bredero Homes Ltd* [1993] 1 WLR 1361 that the only defensible explanation of *Wrotham Park Estate* is restitution. Loss of bargaining opportunity was a fiction. The aim of the award in *Wrotham Park Estate* was to deprive the defendants of an unjustly acquired gain. Steyn LJ thought that cases involving the invasion of property rights such as *Wrotham Park Estate* and the tortious cases represented a useful development in the law. He suggested that the word 'property' in this context should be interpreted in a wide sense.

However, in contrast in *Jaggard v Sawyer* [1995] 1 WLR 269, a differently constituted Court of Appeal disagreed. Sir Thomas Bingham MR insisted that *Wrotham Park Estate* was based on compensatory principles. What was awarded was 'the sum which the defendants would reasonably have been willing to pay to secure release from the covenant' (at 282). Millett LJ agreed that the award was compensatory, not restitutionary. His formulation differed slightly from that of Sir Thomas Bingham MR. Millett LJ stated that Brightman J in *Wrotham Park Estate* 'did not award the plaintiff the profit which the defendant had made by the breach, but the amount which he judged the plaintiff might have obtained as the price of giving its consent' (at 291).

It is worth contrasting the facts in *Surrey County Council v Bredero Homes Ltd* with those in *Jaggard v Sawyer*. In the *Bredero Homes* case, two councils sold land for development and granted planning permission to the developers for 72 homes. The developer subsequently obtained planning permission to build 77 rather than 72 houses, but failed to renegotiate the covenant to build only 72 homes. The councils did not seek an injunction to prevent the developer proceeding in accordance with the second planning permission. The councils claimed to recover all the profit or part of the profit made in building the extra houses as damages for breach of contract. That claim was rejected. In *Jaggard v Sawyer*, Millett LJ stressed that in *Bredero Homes* proceedings were brought after the developers had sold the houses and were no longer amenable to an injunction. The councils had lost their vital bargaining chip. In contrast, on the facts of *Jaggard v Sawyer* the *Wrotham Park Estate* approach to compensating the plaintiff for continuing breaches of covenant and acts of trespass in lieu of an injunction was appropriate.

Most recently, in *Attorney-General v Blake* [1998] Ch 439, the Court of Appeal said of the damages awarded in *Wrotham Park Estate* and its sequels (at 457):

> In such cases the measure of damages is the same, whether they are calculated by reference to the loss sustained by the plaintiff or the saving of expense by the defendant, with the result that their classification as compensatory or restitutionary has been controversial. Those who insist that they are restitutionary, but reject any

further departure from the general rule, justify them by reference to the proprietary nature of a claim to enforce restrictive covenants annexed to land. This is hardly convincing, seeing that the measure of damages cannot depend on whether the proceedings are between the original parties to the contract or their successors in title.

26.6   SKIMPED PERFORMANCE

In *Attorney-General* v *Blake* [1998] Ch 439, the Court of Appeal suggested in dicta that a restitutionary award would be appropriate in a case where a contractor saved expense by not supplying goods or rendering services properly in accordance with his obligation. This provides a neat solution to corner-cutting breaches, common in construction contracts, where a particular feature is specified for by the employer. The usual measure for breach of a construction contract is expectation damages measured on a cost of cure basis (*East Ham Corp* v *Bernard Sunley & Sons Ltd* [1966] AC 406). However, the courts have hesitated to award damages on a cost of cure basis where it would result in an award grossly disproportionate to the breach, and where they were not satisfied that the employer had a genuine intention to rebuild (*Tito* v *Waddell (No. 2)* [1977] Ch 106; *Radford* v *De Froberville* [1977] 1 WLR 1262). In such circumstances an award based upon diminution in value has been seen as the only alternative.

A particularly striking example is *Ruxley Electronics & Constructions Ltd* v *Forsyth* [1996] AC 344, in which Forsyth contracted for a swimming pool to be constructed adjacent to his house, specifying that the depth should be 7 feet 6 inches at the deep end. The contractors, Ruxley, built a pool with a maximum depth of only 6 feet 9 inches. Forsyth claimed damages on a cost of cure basis for the pool's non-conformity. The first instance judge found that, first, the pool was perfectly safe for diving; secondly, the shortfall in the pool's depth did not decrease its value; thirdly, to increase the pool's depth required complete reconstruction at a cost of £21,650; fourthly, Forsyth had no intention of rebuilding the pool; and fifthly, it would be unreasonable to rebuild the pool as the benefits were wholly disproportionate to the costs. The House of Lords held that it would be completely unreasonable to award cost of cure damages and upheld the judge's award of £2,500 in respect of loss of pleasure and amenity.

The award of damages for loss of amenity is open to criticism on the grounds that it introduces vague consideration into the determination of contractual damages and raises a spectre of indeterminacy of awards. It is submitted that this is a case where an award based upon the expense saved by not building the pool to contractual specification would be appropriate and proportionate. How much longer would it have taken to build the pool properly? What materials (tiles, mortar, etc.) were not utilised as a result of the breach? In economic terms such a remedy would provide a clear disincentive to contractors contemplating cutting corners with regard to specifications. A restitutionary award here should be provided as an alternative to cost of cure or diminution of value measures. See McMeel [1995] LMCLQ 456.

Such an award appears to have been made in *Freeman* v *Niroomand* (1996) 52 Const LR 116, although it was justified by the Court of Appeal on a compensatory, rather than restitutionary, basis. This approach now has the support of the Court of Appeal in *Attorney-General* v *Blake* [1998] Ch 439, at 458, who were sceptical of the need to invoke the 'consumer surplus' to justify this conclusion, as Lord Mustill had done in his speech in *Ruxley* (at 360–61).

26.7   CONCLUSION

The debate in English law is at the moment finely balanced. There is judicial agreement on the central question of profiteering from breach. Such efficient breaches of contract are encouraged and indeed applauded by some jurists, especially those of an economic bent. The theory that one has a right to break a contract in order to make more profits under a new contract dates back to Oliver Wendell Holmes's characterisation of contractual obligation as being one to perform or to pay compensatory damages: 'The Path of the Law' (1897) 10 Harv 457, at 462. Efficient breaches are defended by Richard Posner, *Economic Analysis of Law* (3rd edn, 1986), 105–14. These arguments have been adverted to in the dissenting judgment of Millett LJ in *Co-operative Insurance Society Ltd* v *Argyll Stores Ltd* [1996] Ch 286 (and his Lordship's approach to the availability of specific performance was preferred in the House of Lords: [1998] AC 1). It is clear that such breaches do not receive a restitutionary response in English law. Neither is there any appetite for a discretion to single out the deliberate or cynical contract-breaker.

Currently there are pockets of case law where there is an overlap with fiduciary duty or property rights. More recently the case of skimped performance has been reinterpreted on a restitutionary basis. Arguments in the future will be better informed by the academic literature to date, rather than the sporadic, domestic authority. Also of interest is the recognition of restitutionary damages for breach of contract by two jurisdictions whose direct links with English law were formally broken only within the last 50 years. See, for example, the decisions of the Irish High Court in *Hickey and Co. Ltd* v *Roches Stores (Dublin) Ltd* (1976), reported in [1993] RLR 196, and of the Supreme Court of Israel in *Adras Building Material Ltd* v *Harlow & Jones Gmbh* (1988), translated and reported in [1995] RLR 235 awarding restitutionary damages against deliberate contract-breakers. The discussion of Deane J of the High Court of Australia in *Hospital Products Ltd* v *United States Surgical Corporation* (1984) 156 CLR 41 may prove influential (as it did in *Attorney-General* v *Blake* [1998] Ch 439, at 457). At the time of writing, *Blake* is on appeal to the House of Lords, which should provide an opportunity for the UK's highest court to consider this issue.

FURTHER READING

Asterisks indicate especially useful works.

Goff and Jones, 518–23
Birks, 334–36

J. Dawson, 'Restitution or Damages?' (1959) 20 Ohio State LJ 175

D. Friedmann, 'Restitution of Benefits Obtained Through the Appropriation of Property or the Commission of a Wrong?' (1980) 80 ColLR 504, at 513–29

Sharpe and Wadhams, 'Damages for Lost Opportunity to Bargain' (1982) 2 OJLS 290

*G. Jones, 'The Recovery of Benefits Gained from a Breach of Contract' (1983) 99 LQR 443

E. Farnsworth, 'Your Loss or My Gain? The Dilemma of the Disgorgement Principle in Breach of Contract' (1985) 94 Yale LJ 1339

*Birks, 'Restitutionary damages for breach of contract: *Snepp* and the fusion of law and equity' [1987] LMCLQ 421

D. Friedmann, 'Restitution of Profits Gained by Party in Breach of Contract' (1988) 104 LQR 383

D. Friedmann, 'The Efficient Breach Fallacy' (1989) 18 J of Leg St 1

R. O'Dair, 'Restitutionary Damages for Breach of Contract and the Theory of Efficient Breach: Some Reflections' (1993) 46 CLP 113

R. O'Dair, 'Remedies for Breach of Contract: A Wrong Turn' [1995] *Restitution Law Review* 31

A. Burrows, 'No Restitutionary Damages for Breach of Contract' [1993] LMCLQ 453

W. Goodhart, 'Restitutionary Damages for Breach of Contract: the Remedy that Dare Not Speak its Name' [1995] *Restitution Law Review* 3

G. McMeel, 'Common Sense on Cost of Cure' [1995] LMCLQ 456

H. McGregor, 'Restitutionary Damages' in Birks (ed.), *Wrong and Remedies in the Twenty-First Century* (1996) 203, esp. at 210

H. Beale, 'Exceptional Measures of Damages in Contract', in Birks (ed.), *Wrongs and Remedies in the Twenty–First Century* (1996), 217

I. Jackman, 'Restitution for Wrongs' [1989] CLJ 302, at 318–21

*Law Commission, *Aggravated, Exemplary and Restitutionary Damages* (Law Com. No. 247, 1997), paras 3.33–3.38, 3.45–3.47, 3.82–3.84

PART G

TRACING, CLAIMING AND PROPRIETARY RESTITUTION

27   Tracing and Claiming at Common Law

27.1   INTRODUCTION

The power of a claimant to pursue wealth derived from the claimant's assets has been recognised both at common law and in equity. The power has been extended to assets the value of which identifiably derives (at least in part) from his original property. The differences of approach of the two jurisdictions has caused difficulties of exposition and has provoked judicial and juristic calls for harmonisation. Most recently, it has been argued that there is only one set of rules for tracing in English law. Tracing and claiming are distinct exercises. It must be stressed that tracing is a power or process and not a claim of itself: it is the precursor to a claim. The key advantage of tracing is that it allows a claimant to follow value derived from his assets through substitutions. For example, suppose B steals £10,000 from A and gives the money to C, who uses it to purchase a car. The law permits A to regard the value inhering in the car as derived from his money. Accordingly the reach of restitution is extended. Tracing at common law is easily defeated in that the good faith purchaser of money obtains good title to it. Therefore, contrast a second hypothetical: B steals £10,000 from A and buys a car from C with the money. Where C is a good faith purchaser there can be no recourse in restitution against him. Here the tracing rules overlap with the defence of good faith purchase and the character of money as currency (see Chapter 31). Entitlement to other property at common law is robustly protected by the maxim *nemo dat quod non habet*, and the limited exceptions thereto (see 31.2).

Given the central importance of good faith purchase, the cases where a claimant has completed a successful tracing exercise at common law are rare. Such claims succeed only against volunteers and those who can be shown to lack good faith. Generally the successful claim took the form of the *action for money had and received*. The common law's only remedial option was a purely personal action for an equivalent sum to the money traced. However, successful claims have been made to the actual product in the hands of the recipient at common law, in exceptional circumstances.

27.2   THE EARLY CASES

In *Clarke* v *Shee and Johnson* (1774) 1 Cowp 197, 98 ER 1041, a servant of the plaintiff misappropriated money from his master's business and entered into gaming contracts with the defendants. Those contracts were void and illegal under the Lottery Act 1772. Lord Mansfield commenced with a famous exposition of the rationale of the action for money had and received (at 199–200): 'This is a liberal action in the nature of a bill in equity; and if, under the circumstances of the case, it appears that the defendant cannot in conscience retain what is the subject-matter of it, the plaintiff may well support this action.' The Court of King's Bench held that the master could recover the sums paid to the defendants by his servant and was not implicated in the illegality of the underlying contract. Lord Mansfield concluded (at 200–201) that the bank notes:

> are in the nature of specific property; and if their identity can be traced and ascertained, the party has a right to recover. It is of public benefit and example that he should: but otherwise, if they cannot be followed and identified because there it might be inconvenient and open a door to fraud.... Here the plaintiff sues for his identified property, which has come into the hands of the defendants iniquitously and illegally, in breach of the Act of Parliament. Therefore they have no right to retain it.

Accordingly identification is the key, and it appears for the personal claim for money had and received that it is sufficient that the money can be identified as passing into the hands of the defendant. Events after receipt by the defendant are not relevant and do not preclude a personal claim. However, the claim is maintainable only against defendants who are not good faith purchasers. See further 31.3.

The law was pushed a stage further in *Taylor* v *Plumer* (1815) 3 M & S 562, 105 ER 721, in which Plumer entrusted his stockbroker with a banker's draft for £22,200 to be invested in Treasury Bills. The stockbroker absconded with the majority of the money, which he swapped for American shares, stocks and bullion. However, he was overtaken at Falmouth on his way to America, where he surrendered those assets to Plumer's attorney. A claim brought by the stockbroker's assignee in bankruptcy for wrongful interference with goods was dismissed. The Court of King's Bench accepted that Plumer was entitled to the assets which his agent had wrongfully obtained in substitution for his money. Lord Ellenborough CJ articulated what has become known as the 'exchange-product theory' of common law tracing (at 575):

> the product of or substitute for the original thing still follows the nature of the thing itself, as long as it can be ascertained to be such, and the right only ceases when the means of ascertainment fail, which is the case when the subject is turned into money, and mixed and confounded in a general mass of the same description.

First, it is clear from this that the process of tracing at common law extends to substituted assets in which the value derived from the claimant inheres. Secondly, the case is traditionally understood as authority for the proposition that money cannot be followed at common law when it is mixed with other money. This was described by Lord Ellenborough as a 'difficulty of fact and not of law', and he distinguished the case where particular notes or coins are kept separate or are identifiable, which it seems can be traced. This proposition appears to be more a rule of evidence than a substantive legal rule. However, its subsequent legal reception has hardened it into a general rule, thereby depriving tracing at common law of much practical signifi-cance. It has been argued that the standard interpretation of *Taylor* v *Plumer* does not pay sufficient attention to the stockbroker's fiduciary position and the equitable proprietary rights which the court alluded to: Khurshid and Matthews (1979) 95 LQR 78, at 79–82; Smith [1995] LMCLQ 240. However, as Millett LJ has observed, what matters as far as precedent is concerned is how the case is understood, rather than what was originally intended (*Trustee of the Property of F. C. Jones & Sons Ltd* v *Jones* [1997] Ch 159, at 169). Accordingly, *Taylor* v *Plumer* is good authority for a common law version of the exchange-product theory.

27.3   THE PROSPECT OF FUSION

In *Banque Belge pour l'Etranger* v *Hambrouck* [1921] 1 KB 321, a clerk misappropriated money by drawing cheques on his employer's account at the plaintiff bank. He paid the money into his bank, and paid various sums totalling some £465 to his Belgian mistress, Mlle Spanoghe, which she in turn paid into her bank account. The plaintiff bank sought restitution of some £315 which remained in Mlle Spanoghe's account. Her bank paid the money into court. The payments to her were treated as gifts, or not made for valuable consideration (her past or future cohabitation being described as an immoral consideration). All the judges held that the plaintiff bank was entitled to the money. The plaintiff appeared to be content with the claim to the value surviving.

The Court of Appeal appear, to have adopted three different routes to a successful claim. Bankes LJ saw no difficulty in the plaintiff recovering without having recourse to the more liberal rules of equity. However, he added that if it were necessary he saw no difficulty with applying the equitable rules to the facts of the case. A discussion of the detail of the equitable rules is postponed to Chapter 29, but this appears to be correct in that the clerk was in a fiduciary position. Equity could easily trace through the successive bank accounts. Scrutton LJ was more impressed with the argument that the value derived from the plaintiff had changed its identity in its passage through successive bank accounts (at 330):

I am inclined to think that at common law this would be a good answer to a claim for money had and received, at any rate if the money was mixed in Hambrouck's bank with other money. But it is clear that the equitable extension of the doctrine as based on *In re Hallett's Estate* 13 Ch D 696 and explained in *Sinclair* v

Brougham [1914] AC 398 enables money though changed in character to be recovered, if it can be traced.

This is an authoritative statement that the common law is unable to trace money which is mixed with other funds in a bank account.

Atkin LJ explicitly assumed that the transaction under which the clerk obtained the money was a voidable one, necessitating an election by the plaintiff to avoid his title which would then revest in him subject to any intervening claim by a good faith purchaser. Atkin LJ held on the basis of equitable tracing that the plaintiff was entitled to a specific order for the return of money in question. This was in fact the relief prayed for by the plaintiff, but his Lordship went on to consider whether the money could have been recovered in any action for money had and received. Atkin LJ observed (at 333–34): 'the common law rights are large and are admirably stated in *Taylor* v *Plumer*.' Atkin LJ voiced doubts about a restrictive reading of that case by Viscount Haldane LC in *Sinclair* v *Brougham* [1914] AC 398, at 419, and proceeded to promote a fusionist solution (at 335):

> I venture to doubt whether the common law ever so restricted the right as to hold that the money became incapable of being traced, merely because paid into the broker's general account with his banker. The question always was, Had the means of ascertainment failed? But if in 1815 the common law halted outside the bankers' door, by 1879 equity had had the courage to lift the latch, walk in and examine the books: *In re Hallett's Estate* 13 Ch D 696. I see no reason why the means of ascertainment so provided should not now be available for both common law and equity proceedings.

Explicitly distinguishing tracing from claiming, Atkin LJ held that either common law or equitable tracing could support a common law claim to money had and received. There were fewer difficulties in this case because 'substantially no other money has ever been mixed with the proceeds of the fraud' (at 336). A similar fusionist project was pursued by Denning J in *Nelson* v *Larholt* [1948] 1 KB 339 (see 33.3). Despite these bold statements by two of the twentieth century's greatest judges, to date there has been little judicial effort to assimilate the rules of law and equity. One modern tendency is to side-line tracing at common law as far as possible.

27.4 MARGINALISATION?

In *Agip (Africa) Ltd* v *Jackson* [1990] Ch 265, [1991] Ch 547, the chief accountant of the plaintiff company had systematically defrauded them of millions of US dollars over a number of years. A claim was made for some $588,000 which the fraudster sought to launder through various shell bank accounts with the assistance of the defendant firm of accountants. The claim was advanced *inter alia* on the basis of common law tracing (for the claims in equity see Chapters 29 and 30). Millett J stressed that a common law claim for money had and received was a personal one, which was complete upon receipt of the money. The liability of the recipient was strict and it was generally no defence that the recipient had parted with the money. The process of tracing identified a recipient as a potential defendant, whose measure of liability was determined by the value received. More controversially, Millett J asserted that the common law 'can only follow a physical asset, such as a cheque or its proceeds, from one person to another. It can follow money but not a chose in action' (at 285). It should be noted that the insistence on a *physical* substitute cannot stand in the wake of *Lipkin Gorman* v *Karpnale Ltd* [1991] 2 AC 548, where the House of Lords permitted tracing through a chose in action at common law. In *Agip*, Millett J repeated the modern orthodoxy that the power to trace at common law would be lost where it was mixed with other money in a bank account. However, the learned judge drew an important distinction between mixing prior to receipt by the defendant recipient, which can defeat a claim, and subsequent mixing by the defendant recipient, which is irrelevant as the cause of action is constituted upon receipt. The crucial obstacle was, in the view of Millett J, that the money was transferred prior to receipt by the defendants by means of telegraphic transfer: 'Nothing passed between Tunisia and London but a stream of electrons' (at 286). Further, the bank receiving the transfer took a delivery risk, by complying with the payment order before it was itself reimbursed. At common law, it was held, it was impossible to trace the money when it was inevitably mixed with other funds in the New York clearing system. Accordingly, the case is clear authority that modern banking technology and techniques raise insuperable obstacles to common law tracing.

Millett J was explicit that his marginalisation of the common law was deliberate, and policy-driven. He concluded that equity provided a better solution (at 289): 'There is certainly no need for recourse to the common law action for money had and received, which is not well equipped for the task. In my judgment, the plaintiffs' attempted reliance on the common law was unnecessary and misplaced.' Sir Peter Millett was more explicit, writing extra-judicially, when he concluded in (1991) 107 LQR 71, at 71:

> in all but the simplest cases recourse to the common law should be abandoned, that attempts to rationalise and develop the common law rules are unlikely to succeed and should no longer be pursued, and that attempts should be made instead to develop a unified restitutionary remedy based on equitable principles.

The Court of Appeal in *Agip* agreed that tracing at common law was precluded by the mixing in the New York clearing system. However, on appeal, Millett J's controversial view about the common law's inability to cope with telegraphic transfer did not appear to commend itself to the Court. Fox LJ stated that it did not matter that the order in the case was not a cheque ([1991] Ch 547, at 565).

Nevertheless, Millett J's view was followed in *Bank Tejerat* v *Hong Kong and Shanghai Banking Corp. (CI) Ltd* [1995] 1 Lloyd's Rep 239, where a bank mistakenly paid pursuant to a letter of credit, as a result of the tender of forged shipping documents. While it was common ground that the bank had a prima facie claim on the basis of mistake of fact, it was not possible to trace at common law into the hands of the original payee. First, it was stated that the money had been mixed with other moneys as it passed through the hands of correspondent banks (at 245). Secondly, the payment was made by telex instruction (a stream of electrons), and accordingly could not be traced at common law (at 246). It must recalled that the latter reason had not impressed the Court of Appeal in *Agip*. Also, it is hard to see why the rules of tracing needed to be invoked at all where here there was in essence a simple direct payment (although complicated by the machinery of modern banking). The *Tejerat* case is better explained on the basis of its alternative ratio of ministerial receipt (at 246–47; see further 33.5). For discussion, see Birks in Birks (1995), at 302–304.

27.5 CONTINUING RELEVANCE?

Despite attempts to marginalise the power to trace at common law, two significant recent cases have confirmed its significance in appropriate situations.

27.5.1 *Lipkin Gorman* v *Karpnale*

In the leading case of *Lipkin Gorman* v *Karpnale Ltd* [1991] 2 AC 548, Cass was by day an apparently respectable solicitor, but by night a compulsive gambler. He raided the client account of the firm of which he was a partner to feed his addiction. Ultimately there was a shortfall in the client account of £222,908.98. Cheques were drawn upon the account by the firm's cashier and made payable to cash. During the relevant period Cass gambled over half a million pounds at the Playboy Club, in Park Lane, Mayfair. Ultimately the club won and Cass lost some £150,960. Cass's own resources for this period were some £20,000. However, it was conceded by the club that the plaintiff firm's title to the money was not defeated by being mixed with Cass's own money. Lord Goff accepted an argument that the case was effectively indistinguishable from *Clarke* v *Shee and Johnson* (1774) 1 Cowp 197, 98 ER 1041. The cause of action was distinct from the usual claim for money had and received, where money was paid by mistake of fact or upon a failure of consideration to a direct recipient. Where money is misdirected by a third party, the claimant has to establish a basis on which he is entitled to the money. This is done by proving that the money is the plaintiff's legal property and has not been received by a good faith purchaser. Despite the proprietary basis of the claim, Lord Goff said it arose in unjust enrichment and yielded a personal, not a proprietary, claim.

This classification of the cause of action has proved controversial. Whereas, prima facie, the money in the hands of Cass as a partner of the law firm became his legal property, the owner of the original property was entitled to trace it into its product. This involved a decision by the owner of the original property to assert title to the product in exchange for what he was originally entitled to. The solicitors were entitled to trace from their chose in action at the bank into the cash drawn upon it by Cass. This approach identifies tracing as a power which ultimately depends upon an election by the claimant to identify a product as representing value which has been subtracted by him. According to Birks ([1991] LMCLQ 473, at 478):

On this analysis what the solicitors had was not an immediate property in the money but a right — more accurately a power — to trace and claim. That power was a sufficient interest to support the claim against the club. The power itself evidently sufficed, for there was no attempt to exercise it in relation to any traced asset. It was not that the solicitors did vest the money in themselves but that it was money which was liable to be vested in them on their election.

This conception of tracing as a power, hovering or floating over substituted assets (with some superficial similarity to consensual floating securities over classes of corporate assets), appears to be the only defensible explanation of the process, whether at common law or in equity. Tracing necessarily has a flavour of artificiality. It seems the dormant power to trace descends and fixes upon particular substituted assets only when a particular claim is made. Lastly, it should be observed that Birks does not accept the 'proprietary' nature of the claim. The cause of action is non-voluntary transfer, in particular the unjust factor is ignorance: [1991] LMCLQ 473, at 482–83. See 27.6 and further Chapter 5.

27.5.2 Tracing profits

The remarkable case of *Trustee of the Property of F. C. Jones & Sons Ltd* v *Jones* [1997] Ch 159, pushed the exchange-product theory to the limit. A firm of potato growers became bankrupt. The wife of one of the partners invested some £11,700 in potato futures. That sum had been diverted from a partnership bank account. The investment proved profitable and she eventually received some £50,760 which was paid into a deposit account. The funds had been paid away after the act of bankruptcy, but before adjudication. The official receiver laid claim to the money under ss. 37 and 38 of the Bankruptcy Act 1914 (now repealed) and the account-holder interpleaded and paid the money into court. It was held that the result of the doctrine of relation back under the 1914 Act was that the husband had no property in the money paid away, which had retrospectively vested in the trustee-in-bankruptcy. Accordingly he could confer no title upon his wife. Therefore the claim lay exclusively at common law. Millett LJ stated (at 168):

It follows that, if he has to trace his money, he must rely on common law tracing rules, and that he has no proprietary *remedy*. But it does not follow that he has no proprietary *claim*. His claim is exclusively proprietary. He claims the money because it belongs to him at law or represents profits made by the use of money which belonged to him at law.

Here the trustee-in-bankruptcy could trace from the bank account of the partnership into the chose in action which resulted between the wife and the potato futures dealers, following *Lipkin Gorman* v *Karpnale Ltd* [1991] 2 AC 548. The trustee-in-bankruptcy was entitled to a declaration that the money standing in court (now totalling over £100,000 with interest) should be paid out to him. As Nourse LJ recognised, the decision went further than *Lipkin Gorman* in that it held the original owner entitled 'to trace his property into its product, not only in the sense of property for which it is exchanged, but also in the sense of property representing the original and the profit made by the defendant's use of it' (at 172).

It seems that the case cannot be restricted to situations where the doctrine of relation back as applied under the old bankruptcy law applies. Wherever money is misappropriated and reaches the hands of a volunteer, it seems that tracing at common law may entitle a claim to be brought not only to the value received but to the value surviving, including profits derived from the original receipt.

27.6   WHAT IS THE GROUND FOR RESTITUTION?

The cases on tracing at common law have been sporadic over the years due to the perceived greater liberality of the rules for tracing in equity. However, the equitable rules have been hampered by the insistence upon a breach of fiduciary duty or trust as a pre-condition to the power being exercised. Recourse to the common law has in appropriate cases circumvented that requirement. The case law currently stands at a crossroads. It now appears to be accepted in the wake of *Lipkin Gorman* v *Karpnale* that tracing at common law is a power or a process, resembling the right to avoid a transaction on the grounds of misrepresentation. However, that leaves unanswered the underlying ground for restitution or unjust factor. Almost all the cases concern the misappropriation of money which is then diverted to a defendant recipient. The rules operate back-to-back with the recognition that a good faith purchaser takes good title to money, therefore passing it into currency. Claims have succeeded only against recipients lacking in good faith or volunteer recipients. The cause of action relied upon in judicial discussion is explicitly *proprietary*, although the claim for money had and received is recognised as being a personal one. The common law developed no remedy to vindicate rights in personal property. However, in a number of the cases the machinery for payments into courts or the interpleader procedure have effectively allowed proprietary relief. Otherwise the claim is a purely personal one.

This apparently anomalous proprietary ground for restitution has been criticised as not aligning with other unjust factors which depend upon vitiated or qualified intention. Birks has been prominent in advocating recognition of ignorance as the appropriate ground for restitution: [1989] LMCLQ 296. Indeed, in *Agip* v *Jackson* the payments were explicitly said to be made under an operative mistake. The coherence of the law would be enhanced if the ground for restitution were explicitly recognised as being for mistake or ignorance. The proprietary theory is incoherent. It either explains too much — all the law of restitution, including, for example, straightforward mistaken payments, could be explained on a proprietary analysis — or it explains too little — why precisely is wealth recoverable? The answer, it is submitted, is that the transferor's intention was defective or non-existent. See further Chapter 5.

27.7 CONCLUSION

It is submitted that rationality can be brought to this area of the law only if there is reconciliation with the rules of equity which are discussed in the following chapters. However, there are a number of preliminary conclusions. First, tracing is a process or technique for identifying wealth subtracted from a claimant through substitution with other assets in order to locate value derived from the claimant in wealth received or retained by a defendant. Secondly, tracing is usually seen as relevant only where the defendant is an indirect or remoter recipient. However, the defendant in *Jones* v *Jones* was a direct recipient of the claimant's wealth (see 27.5.2). Tracing should not be seen as requiring detailed investigation of banking mechanisms where there is a straightforward payment through the banking system to a direct payee. A common-sense causal approach is sufficient. The confusion introduced in *Bank Tejerat* should be avoided in the future. That confusion can be avoided if the process of tracing is properly related back to the underlying questions in unjust enrichment.

It is submitted that the process can be relevant to three of the key structural questions.

The first question in restitution is whether the defendant is enriched at all? A successful tracing exercise answers this question in the affirmative and supplies the prima facie value of the defendant's enrichment by reference to actual value received.

The second question in restitution is whether the enrichment was received at the claimant's expense. A successful tracing exercise supplies the steps whereby a minus in the account of the claimant is shown to correspond causally to a plus in the assets of the defendant. In cases of direct receipt, this will normally be answered by applying common-sense notions of causation, which should cope adequately with the modern dematerialisation of much wealth. However, it was allowed unnecessarily to cloud the picture in the straightforward mistaken payment case of *Bank Tejerat*, which was demonstrably wrongly decided in relation to these first two questions. The language of tracing is more habitually used in relation to remoter recipients where the exercise of linking the claimant to the defendant is more difficult. Hence the need for evidential rules and presumptions dealing with mixtures and substitutions which may occur *en route*. As we shall see in Chapters 28–30, equity has developed a more sophisticated approach to this than the common law.

Thirdly, a restitutionary claimant must elect between the value received and the value surviving. This election will determine the scope of the tracing exercise. If the claimant is content with a personal claim to the value received, the tracing exercise is complete upon receipt by the defendant. Subsequent events are irrelevant to what is now a constituted cause of action (if an unjust factor is proven), although post-receipt events may be relevant to defences. In contrast, if a claimant wishes to lay claim to the value surviving (the motive usually being priority upon insolvency or a claim to profits) the tracing exercise will need to extend beyond the veil of receipt and identify property retained by the defendant in which value derived from the claimant's assets identifiably inheres.

A further question then arises, which the mechanistic rules of tracing cannot answer: namely, should the claimant be entitled to personal or proprietary relief? As we have seen, the common law never devised a remedy for vindicating property rights. Such claimants must resort to equity.

It is submitted that it is a failure to distinguish the separate enquiries underlying the tracing exercise which has caused confusion. If these are kept clearly in mind, future developments should proceed more smoothly.

FURTHER READING

Asterisks indicate especially useful works.

Goff and Jones, 94–103

R. Pearce, 'A Tracing Paper' (1976) 40 Conv 277

R. Goode, 'The Right to Trace and its Impact on Commercial Transactions' (1976) 92 LQR 360–401, 528–68

Sir Peter Millett, 'Tracing the Proceeds of Fraud' (1991) 107 LQR 71

S. Khurshid and P. Matthews, 'Tracing Confusion' (1979) 95 LQR 78

P. Birks, 'Mixing and Tracing: Property and Restitution' (1992) 45 CLP 69, at 84–98

*P. Matthews, 'The Legal and Moral Limits of Common Law Tracing' in Birks (1995), 23–71

L. Smith, 'Tracing in *Taylor* v *Plumer*: Equity in the Court of King's Bench' [1995] LMCLQ 240

L. Smith, 'The Stockbroker and the Solicitor-General: the Story Behind *Taylor* v *Plumer* (1994) 15 J Legal History 2 (historical)

P. Birks, 'The English Recognition of Unjust Enrichment' [1991] LMCLQ 473

P. Birks, 'Overview' in P. Birks (ed.), *Laundering and Tracing* (1995), 289–322

*L. Smith, *The Law of Tracing* (1997), 160–74, 277–79, 320–39, 370–72

*P. Birks, 'The Necessity of a Unitary Law of Tracing' in R. Cranston (ed), *Making Commercial Law — Essays in Honour of Roy Goode* (1997) 239–58

D. Fox, 'The Transfer of Legal Title to Moneys' [1996] *Restitution Law Review* 60

D. Fox, 'Common Law Claims to Substituted Assets' [1999] *Restitution Law Review* 55

28   *Tracing in Equity*

28.1   THEORETICAL FOUNDATIONS

Tracing at common law has been overshadowed in practice by the more liberal (or more accurately, claimant-friendly) regime developed in equity. Both techniques are concerned with the identification of wealth subtracted from a claimant even though the trail is complicated by substitutions with other assets. Both the common law and equitable species of tracing are merely a pre-condition to establishing a successful restitutionary claim. They are similarly concerned with satisfying the requirements that the defendant be enriched and that it be demonstrated to be at the expense of the claimant. Further, the process of tracing identifies both value received and value surviving and is therefore relevant to the issue of quantum. The technique as developed at common law was regarded as primitive, in particular being unable to cope with the evidential problems thrown up by money being mixed with other property. It should be noted that this characterisation of common law tracing as short-sighted and easily defeated, falls most readily from the mouths of judges with a penchant for equity.

Indeed, equity has developed sophisticated and perhaps over-technical rules for coping with the mixture and substitution of assets. These rules constitute a complex web of entitlements where funds are misdirected and there are competing claims to diminished resources. However, it must be stressed that the rules discussed in this chapter provide no final answer to the question whether a restitutionary claimant should succeed. The rules are no substitute for establishing an appropriate ground for restitution or unjust factor. Further, the rules provide no solution of themselves to the vexed questions of the nature and quantum of any relief (which are considered in the next two chapters). The rules on equitable tracing are evidential, rather than substantive, in their nature. When wealth goes astray there are often insuperable difficulties in conclusively establishing what has become of the value subtracted from the claimant. The so-called rules on tracing cut the Gordian knot, by supplying rules and presumptions which resolve evidential difficulties (usually in favour of claimants) where the ordinary means of proof fail.

The paradigm nineteenth-century case for equitable intervention involved a solicitor or trustee who confused assets entrusted to him with his own. Goff and Jones comment (4th edn, 1993, 75):

> Equity's rules and presumptions were created in the context of litigation between beneficiaries of a trust and a bankrupt trustee who, having mixed his own money and trust money in a bank account, had dissipated part of the funds. The sums involved were small and the activity of the bank account modest.

The paradigm later twentieth-century case concerned the misappropriation of corporate assets by agents or employees of the company. The modern cases concern the fall-out of the collapse of the corporate empires of Robert Maxwell and Asil Nadir, and the catastrophic implosions of the Bank of Commerce and Credit International and Barlow Clowes International. Given the comparatively humble origin of equitable tracing, it is perhaps surprising that its rules and presumptions have coped adequately with sophisticated, modern money-laundering techniques and ingenious commercial fraud. Equity's jurisdiction has traditionally turned upon the need to establish that assets were misapplied in breach of trust or in breach of a fiduciary relationship. This jurisdictional trigger has been much criticised, and in any event has recently been said to be more appropriately concerned with the issue of claiming rather than tracing: Smith, 120–30. The status of the fiduciary relationship requirement is considered further below. The resulting claims, in the shape of personal receipt-based claims, equitable liens and constructive trusts, are properly postponed to the next two chapters. However, it will become obvious that there is an inevitable interdependence with the claims which can be made upon the conclusion of the tracing exercise.

28.2   THE BASIC CONCEPTS INTRODUCED

Equity can trace value though the original asset has been substituted for another, or indeed through a chain of substitutions. Accordingly, it can trace into the proceeds where trust money is misappropriated and used to purchase company shares, or where moneys which have been entrusted to a person for investment are wrongfully used to buy a luxury yacht. The metamorphoses of the underlying value usually pose little problem. But there are two major obstacles to overcome. First, as a pre-condition it still appears to be necessary to establish that money was misapplied in breach of trust or in breach of fiduciary duty (*Sinclair* v *Brougham* [1914] AC 398, as interpreted by the Court of Appeal in *In re Diplock* [1948] Ch 465). Contrast Smith, 120–30. This restriction appears to have escaped intact after the decision of the House of Lords in *Westdeutsche Landesbank Girozentrale* v *Islington London Borough Council* [1996] AC 669, although there are differing interpretations of that ruling. Secondly, at the other end of the claims process tracing is defeated by a bona fide purchaser for value without notice. These restrictions are well-established, and despite academic criticism of the former it appears to be entrenched as a pre-condition of the exercise of the equitable jurisdiction. However, as a matter of practice it can be readily overcome. In *Agip (Africa) Ltd* v *Jackson* [1990] Ch 265, Millett J observed that the requirement depended upon authority rather than principle. Further, in any event (at 290): 'The requirement is, however, readily satisfied in most cases of commercial fraud, since the embezzlement of a company's funds almost inevitably involves a breach of fiduciary duty on the part of one of the company's employees or agents.'

On the burden of proof, see Goff and Jones, 117–19 and Smith (1994) 8 *Trust Law International* 102, at 105.

28.2.1 Presumption against the wrongdoer

The main tracing rules and presumptions are concerned with ascertaining the whereabouts of value when it is mixed with other assets. The main presumption of significance is the presumption against the wrongdoer's interest. Where the competition to entitlement to an asset or assets is between an innocent claimant and a wrongdoer (usually a recalcitrant fiduciary), the courts resolve difficulties of evidence against the wrongdoer's self-interest. This presumption is highly sensitive to context, sometimes resulting in a finding that the wrongdoer intended to withdraw his own money first from a blended fund, and sometimes resulting in an artificial presumed intention honestly to preserve the claimant's assets.

28.2.2 *Pari passu*

Where value derived from a claimant is mixed with that of other innocent parties, a *pari passu* rule of distribution obtains. Accordingly, any interest in a blended asset will be held to decline (or increase) proportionately to each parties' share.

28.2.3 The rule in *Clayton's Case*: first in, first out

Where the blended fund is encountered in a current banking account, an artificial rule of convenience termed 'first in, first out' applies. This derives from an early nineteenth-century case providing guidance on the appropriation of payments into and withdrawals from a bank account. In *Clayton's Case, Devaynes* v *Noble* (1817) 1 Mer 572, 35 ER 781, Sir William Grant MR laid down what became the eponymous rule (at 608):

> there is no room for any other appropriation than that which arises from the order in which the receipts and payments take place, and are carried into the account. Presumably, it is the sum first paid in, that is first drawn out. It is the first item on the debit side of the account, that is discharged, or reduced, by the first item on the credit side.... Upon that principle, all accounts current are settled, and particularly cash accounts.

This rule of convenience is generally applied where there are competing innocent claimants to funds in an active current banking account. However, the courts sometime strive to avoid this drastic and mechanistic solution (see 28.5).

28.2.4 The lowest intermediate balance rule

Where the exercise of identification reaches no further than an account or fund which is subsequently dissipated, a claimant's potential interest in the fund is his share of the lowest intermediate balance. This is so even if the fund is subsequently topped up by the fiduciary, unless it can be shown that there was an intention to restore the fund.

28.2.5 Overdrawn bank accounts

By analogy to the lowest intermediate balance rule, it is not possible to trace through an overdrawn bank account. It must be observed, even at this stage, that the rules which have been developed demonstrate primitive notions of the juridical nature of banking accounts. It is trite law that the relationship which obtains between a banker and customer is that of debtor and creditor where an account is in the black (credit), and of creditor and debtor where an account is in the red (debit). Money paid to a banker becomes the property of the bank (*Foley* v *Hill* (1848) 2 HL Cas 28, 9 ER 28; *Libyan Arab Foreign Bank* v *Bankers Trust Co.* [1989] QB 728, at 748 *per* Staughton J). It is only in a metaphorical, and not literal, sense that money can be said to be mixed with other assets in an account. It may well be that authorities will need to be revisited where metaphorical mixing has been treated as analogous to literal mixing of assets. By way of contrast, two cases in the 1990s on tracing at common law demonstrated a more realistic appreciation of the status of the bank account as being a chose in action: *Lipkin Gorman* v *Karpnale Ltd* [1991] 2 AC 548; *Trustee of the Property of F. C. Jones & Sons Ltd* v *Jones* [1997] Ch 159.

28.3 VICTORIAN DEVELOPMENT AND *IN RE DIPLOCK*

The two leading cases in establishing the rules and presumptions of equitable tracing are *In re Hallett's Estate, Knatchbull* v *Hallett* (1880) 13 Ch D 696 and *In re Diplock, Diplock* v *Wintle* [1948] Ch 465 (CA); affd *sub nom Ministry of Health* v *Simpson* [1951] AC 251.

28.3.1 *In re Hallett*

In *In re Hallett* a solicitor had been entrusted with some Russian bonds by a client. He subsequently, without the client's authority, sold the bonds and paid the proceeds, some £2,994, into his own general bank account which was then in credit as a result of payments in of his own money. After he died the account stood at some £3,000 in credit. It was held that the client could identify in accordance with the rules of tracing the full sum of £2,994 in the account. She was further held entitled to an equitable lien over the account to secure her claim for the value received. A fiduciary relationship was clearly established, the solicitor being at least a bailee of the bonds. Thesiger LJ stated the principle in the following terms (at 723):

> wherever a specific chattel is intrusted by one man to another, either for the purposes of safe custody or for the purpose of being disposed of for the benefit of the person intrusting the chattel; then, either the chattel itself, or the proceeds of the chattel, whether the chattel has been rightfully or wrongfully disposed of, may be followed at any time, although either the chattel itself, or the money constituting the proceeds of that chattel, may have been mixed and confounded in a mass of the like material.

A second question arose on appeal. The deceased solicitor had been a trustee of some bonds and without authority sold them, paying the proceeds into his bank account which had a credit balance representing payments of his own money. He drew money upon the account which he used for his own purposes. At his death the balance of the account was greater than the trust money paid in; however, if payment out of the account were allocated on a 'first in, first out' basis the value surviving attributable to the trust would be greatly diminished. The majority of the Court of Appeal held that the rule in *Clayton's Case* had no application. Sir George Jessel MR employed the presumption against the wrongdoer's interest (at 727):

> where a man does an act which may be rightfully performed, he cannot say that that act was intentionally and in fact done wrongly.... Wherever it can be done rightfully, he is not entitled to say, against the person entitled to the property or the right, that he has done it wrongfully.... When we come to apply that principle to the case of a trustee who has blended trust moneys with his own, it seems to me perfectly plain that he cannot be heard to say that he took away the trust money when he had a right to take away his own money.

Accordingly, where a trustee's account is credited with £100 derived from misappropriated trust assets, and with £100 of his own money, a withdrawal of £100 is presumed to be a withdrawal by the trustee of his own entitlement. Accordingly, £100 of value derived from the trust assets traceably survives in the account. The rule in *Clayton's Case* (1817) 1 Mer 572, 35 ER 781 was trumped where a contrary intention could be shown or presumed. In the hierarchy of norms the presumption against the wrongdoer is stronger than the 'first in, first out' rule. As between innocent claimants, at first instance Fry J held that the rule in *Clayton's Case* did apply, and this was not dissented from on appeal.

The application of the presumption against the wrongdoer in *In re Hallett* should immediately be contrasted with its employment in *Re Oatway, Hertslet* v

Oatway [1903] 2 Ch 356, in which a trustee misappropriated £3,000 in breach of trust, which was paid together with other moneys into his bank account, which immediately prior to receipt had been £78 in credit. Just over a week later he purchased shares in the Oceana company for £2,138 by a cheque drawn upon the account. At that stage the balance was £6,635. The trustee subsequently dissipated the rest of the funds in the account. After his death, the shares were realised for £2,475. Joyce J held that the proceeds of the shares represented the traceably surviving value subtracted from the beneficiary. A wrongdoer was not entitled to have the 'first in, first out' rule applied so as to diminish the proceeds of trust assets wrongfully paid into a bank account. Further (at 360):

> when any of the money drawn out has been invested, and the investment remains in the name or under the control of the trustee, the rest of the balance having been afterwards dissipated by him, he cannot maintain that the investment which remains represents his own money alone, and that what has been spent and can no longer be traced or recovered was the money belonging to the trust.

Hayton concludes in Birks (1995), at 8: 'Once a trustee steps out of line by transferring moneys to his personal account in breach of trust everything is presumed against him until he reinstates the trust fund.' It has been commented that Joyce J 'rightly understood *Hallett* to be authority, not for a presumption that the wrongdoer withdrew his own money first, but rather for a presumption that he intended honestly to preserve the other's property': Birks, 370. The proceeds of the shares were the identifiable value surviving of what had been misappropriated from the trust assets. The beneficiaries were held entitled to a claim to that value surviving, secured by an equitable lien. It should be noted that as with the common law power to trace, the equitable process entitles a claimant to a floating interest over all the assets which might arguably derive from the value subtracted from him. As a matter of theory this involves the potential geometric increase in value traceably surviving. As a matter of practice, most of the wrongdoer's assets have usually been dissipated and the potential targets for a claim, as in this case, are rapidly narrowed.

28.3.2   The *Diplock* case

The other leading authority is the discussion of the Court of Appeal in *In re Diplock* [1948] Ch 465. The authoritative nature of the principles stated therein has recently been confirmed by the House of Lords in *Westdeutsche Landesbank Girozentrale* v *Islington London Borough Council* [1996] AC 669, even though the Court of Appeal's analysis rested upon the shaky foundations of the difficult earlier House of Lords case of *Sinclair* v *Brougham* [1914] AC 398, which was overruled in *Westdeutsche*. In *Sinclair* v *Brougham*, the House of Lords, upon the winding-up of a building society which had conducted an *ultra vires* banking business, held that after the payment of the outside creditors, the depositors of money under the invalid contracts could trace in equity the value they had given and were entitled to rank *pari passu* with the society's shareholders to its remaining assets. Lord Parker of Waddington stated that it was well-settled that the lender, though the underlying loan transaction be *ultra vires*, was entitled to trace his payment into the society's assets. Indeed the case went further in that it was not possible to identify what had become of the respective contributions of shareholders and depositors. There were only two groups of claimants left to the remainder of the society's assets. The point was best expressed by Lord Sumner (at 459–60):

the principle on which *Hallett's case* is founded justifies an order allowing the appellants to follow the assets, not merely to the verge of actual identification, but even somewhat further in a case like the present, where after a process of exclusion only two classes or groups of persons, having equal claims, are left in and all superior claims have been eliminated. Tracing in a sense it is not, for we know that the money coming from A went into one security and that coming from B into another and that the two securities did not probably depreciate exactly in the same percentage, and we know further than no one will ever know any more. Still I think this well within in the 'tracing' equity, and that among persons making up these two groups the principle of rateable division of the assets is sound.

The Court of Appeal in *In re Diplock* treated *Sinclair* v *Brougham* as a fundamentally important case, which explained rather than extended *In re Hallett*. This must be qualified by Lord Greene MR's frank observation, which has attracted the empathy of law students ever since, that (at 518): 'We should, however, be lacking in candour rather than showing respect if we refrained from saying that we find the opinions in *Sinclair* v *Brougham* in many respects not only difficult to follow but difficult to reconcile with one another.'

Diplock's will was held to be invalid on the grounds of uncertainty, but not before his executors had distributed some £200,000 to 139 charities. The successful *in personam* claim by the next-of-kin has already been mentioned (see 3.3). It was further held that the next-of-kin were entitled to bring claims *in rem* where the money could be traced. Lord Greene MR, delivering the judgment of the Court, identified three defects of the common law's approach to tracing and claiming. First, it did not recognise equitable claims to property. Secondly, it had a limited remedial arsenal; in particular, specific relief such as the declaration of a charge was unavailable. Thirdly, the 'materialistic' approach of the common law prevented it from identifying money in a mixed fund. In contrast, equity adopted a more 'metaphysical' approach and accordingly, in the case of a composite fund, 'regarded the almagam as capable, in proper circumstances, of being resolved into its component parts' (at 520). In its most important holding the Court of Appeal insisted that the tracing process required the establishment of two key factors. First, the misapplication of trust money or misappropriation in breach of fiduciary duty. Lord Greene MR spoke of 'the necessity of establishing as a starting point the existence of a fiduciary or quasi-fiduciary relationship or of a continuing right of property recognized in equity' (at 520). Secondly, it was essential to establish what was later termed a proprietary base (Birks, 378–79) and that the property to be traced is identifiably derived from that source. But Lord Greene MR insisted (at 521):

> The equitable remedies pre-suppose the continued existence of the money either as a separate fund or as a part of a mixed fund or as latent in property acquired by the means of such a fund. If, on the facts of any individual case, such continued existence is not established, equity is as helpless as the common law itself.

It was held that the principle in *In re Hallett* was not confined to cases where it was the recalcitrant fiduciary who was responsible for confounding trust money with his own money. Where an innocent volunteer was the defendant, and there was a fund consisting of contributions from the defendant and the claimant, each was entitled to an interest ranking *pari passu* in the resulting fund. Lord Greene MR summarised the position as follows (at 539):

> [1] Where one claimant is a person in a fiduciary relationship to another and has mixed moneys of that other with moneys of his own, that other takes priority. The same result follows where a person taking that other claimant's money from the person in a fiduciary relationship, with notice that it is money held in a fiduciary capacity, proceeds to mix it with money of his own.
>
> [2] Where the contest is between two claimants to a mixed fund made up entirely of moneys held on behalf of the two of them respectively and mixed together by the fiduciary agent, they share *pari passu*, each being innocent.
>
> [3] Where the moneys are handed by way of transfer to a person who takes for value without notice, the claim of the owner of the moneys is extinguished. . . .
>
> [4] In the case, however, of a volunteer who takes without notice, e.g., by way of gift from the fiduciary agent, if there is no question of mixing, he holds the money on behalf of the true owner whose equitable right to the money still persists as against him.
>
> [5] On the other hand, if the volunteer mixes the money with money of his own, or receives it mixed from the fiduciary agent, he must admit the claim of the true owner, but is not precluded from setting up his own claim in respect of the moneys of his own which have been contributed to the mixed fund. The result is that they share *pari passu*.

Where an individual charity had used Diplock money in alterations or improvements of buildings which they already owned, the Court had doubts whether the next-of-kin could trace into the altered assets. It might in some cases be that the alterations added no value to the property, or may indeed have decreased the value. In any event, even if the money could be traced the Court of Appeal would not allow a proprietary claim to charity assets (see 30.4). It is difficult to agree with the conclusion of the Court of Appeal that the Diplock money in such cases could not be traced in any true sense (at 548). In the case of one charity, the Diplock money was paid into a current account which was continuously overdrawn. It seems clear that nothing traceably survived of the Diplock money in that case (at 551). Where a charity paid money into an active banking account, it was held that the rule in *Clayton's Case* should be applied, and that debits and credits should appropriated on a first in, first out basis (at 554).

28.4   THE LOWEST INTERMEDIATE BALANCE RULE

It commonly happens that the proceeds of trust funds are paid into a bank account and the vast majority of the fund is dissipated. Tracing, the characteristic function of which is identification, can do little in the face of the disappearance of the claimant's wealth. This is illustrated by *James Roscoe (Bolton) Ltd v Winder* [1915] 1 Ch 62, in which the purchaser of a business agreed to account for receivables due before a certain date to the purchaser. This he failed to do. Some £155, presumably representing receivables, was paid into the purchaser's general banking account. Within days the balance of the account shrank to some £25, the purchaser having spent the money withdrawn on his own purposes. Subsequently the account was topped up by payment in of other moneys yielding a balance at the purchaser's death of some £358. The vendor company made a claim to the fund. It was held that as in *In re Hallett*, the presumption of honesty trumped the rule in *Clayton's Case*. However, the value traceably surviving, and accordingly any claim, was limited to the lowest intermediate balance of £25. Despite the presumption of honesty, Sargant J observed (at 68–69):

> when the drawings out had reached such an amount that the whole of his private money part had been exhausted, it necessarily followed that the rest of the drawings must have been against trust moneys.... You must, for the purpose of tracing, which was the process adopted in *In re Hallett's Estate*, put your finger on some definite fund which either remains in its original state or can be found in another shape.

It was further held that the only way of circumventing this conclusion, was if it could be demonstrated that the circumstances evinced an intention by the fiduciary to restore the trust moneys. There was nothing on the facts of the present case to suggest a desire for redemption. Here the moneys were paid into a general trading account. It would have been different if there were a separate trust account which had been restored. In contrast, the mere payment of money into a current account was insufficient to support an intention to restore. With regard to the case's clear enunciation of the lowest intermediate balance rule, Birks comments (at 365):

> This seems absolutely correct since, however artificial the rules are, once the court reaches a point in the story at which it is bound to say that the enrichment has disappeared, it is impossible for it to affirm that it has subsequently reappeared.

While not adverting to *Roscoe* v *Winder* by name (although it was referred to in skeleton arguments), Woolf LJ in *Barlow Clowes International Ltd* v *Vaughan* [1992] 4 All ER 22 neatly summarised the rule (at 42):

> It must however be remembered that any solution depends on the ability to trace and if the fund had been exhausted (i.e. the account became overdrawn) the investors whose moneys were in the fund prior to the fund being exhausted will not be able to claim against moneys which were subsequently paid into the fund.

This limitation upon the reach of tracing was approved of by the Privy Council in *Re Goldcorp Exchange Ltd* [1995] 1 AC 74, in which Lord Mustill accepted that it was possible to trace into a mixed but not into a non-existent fund (at 105).

Similarly, in *Bishopsgate Investment Management Ltd* v *Homan* [1995] Ch 211, claims arose out of the death of Robert Maxwell. It transpired that large amounts of money had been misdirected from the pension funds of employees of Maxwell's companies, of which the trustee was BIM, into the bank accounts of various companies with which Maxwell was associated. Those accounts were, or subsequently became, overdrawn and the Maxwell companies were hopelessly insolvent. Leggatt LJ insisted (at 221) that 'it is only possible to trace in equity money which has continued existence, actual or notional'. Dillon LJ affirmed that trust money could not be pursued through overdrawn funds. *Roscoe* v *Winder* was expressly applied. Two further arguments were also rejected. First, the mysterious circumstances of Robert Maxwell's final days were held insufficient to provide evidence of an intention to restore the trust assets. The fact that the account into which the trust moneys had been paid was in credit shortly before the companies were put into administration, was insufficient to evince an attempt at redemption (see Dillon LJ, at 220). Secondly, it was suggested that what has been termed 'backward tracing' was not permissible. Where an asset was acquired before the misappropriation of trust money by means of a bank overdraft, and that overdraft is subsequently discharged using trust moneys, it might be thought there was a causal link between the trust moneys and the acquisition. This may be particularly so if the asset was used as security for an overdraft which was subsequently discharged by the use of misappropriated money. In such circumstances a claim might be made by way of subrogation. However, Leggatt LJ observed (at 221–22): 'there can ordinarily be no tracing into an asset which is already in the hands of the defaulting trustee when the misappropriation occurs.' In contrast, Dillon LJ was more cautious as to the possibility of backward tracing, accepting that it was clearly arguable that if it could be demonstrated that there was a causal connection between a particular misappropriation and the acquisition of an asset, a claim could be made to the asset (at 217). Henry LJ simply concurred with both. See also *Foskett* v *McKeown* [1998] Ch 265, at 283 *per* Sir Richard Scott V-C, and at 289 *per* Hobhouse LJ. It is submitted that where a sufficiently close causal connection can be demonstrated the court should not consider itself hampered by a strict criterion of contemporaneity.

Modern financing methods and transaction structuring do not closely resemble primitive barter or immediate exchange of the type often encountered in textbook examples of tracing.

28.5   MODERN EVASION OF *CLAYTON'S CASE*

Recourse to *Clayton's Case* (1817) 1 Mer 572, 35 ER 781, would have affronted ordinary notions of equity in *Barlow Clowes International Ltd* v *Vaughan* [1992] 4 All ER 22. The case arose out of the notorious sham investment scheme operated by BCI, a Gibraltar-based company. Its promotional literature promised the investment of depositors' money in gilt-edged stock resulting in very high returns, and such returns were apparently achieved. As a result BCI attracted some 11,000, mostly elderly, residents of the UK as investors. It was a fraud and a sham. What little of the investors' money was actually invested in gilts in fact achieved a loss. The very high returns were achieved simply by returning a proportion of the investors' money to them as supposed gains from investments. Most of the money was misapplied and dissipated by BCI's managers, including the purchase of a luxury yacht. By the time of liquidation of BCI, some £140 million was due to investors on their contracts, but only certificates of gilts worth some £1.8 million could be found. In litigation concerned with the distribution of the meagre available funds (including sums in bank accounts, the gilts and the proceeds of the sale of the yacht), competing arguments were raised by early investors and later investors. The early investors argued the funds should be distributed on a proportionate share basis. Later investors argued for the application of the 'first in, first out' rule. *Clayton's Case* would clearly favour the latter group. (In fact the investors were eventually compensated by the Government, and the appeal was brought by the Secretary of State for Trade and Industry by way of subrogation.) The case yields the most sophisticated discussion of the relationship between tracing and *Clayton's Case* to date. The Court of Appeal ultimately held for a rateable distribution between the investors on a *pari passu* basis.

Dillon LJ stressed that the rule in *Clayton's Case* was not invariably applied, citing *The Mecca* [1897] AC 286 and two cases on resulting trusts: *Re British Red Cross Balkan Fund* [1914] 2 Ch 490; and *Re Hobourn Aero Components Ltd's Air-Raid Distress Fund* [1946] Ch 86, at 194. Dillon LJ accepted, by reference to BCI's promotional literature, that it was envisaged that each depositor would participate in a global investment fund. Accordingly it would be inappropriate to apply *Clayton's Case* in the face of such evidence of contrary intention. Dillon LJ rejected a wider submission that the court had a discretion to disapply the rule in *Clayton's Case* simply on the grounds that this application would be unfair in the present case. The authorities on tracing established a clear rule of practice that the 'first in, first out' method was to be applied where several innocent claimants' money had been blended in one account.

Woolf LJ commenced with a dictum of Judge Learned Hand in *Re Walter Schmidt & Co. ex parte Feuerbach* 298 F 314 (1923), at 316:

When the law adopts a fiction, it is, or at least it should be, for some purpose of justice. To adopt [the fiction of 'first in, first out'] is to apportion a common misfortune through a test which has no relation whatever to the justice of the case.

As a matter of principle Woolf LJ expressed clear support for what he termed the '*pari passu ex post facto*' solution (which was modelled on the award of the House of Lords in *Sinclair* v *Brougham* [1914] AC 389). Woolf LJ's assessment of the stringency of the rule in *Clayton's Case* was more flexible than Dillon LJ's. Woolf LJ held that the 'first in, first out' rule would not be applied in a number of situations. First, it is displaced where its application would benefit the trustee to the detriment of the claimant. Secondly, it does not apply if a contrary intention or presumed intention by the claimants can be identified. In summary (at 42): 'the use of the rule is a matter of convenience and if its application in particular circumstances would be impracticable or result in injustice between the investors it will not be applied if there is a preferable alternative.' Woolf LJ also accepted that the promotional literature of BCI indicated a contrary intention. Alternatively, given the fact that no genuine common investment fund was created, he was prepared to construct a hypothetical intention on behalf of all the investors to salvage what they could from the common misfortune they had suffered.

Leggatt LJ also accepted that the depositors' money should be treated as part of a common fund, thereby displacing the 'first in, first out'. Further, the application of that rule would be inconvenient. It is submitted that the reasoning of Woolf LJ is to be preferred to the extent that it goes further than his fellow judges. The application of the first in, first out rule on the facts of *Barlow Clowes* would have yielded capricious results, with the later investors potentially being entitled to all the proceeds of the sale of the yacht. A point which does not seem to have been made is that the resulting fund collected by BCI was not in the nature of an active current banking account of the sort to which *Clayton's Case* is usually supposed to be confined.

Lastly, a third solution to the entitlements of the complete competing claimants which was adverted to, but not argued for by any of the parties, was the 'rolling charge' or 'North American' method. In essence this treats all withdrawals from a blended fund as borne by all the depositors proportionately, rather than visiting the whole loss upon the earliest investors. This was accepted to be a fairer result than *Clayton's Case*, but the consensus of the Court was that its application, though possible with the benefit of modern technology, would involve costs out of all proportion to the sums involved. As a method of measuring competing entitlements it was not rejected outright. For further discussion, see the decision of the Supreme Court of Canada in *Re Ontario Securities Commission and Greymac Creditcorp* [1988] 2 SCR 172; Hayton, in Birks (1995), at 14–15 and Handley (1999) 115 LQR 186.

28.6 TRACING PROFITS

In the usual case the exercise of tracing results in the identification of assets derived from the claimant's wealth which represent only a fraction of the original value subtracted. Nevertheless, the tracing process will occasionally yield an asset which has increased in value. Whether a claim can be made to the increased value of the asset is a question for Chapter 30.

However, the factual possibility is neatly illustrated by *In re Tilley's Will Trusts, Burgin v Croad* [1967] Ch 1179. A widow and executrix confused £2,237 of trust moneys with her own private fund. Over several years she participated in a number of speculative property transactions, yielding substantial profits. One of the beneficiaries under the will trust claimed the share of the profits made by the widow, to the extent that it could not be shown that property purchases were not made out of her own resources. The case clearly illustrates the power to trace and lay claim to profits in the hands of a fiduciary. However, on the facts, given the widow's extensive overdraft facility, Ungoed-Thomas J held that even on an objective test it could not be said that the trust moneys were used to acquire the properties. The widow's breach of trust halted at the mixing of trust moneys with her own resources. The traceable value of the beneficiaries' money was limited to the value received of £2,237.

Compare *Jones v Jones* [1997] Ch 159 (decided at common law) and the decision in the Court of Appeal in *Foskett v McKeown* [1998] Ch 265 (currently on appeal to the House of Lords). See 30.5.

28.7 SWOLLEN ASSETS

Tracing's insistence upon the identifiability of assets received or retained by the defendant which can be linked back to the claimant is often said to be fundamental. However, the strict logic of tracing is not insisted on where what remains is a blended fund to which only innocent claimants are entitled (*Sinclair v Brougham* [1914] AC 398 and *Barlow Clowes International Ltd v Vaughan* [1992] 4 All ER 22). Attempts have been made to take this a step further in another approach which also emanated from North America. The 'swollen assets' theory advocates that where a defendant receives value derived from another, all his assets should be treated as representing the traceable value of what has been derived from the claimant. Accordingly the whole pool of the defendant's wealth is potentially traceable, and claims can be laid to any surviving asset. In a nutshell, this approach would dispense with all the artificial rules of tracing. Once it is shown that a defendant has been enriched by value attributable to the claimant, the court would have the power to impose a restitutionary proprietary remedy over any or all of the defendant's assets.

Desirable though simplification is, this is generally seen as going too far. The court is able to fashion new proprietary rights without any clear linkage being demonstrated between the defendant and what was derived from the claimant. The arguments are more fully considered in Chapter 30. The swollen assets theory as a means of by-passing the tracing exercise has to date been rejected in England. The authorities already discussed demonstrate the importance of identifiability. This is not to say that arguments of a swollen assets nature have not been advanced to the courts. Such arguments usually commence with a notorious obiter discussion by Lord Templeman delivering the advice of the Privy Council in *Space Investments Ltd* v *Canadian Imperial Bank of Commerce Trust Co. (Bahamas) Ltd* [1986] 1 WLR 1072. The actual decision in that case was that a bank trustee was authorised to deposit trust moneys with itself by the terms of the trust instrument. Accordingly the interest for the beneficiaries of the trust ranked *pari passu* with, not prior to, other unsecured creditors of the bank when it became insolvent. However, it was said (at 1074) that where a bank trustee deposited money with itself without authority, 'equity allows the beneficiaries, or a new trustee appointed in place of an insolvent bank trustee to protect the interests of the beneficiaries, to trace the trust money to all the assets of the bank and to recover the trust money by the exercise of an equitable charge over all the assets of the bank'. This was apparently regarded by the Board as a straightforward application of *In re Hallett's Estate* (1880) 13 Ch D 696. The width of the dictum did not escape criticism, but it was applied by the Court of Appeal of New Zealand in *Liggett* v *Kensington* [1993] 1 NZLR 257 (led by Sir Robin Cooke P, who was a member of the Board in *Space Investments*). However, on appeal to the Privy Council in *Re Goldcorp Exchange Ltd* [1995] 1 AC 74, it was held that the investors' reliance upon the earlier case did not assist them (at 105):

> to overcome the difficulty that the moneys said to be impressed with the trust were paid into an overdrawn account and thereupon ceased to exist: see, for example, *In re Diplock* [1948] Ch 465. The observations of the Board in the *Space Investments* case were concerned with a mixed, not a non-existent, fund.

The discussion in *Space Investments* and the idea of tracing to 'swollen assets' was said to require closer examination and further argument (at 109–10). The latter Privy Council decision was followed by the English Court of Appeal in *Bishopsgate Investment Management Ltd* v *Homan* [1995] Ch 211. For discussion, see Smith (1994) 8 *Trusts Law International* 102.

28.8   CONCLUSION: FUSION OF LAW AND EQUITY?

Tracing is an artificial exercise which commences with a proprietary entitlement of a claimant. By rules and presumption the process identifies the links between the claimant's entitlement and an asset received or retained by the defendant. Somewhat artificially, tracing, particularly in its equitable guise, purports to identify value despite mixtures and substitutions. As such it is vital both to claims against remoter recipients and as a foundation to proprietary claims. The current dualism evidenced by the authorities between the common law and equity is impossible to defend as a matter of principle. It seems that history is to blame. The dichotomy between the approaches has often been the subject of judicial lament. In *Lipkin Gorman* v *Karpnale Ltd* [1991] 2 AC 548, Lord Goff envisaged that a beneficial consequence of the recognition of the defence of change of position might be a fused approach to this topic (at 581):

while recognising the different functions of property at law and in equity, there may also in due course develop a more a consistent approach to tracing claims, in which common defences are recognised as available to such claims, whether advanced at law or in equity.

In *Agip (Africa) Ltd* v *Jackson* [1990] Ch 265, Millett J opined that rather than perpetuate the distinction, 'it would be preferable to develop a unified restitutionary remedy for the recovery of property transferred without consideration to a recipient with no legitimate justification for receiving it' (at 289). See further Sir Peter Millett (1991) 107 LQR 71. Similarly, in *Trustee of the Property of F. C. Jones & Sons Ltd* v *Jones* [1997] Ch 159, at 170, Millett LJ insisted that the differences between the common law and equitable species of tracing should not be exacerbated.

In contrast, recent academic work by Lionel Smith and Professor Birks has sought to reinterpret the authorities both at common law and in equity to demonstrate that a unified system of rules already exists. As has been observed, the rules and presumption were devised in order to resolve what would otherwise be evidential impasses. Close reading of the older authorities suggests much cross-fertilisation of ideas. Birks has accordingly argued that the three core rules obtained both at common law and in equity.

First, with regard to the presumption against the wrongdoer's interest, this has its roots in the well-known common law authority on wrongful interference with goods of *Armory* v *Delamirie* (1772) 1 Str 505, 93 ER 664, which was in turn relied upon in the leading equity case of *Lupton* v *White* (1808) 15 Ves Jun 432, 33 ER 817; both of which were cited in *In re Tilley's Will Trusts* [1967] Ch 1179. The presumption has recently been applied to resolve evidential difficulties where two quantities of oil were wrongfully mixed on the basis of common law rules in *Indian Oil Corp. Ltd* v *Greenstone Shipping Company SA, The Ypatianna* [1988] QB 345.

Secondly, the 'first in, first out' rule had its origins in the common law rules for the appropriations of payments of debts and is still widely used in the banking context. The rule in *Clayton's Case* (1817) 1 Mer 572, 35 ER 781 operates both at common law and in equity.

Thirdly, the '*pari passu*' rule is not exclusively equitable. It will be recalled that in *Sinclair* v *Brougham* [1914] AC 398, Lord Sumner relied upon analogous cases in relation to tangible personal property (see 28.3.2). His Lordship referred to *Buckley* v *Gross* (1863) 3 B & S 566, 122 ER 213 (mass of molten tallow) and *Spence* v *Union of Marine Insurance Co. Ltd* (1868) LR 3 CP 427 (confused cargo of cotton). In each of these cases, as in the more recent *Indian Oil Corporation* case, the common law has adopted a rule recognising tenancies in common with respect to confused assets.

For discussion see Birks, 'The Necessity of a Unitary Law of Tracing' in R. Cranston (ed.), *Making Commercial Law — Essays in Honour of Roy Goode* (1997) 239 especially at 253–57; see also Birks, 'On Taking Seriously the Difference Between Tracing and Claiming' (1997) 11 *Trusts Law International* 2, at 4–6; Smith, 'Tracing, "swollen assets" and the lowest intermediate balance' (1994) 8 *Trusts Law International* 102; Smith, 'Tracing into the Payment of Debt' [1995] CLJ 290; Smith, 277–79 and *passim*.

This project has not yet won acceptance in the courts, but it is attractive in principle and eliminates the unnecessary multiplication of concepts in this area of law. This recent juristic exercise demonstrates that the obstacle to a fusion of the principles of tracing at common law and at equity are not as insuperable as has been commonly supposed. Consistently with their shared characteristic of resolving evidential problems of identification, there is no justification in principle or in common sense for persisting with divergent approaches.

FURTHER READING

Asterisks indicate especially useful works.

Goff and Jones, 93–119
Birks, 363–70
*L. Smith, *The Law of Tracing* (1997)
R. Pearce, 'A Tracing Paper' (1976) 40 Conv 277
R. Goode, 'The Right to Trace and its Impact in Commercial Transactions' (1976) 92 LQR 360, 528
G. Jones, 'Tracing Claims in the Modern World' (1987) 37 *King's Counsel* 15
*Sir Peter Millett 'Tracing with Proceeds of Fraud' (1991) 107 LQR 71
P. Birks, 'Mixing and Tracing: Property and Restitution' (1992) 45 CLP 69, especially at 84–98
P. Birks, 'Persistent Problems in Misdirected Money: A Quintet' [1993] LMCLQ 218
Sir Peter Millett, 'Equity — The Road Ahead', (1995) 9 *Trusts Law International* 35, at 38–42
*D. Hayton, 'Equity's Identification Rules' in Birks (1995), 1–21
S. Moriarty, 'Tracing, Mixing and Laundering' in Birks (1995), 73–94
H. Norman, 'Tracing the Proceeds of Crime: An Inequitable Solution?' in Birks (1995), 95–113
P. Birks, in Birks (1995), 289–322
L. Smith, 'Tracing, 'Swollen Assets' and the Lowest Intermediate Balance' (1994) 8 *Trusts Law International* 102
L. Smith, 'Tracing into the Payment of a Debt' [1995] CLJ 290
*P. Birks, 'The Necessity of a Unitary Law of Tracing' in R. Cranston (ed), *Making Commercial Law — Essays in Honour of Roy Goode* (1997), 239
P. Birks, 'On Taking Seriously the Difference Between Tracing and Claiming' (1997) 11 *Trusts Law International* 2, especially 4–6
C. Band, 'The development of tracing rules in commercial cases' [1997] LMCLQ 65 (practical)

29   *Personal Claims in Equity*

29.1   THEORETICAL FOUNDATIONS

A major theme of recent judicial and juristic analysis is the need to distinguish sharply between tracing and claiming. The two preceding chapters focussed on tracing (respectively at common law and in equity), whereas this chapter and the next concentrate upon the potential resulting claims in equity. The concern of this chapter is with personal claims, and the concern of the next is with proprietary claims.

Tracing is a process or technique which identifies value derived from the claimant which has been received or retained by a defendant. Generally, therefore, the tracing exercise establishes that the defendant is enriched at the claimant's expense. It does not of itself provide the ground for restitution, or determine the nature and measure of relief. The only remedy developed at common law where tracing was successful was the action for money had and received. Some cases went further in providing a defrauded party with a defence where he had stripped the wrongdoer of his ill-gotten gains (as in *Taylor* v *Plumer* (1815) 3 M & S 562, 105 ER 721), or where the intepleader procedure allowed the courts to grant appropriate declaratory relief (as in *Trustee of the Property of F. C. Jones Ltd & Sons* v *Jones* [1997] Ch 159). However, otherwise the common law's remedial arsenal was limited to the action for money had and received, and accordingly claimants turn to equity in relation to claims, just as they habitually do in relation to tracing itself. On the importance of distinguishing tracing and claiming, see Smith, 6–14.

In addition to a successful tracing exercise, claiming requires the identification of an appropriate ground for restitution and the selection of a suitable restitutionary remedy. It would be a mistake to think that equitable relief is necessarily proprietary (even ignoring the incoherent but oft-repeated 'rule' that equity only acts *in personam*). Equity developed a personal claim analogous to the claim for money had and received, which is available to a claimant after the successful completion of the tracing exercise, termed 'knowing receipt'.

Two pre-conditions are laid down for a successful claim once tracing is complete. First, there is a much criticised requirement that the claimant's money must have been misappropriated by an initial breach of trust or breach of fiduciary duty. This is usually easily satisfied in the factual configurations in which claims have hitherto been made, but it is seen as unprincipled and an unnecessary limitation upon the reach of restitution. Secondly, the equity case law insists that the defendant recipient be tainted with knowledge, or at least constructive knowledge, of the circumstances in which the claimant's money was misappropriated. The onus is therefore upon the claimant to demonstrate affirmatively by evidence unconscionable receipt by the defendant.

This makes the equitable claim one based on fault, in contrast to the general rule of strict liability which applies in the common law branch of restitution. Accordingly, this requirement has also been criticised as irreconcilable with common law attitudes. It has been suggested that the equity cases could be reinterpreted on a strict liability basis, subject to a defence of good faith purchase: Birks [1989] LMCLQ 296. However, the current judicial trend in cases of remoter recipients is to continue to insist on knowledge, and indeed in some cases a high degree of knowledge, where liability is alleged against remoter recipients in a commercial context. Further confusion is provided by the fact that the cases do not speak with one voice on the requisite degree of knowledge.

29.2   THE INGREDIENTS OF THE RECEIPT-BASED CLAIM

In *El Ajou* v *Dollar Land Holdings plc* [1994] 2 All ER 685, at 700, Hoffmann LJ identified three ingredients of a 'knowing receipt' claim:

(a)   a disposal of the claimant's assets in breach of fiduciary duty;
(b)   the beneficial receipt by the defendant of assets which traceably represent those of the claimant;
(c)   knowledge on the part of the defendant that the assets received are traceable to a breach of fiduciary duty.

Breach of fiduciary duty is sometimes treated as a pre-condition to the exercise of equitable tracing, but while the requirement is insisted upon, it is preferable to treat it as an ingredient of the claim based on knowing receipt. As Millett J observed in *Agip (Africa) Ltd* v *Jackson* [1990] Ch 265, at 290, the requirement depends on authority rather than principle. In reality: 'The requirement is, however, readily satisfied in most cases of commercial fraud since the embezzlement of a company's funds almost inevitably involves a breach of fiduciary duty on the part of one of the company's employees or agents.' The misappropriation of wealth generally requires disloyalty on the part of a senior employee or agent. This was certainly the case in *Agip* v *Jackson* and *El Ajou*. However, there is no need for an employee to be particularly senior, if he occupies a vital position of trust, such as a security guard (*Brinks Ltd (formerly Brink's Mat Ltd)* v *Abu-Saleh (No. 3)* [1996] CLC 133).

The second requirement of beneficial receipt appears to be an equitable equivalent of the established defence in common law of ministerial receipt, except that it is built into the cause of action. In *Agip* v *Jackson*, Millett J insisted that it was an essential feature of the knowing receipt claim that the recipient must have received the assets for his own use and benefit. This explained the immunity of a paying or collecting bank where it acted only ministerially. Accordingly, Millett J reached the conclusion that the defendant firm of accountants were not accountable on the grounds of knowing receipt. There was no cross-appeal from this finding to the Court of Appeal. In the result, the accountants were held liable for what is now termed dishonest accessory liability. The holding that the accountancy firm were dishonest accessories to fraud must as a matter of principle have disentitled them to raise a defence analogous to ministerial receipt. It is submitted that ministerial receipt, like change of position and good faith purchase, is only available to innocent recipients. It should make no difference whether ministerial receipt is conceived of as a defence (as at common law), or whether a requirement that receipt is beneficial is built into the cause of action (as appears to be the trend in the equity cases). Accordingly the firm of accountants in *Agip* v *Jackson* should also have been liable in restitution at common law. The dishonest accessory claim is considered below at 29.6. For ministerial receipt see 32.6.

29.3 THE CATEGORIES OF KNOWLEDGE

The debate as to the requisite degree of knowledge for a successful claim is often conducted by reference to a hierarchy of states of mind devised by counsel in *Baden, Delvaux and Lecuit* v *Société Générale pour Favoriser le Développement du Commerce et de l'Industrie en France SA* [1983] BCLC 325, [1993] 1 WLR 509 (in fact a 'knowing assistance' or 'dishonest accessory liability' case):

    (a)   actual knowledge;
    (b)   wilfully shutting one's eyes to the obvious;
    (c)   wilfully and recklessly failing to make such enquiries as an honest and reasonable man would make;
    (d)   knowledge of circumstances which indicate the facts to an honest and reasonable man;
    (e)   knowledge of circumstances which would put an honest and reasonable man on enquiry.

There is confusion in the case law as to which of these is sufficient to generate a claim in knowing receipt. There is further confusion in older case law, where it is not clear on occasion whether the liability is being imposed on the basis of knowing receipt, or upon the basis of what used to be termed knowing assistance (now called dishonest accessory liability; see 29.6). Dishonest accessory liability, as its new nomenclature suggests, requires dishonesty, although objectively ascertained (*Royal Brunei Airlines Sdn Bhd* v *Tan* [1995] 2 AC 378).

29.3.1   Authority supporting a higher degree of knowledge

In the context of knowing receipt, a stringent standard was set in *Carl Zeiss Stiftung* v *Herbert Smith & Co. (No. 2)* [1969] 2 Ch 276, in which a company in former East Germany claimed to be beneficially entitled to the assets of a company based in former West Germany. The East German plaintiffs sought to make the defendant solicitors accountable for legal fees received from the West German company. Edmund Davies LJ opined that 'want of probity' would need to be alleged (at 304), whereas Sachs LJ tentatively suggested that dishonesty or conscious wrongdoing was required (at 298). In the event it was conceded by counsel for the plaintiffs that the solicitors were under no duty of enquiry because of the complexity of the underlying dispute between the two German companies, and accordingly the claim was struck out.

A similar insistence on dishonesty, or at least a high degree of knowledge, was voiced on the somewhat more genteel facts of *In re Montagu's Settlement Trusts* [1987] Ch 264. In 1948, the tenth Duke of Manchester received a number of items of furniture and paintings which unbeknown to him were subject to a family settlement. These were disposed of by him during his lifetime. After the tenth Duke's death in 1977, the eleventh Duke brought an action against the trustees for the settlement alleging breach of trust by the trustees, and alleging that the tenth Duke in disposing of the assets was accountable as a constructive trustee. Sir Robert Megarry V-C held that there was nothing to suggest that at the time when he received the chattels the tenth Duke had any knowledge that they constituted trust property. The learned judge accepted that it was impossible to attempt to reconcile all the authorities or dicta on the question of personal liability in equity. However, he opined that the basic question in knowing receipt was whether the conscience of the recipient was sufficiently affected to justify making him accountable. It was stressed that knowledge was not equivalent to notice. Sir Robert Megarry V-C was prepared to hold that what was required was some want of probity corresponding to categories (a), (b) and (c) in the *Baden Delvaux* case, but the types that (d) and (e) represented would not suffice. The Duke was simply a layman and had accepted and acted upon the advice given to him by his solicitor, the trustees and the solicitor to the trustees. A factor not expressly adverted to in the case, but which might support a high degree of knowledge for liability in the particular circumstances, was the extreme staleness of the claim: Birks (1992), 35.

Subsequently, Knox J in *Cowan de Groot Properties Ltd* v *Eagle Trust plc* [1992] 4 All ER 700, while conceding that there was a substantial body of authority favouring liability on the basis of constructive knowledge falling short of want of probity, preferred the view of Sir Robert Megarry V-C that knowledge in the first three categories of the *Baden Delvaux* scale should be required in a knowing receipt claim. In the event the defendant in that case was held not to have knowledge or constructive knowledge within any of the five categories. Similarly, in *Polly Peck International plc* v *Nadir (No. 2)* [1992] 4 All ER 769, Scott LJ, in considering a claim to a worldwide *Mareva* injunction against a bank on the basis of what his

Lordship characterised as a knowing receipt claim, appeared to prefer a standard based on want of probity, while acknowledging that an interlocutory appeal was not the correct place to settle the issue. His Lordship warned that the categories of mental state identified in *Baden Delvaux* are 'not rigid categories with clear and precise boundaries. One category may merge imperceptibly into another' (at 777). The obvious policy underlying such a pronouncement is a concern not to unsettle ordinary commercial transactions by too readily imposing restitutionary obligations upon banks and others who deal with corporate bodies. Those concerned by this policy factor have ready recourse to the well-known dictum of Lindley LJ in *Manchester Trust* v *Furness* [1895] 2 QB 539, at 545 (see 31.5).

29.3.2 Authority supporting a lesser degree of knowledge or strict liability

In startling contrast to this judicial squeamishness about restitutionary liability is the academic assertion that the liability of the recipient of misdirected funds should generally be strict, though subject to generous defences including good faith purchase: Birks [1989] LMCLQ 296. In a similar vein, some judicial authority has been prepared to loosen the reins and allow the imposition of liability for knowing receipt for all categories of knowledge, including constructive knowledge: that is, all five points identified on the *Baden Delvaux* scale. In *Belmont Finance Corporation* v *Williams Furniture Ltd (No. 2)* [1980] 1 All ER 393, a company received money from its subsidiary as part of an unlawful scheme by the directors of the subsidiary to provide financial assistance for the purchase of its own shares contrary to the prohibition then contained in s. 54 of the Companies Act 1948 (now s. 151 of the Companies Act 1985). Buckley LJ was prepared to hold the recipient liable on the basis of actual or constructive knowledge of the breach of fiduciary duty by the directors to the subsidiary. Goff LJ held that it was sufficient if the money was received 'knowing, or in circumstances in which it ought to know, that it was in breach of trust' (at 410). In *International Sales and Agencies Ltd* v *Marcus* [1982] 3 All ER 551, Lawson J was prepared to hold that knowing receipt would be satisfied 'if an ordinary reasonable person in his position and with his attributes ought to have known of the relevant breach' (at 558).

Most importantly, two leading first instance decisions by Millett J on the civil consequences of money-laundering support a broad approach to liability and a correspondingly expansive approach to what constitutes requisite constructive knowledge. In *Agip (Africa) Ltd* v *Jackson* [1990] Ch 265, Millett J was prepared to hold the defendant accountants liable if they received money with notice, actual or constructive, that it was trust property, or if they discovered the facts subsequent to receipt but before the money was parted with. However, he also controversially held that the liability applied only to beneficial recipients. This has been criticised above (29.2). In *El Ajou* v *Dollar Land Holdings plc* [1993] 3 All ER 717, the plaintiff was the victim of an elaborate fraud. A claim was brought against a London-based property development company which had received the proceeds of the fraud. Millett J adopted a test (at 739; although disclaiming an intention to lay down an authoritative rule) that:

dishonesty or want of probity involving actual knowledge (whether proved or inferred) is not a precondition of liability; but that a recipient is not expected to be unduly suspicious and is not to be held liable unless he went ahead without further enquiry in circumstances in which an honest and reasonable man would have realised that the money was probably trust money and was being misapplied.

This appears to correspond to (d) on the *Baden Delvaux* scale.

In his extra-judicial writings, Sir Peter Millett has also favoured the conclusion that liability as a matter of principle should be prima facie strict, though subject to defences: (1991) 107 LQR 71. More recently, Lord Nicholls of Birkenhead has added his voice to this debate. In 'Knowing Receipt: The Need for a New Landmark' in Cornish, 231, at 244, he concludes:

> If recipient liability is to have a firmer basis for the future, the attempt to formulate one single principle of personal liability should be abandoned. Instead, personal liability should be based on the combination of two separate principles of liability. First, recipient liability should cover all third party recipients. This would be a principle of strict liability in that it would apply to every recipient with an impeachable title irrespective of fault, but it would be restitutionary in nature. It would be confined to restoring an unjust gain. Change of position would be available as a defence accordingly. Secondly, dishonest recipients should be personally liable to make good losses as well as accounting for all benefits.

As a matter of principle, it is submitted that the prevailing academic view should be adopted as this promotes consistency between the common law and equity. Accordingly, liability should be strict but the defences should be generous.

29.4   KNOWLEDGE IN THE CORPORATE CONTEXT

In the leading case of *El Ajou* v *Dollar Land Holdings plc*, there was a division of opinion between Millett J at first instance and the Court of Appeal as to the proper application of the 'directing mind and will' test for establishing corporate liability. Millett J had held ([1993] 3 All ER 717), that a Mr Ferdman, the chairman of the recipient company, who generally played no active part in its management, but had arranged the transaction under which the money was paid to the company, was not the directing mind and will of the company such as to fix it with sufficient knowledge to be liable on the ground of knowing receipt. It was clear that Mr Ferdman had the requisite knowledge. Millett J wryly commented (at 740): 'Wilful blindness was part of his job description.' The Court of Appeal disagreed ([1994] 2 All ER 685). It was necessary to identify the natural person having management and control in relation to the particular act in question. It was crucial that Mr Ferdman had made all the arrangements in relation to the transaction. It was sufficient for the purpose of liability to treat Mr Ferdman as the company's directing mind and will for the transaction under which the money was received.

29.5 KNOWING RECEIPT AND THE DISSIPATION OF CORPORATE ASSETS

The *ultra vires* rule, which deduced lack of corporate capacity by strict construction of a company's object clause in its articles of association, was finally excised from English company law by the 1989 amendments to the Companies Act 1985, at least as regards outsiders dealing with the company in good faith (s. 35). However, directors may still exceed or abuse their powers under the constitution. Such conduct is properly characterised as *intra vires*. As regards the board of directors, its power to bind the company cannot be impugned in respect of transactions entered into with persons dealing with the company in good faith (s. 35A(1)). Good faith is presumed (s. 35A(2)(c)).

As regards individual directors the leading case is *Rolled Steel Products (Holdings) Ltd v British Steel Corporation* [1986] Ch 246. The case pre-dates the recent reforms, but it still provides the principles which apply to restitution claims against third parties. A director and majority shareholder of a company caused it to enter into a number of transactions, including a guarantee for the benefit of another company which he controlled. The result was to reduce his own liability under a personal guarantee for that company. However, he failed to disclose this matter in accordance with the articles of association. In this action the guarantor company reclaimed moneys paid under the guarantee as money had and received, or moneys which had been misapplied.

Slade LJ insisted that the phrase *ultra vires* be confined to acts which are beyond the corporate capacity of the company. Here the transactions were entered into without authority by the director, because they were not for the purposes of the company. On the evidence, the defendant company knew of this and therefore could not rely upon the guarantee, on the basis of ordinary principles of the law of agency. Presumably it was aware that the director was acting outside the scope of his actual authority, and was therefore disentitled from relying on any apparent authority. With regard to recovery of the moneys paid out, Slade LJ relied upon *Belmont Finance Corporation Ltd v Williams Furniture Ltd (No. 2)* [1980] 1 All ER 393. Slade LJ concluded (at 298):

> The *Belmont* principle thus provides a legal route by which a company may recover its assets in a case where its directors have abused their fiduciary duties and a person receiving assets as a result of such abuse is on notice that they have been misapplied. The principle is not linked in any way to the capacity of the company; it is capable of applying whether or not the company had the capacity to do the acts in question.

Browne-Wilkinson LJ agreed, insisting that the *ultra vires* rule concerned transactions beyond the capacity of the company, which were accordingly wholly void. The crucial distinction was between acts done in excess of a company's capacity (*ultra vires*) and acts done in excess or abuse of the powers of the company (*ultra vires*). Where a transaction was *ultra vires* and wholly void it was irrelevant whether or not the party transacted with had notice of that fact. Browne-Wilkinson LJ summarised his conclusions on *intra vires* transactions (at 306–307):

[1] If a company enters into a transaction which is *intra vires* (as being within its capacity) but in excess or abuse of its powers, such transaction will be set aside at the instance of the shareholders. [2] A third party who has notice — actual or constructive — that a transaction, although *intra vires* the company, was entered into in excess or abuse of the powers of the company cannot enforce such transaction against the company and will be accountable as constructive trustee for any money or property of the company received by the third party.

With respect to transactions which are void as a result of true *ultra vires* (which are less likely to occur in the light of the statutory reform), restitution would not follow automatically, but in most cases there would be a ground for restitution in the shape of mistake or failure of consideration. Presumably a good faith recipient would be entitled to plead bona fide purchase or change of position.

It does sometimes seem to have been assumed that where money is paid *ultra vires*, it can be recovered without more. Such an assumption seems to underlie *Simmonds* v *Heffer* [1983] BCLC 298. The League Against Cruel Sports Ltd, a company limited by guarantee, campaigned to prevent and oppose cruelty to animals. It donated £30,000 to the Labour Party on the understanding that it would be used specifically to promote animal welfare, and a further £50,000 was paid over without any restriction on its use. Mervyn Davies J held that the constitution of the League did not allow the £50,000 donation, and accordingly declared that it was returnable. The absence of any explicit ground for restitution makes the case difficult to explain and anomalous.

Knowing receipt claims are common where corporate powers have been exceeded or abused. *Belmont Finance* is typical of much case law concerned with what is now s. 151 of the Companies Act 1985, which prima facie prohibits a company from providing financial assistance for the purchase of its own shares. Another example of recovery is the case of unauthorised dividend payments, as occurred in *Precision Dippings Ltd* v *Precision Dippings Marketing Ltd* [1986] Ch 1047. A dividend was declared and paid before the auditor's statement was available. The defendant, a subsidiary company of the plaintiff, received some £60,000. It had given no valuable consideration for the money and was accordingly a volunteer. Further, it had notice of the facts surrounding the payment and was therefore liable to refund the £60,000 on an application for summary judgment, following *Rolled Steel Products (Holdings) Ltd* v *British Steel Corporation* [1986] Ch 246.

29.6   DISHONEST ACCESSORY LIABILITY

In the seminal case of *Barnes* v *Addy* (1875) LR 9 Ch App 244, the restitutionary cause of action for knowing receipt was juxtaposed with what became known as 'knowing assistance'. Lord Selborne LC observed (at 251–52, emphasis added):

strangers are not to be made a constructive trustee merely because they act as the agents of trustees in transactions within their legal powers, transactions, perhaps of which a Court of Equity may disapprove, unless those agents *receive* and become chargeable with some part of the trust property, or unless they *assist* with knowledge in a dishonest and fraudulent design on the part of the trustees.

These two causes of action were often pleaded in the alternative, and sometimes were imperfectly distinguished in judicial discussion so that the fundamental differences between them become obscured. This obfuscation was corrected by the leading Privy Council case of *Royal Brunei Airlines Sdn Bhd* v *Tan* [1995] 2 AC 378.

An example of knowing assistance was demonstrated in *Agip (Africa) Ltd* v *Jackson* [1990] Ch 265, [1991] Ch 547, in which the defendant firm of accountants assisted in the laundering of funds misappropriated from the plaintiff company. Millett J stressed that it was not necessary for this head of liability that the defendant should have received any part of the trust property. He concluded (at 292): 'The basis of the stranger's liability is not receipt of trust property but participation in a fraud.' Dishonesty was essential: at least categories (a), (b) or (c) on the *Baden Delvaux* scale. Millett J considered the facts and the use of shell bank accounts and 'cut-outs', and concluded (at 294):

> [The defendants] are professional men. They obviously knew that they were laundering money. They were consciously helping their clients to make arrangements designed for the purpose of concealment from, *inter alios*, the plaintiffs. It must have been obvious to them that their clients could not afford their activities to see the light of day. Secrecy is the badge of fraud. They must have realised at least that their clients *might* be involved in a fraud on the plaintiffs.

The Court of Appeal agreed.

Birks has consistently and vigorously argued that whereas knowing receipt is a cause of action in unjust enrichment, knowing assistance is a cause of action in the law of wrongs. He concludes ([1989] LMCLQ 296, at 334): 'The equitable liability for assisting fraud is virtually unintelligible without fault.' In *Royal Brunei Airlines Sdn Bhd* v *Tan* [1995] 2 AC 378, the airline appointed a travel company to act as its agent. Under the agreement the travel company was required to account to the airline for all the amounts received from the sale of tickets, and it expressly constituted was trustee of those moneys. In practice the company did not pay airline moneys into a separate account; rather they were paid into its current account and utilised in the ordinary course of business. When the travel company became insolvent, the airline sought to make good the shortfall in an action against the managing director and principal shareholder of the company, on the ground of knowing assistance. It was held that the company was in breach of trust in so using the money, that the managing director assisted in that breach of trust and that both the company and the managing director had acted dishonestly. The Privy Council, in an advice delivered by Lord Nicholls of Birkenhead, greatly clarified the law, insisting (at 386): 'Different considerations apply for the two heads of liability. Recipient liability is restitution-based: accessory liability is not.' The Privy Council rejected the traditional requirement, that the breach of trust or fiduciary duty was dishonest, as irrelevant to the liability of the accessory.

With regard to the state of mind of the accessory, the Privy Council accepted the majority judicial and juristic view that dishonesty or want to probity was required, effectively overruling *Selangor United Rubber Estates Ltd* v *Cradock (No. 3)* [1968] 1 WLR 1555, *Karak Rubber Co. Ltd* v *Burden (No. 2)* [1972] 1 WLR 602 and Peter Gibson J's view in *Baden Delvaux* [1993] 1 WLR 509, that all five points on the scale of knowledge would suffice for knowing assistance. Consistently with the approach in modern transactions in commercial law, the Privy Council insisted that honesty was an objective standard (at 389):

> Honesty, indeed, does have a strong subjective element in that it is a description of a type of conduct assessed in the light of what a person actually knew at the time, as distinct from what a reasonable person would have known or appreciated. Further, honesty and its counterpart, dishonesty, are mostly concerned with advertent conduct, not inadvertent conduct. Carelessness is not dishonesty. Thus for the most part dishonesty is to be equated with conscious impropriety. However, these subjective characteristics of honesty do not mean that individuals are free to set their own standards of honesty in particular circumstances. The standard of what constitutes honest conduct is not subjective. Honesty is not an optional scale, with higher or lower values according to the moral standards of each individual.

Most significantly in this factual context, the Privy Council concluded that an honest person does not 'deliberately close his eyes and ears, or deliberately not ask questions, lest he learn something he would rather not know, and then proceed regardless' (at 389).

Accordingly the Privy Council rechristened knowing assistance, *dishonest accessory liability*. It made it clear that the cause of action did not arise in unjust enrichment and that the usual response would be a presumably personal liability to make good the deficiency in the fund. Lord Nicholls concluded (at 392):

> Drawing the threads together, their Lordships' overall conclusion is that dishonesty is a necessary ingredient of accessory liability. It is also a sufficient ingredient. A liability in equity to make good resulting loss attaches to a person who dishonestly procures or assists in a breach of trust or fiduciary obligation. It is not necessary that, in addition, the trustee or fiduciary was acting dishonestly, although this will usually be so where the third party who is assisting him is acting dishonestly. 'Knowingly' is better avoided as a defining ingredient of the principle, and in the context of this principle the *Baden* [1993] 1 WLR 509 scale of knowledge is best forgotten.

It has therefore been authoritatively laid down that dishonest accessory liability is not a cause of action in subtractive unjust enrichment. It is an equitable wrong, analogous to the common law torts of deceit or inducing breach of contract. Accordingly, a compensatory measure, in the form of equitable compensation, will usually be the appropriate response. However, as an equitable wrong, a claim to benefits received as a result of dishonest assistance would in principle be available. For example, any fees earned by the defendant firm of accountants in *Agip* v *Jackson* might be the subject of a disgorgement order. The *Tan* test was applied *Brinks Ltd (formerly Brink's Mat Ltd)* v *Abu-Saleh (No. 3)* [1996] CLC 133, with the result that a wife who assisted her husband in what she believed were tax-evasion motivated trips to Switzerland, but was unaware she was helping to launder the proceeds of the well-known bullion robbery, was exculpated. For discussion, see Birks [1996] LMCLQ 1.

29.7 PRACTICAL ISSUES

Allegations of knowledge or notice, actual or constructive, such as are alleged to render a defendant liable to account, are matters which must be specifically pleaded, with full particulars of the fact and matters which are said to given rise to the actual or constructive knowledge/notice: CPR, PD 16, para. 10.2(5). The onus of proof may be crucial in these cases. The weight of authority in equity is that to render a party liable for what is called knowing receipt there must be affirmative proof by the claimant that that party had such knowledge, actual or constructive. The issue is not finally settled as there much academic support that the burden of proof should be reversed, and that the relevance of the defendant's state of mind is pertinent to the availability or otherwise of a defence of good faith purchase. Accordingly, the onus of proof appears to be a battleground for all future cases concerned with receipt-based liability. In contrast, with respect to dishonest accessory liability, it seems clear from the tenor of *Royal Brunei Airlines Sdn Bhd* v *Tan* that the onus of proof is upon the claimant. Further, this must be correct as a matter of principle if the true analogy is with torts such as deceit.

29.8 CONCLUSION

Dishonest accessory liability has been properly characterised as falling outside the rules of subtractive unjust enrichment. This brings some clarity to this corner of the law. In contrast, receipt-based liability in equity requires more fundamental consideration. However, the Law Commission's review has been put on hold: Harpum, in Cornish, 247, at 249. It seems that the cause of action is constituted upon receipt as with the common law action for money had and received. The trail from the claimant to the defendant is normally supplied by a successful application of the equitable rules of tracing, at least in the case of remoter recipients. What has proved most difficult is discerning the relevant state of mind of the recipient, and indeed what particular states of mind are relevant.

For Birks, the equity cases sew confusion in that the main concern of the law of subtractive unjust enrichment is the integrity of the claimant's decision to transfer wealth. The equity cases ignore this claimant-sided concern, switching to a defendant-sided or fault-orientated strategy. Birks argues for a fundamental reformulation of the authorities at common law and in equity to support a general principle of strict liability (with the cause of action being ignorance or mistake), subject to generous defences of good faith purchase and change of position. The state of the defendant's mind should be relevant only to defences: [1989] LMCLQ 296. In contrast, the judicial instinct when faced with claims to set aside transactions with those not party to the misappropriation of assets has been to insist upon affirmative proof of knowledge, meaning actual knowledge or want of probity. It may be that the policy favouring transactional security which underlies this approach may prevail in the context of remoter recipients. Strict liability does not have the support of all academic commentators: Cranston, *Principles of Banking Law* (1997), 205–12.

In conclusion, it is submitted that it is necessary to draw a distinction between volunteer recipients of misapplied funds, and those who have received benefits in return for valuable consideration. The former should be strictly liable to refund the moneys (the cause of action being mistake or ignorance), subject to the application of change of position. The latter should also be prima facie strictly liable, though entitled to the protection of the defence of good faith purchase. In ordinary commercial transactions with those not implicated in the misapplication of funds, it is submitted that the standard should be one also of honesty, although an objective approach to honesty as essayed in *Tan* should be adopted. If it were felt necessary, the policy of promoting transactional security could be further enhanced by a presumption of good faith, where it is pleaded, requiring the claimant to rebut the plea by leading affirmative evidence of bad faith. This would be consistent with the analogous statutory presumptions in the Bills of Exchange Act 1882, s. 90 and the Companies Act 1985, s. 35A(2)(c).

FURTHER READING

Asterisks indicate especially useful works.

Goff and Jones, 742–46
C. Harpum, 'The Stranger as Constructive Trustee' (1986) 102 LQR 114; 267
*P. Birks, 'Misdirected Funds: Restitution from the Recipient' [1989] LMCLQ 296
Sir Peter Millett, 'Tracing the Proceeds of Fraud' (1991) 107 LQR 71
P. Birks, 'Persistent Problems in Misdirected Money: A Quintet' [1993] LMCLQ 218
*C. Harpum, 'The Basis of Equitable Liability' in P. Birks (ed) *The Frontiers of Liability: Volume 1* (1994), 9, at 17–25
R. Cranston, *Principles of Banking Law* (1997), at 205–12
*Lord Nicholls, 'Knowing Receipt: The Need for a New Landmark' in Cornish, 231–45
P. Birks, 'Accessory Liability' [1996] LMCLQ 1

30   Proprietary Claims in Equity

30.1   INTRODUCTION

It would be perfectly possible for the law of restitution to be exclusively part of the law of obligations. Indeed, the discussion so far in this book has been largely concerned with *in personam* claims. However, in recent years English law has been increasingly promiscuous in its recognition of restitutionary proprietary claims. A key factor in this has been a tendency to conflate the measure of relief question with the nature of relief question. Some of the cases concern claims to the value surviving where that sum exceeds the value received. The desire to strip both wrongdoers and volunteer recipients of what are considered undeserved benefits has been seen as necessarily linked to the award of a proprietary remedy. This is fallacious. It is perfectly possible as a matter of principle to award a claimant the value surviving including profits in a purely personal claim. The other motive for claiming a proprietary remedy is the claimant will obtain priority upon the insolvency of the defendant. Again the restitutionary claimant has won favour, often being character-ised as not having taken the risk of the defendant's insolvency.

It must be recalled that what are being advanced are claims that a new proprietary interest should be recognised by the court. The distinction between *pure* proprietary claims and *restitutionary* proprietary claims is fundamental. The former concern recovery of the very same asset which the claimant has lost, and as a matter of classification are the concern of the law of property. In respect of the latter, it is axiomatic that the asset being claimed was not previously the property of the claimant. The recognition of such a brand new interest at the end of the tracing process adds yet one more level of artifice. It will be seen that the development of restitutionary proprietary remedies has developed in an instrumental and haphazard way, often simply rewarding the claimant in his or her pursuit of profits or in his or her desire to escape the status of being an unsecured creditor. The sceptical view that the very existence of restitutionary proprietary claims detracts from the much trumpeted rationality of the law of unjust enrichment has much to commend it. It will be necessary to consider separately three branches of the subject in which proprietary claims have succeeded:

(a)   subtractive unjust enrichment;
(b)   restitution for wrongs; and
(c)   complex entitlements.

A necessary contextual starting point is to consider the relevant principles and policies of insolvency law.

30.2   THE PHILOSOPHY OF INSOLVENCY LAW

Professor Goode has recently subjected the vexed topic of restitutionary proprietary claims to a sophisticated analysis in the context of the general principles of insolvency law. Goode stresses the fundamental significance of the distinction between property and obligations. He argues (in Cornish, 63, at 65):

> At the heart of insolvency law lies the principle of *pari passu* distribution: all creditors share and share alike. Every proprietary right given against assets held by the debtor reduces the value of its estate available for distribution and, as a corollary, the interest of unsecured creditors in the liquidation process and the value of insolvency law itself.

In respect of consensual transactions, insolvency law provides clear regulation of permissible proprietary rights and remedies. A secured creditor in consensual transactional law is one who has bargained for security. The presence of bargain, value and notice provides the justification for his proprietary entitlement in the event of insolvency. Consensual charges over corporate assets are liable to be set aside if no new value is provided, or if the charge is not perfected by registration (Insolvency Act 1986, ss. 238–245, 423; Companies Act 1985, s. 395, 420–421). In stark contrast, no similar statutory regulation of non-consensual proprietary interests exists. It is a matter for judge-made law. There is always a danger that by awarding a restitutionary proprietary remedy, especially where a defendant is solvent, a judge may overlook the implications of his decision in the wider context of insolvency law. Every recognition of a new form of restitutionary proprietary claim shrinks the assets of insolvent estates and diminishes the centrality of the cardinal principle of insolvency law that creditors should be treated alike and should share rateably their common misfortune.

  For discussion, see R. Goode, 'Proprietary Restitutionary Claims' in Cornish, 65–77, especially at 64–67; F. Oditah, 'Assets and the Treatment of Claims in Insolvency' (1992) 108 LQR 459; D. Paciocco, 'The Remedial Constructive Trust: A Principled Basis for Priorities Over Creditors' (1989) 68 Can Bar Rev 314. A recent decision of the Court of Appeal suggests increasing judicial sensitivity to those issues (*Re Polly Peck International plc (in administration) (No. 2), Marangos Hotel Co. Ltd* v *Stone* [1998] 3 All ER 812).

30.3   THE PROPRIETARY REMEDIES INTRODUCED

There are three main remedies which may be claimed. First, the constructive trust. As its name suggests, this is a trust imposed by law which reverses the unjust enrichment of the defendant by constituting him constructive trustee of an asset for the claimant as beneficiary. It bears little resemblance to an express trust (indeed it shares the same absence of family resemblance as between so-called quasi-contract and genuinely consensual bargains). The main trustee-like obligation on the defendant is to transfer the beneficial interest to the claimant in accordance with the principle in *Saunders* v *Vautier* (1841) 4 Beav 115, 49 ER 282; aff'd Cr & Ph 240, 41 ER 482. With regard to the motives for seeking a proprietary claim, the constructive trust fully rewards both by granting both priority upon insolvency and an entitlement to any profits. English equity lawyers still cling to the pretence that what is created by operation of law is an *institutional* constructive trust, rather than the remedial conception of the constructive trust which obtains in North America: compare *Restatement of the Law of Restitution*, §160, with Sir Peter Millett in Cornish, at 199–200. The view taken in this text is that where constructive trusts are imposed to reverse the unjust enrichment of the defendant, and it is done for instrumental reasons to impose a more stringent burden on the defendant than a merely personal duty to account, such trusts are accordingly operating as a remedy. This is consistent with the dichotomy introduced by our sixth question as to the nature of appropriate relief (see 1.2).

It should be observed that the constructive trust has proved to be a such a flexible judicial device that its boundaries cannot be regarded as fixed within the province of the law of restitution. In *Carl-Zeiss Stiftung* v *Herbert Smith & Co. (No. 2)* [1969] 2 Ch 276, Edmund-Davies LJ stated (at 300–301):

> English law provides no clear and all-embracing definition of a constructive trust. Its boundaries have been left perhaps deliberately vague, so as not to restrict the court by technicalities in deciding what the justice of a particular case may demand. But it appears that in this country unjust enrichment or other personal advantage is not a *sine qua non*. . . . Nevertheless, the concept of unjust enrichment has its value as providing one example among many of what, for lack of a better phrase, I would call 'want of probity', a feature which recurs through and seems to connect all those cases drawn to the court's attention where a constructive trust has been held to exist.

Elias has advanced a detail taxonomy of constructive trusts as furthering one of three aims:

(a)   'perfection', or the fulfilment of expectations;
(b)   'restitution';
(c)   'reparation', or what one might term protecting detrimental reliance.

It has to be accepted that all manifestations of the constructive trust cannot be seen as restitutionary (*cf* Waters, *Constructive Trusts* (1964)). However, in this text we are concerned only with the restitutionary manifestations of the constructive trust. For discussion, see Elias, *Explaining Constructive Trusts* (1990); Beatson, 254–55.

Less well-known, but of increasing practical significance, is the equitable lien or charge. This corresponds to the consensual floating charge in the same way as the constructive trust corresponds to the express trust. It is a charge imposed by law to prevent the unjust enrichment of the defendant. It resembles a consensual charge in that it entitles the claimant as chargee to look to a particular asset belonging to the defendant chargor as security for the payment of his obligation. The asset must be appropriated to the payment of the debt, and only if the obligation is discharged does any surplus belong to the defendant. The term 'equitable lien' is preferred by some to reflect the fact that it is a security created by law, rather than by consent. However, judges use the words 'charge' and 'lien' interchangeably.

More significantly, there are two distinct manifestations of the equitable lien or charge. First, there is a charge for a quantified amount, which is usually measured by the value received by the defendant at the expense of the claimant (for the sake of clarity referred to as the 'equitable lien'). Secondly, there is a charge which entitles the claimant to a proportionate share expressed as a percentage or a fraction of a particular asset (hereafter referred to as a 'proportionate share claim'). Both manifestations of the equitable charge entitle a claimant to priority upon insolvency. However, the ordinary equitable lien will not entitle a claimant to any share of profits derived from the charged asset, whereas the proportionate share claim will entitle the chargee to a share of any profits (although the charged asset may go down as well as up in value).

Lastly, for completeness, subrogation can operate as a restitutionary proprietary remedy. See Chapter 22.

30.4   CLAIMING AFTER TRACING

It seems to be widely accepted that a restitutionary proprietary claim is most defensible where the claimant's cause of action lies in subtractive unjust enrichment, at least where it is within the *vitiation* branch of non-voluntary transfer. Most of the classic authorities concern the misapplication of trust moneys. Nowadays the ground for restitution would explicitly be mistake or ignorance, and accordingly it cannot readily be said that the claimant has taken the risk of the defendant's insolvency. The paradigm application of restitutionary proprietary remedies has been as a result of the successful conduct of the tracing process by such a claimant.

In the seminal case of *In re Hallett's Estate* (1880) 13 Ch D 696, a solicitor wrongfully confused the proceeds of bonds belonging to a client, which he had sold without authority, with his own money. Sir George Jessel MR discussed the situation where a fiduciary made a purchase using money derived from the claimant (at 709):

> the beneficial owner has a right to elect either to take the property purchased, or to hold it as a security for the amount of the trust money laid out in the purchase; or, as we generally express it, he is entitled at his election either to take the property, or to have a charge on the property for the amount of the trust money. But in the second case, where a trustee has mixed the money with his own, there is this distinction, that the *cestui que trust*, or beneficial owner, can no longer elect to take the property, because it is no longer bought with the trust-money simply and purely, but with a mixed fund. He is, however, still entitled to a charge on the property purchased, for the amount of the trust-money laid out in the purchase; and that charge is quite independent of the fact of the amount laid out by the trustee.

A successful claim here depended on the establishment of, first, the fact that the defendant was in a fiduciary position and, secondly, the successful completion of the tracing exercise. Note that the appropriate remedy was a constructive trust or equitable lien where value traceably derived from the claimant was exclusively used in the purchase of the new property. In contrast, where a blended fund was used to purchase the property, the innocent claimant was entitled to an equitable lien which gave him priority over the fiduciary defendant. Similarly, it is clear that the claimant may establish an equitable lien over a bank account into which value traceably subtracted from him has been paid.

The effect of the equitable lien, which in practice can be as stringent as a constructive trust, is demonstrated by *In re Oatway* [1903] 2 Ch 356, in which the claimant, who had been deprived of some £3,000 in breach of trust, was held entitled to an equitable lien over shares worth some £2,457 which had been purchased with a mixture of the proceeds of trust money and the fiduciary's own money. In effect the claimant was entitled to the full value of the shares, which was less than the value received. The result is different where the defendant is an innocent party. It was held in *In re Diplock* [1948] Ch 465, at 524, that:

> Where an innocent volunteer (as distinct from a purchaser for value without notice) mixes 'money' of his own with 'money' which in equity belongs to another person, or is found in possession of such a mixture, although that other person cannot claim a charge on the mass superior to the claim of the volunteer he is entitled, nevertheless, to a charge ranking *pari passu* with the claim of the volunteer.

Whereas an innocent claimant takes priority over a fiduciary owner, he ranks equally with a competing innocent party. This is an application of the proportionate share remedy.

In *In re Diplock*, it was established that the pre-conditions of breach of fiduciary relationship and a successful completion of the tracing exercise were necessary before the claim could be made. Even where these were satisfied, the *in rem* claims were not wholly successful. Where money had been spent on land or buildings belonging to the charities, it was held that a declaration of charge would not produce an equitable result. One explanation of this is that the money could not properly be traced, although this is not entirely convincing (see 28.3.2). Alternatively, it has been suggested that the alterations to the charities' buildings did not constitute an enrichment; Birks, 371–72. A further view is that expenditure was an early recognition of the defence of change of position: Goff and Jones, 110–11, and contrast Birks, 411–12. For further discussion see 32.4. However, the actual decision in *Re Diplock* was that it was inequitable to grant a restitutionary proprietary remedy in such circumstances, which reinforces the remedial nature of the equitable charge in this context, and reminds us that the exercise of equitable remedies is always discretionary. The equitable lien is clearly a powerful remedy where there has been wrongful mixing and substitution of assets. As Hayton comments in Birks (1995), at 9: 'The charge is all-pervasive over the amalgam and then any constituent elements split off from such amalgam.'

30.5   CLAIMING PROFITS

One potential advantage of laying claim to the value surviving is that the product of what traceably derives from the claimant is worth more than the value received. While it is possible to make a personal claim to the value received (as recently exemplified in *Trustee of the Property of F. C. Jones & Sons Ltd* v *Jones* [1997] Ch 159), most commonly in English law the vehicle for this has been an equitable proprietary remedy. In *In re Tilley's Will Trusts* [1967] Ch 1179, the defendant wrongfully mixed trust money with her own resources. She profited from speculative property transactions. One of the beneficiaries sought to persuade the court to award her the proportionate share of the value surviving (including profits) which exceeded the value received. Ungoed-Thomas J was clearly cautious about the implications of the proportionate share claim. It was rightly conceded by the defendant (at 1189) that:

> if a trustee wrongly uses trust money to pay the whole of the purchase price in respect of the purchase of an asset a beneficiary can elect either to treat the purchased asset as trust property or to treat the purchased asset as security for the recouping of the trust money. It was further conceded that this right of election by a beneficiary also applies where the trust asset is purchased by a trustee in part out of his money and in part out of the trust moneys, so that he may, if he wishes, require the asset to be treated as trust property with regard to that proportion of it which the trust moneys contributed to its purchase.

However, on a close examination of the facts, the judge was satisfied that the trustee was not deliberately using trust moneys in the course of her property speculation. While the moneys were wrongfully mixed in her bank account, it was not relied upon for any of the purchases. The judge held that an objective test was to be preferred to a subjective test, in respect of where the trust money was used in the profitable transaction. Even so, Ungoed-Thomas J was satisfied that the breach of trust went no further than the wrongful mixing. Accordingly he held the trustee liable to account only for the value received, namely £2,237. There was no doubt about the trustee's solvency, and therefore any question about an equitable lien was academic. The case neatly illustrates that the value surviving may exceed the value received: Birks, 76, 366–70. However, it also demonstrates judicial squeamishness about the potential windfall to a claimant who has contributed nothing to the increase in the value of the asset. The case may be regarded as anomalous in that it departs from the usually stringent standards of equity in policing the conduct of trustees. Or, perhaps, preferably, it may be seen as emphatically divorcing the result of the tracing exercise from the resulting remedy. Tracing yielded two different measures, namely the value received and the value surviving. Here, where a trustee was not guilty of any conscious impropriety and the evidence of a causal link between the value received and the resulting profits was weak, the judge was not prepared to grant a with-profits proprietary remedy.

This should be contrasted with the stringent approach in *Boardman* v *Phipps* [1967] 2 AC 46, where the defendants were not even trustees, and the common law case of *Jones* v *Jones* in respect of a recipient whose good faith was not in issue. For discussion, see Hayton, in Birks (1995), 5–6, at 10–11. Most recently the issue divided the Court of Appeal in *Foskett* v *McKeown* [1998] Ch 265, where a trustee misapplied some £20,000 of trust moneys to maintain his life assurance policy. One his death this yielded over £1 million. The majority held that the beneficiaries were entitled only to an equitable lien to secure the sums which could be traced into the payment of the premiums. Sir Richard Scott V-C explicitly rejected a proportionate share claim, stressing that the beneficiaries of the policy were innocent. Hobhouse LJ stressed that the life insurance element of the policy amounting to £1million (as opposed to the investment element) had been met by earlier payments by the trustee out of his own moneys. Morritt LJ dissented, favouring a proportionate share claim. The case is currently on appeal to the House of Lords.

30.6 RETENTION OF TITLE CLAUSES

So far it has been seen that the process of tracing in equity and the proprietary claims that can be advanced as a result have been confined to the familiar territory of equity lawyers in supervising the stewardship of trustees and persons in analogous fiduciary positions. During the twentieth century the principles migrated into ordinary commercial practice. Perhaps the landmark case which speeded this transplantation was *Aluminum Industrie Vaassen BV* v *Romalpa Aluminum Ltd* [1976] 1 WLR 676. The explosive impact of the decision was noted at the time in influential articles in the *Law Quarterly Review* by Goode and the *Modern Law Review* by Goodhart and Jones. In the case, a Dutch seller supplied aluminum foil to an English buyer upon its standard terms. These reserved title to the goods until the buyer had met all the liabilities it owed to the seller, and further made elaborate provision for the storage of the goods, any product manufactured with the goods and the proceeds of any sub-sale. Upon the insolvency of the English buyer, the Dutch company claimed the return of unprocessed aluminum foil and the proceeds of sub-sales.

The first holding was that it could reclaim the unprocessed foil and that it had a superior claim over the receiver. This holding was novel but as a matter of legal principle is relatively uncontroversial, as a right to reserve property in the goods is contained in s. 19 of the Sale of Goods Act 1979. Such clauses, whether confined to the debt generated by the original contract of sale or (as in the *Romalpa* case), covering all the liabilities of the buyer, are now common in practice and enforced by the courts (*Armour* v *Thyssen Edelstahlwerke AG* [1991] 2 AC 339).

The second holding was more controversial and has received a frostier judicial and juristic reception. It was held on the basis of *In re Hallett's Estate* (1880) 13 Ch D 696, that the sellers were entitled to trace the proceeds into the receiver's bank account and further to a charge over that account to the extent of some £35,000 received in respect of the sale of its property. It was conceded by the buyers that they were bailees of the goods under the terms of the retention of title clause. This was held to give rise to a sufficient fiduciary relationship to trace and claim in equity. Mocatta J felt obliged to follow the passage in *In re Hallett* (at 710–11): 'If the bailee sells the goods bailed, the bailor can in Equity follow the proceeds, and can follow the proceeds wherever they can be distinguished, either being actually kept separate, or being mixed up with other moneys.' Nothing in *In re Diplock* [1948] Ch 465 detracted from this. Further, s. 95 of the Companies Act 1948 (now s. 395 of the Companies Act 1985) had no application because the proceeds of the sub-sales always belonged in equity to the plaintiffs. It was not a registrable charge over the debt. The decision was upheld by the Court of Appeal, Roskill LJ finding no difficulty in applying the principles in *In re Hallett* to the present facts. (It should be observed that the judgments in the case were given by commercial lawyers rather than equity lawyers, and that rather more time was spent on the issues of the incorporation of terms and contractual interpretation than on the issues of tracing and claiming in equity.)

The immediate reaction can be found in Goode, 'The Right to Trace and Its Impact in Commercial Transactions' (1976) 92 LQR 360, 528, at 547–52, 563–68, and Goodhart and Jones, 'The Infiltration of Equitable Doctrine into English Commercial Law' (1980) 43 MLR 489, at 501–13. A significant difference between the *Romalpa* case and the traditional equity authority is that the fiduciary relationship was constituted by the contractual matrix. The concession that the buyers were fiduciary bailees has subsequently been treated as a crucial factor, and therefore as a reason for not following the case. The intellectual assault upon the second holding in *Romalpa* began with *Re Bond Worth Ltd* [1980] Ch 228, which decided that a claim to resale proceeds was in effect a consensual floating charge and as such required registration under s. 95 of the Companies Act 1948 (now s. 395 of the Companies Act 1985).

It must be observed that most of the retention of title cases turn upon the particular interpretation of the clause. However, the clear trend of modern authority is to permit the supplier to reclaim unmixed and unmanufactured goods supplied. In contrast, the courts construe any claim to resale proceeds or to mixed and manufactured goods as an equitable floating charge which is void if not registered under the Companies Act. Perhaps the fundamental error in the second limb of the *Romalpa* case was the extension of doctrines used to reverse subtractive unjust enrichment (which are obligations imposed by law) to the arena of consensually created quasi-security devices. The modern approach is to treat proceeds and product claims as attempts to create security which are void if not perfected by notice to other creditors (*E. Pfeiffer Weikellerie-Weineinkauf GmbH* v *Arbuthnot Factors Ltd* [1988] 1 WLR 150; *Tatung (UK) Ltd* v *Galex Telesure Ltd* (1989) 5 BCC 325; *Compaq Computers Ltd* v *Abercorn Group Ltd* [1991] BCC 484). For discussion from the insolvency perspective see Goode in Cornish, at 66–67. See generally, G. McCormack, *Reservation of Title* (2nd edn, 1995) at 73–91 (on proceeds claims).

Accordingly, the conclusion is that the attempt in the *Romalpa* case to use the equitable charge to capture the proceeds of sub-sales of goods supplied on retention of title terms has foundered. The charge is seen more properly as a consensual floating one, which depends for its enforceability upon compliance with the companies legislation. In this particular context at least, the principles of insolvency law are respected.

30.7 PROPRIETARY CLAIMS IN CASES OF SUBTRACTIVE UNJUST ENRICHMENT

It seems to be widely accepted that a legitimate role for restitutionary proprietary remedies is to reverse unjust enrichment by subtraction, at least where the transfer was non-voluntary in the sense that the transferor's intention was vitiated. The policy rationale for this is to allow the restitutionary claimant to escape the consequences of the defendant's insolvency, because he is an involuntary creditor. The claimant has not taken the risk that the defendant will become insolvent in contrast, for example, to ordinary trade creditors who have contracts with the defendant, advancing sale credit or loan credit, knowing the risks. Such trade creditors could always bargain for security under the law of consensual security transactions. Similarly, suppliers of goods could sell only on retention of title terms. In the absence of bargained-for security, such creditors fall to be considered as part of the common body of unsecured creditors. The transferor who pays by mistake (see 30.7.1), or who is ignorant that wealth has haemorrhaged away, is therefore preferred as a matter of risk analysis.

The preferential position of this class of restitutionary claimant is sometimes contrasted with the position of other involuntary creditors, such as the victims of torts by the insolvent person. Such obligations, as with unjust enrichment, are imposed by law rather than voluntarily assumed. This argument proves not to be as strong as it may first appear to be, as it overlooks the statutory provisions which insolvency law has already made where an insolvent tortfeasor has insurance to cover his liabilities. In such cases statute grants the victim of the tort a direct claim against the insurance company: see the Third Parties (Rights Against Insurers) Act 1930 and s. 151 of the

Road Traffic Act 1988. It is probably the immaturity of the law of restitution which has meant that the priority of restitutionary claimants has not received the same attention in the statutory regime for insolvency as the rights of consensual creditors and the victims of torts.

The position of the mistaken payer must be contrasted with the claimant for failure of consideration (see 30.7.2). The latter claim is treated analogously to contractual claims for debt and damages. A person who advanced credit in the expectation of some bargained for counter-performance can be seen as having taken the risk of the payee's insolvency. The failure of consideration claimant is not an involuntary creditor.

For discussion, see Goff and Jones, 76–93; Paciocco, 'The Remedial Constructive Trust: A Principled Basis for Priorities Over Creditors' (1989) 68 Can Bar Rev 315; and Sherwin, 'Constructive Trusts and Bankruptcy' [1989] U Ill L Rev 297.

30.7.1 Mistaken payments

The sympathy to the restitutionary claimant whose intention to transfer has been vitiated was in evidence in the case of *Chase Manhattan Bank NA* v *Israel British Bank (London) Ltd* [1981] Ch 105. Chase, a New York bank, acting upon instructions, paid US\$ 2,000,687.50 to another bank via the New York clearing house system, for the defendant's account. Later on the same day, a second identical payment was made due to a clerical error on the part of an employee of Chase. The defendant, which was a bank based in London, learned of the mistaken payment two days later, and was found either to know that it was a mistaken payment or must have been put on enquiry that there had been a mistake. Within a month of the payment a petition was brought to wind up the defendant which was insolvent. If the plaintiff was confined to a merely personal claim, it had little hope of recovering the whole of its loss. The case obviously yielded a conflicts of law dimension, but it was common ground that the consequences of mistaken payment were to be determined in accordance with New York law as the *lex causae*, and that the procedural rights and remedies must be ascertained by English law as the *lex fori*. In the result, Goulding J held that the appropriate rules are the same under English law and New York law.

The case is a striking example of the dichotomy between tracing and claiming. However, it may be criticised in that Goulding J was asked to decide that a restitutionary proprietary claim would be available if the proceeds of the mistaken payment could be traced. The judge was not asked to decide whether on the facts of the particular case they could be traced. Goulding J accepted the plaintiff's case that the pleading of a mistake and the payment were sufficient. It was not necessary to plead and prove in detail the operation of the clearing house inter-bank payments system in New York, neither was it necessary to identify any particular chose in action or other property to which the plaintiff laid claim. Goulding J commented (at 121): 'when equitable rights are in question, the court does not encourage fine distinctions founded on the technicalities of financial machinery.' It is unsatisfactory that the court was prepared to hold that a restitutionary proprietary remedy was available when there was no evidence before it that anything could be identified as traceably derived from the plaintiff's wealth. It may well be that tracing was not the problem in this case, hence the focus upon the availability of a restitutionary proprietary claim.

The case is striking for two points in relation to the law of restitution. First, it supports the assertion that the fiduciary relationship requirement is an element of claiming rather than tracing. Goulding J found it necessary, in accordance with *In re Diplock* [1948] Ch 465 and *Sinclair v Brougham* [1914] AC 398, to treat it as an element of the claim. It is submitted that if the fiduciary relationship requirement still obtains, it makes more sense in relation to the claiming rather than the tracing part of the cause of action. Secondly, Goulding J was prepared to hold that it was not necessary that the breach of fiduciary duty took place before the value traced reached the defendant. Neither was it necessary that the fiduciary relationship should be based on a consensual transaction. Goulding J stated (at 119): 'It is enough that, as in *Sinclair v Brougham* [1914] AC 398, the payment into wrong hands itself gave rise to a fiduciary relationship.' No case better illustrates the instrumental use of the fiduciary relationship requirement. It is hard to see how the defendant bank became a fiduciary, especially given Goulding J's conclusion that it effectively became a trustee on the day of the payment, not on the day that it learnt of the mistaken payment. Goulding J accordingly concluded (at 119–20):

> a person who pays money to another under a factual mistake retains an equitable property in it and the conscience of that other is subjected to a fiduciary duty to respect his proprietary right.... Thus, in the belief that the point is not expressly covered by English authority and that *In re Diplock* does not conclude it by necessary implication, I hold that the equitable remedy of tracing is in principle available, on the ground of continuing proprietary interest, to a party who has paid money under a mistake of fact.

This case neatly illustrates both the incoherence and unprincipled nature of the fiduciary relationship requirement, and further the ability of judges to circumvent its restrictive approach in practice.

The better view is that in accordance with the principles outlined above, where a restitutionary claimant can traceably identify the value subtracted from him which he has paid as a result of the mistake, there is a strong case for awarding a restitutionary proprietary remedy if the defendant is insolvent. It may also be desirable that such a remedy should be capped at the level of the value received and should not yield any profits that have resulted from the receipt of the money (which should be kept for the defendant's general creditors). However, this straightforward approach is not yet English law.

Chase Manhattan has received much academic attention. In addition, in the leading case of *Westdeutsche Landesbank Girozentrale v Islington London Borough Council* [1996] AC 669, Lord Browne-Wilkinson attempted to reinterpret *Chase*

Manhattan in accordance with his own views. Lord Browne-Wilkinson concentrated on a fact which Goulding J had thought of little significance, that the mistake had been discovered almost immediately by the recipient bank. Lord Browne-Wilkinson did not accept that a fiduciary relationship arose upon receipt of the money, but believed the case might be defensible on the basis that the conscience of the recipient was affected when it discovered the mistake and failed to take immediate steps to rectify the error (at 715). The result of *Westdeutsche* is that the authority of *Chase Manhattan* on the fiduciary relationship point is now highly suspect. That case also suggests a restrictive approach to proprietary claims where the cause of actions is based upon failure of consideration.

30.7.2   Failure of consideration

Whereas it has been argued that the restitutionary claimant whose intention has been vitiated has a strong argument in favour of a proprietary remedy in the event of the defendant's insolvency, the position of the claimant whose intention was qualified is less compelling. As has been stated at 30.7 above, a person who advances his claim on the basis of failure of consideration is more analogous to the ordinary trade creditor who has extended sale credit or loan credit to the defendant. This is illustrated by recent leading discussion by the Privy Council in *Re Goldcorp Exchange Ltd* [1995] 1 AC 74. Goldcorp was a New Zealand company dealing in gold coins and ingots as consumer products. More than a thousand small investors entered into contracts with *Goldcorp* for the purchase of gold bullion for future delivery. They received a 'certificate of ownership' stating that they had the right to delivery of their purchases on seven days' notice and payment of delivery charges. The contracts provided that *Goldcorp* would store and insure the bullion for free. The metal was stored on an unallocated basis, but it was represented that Goldcorp's stocks of bullion were always sufficient to meet all the contracts and that they were audited by Peat Marwick, the well-known firm of accountants. The company became hopelessly insolvent. Its bank held a floating charge over all the company's assets securing the liabilities of the company to it. The bank called in the receivers and its floating charge crystallised. The bank's secured debt exceeded all the assets of the company, including the unallocated bullion. There had been no appropriation to particular non-allocated investors' contracts. Accordingly the Privy Council held that no property passed to the non-allocated claimants in the bullion under the contract of sale in accordance with s. 18 of the Sale of Goods Act 1908 (New Zealand) corresponding to s. 16 of the Sale of Goods Act 1979 (UK), which provided that property cannot pass in unascertained goods.

The claimants further argued that they were entitled to a remedial constructive trust or restitutionary proprietary remedy over the company's bullion stocks, representing the value of the purchase moneys paid. Lord Mustill was sceptical of the claimants' attempt to label the company as a fiduciary. He observed (at 98): 'the essence of a fiduciary relationship is that it creates obligations of a different character from those deriving from the contract itself.' Even if the company were a fiduciary, it was difficult to circumvent the fact that the company had not done what it had promised to do, i.e., to maintain a separate and sufficient stock of bullion. The contractual matrix did not require the company keep separate all its stocks of bullion to fulfil the contracts of the unallocated claimants. The company was not unjustly enriched by the obtaining of bullion. Neither did it wrongfully interfere with any subsisting trust. Accordingly there was no claim of a restitutionary proprietary character over the company's assets in order to remedy the fact that the company was unable to do what it had promised to do because of its intervening insolvency.

Alternatively the claimants sought to pursue their purchase moneys into the general assets of the company. First, the Privy Council rejected an argument, by analogy with *Barclays Bank Ltd* v *Quistclose Investments Ltd* [1970] AC 567 and in *In re Kayford Ltd* [1975] 1 WLR 279, that the payments were impressed with a continuing beneficial interest in favour of the claimants, as there was nothing in the contractual matrix to support such a finding. The company was free to dispose of purchase moneys as it saw fit. Secondly, an argument based on three vitiating factors, namely misrepresentation, mistake and total failure of consideration, also failed. The misrepresentation claim was flawed as there had been no attempt to avoid the contract; indeed to date the claimants had been clamouring to enforce the contract. Similar considerations applied to mistake, of which it could also be said that there was no operative mistake in that the claimants were correct in believing that they were bound to pay the company the purchase moneys. Presumably, there was simply a misprediction: that the company would perform. Lastly, with regard to total failure of consideration, Lord Mustill said that in the meantime the claimants did have the benefit of a contract for the sale of unascertained goods. On this point the reasoning of the Privy Council is flawed in that it appears to assume the correctness of the fallacy in *Chandler* v *Webster* [1904] 1 KB 493. As is now recognised, the appropriate consideration is not the promise, but rather the promised performance. Here the claimants had received nothing of what they had bargained for. The inability of the defendant company to perform its obligations due to its insolvency, did give rise to a failure of consideration.

However, the decision of the Privy Council can be supported on two distinct grounds. First, there had been no termination for breach by the claimants. Rather, they had sought to enforce their contractual entitlements through the courts. Secondly, and more pertinently in this context, a restitutionary claimant on the ground of failure of consideration should not as a matter of principle be entitled to a restitutionary proprietary claim. The claimants were voluntary creditors who, by not bargaining for security, had taken the risk of the defendant's insolvency.

Lastly, it should be observed that Lord Mustill on behalf of the Privy Council could not see any room for the operation of a remedial constructive trust in this context, while recognising that there was room for further development: 'remedial restitutionary rights may prove in the future to be a valuable instrument of justice' (at 104).

The reasoning of *Goldcorp* reproduces the decision in *Re Wait* [1927] 1 Ch 656, in which the Court of Appeal held that the pre-paying buyer of an identified quantity of wheat forming part of a bulk cargo had no claim to the wheat upon the insolvency of the defendant seller. The Court of Appeal further rejected arguments that the buyer had obtained some kind of equitable interest in the cargo. In the absence of any manifestation to create a distinct equitable interest, the provisions of ss. 16–18 of the Sale of Goods Act 1893 exhaustively stated that the proprietary relationships between the sellers and buyers. The case is a well-known rejection of the infiltration of equitable principles into ordinary commercial transactions. However, the result in the case would be different in the light of statutory reform of the relevant rules of sale of goods and property law introduced by the Sale of Goods (Amendment) Act 1995, which introduced new ss. 20A and 20B into the Sale of Goods Act 1979. These constitute the pre-paying purchaser of part of an identified bulk a tenant in common of the bulk and provide detailed rules in relation to disputes between sellers and competing buyers. The detail will be found in discussions of sale of goods and property law. However, it can be observed that such provisions would not assist claimants like those in *Goldcorp*, or in the similar English case of *In re London Wine Co. (Shippers) Ltd* [1986] PCC 121, as there was no identified bulk in those cases. In both cases the goods were wholly unascertained. The boundaries of the property law identified in the *London Wine* case have been stretched in *Re Staplyton Fletcher Ltd* [1995] 1 All ER 192.

In relation to the law of unjust enrichment and restitutionary proprietary claims, however, it is clear that where the claim is one for failure of consideration, arising out of breach of contract, a constructive trust or an equitable charge should not be readily available.

30.7.3   Void contracts

The leading discussion is that of the House of Lords in *Westdeutsche Landesbank Girozentrale* v *Islington London Borough Council* [1996] AC 669, which concerned a void interest rate swap agreement. As has been argued above (see 12.2.1), the cause of action in that case is best seen as being failure of consideration or mistake. The House of Lords unanimously held that the claimant bank should not be entitled to a restitutionary proprietary remedy, this time advanced under the guise of a resulting trust. Lord Goff of Chieveley commented that both parties entered into a commercial transaction, which had for technical reasons been found to be void *ab initio*. Accordingly each party which entitled to recover money at common law, on the ground in his Lordship's view of failure of consideration. Lord Goff continued (at 684):

> why should the plaintiff bank been given the additional benefits which flow from a proprietary claim, for example the benefit of achieving priority in the event of the defendant's insolvency? After all, it has entered into a commercial transaction, and so taken the risk of the defendant's insolvency, just like the defendant's other creditors who have contracted with it, not to mention other creditors to whom the defendant may be liable to pay damages in tort.

Lord Goff further observed that where money was paid on a conditional basis the payee was free to use it as he saw fit, and may well have disposed of the value received before failure of consideration. The money would presumably be untraceable in such circumstances. See also Lord Browne-Wilkinson (at 707).

After *Kleinwort Benson Ltd* v *Lincoln City Council* [1999] 2 AC 349, the money was presumably recoverable on the alternative basis of mistake of law. Despite this alternative analysis, it is submitted that in such circumstances the transferor was a risk-taker, for the reasons adumbrated by Lord Goff, and accordingly should not be entitled to a proprietary claim. First, the 'voluntary assumption of risk' argument still applies despite re-characterisation of the claim as based on mistake of law. Secondly, the mistake of law identified by the majority in that case has itself proven controversial.

30.8 RESTITUTION FOR WRONGS AND CONSTRUCTIVE TRUSTS

Restitutionary proprietary remedies have not been confined to the realm of subtractive unjust enrichment. The constructive trust has been used to strip wrongdoers of their ill-gotten gains within the law of restitution for wrongs. The leading case is now *Attorney-General for Hong Kong* v *Reid* [1994] 1 AC 324. In *Macmillan Inc.* v *Bishopgate Investment Trust plc (No. 3)* [1995] 1 WLR 978, Millett J stated (at 988–89):

> The English law of restitution makes a fundamental distinction between the unjust enrichment of the defendant which is occasioned by depriving the plaintiff of his property and enrichment which results from a wrong done to the plaintiff by the defendant. In the first category of case the plaintiff's restitutionary claim is said to have a proprietary base. The enrichment of the defendant is at the direct expense of the plaintiff and is matched by a corresponding diminution of his assets. The plaintiff brings the claim in order to recover his own property and must succeed, if at all, by virtue of his own title. In the latter class of case his claim arises from a breach of fiduciary or other obligation on the part of the defendant. The distinction is that drawn by equity between a claim of an equitable owner to recover his property, or compensation for the failure to restore it, from a person into whose hands it has come and the claim by a plaintiff in respect of a breach of fiduciary obligation owed to him. In the former case he relies upon his continuing equitable interest in the property under an express or resulting trust; in the latter, upon an equity between the parties which may in appropriate circumstances give rise to a constructive trust. The distinction, which is crucial, may have been lost sight of in the language of some of the more recent decisions on knowing receipt.

Leaving to one side Lord Millett's individual views on the precise characterisation of the trust arising by operation of law, it is clear that the constructive trust has been used as a tool of disgorgement within restitution for wrongs. There is some confusion caused by the loose terminology sometimes employed, whereby a personal account is misleadingly said to render the defendant accountable *as a constructive trustee.* The italicised words appear to add nothing of substance which detracts from the personal nature of the liability to account. However, the reference to constructive trusteeship has sometimes been mistaken for a reference to a substantive constructive trust. This has made little difference in the cases where the error has occurred, as the solvency of the defendant was not in question. However, it cannot be supported in principle as accountability as a constructive trustee is distinct from a constructive trust. In the former category there is no trust property and no particular asset or assets to which a constructive trust could attach.

There have been attempts to justify the use of constructive trust as a weapon of disgorgement on the basis of principle. These have proved unsuccessful. The only justifications for the use of constructive trust in this area are the policies of punishment and deterrence. The courts are motivated to punish the individual recalcitrant fiduciary and to set an example for others in the same position. Whether these policies support some of the broader propositions in the cases is a matter for debate.

30.8.1   Breach of fiduciary duty

Breach of fiduciary duty can give rise to a number of remedial responses. Equity's particular concern with those who manage the affairs or property of others, such as trustees and company directors, made it particularly suspicious of the temptations open to those it labelled fiduciaries. The factor of deterrence has weighed heavily, to the extent of having worked injustice in some individual cases. The question here is to what extent proprietary relief is available. Clearly, where a transaction between a fiduciary and his principal is rescinded as a result of breach of fiduciary duty, rescission may have proprietary effect. However, the proprietary nature of rescission is limited by the bars which are characteristic of the operation of that remedy, including the intervention of third party rights and lapse of time. These reduce the impact of proprietary relief on third parties. Further, rescission here could be alternatively analysed as proceeding on the basis of vitiated voluntariness, usually misrepresentation or non-disclosure by the fiduciary. Such relief would be consistent with the principles outlined above. The cause of action can equally been seen as arising in subtractive unjust enrichment, as in restitution for wrongs.

It is a different matter when we consider the fiduciary's duty to account for secret profits which is explicable only in terms of restitution for wrongs. This was considered to be either a liability to account in equity, or an action for money had and received in *Regal (Hastings) Ltd* v *Gulliver* [1942] 1 All ER 378. However, in the leading case of *Boardman* v *Phipps* [1967] 2 AC 46, in addition to the language of account, the language of constructive trusteeship was also used. Nothing seemed to turn on this in the case. The personal liability was clearly one to disgorge profits. Constructive trusteeship would not alter the quantum of relief. Further, there was no suggestion that the defendants were insolvent (indeed Lord Boardman was a millionaire) and a personal duty to account would have sufficed. However, the case is often understood as imposing a proprietary liability: e.g., Sir Peter Millett, 'Bribes and Secret Commissions' [1993] RLR 7; Goode, 'The Recovery of a Director's Improper Gains: Proprietary Remedies for the Infringement of Non-proprietary Rights' in E. McKendrick (ed.), *Commercial Aspects of Trusts and Fiduciary Obligations* (1992), 137–48; Goode, in Cornish, 73–74. It is submitted that there is little in these cases to support the proprietary interpretation of them and the law would be greatly clarified if it were made clear that they imposed only a personal liability.

An analogous question has arisen in respect of the equitable wrong of breach of confidence. In *LAC Minerals Ltd* v *International Corona Resources Ltd* (1989) 61 DLR (4th) 14, the Supreme Court of Canada awarded a restitutionary proprietary remedy in the shape of a constructive for a breach of confidence. Contrast the welcoming reception of Davies ([1990] LMCLQ 4) with the rigorous analytical critique of Birks ([1990] LMCLQ 460).

All of these cases must now be considered in the light of *Attorney-General for Hong Kong* v *Reid*, discussed below.

30.8.2 Bribes and secret commissions

In the leading English case of *Lister & Co.* v *Stubbs* (1890) 45 Ch D 1, a strong Court of Appeal decided that the liability of the recipient of a bribe was personal only. Lister & Co. were silk screeners, dyers and manufacturers in Bradford. Stubbs was their foreman dyer responsible for purchasing the raw materials for dyeing. It was alleged that over a 10-year period he had received some £5,541 in commissions from Varley & Co., a dry salters in Leeds, the figure being based upon the quantity of goods ordered by Listers. It was further alleged that the money had been invested by Stubbs in land in Yorkshire and in other investments. Lister & Co. brought an action seeking to follow the secret profits into the investments. They sought an interlocutory injunction (now a freezing order) seeking to restrain Stubbs from dealing with those assets. Such relief was only available before the Court of Appeal decision in *Mareva Compañia Naviera SA* v *International Bulkcarriers SA* [1975] 2 Lloyd's Rep 509 if the claimant could show some proprietary entitlement. Lindley LJ was emphatic that the liability was one to account for the bribe the moment it was received. However, in a classic passage he observed (at 15):

> One consequence, of course, would be that, if Stubbs were to become bankrupt, this property acquired by him with the money paid to him by Messrs Varley would be withdrawn from the mass of his creditors and be handed over bodily to Lister & Co. Can that be right? Another consequence would be that, if the Appellants are right, Lister & Co. can compel Stubbs to account to them, not only for the money with interest, but for all the profits which he might have made by embarking on trade with it. Can that be right?

The logical fallacy simply was 'confounding ownership with obligation' (at 15). See also 23.7. Despite its obvious logic, the decision was often criticised as being anomalous: Sir Peter Millett [1993] RLR 7. It had its defenders: from an insolvency context, see Goode, 'Ownership and Obligation in Commercial Transactions' (1987) 103 LQR 433, at 441–45; and Birks, 387–89.

The decision must now be contrasted with the opposite view taken by the Privy Council in *Attorney-General for Hong Kong* v *Reid* [1994] 1 AC 324. Reid was acting Director of Public Prosecutions in the former colony, but appears to have been in the pocket of the Triads. Before his corruption was exposed he had received some HK$12.4 million in bribes, presumably to stifle prosecutions. He was sentenced to eight years' imprisonment and ordered to pay the Crown that sum in compensation, being the value of his assets which had only been derived from bribes. Reid was the beneficial owner of three freehold properties in his native New Zealand, two held jointly with his wife and one in the name of his solicitor. The Attorney-General sought to register caveats against those properties, on the ground that they were held on constructive trust for the Crown. The Court of Appeal in New Zealand, following *Lister & Co.* v *Stubbs*, held that the Crown had no proprietary interest in the property. The Privy Council disagreed. In a trenchant advice delivered by Lord Templeman, two lines of reasoning can be discerned. First, the policies of punishment or deterrence. Lord Templeman bemoaned the circumstances (at 330–31):

> Bribery is an evil practice which threatens the foundations of any civilised society. In particular bribery of policemen and prosecutors brings the administration of justice into disrepute. Where bribes are accepted by a trustee, servant, agent or other fiduciary, loss and damage are caused to the beneficiaries, master or principal whose interests have been betrayed. The amount of loss or damage resulting from the acceptance of a bribe may or may not be quantifiable. In the present case the amount of harm caused to the administration of justice in Hong Kong by the first respondent in return for bribes cannot be quantified.

In addition to this policy-based reasoning, there is an argument from principle. Lord Templeman stated (at 331):

> As soon as the bribe was received it should have been paid or transferred instanter to the person who suffered from the breach of duty. Equity considers as done that which ought to have been done. As soon as the bribe was received, whether in cash or in kind, the false fiduciary held the bribe on a constructive trust for the person injured.

This is a novel application of the well-known equitable maxim. As is clearly argued by Professor Goode, its application is entirely circular: Goode, in Cornish, 69–73. Its conclusion is stated as the premise. It adds no independent logical route to the conclusion reached. However, when confronted with Lindley LJ's two key questions from *Lister & Co.* v *Stubbs*, Lord Templeman was content to answer both in the affirmative. Accordingly both the profit-seeking and the priority in insolvency motives for restitutionary proprietary remedies were encouraged by the Privy Council in this case. Lord Templeman cited with approval the arguments of Sir Peter Millett in [1993] RLR 7.

30.8.3   Tortious wrongdoing

Reid appeared to signal the greater willingness of the courts to impose restitutionary proprietary remedies in the context of restitution for wrongs. However, the case has not been greeted with great enthusiasm. As a matter of strict precedent it can be argued that English courts up to and including the Court of Appeal are still bound by the decision in *Lister & Co. v Stubbs*. The opinions of the Privy Council are only of persuasive authority. However, a more realistic version of the doctrine of precedent suggests that English courts generally do follow the Privy Council.

Reid received a lukewarm response in the recent English Court of Appeal case of *Halifax Building Society v Thomas* [1996] Ch 217, which concerned the claim, *inter alia*, for a constructive trust in response to the tort of deceit. In the circumstances of the case, where there were competing claims by the Crown Prosecution Service and the plaintiff building society, it was decided that the building society had neither a personal claim nor a proprietary claim. However, the Court of Appeal did reject explicitly the claim to a constructive trust after consideration of *Attorney-General for Hong Kong v Reid* (at 228–29). See also *Attorney-General v Blake* [1997] Ch 84, at 96–97 *per* Sir Richard Scott V-C. For discussion, see Birks (1996) 10 *Trust Law International* 2; Goode, in Cornish, 69–73.

More recently, the Court of Appeal in *Re Polly Peck International (in administration) (No. 2), Marangos Hotel v Stone* [1998] 3 All ER 812, rejected a claim to a constructive trust over profits made as a result of trespass to land. The defendant was insolvent and to grant a remedial constructive trust in such a case would contradict the statutory insolvency regime of *pari passu* (*per* Mummery LJ at 826–27).

30.9   COMPLEX ENTITLEMENTS AND PROPRIETARY RESTITUTIONARY CLAIMS

The question has rarely arisen. Where a claimant recovers in excess of his own interest in a cause of action arising in contract or tort, he is often subject to a restitutionary duty to account over to his co-entitled party. The metaphor of the conduit pipe often proves irresistible. The courts have shown some willingness to reinforce the personal duty with a proprietary claim. The leading case is now *Lord Napier and Ettrick v Hunter* [1993] AC 713. For discussion see 19.4.3, 19.5.2 and 19.9.

30.10   CONCLUSION

A sceptical view has been taken in this chapter as to the greater liberality with which the courts award restitutionary proprietary remedies. The view advanced is that such claims are most defensible in the context of subtractive unjust enrichment, and in particular cases of vitiated voluntariness, and also in the context of complex entitlements where one party recovers in respect of another's interest and it is inappropriate that he should retain a windfall, or that his general creditors should share in it. The expansion of the remedial constructive trust and other restitutionary proprietary remedies into restitution for wrongs, or in cases of qualified intention to benefit the defendant should be resisted as far as possible. Even where the innocent defendant is insolvent, regard should be had to the principles and policies of insolvency law and whether the imposition of restitutionary proprietary relief will diminish the general pool of assets available to unsecured creditors.

FURTHER READING

Asterisks indicate especially useful works.

Goff and Jones, 76–93

L. Smith, *The Law of Tracing* (1997), 283–369

R. Chambers, *Resulting Trusts* (1997)

G. Elias, *Explaining Constructive Trusts* (1990)

A. Oakley, *Constructive Trusts*, 3rd edn (1997)

R. Goode, 'Ownership and Obligation in Commercial Transactions' (1987) 103 LQR 433, at 441–45

Sir Peter Millett, 'Bribes and Secret Commissions' [1993] *Restitution Law Review* 7

*D. Paciocco, 'The Remedial Constructive Trust: A Principled Basis for Priorities Over Creditors'(1989) 68 Can Bar Rev 315

*E. Sherwin, 'Constructive Trusts in Bankruptcy' [1989] U Ill L Rev 297

R. Goode, 'The Recovery of a Director's Improper Gains: Proprietary Remedies for the Infringement of Non-proprietary Rights' in E. McKendrick (ed), *Commercial Aspects of Trusts and Fiduciary Obligations* (1992), 137–48

*R. Goode, 'Proprietary Restitutionary Claims' in Cornish, 63–77

*Sir Peter Millett, 'Restitution and Constructive Trusts' in Cornish, 199–217

D. Hayton, 'Equity's Identification Rules' in Birks (1995), 1–21

*P. Birks, 'The End of the Remedial Constructive Trust' (1998) 12 *Trusts Law International* 202

D. Wright, 'Professor Birks and the Demise of the Remedial Costructive Trust' [1999] *Restitution Law Review* 128

PART H

DEFENCES

31 Good Faith Purchase

31.1 THEORETICAL FOUNDATIONS

The defence of good faith purchase is crucial to the coherence of the modern law of restitution. It straddles the boundaries of contract, unjust enrichment and property. Its prominence in the modern law was secured by the leading case of *Lipkin Gorman* v *Karpnale Ltd* [1991] 2 AC 548. That case also yielded appellate recognition for the restitutionary defence of change of position. The campaign for such recognition had led to attempts to assimilate good faith purchase to change of position. See Birks [1991] LMCLQ 473, at 490–91 and Sir Peter Millett (1991) 107 LQR 71, at 82 ('it may come to be recognised that the defence of bona fide purchaser for value is simply the paradigm change of position defence').

However, it is submitted that such purported rationalisation would be an error. Good faith purchase and change of position are distinct defences with wholly different normative underpinnings. It has been convincingly argued that good faith purchase is an instrumental defence which 'deploys a broad policy of transactional security in exchange dealings, with the primary (economic) objective of facilitating the free transfer of wealth': Barker, in Birks (1995), 191, at 192–93. In contrast, change of position is concerned with the perceived unfairness of compelling an innocent recipient to disgorge in full where there has been intermediate expenditure on the faith of receipt.

These differing foundations yield markedly differing results. Where good faith purchase is available and is proved, the defendant establishes a complete defence to the claim. In contrast, change of position operates proportionately to the expenditure in reliance upon receipt, usually diminishing the claim *pro tanto* rather than extinguishing the whole claim as a matter of course.

It is obvious from the foregoing that good faith purchase is concerned with the well-known tension between two potentially conflicting principles of law. The first favours the protection of ownership and the preservation of wealth. The second promotes and facilitates the consensual transactions which constitute the market economy. Precisely where the law draws the line between the former and the latter is controversial, and it will be seen that the defence is not a general one. Further, the defence of good faith purchase shares its normative underpinning with foundational rules of the law of unjust enrichment, that wealth passing pursuant to an apparently consensual arrangement is governed by the terms of that transaction, unless or until the transaction is held to be legally ineffective. The availability of and ingredients of good faith purchase will now be considered.

31.2   HISTORY AND DIFFERENT MANIFESTATIONS OF WEALTH

Distinct species of good faith purchase developed at common law and in equity. It is necessary to identify with precision the claims which can be met by the defence. Ownership of tangible property is rigorously protected at common law. The general principle is that a common law proprietary interest is not lost unless there is an act of apparent transmissive consent or some other conduct attributable to the owner.

In relation to tangible personal property this general rule is expressed in the maxim *nemo dat quod non habet* (encapsulated in s. 21 of the Sale of Goods Act 1979). The exceptions to *nemo dat* are exhaustively identified by statute, and are all particular examples of the true owner being precluded from asserting his proprietary interest because he has entrusted the property to another or assented to its remaining in the possession of another. Therefore property will pass if goods are sold by a person with the authority or consent of the owner, or if there are facts estopping the owner from denying that other's authority to sell (Sale of Goods Act 1979, s. 21(1)). Similarly, sale by a mercantile agent in possession of the goods (s. 2(1) of the Factors Act 1889), by a seller in possession (s. 24 of the 1979 Act and s. 8 of the 1889 Act) or by an unpaid seller (under s. 48 of the 1979 Act), or by a buyer in possession (s. 25 of the 1979 Act and s. 9 of the 1889 Act) will all result in a transfer of common law property to a good faith purchaser at the expense of the true owner. Further, a sub-sale of property by a person who obtained a defeasible title to the goods by conduct which amounted to an operative vitiating factor, usually misrepresentation, will be effective to pass common law title to the sub-buyer if the transaction takes place before the original owner can rescind (s. 23 of the 1979 Act; *Lewis* v *Averay* [1972] 1 QB 198; *Car & Universal Finance Co. Ltd* v *Caldwell* [1965] 1 QB 525). A further policy-driven exception to *nemo dat* is recognised for the private purchaser of a motor vehicle bought from the hirer under a hire-purchase agreement (Part III of the Hire-Purchase Act 1964).

It will be seen from this branch of the law that good faith purchase is not seen as sufficient to defeat the rights of the party originally entitled to chattels. In contrast, a situation in which the common law recognises good faith purchase as sufficient is where a claim was based upon continuing title to money or negotiable instruments. Here it has been held that proof of good faith purchase has the effect of passing money into currency. This is discussed further at 31.3 below.

In equity, the bona fide purchaser for value without notice is able to defeat any personal or proprietary claim based upon a continuing equitable proprietary interest in the asset received. Here, it is a general defence. Historically, this was treated as a matter of jurisdiction. The purchaser for value in good faith possessed a clear conscience and was accordingly immune from any claim. Confusion is created by the related body of law in which claims are made to misdirected funds on the basis that the recipient received them with knowledge (including constructive knowledge) of their suspicious provenance.

31.3 MONEY AS CURRENCY

Money's 'basic function is that of serving as a universal medium of exchange': F.A. Mann, *The Legal Aspect of Money* (5th edn, 1992). It is the character of money as a universal medium of exchange which for policy reasons leads to the recognition of good faith purchase in this context.

In *Miller* v *Race* (1758) 1 Burr 452, 97 ER 398, a bank note came into the possession of the plaintiff for valuable consideration in the usual course of business without any notice of its having been stolen. The court treated the bank note as equivalent to coinage. The Court of King's Bench, led by Lord Mansfield, emphatically upheld the plaintiff's ownership of the note, explicitly referring to the need to protect trade and commerce. Lord Mansfield stated (at 457–58):

> It has been quaintly said 'that the reason why money cannot be followed is, because it has no ear-mark': but this is not true. The true reason is, upon account of the currency of it: it can not be recovered after it has passed in currency. So, in the case of money stolen, the true owner can not recover it, after it has been paid away fairly and honestly upon a valuable and bona fide consideration: but before money has passed in currency, an action may be brought for the money itself.

The rule applies to money in the forms of notes and coinage and to other negotiable instruments. The burden of proving good faith purchase is upon the defendant, but in the case of bills of exchange both value and good faith are presumed (s. 30 of the Bills of Exchange Act 1882). Accordingly, the original owner will be able to recover only against the volunteer (such as a finder) or against a recipient in bad faith (the thief or one taking with knowledge of the circumstances). The common law requires actual knowledge or dishonesty: compare s. 90 of the Bills of Exchange Act 1882.

There are few reported incidences of successful recovery. In *Clarke* v *Shee and Johnson* (1774) 1 Cowp 197, 98 ER 1041, a servant of the plaintiff misapplied his master's money, paying some £459 to the defendants on what appeared to have been bets upon the outcome of the State Lottery (which derivate transactions were outlawed by the Lottery Act 1772). The statutory prohibition meant that the defendants did not provide valuable consideration, and it was held that the plaintiff was not tainted by his servant's participation in an illegal contract. Accordingly he could recover. Lord Mansfield stated (at 200):

Where money or notes are paid bona fide, and upon a valuable consideration, they never shall be brought back by the true owner; but where they come mala fide into a person's hands, they are in the nature of specific property; and if their identity can be traced and ascertained, the party has a right to recover.

In *Nelson* v *Larholt* [1948] 1 KB 339, an executor misappropriated funds from the estate by drawing cheques from the estate bank account in favour of his bookmaker. The cheques were delivered out of office hours and were signed explicitly as executor of the estate. The co-executor and the beneficiaries of the estate were held entitled to recover the sum misapplied from the bookmaker. Denning J, in a bold judgment, sought to fuse principles which had developed separately at law and in equity into a unified restitutionary solution. He stated (at 342–43):

> If [money] is taken from the rightful owner, or, indeed, from the beneficial owner, without his authority, he can recover the amount from any person into whose hands it can be traced, unless and until it reaches one who receives it in good faith and for value and without notice of the want of authority. Even if the one who received it acted in good faith, nevertheless if he had notice — that is, if he knew of the want of authority or is to be taken to have known of it — he must repay.

While good faith and value were admitted, Denning J held that the bookmaker knew or must be taken to have known of the want of authority of the executor.

Clarke v *Shee and Johnson* was following the leading case of *Lipkin Gorman* v *Karpnale Ltd* [1991] 2 AC 548, where the partner of a law firm misappropriated money from a client account and gambled it away at a casino. The gaming contracts were void under s. 18 of the Gaming Act 1845 and therefore the casino, while a recipient in good faith, provided no consideration of value in the eyes of the law. The interposition of chips as a mechanism for gambling made no difference to this conclusion. In the case of unsuccessful bets the casino provided no consideration because its promise to pay upon a successful bet was void, and in the case of successful bets the payment to the gambler is treated in law as a gift. In addition, Lord Goff of Chieveley made an important observation on the relationship of the two leading restitutionary defences (at 580–81):

> The defence of change of position is akin to the defence of bona fide purchase; but we cannot simply say that bona fide purchase is a species of change of position. This is because change of position will only avail a defendant to the extent that his position has been changed; whereas, where bona fide purchase is invoked, no enquiry is made (in most cases) into the adequacy of consideration.

The reference to adequacy of consideration appears to incorporate by reference technical rules governing the requirements for a binding contract (whereby, for example, a peppercorn is said to be sufficient consideration). Generally there is no enquiry into the substantive equivalence of exchange. However, the words in parenthesis emphasise that this is not without exception. The exception which applied, in *Lipkin Gorman*, is that the consideration must be of value in the eyes of the law, that is not pursuant to an illegal or illicit transaction. Such was the effect of the Gaming Act 1848 on the services provided by the casino. Similarly, in *Banque Belge pour l'Etranger* v *Hambrouck* [1921] 1 KB 321, the mistress of a clerk who misappropriated money belonging to his employer, had no defence to a claim in respect of proceeds which she retained. Her illicit cohabitation was described as an immoral consideration of no value in the eyes of the law. Changes in social morality may render the language inappropriate, but the substantive point appears still to be sound.

31.4 MISTAKEN PAYMENTS AND GOOD FAITH PURCHASE

This derives from the difficult case of *Aiken* v *Short* (1856) 1 H & N 210, 156 ER 1180. The facts and holding were discussed above in 3.5.2. Pollock CB and Platt B stressed that the defendant had a valid debt and a clear right to the money as against Carter. Given that the defendant had approached Carter first and he had referred her to the bank, 'the money was, in fact, paid by the Bank as the agents of Carter' (at 214, *per* Pollock CB).

Goff and Jones, who in earlier editions had accepted the characterisation of this defence as good faith purchase, now treat *Aiken* v *Short* as an example of change of position: Goff and Jones, 204–205. The concern appears to be that the ground of restitution is mistake, not a claim based on title. The strict view is taken that good faith purchase should be a defence only where a claim is based upon title either at common law or in equity. This reasoning should not be accepted. First, it is clear from *Aiken* v *Short* and dicta in the subsequent House of Lords of *Kerrison* v *Glyn, Mills, Currie & Co.* (1911) 81 LJKB 465, that good faith purchase is an autonomous defence here. Secondly, good faith purchase extinguishes a restitutionary claim in full, and not merely *pro tanto* as is the case with change of position. Thirdly, and most crucially, payment in such circumstances amounts to a valid accord and satisfaction, which can only be set aside in accordance with the rules of contract law. The primacy of contract ousts the possibility of restitutionary recovery here, unless the contractual matrix can be set aside.

Barclays Bank Ltd v *W. J. Simms, Son & Cooke (Southern) Ltd* [1980] QB 677, at 695, canonised the role of good faith purchase in proposition 2(b), as a limitation upon recovery in Robert Goff J's classic formulation. *Barclays Bank* was followed and actual authority found in *Lloyds Bank plc* v *Independent Insurance Co. Ltd* [1999] 2 WLR 986. Its recognition by a modern Court of Appeal authority entrenches the defence as autonomous in the context of mistaken payments. Contrast Baker [1999] RLR 75, 87–89. See generally 3.5.2.

31.5 EQUITABLE CLAIMS

Equitable claims to misappropriated wealth may either be personal (as in so-called knowing receipt) or proprietary (seeking the imposition of a constructive trust or equitable lien after a successful tracing exercise). Both personal and proprietary claims are liable to be defeated by a bona fide purchaser for value without notice. In respect of the personal claim, some of the authorities have treated knowledge or notice of the circumstances as constituent parts of the claimant's cause of action, rather than relevant to the defence of good faith purchase (e.g., *In re Montagu's Settlement Trusts* [1987] Ch 264; *Cowan de Groot Properties Ltd* v *Eagle Trust plc* [1992] 4 All ER 700; *Polly Peck International plc* v *Nadir (No. 2)* [1992] 4 All ER 769). In contrast, there is a respectable academic argument that claims to misdirected funds should be governed by a yardstick of strict liability both at common law and in equity: Birks [1989] LMCLQ 296. (For discussion see Chapter 5.)

In this context the key practical issue is in relation to the burden of proof. Where it is accepted that liability is strict subject to a defence of good faith purchase, both principle and the majority of case law places the onus upon the defendant to make out affirmatively good faith purchase (*Re Nisbet and Potts' Contract* [1906] 1 Ch 386; *G. L. Baker Ltd* v *Medway Building and Supplies Ltd* [1958] 1 WLR 1216; *Lipkin Gorman* v *Karpnale Ltd*; for discussion, see Barker, in Birks (1995) at 205–209). Whereas the common law is concerned with actual notice, dishonesty and knowledge of want of authority, it seems that equity may extend to various species of constructive notice. The debate about the level of knowledge required in recent equity cases is discussed in Chapter 29. However, it is always wise to remember the words of Lindley LJ in *Manchester Trust* v *Furness* [1895] 2 QB 539, at 545:

As regards the extension of the equitable doctrines of constructive notice to commercial transactions, the Courts have always set their faces resolutely against it. The equitable doctrines of constructive notice are common enough in dealing with land and estates, with which the Court is familiar; but there have been repeated protests against the introduction into commercial transactions of anything like an extension of those doctrines, and the protest is founded on perfect good sense. In dealing with estates in land title is everything, and it can be leisurely investigated; in commercial transactions possession is everything, and there is no time to investigate title; and if we were to extend the doctrine of constructive notice to commercial transactions we should be doing infinite mischief and paralyzing the trade of the country.

31.6 RELATED ISSUES

As was stated at 31.1 above, the defence of good faith purchase shares the same normative underpinnings as the rule in unjust enrichment which precludes recourse to restitutionary rights where the transfer of wealth is governed by an apparently binding consensual transaction, unless or until that transaction is held to be ineffective. In the context of compulsion (*Dimskal Shipping Co. SA* v *International Transport Workers' Federation, The Evia Luck (No. 2)* [1992] 2 AC 152, at 165) and failure of consideration (*Pan Ocean Shipping Co. Ltd* v *Creditcorp Ltd, The Trident*

Beauty [1984] 1 WLR 161) restitutionary claims were said to be precluded where there was an effective contractual matrix governing the transfer of benefits.

Similar considerations to those which give rise to the defence of good faith purchase appear to underlie the principles governing whether a third party is tainted by the wrong or vitiating factor of another (such as misrepresentation or undue influence). The leading cases of *Barclays Bank plc* v *O'Brien* [1984] 1 AC 180, *CIBC Mortgages plc* v *Pitt* [1984] 1 AC 200, *Royal Bank of Scotland* v *Etridge (No. 2)* [1998] 4 All ER 705 and *Barclays Bank plc* v *Boulter* [1999] 4 All ER 513 treat the notice of the third party as an ingredient of the claim against the third party and not as an application of the defence of good faith purchase. Contrast O'Dell [1997] CLJ 71 and Barker [1999] RLR 75, 89–91. See 7.6.

31.7 PRACTICAL ISSUES

Where bona fide purchase is available it must be explicitly pleaded as a defence by the defendant. The onus of proof lies on the defendant, although in cases governed by the Bills of Exchange Act 1882 both good faith and value are presumed. Where the claimant wishes to question value, good faith or absence of notice, this too must be explicitly pleaded in a reply. Allegations of lack of good faith or notice (constructive or otherwise) must be specifically pleaded: CPR Part 16, PD 16, para. 10.2(5).

FURTHER READING

Asterisks indicate especially useful works.

Goff and Jones, 842–45
P. Birks, 'Misdirected Funds: Restitution from the Recipient' [1989] LMCLQ 296, at 301–303
P. Birks, 'The English Recognition of Unjust Enrichment' [1991] LMCLQ 473, at 486–92
Sir Peter Millett, 'Tracing the Proceeds of Fraud' (1991) 107 LQR 71, at 82
P. Birks, (1992), 123–47, at 132–35
*F. A. Mann, *The Legal Aspect of Money*, 5th edn (1992), 1–14
P. Key 'Bona fide purchase as a defence in the law of restitution' [1994] LMCLQ 421
*K. Barker, 'After Change of Position: Good Faith Exchange in the Modern Law of Restitution' in P. Birks, *Laundering and Tracing* (1995), 191–215
P. Birks, 'Overview — Defences' in Birks (1995), 332–36
D. Fox, 'The Transfer of Legal Title to Money' [1996] *Restitution Law Review* 60
D. Fox, 'Bona fide Purchase and the Currency of Money' [1996] CLJ 547
*K. Barker, 'Bona Fide Purchase as a Defence to Unjust Enrichment Claims: A Concise Restatement' [1999] *Restitution Law Review* 75

32 Change of Position, Estoppel and Ministerial Receipt

32.1 THEORETICAL FOUNDATIONS

The development of restitutionary defences has proceeded in a rather haphazard way, in the shadow of doubts about the conceptual basis and unity of the substantive part of the subject. With unjust enrichment firmly entrenched in the underlying principle behind restitutionary causes of action, it is now possible for the law on defences to develop on a more rational basis. *Lipkin Gorman* v *Karpnale Ltd* [1991] 2 AC 548 not only took the giant step of recognising unjust enrichment as a touchstone of liability, it also gave explicit appellate recognition to the defence of change of position. This protects the security of receipt of the defendant who is enriched, but whose circumstances change as a result of being benefited so that it would inequitable to order restitution of some or all of the enrichment. An important feature of change of position is that it may operate *pro tanto*. That is, it operates proportionately to the expenditure or loss suffered by the defendant upon the faith of receipt.

Prior to *Lipkin Gorman*, a defence of estoppel was prominent in the mistaken payments cases. Estoppel required two elements:

(a) either a representation by the payer that the payment was a correct one, or a breach of duty by the payer accurately to state the account between payer and payee;

(b) detrimental reliance by the payee upon that representational breach of duty.

Estoppel was open to criticism on two grounds. First, the insistence upon an active misrepresentation or breach of the duty of accuracy could be regarded as favouring the payer too much. Secondly, the defence operated as an all-or-nothing defence. It completely precluded the restitutionary claim. Accordingly, expenditure of £500 in reliance upon receipt would be a complete defence to a claim for an overpayment of £1,000 (*Avon County Council* v *Howlett* [1983] 1 WLR 605).

A general defence of change of circumstances was first explicitly recognised in the US *Restatement of the Law of Restitution*, §142:

(1)   The right of a person to restitution from another because of a benefit received is terminated or diminished if, after the receipt of the benefit, circumstances have so changed that it would be inequitable to require the other to make full restitution.

(2)   Change of circumstances may be a defense or a partial defense if the conduct of the recipient was not tortious and he was no more at fault for his receipt, retention or dealing with the subject-matter than was the claimant.

(3)   Change of circumstances is not a defense if

(a)   the conduct of the recipient in obtaining, retaining or dealing with the subject-matter was tortious, or

(b)   the change occurred after the recipient had knowledge of the facts entitling the other to restitution and had an opportunity to make restitution.

In English law, prior to *Lipkin Gorman*, two House of Lords cases proved obstacles to the recognition of change of position: *R. E. Jones Ltd* v *Waring & Gillow Ltd* [1926] AC 670 and *Ministry of Health* v *Simpson* [1951] AC 251. Sympathetic judges in the lower courts, though, had 'smuggled *dicta* into the cases in support': Birks, 414. These included Denning LJ in *Larner* v *London County Council* [1949] 2 KB 683, at 688; Robert Goff J in *BP Exploration (Libya) Ltd* v *Hunt (No. 2)* [1979] 1 WLR 783 (QBD), at 800, 804 and in *Barclays Bank Ltd* v *W. J. Simms, Son & Cooke (Southern) Ltd* [1980] 2 QB 677, at 695–96; and Lord Goff of Chieveley in *R* v *Tower Hamlets London Borough Council ex parte Chetnik Developments Ltd* [1988] AC 858, at 882.

Further, a number of cases have been rationalised as being based on change of position. For example, some of the restrictions upon recovery in *In re Diplock* [1948] Ch 465 have been explained on this basis.

From the practical point of view, a major difficulty is posed by the fact that the House of Lords in *Lipkin Gorman* deliberately left open the scope of the defence to be decided on a case-by-case basis. This makes it difficult to say anything definitive about the boundaries of the defence, or to predict how it will operate in practice. It can also be observed that an explicit plea of change of position has not been successful in a single reported case since *Lipkin Gorman*. In advising on this topic, it will often be more rewarding to consider academic writings on the topic, rather than the case law to date which provides few pointers. An important structural question is whether the defence goes to the issue of enrichment, or whether it goes to the issue of whether it is unjust to order the defendant to make restitution. First, we should consider *Lipkin Gorman* and subsequent authority. Secondly, there will be a brief review of academic discussion on the defence. Thirdly, the related agency defence of ministerial receipt will be discussed.

32.2 THE RECOGNITION OF CHANGE OF POSITION

It will recalled that in *Lipkin Gorman* v *Karpnale Ltd* [1991] 2 AC 548, the recalcitrant solicitor gambled in total some £561,014.06 at the Playboy Club. This global figure included sums won and restaked. The gambler won some £378,294.04. The total shortfall on the client account was £222,908.98. The solicitors' claim in the action for money and received was for some £219,173.98. However, the net position as between the club and the gambler was that the club won some £150,960 as a result of his compulsive behaviour. In *Lipkin Gorman*, Lord Templeman stated that it was a requirement of the claim that 'the defendant was unjustly enriched and remained unjustly enriched' (at 560). Lord Templeman examined what would happen where the defendant was the innocent donee of £20,000 of stolen money. The recipient was prima facie liable to a claim in restitution for the full amount. However, if the donee spent £20,000 on a car which would not have been purchased but for the gift of stolen money, the donee could plead change of position. He would remain enriched only to the extent of the second-hand value of the car. Further, if the donee had spent £20,000 on a trip around the world which he would not have taken but for the gift, the donee would have a complete defence for the claim in restitution. On the facts of the case, the club remained enriched to the extent of its net winnings. Lord Bridge agreed with Lord Templeman.

Lord Goff of Chieveley surveyed the history of, and the arguments for, the recognition of change of position in English law. His Lordship noted the weaknesses in the defence of estoppel: namely, the insistence upon a representation and the fact that estoppel did not operate *pro tanto*. Lord Goff observed that change of position had obtained partial recognition in English law in two groups of cases. First, ministerial receipt, where an agent had paid over to his principal without notice of a claim: see Goff and Jones, 833–38. Secondly, where money has been paid out under a forged bill of exchange: see Goff and Jones, 838–41. Accordingly, Lord Goff was prepared to forge a new defence of change of position free from the shackles of the old restrictive approach to estoppel.

One striking question is whether the case law in estoppel survives this recognition of change of position. It is submitted that the better view is that the decision in *Lipkin Gorman* effectively excludes the operation of estoppel in this context. Therefore estoppel no longer has any role to play here. There are a number of reasons for this. First, to allow estoppel completely to exclude a claim in restitution where the expenditure in reliance is less, even considerably less, than the total claim would operate an injustice at the expense of the transferor. The availability of the more proportionate defence means that the court must necessarily disregard the earlier primitive defence. Accordingly, *Lipkin Gorman* can be seen as having impliedly overruled the decision of the Court of Appeal in *Avon County Council* v *Howlett* [1983] 1 WLR 604. Secondly, support for this position can be garnered from the speech of Lord Goff, where his Lordship commented (at 579) 'that, in many cases, estoppel is not an appropriate concept to deal with the problem'. In Newfoundland the courts have rejected estoppel completely in this context (*RBC Dominion*

Securities Inc. v *Dawson* (1994) 111 DLR (4th) 230, at 237). The case law on estoppel is preserved, for the avoidance of doubt, by Goff and Jones, 828–33. Even if estoppel does survive, it is submitted that it will have only limited operation, in circumstances where there is an *express* representation by the transferor that the transferee is entitled to the money, and where it would be difficult for the transferee to quantify his expenditure in reliance.

Lord Goff proceeded to state the rationale of the new defence, and suggested some situations in which it would apply (at 579):

> why do we feel that it would be unjust to allow restitution in cases such as these? The answer must be that, where an innocent defendant's position is so changed that he will suffer an injustice if called upon to repay or to repay in full, the injustice of requiring him so to repay outweighs the injustice of denying the plaintiff restitution. If the plaintiff pays money to the defendant under a mistake of fact, and the defendant then, acting in good faith, pays the money or part of it to charity, it is unjust to require the defendant to make restitution to the extent that he has so changed to his position. Likewise, on facts such as those in the present case, if a thief steals my money and pays it to a third party who gives it away to charity, that third party should have a good defence to an action for money had and received. In other words, bona fide change of position should of itself be a good defence in cases such as these.

This is a broad statement of principle. Two points should be noted. First, the defence only avails a party acting in good faith. Secondly, there is no explicit insistence upon the need for the defendant's circumstances to have changed as a result of his reliance upon the payment. Accordingly on this formulation the defence may be available to one who receives value which is subsequently destroyed or stolen. Lord Goff was keen to avoid saying anything which would prejudice the development of the defence on a case-by-case basis. His Lordship was even reluctant to consider in detail the requirement that the defendant should neither be a wrongdoer, nor act in bad faith. The defence will be available most commonly in cases of mistake, but was also available against the cause of action in *Lipkin Gorman* where a thief transferred stolen money to an innocent party. Lord Goff concluded (at 580):

> At present I do not wish to state the principle any less broadly than this: that the defence is available to a person whose position has so changed that it would be inequitable in all the circumstances to require him to make restitution, or alternatively to make restitution in full. I wish to stress however that the mere fact that the defendant has spent the money, in whole or in part, does not of itself render it inequitable that he should be called upon to repay, because the expenditure might in any event have been incurred by him in the ordinary course of things.

Accordingly the defence would be available only on 'comparatively rare occasions'.

The application of this new-found principle to the instant facts was difficult. As has already been observed, Lord Templeman broadly stated that the club remained enriched to the extent of its net winnings. In contrast, Lord Goff subjected the question to more detailed scrutiny. The problem arose from the fact that the gambler might have won his first bet one evening, but then gone on to lose subsequent bets. There was an obvious difficulty in seeing how the numerous bets could be aggregated together. The problem here was one of anticipatory expenditure by the club, prior to any receipt of money from the gambler. Could change of position apply even though some of the expenditure must have taken place, on the balance of probabilities, before the club received the stolen money? Lord Goff examined numerous possible alternative routes on the facts of this case, but eventually returned to the net winnings position. At root, this was a matter of fairness. If the gambler had simply placed a large bet of £100,000 each night, which he had lost, the club would be bound to repay. However, more commonly the gambler would have won a number of bets over an evening, while losing many. Lord Goff acknowledged that the application of the principle to the facts of the case was necessarily makeshift (at 582–83):

> It is the totality of the bets which yields, by the laws of chance, the occasional winning bet; and the occasional winning bet is therefore, in practical terms, the result of the casino changing its position by incurring the risk of losing on each occasion when a bet is placed with it by the gambler. So, when in such circumstances the plaintiff seeks to recover from the casino the amount of several bets placed with it by a gambler with his money, it would be inequitable to require the casino to repay in full without bringing into account winnings paid by it to the gambler on any one or more the bets so placed with it. The result may not be entirely logical; but it is surely just.

Lord Griffiths and Lord Ackner agreed with both Lord Goff and Lord Templeman. The practical difficulties of applying the principle of change of position to the sequence of transactions in *Lipkin Gorman* perhaps supports their Lordships' caution in not fleshing out the detail of the defence. As a practical matter, perhaps the most helpful guide in *Lipkin Gorman* itself is Lord Goff's statement that the defence will succeed only in comparatively rare cases. Subsequent case law suggests that this is correct.

32.3   CASE LAW AFTER *LIPKIN GORMAN*

The following year, the High Court of Australia in *David Securities Pty Ltd* v *Commonwealth Bank of Australia* (1992) 175 CLR 353 added its support to the recognition of change of position. The High Court stressed (at 385–86) that in common law jurisdictions where the defence was already recognised:

> the common element in all cases is the requirement that the defendant point to expenditure or financial commitment which can be ascribed to the mistaken payment. In Canada and in some United States decisions, the defendant has been required to point to *specific* expenditure being incurred because of the payment.

Other cases in the United States allow a wider scope to the defence, such that a defendant can rely upon it even though he or she cannot precisely identify the expenditure caused by the mistaken payment. In no jurisdiction, however, can a defendant resort to the defence of change of position where he or she has simply spent the money received on ordinary living expenses.

The interest rate swap cases have provided some further authority on the question of change of position. At first instance Hobhouse J considered the position in *Westdeutsche Landesbank Girozentrale v Islington London Borough Council* [1994] 4 All ER 890, at 946–54, where Westdeutsche had made a back-to-back swap agreement with another bank. The bank's attempt to rely upon the defence against the counterclaim brought by Islington was considered to be misconceived for a number of reasons. Hobhouse J stated (at 948–49):

> First, Islington has no counterclaim against Westdeutsche. Westdeutsche has not been enriched at the expense of Islington. Therefore the allegation of such a defence has no relevance. Secondly, there has been no alteration of the position of Westdeutsche since it received the sums paid to it by Islington. The change of position of Westdeutsche occurred on 16 June 1987, when it entered into the contract with Morgan Grenfell. That contract was, as a legal transaction, wholly independent of Westdetusche's transaction with Islington. The supposed existence of the contract between Westdeutsche and Islington had provided the motive for Westdeutsche to enter into a contract with Morgan Grenfell, but that was all. Therefore there has been no change of position of Westdeutsche relevant to any claim which Islington might have had against it. Thirdly, whilst it is presently correct that Westdeutsche as the floating rate payer under its contract with Morgan Grenfell is presently out of pocket, it does not follow that this will be the final outcome of that contract.... To assert that Westdeutsche will have made a loss through entering into the Morgan Grenfell contract is simply a speculation.

Hobhouse J similarly rejected a plea of change of position by Islington. It might perhaps be better to characterise this defence as one based upon disruption to public finances and accordingly an aspect of public policy as a defence to a restitutionary claim. Indeed, it was so advanced on this basis. It was argued (at 949) that it would be:

> inconsistent with a statutory policy that the finances of local authorities should be regulated on an annual basis. In my judgment this argument is better considered as an aspect of change of position. At the time that the payment of £2.5m was made, this argument would not have provided any defence to a claim for its repayment. It is only because subsequent accounting years have come and gone that the factual basis of the defence arises.

Hobhouse J regarded the proposed change of position as more theoretical than real. The council had in fact budgeted, once the difficulty about incapacity had become clear, to make repayments to the bank. In any event, the relevant years of accounts would need to be rectified as a result of the impermissible swaps trading.

A similar argument arose in *South Tyneside Metropolitan Borough Council* v *Svenska International plc* [1995] 1 All ER 545, in which unusually the council was plaintiff. The bank and the council entered into an interest rate swap commencing 2 June 1988 and terminating on 3 February 1995. The notional principal sum was £15 million; the bank was the fixed rate payer and the council was the floating rate payer. All of the bank's deals were 'hedged'. On hearing the provisional view of the House of Lords that such transactions were *ultra vires* and void in November 1990, the bank closed down its position and unwound its hedges. It was agreed that it had sustained a loss of £1.2 million by that date. The council sought restitution of the net sum it had paid under the transaction, and the bank argued that it had changed its position. It was argued for the bank that change of position was not limited to events occurring after receipt of the money. Clarke J referred expressly to §142(1) of the American *Restatement* which is explicitly confined to circumstances changing 'after receipt and benefit'. Clarke J concluded, however (at 566):

> that in the light of the actual decision in *Lipkin Gorman* there can be no rigid rule that events prior to receipt of the money or benefit are always irrelevant. Nevertheless the earlier statements of principle in the speech of Lord Goff and in the statutes and authorities to which he refers support the conclusion that, save perhaps exceptional circumstances, the defence of change of position is designed to protect a person who receives money in good faith and who thereafter changes his position in good faith so that it would be inequitable to require him to repay part or all of the money to its rightful owner.

Clarke J also held that in the circumstances of the void swap agreements, the defence of change of position was unavailable because the bank would be relying upon the supposed validity of a void contract. The case is discussed by Nolan [1995] LMCLQ 313 and is criticised by Goff and Jones, 823–24. It is submitted that Clarke J was correct to say that change of position will generally avail a defendant who circumstances change only after receipt, although in the light of *Lipkin Gorman* it is not desirable to draw a hard-and-fast rule. Clarke J's holding that it was impermissible for the bank to rely upon the supposed obligations under the void contract to have found the change of position should be treated with more circumspection. It should be remembered that all the transactions in *Lipkin Gorman* were void and unenforceable, and the House of Lords had no difficulty with having regard to the casino's supposed obligation in honour to meet winning bets.

Lastly, it is clear that change of position is equally applicable to the new right of recovery based upon mistakes of law (*Kleinwort Benson Ltd* v *Lincoln City Council* [1998] 3 WLR 1095, at 1122 *per* Lord Goff of Chieveley; at 1139 *per* Lord Hoffmann and at 1149–50 *per* Lord Hope of Craighead). In *Nurdin & Peacock plc* v *D. B. Ramsden & Co. Ltd* [1999] 1 All ER 941, Neuburger J rejected an attempted reliance upon change of position by the landlord in respect of overpayments of rent. The cause of action was mistake of fact or law. The landlord argued that the overpayments had caused it to refrain from exercising its right to institute the operation of the upwards-only rent-review clause. The argument was rejected, not least because it was unclear that the rental market justified the conclusion that the landlord would have succeeded in having the rent increase pursuant to the clause. In any event, Neuburger J was satisfied that any prejudice suffered was slight and insufficient to constitute change of position (at 956–57). Neuburger J appears to be correct to have rejected this ingenious, but ultimately misconceived, plea of change of position on these facts.

32.4   REINTERPRETATION OF AUTHORITY

In addition to its partial recognition in the agency and bills of exchange cases, and through the doctrine of estoppel, it has also been argued that earlier leading case law is best reinterpreted as an application of the change of position defence. In earlier editions Goff and Jones described the supposed limitation on the right to trace in equity — that the process would not be allowed where it was inequitable to do so as recognised in *In re Diplock* [1948] Ch 464 — as a primitive application of the defence of change of position: see now Goff and Jones, 110–11. First, the limitation was held to apply where some of the recipient charities had used the money to make alterations to their premises. The Court of Appeal asked (at 547): 'What would be the value of a building in the middle of Guy's Hospital without any means of access through other parts of the hospital property?' The use of the Diplock money may not have added any value to the hospital premises. In the circumstances it was inequitable to grant a charge over the new ward, or the hospital as a whole. Secondly, in the case of the Leaf Homœpathic Hospital the Diplock money was used to pay off an existing incumbrance upon property owned by the charity. The Court refused to allow subrogation to the earlier charge. The previous security had been discharged. The case was regarded as analogous to the cases where Diplock money was spent on improvements to the charity's property (at 549–50). Goff and Jones continue to analyse these exceptions to the right to trace and claim in equity in terms of change of position, but strike a note of caution (at 111):

> The defence of change of position should not be narrowly defined and should be allowed to grow in a flexible and pragmatic fashion. In each case it is a question of fact whether it is inequitable, given the change of position, to reject the particular restitutionary claim. It should not necessarily be a defence that the defendant is an innocent volunteer who has improved land or paid off a secured debt.

With regard to the first group of charities, the rationalisation in terms of change of position is not accepted by Birks. In his view the alterations to land exception is an illustration of a case in which the surviving enrichment has been extinguished. This is because where someone mistakenly improves land with another's money, he can rarely be said to have freely accepted the end-product of the work so as to overcome the argument from subjective devaluation: Birks, 371–72. There is clearly no enrichment where the alterations to the land are so eccentric as to have no value, or possibly devalue the property. In any event, unless an objective test of value is to be deployed, it is safe to say that there is no surviving enrichment where money is used in such alterations. Accordingly Birks rejects change of position as an explanation of the improvement to hospitals cases: Birks, 411–12.

With respect to the case of the Leaf Homœpathic Hospital, the reasoning of the Court of Appeal in *In re Diplock* has been subjected to a significant critical reappraisal by Millett LJ in *Boscawen v Bajwa* [1996] 1 WLR 328, at 340–41. Millett LJ appeared to accept Goff and Jones' rationalisation of the case on the basis of change of position:

> It may be doubted whether in its anxiety to avoid injustice to the hospital the court may not have done an even greater injustice to the next of kin, who were denied even the interest on their money. Justice did not require the withholding of any remedy, but only that the charge by subrogation should not be enforceable until the hospital had had a reasonable opportunity to obtain a fresh advance on suitable terms from a willing lender, perhaps from the bank which had held the original security.

> Today, considerations of this kind would be regarded as relevant to a change of position defence rather than as going to liability.

Similarly, Birks agrees that the restriction on tracing and claiming in *In re Diplock* where the money had been employed to discharge a secured debt is open to review: Birks, 372–75.

More recently, the decision of *Cheese v Thomas* [1994] 1 WLR 129, which was decided after the *Lipkin Gorman* case but not explicitly in terms of change of position, has been re-analysed in terms of that defence. Cheese, aged 88, wished to move back to his native Middlesex. He arranged to buy a house together with his great-nephew, Thomas. Cheese provided £43,000 and Thomas the balance of £40,000 by way of a mortgage for a house worth £83,000. The house was in Thomas's sole name, but it was understood that Cheese would have a licence to stay there for life. Thomas failed to keep up the mortgage repayments, so Cheese tried to escape the transaction. It was held that the transaction was vitiated by undue influence. In the meantime, the property crash intervened and the value of the house had fallen from £83,000 to £55,400. The question arose on whom the loss should fall. The judge held that the loss brought about by the fall in the property market should be shared between the two in the same proportions (43:40) as they had contributed to the purchase price. Accordingly, Cheese would bear £14,300 of the loss and Thomas £3,300.

The Court of Appeal upheld that finding. Sir Donald Nicholls V-C stressed (at 135): 'Restitution has to be made, not damages paid.' He also emphasised that the aim of the court was to do practical justice (citing *Erlanger* v *New Sombrero*

Phosphate Co. (1878) 3 App Cas 1218, at 1278–79 *per* Lord Blackman). The proper characterisation of the transaction was that both great-uncle and great-nephew were making a financial contribution to the acquisition of a new asset from which both hoped to benefit. Nicholls V-C considered the award of an equitable allowance to a pop music manager in respect of the benefits conferred upon a young pop performer by the Court of Appeal part of the process of rescinding the contractual arrangements on the grounds of undue influence in *O'Sullivan* v *Management Agency and Music Ltd* [1985] QB 428. Nicholls V-C stressed: 'What is true of profits must also be true of losses' (at 138). The gist of the issue was that each party should get back a proportionate share of the net proceeds of the house, after deducting the amount paid to the building society. What turned out to be crucial was the judge's finding that Thomas had not acted in a morally reprehensible way. It seems that Thomas was not a conscious wrong-doer. The case was one of presumed undue influence: Thomas had conceded that the presumption of undue influence applied to the facts of the case. There was no attempt to show that Cheese had been independently advised. The only issue in dispute was as to whether the transaction was manifestly disadvantageous to Cheese. The case was not one of improper behaviour or trickery.

Cheese v *Thomas* can be seen as working out the detail of the principle that restitution must be accompanied by counter-restitution where benefits have been transferred by both parties. Alternatively, the case has been ingeniously analysed in terms of change of position by Chen-Wishart (1994) 110 LQR 173. If the case is accepted as one based on change of position, it illustrates that the restriction of change of position to defendants who act in good faith and are not at fault, does not preclude defendants in presumed undue influence cases from seeking to rely upon the defence.

32.5 ACADEMIC ANALYSIS OF CHANGE OF POSITION

Richard Nolan, in 'Change of Position' in Birks (1995), at 135–89, analyses which of the ingredients of the claimant's cause of action is defeated by the assertion of change of position. Following Birks (Birks (1992), 125), Nolan argues 'that, by far and way most often and most obviously, the defence counters the assertion that the defendant is still enriched at the time of the action' (at 136). Only in limited circumstances might the defence of change of position go to the *injustice* of the defendant's receipt (at 172–75). Nolan concludes (at 189):

A two-stage model of change of position is proposed. First, a causal link must be demonstrated between the enrichment of the defendant and the erasure of enrichment put by way of defence to the plaintiff's claim; and, it is submitted, that link may be demonstrated in more ways than may have been thought hitherto. Further, it should be possible to base the defence of change of position on events which are the result of an anticipation of the receipt, though there is first instance authority to the contrary. Secondly, after the necessary causal link has been established, the court must decide whether there are any reasons why the defence might be withheld; principal among such considerations is whether there is any fault on the part of the defendant which might deny him a defence. Fault can render the defence unavailable, but it is submitted that the acts and defaults of the defendant which are to be regarded as culpable should not constitute too broad a category. A similar two-stage model is proposed for any injustice-related defence of change of position.

Nolan further argues that the defence should be available in both personal and proprietary claims. Further, he insists that the defence of change of position is distinct from good faith purchase and the need to insist upon counter-restitution. See further, Birks in Birks (1995), 322–32. Birks accepts that the focus of the defence of change of position will be on expenditure in reliance upon the security of the receipt. He also agrees that theft and casual destruction must count as relevant changes of position. Birks, however, remains sceptical of any unjust related version of change of position.

A further general survey is again by Birks, 'Change of Position: The Nature of the Defence and its Relationship to Other Restitutionary Defences' in McInnes, 49–74. The rationale of the defence is firmly located in the competition between the principle of unjust enrichment and the public interest in the security of receipts. Birks insists that the defence relates to the enrichment aspect, not the injustice aspect of the restitutionary enquiry. Birks draws parallels with *Wegfall Der Bereicherung*, the falling away of enrichment, which under the German Civil Code, BGB § 816(3), reduces the measure of recovery in German law. Birks further reiterates his resilement from earlier attempts to merge the defence of change of position with the clearly autonomous neighbouring defences of good faith purchase, ministerial receipt and the need to insist upon counter-restitution. Most importantly, Birks draws an illuminating distinction between the *abstract survival* of enrichment as part of the notional fund of the defendant's assets (which is the concern of change of position) and the peculiar common law notion of *specific or traceable* survival of wealth, where a claimant seeks to establish a proprietary remedy to value surviving rather than making a personal claim to value received (at 68–74). For a comparative survey see Hellwege [1999] RLR 92.

32.6 THE AGENT'S DEFENCE OF MINISTERIAL RECEIPT

32.6.1 Requirements and history

An agent who has paid over money to his principal has a complete defence to a claim in restitution brought against him. The appropriate defendant is the principal. On one view, this is not so much a defence as a means of identifying the correct defendant. There are a number of requirements. First, the receipt must be in a ministerial capacity, that is a receipt *qua* agent. Accordingly, the claim of ministerial receipt failed in *Baylis* v *Bishop of London* [1913] 1 Ch 127, where Hamilton LJ observed (at 141): 'No answer is forthcoming to the question "Who is the Bishop's principal?''' Secondly, the defence only avails an agent acting for a disclosed, as opposed to an undisclosed, principal (*Agip (Africa) Ltd* v *Jackson* [1990] Ch 265, at 288). Thirdly, the agent must have paid over the money, or otherwise acted to his detriment (*Holland* v *Russell* (1861) 1 B & S 421, 121 ER 773; aff'd (1863) 4 B & S 514, 122 ER 365). Fourthly, the payment over must precede any notice of the claimant's right of recovery (*Continental Caoutchouc and Gutta Percha Co.* v *Kleinwort, Sons & Co.* (1904) 90 LT 474, at 477). Fifthly, the agent must not have knowledge of or be privy to any wrongdoing which resulted in the benefit (*Snowdon* v *Davis* (1808) 1 Taunt 359, 127 ER 727).

The principle underlying ministerial receipt has been explained by the High Court of Australia in *Australia & New Zealand Banking Group Ltd* v *Westpac Banking Corp.* (1988) 164 CLR 662, in the following terms (at 682):

> The rationale of such a general rule can be identified in terms of the law of agency and of notions of unjust enrichment. If money is paid to an agent on behalf of a principal and the agent receives it in his capacity as such and, without notice of any mistake or irregularity in the payment, applies the money for the purpose for which it was paid to him, he has applied it in accordance with the mandate of the payer who must look to the principal for recovery.

Ministerial receipt has a long history. In *Sadler* v *Evans, Lady Windsor's case* (1766) 4 Burr 1984, 98 ER 34, a claim was brought against an agent and receiver of Lady Windsor to contest some customary dues. The money (one shilling and sixpence) was paid to the defendant, who provided a receipt acknowledging its receipt on behalf of Lady Windsor. It was alleged that the sums were not due and an action of money had and received was brought against the agent. The Court of King's Bench held, according to the report (at 1986):

> the plaintiff ought not recover against the defendant, in this action, and that the action ought to have been brought against Lady Windsor herself, and not against her agent. ... And Lord Mansfield ... said, he kept clear of all payments to third persons, but where 'tis to a known agent; in which, the action ought to be brought against the principal, unless in special cases (as under notice, or mala fide).

Conversely in *Buller* v *Harrison* (1777) 2 Cowp 565, 98 ER 1234, the plaintiff paid £2,100 to the defendant in respect of a claim brought upon a policy of insurance, in respect of which the defendant was acting as agent for the insured in New York. The plaintiff believed the loss be one which arose under the policy. Upon receipt of the money, the defendant credited the sum received against the sum of £3,600 which the insured owed to him. Less than two weeks later the plaintiff gave the defendant notice that it was a foul loss and sought restitution of the money. Lord Mansfield held there was no payment over, because there was no fresh credit advanced to the principal. It was wrong that the defendant should have the benefit of moneys obtained by misrepresentation by his principal.

In *Holland* v *Russell* (1861) 1 B & S 424, 121 ER 773, a plaintiff insurer paid the defendant agent under a policy, before discovering there had been some material non-disclosure on the part of the principal. The insurer sued to recover the money paid to the defendant agent. The money received had been used for three purposes:

(a)   some had been remitted to the principal;

(b)   some had been applied in respect of the agent's own claim for disbursements and commissions; and

(c)   the remainder had been applied to meet other expenses of the principal in relation to the insurance, at the principal's direction.

Buller v *Harrison* was distinguished as being a case where there was a running account between agent and principal, whereas here there was a settled account, which was equivalent to the agent having paid over the full sum. The defendant, who had acted all along in good faith without knowledge of any objection, was entitled to a complete defence of ministerial receipt. The judgment was upheld in the Court of Exchequer Chamber: (1863) 4 B & S 514, 122 ER 365. The latter case is more favourable to the agent, apparently on the ground that the majority of the money had been paid over to the principal.

Snowdon v *Davis* (1808) 1 Taunt 359, 127 ER 872 illustrates that ministerial receipt is not available to an agent who is a wrongdoer. The plaintiff paid money under duress of goods levied by the defendant bailiff in excess of his powers under a writ of distress. The bailiff paid the money over to the sheriff and resisted a claim for action for money had and received on the grounds that he had paid over. The defence was rejected in the circumstances. It did not apply in cases of compulsion or extortion of money *colore officii* in excess of authority. Sir James Mansfield CJ observed (at 363): 'The plaintiff pays it under the terror of process, to redeem his goods, not with an intent that this should be delivered over to anyone in particular.'

32.6.2   Modern applications

A curious recent application of ministerial receipt was to defeat the common law claim for money had and received against the money laundering accountants in *Agip (Africa) Ltd* v *Jackson* [1990] Ch 265. Millett J concluded (at 288):

> there is a clear answer to the plaintiff's claim for money had and received. Jackson & Co. must be treated as being in the same position as an agent who has accounted to his principal. Money paid by mistake to such an agent cannot afterwards be recovered from the agent but only from the principal. In every previously decided case the agent has received the money directly from the plaintiff, and it is well established that to obtain the benefit of the defence the recipient must have been known to the plaintiff to have been acting for a disclosed principal. In such a case the agent is treated as a mere conduit pipe and the money is taken as having been paid to the principal rather than the agent.

Millett J treated the shell payee company as the principal, and said that the defence would not avail it. However, he appeared to allow the accountants to benefit from the defence. He observed that the defence was not available to somebody who was implicated in the principal's fraud. However, the detailed principles were not a matter of common law. Rather, Millett J only treated the state of mind of the defendant accountants as relevant to the equitable claims for knowing receipt and knowing assistance. It will be recalled that ultimately Millett J held that the accountants must have known they were laundering money, and were accordingly accountable on that basis. On this basis it seems unclear why Millett J rejected the claim at common law. He suggests that the plaintiffs had failed to discharge the burden of proof, which they bore, that the defendants knew of their claim before they made the payments over. The unsatisfactory handling of this issue in *Agip* must be due to Millett J's explicit hostility to utilising common law principles as a vehicle for restitutionary recovery. See also *Bank Tejerat* v *Hong Kong and Shangai Banking (CI) Ltd* [1995] 1 Lloyd's Rep 239, at 246–47.

Even more recently, in *Portman Building Society* v *Hamlyn Taylor Neck* [1998] 4 All ER 202, Millett LJ has considered the operation of ministerial receipt in respect of a claim brought against a firm of solicitors by a lender arising out of a mortgage fraud. Millett LJ denied that the solicitors were ever enriched by the receipt of the mortgage moneys, which they did not receive for their own use and benefit but for the use of the plaintiff building society. Millett LJ observed (at 207):

> Save in strictly limited circumstances it is no defence the defendant has parted with the money. All that is true. But it is, of course, a defence that he has parted with it by paying it to the plaintiff or *to the plaintiff's order....* That is what the firm did in the present case.

Millett LJ rejected attempts to merge the defence of ministerial receipt with change of position (at 207):

> I myself do not regard the agent's defence in such a case as a particular instance of the change of position defence, nor is it generally so regarded. At common law the agent recipient is regarded as a mere conduit for the money, which is treated as paid to the principal, not to the agent. The doctrine is therefore not so much a defence as a means of identifying the proper party to be sued. It does not, for example, avail the agent of an undisclosed principal; though today such an agent would be able to rely on a change of position defence.
>
> The true rule is that where the plaintiff has paid money under (for example) a mistake to the agent of a third party, he may sue the principal whether or not the agent has accounted to him, for in contemplation of law the payment is made to the principal and not to his agent. If the agent still retains the money, however, the plaintiff may elect to sue either the principal or the agent, and the agent remains liable if he pays the money over to his principal after notice of the claim. If he wishes to protect himself, he should interplead. But once the agent has paid the

money to his principal or to his order without notice of the claim, the plaintiff must sue the principal.

In addition, it was also fatal to the claim that the money was paid pursuant to an operative binding contract whereby the defendant solicitors were required to transfer the money in accordance with the instruction of the lender.

32.6.3 Theoretical foundations

There are several possible explanations for the doctrine of ministerial receipt. There is a view consistently expressed by Goff and Jones that it is a species of change of position, albeit with special features because of the agency context in which it operates: Goff and Jones, 833–38. Secondly, Swadling argues in Birks (1995), at 243, that 'the real reason for the defence is that the plaintiff is in certain circumstances estopped from bringing a claim against an agent who has done no more than follow his (i.e. the plaintiff's) instruction and make a payment over to his principal'. Swadling argues that there are four elements to the defence:

(a)   the receipt must be ministerial, not beneficial;
(b)   the recipient must have passed on the benefit to his principal;
(c)   the recipient must not be tainted by wrongdoing; and
(d)   the claimant must have known he was making a payment to an agent.

Accordingly Swadling argues that the defence can only operate in the context of unjust factors such as mistake or failure of consideration. In cannot be relied upon in cases of duress or restitution for wrongs, nor significantly in cases of ignorance, where the claimant gave no consent to the transfer. In such a case the claimant cannot fulfil Swadling's fourth requirement and knowingly make a payment to an agent. See Swadling, in Birks (1995), 243–60, at 259–60.

Birks strikes a more cautious note, suggesting further fine-tuning is required. He suggests that ministerial receipt may simply be a rule for ascertaining the correct defendant: Birks [1989] LMCLQ 296, at 303–4. More recently, in response to Swadling, Birks envisages an expansive role for the defence. Birks stills sees the defence as more closely tied to change of position than to estoppel. Where contracts have been formed, English law readily allows the agent to drop out of the picture. Birks supports a similar policy in respect of restitutionary liability. Birks, in Birks (1995), 341, concludes (at 345):

> the real payee is the principal, and the principal should be the defendant in the light of that reality. It is not clear why the payer should be able to have an alternative recourse in this situation. Lastly, the basic concepts of the law of agency seem to be confounded by the liability of the agent. The agent should drop out.

Then there is the position advocated by Millett LJ in *Portman Building Society*, that the defence of ministerial receipt should be seen as autonomous, and not as a species of change of position. Millett LJ was emphatic that the doctrine was aimed at identifying the appropriate defendant.

Lastly, it should be recalled that the case law to date on ministerial receipt is exclusively concerned with common law claims. In contrast, the position of the agent is not treated in equity claims as giving rise to a special defence. Rather, liability in knowing receipt is treated as only attaching to one who receives beneficially, rather than ministerially. Agents are excluded by the definition of the cause of action. In *Agip (Africa) Ltd* v *Jackson* [1990] Ch 265, Millett J, in considering a claim based on knowing receipt, observed (at 292):

> the recipient must have received the property for his own use and benefit. This is why neither the paying nor the collecting bank would normally be brought within it. In paying or collecting money for a customer the bank acts only as his agent. It is otherwise, however, if the collecting bank uses the money to reduce or discharge the customer's overdraft. In doing so it receives the money for its own benefit.

Accordingly, the defendant firm of accountants were acquitted of knowing receipt because they did not receive beneficially. However, Millett J went on to find that they had sufficient knowledge to be accountable on the grounds of knowing assistance (or as we now say, dishonest accessory liability). Millett J's willingness to recognise the defence of ministerial receipt on the facts of *Agip* must be criticised on the basis that he made it available to a wrongdoer, whereas a restitutionary defence such as ministerial receipt (whether expressed as an ingredient of the cause of action or a special defence) should never be available to one who lacks good faith. For the position of banks, see Bryan in Rose (1998), 161–88.

32.7 PRACTICAL ISSUES

As a matter of principle, and good practice, change of position or ministerial receipt should be specifically pleaded. Advisers acting for defendants whose circumstances have changed should ascertain and enumerate as far as is practically possible any actual expenditure or loss incurred by the defendant in relation to the receipt. Where possible this should be incorporated as a schedule in the defence. In some circumstances, it may not be possible to point to precise items of expenditure in reliance upon the receipt. In such cases, the pleadings should particularise as far as possible the change in the mode of living of the defendant. In replying to a plea of change of position, those acting for the claimant may often wish to allege that the defendant knew or ought to have known that he was unjustly enriched at the claimant's expense. By analogy with CPR PD 16 on statements of case, the claimant should specifically particularise any allegations of notice or knowledge of a fact: CPR Part 16, PD 16, para. 10.2(5).

FURTHER READING

Asterisks indicate especially useful works.

Change of position and estoppel

*Goff and Jones, 818–41

G. Jones, 'Change of Circumstances in Quasi-Contract' (1957) 73 LQR 48

P. Birks, 'The Recovery of Carelessly Mistaken Payments' [1972] CLP 179

J. Beatson and W. Bishop, 'Mistaken Payments in the Law of Restitution' (1986) 36 U Toronto LJ 149; also in Beatson, 137–76

P. Butler, 'Mistaken Payments, Change of Position and Restitution' in Finn, 87–137

P. Birks, in Birks (1992), 123–47

*R. Nolan, 'Change of Position' in Birks (1995), 135–89

*P. Birks, in Birks (1995), 322–32

M. Chen-Wishart, 'Loss-sharing, Undue Influence and Manifest Disadvantage' (1994) 110 LQR 173

*P. Birks, 'Change of Position — The Nature of the Defence and Its Relationship to Other Restitutionary Defences', in McInnes, 49–74

M. Bryan, 'Change of Position: Commentary', in McInnes, 75–85

R. Nolan, 'Change of Position in Anticipation of Enrichment' [1995] LMCLQ 313

P. Key, 'Excising Estoppel by Representation as a Defence to Restitution' [1995] CLJ 525

P. Hellwege, 'The Scope of Application of Change of Position in the Law of Unjust Enrichment: A Comparative Study' [1999] *Restitution Law Review* 92

Ministerial receipt

*Goff and Jones, 833–38

*W. Swadling, 'The Nature of Ministerial Receipt' in Birks (1995), 243–60

P. Birks, in Birks (1995), 341–47

*M. Bryan, 'Recovering Misdirected Money from Banks: Ministerial Receipt at Law and in Equity' in Rose (1998), 161–88

33 Compromise and Submission to an Honest Claim

33.1 THEORETICAL FOUNDATIONS

Goff and Jones have consistently argued that restitutionary rights are defeated where the payment was made as part of a compromise, or in submission to an honest claim. Goff and Jones state (at 53–54):

> The plaintiff confers a benefit on the defendant, in pursuance of the defendant's honest claim and with the intention of compromising that claim. The general principle is that the plaintiff's restitutionary claim must fail. The compromise cannot be set aside, whether or not the claim was accompanied by the threat of legal proceedings.
>
> A person upon whom a claim is made is not allowed to choose his own time for litigation; moreover, the courts lean in favour of settlements, and to allow a party to reopen a transaction of this kind serves to promote rather than to allay disputes.

The operation of submission to a honest claim will be most prominent where a claim of restitution is based upon mistake of law, duress or compulsion, or is a claim to recover money paid pursuant to an *ultra vires* demand by a public authority. The topic has already been addressed in the appropriate parts of this book. It should be noted that Goff and Jones treat submission to an honest claim as a 'limitation' upon the right to restitution, rather than a defence: Goff and Jones, 53–58. It is submitted that as the doctrine is more explicitly recognised, it will be treated as a defence alongside good faith purchase and change of position, as indeed it was by Robert Goff J in *Barclays Bank Ltd* v *W. J. Simms, Son & Cooke (Southern) Ltd* [1980] QB 677, at 695.

The terminology in relation to this topic has not yet settled down, and the concept of settlement or submission to an honest claim has only recently surfaced explicitly in the authorities. First, it is best to separate out contractual compromises, where there is clear offer, acceptance and consideration. This excludes any recourse to restitution by the operation of the principle of the primacy of contract, or subsidiarity, in accordance with the third stage of the restitutionary enquiry (see 1.2). Compromises may be set aside, but only by establishing the standard contractual vitiating factors such as duress, misrepresentation or a mistake which renders the subject-matter of the transaction essentially and radically different to what the parties supposed it to be. The leading case of *Callisher* v *Bischoffsheim* (1870) LR 5 QB 449 emphasises the courts' reluctance to interfere with binding compromises. This principle or policy is now even more prominent in the light of the current reforms to civil justice.

Leaving to one side the contractual cases, the difficult question is whether there is any role for a separate doctrine of non-contractual submission to an honest claim. Some leading writers are sceptical: Burrows, 101–103, 118. The situation is complicated by Goff and Jones's use of a number of different terminological expressions to cover this point. In addition to settlement of or submission to a honest claim, Goff and Jones also use the language of 'waiver of enquiries', 'assumption of risk' (Goff and Jones, 54) and 'voluntary payments' (Goff and Jones, 197). Here the language of voluntary payments will be eschewed because of the difficulties which that phrase has caused in the past. However, the core of this defence appears to be that the payer who has settled an honest claim, has clearly accepted the risk that had he chosen to dispute it and litigate, he would have established that the payment was not due and owing.

Perhaps the best statement of the defence is by Hobhouse J in *Westdeutsche Landesbank Girozentrale* v *Islington London Borough Council* [1994] 4 All ER 890, at 934:

> If the facts were that these payments had been made with a conscious appreciation that the contracts were or might be void, that would normally suffice to negative any right of recovery. They would be voluntary payments. But, unless there was such an actual conscious appreciation, the principle cannot be applied. It does not suffice that a fully informed investigation of the legal position leading to the correct conclusions in law would have disclosed that the councils did not have the capacity to enter into the contracts. A situation has to be disclosed which is tantamount to a willingness to make a gift of the money to recipient.

This formulation and the insistence upon a conscious appreciation by the payer was approved of by Lord Hope of Craighead in *Kleinwort Benson Ltd* v *Lincoln City Council* [1998] 3 WLR 1095, at 1150. It is submitted that certainly in the wake of the *Kleinwort Benson* case, the concept of a non-contractual submission to a honest claim does operate as an autonomous restitutionary defence. However, as the formulation of Hobhouse J in *Westdeutsche* suggests, it will not be easy to establish.

In an interesting article, Neil Andrews has argued that the law in this area should be reformulated to give greater prominence to the concept of a settlement, including an implied settlement: 'Mistaken settlements of disputable claims' [1989] LMCLQ 431. This would supersede the current profusion of, and confusion in, the terminology used. The argument posits a broad approach to the question of what amounts to a settlement. A settlement is seen as a vehicle for allocating the risk in relation to the dispute between the parties. The parties having accordingly assumed the risks, they should not easily be allowed to escape. Accordingly it is the stringent rule of contractual mistake which should be applied rather than the more generous tests for the recovery of mistaken payments in the law of restitution. Andrews reinterprets a number of leading cases, such as *Bell* v *Lever Brothers Ltd* [1932] AC 161 and *McGee* v *Pennine Insurance Co. Ltd* [1969] 2 QB 507, in terms of an implied settlement. Most strikingly, he interprets *Kelly* v *Solari* (1841) 9 M & W 54, 152 ER 24, as evidencing an implied settlement, and therefore as wrongly decided unless it could be shown that the payee knew of the mistake being made. The argument is an impressive one. However, ultimately it appears to stretch too far the concept of the settlement, and runs the risk of introducing unnecessary fiction into this area of the law. The better view appears to be that it is proper to distinguish between genuinely contractual compromises, which can only be set aside in accordance to the rule of contract law, and the separate restitutionary doctrine of the settlement of an honest claim. If the courts are to insist upon a conscious appreciation of the risk taken by the payer, the defence will not operate as widely in the restitutionary context as Andrews considers.

In the other leading academic discussion of this topic, Arrowsmith also rejects the concept 'submission to an honest claim' in the context of mistaken payments. She prefers the language of waiver. Accordingly she concludes, in 'Mistake and the Role of the "Submission to an Honest Claim"' in Burrows (1991), 17, at 38:

> restitution should normally be refused whenever the payer had doubts on the issue on which he claims to be mistaken at the time he paid. Although he can still be said to be mistaken, he can be said to have waived his right to recover in such circumstances, since he ought not to pay unless the payee agrees to accept a payment which is conditional. The principle is of some importance, since, it has been argued, even where the payment is made in response to a legal claim, there is not normally a contractual settlement of the parties' rights. On the other hand, there should generally be a right to restitution where there are no doubts existing, whether the mistake is one of fact or law.

33.2 MISTAKEN PAYMENTS

The liberalisation of the ground for recovery for mistake of law by the House of Lords in *Kleinwort Benson Ltd* v *Lincoln City Council* [1999] 2 AC 349, may appear to constitute too great an interference with the stability of transactions. However, on a close reading of the speeches of the majority of the House of Lords it is clear that the intention of their Lordships was to switch attention from unprincipled restrictions on the cause of action to a more sensitive regime of appropriate defences. Of great significance in the context of claims for the return of money paid under a mistake, especially of law, is the policy upholding compromises entered into in good faith and the defence of in submission to an honest claim. Goff and Jones have consistently argued that the cases on payment under a mistake of law should be reinterpreted on the basis that the courts were upholding payments made in submission to a honest claim (at 214). They suggest that the only practical consequence of the distinction between facts and law is the greater likelihood of the payer under a mistake of law assuming the risk that he is mistaken, whereas this is uncommon in relation to mistakes of fact (at 215).

The principle is well established. Robert Goff J explicitly based his proposition 2(a) in *Barclays Bank Ltd* v *W. J. Simms, Son & Cooke (Southern) Ltd* [1980] QB 677 upon the dictum of Parke B in *Kelly* v *Solari* (1841) 9 M & W 54, 152 ER 25. There, the learned Baron suggested the following limit on recovery for a mistake of fact (at 59):

> If, indeed, the money is intentionally paid, without reference to the truth or falsehood of the fact, the plaintiff meaning to waive all enquiry into it, and that the person receiving shall have the money at all events, whether the fact be true or false, the latter is certainly entitled to retain it.

The practical problem remains that while it appears that the law now recognises the defence of submission to an honest claim, it has never been explicitly applied in the cases. Therefore it is hard to state with certainty the circumstances in which it will be established. Goff and Jones are agnostic whether submission to an honest claim is properly described as a defence or a limit upon the availability of restitution: Goff and Jones, 234. It is submitted on the basis of the ordinary principle that he who asserts must prove, that it is best recognised as a defence. Accordingly the burden of proof for establishing a binding settlement on payment and submission to an honest claim is upon the recipient. This would also be consistent with Robert Goff J's classification of submission to an honest claim alongside the defences of good faith purchase and change of position in *Barclays Bank* v *Simms*. The leading discussion of the majority in *Kleinwort Benson Ltd* v *Lincoln City Council* is discussed above in 3.5.1.

33.3   DURESS AND *ULTRA VIRES* DEMANDS

Arrowsmith has argued that it is inappropriate to apply the same test to cases of mistake where the payee is usually blameless to cases involving duress where there is misconduct by the payee: Arrowsmith, in Burrows (1991), 17, at 20–21. However, the principle of submission to an honest claim was recognised by the Court of Appeal in *Maskell* v *Horner* [1915] 3 KB 106 (see Goff and Jones, 347–51). It has been argued above that while the test of duress will be applied objectively, there is still room for the operation of submission to an honest claim in duress cases. Indeed this appears to be the best explanation of *CTN Cash and Carry Ltd* v *Gallaher Ltd* [1994] 4 All ER 714 (see 6.6 above).

In the context of *ultra vires* demands by public authorities, it has been recognised that submission to an honest claim may operate to bar the right to recovery (*Woolwich Equitable Building Society* v *Inland Revenue Commissioners* [1993] AC 70). See 17.2.

FURTHER READING

Asterisks indicate especially useful works.

Goff and Jones, 53–58, 197–200, 214–15, 234–35, 347–51, 683
*N. Andrews, 'Mistaken Settlements of Disputable Claims' [1989] LMCLQ 431
*S. Arrowsmith, 'Mistake and the Role of the "Submission to an Honest Claim"' in Burrows (1991), 17–38
D. Foskett, *The Law and Practice of Compromise*, 4th edn (1996)

34 Passing On

34.1 INTRODUCTION

It seems safe to assert that passing on is not a general defence in the law of unjust enrichment. The premise upon which it rests is flawed. The defendant says to the claimant: 'I have not been enriched at your expense. You have passed on the diminution in your wealth to your customers, by increasing your prices.' The defence has been argued vigorously by revenue authorities who have imposed unlawful or *ultra vires* taxation upon businesses. The fallacy in the argument is that every restitutionary claimant must adjust his financial position, pending the successful outcome of the recovery exercise. The claimant is entitled to say to the defendant: 'This is none of your business; in any event I may pass on the benefit of what I recover from you to my customers in the future.' In traditional terms, what the claimant does to provide for the loss is *res inter alios acta*.

There are two almost insuperable objections to its recognition. First, it contradicts the underlying principle of unjust enrichment. The subject is concerned with the reversal of unjust gains. It is not focussed on loss or deprivation. It is never said in cases of acquisitive wrongdoing that the absence of a correlation between the gain and loss negates the enrichment of the defendant. Passing on is not said to go to the issue of enrichment. Rather it is said to defeat the claimant's assertion that the enrichment was *at his expense*. This appears to be an unmeritorious attempt to utilise the claimant's prudential measures in order to exculpate the defendant. Secondly, and more practically, the application of the defence appears to require almost inscrutable economic and evidential considerations: see Rudden and Bishop (1981) 6 ELR 243. For this reason the proposed defence should be rejected. It may be that different considerations apply where taxes are overpaid and the claimant is acting in the capacity of tax collecter rather than taxpayer.

34.2 THE TAXATION CASES

The context in which the proposed defence is most commonly encountered is the imposition of *ultra vires* taxes. The defence received support in the Supreme Court of Canada in *Air Canada* v *British Columbia* (1989) 59 DLR (4th) 161. LaForest J stated (at 193–94):

> The law of restitution is not intended to provide windfalls to plaintiffs who have suffered no loss. . . . If the airlines have not shown that they bore the burden of the tax, then they have not made out the claim. What the province received is relevant only insofar as it was received at the airlines' expense.

Additionally the European Court of Justice has sanctioned the defence, provided its operation in the Community sphere is no more stringent than that which would apply in domestic law. The leading discussion is *Amministrazione delle Finanze dello Stato* v *SpA San Giorgio* [1983] ECR 359. The court proclaimed (at 362–63):

> Community law does not prevent a national legal system from disallowing the repayment of charges which have been unduly levied where to do so would entail unjust enrichment of the recipient. There is nothing in Community law therefore to prevent the courts from taking account, under the national law, the fact that the unduly levied charges have been incorporated in the price of the goods and must have passed that on to customers.

To date, in domestic law, consideration of the supposed defence has received only passing consideration. In *Woolwich Equitable Building Society* v *Inland Revenue Commissioners* [1993] AC 70, Lord Goff observed (at 177–78):

> It will be a matter of consideration whether the fact that the plaintiff has passed on the tax or levy so that the burden has fallen on another should provide a defence to his claim. Although this is contemplated by the European Court of Justice in the *San Giorgio* case, it is evident from *Air Canada* v *British Columbia* 59 DLR (4th) 161 that the point is not without its difficulties; and the availability of such a defence may depend upon the nature of the tax or other levy. No doubt matters of this kind will in any event be the subject of consideration during the current consultations with the Law Commission.

More recently, the High Court of Australia has emphatically rejected passing on in *Commissioner of State Revenue (Vic)* v *Royal Insurance Australia Ltd* (1994) 182 CLR 51. The defence has been rejected as a matter of English common law in the swaps cases, which will be considered at 34.3 below. However, it should be noted that the defence has been applied in certain statutory contexts, where restrictions are placed upon the right to recover overpaid taxes and other levies. For discussion of s. 20 of the Finance Act 1995 and s. 80(3) of the Value Added Tax Act 1994, see Law Commission, *Restitution: Mistakes of Law and Ultra Vires Receipts and Payments* (Law Com. No. 227), paras 10.44 to 10.48 and Appendix B.

34.3   PRIVATE TRANSACTIONS

Outside the special context of the taxation cases, passing on has been relied on only in the void interest rate swap agreement cases, which were decided as a matter of private law (although admittedly the defendants were usually public authorities). In an earlier case, *Kleinwort Benson Ltd v South Tyneside Metropolitan Borough Council* [1994] 4 All ER 972, Hobhouse J had to decide whether a local authority, which was the net recipient of benefits under a void contract, could raise as a defence the bank's strategy of hedging transactions. Hobhouse J observed that this was the flipside of the coin to the issues which arise where a defendant says he has changed his position as a result of the enrichment. Here, the defendants argued that the paying bank must have recouped its losses under the hedging transaction. Hobhouse J rejected the idea of passing on as having any relevance in the private law of transactions (at 984–85):

> What is the legal principle which the defendants invoke? It can only be some unspecific principle which derives not from the law of restitution, but from some concept of compensation. The essential feature in what the defendants here are asking the court to do (and other defendants in similar actions) is to make an assessment of loss suffered by the relevant plaintiff as if one were investigating a right to compensation. The argument involves problems of remoteness. Even the simplest cases where parties are dealing on a market, other individual contracts are in principle too remote to be taken into account.

Hobhouse J did not regard passing on a providing any defence to the prima facie claim of unjust enrichment. He rejected the approach of the majority in the *Air Canada* case, while accepting that special considerations may apply in the taxation cases. Hobhouse J concluded (at 987):

> If the plaintiff is to be denied his remedy in respect of this sum which he has paid to the defendant and which it is unjust that the defendant should retain, it must be upon a basis that is relevant to the law of restitution and not some principle borrowed from the law of compensation. Further, the application of the principle, if it is to be adopted, must respect the principles of remoteness recognised in the law of compensation.

This approach was subsequently approved of by the Court of Appeal in *Kleinwort Benson Ltd v Birmingham City Council* [1997] QB 380. The Court thoroughly reviewed authorities throughout the common law world on passing on. Evans LJ too distinguished the taxation cases as being of 'limited assistance' because of the public law element, and further because in some cases the claimant might be acting as tax collector rather than taxpayer (at 389). Evans LJ stressed that the bank was under no duty to hedge its risk, and in any event such hedging arrangements were separate and independent contracts which were too remote from the swaps agreements to set off against the bank's loss. Morritt LJ considered the view of La Forest LJ in *Air Canada* v *British Columbia* (1989) 59 DLR (4th) 161, at 193, that: 'The law of restitution is not intended to provide windfalls to plaintiffs who have suffered no loss.' Morritt LJ rejected the proposition that even where the loss had been passed on, it would be unjust for the claimant to recover. As between the claimant and the defendant, the former had a better right to any windfall (at 401).

34.4 CONCLUSION

It is submitted that the courts are correct, at least in the law of private transactions, to reject the alleged defence of passing on. The supposed defence is inconsistent with the underlying principle of unjust enrichment. The situation is properly judged as between claimant and defendant. As between the two the claimant has the better right, and should not be prejudiced by efforts to rearrange its finances pending recovery of the benefits from the defendant. As has been acknowledged, the taxation cases may involve special issues. First, it may be thought that too much restitution would be disruptive to public finances. This argument should be rejected as being inconsistent with the Rule of Law. Secondly, certain taxes, such as value added tax, may raise additional complications in that the claimant may be operating as a tax collector rather than a taxpayer. It must be acknowledged that special considerations arise here. See the Law Commission, *Restitution: Mistakes of Law and Ultra Vires Receipts and Payments* (Law Com. No. 227, 1997), paras 10.44 to 10.48 and Appendix B. Accordingly, passing on has no place in the modern law of unjust enrichment at least as far as private transactions are concerned.

FURTHER READING

Asterisks indicate especially useful works.

Goff and Jones, 658–59, 684–88
B. Rudden and W. Bishop, 'Gritz and Quellmehl: Pass It On' (1981) 6 ELR 243
*F. Rose, 'Passing On' in Birks (1995), 261–87
Law Commission, *Restitution: Mistakes of Law and Ultra Vires Receipts and Payments* (Law Com. No. 227, 1997)

35 Illegality and Public Policy as Defences

35.1 INTRODUCTION

We saw in Chapter 13 that illegality will generally prevent both parties from enforcing a tainted transaction or seeking other relief, including restitution of benefits transferred under it. There we have already discussed two possible exceptions to the general preclusion of restitutionary claims in this context, namely the *locus poenitentiae* and *non in pari delicto* cases. This chapter is concerned with the operation of illegality, and by extension public policy, in precluding restitutionary claims.

A contract or other transaction may be illegal in three ways. First, statute may expressly prohibit both the formation and the performance of the contract. This will be the case where, for example, the statute provides: 'No action shall lie ....' Secondly, statute might impliedly prohibit enforcement of the contract. In *Phoenix General Insurance Co. of Greece SA* v *Halvanon Insurance Co. Ltd* [1988] QB 216, Kerr LJ summarised the position (at 273):

> (i) Where a statute prohibits both parties from concluding or performing a contract when both or either of them have no authority to do so, the contract is impliedly prohibited ... (ii) But where a statute merely prohibits one party from entering into a contract without authority, and/or imposes a penalty upon him if he does so (i.e. a unilateral prohibition) it does not follow that the contract itself is impliedly prohibited so as to render it illegal and void. Whether or not this statute has this effect depends upon considerations of public policy in the light of the mischief which the statute is designed to prevent, its language, scope and purpose, the consequences for the innocent party, and any other relevant considerations.

Thirdly, the transaction may be illegal where it contemplates the commission of a crime at common law, or another act which the common law deems to be contrary to public policy. We are not here concerned with the general rules of illegality in relation to transactions, which can be found in the contractual texts (e.g., Anson, 333–37; 348–81) and the texts on trusts. We are concerned with the effect of express or implied statutory prohibition or the fact that a transaction is contrary to public policy, upon a claim to restitution. It is a difficult question whether an express or implied statutory prohibition of the enforcement of a transaction, necessarily precludes any relief in restitution.

35.2 THE SCOPE OF THE PROHIBITION OF RESTITUTIONARY CLAIMS

The true scope of the *in pari delicto* principle in relation to restitutionary claims is difficult to state. The issues here are the same as those discussed in Chapter 13 above. The question is, when does illegality preclude the restitutionary claim? In identifying exceptions to the *in pari delicto* principle, does this create a new ground for restitution? Birks argues that where the parties are held not be *in pari delicto*, the ground for restitution can usually be found elsewhere in the law of restitution, usually in cases of vitiated voluntariness such as mistake or compulsion: Birks, 424–32.

35.2.1 Mistake

In *Oom* v *Bruce* (1810) 12 East 225, 104 ER 87, the plaintiff entered into an insurance policy for goods to be carried from Russia to England. The contract was made after the commencement of hostilities between the two countries but before the plaintiff had knowledge of the fact, and after the ship had sailed and been seized and made to return to Russia. The plaintiff sought to recover the premium paid. The contract was presumably illegal at common law on the basis that it involved trading with the enemy. The Court of King's Bench stressed that the plaintiff had no knowledge of the circumstances giving rise to the illegality. Accordingly, Lord Ellenborough CJ held (at 226): 'there is no reason why they should not recover back the premiums which they have paid for an insurance from which, without any fault imputable to themselves, they could never have derived any benefit.'

Induced mistake caused the transfer in *Hughes* v *Liverpool Victoria Legal Friendly Society* [1916] 2 KB 482, where the plaintiff was fraudulently persuaded by a representative of the insurer that a life insurance policy, in which he had no insurable interest, was valid. Upon the plaintiff discovering the policy was illegal and void, she claimed recovery of the premiums paid. Phillimore LJ stated the principle (at 492):

> where an illegal contract of insurance is entered into, and the assured is ignorant of the law and is induced to enter into it by the fraudulent misrepresentation of the law by the agent of the assurance company, the parties are not *in pari delicto* and the assured may recover the premiums paid.

The unsatisfactory earlier decision of *Harse* v *Pearl Life Assurance Co.* [1904] 1 KB 558 insists that an innocent misrepresentation would not suffice. This is probably not good law. The leading case is *Kiriri Cotton Co. Ltd* v *Dewani* [1960] AC 192, which has been discussed at 13.4. This case requires reinterpretation in the light of *Kleinwort Benson Ltd* v *Lincoln City Council* [1999] 2 AC 349.

35.2.2   Duress and imposition

The facts of *Smith* v *Bromley* (1760) 2 Doug 696 (note), 99 ER 441, are reminiscent of the fiction of Fanny Burney. A lady was imposed upon by her brother's chief creditor to pay an extra sum to him, before he would sign a certificate of discharge releasing the brother from bankruptcy. The money was paid and the defendant creditor signed the discharge. The lady then sought recovery of the £40 she had paid. The Court of King's Bench awarded her restitution. Lord Mansfield stated (at 697):

> If the act is in itself immoral, or a violation of the general laws of public policy, there, the party paying shall not have this action; for where both parties are equally criminal against such general laws, the rule is, *potior est condito defendentis.* But there are other laws which are calculated for the protection of the subject against oppression, extortion, deceit &c. If such laws are violated, and the defendant takes advantage of the plaintiff's condition or situation, there the plaintiff shall recover.

That case was followed in *Smith* v *Cuff* (1817) 6 M & S 160, 105 ER 1203 on similar facts. Lord Ellenborough CJ commented that the parties were never equally guilty 'when one holds the rod, and the other bows to it' (at 164).

35.2.3   Failure of consideration

In *Parkinson* v *College of Ambulance Ltd* [1925] 2 KB 1, the plaintiff somewhat foolishly paid £3,000 to the defendant charity, relying upon a representation by the secretary of the charity that a knighthood would be forthcoming in return. Unsurprisingly, the representation turned out to be fraudulent and Mr Parkinson sought restitution from the charity. This was held to be a case where the parties were *in pari delicto*, because even if the secretary of the charity was more at fault, the plaintiff had made a contract which he ought never have entered into. One can have more sympathy for the plaintiff in *Berg* v *Sadler & Moore* [1937] 2 KB 158. The plaintiff was on the stop list of the Tobacco Trade Association as a result of a breach of their price-fixing rules. He attempted to obtain cigarettes using the name of a friend. The money was paid, but when the defendant suppliers discovered the true purchaser they refused to supply the cigarettes or return the purchase price. The plaintiff's claim for restitution was rejected by the Court of Appeal. The Court stridently held that it amounted to an attempt to obtain goods by false pretences, and accordingly the Court refused to lend its aid to the plaintiff (but happily lent its aid to the anti-competitive practice of the trade association).

There is a paucity of authority of situations where a party has recovered on the ground of failure of consideration on the basis that he was not equally guilty in respect of the illegal transaction. Perhaps an example is *Hermann* v *Charlesworth* [1905] 2 KB 123, in which the plaintiff was a single lady desirous of getting married. She agreed to pay the defendant marriage advertising agent £250 if an introduction arranged by the defendant led to matrimony. The plaintiff paid £52, of which £47 would be returned if no marriage followed within nine months. Various introductions led to nothing, and the plaintiff claimed the return of her money. The Court of Appeal held that the transaction was illegal (which must be of interest to the numerous dating agencies which proliferate these days). Collins MR acknowledged that the plaintiff had had the benefit of a number of introductions, but was prepared to treat these as actions taken by the defendant in his own interest in order to improve his chances of winning what was characterised as a wager. Collins MR felt that equity was not precluded from ordering the recovery of money under an illegal transaction simply because the defendant had incurred and taken some steps towards performance in carrying out his side of the contract. The case is explicable either on the ground of failure of consideration (and a very beneficial interpretation of failure of consideration at that), or on the basis that the plaintiff fell within the protected class of vulnerable people, whom the policy of outlawing marriage-brokering contracts was aimed at protecting. Compare Birks, 210.

35.3 RESTITUTION PROHIBITED IF IT IS TANTAMOUNT TO CONTRACTUAL ENFORCEMENT

An important principle is that restitution is impermissible where an award would be equivalent to the enforcement of the illegal contract. In *Taylor* v *Bhail* [1996] CLC 377, the headmaster of a school which had suffered storm damage, agreed to award a contract to the plaintiff builder on the basis that the builder would inflate his estimate by £1,000 in order that the defendant could pocket the additional £1,000 recouped from the school's insurers. The work being done, the plaintiff claimed alternatively upon the contract, or for a *quantum meruit* in respect of work done. The ground of restitution was not identified, but was presumably failure of consideration or free acceptance. The Court of Appeal refused to enforce either the contractual or the restitutionary claim.

Millett LJ held that the transaction was illegal. Whereas the defendant was enriched at the plaintiff's expense, it could not be said to be unjust because of the illegality of the transaction into which both entered. Further, the existence of the illegal contract excluded recourse to the law of restitution. This is an application of the primacy of contract principle. To have succeeded, the plaintiff should have repudiated the contract. But this could have been done only if there had been no partial performance of the illegal purpose. It was now too late to withdraw (at 383). This decision may take the primary of contract argument too far. See Rose, 'Confining Illegality' (1996) 112 LQR 545.

More recently, in *Mohamed* v *Alaga & Co.* [1999] 3 All ER 699 the plaintiff entered into a fee-sharing agreement with the defendant solicitor, whereby the plaintiff would refer asylum-seekers to the solicitor in return for a proportion of the fees contrary to the Solicitors' Practice Rules. The plaintiff again claimed alternatively under the contract or in restitution. The Court of Appeal would not enforce the illegal contract. However, the plaintiff was allowed to pursue a *quantum meruit* claim, sounding in restitution, as he was apparently unaware of the illegality of the transaction (at 707–708). These recent decisions of the Court of Appeal are difficult to reconcile. Presumably in the latter case the award of reasonable remuneration would not have been equivalent to contractual enforcement.

35.4 PROPRIETARY CLAIMS UNDER ILLEGAL TRANSACTIONS

This is the province of the law of property, but will be briefly discussed here. The leading cases are *Tinsley* v *Milligan* [1994] 1 AC 340 and *Tribe* v *Tribe* [1996] Ch 107. In *Tinsley* v *Milligan*, the plaintiff, aged 19, and the defendant, aged 38, were lesbian lovers. They purchased a property in the sole name of the plaintiff, but on a common understanding that they would be joint beneficial owners. The house was in the plaintiff's name in order to enable the defendant to make fraudulent claims upon the Department of Social Security (DSS). The money obtained by the fraud contributed only in a small way to the acquisition of the equity in the home. Subsequently the defendant repented of the fraud and disclosed this to the DSS. The parties quarrelled and the plaintiff moved out. The plaintiff claimed possession of the property, asserting sole ownership. The defendant counterclaimed for a declaration that the property was held in equal shares. The House of Lords by a majority held for the defendant. The claimant was entitled to vindicate her interest in the property, whether legal or equitable, if she was not forced to plead or rely on any illegality, even though it transpired that the title relied upon was acquired in the course of carrying through an illegal transaction. On the facts there was no evidence to rebut the presumption of the resulting trust over the property.

Lord Goff of Chieveley and Lord Keith of Kinkel dissented. Lord Goff, with Lord Keith agreeing, insisted that a court of equity would not assist a claimant who does not come with clean hands (at 362). Lord Browne-Wilkinson gave the main speech of the majority. It was clearly established at law that property in goods or land can pass under or pursuant to an illegal contract (*Bowmakers Ltd* v *Barnet Instruments Ltd* [1945] KB 65). The same should apply in equity given that there was now a single law of property. All that was necessary in this case was for the defendant to plead the common intention that the property should be shared between them and that she had contributed to the purchase price. Only in the reply, and during cross-examination of the defendant, would any illegality emerge. This did not preclude the claim. The party claiming title could recover as long as she did not need to plead or rely upon the illegal acts.

In *Tribe* v *Tribe*, the plaintiff transferred shares to his son with the intention of deceiving his creditors. The illegal purpose was never carried into effect, but the son refused to re-transfer the shares. The Court of Appeal held that the father was entitled to lead evidence to rebut the presumption of advancement, without relying upon illegality. Millett LJ, in the leading judgment, pointed out that if the transfer had been to a nephew or friend the presumption of resulting trust would have arisen. There the burden of proof that the transfer was intended to be by way of gift was upon the transferee. Given that the transferee was the son, the presumption of advancement applied, placing the burden of proving that the transfer of shares was not intended as a gift upon the father. Millett LJ relied upon *Tinsley* v *Milligan* [1994] 1 AC 340, and in particular on Lord Browne-Wilkinson's recognition of the existence of the doctrine of *locus poenitentiae* (at 374). Millett LJ concluded (at 126):

> The *locus poenitentiae* is not therefore an exclusively contractual doctrine with no place in the law of restitution. It follows that it cannot be excluded by the mere fact that the legal ownership of property has become lawfully vested in the transferee. It would be unfortunate if the rule in equity were different. It would constitute a further obstacle to the development of a coherent and unified law of restitution.

The *locus poenitentiae* operated to mitigate the harshness of a primary rule prohibiting enforcement of illegal transactions. However, the plaintiff must have withdrawn from the transaction before any further steps were taken. Millett LJ concluded by summarising the present law (at 134–35):

> (1) Title to property passes both at law and in equity even if the transfer is made for an illegal purpose. The fact the title has passed to the transferee does not preclude the transferor from bringing an action for restitution.
> (2) The transferor's action will fail if it would be illegal for him to retain any interest in the property.
> (3) Subject to (2) the transferor can recover the property if he can do so without relying on the illegal purpose. This will normally be the case where the property was transferred without consideration in circumstances where the transferor can rely on an express declaration of trust, or a resulting trust in his favour.
> (4) It will almost invariably be so where the illegal purpose has not been carried out. It may be otherwise where the illegal purpose has been carried out and the transferee can rely on the transferor's conduct as inconsistent with his retention of a beneficial interest.
> (5) The transferor can lead evidence of the illegal purpose whenever it is necessary for him to do so provided that he has withdrawn from the transaction before the illegal purpose has been wholly or partly carried into effect.

35.5 PUBLIC POLICY PRECLUDING A RESTITUTIONARY CLAIM

Public policy may preclude a restitutionary claim. This is a distinct question, short of a finding that a transaction is illegal. The source of the public policy may be statute, or common law. Goff and Jones argue for a general principle that public policy may bar a restitutionary claim: Goff and Jones, 67–72. There is a general principle that restitution will not be allowed if it would in effect enforce a transaction which statute or common law prohibits. This is one explanation of the failure of the common law claim in *Sinclair* v *Brougham* [1914] AC 398. The House of Lords held that the policy of *ultra vires* prohibited the depositors' claims at common law. To allow the common law claim would be indirectly to sanction the *ultra vires* borrowings by the building society. This was the explanation given by Lord Goff of Chieveley of *Sinclair* v *Brougham* in *Westdeutsche Landesbank Girozentrale* v *Islington London Borough Council* [1996] AC 669, at 688. In contrast, the majority of the House of Lords held that the decision on the common law claim in *Sinclair* v *Brougham* was wrong, and that the money could be recovered in restitution. Presumably the majority of the House of Lords in *Westdeutsche* did not think that the allowance of a restitutionary remedy would have the indirect effect of enforcing an *ultra vires* contract.

The question also arises in respect of contracts which are unenforceable for want of formality. The leading modern discussion is that of the High Court of Australia in *Pavey & Matthews Pty Ltd* v *Paul* (1987) 162 CLR 221 (see 12.5). The High Court held that the enforcement of a restitutionary *quantum meruit* would not frustrate the policy of a statute prohibiting enforcement of a binding contract not reduced to writing, by the builder. Where the work had been completed the claim was maintainable. Mason and Wilson JJ attempted to identify the purpose behind the statutory provision. It protected the building owner against claims where the contract failed properly to identify the work, even where the building was completed. However, the statutory protection did not extend to a case where the building owner requested and accepted work but declined to pay for it purely on the grounds of non-compliance with the statutory formalities. Such a contention was 'Draconian', and could not have been the intention of the legislature (at 229). Deane J, delivering the leading judgment, could identify no statutory intention to penalise the builder (at 262). It is submitted that the dissenting judgment of Brennan J is to be preferred. Recourse to restitution would frustrate the policy of the statute which was to render such obligations unenforceable. This was particularly so on the facts of *Pavey*, where the oral unenforceable contract was to pay a reasonable rate. The enforcement of the restitutionary *quantum meruit* exactly imitated the enforcement of the contract. In discussing the case, Ibbetson has observed ((1998) 8 OJLS 312, at 326):

> The more profitable approach — in reality the whole crux of the problem — is to determine whether the purpose at the base of the statutory prohibition of the contractual action would be frustrated by the allowance of the restitutionary remedy.

A different problem has arisen in the context of industrial action, where statute confers an immunity from actions in respect of civil wrongs. In *Universe Tankships Inc. of Monrovia* v *International Transport Workers' Federation, The Universe*

Sentinel [1983] 1 AC 366, the ITF had blacked a vessel flying under a flag of convenience at Milford Haven. Causes of action in tort against the ITF were within the scope of the immunity granted by ss. 13 and 14 of the Trade Union and Labour Relations Act 1974. A claim in restitution for the return of a contribution to the ITF's welfare fund under duress was allowed by a majority of the House of Lords. Lord Diplock, in the leading majority speech, stressed the autonomy of the claim for money had and received on the basis of illegitimate pressure. It was not dependent upon the existence of any tort. Accordingly the statutory immunities were not directly applicable to the claim in restitution. However, that was not the end of the statute's role in the dispute. Lord Diplock observed (at 385):

> Nevertheless, these sections ... afford an indication, which your Lordships should respect, of where public policy requires the line should be drawn between what kind of commercial pressure by a trade union upon an employer in the field of industrial relations ought to be treated as legitimised despite the fact that the will of the employer is thereby coerced, and what kind of commercial pressure in that field does amount to economic duress that entitles the employer victim to restitutionary remedies.

The majority held that there was no public policy bar to recovering restitution, by analogy with the Trade Unions and Labour Relations Act 1974, because on the facts of a particular dispute the pressure complained of was insufficiently connected with the terms and conditions of the employment of the crew under s. 29. For discussion, see Birks, 349–51.

The Universe Sentinel was replayed in Sweden in *Dimskal Shipping Co. SA v International Transport Workers' Federation, The Evia Luck (No. 2)* [1992] 2 AC 152. The case gave rise to conflicts problems which are discussed at 37.5. The blacking of the ship was lawful by Swedish law. However, the majority of the House of Lords held that the governing law was a proper law of contract which was English law. Accordingly, sums paid were recoverable in restitution on the grounds of economic duress. Lord Goff of Chieveley, delivering the speech of the majority, referred to the passage in Lord Diplock's speech in *The Universe Sentinel* quoted above, and stated (at 167):

> It is not necessary for present purposes to explore the basis of this decision. It appears to bear some affinity to the principle underlying those cases in which the courts have given effect to the inferred purpose of the legislature by holding a person entitled to sue for damages for breach of statutory duty, though no such right of suit has been expressly created by the statute imposing the duty. It is enough to state that, by parity of reasoning, not only may an action of restitution be rejected as inconsistent with the policy of a statute such as that under consideration in *The Universe Sentinel* [1983] 1 AC 366, but in my opinion the claim that a contract is voidable for duress by reason of pressure legitimised by such a statute may likewise be rejected on the same ground.

It is submitted that the approaches of Lords Diplock and Goff provide model guidance on how judges should reason by analogy from statutory prohibitions and statutory immunities. The immaturity of the law of restitution has had the unfortunate consequence that, whereas statute often provides for the consequence of certain transactions or acts, the question of the recovery of benefits transferred is not explicitly addressed. The courts will need to be sensitive to whether recovery in restitution is consistent with the scheme of the legislation, and that allowing recovery does not frustrate the policy behind the statute.

FURTHER READING

Asterisks indicate especially useful works.

Birks, 424–32
Goff and Jones, 607–35
Anson, 381–98
*F. Rose, 'Restitutionary and Proprietary Consequences of Illegality' in Rose (1996), 203–34

Repentance

J. Grodecki, 'In Pari Delicto Potior est Conditio Defendentis' (1955) 71 LQR 254
J. Beatson, 'Repudiation of Illegal Purpose as a Ground for Restitution' (1975) 91 LQR 313
R. Merkin, 'Restitution by Withdrawal from Executory Illegal Contracts' (1981) 97 LQR 420
Law Commission Consultation Paper No. 154, paras 2.49 to 2.56
N. Enonchong, 'Title Claims and Illegal Transactions' (1995) 111 LQR 135
M. Clarke, 'Illegal Insurance' [1987] LMCLQ 201
M. Furmston, 'The Analysis of Illegal Contracts' (1966) 16 U Toronto LJ 267
N. Enonchong, *Illegal Transactions* (1998)

Public policy

Goff and Jones, 67–72
*D. Ibbetson, 'Implied Contracts and Restitution: History in the High Court of Australia' (1988) 8 OJLS 312

36 Limitation

36.1 INTRODUCTION

Limitation is the foremost example of a policy-motivated defence. The practical disadvantages of reopening transactions many years later — including the availability of records, the availability of witnesses and the accuracy of their recall, and so on — are well known. In particular in the context of restitution, the policy of security of receipt entitles a defendant whose right to money or other benefits has gone unchallenged for a lengthy period, to retain that money even though he may not be able to demonstrate a change of position. These factors led Lord Sumner to the view that the limitation period in respect of claims for the recovery of mistaken payments should be 'cut down to a very short period' (*R. E. Jones Ltd v Waring & Gillow Ltd* [1926] AC 670, at 696). However desirable shorter limitation periods for actions in restitution may be as a matter of policy, though, the present situation is more confused.

The Limitation Act 1980 still exhibits the assumptions of its 1939 predecessor that civil obligations are derived from just two sources: contract and tort. The immaturity of the law of unjust enrichment is here manifested by the problems caused because the relevant statute makes no explicit provision for it. There are two possibilities. First, the absence of an express limitation defence in respect of most claims in unjust enrichment entails that there is no such defence. Limitation defences are statutory, and if Parliament has not provided for one there is no time bar. Secondly, and alternatively, the courts could pursue a strategy of forcing claims in unjust enrichment into the statutory scheme, however awkward the language may be. As we shall see, the latter has been the favoured approach. As Robert Goff J stated in *BP Exploration (Libya) Ltd v Hunt (No. 2)* [1979] 1 WLR 783 (QBD) (at 836–37): 'when the claim in question is a claim to restitution, the courts have in the past placed a benevolently broad construction upon Acts of Parliament in order to make them applicable to such claims when the legislature has failed to provide expressly for them.'

It is necessary to recall the bifurcation of the law of restitution into subjective unjust enrichment and restitution for wrongs. In the latter category, the cause of action arises outside the law of unjust enrichment, in contract, tort or equitable wrongs. Accordingly, as a matter of principle, such claims should be governed by the appropriate limitation period for the cause of action regardless of the restitutionary character of the remedy. However, there are some authorities which cause difficulties for this simple, principled approach. Most recently, the Law Commission has issued a consultation paper on the reform of limitation, which explicitly deals with the position of claims in unjust enrichment: Law Commission, *Limitation of Actions* Consultation Paper, No. 151 (1998), paras 5.1 to 5.19 and 13.77 to 13.83.

36.2   THE SCHEME OF THE ACT

Section 2 of the Limitation Act 1980 provides a six-year limitation period for claims founded upon tort from the date of the accrual of the cause of action. Thus, as a matter of principle, where a claim is brought to force a tortfeasor to disgorge benefits obtained at the expense of a claimant, this period should apply. However, the case of *Chesworth* v *Farrar* [1967] 1 QB 407 suggests a more complicated solution. A landlord took possession of the premises and also, as a consequence, of a large amount of personal property belonging to the plaintiff tenant. Subsequently a claim was brought against the estate of the landlord claiming nearly £60,000 for the value of goods lost as a result of a breach of bailment by the landlord. In the alternative there was a claim for nearly £3,000 as money had and received, being the proceeds of the sale of some antiques of the plaintiff. Edmund Davies J held that in respect of the claim in bailment, it was in substance an action in tort and accordingly time-barred under the then short period for claims against an estate under the Law Reform (Miscellaneous Provisions) Act 1934 (see now the Proceedings Against the Estates Act 1970). However, in respect of the claim for money had and received, based on waiving the tort of conversion, this was held to be 'founded on simple contract' under s. 2(1)(a) of the Limitation Act 1939 (now s. 5 of the 1980 Act). The latter claim therefore succeeded. Birks argues that the claim for the proceeds of the sale of the antiques can only be seen as arising in tort, despite the fact that the plaintiff sought a restitutionary rather than a compensatory measure: Birks, 348–49. See also 25.3.

Turning to s. 5 of the 1980 Act, this provides that actions 'founded on simple contract' also carry a six-year limitation period from the date of accrual of the cause of action. Most common law restitutionary actions are treated as falling within this section. Influential dicta of the Court of Appeal in *In re Diplock* [1948] Ch 465, at 514, on the predecessor of s. 5 (s. 2(1)(a) of the 1939 Act) are often cited:

We assume ... that the words 'action founded on simple contract' must be taken to cover actions for money had and received, formerly actions on the case, and, as such, covered in express terms by the Statute of James I [Limitation Act 1623].

The assumption must we think be made though the words cannot be regarded as felicitous.

These words proved influential with Edmund Davies J in *Chesworth* v *Farrar*. More recently they have been followed by Hobhouse J in *Westdeutsche Landesbank Girozentrale* v *Islington London Borough Council* [1994] 4 All ER 890, at 942 and *Kleinwort Benson Ltd* v *South Tyneside Metropolitan Borough Council* [1994] 4 All ER 972, at 978. For comment, see Birks in Cornish, 26–27. It seems likely that these cases would now be decided differently in the light of *Kleinwort Benson Ltd* v *Lincoln City Council* [1999] 2 AC 349.

While open to attack on the basis of disloyalty to the statutory words, as a matter of practice it is unlikely that a judge will be deterred under the current statutory arrangements from following the *Diplock* fiction and squeezing common law restitutionary actions into s. 5 of the 1980 Act. The alternative of no limitation period does not commend itself to the courts. In most cases, such as mistaken payments, the accrual of the cause of action will be the date of receipt (*Baker* v *Courage & Co.* [1910] 1 KB 56). However, where the claim is one based on failure of consideration, the relevant date is when the consideration failed (*BP Exploration (Libya) Ltd* v *Hunt (No. 2)* [1979] 1 WLR 783 (QBD), [1981] 1 WLR 232 (CA), [1983] 2 AC 352 (HL); *Guardian Ocean Cargoes Ltd* v *Banco de Brasil (No. 3)* [1992] 2 Lloyd's Rep 193, at 200 *per* Hirst J, [1994] 2 Lloyd's Rep 152, at 160 *per* Saville LJ).

Section 9 of the 1980 Act provides that an 'action to recover any sum recoverable by virtue of any enactment' has a six-year limitation period from the date on which the cause of action accrued. This arguably extends to claims under the Law Reform (Frustrated Contracts) Act 1943. In favour of such an interpretation is the clear statutory language. For example, a claim to recover benefits conferred pursuant to a frustrated contract where there has been a partial failure of consideration is (as the law currently stands) maintainable only by reason of the statute, and not at common law. The counter-argument is that it is far from clear that the section is intended to cover statutory claims brought by one private individual against another, such as under the Misrepresentation Act 1967 or the 1943 Act. Further, such claims are unliquidated rather than liquidated and may not fall within the statutory language. See McGee, *Limitation Periods*, paras 4.018 to 4.020.

Section 10 provides a special two-year limitation period for claims under s. 1 of the Civil Liability (Contribution) Act 1978. For consideration of such claims see 21.1.

Section 21 provides a six-year limitation period for an action by beneficiaries to recover trust property or any other claims in respect of breach of trust. There is an exception for cases where the claim involves fraud or fraudulent breach of trust to which the trustee was party or privy, or where the claim is one to recover from the trustee himself trust property or the proceeds of trust property, where there is no limitation period.

Section 22 provides a 12-year limitation period in respect of claims, such as that in *In re Diplock* [1948] Ch 465, for recovery in respect of the personal estate of the deceased person.

Section 23 provides in respect of claims for an account, that the appropriate time limit is that of the claim which is the basis of the duty to account. Accordingly, a contractual duty to account is subject to the contractual period (*Paragon Finance plc v D. B. Thakerar & Co.* [1999] 1 All ER 400).

Section 29 provides for fresh accrual of the cause of action on an acknowledgement of a debt or a part payment, which could extend to restitutionary cases.

More significant is s. 32, which postpones the running of the limitation period in cases of fraud (s. 32(1)(a)) or deliberate concealment by the defendant (s. 32(1)(b)) and also where 'the action is for relief of the consequences of mistake': s. 32(1)(c)). The period runs only from the time the plaintiff discovers the fraud, concealment or mistake, or could have done so with reasonable diligence. Section 32(1)(a) (or rather its predecessor) was utilised in the restitutionary action in *G. L. Baker Ltd* v *Medway Building and Supplies Ltd* [1958] 1 WLR 1216. Subsection (1)(c) on its terms applies only where mistake is an essential ingredient of the cause of action, for example where relief is sought from entering into a contract on the grounds of mistake (*Phillips-Higgins* v *Harper* [1954] 1 QB 411). As such, it clearly applies to restitutionary actions to recover money paid under a mistake of fact or a mistake of law. Indeed, the decision of the House of Lords in *Kleinwort Benson Ltd* v *Lincoln City Council* [1999] 2 AC 349 makes this subsection of great practical relevance for two reasons. First, the decision of the House of Lords to abrogate the mistake of law rule introduces a new cause of action which clearly falls within the terms of the subsection. Secondly, the wide definition given to mistake of law, to include the subsequent overruling of earlier authority, means that time will start to run only from the date of the appellate authority which overruled the old case law. See 3.6.

36.3 EQUITABLE CLAIMS AND LACHES

It is difficult to give definitive advice on the scope of the doctrine of laches. 'Laches' is the doctrine whereby equitable remedies are refused because of delay in the bringing of suit. Claims in equity, such as for rescission, are not always covered by the statute. Often, equity follows the law by imposing by analogy the statutory limitation period which would apply to a corresponding common law cause of action. For a recent discussion, see *Coulthard* v *Disco Mix Club Ltd* [1999] 2 All ER 457.

In *Lindsay Petroleum* v *Hurd* (1874) LR 5 PC 221, Sir Barnes Peacock, delivering the advice of the Privy Council, laid down the classic test for laches (at 239–40):

> Where it would be *practically unjust* to give a remedy, either because the party has, by his conduct done that which might fairly be regarded as equivalent to a waiver of it, or where, by his conduct and neglect he has though perhaps not waiving that remedy, yet put the other party in a situation in which it would not be reasonable, in either of these cases, lapse of time and delay are most material.

In *Erlanger* v *New Sombrero Phosphate Co.* (1878) 3 App Cas 1218, Lord Blackburn laconically remarked of this test (at 1279):

I have looked in vain for any authority which gives a more distinct and definite rule than this; and I think, from the nature of the enquiry, it must always be a question of more or less, depending on the degree of diligence which might reasonably be required, and the degree of change which has occurred, whether the balance of justice or injustice is in favour of granting a remedy or withholding it.

Laches were held to bar a remedy for undue influence on the facts of *Allcard* v *Skinner* (1887) 36 Ch D 145, by the majority of the Court of Appeal. A claim to value surviving in the hands of the influencer was barred, because the plaintiff freed herself from his influence in 1879 but made no claim for its return until over six years later. This case suggests that time starts to run from the time the vitiating factor ceased to operate.

A recent application of the defence was in *Nelson* v *Rye* [1996] 1 WLR 1378. The plaintiff, a popular musician, sought an account from his former manager. The manager sought to bar the remedy in respect of matters more than six years before the issue of the writ, on the grounds of limitation laches. Laddie J somewhat controversially held that the liability to account was for a breach of a fiduciary relationship which gave rise to a constructive trust. Accordingly, it was held, no limitation applied by reason of s. 21(1)(b) of the 1980 Act. This has been doubted by Sir Peter Millett, writing extra-judicially, in Cornish, 199, 207, and the case has been overruled by the Court of Appeal on the limitation point (*Paragon Finance plc* v *D. B. Thakerer & Co.* [1999] 1 All ER 400, at 415–16 *per* Millett LJ; see also *Coulthard* v *Disco Mix Club Ltd* [1999] 2 All ER 457). However, in any event Laddie J held that the claim in respect of the period in excess of six years before the writ was barred by laches. The wide-ranging consideration of the evidence demonstrates the flexible and discretionary nature of the bar. For example, Laddie J commented (at 1394) that:

> In my view there was a wilful refusal by Mr Nelson to involve himself in his financial affairs. . . . He was happy to drive his Rolls Royce, live in a mansion and take far more out of [the business] than could be justified on the basis of its receipts but he did not want to know the details of how the sums added up — or failed to add up. He rejected all advice.

To insist on an account ranging over so wide a period would cause substantial prejudice to the defendant. Whereas fixed limitation periods can be criticised as arbitrary, at least they promote certainty. The wide-ranging enquiry required by the doctrine of laches essentially involves considering the merits of the whole case simply in order to inform the judge in the exercise of his discretion.

36.4 REFORM

The Law Commission's Consultation Paper No. 151 (1998) suggests, in general, a uniform limitation period of three years, running from the date of discoverability of the cause of action, subject to a long-stop of 10 years. This would encompass claims in unjust enrichment. See McGee, *Limitation Periods*, 3rd edn (1998), 19–20. The desirability of a coherent limitation statute to deal with the modern development in restitution was stressed by Brooke LJ in *Portman Building Society* v *Hamlyn Taylor Neck* [1998] 4 All ER 202, at 209. Perhaps the most pressing issue is mistake of law. The abrogation of the bar on recovery post-dated the Law Commission paper. In *Kleinwort Benson Ltd* v *Lincoln City Council* [1999] 2 AC 349, Lord Goff discussed the impact of the holding of the majority when combined with s. 32(1)(c) of the 1980 Act (at 389):

> I recognise that the effect of section 32(1)(c) is that the cause of action in a case such as the present may be extended for an indefinite period of time. I realise that this consequence may not have been fully appreciated at the time when this provision was enacted, and further that the recognition of the right at common law to recover money on the ground that it was paid under a mistake of law may call for legislative reform to provide for some time limit to the right of recovery in such cases. The Law Commission may think it desirable, as the result of a decision in the present case, to give consideration to this question; indeed they may think it wise to do so as a matter of some urgency.

See also Lord Hoffmann at 401, and Lord Hope of Craighead at 416–18 and on behalf of the minority, Lord Browne-Wilkinson at 364.

It is certainly preferable that the limitation period question in respect of these cases should be revisited by Parliament. Indeed, the best course would be for the general reforms advocated by the Law Commission to put into practice. The position reached after *Kleinwort Benson* is obviously unsatisfactory, but the view taken here, which is similar to that of Lord Hope, is that in practice there will not be a flood of litigation after the *Kleinwort Benson* case. Given the other important restitutionary defences of good faith purchase, change of position and submission to a honest claim, the need for a stringent limitation period is not that pressing. See 3.6.

FURTHER READING

Asterisks indicate especially useful works.

Goff and Jones, 846–62
*H. McLean, 'Limitation of Actions in Restitution' [1989] CLJ 472
A. McGee, *Limitation Periods*, 3rd edn (1998), 19–20, 41–58
Law Commission, *Limitation of Actions* (Consultation Paper No. 151, 1998) paras 5.1 to 5.19 and 13.77 to 13.83

PART I

PRACTICAL MATTERS

37 Conflict of Laws

37.1 INTRODUCTION

The intersection of unjust enrichment and the conflict of laws is one of immense theoretical difficulty, but also one of growing practical significance. As with other practical matters, the immaturity of the law of restitution has resulted in there being little explicit provision for it in the governing treaties and statutes. Similar questions are therefore posed as arise in relation to limitation (see 36.1 above) and interest (see 38.1 below), as to how restitution can be accommodated within the existing structure.

There are two key questions in private international law:

(a) which is the appropriate jurisdiction for the particular dispute? (the 'jurisdiction question'); and
(b) what is the governing law of the dispute in question? (the 'choice of law question').

Traditionally, the latter was the focus of most academic discussion and the subject of the majority of disputes. In recent decades, the jurisdiction question has assumed greater prominence. The jurisdiction question must be sub-divided into the appropriate rules governing those disputes which fall within the Brussels Convention (and related conventions) and those which do not. The following is not intended to be a comprehensive discussion, but simply seeks to highlight the key practical issues of which advisers should be aware.

37.2 JURISDICTION IN NON-BRUSSELS CONVENTION CASES

The rules relating to service of process out of the jurisdiction under the well-known RSC Ord. 11 have now been re-enacted in Sch. 1 to the Civil Procedure Rules (CPR)

1998. The familiar numbering and lettering remain the same, although the language has been modified to include references to 'claim forms', and so on. The claimant must satisfy a two-stage process. First, he must persuade the court that the claim falls within one of the heads under Ord. 11(1). Secondly, he must persuade the court that England is the most appropriate jurisdiction for the dispute to be litigated in. This is the *forum conveniens* test (see the leading discussion in *Spiliada Maritime Corp.* v *Cansulex Ltd* [1987] 1 AC 460, at 478 and *Seaconsar Far East Ltd* v *Bank Markazi Johmouri Islami Iran* [1994] 1 AC 438). The most appropriate heads in relation to restitution disputes will often be Ord. 11(1)(d) and (e) in relation to contractual disputes. There was a tendency in the old case law to force all restitution disputes within these heads (*Bowling* v *Cox* [1926] AC 751; *cf In re Jogia* [1988] 1 WLR 484). In 1993, a new head (t) was introduced into Ord. 11 which may render this approach both unnecessary and inappropriate. Ord. 11(1)(t) provides:

> the claim is brought for money had and received or for an account or other remedy against the defendant as constructive trustee, and the defendant's alleged liability arises out of acts committed, whether by him or otherwise, within the jurisdiction....

The provision is not felicitously worded and it is somewhat surprising that it was added as late as 1993 given its anachronistic reference to the action for money had and received, and its reliance upon the convoluted and confusing notion of accountability as a constructive trustee. However, if it is given a wide interpretation so as to include all common law restitutionary actions (including those previously brought under the action for money paid, or for a *quantum meruit*, which are not explicitly referred to) and all equitable restitutionary claims, it should prove appropriate in practice. It is not entirely clear what the connecting factor is with the jurisdiction where a claim is based upon, for example, a mistaken payment, which requires no conduct on behalf of the defendant. Arguably the fact that the defendant is enriched in the jurisdiction should suffice.

37.3 JURISDICTION UNDER THE BRUSSELS CONVENTION

The Brussels Convention on Jurisdiction and the Enforcement of Judgments in Civil and Commercial Matters is implemented by the Civil Jurisdiction and Judgments Act 1982, and appears as Sch. 1 to that enactment. The Brussels Convention provides a scheme of jurisdiction for the members of the European Union in respect of civil and commercial disputes. The basic principle is that where a defendant is domiciled in a Member State he is entitled to be sued in the country in which he is domiciled (Article 2). As an exception to this general principle, the Convention provides for special jurisdiction in a number of cases, of which the relevant ones for present purposes are contained in Article 5:

> A person domiciled in a Contracting State may, in another Contracting State, be sued:

(1)   in matters relating to a contract, in the courts for the place of performance of the obligation in question;

...

(3)   in matters relating to tort, delict or quasi-delict, in the courts for the place where the harmful event occurred or in the case of a threatened wrong is likely to occur.

There is no explicit provision for claims for restitution. To date there has been no guidance from the European Court of Justice on how unjust enrichment relates to this scheme. However, there is now English authority on the role of restitution in relation to the Modified Convention (see 37.4) which distributes jurisdiction between the constituent parts of the United Kingdom.

37.4   JURISDICTION UNDER THE MODIFIED CONVENTION

The Modified Convention allocates jurisdiction between the constituent parts of the United Kingdom in a manner virtually identical to the overall Brussels Convention. The Modified Convention appears as Sch. 4 to the Civil Jurisdiction and Judgments Act 1982. A dispute between an English-based bank and a Scottish local authority gave rise to the longest-running, and presumably most expensive, saga in the swaps fiasco.

In *Kleinwort Benson Ltd* v *Glasgow City Council* [1999] 1 AC 153, an English bank sought restitution from a Scottish local authority in respect of seven void swaps transactions. The council claimed to be entitled to be sued in its country of domicile (Scotland) under Article 2 of Sch. 4 of the 1982 Act. The bank argued that it was entitled to sue in England on the basis of special jurisdiction under either Article 5(1) or Article 5(3) of the Modified Convention. In February 1992, Hirst J found for the council on the basis that, the transactions having been declared void, it would be artificial to say that they fell within the language of Article 5(1). Further, it would be an even greater strain upon the language to bring them within Article 5(3) (*sub nom Barclays Bank plc* v *Glasgow City Council* [1993] QB 429). The Court of Appeal referred the matter for interpretation to the European Court of Justice ([1994] QB 404). The European Court of Justice, despite written submissions by the parties, the European Commission, the United Kingdom, France, Germany and Spain, declined jurisdiction over the interpretation of the Modified Convention, as it was a matter of national law, although based on the Brussels Convention ([1996] QB 57).

A differently constituted Court of Appeal accordingly had to consider the matter without the assistance of the European Court of Justice (*Kleinwort Benson Ltd* v *Glasgow City Council* [1996] QB 678). By a majority it held that the claim fell within Article 5(1). In the leading majority judgment Millett LJ could see no reason why 'contract' in Article 5(1) should not include a void contract, nor why the 'place of performance of the obligation in question' should not mean the intended place of performance of the supposed obligation. Millett LJ considered that the approach contended for by the council would lead to inconsistencies and anomalies. He sketched the following example (at 701):

Suppose P agrees to buy goods from D, the goods are to be delivered in London and payment to be made in Frankfurt. P pays for the goods, but the goods are not delivered. P has a choice of remedies. He can sue D for damages for breach of contract, bringing the action in England, the place where the obligation to deliver the goods should have been performed. Or he can treat the contract as discharged by breach and sue to recover the payment for a total failure of consideration. The nature of the remedy sought does not prevent the action from being tried in England, the place of performance of contractual obligation, the breach of which has given rise to the relief claimed. Next, suppose that after one consignment has been delivered D refuses to deliver any more, and alleges want of contractual capacity. P may accept this or dispute it. If he accepts it, or it is established, he is entitled to recover the payment after giving credit for the value of the consignment delivered. It makes no sense to deprive the court in England of jurisdiction to try the action, England being the intended place of performance of the supposed obligation the failure to perform which has given rise to the relief sought. The factor which connects the dispute with England is the same whether D's contention that he lacked contractual capacity is right or wrong.

On appeal, the majority of the House of Lords disagreed ([1999] 1 AC 153). In the leading speech, Lord Goff of Chieveley stressed the need to have regard to any relevant decisions of the European Court of Justice (s. 16(3) of the 1982 Act). First, the general rule was the principle of domicile under Article 2. Further, it was well established in the European jurisprudence that provisions such as Article 5, derogating from Article 2, are to be construed restrictively. Secondly, what is important for the provisions of Article 5 is the existence of a particularly close connecting factor between the relevant dispute and the court which is to hear it. Thirdly, it is necessary to identify the obligation in question which forms the basis of the claim. In Lord Goff's view the case was a very simple one. He concluded (at 167):

I have to confess that I find it very difficult to see how such a claim can fall within article 5(1). It can only do so if it can properly be said to be based upon a particular contractual obligation, the place of performance of which is within the jurisdiction of the court. Where, however, as here, the claim is for the recovery of money paid under a supposed contract which in law never existed, it seems impossible to say that the claim for the recovery of the money is based upon a particular contractual obligation.

In truth, the claim in the present case is simply a claim to restitution, which in English law is based upon the principle of unjust enrichment; and claims of this kind do not *per se* fall within article 5(1). It is not necessary for the purposes of the present case to hold that a claim to restitution can never fall within article 5(1). Very exceptionally, there may be particular circumstances in which it can properly be said, at least in cases arising under the Convention, that the claim in question, although a claim to restitution, is nevertheless based on a contractual obligation and so falls within the article. ... But no such circumstances arise in the vast majority of claims to restitution, which are founded simply upon the principle of unjust enrichment. Such is, in my opinion, the present case. No express provision is made in article 5 in respect of claims for unjust enrichment as such; and it is legitimate to infer that this omission is due to the absence of any close connecting factor consistently linking claims to any jurisdiction other than the defendant's domicile. Article 2 therefore provides the appropriate jurisdiction for such claims.

The view of the majority of the Court of Appeal was inconsistent with the jurisprudence of the European Court of Justice. Lords Clyde and Hutton delivered concurring speeches.

Lords Nicholls of Birkenhead and Mustill dissented, foreseeing practical difficulties with the arguments of the local authority. Disputes as to the existence of a contractual obligation, and the consequences of ineffectiveness fell within the meaning of 'matters relating to a contract'. Lord Nicholls pointed out that the same conclusion was reached in the written observations to the European Court by the United Kingdom, France, Spain and the Commission of the European Communities, with Germany alone a dissenting voice. Lastly, the House of Lords was unanimous that restitution claims did not fall within Article 5(3) of the Modified Convention. For discussion, see Peel [1998] LMCLQ 22.

This was a finely balanced dispute which provoked vigorous disagreement. Given the general principle espoused in Article 2 of the Convention, there was no necessity to force restitution into a particular slot such as Article 5(1) elsewhere in the Convention. The importance of the general principle of domicile weighed heavily with the majority of the House of Lords. This is consistent with the tenor of the case law of the European Court of Justice. However, that court has not yet had to face up to the problems posed by the failure to provide explicitly for restitutionary disputes within the Convention. On balance, it is submitted that the more practical approach of the majority of the Court of Appeal and the minority of the House of Lords is to be preferred. Disputes arising out of contracts, even void contracts, can be seen as fitting within the language of Article 5(1). Indeed, it is desirable to avoid a situation where the allegation of nullity leads to a change in the jurisdictional venue. It should be recorded that the reason behind the vigour with which this jurisdictional dispute was waged was the more attractive limitation period in England, as opposed to that in Scotland. Further, Kleinwort Benson hoped to rely upon s. 32(1)(c) of the English Limitation Act 1980, as it eventually did in *Kleinwort Benson Ltd v Lincoln City Council* [1998] 3 WLR 1095.

37.5 CHOICE OF LAW

It is commonly stated that the law of restitution divides into subtractive unjust enrichment and restitution for wrongs. In the latter category, where the claim for restitution is based upon a cause of action in contract or tort, the respective provisions of the Contracts (Applicable Law) Act 1990 and the Private International Law

(Miscellaneous Provisions) Act 1995 would appear to govern. Within subtractive unjust enrichment many disputes arise out of failed contracts. In such situations the appropriate starting point also appears to be the Contracts (Applicable Law) Act 1990, which implements the Convention on the Law Applicable to Contractual Obligations (the 'Rome Convention') (which appears as Sch. 1 to the Act). By Article 10(1)(e) of the Rome Convention, the applicable law of the contract also governs 'the consequences of nullity of the contract'. However, English law has expressly derogated from this aspect of the Rome Convention by s. 2(2) of the 1990 Act. The background to this appears to be concerns about the immaturity of the law of unjust enrichment. Accordingly, the consequences of a void contract remain a matter for common law as regards the choice of law rule.

Outside of the statutory provisions, the best starting point is rule 200 of *Dicey and Morris on the Conflict of Laws*, 13th edn (2000) (at 1485):

(1)   The obligation to restore the benefit of an enrichment obtained at another person's expense is governed by the proper law of the obligation.

(2)   The proper law of the obligation is (*semble*) determined as follows:

(a)   If the obligation arises in connection with a contract, its proper law is the law applicable to the contract;

(b)   If it arises in connection with a transaction concerning an immovable (land), its proper law is the law of the country where the immovable is situated (*lex situs*);

(c)   If it arises in any other circumstances, its proper law is the law of the country where the enrichment occurs.

In many cases this rule will favour the proper law or the putative proper law of the contract as appropriate for the resolution of restitutionary claims. This is the approach of the Law Reform (Frustrated Contracts) Act 1943, which applies, on its terms, only to contracts governed by English law.

Support for the application of the proper law or the putative proper law of the contract to disputes concerning the validity of the contract and restitution of benefits conferred thereunder is also provided by the decision of the House of Lords in *Dimskal Shipping Co. SA* v *International Transport Workers' Federation, The Evia Luck (No. 2)* [1992] 2 AC 152. The shipowners sought to avoid contracts with the ITF and to seek restitution of benefits conferred thereunder on the basis that the contracts were procured by the economic duress of the ITF by blacking one of the company's vessels in Sweden. The proper law of the contracts was English law. The conduct amounting to economic duress was not legitimised under English law as it constituted secondary industrial action. In contrast, the conduct would have been legitimised by Swedish law, the place where it in fact occurred. In the leading speech, Lord Goff of Chieveley stressed that the cause of action was not one which depended upon the commission of any tort. The proper law of the contract governed the material or essential validity of the contract. There was no reason for rejecting the application of English law; where the conduct amounted to economic duress within

English law, it was of no importance where the actual conduct took place. For discussion, see O'Dair [1992] LMCLQ 145. Lastly, there is support for Dicey and Morris's rule 200(2)(c) in *In re Jogia* [1988] 1 WLR 484, although that case was mainly decided on jurisdictional grounds.

Conflicts has given rise to some difficult problems in cases arising out of the tracing and claiming of misdirected funds. The problem was side-stepped in *Chase Manhattan Bank NA v Israel British Bank (London) Ltd* [1981] Ch 105, by Goulding J's finding that there was no difference between the law of New York and the law of England as to whether a mistaken payer was entitled to a proprietary remedy at the conclusion of a successful tracing exercise.

In *El Ajou v Dollar Land Holdings plc* [1993] 3 All ER 717, Millett J was able to reject an argument that it was impossible to conduct an equitable tracing exercise where money had passed through civil law jurisdictions which did not recognise the concept of equitable ownership, because foreign law had not been pleaded and proved. In any event, Millett J would have rejected the submission because the appropriate governing law, in accordance with Dicey and Morris's rule 200(2)(c), was the law of the country where the defendant received the money. English law would govern, and it was irrelevant that some of the bank accounts were located in civil law countries: 'This is because the plaintiff's ability to trace money in equity is dependent on the power of equity to charge a mixed fund with the repayment of trusts money, *not upon any actual exercise of that power*. The charge itself is entirely notional.' Millett J concluded (at 737):

An English court of equity will compel a defendant who is within the jurisdiction to treat assets in his hands as trust assets if, having regard to their history and his state of knowledge, it would be unconscionable for him to treat them as his own. Where they may have passed through many different hands in many different countries, they may be difficult to trace; but in my judgment neither their temporary repose in a civil law country nor their receipt by intermediate recipients outside the jurisdiction should prevent the court from treating assets in the legal ownership of a defendant within the jurisdiction as trust assets. In the present case, any obligation on the part of DLH to restore to their rightful owner assets which it received in England is governed exclusively by English law, and the equitable tracing rules and the trust concept which underlies them are applicable as part of that law. There is no need to consider any other system of law.

The decision was varied by the Court of Appeal on a different point ([1995] 2 All ER 685).

The other major authority on restitution and the conflict of laws concerns the misapplication of securities by the late Robert Maxwell: *Macmillan Inc. v Bishopsgate Investment Trust plc (No. 3)* [1995] 1 WLR 978 (Millett J); [1996] 1 WLR 387 (CA). The case concerned the disputed ownership of the large tranche of shares in Berlitz, a company incorporated in New York. Macmillan was the beneficial owner, whereas Bishopsgate held the shares on trust for it. In breach of trust, the shares were repeatedly used as security for debts owed by private companies controlled by Mr Maxwell. The plaintiff argued that its claim against those who accepted the shares as security should be characterised as restitutionary, which pointed towards English law. In contrast, the defendants insisted that it was the issue which should be characterised. The issue was one of priorities, and whether they were bona fide purchasers for value without notice of the shares. This pointed towards New York which was the *lex situs* of the shares, the place of incorporation of the company, the place where the share register was kept and the place of the transaction. The Court of Appeal preferred the approach of the defendant. Therefore, even if the claim was characterised as a restitutionary one, as Millett J had done, the characterisation question focussed upon a particular issue, not the type of claim. Millett J had also ultimately preferred the law of New York as the law of the transaction in question. The Court of Appeal favoured the law of New York as the law of the place where the shares were situated (the *lex situs*), which is the law of the place where the share register was kept or the place of incorporation (which was the same in this case). For discussion, see Bird [1996] LMCLQ 57.

FURTHER READING

Asterisks indicate especially useful works.

*L. Collins, *Dicey and Morris on the Conflict of Laws*, 13th edn (2000), 1485–1506
*F. Rose (ed), *Restitution and the Conflict of Laws* (1995) (2nd edn forthcoming)
A. Dickinson, 'Restitution and the Conflict Laws' [1996] LMCLQ 556

Jurisdiction

E. Peel, 'Non-Admissibility and Restitution in the European Court of Justice' [1996] LMCLQ 8
J. Riley, 'Void Contracts, Restitution and Jurisdiction' [1996] LMCLQ 182
G. Virgo, 'Restitution and Private International Law — Square Pegs and Round Holes' [1996] *Restitution Law Review* 109
*A. Dickinson, 'Restitution and the Conflict of Laws in the House of Lords' [1998] LMCLQ 104
*E. Peel, 'Jurisdiction over Restitutionary Claims' [1998] LMCLQ 22

Choice of law

J. Bird 'Bribes, Restitution and the Conflict of Laws' [1995] LMCLQ 198
A. Briggs, 'Restitution meets the Conflict of Laws' [1995] *Restitution Law Review* 94
J. Bird, 'Restitution's uncertain progress' [1995] LMCLQ 308
A. Briggs, 'From Complexity to Anticlimax: Restitution and Choice of Law' [1996] *Restitution Law Review* 88
J. Stevens, 'Restitution or Property? Priority and Title to Shares in the Conflict of Laws' (1996) 59 MLR 741

J. Bird, 'Choice of law rule for priority disputes in relation to shares' [1996] LMCLQ 57

G. Virgo, 'Reconstructing the law of restitution' (1996) 11 *Trusts Law International* 20

G. Moss QC and F. Toube, 'Cross-Border Security Enforcement and the Conflict of Laws' in Rose (1998), 89–98

N. Segal, 'Cross-Border Security Enforcement, Restitution and Priorities' in Rose (1998), 99–119

38 Interest

38.1 INTRODUCTION

The purpose of an award of interest on the principal sum claimed in an action is to provide additional relief to a claimant who has been kept out of the money to which he or she was entitled. The power to award interest is contained in s. 35A of the Supreme Court Act 1981 and s. 69 of the County Courts Act 1984. The court has a discretion over the following questions: Should interest be awarded? At what rate? And for what period? As a matter of practice, the courts almost invariably award interest. A claim for interest must be pleaded with some particularity under CPR Part 16, rr. 16.4(1)(b) and 16.4(2). The particulars of claim must set out the relevant enactment, the percentage rate claimed, the date from which it is claimed, the date to which it is calculated (which should be no later than the date of the claim form), the total amount of interest claimed up to the date of calculation, and the daily rate thereafter. Courts generally adopt the 8 per cent simple rate of interest payable on judgment debts as a matter of practice. Interest is payable on judgments from the date of judgment (Judgments Act 1838, s. 17, and County Courts Act 1984, s. 74). It should be noted that the county court does not award interest on judgments of less than £5,000 (County Court (Interest on Judgments) Order 1991 (SI 1991 No. 1184)).

Given the large sums of money involved in many recent restitutionary cases, the issue of interest has loomed large. It should be recalled that the claim in *Woolwich Equitable Building Society* v *Inland Revenue Commissioners* [1993] AC 70 was concerned solely with the issue of interest which amounted to some £6.73 million. Further, interest has been crucial in some of the swaps cases. The only issue before the House of Lords in *Westdeutsche Landesbank Girozentrale* v *Islington London Borough Council* [1996] AC 669 was the type of interest and the date from which it should be awarded. In addition to the statutory powers to award interest, there had developed a jurisdiction in equity to award compound interest in cases of fraud or breach of fiduciary duty. The limits of this jurisdiction divided the House of Lords in

Westdeutsche. A minority favoured developing the jurisdiction to all cases where the claimant had been kept out of his money, that is all restitutionary claims. The majority ultimately preferred the orthodox position. Other recent cases in unjust enrichment illustrate how the courts will exercise their discretion in determining the appropriate dates from which interest should be awarded.

38.2 THE *WESTDEUTSCHE* CASE IN THE HOUSE OF LORDS: SIMPLE OR COMPOUND INTEREST?

In *Westdeutsche Landesbank Girozentrale* v *Islington London Borough Council* [1994] 4 All ER 890, [1996] AC 669, Hobhouse J and the Court of Appeal both held that the defendant received the money in a fiduciary capacity and accordingly a proprietary claim was available in equity. Therefore the jurisdiction to award compound interest was available. They differed in that Hobhouse J confined the award of compound interest to the beginning of April 1990 when it had become clear, in the wake of the judgment of the Divisional Court in *Hazell*, that the underlying transaction was void. In contrast, the Court of Appeal awarded interest from the date of the payment, namely 18 June 1987. Dillon LJ relied upon *BP Exploration (Libya) Ltd* v *Hunt (No. 2)* [1979] 1 WLR 783 (QBD), at 846, for the principle that the date of receipt was prima facie the date from which interest should run. For Dillon LJ the overriding factor was that the council had had the use of the whole of Westdeutsche's £2.5 million from the date of payment. The Court of Appeal was also of the view that an award of compound interest reflected better the commercial reality, that if Islington had not received the money under the swap agreement it would have had to borrow it elsewhere at a commercial rate. The House of Lords unanimously held that Westdeutsche only had a personal claim to recover the money at common law, and that there was no equitable proprietary claim or breach of fiduciary duty which could justify the equitable jurisdiction to award compound interest as traditionally understood. However, the House of Lords split upon the development of that jurisdiction.

The majority held that it would inappropriate to develop the equitable jurisdiction to award compound interest in support of the common law claim. It was common ground in the absence of agreement or custom that the court had no jurisdiction to award compound interest at common law or under s. 35A of the Supreme Court Act 1981. Lord Browne-Wilkinson summarised the position of the equitable jurisdiction (at 701): 'In the absence of fraud courts of equity have never awarded compound interest except against a trustee or other person owing fiduciary duties who is accountable for profits made from his position.' This followed the leading case of *President of India* v *La Pintada Compania Navigacion SA* [1985] AC 104, at 116. Having rejected the equitable proprietary claim and the characterisation of the council as a fiduciary (see 30.8), Lord Browne-Wilkinson in the leading majority speech held that interest must therefore be simple under the Act. His Lordship agreed with the Court of Appeal that the appropriate date should be the date of the receipt of the money, namely 18 June 1987. There was no good ground for departing from the general rule that interest was payable from the date of the accrual of the cause of action. Lord Browne-Wilkinson rejected any development of the power to award compound interest in respect of all restitutionary claims as an example of 'usurping in the function of Parliament' (at 717). Parliament had considered the matter twice since 1934 and had made it clear that there was no power to award compound interest on common law claims.

Lord Lloyd of Berwick similarly rejected any extension of the jurisdiction for three reasons. First, the point was scarcely argued before the House of Lords. Secondly, it was inconsistent with the ratio decidendi of the House of Lords in *La Pintada* [1985] AC 104. Lord Lloyd commented (at 740):

Parliament has on two occasions, first in 1934 and then in 1981, remedied injustices which had long been apparent in the power to award interest at common law. On the latter occasion it did so in the light of the view expressed by the Law Commission that the equitable jurisdiction to award interest was working satisfactorily, and called for no change. To extend the equitable jurisdiction for the first time to cover a residual injustice at common law, which Parliament chose not to remedy, would, I think, be as great a usurpation of the role of the legislature, and as clear an example of judicial law-making, as it would have been in *La Pintada*.

Lastly, Lord Lloyd was not convinced that policy reasons in favour of change were made out. Certainty was essential in commercial transactions in which the new alleged discretion would operate.

Lord Goff in his dissenting speech started with the recent recognition in *National Bank of Greece SA* v *Pinios Shipping Co. (No. 1)* [1990] 1 AC 637, that by the custom of bankers, banks were entitled to compound interest on advances made to their customers. Further, his Lordship quoted Hobhouse J at first instance ([1994] 4 All ER 890, at 955):

Anyone who lends or borrows money on a commercial basis receives or pays interest periodically and if that interest is not paid it is compounded ... I see no reason why I should deny the plaintiff a complete remedy or allow the defendant arbitrarily to retain part of the enrichment which it has unjustly enjoyed.

Lord Goff agreed: full restitution required the award of compound interest. It was wrong in principle to confine the jurisdiction to certain restrictive categories such as proprietary claims. Lord Woolf proceeded on the basis that equity's role was to remedy the inadequacies of common law. His Lordship cited criticism of *La Pintada* by Mann (1985) 101 LQR 30. On the whole, Lord Woolf was of the view that the extension of the jurisdiction would be a further improvement of the powers of English courts.

The arguments are finely balanced, but it is submitted that the approach of the majority is to be preferred. To introduce what was effectively a brand new judicial form of relief for restitutionary causes of action, would have been too much like judicial legislation, given the Parliamentary interventions this century. The view that questions as to whether interest is payable, and in what form, are more appropriate for Parliament than the courts, is confirmed by the recent Late Payment of Commercial Debts (Interest) Act 1998.

In summary, the position after *Westdeutsche* is the same as it was after *La Pintada* [1985] AC 104, where Lord Brandon of Oakbrook stated that the power to award compound interest in equity was confined to 'cases where the money had been obtained and retained by fraud, or where it had been withheld or misapplied by a trustee or anyone else in a fiduciary position' (at 116). A leading example of the deployment of the jurisdiction against a recalcitrant fiduciary is *Wallersteiner* v *Moir (No. 2)* [1975] QB 373. However, even where the jurisdiction exists, the award of compound interest will not always be appropriate. See *O'Sullivan* v *Management Agency and Music Ltd* [1985] QB 428, where the Court of Appeal held that it would be awarded only where it could be shown that the fiduciary had use of the benefit received in the course of trade (at 461–62). As a practical matter it is still necessary to establish a fiduciary relationship or fraud in order to come within this jurisdiction.

38.3 STATUTORY AWARDS OF INTEREST

Section 35A of the Supreme Court Act 1981 (as inserted by the Administration of Justice Act 1982) empowers the High Court in proceedings for the recovery of debt or damages to award simple interest. The rate is at the discretion of the court, though it is usually the same rate as that applicable for judgment debts. The court has a number of options in the exercise of discretion. First, as to whether interest should be awarded at all. Secondly, as to the rate which is appropriate. Thirdly, as to whether the interest should attach to all or only a part of the debt or damages. Fourthly, the period during which interest is payable. The appropriate dates must be between the date of the accrual of the cause of action, and either the date when the money was paid prior to judgment or the date of judgment. The Act empowers the court to award interest only where proceedings have begun, whether or not they have been pursued to judgment. The statutory powers supersede s. 3(1) the Law Reform (Miscellaneous Provisions) Act 1934.

The leading guidance on the question of how the court should exercise its discretion as to interest is *BP Exploration (Libya) Ltd* v *Hunt (No. 2)* [1979] 1 WLR 783 (QBD), which was decided under the 1934 Act. This was a claim under s. 1(3) of the Law Reform (Frustrated Contracts) Act 1943. Robert Goff J was under no doubt that claims under s. 1(2) and (3) of the 1943 Act were claims for the recovery of a debt. The former was a statutory version of the action for money had and received, and the latter was closely analogous to a *quantum valebat* or *quantum meruit* claim, which were themselves superseded by claims in *indebitatus assumpsit*. These were all claims for the recovery of a debt. Robert Goff J explicitly drew an analogy with the approach of the courts to the application of statutory limitation periods. He commented (at 836–37):

Certainly, when the claim in question is a claim to restitution, the courts have in the past placed a benevolently broad construction upon Acts of Parliament in order to make them applicable to such claims, when the legislature has failed to provide expressly for them.

The date at which the cause of action accrued was the date of the frustration of the contract, namely 7 December 1971 (at 809). This highlights an important difference between cases where the intention of the transferor is vitiated, such as cases of mistake, where the cause of action accrues upon the receipt of the benefit, and cases where the intention of the transferor is qualified, and the ground of recovery is failure of consideration, in which the cause of action does not accrue until the consideration has failed. Robert Goff J summarised the principle upon which interest should be awarded (at 845): 'The fundamental principle is that interest is not awarded as a punishment, but simply because the plaintiff has been deprived of the use of the money which was due to him.' Generally interest will run from the date of the accrual of the cause of action, but there is no general rule to that effect.

However, there are three main groups of cases in which the courts do depart from the general rule of awarding interest from the date of the accrual of cause of action. First, cases involving the position of the defendant. In these cases the defendant did not know, or could not reasonably have known, that a claim was likely to be made against him. In such cases the court will grant interest only from the date of the demand by the claimant. Secondly, where the claimant has been guilty of unreasonable delay, the court may decline to award interest for the full period. This is done to encourage claimants to proceed with reasonable dispatch in pursuing claims. Thirdly, there are miscellaneous cases in which the courts did not consider it just to award interest for the whole period between the date of the accrual of the cause of action and the date of payment or judgment (at 846-47). In the circumstances of the case, Robert Goff J held that this was an appropriate case where the period of interest should run from the date at which the plaintiff made it clear that he was making a claim, namely 14 June 1974 (at 848). The Court of Appeal upheld the judge's exercise of his discretion ([1981] 1 WLR 232, at 245), as did the House of Lords ([1983] 2 AC 352, at 373–74).

It can often be argued in respect of claims for restitution, especially with regard to mistaken payments, that there should be no interest awarded until the date of the demand by the claimant. Indeed, this was the old practice of the Courts of Equity. Where the defendant is not at fault in receiving the money, and may even be unaware of the circumstances surrounding the payment and the mistake, there is much to be said for the view of the date when the claim is first manifested as a more appropriate date than the date of the accrual of the cause of action.

The *BP* v *Hunt* guidance was approved of in the higher courts in *Westdeutsche*. Most recently this was the approach of Neuberger J in *Nurdin & Peacock plc* v *D. B. Ramsden & Co. Ltd* [1999] 1 All ER 941. Interest on the first five overpayments was awarded from 21 May 1987, which was seven days after a letter before action demanding repayment by the plaintiff's solicitors, giving seven days to make the payment. With regard to the last four overpayments, Neuberger J had held that these were recoverable under a contractual agreement and accordingly interest was payable only from seven days after his earlier judgment in the rectification proceedings. The judge further held that if they had been recoverable in restitution on the ground of mistake of law, he would have awarded interest on them from the date of the payment (at 966–68).

39 Practice and Procedure

39.1 INTRODUCTION

This chapter is intended to introduce some aspects of civil procedure and practice of particular relevance to restitutionary claims. Indeed, it can be said that claims which are now classified as arising out of unjust enrichment, have been the driving force behind a number of the most important innovations in modern civil justice, such as freezing orders and search orders. It can be observed that English law developed and refined the procedural mechanisms to cope with the growing number of claims in respect of misdirected funds earlier (in the 1970s and 1980s) than it began to develop and refine the substantive principles of restitution (in the late 1980s and 1990s). Further, restitutionary disputes are often litigated by way of the various accelerated procedures, such as summary judgment. The cheque rule and its exceptions to some extent reflect restitutionary language. Lastly, the Bankers' Books Evidence Act 1879 is most commonly utilised in the restitutionary context.

Obviously, a revolution overtook civil justice on 26 April 1999 with the implementation of the Woolf reforms. For detailed commentary on the reforms, and the new Civil Procedure Rules and accompanying Practice Directions, see *Blackstone's Civil Practice* (2000). The principles underlying the subject are best distilled in Neil Andrews, *Principles of Civil Procedure* (1994). This pre-dates the new Civil Procedure Rules, but it is still an excellent source of reference and I have borrowed some of its terminology, such as 'pre-emptive justice' and 'accelerated justice'.

39.2 PRE-EMPTIVE JUSTICE

39.2.1 Freezing orders

According to CPR Part 25, r. 25.1(f), a freezing injunction is an order:

(i) restraining a party from removing from the jurisdiction assets located there; or

(ii)   restraining a party from dealing with any assets whether located within the jurisdiction or not. . . .

The impetus for the development of freezing injunctions (or *Mareva* injunctions as they were known before the recent civil justice reforms) was often driven by cases with a restitutionary flavour. In *Lister & Co.* v *Stubbs* (1890) 45 Ch D 1, an employer sought an interlocutory injunction restraining its former employee from dealing with land and investments which it alleged represented the proceeds of bribes and secret commissions. The Court of Appeal refused to grant any such order on the basis that the courts, at that time, only had the jurisdiction to grant injunctions in respect of property which the plaintiff alleged belonged to him. The procedural dimension of this case was eventually superseded by the recognition of asset-freezing injunctions in the seminal Court of Appeal decisions of *Nippon Yusen Kaisha* v *Karageorgis* [1975] 1 WLR 1093 and *Mareva Compañia Naviera SA* v *International Bulkcarriers SA* [1975] 2 Lloyd's Rep 509. The award of *Mareva* (or freezing) injunctions was subsequently given statutory authority by s. 37(3) of the Supreme Court Act 1981:

The power of the High Court to grant an interlocutory injunction restraining a party to any proceedings from removing from the jurisdiction of the High Court, or otherwise dealing with, assets located within that jurisdiction shall be exerciseable in all cases where the party is, as well as in cases where he is not, domiciled, resident or present with that jurisdiction.

The development of and principles in respect of *Mareva* injunctions, including world-wide *Mareva* injunctions, are traced in Andrews, paras 8-023 to 8-049. The significance of the *Mareva* injunction is that it helps to prevent the dissipation of assets, even where the claimant's action is a *personal* one. Indeed, where the claim is one for proprietary relief, different principles apply.

In *Polly Peck International plc* v *Nadir (No. 2)* [1992] 4 All ER 769, the administrator of PPI sought a *Mareva* injunction against IBK, a northern Cyprus bank, alleging that it was responsible for misdirecting £142 million of PPI's assets. Further, the administrators claimed a *Mareva* injunction against the Central Bank of Northern Cyprus in respect of some £44 million which it had received from IBK, alleging that it was a constructive trustee for the whole sum, and further a tracing claim to some £8.9 million standing in its London account. At first instance, Millett J granted the injunctions. The Central Bank appealed. The claim in respect of the £44 million was explicitly pleaded on the basis of a liability as a constructive trustee (a personal claim). In contrast, the claim to the £8.9 million was based upon an exercise in equitable tracing which had identified money standing in the London account derived from PPI's assets, and was accordingly a proprietary claim. Scott LJ stressed the 'important difference' between the two (at 776):

Equitable tracing leads to a claim of a proprietary character. A fund is identified that, in equity, is regarded as a fund belonging to the claimant. The constructive trust claim, in this action at least, is not a claim to any fund in specie. It is a claim to monetary compensation. The only relevant interlocutory protection that can be sought in aid of a money claim is a Mareva injunction, restraining the defendant from dissipating or secreting away his assets in order to make himself judgment proof. But if identifiable assets are being claimed, the interlocutory relief sought will not be a Mareva injunction but relief for the purpose of preserving intact the assets in question until their true ownership can be determined. Quite different considerations arise from those which apply to the Mareva injunction.

Accordingly, Scott LJ treated the two applications separately.

He rejected the *Mareva* injunction on the basis that the claim against Central Bank was no more than speculative. On the basis of the principle that there should be no interference with the ordinary business of the defendant, it would be positively unfair to maintain the injunction which had already seriously interfered with the Central Bank's business.

In contrast, the injunction sought in respect of the £8.9 million was not a *Mareva* injunction. For example, there would be no provision entitling the money to be used for normal business purposes, the payment of legal fees, and so on. The governing principles were those in respect of interlocutory injunctions in general laid down in *American Cyanamid Co.* v *Ethicon Ltd* [1975] AC 396. PPI had, first, to demonstrate an arguable case and, secondly, to demonstrate that the balance of convenience favoured granting the order. The late stage at which the tracing claim was put forward (not until the ninth and tenth affidavits sworn on behalf of the plaintiff) tipped the balance of convenience against granting the wide injunctions sought. However, the Court did grant a limited order restraining the bank from dealing with the fund otherwise than in its normal course of business and unless and to the extent that there were no funds in England available to be used (at 782–85). In the result, this form of relief appears to resemble more a *Mareva* injunction than an order preserving property until its ownership is resolved in proceedings. There is a crucial difference between *Mareva* relief and an interlocutory injunction preserving property. The *Mareva* injunction does not give security or priority upon the insolvency of the defendant. In contrast, proprietary relief accompanied by an interlocutory order preserving the asset will ensure priority.

Banks must comply with a *Mareva* injunction once they have knowledge of it. In *Z Ltd* v *A-Z and AA-LL* [1982] QB 558, the London office of a large foreign corporation was subjected to a massive fraudulent conspiracy. It sought to trace £2 million into various bank accounts and other property. It obtained *Mareva* injunctions and orders for specific discovery against 19 conspirator defendants, and a further 18 defendants who had received assets, including five clearing banks. The banks sought guidance on their obligations under such injunctions. Lord Denning MR concluded (at 574):

As soon as a bank is given notice of a *Mareva* injunction, it must freeze the defendant's bank account. It must not allow any further drawings to be made on it, neither by cheques drawn before the injunction nor by those drawn after it. The reason is because, if it allowed any such drawings, it would be obstructing the course of justice — as prescribed by the court which granted the injunction — and it would be guilty of a contempt of court.

The development of world-wide *Mareva* injunctions was promoted in the extensive *Derby* v *Weldon* litigation: *Derby* v *Weldon* [1990] Ch 48; *Derby* v *Weldon (Nos 3 & 4)* [1990] Ch 65; *Derby* v *Weldon (No. 6)* [1990] 1 WLR 1139.

Ancillary orders are often made in support of such injunctions, requiring the defendant to disclose material about his assets. Sometimes, such orders are made against banks and others, who are not defendants. The jurisdiction to seek pre-action disclosure against the bank, as a non-party, appears to be based upon the principle in *Norwich Pharmacal Co.* v *Customs and Excise Commissioners* [1974] AC 133, that where an innocent party has got mixed up in another's wrongdoing, they are liable to make disclosure (see *Bankers Trust Co.* v *Shapira* [1980] 1 WLR 1274). See below at 39.4.

39.2.2 Search orders

A search order requires a party to admit another party to premises for the purpose of preserving evidence and is now granted under s. 7 of the Civil Procedure Act 1997 and CPR Part 25, r. 25.1(h). These were formally known as *Anton Piller* orders, after the leading case of *Anton Piller KG* v *Manufacturing Processes Ltd* [1976] Ch 55. See Andrews, paras 8-001 to 8-022. The Draconian nature of the order had led to it being applied with greater circumspection in recent years. The essence of the jurisdiction is that the defendant has in his possession evidence which there is a real possibility will be destroyed when he hears of the proceedings. Such orders have often been granted in disputes with a restitutionary flavour, especially breach of intellectual property torts, breach of fiduciary duty and breach of confidence.

One of the leading modern cases involved former employees dishonestly taking customer lists and pricing information with them to their new business. An *Anton Piller* order was sought in support of a claim based on breach of confidence. Sir Donald Nicholls V-C took the opportunity in *Universal Thermosensors Ltd* v *Hibben* [1992] 1 WLR 840 to issue general guidelines as to the granting an execution of *Anton Piller* orders. The effect of the grant of the injunction was to stifle the fledgling business, effectively putting the plaintiff into a better position than if there had been no breach of confidence. Sir Donald Nicholls V-C cited with approval an influential article by Dockray and Laddie ((1990) 106 LQR 601) and the earlier judgments of Scott J in *Columbia Picture Industries Inc* v *Robinson* [1987] Ch 38 and Hoffmann J in *Lock International plc* v *Beswick* [1989] 1 WLR 1268. He observed that such orders 'are rightly made much more sparingly than previously' (at 860). The detailed guidance is to be found at 860–61. Sir Donald Nicholls V-C concluded (at 861):

it must be appreciated, and certainly it is my view, that *in suitable and strictly limited cases, Anton Piller* orders furnish courts with a valuable aid in their efforts to do justice between two parties. Especially is this so in blatant cases of fraud. It is important therefore that these orders should not be allowed to fall into disrepute.

39.3   ACCELERATED JUSTICE

39.3.1   Summary judgment

The old RSC Ord. 14 was much in evidence in restitutionary cases. For example, the following House of Lords decisions were vindicated using the process of summary judgment: *Guinness plc* v *Saunders* [1990] 2 AC 663; *Hyundai Heavy Industries Co. Ltd* v *Papadopoulos* [1980] 1 WLR 1129; and *Stocznia Gdanska SA* v *Latvian Shipping Co.* [1998] 1 WLR 574. The procedure was also used extensively in the swaps cases once the initial lead cases had been decided. The new procedure under CPR Part 24 should be even more useful in the context of restitution cases. First, summary judgment is now available to a defendant as well as to a claimant, enabling weak claims to be disposed of on a summary basis. The test under the new rule is more applicant-friendly than under the old rules which required a defendant to show only that he had 'a triable issue'. It is now necessary to show that a claim or defence 'has a real prospect of success', which is clearly modelled upon the old test for setting aside a default judgment in *Alpine Bulk Transport Co. Inc.* v *Saudi Eagle Shipping Co. Inc, The Saudi Eagle* [1986] 2 Lloyd's 221.

39.3.2   The cheque rule

The power to award summary judgment was first granted in respect of dishonoured bills of exchange. The special position of cheques and other bills of exchange is now reflected in the 'cheque rule'. Where a cheque or other bill of exchange is dishonoured, the payee may seek summary judgment upon the contract contained in the bill of exchange. This readily leads to summary judgment. The defendant can raise only limited defences. First, where the defendant can show fraud, duress or illegality tainting the bill. Secondly, where defendant can show a total failure of consideration he can resist summary judgment. See the leading House of Lords case of *Nova (Jersey) Knit Ltd* v *Kammgarn Spinnerei GmbH* [1977] 1 WLR 713. An explanation for this is that bills of exchange (and also letters of credit) are treated as cash. They are often described as the 'life-blood of commerce'. The courts are reluctant, as a matter of policy, to allow a defence to operate as a set-off to the main claim. Accordingly, no set-off is allowed of unliquidated sums, such as a claim for damages. However, where the claim is liquidated, such as a claim for restitution of the price, the defence of set-off can be raised. See Andrews, paras 6-016; paras 6-018 to 6-021. Accordingly, where the seller of goods seeks summary judgment in respect of a dishonoured cheque, the defendant will be able to resist the application only if he has validly rejected the goods, for example on the grounds of breach of the obligation with regard to satisfactory quality, and is counter-claiming restitution of the price on the basis of a total failure of consideration.

The restrictive approach of the substantive English law to when a claimant can recover on the basis of failure of consideration, namely by insisting upon the requirement of *totality*, is here reinforced by the rules of procedure. If the requirement of totality were to be abandoned in the substantive law, it would also have to be considered what impact this would have upon the traditional cheque rule. While there is no authority as yet, it is clear that the cheque rule is an aspect of practice which will survive the introduction of the new rules on summary judgment.

39.4 OBTAINING EVIDENCE

Search orders could obviously be included under this heading too. In simple, two party cases the usual rules of disclosure (formerly discovery) apply. See CPR Part 31. In a case of wrongdoing, where the claimant has an election between a compensatory and a restitutionary measure of relief and he lacks the information as to which will yield the higher sum, the court can order disclosure by the defendant of the necessary information, although it will not make an oppressive order (*Island Records Ltd* v *Tring International plc* [1995] 3 All ER 444 and *Tang Man Sit* v *Capacious Investments Ltd* [1996] 1 All ER 193, at 198).

39.4.1 Third party disclosure

The general rule before the civil justice reforms was that it is not possible to obtain discovery against a non-party. This was known as the 'mere witness' rule. A party could not obtain discovery against a non-party except in certain exceptional cases (*Sunderland Steamship P and I Association* v *Gatoil International Inc., The Lorenzo Halcoussi* [1988] 1 Lloyd's Rep 180, at 184 *per* Steyn J). The new Civil Procedure Rules envisage disclosure orders against non-parties becoming more available and provide a distinct procedure (CPR Part 31, r. 31.17). However it is likely that the former practice will be followed so that the orders are not oppressive to third parties. The former practice is explicitly preserved: CPR Part 31.18.

An important exception to the 'mere witness' rule was the leading House of Lords case of *Norwich Pharmacal Co.* v *Customs and Excise Commissioners* [1974] AC 133, in which the plaintiffs became aware that goods were being imported which infringed their patent. They sought discovery of the names of the importers from the Commissioners for Customs and Excise. It was held that the applicant must demonstrate the existence of a prima facie case against the intended defendant. Further, it must be demonstrated that the party against whom the order is sought has the relevant information. The gist of the claim is that the party with the information has become mixed up with the alleged wrongdoing, or has somehow facilitated it. It was not necessary that the non-party's involvement in the wrongdoing was not contemporaneous.

Accordingly discovery was ordered against the wife of a judgment debtor where she was involved in the dissipation of the proceeds of the misdirected funds (*Mercantile Group (Europe) AG* v *Aiyela* [1994] QB 366). The 'mere witness' rule was irrelevant where discovery was sought against a third party in aid of a post-judgment *Mareva* injunction. All that had to be shown was that the third party had become mixed up in the relevant transaction, and that it was just and convenient to make the order. There was evidence that the defendant's wife held assets which in truth belonged to her husband. 'She was therefore ''mixed up'' in her husband's attempts to make himself judgment proof' (*per* Steyn LJ, at 376).

The established jurisdiction to order disclosure against a third party is of particular assistance where a claimant seeks to trace and claim misdirected funds. This is known as the *Bankers Trust* order after the leading case of *Bankers Trust Co.* v *Shapira* [1980] 1 WLR 1274. The order compels a non-party, usually a bank, to give disclosure of information and documentation in relation to the defendant's financial affairs. In *Shapira*, two men defrauded a New York bank of US$1 million by means of two forged cheques drawn on a Saudi Arabian bank. On their orders the American bank transferred over US$700,000 of the proceeds of the fraud to the London branch of a Swiss bank. Having obtained a *Mareva* injunction against the Swiss bank, the plaintiff bank sought discovery of documentation relating to the fraudsters and the money. The Court of Appeal granted the order, explicitly recognising the novelty of the jurisdiction. Lord Denning MR stated (at 1282): 'If the plaintiff's equity is to be of any avail, he must be given access to the bank's books and documents — for that is the only way of tracing the money or knowing what has happened to it.' Waller LJ agreed, while apparently acknowledging that the relief was wider that that available under the Bankers' Books Evidence Act 1879 (see 39.4.2). The principle has been applied in relation to a claim arising out of a massive commercial fraud: *Arab Monetary Fund* v *Hashim (No. 5)* [1992] 2 All ER 911. However, in that case Hoffmann J cautioned (at 916): 'Orders for discovery before trial in aid of *Mareva*s or in the *Bankers Trust* form against third parties are extraordinary remedies and should not be regarded as the common coin of litigation.' The order appears to be confined to claims of a proprietary character (at 918). Further, such orders will generally not be made against banks located outside the English jurisdiction (*MacKinnon* v *Donaldson Lufkin & Jenrette Securities Corp.* [1986] Ch 482). For discussion, see Andrews, paras 11-028 to 11-045.

39.4.2   The Bankers' Book Evidence Act 1879

Whereas *Bankers Trust* orders are used in urgent cases, often in conjunction with freezing injunctions, in non-urgent cases the appropriate procedure is under the Bankers' Books Evidence Act 1879 (as amended). By section 7:

> On the application of any party to a legal proceeding a court or judge may order that such party be at liberty to inspect and take copies of any entries in a banker's book for any of the purposes of such proceedings.

There must be 'special cause' in order to invoke the jurisdiction where the bank is not a party (s. 6). The order will override the bankers' duty of confidentiality to their customers. The procedure is not often used. It has been held to be an inappropriate means of discovering the whereabouts of the assets of a judgment debtor. Rather, resort should be had to examination of the defendant (*D. B. Deniz Nakliyati Tas* v *Yugopetrol* [1992] 1 WLR 437). There Nolan J stated (at 443):

> For nearly a century now the courts have been concerned to ensure that orders under section 7 should not be allowed to effect more than a strictly limited intrusion into the affairs of third parties, and in particular should not be regarded as the equivalent of fishing licences.

See generally Andrews, para. 11-047.

39.5   MISFEASANCE PROCEEDINGS AND INSOLVENT COMPANIES

A further summary procedure is contained in s. 212 of the Insolvency Act 1986, whereby the liquidator of an insolvent company is empowered to bring summary proceedings for the recovery of money and other property misapplied by its directors and linked persons. Oditah has observed that the section is 'purely enabling and facilitative': [1992] LMCLQ 207. Further: 'Section 212 is primarily concerned with restitution — restoration of corporate property misapplied or retained by the person charged' (at 218). For example, the section has been relied on where a director of the company was the recipient of secret commissions (*Re Derek Randall Enterprises Ltd* [1990] BCC 749). However, the claim failed on the facts of that particular case, where the director subsequently applied the misappropriated money in the discharge of the company's liabilities. For detailed consideration of the jurisdiction, see Oditah, 'Misfeasance Proceedings Against Company Directors' [1992] LMCLQ 207.

FURTHER READING

Asterisks indicate especially useful works.

Search orders and freezing injunctions

Andrews, chap. 8

J. Hill, *The Law Relating to International Commercial Disputes*, 2nd edn (1998), 289–320

*M. Dockray and H. Laddie, 'Piller Problems' (1990) 106 LQR 601

*L. Collins, 'The Territorial Reach of *Mareva* Injunctions' (1989) 105 LQR 262

A. Malek and C. Lewis, 'World-wide *Mareva* injunctions — the position of international banks' [1990] LMCLQ 88

D. Capper, 'Worldwide *Mareva* Injunctions' (1991) 54 MLR 329

A. Zuckerman, '*Mareva* Injunctions and Security for Judgments in a Framework of Interlocutory Remedies' (1993) 109 LQR 432

A. Zuckerman, 'Interlocutory Remedies in Quest of Procedural Fairness' (1993) 56 MLR 325

Obtaining evidence

Andrews, chap. 11
C. Styles and C. Hollander, *Documentary Evidence,* 5th edn (1995), 55–64

Summary judgment

Andrews, paras 6-008 to 6-021; paras 9-019 to 9-032

Misfeasance proceedings

F. Oditah, 'Misfeasance Proceedings Against Company Directors' [1992] LMCLQ 207

40 Drafting Statements of Case

40.1 INTRODUCTION

Under the modern code of English civil procedure it is no longer appropriate to talk about pleadings. However, it still appears to be proper to speak of pleading or drafting the statements of case in which each party makes its allegations of fact. The reforms do not appear to have changed the basic principles of pleading, although it is now possible to refer in the particulars of claim to any point of law on which a claim is based: CPR, PD 16, 'Practice Direction — Statements of Case', para. 10.3(1). The parties' statements of case provide the opportunity for a clear and concise identification of the causes of action relied upon and the defences which are alleged to defeat or diminish the alleged claims. As such the purpose of these documents is to identify and narrow the issues in dispute between the parties at an early stage. Accordingly, the whole of this book so far has been aimed at identifying the ingredients of restitutionary causes of actions and the defences thereto. Given the rapid development of the subject, especially over the last decade since its deeper structure was exposed, it can sometimes be difficult to discern what are the necessary allegations of fact giving rise to an appropriate cause of action or defence. Much painstaking restitutionary scholarship is concerned with identifying those things which need to be proved in order for a claim or a defence to succeed (the essential *probanda*). What follows is some general guidance on particular issues which may be of importance when drafting statements of case.

40.2 HISTORICAL BACKGROUND

No area of the law perhaps better illustrates the famous observation of Maitland: 'The forms of action we have buried, but they still rule us from their graves' (*The Forms of Action at Common Law* (1954), 2). The forms of action and the relevant equitable techniques were introduced in Chapter 2. As a matter of principle, in the modern law of unjust enrichment, the language of the forms of action should wherever possible be eschewed. The story of how the Victorians abolished the forms of action is told by Maitland (at 81):

> The next great step was taken by the Common Law Procedure Act 1852, section 3. Under this statute no form of action is to be mentioned in the writ, which is for the future to be a simple writ of summons. But even after this Act, the form of action remains of vital importance to the pleader for each action retains its own precedents, and although the choice of the proper form of action need no longer be made in the choice of writ it is merely deferred until the declaration.
>
> The last great step comes with the Judicature Acts of 1873–75, the statutes effecting the fusion of equity and law. By these statutes and by the Rules of the Supreme Court made thereunder, a new code of civil procedure was introduced, largely dependent for its working upon wide discretionary powers allowed to the judges. Henceforward not only is the writ a simple writ of summons, but there are no longer any 'forms of actions', in the old sense of the phrase.
>
> A plaintiff is to state his case, not in any formula put into King's mouth but in the plaintiff's own (or his adviser's) words endorsed upon the writ, and his pleader is to say not upon what form of action he relies but merely what are the facts upon which he relies.

We have since moved on a stage further with the abolition of writs of summons and other originating process and their replacement by claim forms. The law is now concerned with causes of action and defences. For example, in contract law pleadings no longer refer to *assumpsit, covenant*, goods bargained and sold or goods sold and delivered. However, with regard to causes of action in unjust enrichment, the practitioner who turns to the leading text may be forgiven for thinking that he is still in the pre-Victorian era. In Sir Jack Jacob and Iain Goldrein (eds), *Bullen, Leake & Jacob's Precedents of Pleadings*, 13th edn (1990), the law and practice are to be found under the impermissible soubriquets of *money had and received* and *money paid*: 654–65, 669–70, 1313–14 and 1317. In the precedent for *money had and received*, the form of action is invoked and the practitioner then encouraged to 'state particulars showing when and how money was received by the defendant, and the facts which are alleged to make such receipt the receipt to the use of the plaintiff' (at 661). Even less helpfully, in the count for *money paid* the draft includes: 'the said request is to be implied from the following circumstances, namely, *state the circumstances*' (at 670). The proposed defence proceeds on the basis that the defendant should deny the request (at 1317). This is wholly unsatisfactory. As Stable J observed in *Dies v British and International Mining and Finance Corporation Ltd* [1939] 1 KB 724, at 738–39:

> The question whether the right exists cannot be determined by inquiring whether the action for money had and received is the appropriate form of plea. If the right

exists, the form of plea is appropriate enough. If the right does not exist, it cannot be enforced, no matter how attractively it be disguised by the pleader.

The question is not now one of the appropriate form in which to clothe the right, but whether or not the right exists, although the absence of any clothing that fits may be an indication of the non-existence of the right.

The modern approach to pleading restitutionary causes of action and defences should be tied into the modern structure of the restitutionary enquiry.

40.3   THE STRUCTURE OF THE UNJUST ENRICHMENT ENQUIRY

The structure of the modern enquiry should inform the structure of the statement of case.

Where the enrichment is not in the form of money, it will be necessary to plead the factors establishing the enrichment. Accordingly the facts supporting a genuine request, free acceptance or a finding of incontrovertible benefit should be pleaded with particularity. The circumstances whereby it is alleged that a debt or other obligation owed by the defendant has been discharged or extinguished by the claimant's conduct should be set out. In the case of profiting by wrongdoing, the benefits which were alleged to have been the result of the breach of primary legal duty owed to the claimant should be identified.

With regard to the 'at the expense of' question, each claimant should clearly identify whether the claim is brought in subtractive unjust enrichment, or restitution for wrongs or in the alternative in both. Further, where a claimant is minded to seek restitutionary damages for wrongdoing, the prayer for relief should state explicitly that damages are sought on a restitutionary or compensatory basis. In *Ministry of Defence* v *Ashman* [1993] 2 EGLR 102, Lloyd LJ complained that the pleaded case was simply a claim for damages for trespass, and did not explicitly request restitution. While this was not seen as an obstacle by the other members of the Court of Appeal, the best practice is to state explicitly that damages are sought alternatively on a compensatory or restitutionary basis. It should be remembered that in appropriate cases the claimant has an election up to the date of judgment as to which basis he prefers, and it is best to keep the option open until that stage.

Turning to the contractual or transactional matrix question, the terms of any contract between the parties, or between one of the parties and a non-party, which are relevant to the transfer of the benefit should be specifically pleaded. In addition, particulars of the invalidity of that transaction, whether void or voidable, must be included. The ground upon which the contract is invalid, whether incapacity, misrepresentation, duress and so on, should be identified with precision. Further, where a claimant had an election to bring the subsisting contract or other transaction to an end, the words, or documents or conduct by which the claimant exercised that right of termination or rescission should be particularised. It is not sufficient that reasons exist which entitle the claimant to terminate or rescind; what is necessary is that the election has been exercised.

The pleading must be explicit as to the ground for restitution or unjust factor. Perhaps the bane of lawyers in this area currently is the general unparticularised allegation that the defendant has been unjustly enriched or should pay on a *quantum meruit* basis. Such generalised allegations do not comply with the requirement that the claimant should identify with precision the cause of action upon which he relies. Accordingly, mistake, compulsion, failure of consideration or wrongdoing must be pleaded.

The claimant must also be explicit about the quantum of relief, whether the claim is confined to the value received, or whether in the alternative there is a claim to the value surviving. Similarly, in restitution for wrongs the relevant benefits must be identified with precision.

Turning to the nature of relief, the claimant must be explicit if a proprietary claim is sought in addition to a personal claim. The extra benefits which flow from a proprietary claim will not be made available unless the basis for it is pleaded and proved. For example, in *Kleinwort Benson Ltd* v *South Tyneside Metropolitan Borough Council* [1994] 4 All ER 972, the plaintiff claimed only a personal judgment rather than a proprietary one. Hobhouse J therefore awarded interest on a simple rather than a compound basis. He would have been prepared to award compound interest if a proprietary claim had been maintained (at 990–95). Of course, this would now be decided differently in the wake of *Westdeutsche Landesbank Girozentrale* v *Islington London Borough Council* [1996] AC 669 in the House of Lords. However, the point remains the same. If a claimant seeks the additional benefits of a proprietary claim, such as profits, priority upon insolvency or compound interest, he must explicitly ask for such a remedy.

Where the process of tracing is relied upon in support of such a proprietary claim the claimant will need to set out the basic stages in the process of identification of the asset moving from himself to the defendant. The level of detail is a matter of debate. A claimant may take some comfort from the words of Goulding J in *Chase Manhattan Bank NA* v *Israel-British Bank (London) Ltd* [1981] Ch 105, where it was argued (at 121):

> that, by not pleading and proving in greater detail the operations of the clearing house inter-bank payment system (known as CHIPS for short) in New York, the plaintiff had failed to identify any chose in action or other particular subject of property to which the plaintiff's alleged equitable interest could attach and from which tracing could begin. I cannot accept that contention. A payment, and a mistake, are alleged in terms by paragraph 2 of the re-amended statement of claim and plainly admitted by paragraph 2 of the re-amended defence; and when equitable rights are in question, the court does not encourage fine distinctions founded on the technicalities of financial machinery.

Despite this, and given the doubtful nature of the *Chase Manhattan* authority, it is best practice to set out as far as the claimant can reasonably ascertain, the path taken by the wealth subtracted from him, with as much particularity as can be obtained before disclosure.

40.4 MISTAKEN PAYMENTS

By way of illustration it is worth considering in more detail how a typical mistaken payment case should be set out. The essentials of the cause of action are that (1) there has been a payment; (2) which was caused; (3) by a mistake. How much detail about the mistake needs to be included? In *Avon County Council* v *Howlett* [1983] 1 WLR 605, the Court of Appeal thought that where human error was responsible for a mistake it was reasonable to expect the claimant to identify the responsible individuals so that they could be called as witnesses. It can be argued that given the liberalisation of recovery for mistake, to encompass mistakes of law, such a detailed approach is no longer necessary. It is submitted that it remains best practice to set out the actual mistake with sufficient particularity, and if possible to identify which individual within an organisation was responsible for the error. Certainly, this cautious approach would be consistent with the concerns of Lord Hope in *Kleinwort Benson Ltd* v *Lincoln City Council* [1999] 2 AC 349, where he bemoaned the fact that there were no details given of the circumstances of the nature of the alleged mistake, while observing that there had equally been no request for further and better particulars (at 403).

It is still incumbent upon the claimant to establish an unjust factor, and he should particularise as far as he can the appropriate ground for restitution. There is obviously no need to plead that the payee knew or ought to have known that the payment was made under mistake. However, advisers acting for claimants may wish to consider at least the latter allegation. The law on this question is still unsettled, but in the light of the reinterpretation of the *Chase Manhattan* case by Lord Browne-Wilkinson in *Westdeutsche Landesbank Girozentrale* v *Islington London Borough Council* [1996] AC 669, there is a possibility that a recipient who knows, or possibly ought to know, that he has received a mistaken payment, may be also accountable under an equitable proprietary remedy. This would bring with it the advantage of profits, priority on insolvency and compound interest. Therefore, while it is not necessary for the common law action, consideration should be given to the question whether such an allegation can be proved.

Turning to the defence, the restitutionary defences such as good faith purchase or good faith change of position must be explicitly pleaded. Indeed, a plea of change of position may be the best way in practice to avoid a speedy application for summary judgment by the claimant. The defendant must particularise and quantify as far as possible in a table or schedule the extent to which his financial position has been changed upon the faith of the receipt. A very general allegation of the defence would not ordinarily be good practice. However, in some exceptional cases the courts may be willing to allow that there has been a change in the mode of living, though as far as possible this should be identified.

40.5 MATTERS THAT NEED TO BE SPECIFICALLY PLEADED

Under the new CPR, PD 16, r. 10(2) provides:

The claimant must specifically set out the following matters in his particulars of a claim where he wishes to rely on them in support of his claim:

(1)   any allegation of fraud,
(2)   the fact of any illegality,
(3)   details of any misrepresentation,
(4)   details of all breaches of trust,
(5)   notice or knowledge of a fact,
(6)   details of unsoundness of mind or undue influence....

Many of these will be relevant factors in restitution cases, especially r. 10.2(5) which will be relevant in cases of unconscionable receipt, whether in the terms of free acceptance or a claim in so-called knowing receipt in equity. It is still common practice to plead matters such as knowledge, constructive knowledge, notice or constructive notice of facts by reference to the *Baden Delvaux* scale of hierarchy of states of mind ([1993] 1 WLR 509, at 575–76; see 29.3 above). For an example, see *Polly Peck International plc* v *Nadir (No. 2)* [1992] 4 All ER 769. It should be noted that the *Baden Delvaux* scale has been rejected in the context of knowing assistance or dishonest accessory liability (*Royal Brunei Airlines Sdn Bhd* v *Tan* [1995] 2 AC 378). Given the current uncertainty as to the level of knowledge or constructive knowledge required to support a claim for knowing receipt, the usual practice is to allege a number of the *Baden Delvaux* heads of knowledge in the alternative. Similar considerations will apply where the defence raises good faith purchase or good faith change of position, and the claimant in a reply wishes to allege sufficient actual or constructive knowledge or notice to disentitle the defendant from making out the defence. Lastly, another practical matter which requires specific pleading is interest: see CPR Part 16, r. 16.4(2).

FURTHER READING

Sir J. Jacob and I. Goldrein (eds), *Bullen, Leake & Jacob's Precedents of Pleadings*, 13th edn (1990), 654–65, 669–70, 1313–14, 1317

K. Mason and J. Carter, *Restitution Law in Australia* (1996), 968–81

Index